PUBLIC BORROWING

PUBLIC BORROWING

Critical Concepts in Finance

Edited by
Tehreem Husain and D'Maris Coffman

Volume II
The Washington Consensus and its Critics

Routledge
Taylor & Francis Group

LONDON AND NEW YORK

First published 2022
by Routledge
2 Park Square, Milton Park, Abingdon, Oxon OX14 4RN

and by Routledge
52 Vanderbilt Avenue, New York, NY 10017

Routledge is an imprint of the Taylor & Francis Group, an informa business

British Library Cataloguing-in-Publication Data
A catalogue record for this book is available from the British Library

Library of Congress Cataloging-in-Publication Data
A catalog record has been requested for this book

ISBN: 978-1-138-90553-5 (set)
ISBN: 978-1-138-90555-9 (volume II)

Typeset in Times New Roman
by Deanta Global Publishing Services, Chennai, India

Publisher's Note
References within each chapter are as they appear in the original complete work

CONTENTS

CONTENTS

VOLUME II ACKNOWLEDGEMENTS

The publishers would like to thank the following for permission to reprint their material:

The authors for permission to reprint Philippe Aghion, Abhijit V. Banerjee and Phillippe Bacchetta, 'Financial Development and the Instability of Open Economies', *NBER Working Paper* No. w10246, (January 2004).

The IMF for permission to reprint S. Amadou, 'Emerging Market Bond Spreads and Sovereign Credit Ratings: Reconciling Market View with Fundamentals', *IMF Working Paper* 01/165, 2001.

The Federal Reserve Bank of New York for permission to reprint R. Cantor and F. Pecker, 'Determinants and Impact of Sovereign Credit Ratings', *Federal Reserve Bank of New York Economic Policy Review* October 1996, 37–54.

The Bank of England for permission to reprint G. Ferrucci, 'Empirical Determinants of Emerging Market Economies' Sovereign Bond Spreads', Working Paper No. 205. Bank of England, London, 2003.

Elsevier for permission to reprint H. D. Gibson, S. G. Hall and G. S. Tavlas, 'The Greek Financial Crisis: Growing Imbalances and Sovereign Spreads', *Journal of International Money and Finance* 31, 2012, 498–516.

University of Chicago Press for permission to reprint Rudiger Dornbusch, 'Expectations and Exchange Rate Dynamics', *Journal of Political Economy* 84, 6, 1976, 1661–1176.

Oxford University Press for permission to reprint Guillermo A. Calvo and Carmen M. Reinhart, 'Fear of Floating', *The Quarterly Journal of Economics* 117, 2, 2002, 379–408.

The American Economic Association for permission to reprint Stanley Fischer, 'Exchange Rate Regimes: Is the Bipolar View Correct?', *Journal of Economic Perspectives* 15, 2, 2001, 3–24.

Elsevier for permission to reprint Paul Krugman, 'Financing vs. Forgiving a Debt Overhang', *Journal of Development Economics* 29, 3, 1998, 253–268.

John Wiley & Sons for permission to reprint Cesar Martinelli and Mariano Tommasi. 'Sequencing of Economics Reforms in the Presence of Political Constraints', *Economics and Politics* 9, 2, 1997, 115–131.

The American Economic Association for permission to reprint Ronald I McKinnnon and Huw Pill, 'Credible Economic Liberalizations and Overborrowing', *American Economic Review* 87, 2, 1997, 189–193.

Springer for permission to reprint Dani Rodrik, Arvind Subramanian and Francesco Trebbi, 'Institutions Rule: The Primacy of Institutions Over Geography and Integration in Economic Development', *Journal of Economic Growth* 9, 2, 2004, 131–165.

Stanford University Press for permission to reprint Stanley L., Engerman and Kenneth L. Sokoloff, 'Factor Endowments, Institutions, and Differential Paths of Growth Among New World Economies: A View from Economic Historians of the United States', in Stephen Haber (ed.) *How Latin America Fell Behind* (Stanford University Press, California, 1997).

Palgrave Macmillan for permission to reprint José Antonio Ocampo, 'Capital-Account and Counter-Cyclical Prudential Regulations in Developing Countries', in Ricardo Ffrench-Davis and Stephany Griffith-Jones (eds), *From Capital Surges to Drought: Seeking Stability for Emerging Markets* (Palgrave MacMillan, London, 2003).

Elsevier for permission to reprint Joseph E. Stiglitz, 'Capital Market Liberalization, Economic Growth, and Instability', *World Development* 28, 6, 2000, 1075–1086.

Oxford University Press for permission to reprint J. Williamson, 'What Should the World Bank Think about the Washington Consensus?', *World Bank Economic Review* 15, 2, 2000, 251–264.

Disclaimer

VOLUME II INTRODUCTION

The Washington Consensus and its Critics

The Latin American debt crisis gave rise to the development of a new reform agenda. Coined the 'Washington Consensus' by John Williamson of the Institute for International Economics, the agenda comprised of ten policy principles that were meant to guide structural adjustment. These were fiscal discipline, redirection of public spending, lower marginal tax rates, interest rate liberalization, competitive exchange rate policy, trade liberalization, privatization of state industries, encouragement of foreign direct investment, deregulation of public monopolies, and securing of private property rights. Adherence to these principles did, to a degree, determine access to bank financing and to international capital markets. Yet there remains considerable disagreement about how far any or all of these are of key importance to markets. This volume covers all these debates in detail.

Financial liberalization remains an important policy principle advocated by the Washington Consensus; it is purported to improve financial market efficiency and thereby generate savings, investment, and higher growth (Akinsola & Odhiambo, 2017). However, a key point of contention in terms of adherence to such policies is the trade-off between gains from financial liberalization (through capital market access) and the risks associated with managing volatility of international capital flows. We start the volume with Aghion, Bacchetta, and Banerjee's (2004), 'Financial Development and the Instability of Open Economies' which attempts to answer this fundamental question. The authors analyze the role of financial factors as a source of instability in small open economies and find that the degree of financial development matters for financial stability. Countries at an intermediate level of financial development are more unstable than either very developed or very underdeveloped economies. Moreover, countries experiencing a new phase of financial development may become more unstable in the short run. Their findings raise concerns about the potential implications that financial liberalization policies have on financial stability.

Implementation of financial liberalization policies as part of a broader reform agenda influences sovereign bond ratings granted by *credit rating agencies*. Sovereign ratings are key determinants of the pricing of sovereign bonds and sovereign spreads incorporate market participants' views of expected credit rating changes (Erb, Harvey & Viskanta, 2000). Sy (2001) studies the relationship between emerging market sovereign spreads and ratings on the performance of their long-term foreign currency denominated debt. Results indicate that sovereign spreads and ratings adjust differently depending on whether spreads are 'excessively high' or 'excessively low'. His chapter also indicates that significant deviations between market and rating agencies' views should result in further scrutiny of country and market fundamentals.

This gives rise to two important questions. First, what country fundamentals are crucial in influencing credit ratings? Second, can we determine the direction of causality between credit ratings and sovereign spreads? Cantor and Packer (1996) answer both these questions through analysing sovereign credit ratings assigned by Moody's Investor Services and Standard and Poor. The authors find six factors in determining a country's credit rating: 'per capita income, GDP growth, inflation, external debt, level of economic development, and default history'. In addition, in this study sovereign ratings have a strong effect on market yields. Ferrucci's study 'Empirical Determinants of Emerging Market Economies' Sovereign Bond Spreads' also reinforces Cantor and Packer's (1996) findings that debtor country's fundamentals and external liquidity conditions are important determinants of market spreads. Furthermore, market assessment of a country's creditworthiness is more broad based than a limited set of fundamentals. Moreover, the chapter shows that under certain conditions country fundamentals can have limited explanatory power in understanding spreads.

Combining Cantor and Packer's (1996) argument that sovereign ratings influence market yields and Ferrucci's (2003) ideas that country fundamentals can be of limited use in understanding spreads leads us to another important question, namely, do credit ratings effectively capture risk premia at different points in the business cycle? Gibson, Hall, and Tavlas (2012) take the case of the Greek financial crisis and the growing fiscal and current account deficits since euro-area entry in 2001. The authors investigate the extent to which credit ratings can capture these premia. The authors estimate a cointegrating relationship between the spreads and their long-term fundamental determinants. Comparing the spreads predicted by this relationship with actual spreads suggests that interest rate spreads did not adequately reflect these imbalances, with significant deviations between predicted and actual spreads. All three studies show that while standard economic fundamentals emphasized in the Washington Consensus significantly affect bond yield spreads, the market's attitude towards risk remains an important determinant.

Besides financial liberalization, a key component of the structural adjustment programme advocated by the Washington Consensus is competitive exchange rate policy and trade liberalization. This has garnered huge debate. A seminal piece covered in the volume is on expectations and exchange rate dynamics by Dornbusch (1976). The author theorizes that large fluctuations in exchange rates can be consistent with the formation of rational expectations. Dornbusch's (1976) model shows that in the short run a monetary expansion induces an immediate depreciation in the exchange rate and accounts for fluctuations in the exchange rate and terms of trade.

In addition to fluctuations in exchange rates as suggested by Dornbusch (1976), specific exchange rate regimes can make countries prone to endemic currency and banking crises. Putting exchange rate regimes on a spectrum, fixed exchange rates sit at one end, whereas floating exchange rates sit at the other extreme. In the middle lie intermediate policy regimes such as soft pegs. A wide body of literature has advocated for adopting either fixed or free exchange rate solutions since intermediate policy regimes can make countries more prone to financial crises (Angkinand & Willett, 2011). Calvo and Reinhart (2002) analyze the behaviour of exchange rates, reserves, monetary aggregates, interest rates, and commodity prices to ask an important question: do 'official labels' of exchange rate arrangements provide an adequate representation of actual country practice? Their findings show that there is a substantial difference between *de jure* and *de facto* exchange rate regimes. The authors term it as an almost epidemic sense of 'fear of floating' and show that many emerging market economies revert to a high degree of exchange rate inflexibility after crisis episodes.

Fischer (2001) also studies country vulnerability to crisis due to exchange rate regimes. He employs the same spectrum of exchange rates with fixed exchange rates at one end and floating exchange rates lying at the other extreme. He argues that the intent of adopting either corner solution or the 'bipolar view' is not to rule out everything but the extremes. Rather it is to show that a segment of that line representing a variety of soft pegging exchange rate arrangements is unsustainable. However, there are a wide variety of possible flexible rate regimes. In practice, cross-country experiences of adopting exchange rate regimes determined at least in part by market forces show huge variation. This is because market determined exchange rate regimes prescribed by the Washington Consensus depend, amongst others, on a deep and liquid foreign exchange market and a coherent policy of central bank intervention in the foreign exchange market (Duttagupta, Karacadag & Fernandez, 2006).

The foremost element of the Washington Consensus was the need to create economic stability by controlling inflation and reducing government budget deficits. Reduction of budget deficits would imply lower borrowing and hence improved macroeconomic fundamentals. However, some countries inherit a large stock of debt which causes them to resort to seeking new borrowing and leaving them highly indebted. This is referred to as a 'debt overhang', where countries have a large debt stock that creditors do not confidently expect to be fully repaid. Krugman (1988) analyzes the trade-off that creditors face in terms of either financing or forgiving a debt overhang. Creditors have two potential choices, either financing the country in the hope that it will eventually be able to repay its debt or to forgive, reducing the debt to a level that the country can repay. Krugman's chapter shows that the choice between financing and forgiveness represents a trade-off, which can be improved if both financing and forgiveness are contingent on exogenous states of nature.

Besides economic considerations, overarching political motivations also influence debt forgiveness. Neumayer (2002) analyzes factors determining the allocation of debt forgiveness giving key emphasis to governance. Results suggest that good governance standards are a significant factor in debt forgiveness. This sheds light on the market consensus about the widespread benefits of implementing economic reforms. Standard recommendations for economic liberalization and transition to a market economy focus on the simultaneous and instantaneous implementation of all relevant reforms (Funke, 1993). Martinelli and Tommasi (1997) present a model where policymakers face political constraints that make big-bang reforms the best and in some cases the only feasible strategy. They show that when governments are unable to pre-commit and societal interest groups have veto power, only far-reaching reforms (even if quite costly) have any hope of success. The model has explanatory power in helping to understand why in recent years several Latin American countries have opted for radical reform.

Radical reform may lead countries to become prone to excessive foreign borrowing. This can lead to a sharp withdrawal of foreign funds, decline in asset values, and economic downturns. While Chile, Mexico, and Argentina faced a depressive aftermath of reform programmes during the 1980s–90s, Indonesia, Malaysia, and Thailand had sizable current account deficits but did not experience any economic debacle. McKinnon and Pill (1997) investigate economies transitioning from economic repression to liberalization and explore when countries become vulnerable to over-borrowing. They emphasize the credibility of the reform process as a tool to ensure sustainability. Poor reform credibility and increased uncertainty of investment returns can result in capital markets malfunctioning or underperforming. The authors lay emphasis on regulations, specifically prudential banking regulations, that are beneficial in protecting financial systems from potential distress. Overall, institutional development is critical in determining how quickly and effectively countries can implement structural reforms.

Differential experiences of countries transitioning from economic repression to liberalization formed the fundamental motivation behind McKinnon and Pill's (1997) chapter. What is the causal factor behind disparate economic outcomes? Is it geography or institutions? Rodrik, Subramanian, and Trebbi's (2004) chapter asks this fundamental question and advocates for the overwhelming importance of institutional quality. Using instrumental variables for institutions and trade, their results show that once institutions are controlled for, conventional measures of geography and trade are almost always insignificant. Starting with the seminal piece by North and Weingast (1989), covered in Volume I, the role of institutions in economic development has been a subject of much debate. Engerman and Sokoloff (1994) emphasize that institutions are not *exogenous*. It is crucial to understand the sources of institutions in order to recognize their relation to development. Taking the case of Spanish colonies in Mexico and Peru and mainland North America, the authors argue that the roots of inequality lay in differences in initial factor endowments. Overall, differences in the degree of inequality in wealth, human capital, and political power accounts for how fundamental economic institutions evolved over time.

Rodrik, Subramanian, and Trebbi (2004) and Engerman and Sokoloff (1994) both analyze the importance of institutions in economic development. McKinnon and Pill's (1997) chapter also advocates the importance of regulatory institutions, in playing a crucial role towards ensuring financial stability. Ocampo (2003) shows that capital account volatility can be effectively managed through two complementary instruments; capital account regulations and counter-cyclical prudential regulation of domestic financial intermediaries. Capital flows are intimately associated with the business cycle. Introducing counter-cyclical elements into prudential regulation and supervision, together with stricter rules to prevent and reduce currency and maturity mismatches, can effectively diminish capital-account volatility. Hence, robust governance and regulatory frameworks are integral to countries undertaking structural reforms and becoming more market-oriented. However, cross-country institutional heterogeneity makes reform success limited.

In the aftermath of a financial crisis, there are vociferous debates on reforming global economic architecture to make crises less frequent and less deep. This volume covers the discussions that ensued post Asian Financial Crisis of 1997 and the Global Financial Crisis of 2007. Stiglitz (2000) takes the case of the Asian Financial Crisis of 1997 and discusses the manner in which hurriedly executed financial and capital market liberalization without putting in place an effective regulatory framework results in crises. Reviewing the arguments for capital market liberalization, he makes the case for intervention in short-term capital flows. He argues that some forms of intervention are likely to be welfare enhancing. This finding is in contrast with the policy prescription advocated by the Washington Consensus.

How successful has the policy set prescribed by the Washington Consensus been? In an article originally published in *The Financial Times* Naim (2002) took account of the Washington Consensus. Adherence to these principles promised imminent prosperity and a flood of foreign money and goods. In his own words, the Washington Consensus 'soon acquired a life of its own, becoming a brand name worldwide and used independently of its original intent and even of its content'. Politicians and multilateral institutions 'selling' the product had no interest in curbing illusions of prosperity or foreign money or, more importantly, nurturing realistic expectations of how quick, painless, and widespread the purported effect of these reforms would be.

Birdsall, de la Torre, and Caicedo (2010) take Naim's (2002) stance and argue that a complete mismatch existed between reformers' expectations and actual reforms in terms of growth, poverty reduction, and inequality. The authors assess three potential explanations for what went wrong with the Washington Consensus-style reform agenda. First, shortfalls existed in the implementation of reforms combined with impatience regarding their expected effects. Second, there were fundamental flaws in either the design, sequencing, or basic premises of the reform agenda. Lastly, the policy reform package of the Washington Consensus did not address volatility, institutional development, knowledge, and technological innovation and inequality.

Williamson (2000), the architect of the principles behind the Washington Consensus, reflects on the conceptual framework behind the consensus and how it evolved. He distinguishes between his original meaning as a summary of the lowest common denominator of policy advice addressed by the Washington-based institutions (including the World Bank) and the subsequent use of the term to signify neoliberal or market-fundamentalist policies. He argues that the ten policy principles could not be expected to provide an effective framework for combating poverty but that the original advice is still broadly valid. He argues that any policy manifesto designed to eliminate poverty needs to go beyond the original version but concludes by cautioning that no consensus on a wider agenda currently exists. In the aftermath of the Global Financial Crisis, there have been calls for a 'post-Washington Consensus'. Volume III explores what that might look like in practice.

References

Akinsola, F. A., & Odhiambo, N. M. (2017). The impact of financial liberalization on economic growth in sub-Saharan Africa. *Cogent Economics & Finance, 5*(1), 1338851.

Angkinand, A. P., & Willett, T. D. (2011). Exchange rate regimes and banking crises: the channels of influence investigated. *International Journal of Finance & Economics, 16*(3), 256–274.

Duttagupta, R., Karacadag, C., & Fernandez, G. C. (2006). *Moving to a flexible exchange rate: how, when, and how fast?* International Monetary Fund.

Erb, C. B., Harvey, C. R., & Viskanta, T. E. (2000). Understanding emerging market bonds. *Emerging Markets Quarterly, 4*, 7–24.

Funke, N. (1993). Timing and sequencing of reforms: competing views and the role of credibility. *Kyklos, 46*(3), 337–362.

Naim, M. (2002). Washington Consensus: a damaged brand. *Financial Times, 28.*

Neumayer, E. (2002). Is good governance rewarded? A cross-national analysis of debt forgiveness. *World Development, 30*(6), 913–930.

North, D. C., & Weingast, B. R. (1989). Constitutions and commitment: the evolution of institutions governing public choice in seventeenth-century England. *The Journal of Economic History, 49*(4), 803–832.

15

FINANCIAL DEVELOPMENT AND THE INSTABILITY OF OPEN ECONOMIES

Philippe Aghion, Philippe Bacchetta, and Abhijit Banerjee

Source: *NBER Working Paper* No. 10246 (January 2004).

ABSTRACT

This paper introduces a framework for analyzing the role of financial factors as a source of instability in small open economies. Our basic model is a dynamic open economy model with a tradeable good produced with capital and a country-specific factor. We also assume that firms face credit constraints, with the constraint being tighter at a lower level of financial development. A basic implication of this model is that economies at an intermediate level of financial development are more unstable than either very developed or very underdeveloped economies. This is true both in the sense that temporary shocks have large and persistent effects and also in the sense that these economies can exhibit cycles. Thus, countries that are going through a phase of financial development may become more unstable in the short run. Similarly, full capital account liberalization may destabilize the economy in economies at an intermediate level of financial development: phases of growth with capital inflows are followed by collapse with capital outflows. On the other hand, foreign direct investment does not destabilize.

1 Introduction

This paper introduces a framework for analyzing the role of financial factors as a source of instability in small open economies. Our basic model is a dynamic open economy model with a tradeable good produced with internationally mobile capital and a country- specific factor. Moreover, firms face financial constraints: the amount they can borrow is limited to μ times the amount of their current level of investible funds.[1] A high μ then represents an effective and developed financial sector while a low μ represents an underdeveloped one.

Our model can provide some answers to a number of important and rather basic questions. First, we show that it is economies at an intermediate level of financial development - rather than the very developed or underdeveloped - that are the most unstable. This is true both in the sense that temporary shocks will have large and persistent effects and also in the sense that these economies can exhibit stable limit cycles. Thus, countries going through a phase of financial development may become more unstable in the short run.

Second, the model allows us to examine the effects of financial liberalization on the stability of the macroeconomy. Once again it turns out that the interesting economies are the ones at an intermediate level of financial development. In these economies, full financial liberalization (i.e., opening the domestic market to foreign capital flows) may actually destabilize, inducing chronic phases of growth with capital inflows followed by collapse with capital flight. On the other hand, foreign direct investment never destabilizes since foreign direct investors come in with their own credit—their ability to invest is unrelated to the state of the domestic economy. Overall, this suggests that economies at an intermediate stage of financial development should consider carefully how they liberalize their capital account. Allowing foreign direct investment while initially restricting portfolio investment may sometimes be a reasonable approach.

Third, our model allows us to assess the macroeconomic effects of specific shocks to the financial sector such as overlending by banks (leading to a phase of bank failures) or overreaction by investors to a change in fundamentals.[2] Once again, our model predicts these shocks to have their most persistent effects when financial markets are at an intermediate stage of development.

The basic mechanism underlying our model is a combination of two forces: on one side, greater investment leads to greater output and ceteris paribus, higher profits. Higher profits improve creditworthiness and fuel borrowing that leads to greater investment. Capital flows into the country to finance this boom. At the same time, the boom in investment increases the demand for the country-specific factor and raises its price relative to the output good (unless the supply of that factor is extremely elastic). This rise in input prices leads to lower profits and therefore, reduced creditworthiness, less borrowing and less investment, and a fall in aggregate output. Of course, once investment falls all these forces get reversed and eventually initiate another boom. It is this endogenous instability which causes shocks to have persistent effects and in more extreme cases leads to limit cycles.

The reason why an intermediate level of financial development is important for this result is easy to comprehend: at very high levels of financial development, most firms' investment is not constrained by cash flow so shocks to cash flow are irrelevant. On the other hand, at very low levels of financial development, firms cannot borrow very much in any case and therefore their response to cash-flow shocks will be rather muted - extra cash means more investment but only a little more. Therefore shocks will die out without causing any great turmoil. It is then at intermediate levels of financial development that shocks to cash flow will have an effect intense enough to be a source of instability.

This last argument also helps us understand why opening the economy to foreign capital may destabilize: essentially, the response of an economy with a closed capital market to a cash flow shock is limited since only so much capital is available to entrepreneurs. Additional funding sources in an open economy potentially increases the response to a shock and therefore the scope for volatility.

The basic mechanics of instability described here - an increase in input price leading to a profit squeeze and eventual output collapse - have been documented in a number of countries. For example, in the years leading up to the crisis of the early 1980s in the Southern Cone countries, there is evidence that profits in the tradeable sector sharply deteriorated due to a rise in domestic input prices (see Galvez and Tybout, 1985, Petrei and Tybout, 1985, or De Melo, Pascale and Tybout, 1985). Moreover, ample anecdotal evidence supports the impact of 'competitiveness' (e.g., a real appreciation) on the financial conditions of firms.

The dynamic impact of a liberalization predicted by the model is also consistent with the experience of several emerging market countries that have liberalized, in particular in Southeast Asia and Latin America, but also in some European countries. In the years prior to their respective crises, these economies had been going through a process of rapid financial sector liberalization, which facilitated borrowing by domestic firms. Partly as a result of this liberalization, capital flowed into these economies in large quantities, allowing rapid growth in lending and a boom in investment. However, episodes of large capital inflows have often been associated with growing imbalances, such as a real currency appreciation[3], an increase in real estate prices (e.g., see Guerra de Luna, 1997), or an increase in non-performing loans (see World Bank, 1997, p. 255). When the crisis came, most of these forces got reversed - capital flowed out, the currency collapsed, real estate prices dropped, lending stopped, and investment collapsed.[4]

It is however important to emphasize that the goal of this paper is not to explain exactly what happened in some particular country, but rather to propose a unified macroeconomic framework that gives a central role to financial constraints and financial development. There are certainly a number of strands of the existing literature anticipating a significant part of what we have done here. Gertler and Rogoff (1990) study an open economy model with credit-market imperfections. However, they do not consider business cycle fluctuations.[5] The idea that financial constraints on firms can play a role in the propagation of the business cycle was modeled in Bernanke and Gertler (1989). Subsequent work by Kiyotaki and Moore (1997), Aghion, Banerjee, and Piketty (1999) and Azariadis and Smith (1998) have shown that these constraints can lead to oscillations, though only in the context of a closed economy. However, none of these papers study the effects of opening up the domestic financial sector to foreign capital flows and none of them, except Aghion, Banerjee, and Piketty (1999), focus on the level of financial development as a factor determining the extent of instability. While the model's structure is in a spirit similar to Aghion, Banerjee, and Piketty (1999), this paper differs in key respects. First, the economic mechanisms at work are of a different nature. Second, the economic questions and the types of policy shocks we focus on are entirely different. Finally, at a methodological level, unlike Aghion, Banerjee, and Piketty (1999) we show that our results are robust to the introduction of forward-looking entrepreneurs.

A separate literature focuses on the case for free capital mobility. Policy interest in the debate has been aroused by the recent, rather mixed, experience of a number of countries that have liberalized their capital account.[6] However, a number of important aspects, including the implications of liberalization on volatility, have not been widely studied.[7] More importantly, none of these papers attempt to relate the effect of liberalization to the functioning of the domestic financial sector.

Finally a number of recent papers stress that specific shocks to the financial sector, such as those brought on by policy mistakes, herd behavior, panics, or corruption in the financial sector, may lead to crises in the real economy. While accepting the validity of these arguments, we feel these models suffer from ignoring some of the interactions between the financial sector and the rest of the economy. As our model makes clear, volatile behavior may arise even in the absence of such shocks; while on the other hand, the presence of such shocks does not automatically imply they will have large and persistent real effects.

The paper is organized as follows. Section 2 represents the core of the paper, with a description of a basic version of the open-economy model and a characterization of the conditions under which macroeconomic volatility arises. Section 3 presents the model under more general assumptions and provides numerical simulations to assess the plausibility for volatility. Section 4 analyzes the impact of a capital account liberalization and contrasts the stabilizing effect of unrestricted FDI with the potentially destabilizing effects of either foreign *indirect* investments or *restricted* foreign direct investments. Section 5 describes various extensions and draws some tentative policy conclusions.

2 The Basic Mechanism

For pedagogical purposes we consider first a simple model with constant saving rates and a Leontief technology involving a inelastic supply of the country-specific factor. In Section 3, we consider a more general model with three main extensions: first the supply of domestic input is elastic; second, the production technology is more general; and third, saving decisions result from intertemporal utility maximization.

2.1 A Simple Framework

We consider a small open economy with a single tradeable good produced with capital and a country-specific factor. One should typically think of this factor as input services such as (skilled) labor or real estate. We take the output good as the numeraire and denote by p the price of the country-specific factor when expressed in units of the output good. The relative price p can also be interpreted as the real exchange rate. In this basic framework we assume that the supply of the country-specific factor is inelastic and equal to Z.

For the sake of presentation, in this subsection we also assume that all agents *save* a fixed fraction $(1 - \alpha)$ of their total end-of-period wealth and thus consume a fixed fraction α. The intertemporal decisions of lenders are of no consequence for output in such an open economy since investors can borrow in international capital markets. They will, however, affect net capital flows.[8]

There are two distinct categories of individuals in the economy. First, the *lenders,* who cannot directly invest in production, but can lend their initial wealth endowments at the international market-clearing interest rate r. Second, the *entrepreneurs* (or *borrowers*) who have the opportunity to invest in production. There is a continuum of lenders and borrowers and their number is normalized to one for both categories.

Output y is given by the following production function:

$$y = \min\left(\frac{K}{a}, z\right),\qquad\qquad(1)$$

where $\frac{1}{a} > r$, i.e., we assume that productivity is larger than the world interest rate. K denotes the current level of capital and z denotes the level of the country-specific input. With perfect capital markets, investment would simply be determined by the international interest rate r.

Credit-market imperfections: Due to standard agency (moral hazard) considerations, an entrepreneur with initial wealth W^B can borrow at most μW^B. The presence of capital market imperfections implies that entrepreneurs cannot borrow up to the net present value of their project; they can only borrow an amount proportional to their current cash-flow (as in Bernanke-Gertler (1989)). The proportionality coefficient, or *credit multiplier* $\mu > 0$, reflects the level of financial development in the domestic economy. In the extreme case where $\mu = 0$, the credit market collapses and investors can only invest their own wealth. Higher values of μ correspond to higher levels of financial development.

A simple justification for relating the capital market to the level of financial development and basing it on moral hazard by the borrower, can be found in Holmstrom-Tirole (1996) and in Aghion-Banerjee-Piketty (1999). In general μ will depend on the rate of interest being charged, which in turn implies a constant credit multiplier in a model where the interest rate is given by the world capital markets. However, in section 4 and the Appendix we compare our basic model with a model with a closed capital market where the interest rate is endogenously determined by domestic investment demand and domestic savings supply. Yet, for convenience, we shall maintain the assumption of a μ that does not depend on the interest rate in that section as well. As shown in Aghion-Banerjee-Piketty

5

(1999), this corresponds to a particular parametrization of the more general model of the credit market presented in that paper. Our results would only be stronger if we allowed the usual negative relation between the interest rate and μ.[9]

Production decision: Denote by L the amount borrowed. The funds available to an entrepreneur with total initial wealth W^B are $I = W^B + L$. When the credit constraint is binding, $I = (1 + \mu) W^B$. Entrepreneurs will choose the level of the country-specific factor z, with corresponding investment $K = I - p \cdot z$, to maximize current profits. Given the above Leontief technology, the optimum involves $z = K/a$, so that:

$$I \quad p \cdot z = a \cdot z \tag{2}$$

Depending on the level of entrepreneurs' wealth, there are three cases:

i) *Binding credit constraint and $p = 0 \cdot W^B$* is low so that the credit constraint is binding ($L = \mu W^B$) and $K/a < Z$. In this case, there is an excess supply of the country-specific input. This immediately gives us $p = 0$. Output at date t is then given by:

$$y_t = \frac{K_t}{a} = \frac{1}{a}(1 + \mu) W_t^B.$$

ii) *Binding credit constraint and $p > 0 \cdot W^B$* is low so that $L = \mu W^B$, but $K/a \geq Z$. Thus, there is excess demand for the immobile factor. Therefore $p > 0$ and output is determined in equilibrium by the supply of the country-specific input: $y_t = z$. From (2) and the definition of I, the equilibrium price of the country-specific input is given by:

$$p_t = \frac{(1 + \mu) W_t^B - aZ}{Z}. \tag{3}$$

Notice that in this case the entrepreneur's entire wealth is invested in the domestic technology since it has returns higher than the world interest rate, i.e., $y - rL > rW^B$.[10]

iii) *Unconstrained entrepreneurs.* W^B is large enough so that $L < \mu W^B$. As in ii), $p > 0$ and $y_t = z$, but p is not affected by the level of investment. When W^B is large, entrepreneurs borrow until profits equal the international interest rate: $y - rL = rW^B$, i.e., until $y = rI$. This determines the maximum price level. Hence, $I = Z/r$ so that the price is given by:

$$p_t = \frac{1}{r} - a.$$

The equilibrium price p_t, i.e., the real exchange rate, which is a positive function of W^B, is the key variable whose movements over time will produce volatility.

The Timing of Events: The timing of events within each period t is the following. Investment, borrowing and lending, and the payment of the country-specific factor services $p \cdot Z$ by entrepreneurs to the owners of that factor, take place at the *beginning* of the period (which we denote by t^-). Everything else occurs at the *end* of the period (which we denote by t^+): the returns to investments are realized; borrowers repay their debt, rL, to lenders; and finally, agents make their consumption and savings decisions determining in turn the initial wealth of borrowers at the beginning of the next period (i.e., at $(t+1)^-$).

Dynamic Equations: Now that we have laid out the basic model, we can analyze the aggregate dynamics of the economy and in particular investigate why open economies with imperfect credit markets may experience macroeconomic volatility. Since both I and p depend on entrepreneurs' wealth W^B, output does too. Thus, output dynamics are determined by the evolution of entrepreneurs' behavior. Let W^B_{t+1} denote the disposable wealth of entrepreneurs (borrowers) at the beginning of period $t+1$. The dynamic evolution of W^B (and therefore of investment and total output) between two successive periods is simply described by the equation:

$$W^B_{t+1} = (1-\alpha)\left[e + y_t - r\mu W^B_t\right] \tag{4}$$

where ε is an exogenous income in terms of output goods, $yt = \min(I/a, Z)$ is output in period t (also equal to the gross revenues of entrepreneurs during that period). The expression in brackets is the *net* end-of-period t revenue of entrepreneurs. The net disposable wealth of entrepreneurs at the beginning of period $t+1$ is what remains of this net end-of-period return after consumption, hence the multiplying factor $(1-\alpha)$ on the right-hand-side of equation (4).

Entrepreneurs invest and borrow only if their profits are larger than or equal to the international return. When μ or W^B are large, entrepreneurs invest only up the point where $y - rL = rW^B$. Any remaining wealth is invested at the international market rate. In this case, no pure profits are earned from production and the evolution of wealth is simply given by:

$$W^B_{t+1} = (1-\alpha)\left[e + rW^B_t\right]. \tag{5}$$

Thus, the dynamics are fully described either by difference equation (4) or by difference equation (5).

2.2 Volatility

When the dynamic evolution of domestic entrepreneurs' wealth is described by equation (4), an increase in entrepreneurs' wealth $W_t{}^B$ at the beginning of period t has an ambiguous effect on next period's wealth W^B_{t+1}. This is due to the fact that the amount of invested wealth itself depends *negatively* on the input price p, whilst p depends *positively* on current wealth. Using the fact that:

$$(a + p_t) y_t = (1 + \mu) W_t^B,$$

we have:

$$\frac{dy_t}{dW_t^B} = \frac{(1 + \mu)}{a + p_t} - \frac{y_t}{a + p_t} \frac{\partial p_t}{\partial W_t^B}.$$

Then, from (4), the impact of last period wealth on current end of period wealth can be decomposed into two effects:

$$\frac{dW_{t+1}^B}{dW_t^B} = (1 - \alpha) \left[\underbrace{\frac{1 + \mu}{a + p_t} - r\mu}_{\text{wealth effect}} - \underbrace{\frac{y_t}{a + p_t} \frac{\partial p_t}{\partial W_t^B}}_{\text{price effect}} \right]$$

On the one hand, there is a positive *wealth effect* of current wealth on future wealth: for a given price of the country-specific factor p_t, a higher inherited wealth W_t^B from period $(t-1)$ means a higher level of investment $(1 + \mu) W_t^B$ in period t which, all else equal, should produce higher revenues and thus higher wealth W_{t+1}^B at the beginning of period $t+1$. On the other hand, there is a negative *price effect* of current wealth on future wealth: more investment in period t also implies a greater demand for the country-specific factor to thus raise its price p_t during that period. This, in turn, has a detrimental effect on period t revenues and therefore on the wealth W_{t+1}^B at the beginning of period $t+1$.

With the above Leontief specification, the price effect is eliminated whenever the current wealth W_t^B is so small that current investment cannot absorb the total supply of the country-specific factor. In this case $p_t \equiv 0$ and:

$$W_{t+1}^B = (1 - \alpha) \left[e + \left\{ \frac{1 + \mu}{a} - r\mu \right\} W_t^B \right], \tag{6}$$

so that $dW_{t+1}^B / dW_t^B > 0$.

On the other hand, the price effect dominates when the current wealth W_t^B is sufficiently large that current investment exhausts the total supply of the country-specific factor. In this case, we simply have:

$$W_{t+1}^B = (1 - \alpha) \left[e + Z - r\mu W_t^B \right], \tag{7}$$

so that $dW_{t+1}^B / dW_t^B < 0$.

Figure 1 shows the relationship between W_{t+1}^B and W_t^B in this basic Leontief setup. This relationship is represented by three segments corresponding to the three cases described in 2.1. The first one is the upward sloping curve described by (6) for $W < \underline{W} = \dfrac{az}{1+\mu}$; this is the case where the wealth effect dominates as $p=0$. The second segment, for $\underline{W} < W < \overline{W} = \dfrac{z}{(1+\mu)r}$; is described by (7); in this case, the price effect always dominates. Finally, the third segment $(W > \overline{W})$ represents equation (5) where entrepreneurs are not credit-constrained. As drawn in the figure, the 45° line intersects the $W_{t+1}^B(W_t^B)$ curve at the point $\hat{W}$ which lies in the second segment. This intersection can also be in either of the other two segments. It will be in the first segment when $\dfrac{(1-\alpha)e}{1-(1-\alpha)\left\{\dfrac{1+\mu}{a}-r\mu\right\}}$, the fixed point of equation (6), is less than $\underline{W}$. Since $\dfrac{(1-\alpha)e}{1-(1-\alpha)\left\{\dfrac{1+\mu}{a}-r\mu\right\}}$ is increasing in μ while $\underline{W}$ is decreasing, it is clear that this can only happen when μ is very small. On the other

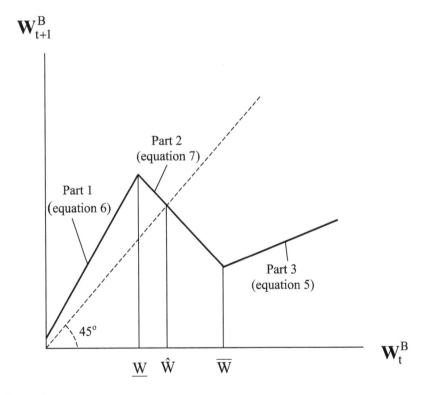

Figure 1

9

hand, the intersection will be in the third segment when the fixed point of equation (5), $\frac{(1-\alpha)e}{1-(1-\alpha)r} > \overline{W} = \frac{Z}{(1+\mu)r}$. This will only happen when μ is sufficiently large. For intermediate values of p, corresponding to an intermediate level of financial development, the case is depicted in Figure 1, the one case where the economy does not converge monotonically to its steady state.

In this case there are two possibilities—*short run fluctuations,* represented by oscillations that eventually converge to the steady state, $\hat{W}$, and *long run volatility,* represented by a system which does not converge to a steady state but instead continues to oscillate forever. A necessary condition for the existence of such a limit cycle is that the steady state at $\hat{W}$ be unstable, true only when the slope of the $W_{t+1}^B(W_t^B)$ schedule at $\hat{W}$ is less than -1, corresponding to when $\hat{W}$ lies in the second segment of that schedule. Thus, for *long run volatility* to occur, we must have $\underline{W} < \hat{W} < \overline{W}$ and $-(1-\alpha)\mu r < -1$.

If these conditions hold, one can easily derive additional sufficient conditions under which long-run volatility actually occurs. For example, a two-cycle (W_1, W_2) will satisfy:[11]

$$W_1 = \frac{(1-a)(e+Z)}{1+r\mu(1-\alpha)^2\left(e+\dfrac{1+\mu}{a}-r\mu\right)}; \quad W_2 = \frac{(1-\alpha)^2\left(e+\dfrac{1+\mu}{a}-r\mu\right)(e+Z)}{1+r\mu(1-\alpha)^2\left(e+\dfrac{1+\mu}{a}-r\mu\right)}$$

with $W_1 < \underline{W} < W_2 < \overline{W}$. This two-cycle will be stable whenever $(1-\alpha)^2 r\mu\left(\dfrac{1+\mu}{a}-r\mu\right) < 1$. Conditions for the existence of longer (and more plausible) cycles can be derived using standard techniques. The dynamic simulations will show that the fluctuations can be complex since wealth can fluctuate between the constrained (the first two segments in Figure 1) and the unconstrained (the third segment) regions.

Intuitively, the basic mechanism underlying this cyclicality can be described as follows: during a boom the demand for the domestic country-specific factor goes up as (high yield) investments increase, thus raising its price. This higher price will eventually squeeze investors' borrowing capacity and therefore the demand for country-specific factors. At this point, the economy experiences a slump and two things occur: the relative price of the domestic factor collapses, while a fraction of the factor available remains unused since there is not enough investment. The collapse in the factor price thus corresponds to a contraction of real output. Of course, the low factor price will eventually lead to higher profits and therefore to more investment. A new boom then begins.

The reason why the level of financial development matters is also quite intuitive: economies at a low level of financial development have low levels of investment and do not generate enough demand to push up the price of the country specific factor while economies at a very high level of development have sufficient demand for that factor to keep its price positive.

2.3 Discussion

Although the above framework is extremely simple, it generates a number of predictions for empirical analysis on emerging markets. In particular, our model predicts: (i) that the investment to GDP and private credit to GDP ratios should increase during a "lending boom";[12] (ii) that lending booms are times of net capital inflows; (iii) that the real exchange rate (p_t in our model) should increase during a lending boom; (iv) that the fraction of defaulting loans should increase towards the end of a lending boom (in a straightforward extension of our model with uncertainty and defaults, which we develop in section 5.1 below). Recent work by Gourinchas, Valdes, and Landerretche (2001) provides an interesting cross-country study of lending booms and examine the pattern of a set a macroeconomic indicators around these booms.[13] The behavior of these indicators is shown to be fully consistent with the above predictions. In particular, by comparing with "tranquil periods", Gourinchas et al. show that during lending booms the output gap is higher, the investment/GDP ratio increases, the proportion of short term debt increases, the current account worsens, the real exchange rate appreciates, especially at the end of the boom period.

When lending declines, all these movements are reversed. In particular, the fact that investment follows a credit expansion and is sharply procyclical is fully consistent with our approach.

The above model is very simple, but simplicity and tractability always come at a cost. In particular, the analysis has been drastically simplified by assuming a Leontief technology, a constant savings rate, and an inelastic supply of the non-tradeable input.

In the next section we relax these three assumptions. Moreover, in the concluding section we discuss mechanisms that lead to a procyclical μ and therefore amplify the underlying volatility.

An important question is whether the basic mechanism leading to volatility depends on the assumption of discrete time. It is well known that volatility occurs more easily under discrete time. However, it is not difficult to show that a similar mechanism can occur under continuous time. First, this can happen with a system of two differential equations. For example, if domestic lenders are also workers paid by the entrepreneurs and use the local input for their consumption, then a second dynamic equation describing the evolution of domestic lenders' wealth must be added to the dynamic equation describing the evolution of domestic entrepreneurs' wealth. If domestic lenders' demand for the local input is not too price elastic, we still get the same type of volatility as in the basic model with a single difference equation. Second, Bruchez (2001) shows that if the lags between the wealth realization in period t and the wealth investment in period $t + 1$ differ across firms, equation (4) becomes an ordinary differential equation that can also exhibit periodic solutions.[14]

3 Assessing Plausibility: Some Simulation Results

The main purpose of this section is to ask whether the analytical conclusions derived in the previous section are empirically plausible. The simulation results are again focused on the possibility of - and the conditions for - long run volatility in economies at intermediate levels of financial development.[15]

We shall first extend our basic model in three respects: first, we allow for elastic supply of the non-tradable factor; second, we replace the Leontief technology by a more general CES technology, thereby allowing for substitutability between the tradable and non-tradable factors; third, we replace the constant savings rate assumption of the basic model with intertemporal utility maximization by entrepreneurs. The implications of each of these, are analyzed in detail in Aghion, Bacchetta, and Banerjee (2001b). Our main conclusion there is that for endogenous fluctuations to obtain in equilibrium, we need: (i) enough inelasticity in the supply of the non-tradable input; (ii) enough complementarity between the two inputs; (iii) a sufficiently low intertemporal elasticity of substitution between current and future consumption. In the simulations presented in this section, the three extensions are being simultaneously considered.

3.1 Generalizing our framework

We modify our previous model by assuming:

1. *Elastic Supply of the Country-Specific Factor:* we relax the assumption of a fixed supply of the country-specific factor and assume that Z is instead produced by (domestic) lenders using the tradeable good at a cost $c(Z) = \varphi Z^v$, where $v > 1$. Maximization of a domestic lender's profit $pZ - \varphi Z^v$, yields the optimal supply of the country-specific factor:

$$Z = \left(\frac{p}{\varphi v} \right)^{\frac{1}{v-1}}. \tag{8}$$

2. *CES Technology:* we replace the Leontief technology by a CES production function, with $f(K, z) = A(K^\theta + \gamma z^\theta)^{1/\theta}$, with $A > r$ and $\gamma > 0$.[16] The parameter θ determines the elasticity of substitution between K and z (we assume $\theta < 1$ for concavity). This CES specification includes as special cases, both the Cobb-Douglas technology when $\theta = 0$, and a Leontief technology when $\theta \to -\infty$.

3. *Optimal Savings by Entrepreneurs*: we replace the constant savings rate assumption in our basic model by the assumption that entrepreneurs are infinitely-lived and maximize their net present utility of consumption, with instantaneous utility being given by: $u(C^B) = C^{B(1-\rho)}/(1-\rho)$, where $1/\rho$ is the elasticity of intertemporal substitution and $\rho > 0$. Then domestic entrepreneurs solve:

$$\max \sum_{t=0}^{\infty} \beta^t u\left(C_t^B\right) \quad s.t. \quad C_t^B = \Pi_t - W_{t+1}^B$$

The first order conditions for this problem give us:

$$\frac{C_{t+1}^B}{C_t^B} = \left(\beta M_{t+1}\right)^{\frac{1}{\rho}} \tag{9}$$

where $M_t = \Pi_t / W_t^B$. It is clear from equation (9) that the ratio $\frac{c_{t+1}^B}{c_t^B}$ approaches 1 as ρ increases. This implies that an increase in ρ (a reduction in the elasticity of intertemporal substitution) reduces consumption changes and gives correspondingly larger intertemporal savings changes, i.e., savings become more pro-cyclical over time. This, in turn, will tend to amplify the cycle as the price of the country-specific input increases more sharply during a boom. True, to the extent that the returns to savings are higher when the economy is in a slump (slumps are typically followed by periods with high investment profitability), there should be a greater tendency to save more in a slump, thereby attenuating the cyclical variations. However, this latter effect is weaker, the higher the cost of intertemporal substitution (i.e., with a larger p).[17]

3.2 Simulations

We present our simulation results by successively varying three parameters: i) the elasticity of substitution between capital and the other factor in the production function, measured by θ; ii) the intertemporal elasticity of substitution $1/\rho$; (iii) the elasticity of country-specific factor supply as measured by v. The other parameters are taken to be constant in these simulations, and we fix them at empirically plausible values. We set the gross interest rate $r = 1.02$ and the productivity factor $A = 1.5$. Whenever it is fully inelastic we set the total supply of the immobile factor $Z = 100$ and its weight in the production function $r = 1$ (these two parameters have little influence on the simulation results). The discount rate of entrepreneurs is $\beta = 0.9$, a value implying that domestic entrepreneurs are impatient relative to the interest rate. Finally, we set the credit multiplier $\mu = 4$, a value implying a cash flow-capital ratio of 0.2 when firms are credit-constrained, a plausible number even for US firms (see Fazzari, Hubbard, and Petersen (1988)). The values considered for θ lie between -0.5 and -4; those for v lie between 4.33 and 7.66 corresponding to elasticities $(1/(v-1))$ of 15 and 30 percent; and those for p are between 0.5 and 10. In all simulations, we assume $e=0$.

In each case, we consider the dynamic impact on output of a negative shock that makes wealth fall by 1% below the steady-state wealth. We normalize output so that it is initially equal to 100 and we look at the dynamic evolution of output over 30 periods after the shock. Figures 2 and 3c and 3d display the simulations in the log utility case where $\rho=1$. It can easily be shown (see the working paper version) that this case is equivalent to the constant savings rate economy analyzed in the previous section.[18]

Figure 2 presents the log utility case with a fixed supply of the country specific factor. The diagrams show four cases corresponding to different values of input substitutability θ, each leading to a different dynamic path. In Figure 2a, where $\theta=-0.5$, there is no instability and output converges smoothly to its initial level. When θ decreases to -1.5 (Figure 2b), output still converges but includes oscillations.

Figure 2c shows a two-cycle, which arises when $\theta=-2$. Finally, when $\theta=-4$ (Figure 2d), more complex dynamics arise due to 'regime switching': large increases in wealth lead the system to the unconstrained region (the third segment in Figure 1), but the system returns to the constrained region since $r<1$. Notice that the fluctuations in 2c and 2d are larger than the initial shock, so that small shocks are amplified (actually infinitesimal shocks would lead to similar fluctuations).

In Figures 3a and 3b, we assume that $\theta=-4$ with an inelastic supply of the country- specific factor, while we depart from log utility by varying the intertemporal elasticity parameter ρ. With a lower elasticity of intertemporal substitution, $\rho=10$, the system tends to be even more unstable and switches more easily across regimes. When entrepreneurs are more ready to substitute intertemporally, which in this figure corresponds to the case where $\rho=0.5$, regime switches are less frequent. The most important conclusion from Figure 3, however, is that the long-run instability results established under constant savings rates (or with optimal intertemporal savings in the log utility case), carry over to a wide range of elasticities of intertemporal substitution.

Finally, in Figures 3c and 3d we show simulations with an elastic supply of the country-specific factor, assuming $\theta=-4$ and log utility. Obviously, with an elastic supply there is less scope for fluctuations. For example, Figure 3d shows that with a supply elasticity of 30 percent fluctuations die out rapidly. However, with an elasticity of 15 percent, which appears reasonable in the short run, we still have fluctuations with a two-cycle.

Thus, even though our model is highly stylized, long-run output volatility and/ or large amplification of shocks occur for empirically reasonable parameter values and are not confined to one particular functional form.

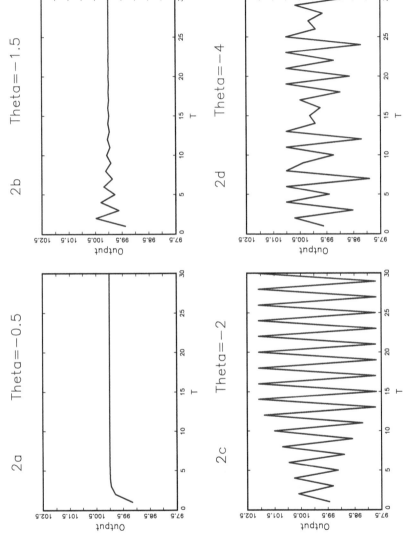

Figure 2

15

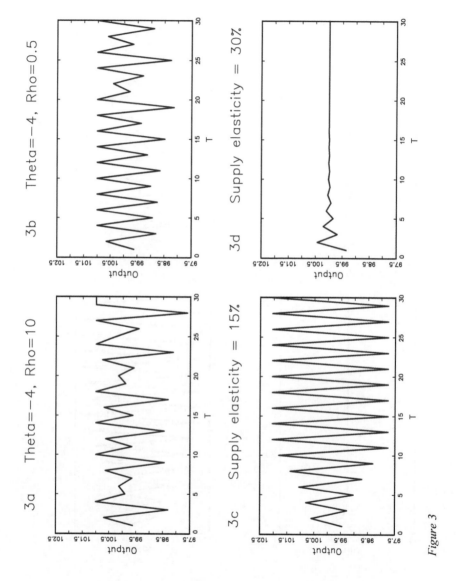

Figure 3

16

4 Financial Liberalization and Instability

The previous analysis shows that a fully open economy with imperfect credit markets can exhibit volatility or a cycle. We show in this section that the same economy can be stable if it is closed to capital flows or if only foreign investment (FDI) is allowed. Thus, a full liberalization to capital movements may destabilize an economy: while it stabilizes the real interest rate, it also amplifies the fluctuations in the price of the country-specific factor. This in turn, increases the volatility in firms' cash-flows and therefore aggregate output. We first consider the case of an economy that opens up to foreign lending. Then, we examine the case of FDI, where foreign investors are equity holders and are fully informed about domestic firms. Even though the results are valid with general production functions, we present the Leontief case for pedagogical reasons.

4.1 Liberalizing Foreign Lending

We consider an economy with low domestic savings, with the Leontief technology specified in Section 2.1, and we first assume that this economy is *not* open to foreign borrowing and lending (this closed economy is described in details in Appendix A). In that case, at each date, the current wealth of domestic lenders W^L matters since domestic investment is constrained by domestic savings $W^B + W^L$. Now suppose that the initial levels of wealth held by entrepreneurs and domestic lenders, W^B and W^L respectively, are sufficiently small so that initially $p_0 = 0$ This corresponds to a situation where domestic entrepreneurs cannot exhaust the supply of country-specific inputs. Let us also assume that at date 0 domestic savings $W_0^B + W_0^L$ are less than the investment capacity $(1 + \mu)W_0^B$.[19] If $\mu > 1$ there will then be excess investment capacity in following periods as long as p_t remains equal to zero. To see this, note that the domestic interest rate r_t, determined in a closed economy by the comparison between W_t^L and μW_t^B, is such that entrepreneurs are indifferent between borrowing and lending, that is: $r_t = \frac{1}{a}$ in the Leontief case. Therefore, if $p_t = 0$ and $W_t^L < \mu W_t^B$, we have:

$$W_{t+1}^B = (1-\alpha)\left[e + \frac{1}{a}W_t^B\right]$$

$$\text{and } W_{t+1}^L = (1-\alpha)\left[e + \frac{1}{a}W_t^L\right]$$

so that $W_t^L < \mu W_t^B$ implies that: $W_{t+1}^L < \mu W_{t+1}^B$ and therefore $r_{t+1} = \frac{1}{a}$. In Appendix A we provide sufficient conditions under which $p_t = 0$ and $r_t = \frac{1}{a}$ for all t. Under these conditions a entrepreneurs' wealth will grow as the (low) rate $\frac{1-\alpha}{a}$, since it is constrained by the (low) level of domestic savings, and the $W_{t+1}^B(W_t^B)$ schedule will intersect the 45° line on its first branch along which $p_t = 0$. This, in turn, implies that there will be no persistent fluctuations in this closed economy.

What happens if this economy is fully opened up to foreign borrowing and lending? The interest rate will be fixed at the international level r. By itself, this could only help stabilize any closed economy that otherwise might (temporarily) fluctuate in reaction to interest rate movements. However, the opening up of the economy to foreign lending also brings net capital inflows as investors satisfy their excess funds demand in international capital markets. The corresponding rise in borrowing in turn increases the scope for bidding up the price of the country-specific factor, thereby inducing permanent fluctuations in p, W^B and aggregate output.

Figure 4 presents an illustration of a liberalization in the Leontief case. The wealth schedule shifts up after a capital account liberalization. $\widehat{W}^B$ refers to the stable steady-state level of borrowers' wealth before the economy opens up to foreign borrowing and lending. After the liberalization W^B progressively increases as capital inflows allow investors to increase their borrowing, investments and profits. During the first two periods following the liberalization, the demand for the country-specific factor remains sufficiently low that $p = 0$. In period 3 (at W_3^B) p increases, but we still have growth. However, in period 4 (at W_4^B) the price effect of the liberalization becomes sufficiently strong as to squeeze investors' net worth, thereby bringing on a recession. At that point, aggregate lending drops, capital flows out and the real exchange depreciates (p drops). The resulting gain in competitiveness allows firms to rebuild their net worth so that growth can eventually resume. The economy ends up experiencing permanent fluctuations of the kind described in the previous section.

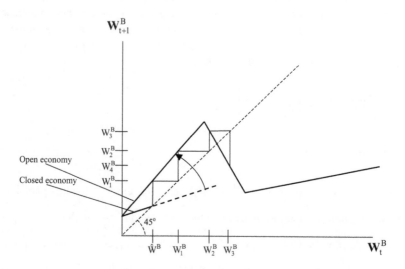

Figure 4

We should stress that the dynamics in Figure 4 occurs only for *intermediate* levels of financial development. As we argued in Section 2, with a large μ there is no volatility in an open economy, as it is the third segment of the curve that cuts the 45° line.[20] When $\mu = 0$, financial opening will not help investment and no capital inflow will occur, so there will be no upward pressure on the price of the country-specific input.[21] The above example therefore suggests that it might be desirable for a country to increase its μ, i.e., to develop its domestic financial sector *before* fully opening up to foreign lending.

4.2 Foreign Direct Investment

Whilst a full liberalization to foreign lending can have destabilizing effects on economies with intermediate levels of financial development, those economies are unlikely to become volatile as a result of opening up to foreign *direct* investment alone. We distinguish FDI from other financial flows by assuming that it is part of firms' equity and that FDI investors have full information about firms.[22] Furthermore, we first concentrate on the benchmark case where the supply of FDI is infinitely elastic at some fixed price greater than the world interest rate, say equal to $r + \delta$.[23]

Starting from a situation in which domestic cash flows are small so that domestic investment cannot fully absorb the supply of country-specific factors, foreign direct investors are likely to enter in order to profit from the low price of the country-specific factors. This price will eventually increase and may even fluctuate as a result of FDI. But these price fluctuations will only affect the distribution of profits between domestic and foreign investors, not aggregate output. For example, in the Leontief case with FDI, aggregate output will stabilize at a level equal to the supply of factor resources Z, whereas the same economy may end up being destabilized if fully open to foreign *portfolio* investment (i.e., to foreign lending).

Consider a closed Leontief economy open to foreign *direct* investment only. Assume also that W^L is large enough so that firms can still borrow their desired amount domestically (otherwise investment is still constrained by savings and the scope for fluctuations is much smaller). Then FDI will flow into the economy as long as the rate of return on that investment remains greater than or equal to $r + \delta$. Thus, if F denotes the net inflow of direct investment, in equilibrium we obtain the free-entry condition:

$$F > 0 \Rightarrow R = r + \delta,$$

where $R = \frac{y - \tilde{r}L}{W^B + F}$ is the net rate of return on foreign direct investment and $\tilde{r}$ is the domestic interest rate. If domestic savings are less than the investment capacity of domestic entrepreneurs (i.e., $W^L < \mu W^B$), we would have $\tilde{r} = \frac{1}{a}$. However, as domestic savings exceed the investment capacity of domestic entrepreneurs, $\tilde{r} = \underline{\sigma}$, where $\underline{\sigma}$ is the return of an alternative, inefficient, storing technology (as in

Aghion, Banerjee, and Piketty (1999)). In a closed economy, lenders will invest their excess savings in this technology.

Assume that $R > r + \delta$ as long as $p=0$ (this implies $r + \delta < \frac{1}{a}(1+\mu) - \mu\underline{\sigma}$), so that there will be a positive flow of FDI as long as $p=0$. Using the fact that $L = \mu(W^B + F)$ and that $y=z$ when $p>0$, we can rewrite the above free-entry condition as:

$$(r+\delta)(W^B + F) = Z - \mu\underline{\sigma}(W^B + F).$$

This, together with the price equation (3), implies that:

$$p = \frac{1+\mu}{r+\delta+\underline{\sigma}\mu} - a,$$

which in turn gives a stable value for p. Thus, even though FDI leads to a price increase it does not generate price and output volatility.

Consider now an economy which has already been opened up to foreign borrowing and lending at rate r, that is to foreign portfolio flows only, and which, as a result has become volatile as in the example depicted in Figure 4. What will happen if this economy is now also opening up to FDI? By the same reasoning as before, opening up to FDI will stabilize the price of the country-specific factor at level p^* such that:

$$(r+\delta)(W^B + F) = Z - r\mu(W^B + F).$$

This again will eliminate investment and output volatility in this economy (assuming that initially the country is attracting FDI). In other words, if there are no limitations on FDI inflows and outflows (and FDI involves complete information on domestic firms), the price of the country-specific factor and therefore aggregate domestic GDP or GNP will remain constant in equilibrium.

The reason why FDI acts as a stabilizing force is again that, unlike foreign lending, it does not depend on the creditworthiness of the domestic firms, and furthermore it is precisely during slumps that foreign direct investors may prefer to come in so as to benefit from the low price of the country-specific factor.

What happens if foreign *direct* investment is *complementary* to domestic direct investment, that is, to W^B? Such complementarity may be due to legal restrictions whereby the total amount of FDI cannot be greater than a fixed fraction x of domestic investors' wealth W^B, or it may stem from the need for local investors to enforce dividend payments or to help exert control. Appendix A shows that foreign direct investments subject to complementarity requirements of the form $F \leq xW^B$ may sometimes *de*-stabilize an emerging market economy. Indeed, in contrast to the unrestricted FDI case analyzed above, such direct investments ultimately will fall during slumps, that is, when investors' wealth W^B_{t+1} is experiencing a downturn. Downturns will also typically be deeper than in absence of FDI since, by amplifying the increase in p_t during booms, FDI increases production costs and thus accentuates the credit-crunch induced on firms. Thus, whilst unrestricted FDI has a stabilizing effect on an open emerging market economy, opening such an economy to restricted FDI may actually have the opposite effect.

5 Extensions and Policy Conclusions

The previous sections have analyzed a stylized model that illustrates how the interaction between credit market imperfections and real exchange rate fluctuations can cause instability in some open economies. We have purposely abstracted from numerous factors making the analysis more realistic which could further affect the dynamics. In this section we examine several directions in which our simple framework can be extended and discuss policy implications.

5.1 Uncertainty and Defaults

The model presented above can easily be extended to incorporate random project returns and defaults. We consider the case of a CES production function. With a risk of default from borrowers, lenders will charge a risk premium on their loans. If we denote the interest rate on a risky loan by R, we have $R>r$ where r is the international interest rate (the interest rate in the absence of default risk); the risk premium is thus $R-r$.

Suppose that the tradeable output technology is random, equal to $\tilde{\sigma} \cdot f(K, z_N)$ where the firm-specific productivity shock $\tilde{\sigma}$ is uniformly distributed on the interval $[\underline{\sigma}, \bar{\sigma}]$ and is realized at the end of the period. The same will be true for the *equilibrium* gross return generated by investors, namely:

$$\tilde{y}_T = \max_{z_N} \tilde{\sigma} \cdot f(I - p \cdot z_N, z_N)$$

$$= \tilde{\sigma} \cdot \psi(p_t) I,$$

where $I = W^B + L$ is the current flow of investment.

Now, if an entrepreneur defaults on his debt, it may be genuine because the revenue $\sigma \psi(p) I$ does not cover the repayment obligation on L (a "*liquidity* default"), or it may be deliberate when the entrepreneur chooses not to repay his debt despite the higher chance of facing a penalty (a "*strategic* default"). Consistent with our earlier modelling approach, we assume *strategic* defaults are *ex ante* decisions whereby defaulting borrowers sink a cost of $c \cdot I$ to hide their investment funds I.

But now additional uncertainty about the productivity parameter $\tilde{\sigma}$ introduces the possibility of *ex post liquidity* defaults, namely whenever $\tilde{\sigma} < \sigma^*$ where σ^* is defined by the zero profit-condition:

$$\sigma^* \psi(p)(W^B + L) - RL = 0, \tag{10}$$

where R is the repayment obligation specified in the loan contracts between lenders and borrowers (borrowers are protected by limited liability, and therefore cannot be asked to repay more than $\min(\sigma^* \psi(p)(W^B + L), RL)$).

Competition among lenders will set the equilibrium repayment schedule R so as to make any lender indifferent between making a (risky) loan on the domestic market and making a safe loan at rate r on the international credit market ($R = r$ in the absence of uncertainty). More formally:

$$rL = \int_{\underline{\sigma}}^{\bar{\sigma}} \min\left(RL, \tilde{\sigma} \psi(p)(W^B + L)\right) \frac{d\sigma}{\bar{\sigma} - \underline{\sigma}} \tag{11}$$

Appendix B shows that the number of defaulting firms, equal to $(\sigma^+ - \underline{\sigma})/(\bar{\sigma} - \underline{\sigma})$, can be easily derived from (10) and (11). It is shown that this number is increasing in p (and thus in W^B) when entrepreneurs are credit constrained. Thus, the number of defaults increases during periods of real appreciations, which in turn happen towards the end of booms. This prediction appears to be consistent with available anecdotal evidence on the dynamics of default rates in emerging market economies.[24]

Once a firm defaults, it is often declared bankrupt. If we assume that bankruptcy is declared one period after the default, then our model predicts a counter-cyclical number of bankruptcies in equilibrium, with the highest number of bankrupted firms being observed in slumps. If we further assume that bankruptcies involve a substantial liquidation or restructuring cost, borne by the entrepreneurial class in the following periods either directly (disruption of supply chains, etc.) or indirectly (because the government needs resources for the clean-up and taxes the entrepreneurs for them), then the slumps may ultimately be significantly deeper and longer-lasting than what our benchmark model predicts. Notice, however, that bankruptcy costs will significantly deepen the slumps only in those economies facing credit constraints.

5.2 Amplifying Factors

Additional destabilizing factors of the kinds discussed in the recent literature on financial crises, which in economies with highly developed financial systems would have little or no impact on the dynamics of real economic activity, are likely to exacerbate output

volatility in economies with intermediate levels of financial development. In the model, this implies that μ can be pro-cyclical. The following discussion is largely informal and suggestive, as a more elaborated analysis would certainly require another paper.

5.2.1 Moral hazard on the lenders' side

Suppose that the bulk of lending activities is performed by banks, which in turn are regulated by the central bank or by the government. Now, in most countries (including such developed countries as Japan or France) banking regulation is imperfect and what we often observe over the cycle is that banks tend to *overlend* during booms. This in turn may be due, either to an *overload* problem (there are too many lending opportunities during booms and banks have limited time and attention to perform adequate screening and monitoring on each project), or to an increase in *bank competition*[25] (which in turn may induce some banks to engage in preemptive lending). This tendency for banks to overlend during booms can be easily captured in our model by assuming that the credit-multiplier μ varies pro-cyclically. A small pro-cyclical variation of μ around a given average $\bar{\mu}$ would have no effect on the dynamics of wealth and output if $\bar{\mu}$ is sufficiently large, in other words if the financial system is sufficiently developed.[26] (For example, the S & L crisis did not produce major macroeconomic effects on the U.S. economy.) However, if $\bar{\mu}$ lies in the intermediate range for which the 45° line intersects the wealth schedule $W_{t+1}^B(W_t^B)$ on its downward sloping part, then pro-cyclical fluctuations of μ will obviously exacerbate volatility in the corresponding economy (as overlending will magnify the price effect during booms). In other words, moral hazard in the financial sector can be an important source of instability, but only in an economy with an intermediate level of financial development.

5.2.2 Investors' overreactions to changes in fundamentals

Consider further a straightforward extension of our model with defaults in which foreign investors have imperfect information about the efficiency of creditors' monitoring (and therefore about the actual value of the credit-multiplier μ).[27] Then, suppose that the economy experiences a negative but temporary productivity shock (i.e., a negative but temporary shock to σ) which will naturally have the effect of increasing the equilibrium amount of defaults in the short-run. Now, given that the lenders are uncertain about μ, if they do not observe the shock to μ, they will not know whether to ascribe these extra defaults to a change in a or to lower value of μ - in other words, they will be unsure of whether most of these are strategic defaults (suggesting incompetence of the financial sector) or rather liquidity defaults (associated with a shock to profits). As a result they will respond in part by adjusting their assessment of μ downwards. From then on, the comparison between an economy with a level of financial development (i.e., a high μ) and an economy with an intermediate level of financial development (i.e., an intermediate level of μ) exactly parallels the previous case: if μ is high, the updating of μ will have no effect on the dynamics of wealth and output, since the 45° line intersects the wealth schedule W_{t+1}^B (W_t^B) on its third-upward-sloping part;[28] on the other hand, if we start from an economy at an intermediate level of financial development, the downward updating in μ will prolong and amplify the initial effect of the temporary productivity shock on a. This implies, for example, that the number of defaults can increase over several periods.

Once again, the model tells us that overreactions by investors, as captured for example in models which stress herd behavior, can only be source of substantial instability in economies at a certain stage of financial development.

5.3 Some Policy Conclusions

Our model provides a simple and tractable framework for analyzing financially-based crises in economies which are at an intermediate level of financial development. The story we tell is based on some very basic features of these economies, in contrast with other more institutionally-based theories which invoke moral hazard among lenders, herd behavior among investors, etc. This is not to say that our model is inconsistent with this class of theories—as shown in the previous subsections. However, our model does suggest a somewhat different policy response: slumps should be seen as part of a normal process in economies like these which are both at an intermediate level of financial development and in the process of liberalizing their financial sectors. We should therefore not overreact to the occurrence of financial crises, especially in the case of emerging market economies. In particular, hasty and radical overhauling of their economic system may do more harm than good.[29]

Second, policies allowing firms to rebuild their credit worthiness quickly will at the same time contribute to a prompt recovery of the overall economy. In this context it is worth considering the role for monetary policy and, more generally, for policies affecting the credit market. Whilst our model in its present form cannot be *directly* used for this purpose since money is neutral (and in any case the interest rate is fixed by the world interest rate), it can be extended to allow for both monetary non-neutrality and a less infinitely elastic supply of foreign loans (see Aghion-Bacchetta-Banerjee (2000, 2001a, 2004)). Once we take our framework in this direction it quickly becomes clear that a low interest rate policy is *not* necessarily the right answer *even in a slump induced by a credit crunch.* The problem is that while such an interest rate reduction may help restore the firms' financial health (and therefore their investment capacity), the net obligations of those who have borrowed in foreign currency will also rise if it leads to a devaluation of the domestic currency. Therefore, the optimal interest rate policy ex post during a financial crisis cannot be determined without knowing more about the details of the currency composition of the existing debt obligations of domestic enterprises.

This emphasis on creditworthiness as the key element in the recovery from a slump, also suggests that a policy of allowing insolvent banks to fail may in fact prolong the slump if it restricts firms' ability to borrow (because of the comparative advantage of banks in monitoring firms' activities[30]). If banks must be shut down, there should be an effort to preserve their monitoring expertise on the relevant industries. Moreover, to the extent that the government has to spend resources on restructuring and cleaning-up after a spate of bankruptcies, it should avoid raising taxes during a slump since doing so would further limit the borrowing capacity of domestic entrepreneurs and therefore delay the subsequent recovery.

Third, our model also delivers *ex ante* policy implications for emerging market economies not currently under a financial crisis. In particular: (i) an unrestricted financial liberalization may actually *destabilize* the economy and engender a slump that would otherwise not have happened. If a major slump is likely to be costly even in the long-run (because, for example, it sets in process destabilizing political forces), fully liberalizing foreign capital flows and fully opening the economy to foreign lending may not be a good idea at least until the domestic financial sector is sufficiently well-developed (that is, until the credit-multiplier p becomes sufficiently large); (ii) foreign *direct* investment does *not* destabilize. Indeed, as we have argued above, FDI is most likely to come in during slumps when the relative price of the country-specific factor is low; furthermore, even if this price ends up fluctuating when the economy is open to FDI, these fluctuations will only affect the distribution of profits between domestic and foreign investors but not aggregate output. Therefore there is no cost a priori to allowing FDI even at low levels of financial development;[31] (iii) what brings about financial crises is precisely the rise in the price of country specific factors. If one of these factors (say, real estate) is identified to play a key role in sparking a financial crisis, it would be sensible to control its price, either directly or through controlling its speculative demand using suitable fiscal deterrents. This, and other important aspects in the design of stabilization policies for emerging market economies, await future elaborations of the framework developed in this paper.

Appendix A: The Analytics of Financial Liberalization

A) Liberalization to Foreign Lending

Here, we construct an example of an economy which, in the absence of foreign borrowing and lending, would be asymptotically stable and actually converge to a permanent boom, but which becomes permanently volatile once fully open to foreign borrowing and lending. The analysis of the closed economy is similar to Aghion, Banerjee, and Piketty (1999).

More specifically, consider an economy in which:

(a) The production technology is Leontief with an inelastic supply of the country-specific factor, that is: $f(K,z) = \min\left(\dfrac{K}{a}, z\right)$, $a < 1$, where $K = I - p \cdot z$.

(b) Financial markets are initially closed to foreign capital inflows so that the aggregate supply of funds available to domestic investors, I_t, is now equal to the min of the investment capacity $(1+\mu)W_t^B$ and of total domestic asvings $W_t^B + W_t^Z$. That is:

$$I_t = m\left\{(1+\mu)W_t^B, W_t^B + W_t^z\right\}$$

(c) Initially, at time $t=0$, the investment capacity of domestic entrepreneurs exceeds the total amount of domestic savings, so that $\mu W_0^B > W_0^z$ (in the opposite case. opening up to foreign borrowing and lending would have no effect on investment and output in the domestic economy).

(d) We impose the following restrictions on the parameters of the economy:
   (i) $\mu > 1$
   (ii) $1 - \alpha < a$
   (iii) W_0^z and W_0^B are leas than $\hat{W} = \dfrac{(1-a)\varepsilon}{1-(1-a)\frac{1}{a}}$

   (iv) $\hat{W} < \dfrac{a}{2}Z.$

We now show that a closed economy which satisfies assumptions (a), (b), (c), (d), *stable*, with constant price $p_t \equiv 0$ and constant interest rate $r_t \equiv \dfrac{1}{a}$, and wealth level W_t^B and W_t^L which both converge monotonically to $\hat{W}$ as $t \to \infty$.

First, assumption (c) implies that $r_0 = \dfrac{1}{a}$, and it also implies that $I_0 = W_0^L + W_0^D$ asaumptions (d)-(iii) and (d)-(iv) then imply that $I_0 < aZ$, so that $p_0 = 0$. Next, on can show that at any date s, $r_s = \dfrac{1}{a}$ and $p_0 = 0$. To see this, suppose that for all $s \leq t$, $r_e = \dfrac{1}{a}$ and $p_s = 0$, and let us ahow that $r_{t+1} = \dfrac{1}{a}$ and $p_{t+1} = 0$. If $r_s = \dfrac{1}{a}$ and $p_s = 0$ for all $s \leq t$, then for all $s \leq t$ the wealth levels W_{s+1}^L and W_{s+1}^B satisfy the equations:

$$W_{s+1}^L = (1-\alpha)\left[e + \frac{1}{a}W_s^L\right] \tag{(1)s}$$

and

$$W_{s+1}^B = (1-\alpha)\left[e + \frac{1}{a}W_s^B\right]. \tag{(2)s}$$

It then follows from assumption (d)-(i), i.e., from $\mu > 1$, and from assuming that $r_t = \frac{1}{\alpha}$ (which implies that $\mu W_t^B > W_t^L$), that $\mu W_{t+1}^B > W_{t+1}^Z$ and therefore $r_{t+1} = \frac{1}{a}$. Furthermore, it follows from assumption (d)-(iii) and equations $(1)_s$ and $(2)_s$ for $s \le t$, that $W_s^L < \hat{W}$ and $W_s^B < \hat{W}$ for all $s \le t+1$; this in turn implies that:

$$I_{t+1} = W_{t+1}^L + W_{t+1}^B < 2\hat{W},$$

so that $I_{t+1} < aZ$ by assumption (d)-(iv) and therefore $p_{t+1} = 0$. We have thus shown: that if $r_s = \frac{1}{a}$ and $p_s = 0$ for all $s \le t$, then $r_{t+1} = \frac{1}{a}$ and $p_{t+1} = 0$. Together with the fact that $r_0 = \frac{1}{a}$ and $p_0 = 0$, this proves by induction that $r_s = \frac{1}{a}$ and $p_s = 0$ for all s, so that the entire wealth trajectory (W_s^L, W_s^B) is determined by (W_0^L, W_0^B) together with the dynamic equations $(1)_s$ and $(2)_s$. But this, together with assumption (d)-(ii), implies that the equilibrium trajectory (W_s^L, W_s^B) is *stable*, with both W_s^L and W_s^B converging monotonically towards $\hat{W}$ when $t \to \infty$. Thus, a closed economy characterized by (a)-(d) will display no volatility in price, interest rate, wealth and (tradeable) output.

Now, a closed economy that satisfies (a)-(d) and therefore is stable, may end up becoming volatile if fully open to foreign borrowing and lending. For example, this will be the case if that same economy satisfies the sufficient conditions provided in Section 2.2 for the existence of two-cycles. And one can easily verify that the two sets of conditions are consistent, in the sense that there exists a non-empty set of parameters which satisfy both sets of condition simultaneously.

B) Restricted FDI

Let F denote the current amount of FDI, and let us impose the constraint: $F \le xW^B$, with the fraction x being initially amall. We assume that foreign investors receive their proportional share of output and that this is always larger than their reservation return $r + \delta$ (given the conatraint x, the aupply is no longer fully elastic as in the preceding case). The equilibrium price for the country-specific factor is now equal to:

$$p_t = m\left(0, \frac{(1+\mu)\left(W_t^B + F_t\right) - aZ}{Z}\right).$$

Let $L_t = \mu(W_t^B + F_t)$. Then the dynamics of investors' wealth is described by the equations:

(I) $\quad W_{t+1}^B = (1-\alpha)\left[e + \frac{1}{a}\left(W_t^B + F_t + L_t\right) - \tilde{r}L_t\right]$

when W_t^B is small and therefore $p_t \equiv 0$ (part 1 of the $W_{t+1}^B(W_t^B)$ curve), and:

(II) $\quad W_{t+1}^B = (1-\alpha)\left[e + \frac{Z}{1+x} - \tilde{r}L_t\right]$

when there is excess demand for the country-specific factor and therefore p_t becomes positive (part 2 of the $W_{t+1}^B(W_t^B)$ curve).

(In (I) and (II) the variable $\tilde{r}$ denotes the domestic interest rate, which is equal to $\underline{\sigma}$ if $\mu(W^B + F) < W^2$ and to the profit rate otherwise.

For x sufficiently small, we have $F_s = xW_s^B$ so that the above equation (II) implies a total level of *direct* investment (domestic and foreign) equal to:

$$W_{t+1}^B + xW_{t+1}^B = (1-\alpha)\left[e(1+x) + Z - \tilde{r}\mu W_t^B(1+x)^2\right]$$

which for e small is *decreasing* in x. In particular, starting from an economy without any FDI, introducing highly constrained FDI may end up *deepening* the slump which it was meant to eliminate.

Appendix B: Uncertainty and Defaults

Here we derive the number of defaulting firms when there is firm-specific uncertainty. Deriving RL from (10) and substituting into (11) gives:

$$rL = \frac{\psi(p)(W^B + L)}{\bar{\sigma} - \underline{\sigma}} \int_{\sigma}^{\bar{\sigma}} m(\sigma^*, \sigma) d\sigma \tag{12}$$

The number of defaulting firms, $(\sigma^* - \underline{\sigma})/(\bar{\sigma} - \underline{\sigma})$, can be derived from (12). When firms are credit constrained, we can use the fact that $L/(W^B + L) = \tau/r$ and get:

$$\sigma^* = \bar{\sigma} - \sqrt{(\bar{\sigma} - \underline{\sigma})\left[\bar{\sigma} + \underline{\sigma} - \frac{2\tau}{\psi(p)}\right]}$$

Thus, σ^* depends positively on p and so does the number of defaulting firms. Since p is a positive function of W^B, σ^* depends also positively on W^B. On the other hand, when entrepreneurs are unconstrained the numbers of defaults depends negatively on W^B (the larger the wealth, the smaller the probability of defaults). In that case we have:

$$\sigma^* = \bar{\sigma} - \sqrt{(\bar{\sigma} - \underline{\sigma})\left[\bar{\sigma} + \underline{\sigma} - \frac{2(I - W^B)}{I}\right]}$$

where I is determined by the world interest rate r.

We are grateful to an anonymous referee, Beatriz Armendariz, Laura Bottazzi, Raquel Fernandez, Ed Glaeser, Urban Jerman, Hélène Rey, David Weil, and seminar participants at Harvard University, the Universitat Autònoma of Barcelona, and the LSE/FMG conference on market liquidity for comments on a previous draft. Pierre-Alain Bruchez provided excellent research assistance. Financial support from the MacArthur Foundation (Banerjee and Aghion) and the NSF (Banerjee) is gratefully acknowledged. Bacchetta's work on this paper is part of a research network on 'The Analysis of International Capital Markets: Understanding Europe's role in the Global Economy,' funded by the European Commission under the Research Training Network Program (Contract No. HPRN-CT-1999-00067). The views expressed herein are those of the authors and not necessarily those of the National Bureau of Economic Research.

Notes

1 The fact that firm level cash-flow is an important determinant of investment is now widely recognized even in the context of economies like the U.S. which have excellent financial markets. (e.g., see Hubbard (1998) or Bernanke, Gertler, and Gilchrist (1999)).

2 Perhaps as a consequence of herd behavior.

3 See, for example, Calvo et al. (1996). The degree of real appreciation varies across countries; for example, it has been more pronounced in Latin America than in Asia.

4 See World Bank (1997) and Milesi-Ferretti and Razin (1998) for systematic descriptions of the link between and capital flow reversals and currency crises. Gourinchas, Valdés, and Landerretche (2001) provide a systematic analysis of lending booms which coincide with movements in output, capital inflows, the current account and the real exchange rate that are fully consistent with our results. See also Honkapohja and Koskela (1999) for an illuminating description of the Finnish crisis of the 1990s, which fits well our analysis: first, an economic environment characterized by a large proportion of credit-constrained enterprises, for which investments are highly elastic w.r.t. current profits; second, a financial market deregulation in the 1980s that leads to a huge expansion of bank lending, to major inflows of foreign capital and to a sharp increase in real asset prices (in particular real estate prices) during the boom; and subsequently in the 1990s, a sharp fall in real asset prices, investments, and real GDP, and the occurrence of a banking crisis that eventually led to a tightening of banking regulations and to a devaluation of the Finnish currency after hopeless efforts to maintain a fixed exchange rate.

5 Caballero and Krishnamurthy (2001) distinguish between credit constraints from foreign investors and constraints from domestic investors to explain the amplification of shocks in an open economy. They also abstract from business fluctuations issues.

6 See, for example, Johnston et al. (1997) or Eichengreen et al. (1998).

7 Obstfeld (1986), McKinnon (1993), Bacchetta (1992), Bartolini and Drazen (1997) analyze capital account liberalizations. McKinnon and Pill (1997) and Bacchetta and van Wincoop (2000) are among the first examining the issue of volatility.

8 Notice that the separation between the decisions of lenders and entrepreneurs does not imply separation between total national savings and investment. Gertler and Rogoff (1990) show that a framework with credit constraints can explain the high correlation between total savings and investment (Feldstein and Horioka, 1980). We obtain a similar result in our framework. However, in general this result also depends on lenders' savings behavior.

9 From Aghion-Banerjee-Picketty, we find $\mu = 1/(1 - \tau/ac)$, where τ is the cost of cheating for the borrower and c is proportional to the debt collection cost in case of default for the lender. With a higher level of financial development, τ is larger and c smaller. This implies that μ is larger.

10 Using $y = Z$ and $L = \mu W^B$, this inequality can be written as $Z > (1 + \mu)rW^B$. Using (3), this implies $\dfrac{1}{a+p} > r$. This holds for p not too large since $1/a > r$. When p is large enough that this inequality does not hold, we are in case iii).

11 This follows immediately from the equations:

$$W_1 = (1 - \alpha)(e + Z - r\mu W_2)$$

$$W_2 = (1 - \alpha)\left(e + \frac{1+\mu}{a} - r\mu\right)W_1.$$

12 In the context of the above model, we have:

$$\frac{I_t}{y_t} = a + p_t,$$

which indeed increases during a lending boom as a result of the price effect.

13 See also Tornell and Westermann (2002).

14 This result obtains when the discrete lags are randomly gamma distributed, as shown in Invernizzi and Medio (1991)

15 When looking at the real world, the distinction between persistent oscillations that eventually die out, and those that never die out, may not be so important as our analysis suggests. This is because in reality, even if oscillations eventually die out, there are always shocks that start them off again.

16 This is to make sure that it pays to produce at least some times and that the country-specific factor is used.

17 To assess the overall effect of a change in the elasticity of intertemporal substitution on volatility, it is instructive to replace C_t^B by $\Pi_t - W_t^B$ in (9), giving a dynamic relationship:

$$W_{t+1}^B = \frac{\left(\beta M_{t+1}\right)^{\frac{1}{\rho}}}{M_{t+1} + \left(\beta M_{t+1}\right)^{\frac{1}{\rho}}} \Pi_t + \frac{1}{M_{t+1} + \left(\beta M_{t+1}\right)^{\frac{1}{\rho}}} W_{t+2}^B$$

Entrepreneurs' wealth available for next period is now a weighted average of past profits and expected future wealth. While this second order (highly non-linear) difference equation dose not lend itself to analytical solutions, it can be resolved numerically as we show in the next subsection.

18 Note that the simulation technique differs between the constant savings rate case and the log-utility case with infinitely lived and forward-looking entrepreneurs. In the former case, we simply need to run a first order difference equation with given initial wealth level. In the latter case, as shown in footnote 17, the dynamic system is described by a forward-looking second order difference equation which requires that we compute the initial consumption level for given initial wealth (e.g., using a shooting algorithm). When $\rho = 1$, however, the two methods generate exactly the same dynamics.

19 If $\mu W^B < W^L$, opening up the economy to foreign lending would make no difference: since the investment capacity of domestic entrepreneurs cannot even absorb domestic savings, there is no need for foreign lending in this case.

20 When several developed countries did liberalize their capital movements in the 1970s and 1980s periods of high instability could not be observed.

21 This may be the case in some of the poorer African and Asian countries.

22 Typically, measured FDI implies participations of more than 10% in a firm's capital so this appears to be a reasonable assumption. Razin et al (1998) make a similar distinction about FDI.

23 This, in turn, implies that in our model FDI is a substitute to domestic investment. The effects of FDI on macroeconomic volatility when domestic and foreign investments are complementary, are discussed at the end of this section.

24 See Mishkin (1996) for the case of Mexico, and World Bank (1997) for capital inflows episodes.

25 Competition may increase because of an increase in the volume of lending - loan officers who fail to make lots of loans at time when everybody else is increasing lending, may fear that they will look inept.

26 When $\bar{\mu}$ is sufficiently high the 45° line intersects the wealth schedule W_{t+1}^B (W_t^B) on its rightward upward sloping part, so that the dynamics of wealth is actually independent of μ.

27 For example, financial liberalization has just occurred and foreign investors cannot yet asses the new monitoring cost c that should result from it.

28 We implicitly assume that the updating on c, and therefore on μ, is relatively small.

29 Indeed, if our model is right, the slump sets in motion forces which, even with little interference, should eventually bring growth back to these economies. The risk is that by trying to overhaul the system in a panic, one may actually undermine those forces of recovery instead of stimulating them. This is not to deny that there is a lot that needs changing in these economies, especially on the institutional side with the establishment and enforcement of disciplinary rules in credit and banking activities. For example, in the context of our model, banks may typically engage in preemptive lending to speculators in domestic inputs and/or to producers during booms. This in turn will further increase output volatility whenever inadequate monitoring and expertise acquisition by banks increases aggregate risk and therefore the interest rate imposed upon domestic producers.

30 See Diamond (1984).

31 This strategy of allowing only FDI at early stages of financial development is in fact what most developed countries have done, in particular in Europe where restrictions on cross-country capital movements have only been fully removed in the late 1980s whereas FDI to - and between - European countries had been allowed since the late 1950s.

References

[1] Aghion, Ph., Ph. Bacchetta, and A. Banerjee (1999), "Financial Liberalization and Volatility in Emerging Market Economies," in P.R. Agenor, M. Miller, D. Vines, and A. Weber (eds.), *The Asian Financial Crises: Causes, Contagion and Consequences,* Cambridge University Press, p. 167-190. Published under the wrong title "Capital Markets and the Instability of Open Economies".

[2] Aghion, Ph., Ph. Bacchetta, and A. Banerjee (2000), "A Simple Model of Monetary Policy and Currency Crises," *European Economic Review* 44, 728-738.

[3] Aghion, Ph., Ph. Bacchetta, and A. Banerjee (2001a), "Currency Crises and Monetary Policy in an Economy with Credit Constraints," *European Economic Review* 45, 1121-1150.

[4] Aghion, Ph., Ph. Bacchetta, and A. Banerjee (2001b), "Financial Development and the Instability of Open Economies," Working Paper, Study Center Gerzensee, http://www .szgerzensee.ch/download/abb2001.pdf.

[5] Aghion, Ph., Ph. Bacchetta, and A. Banerjee (2004), "A Corporate Balance-Sheet Approach to Currency Crises," *Journal of Economic Theory,* forthcoming.

[6] Aghion, Ph., A. Banerjee, and T. Piketty (1999), "Dualism and Macroeconomic Volatility," *Quarterly Journal of Economics,* November, 1357-1397.

[7] Azariadis, C. and B. Smith (1998), "Financial Intermediation and Regime Switching in Business Cycles," *American Economic Review* 88, 516-536.

[8] Bacchetta, Ph. (1992), "Liberalization of Capital Movements and of the Domestic Financial System," *Economica* 59, 465-74.

[9] Bacchetta, Ph and R. Caminal (1999), "Do Capital Market Imperfections Exacerbate Output Fluctuations?," *European Economic Review* 44, *449-468.*

[10] Bacchetta, Ph. and E. van Wincoop (2000), "Capital Flows to Emerging Markets: Liberalization, Overshooting, and Volatility," in S. Edwards (ed.), *Capital Flows and the Emerging Economies - Theory, Evidence, and Controversies,* The University of Chicago Press, 61-98.

[11] Bartolini, L. and A. Drazen (1997), "When Liberal Policies Reflect External Shocks, What Do We Learn?" *Journal of International Economics* 42, 249-73.

[12] Bernanke, B. and M. Gertler (1989), "Agency Costs, Net Worth, and Business Fluctuations," *American Economic Review* 79, 14-31.

[13] Bernanke, B., M. Gertler, and S. Gilchrist (1998), "The Financial Accelerator in a Quantitative Business Cycle Framework," in J. Taylor and M. Woodford (eds), *Handbook of Macroeconomics,* vol. 1C, 1341-1393.

[14] Bruchez, P.-A. (2001), "Discrete and Continuous Time in Financial Accelerator Models," in progress, Study Center Gerzensee.

[15] Caballero, R.J. and A. Krishnamurthy (2001), "International and Domestic Collateral Constraints in a Model of Emerging Market Crises," *Journal of Monetary Economics* 48, 513-548.

[16] Calvo, G.A., L. Leiderman, and C.M. Reinhart (1996), "Inflows of Capital to Developing Countries in the 1990s," *Journal of Economic Perspectives* 10, 123-39.

[17] Diamond, D (1984), "Financial Intermediation and Delegated Monitoring", *Review of Economic Studies,* 62, 393-414.

[18] Eichengreen, B., M. Mussa, G. Dell'Ariccia, G.M. Milesi-Ferretti, and A. Tweedie (1998), "Capital Account Liberalization: Theoretical and Practical Aspects," IMF Occasional Paper No. 172.

[19] Fazzari, S.M., R.G. Hubbard, and B.C. Petersen (1988), "Financing Constraints and Corporate Investment," *Brookings Papers on Economic Activity 1:1998,* 141195.

[20] Feldstein, M. and C. Horioka (1980), " Domestic Saving and International Capital Flows," *Economic Journal* 90, 314-29.

[21] Galvez, J. and J. Tybout (1985), "Microeconomic Adjustments in Chile during 1977-81: The Importance of Being a *Grupo," World Development* 13, 969-994.

[22] Gertler, M. and K. Rogoff (1990), "North-South Lending and Endogenous Capital-Markets Inefficiencies," *Journal of Monetary Economics* 26, 245-66.

[23] Gourinchas, P.-O., R. Valdés, and O. Landerretche (2001), " Lending Booms: Latin America and the World," NBER WP No. 8249.

[24] Guerra de Luna, A. (1997), "Residential Real Estate Booms, Financial Deregulation and Capital Inflows: an International Perspective," mimeo, Banco de México.

[25] Grandmont, J.-M. (1988), " Non-Linear Difference Equations, Bifurcations and Chaos: An Introduction," CEPREMAP Working Paper No. 8811, Paris.

[26] Holmstrom, B. and J. Tirole (1997), "Financial Intermediation, Loanable Funds and the Real Sector," *Quarterly Journal of Economics* CXII, 663-691.

[27] Honkapohja, S. and E. Koskela (1999), "The Economic Crisis of the 1990s in Finland," *Economic Policy* 14, 401-436.

[28] Hubbard, R. G. (1998), "Capital Market Imperfections and Investment," *Journal of Economic Literature* 36, 193-225.

[29] Invernizzi, S. and A. Medio (1991), "On Lags and Chaos in Economic Dynamic Models," *Journal of Mathematical Economics* 20, 521-550.

[30] Johnston, R.B., S.M. Darbar, and C. Echeverria (1997), "Sequencing Capital Account Liberalizations: Lessons from the Experiences in Chile, Indonesia, Korea, and Thailand," IMF Working Paper 97/157.

[31] Krugman, P. (1979), "A Model of Balance of Payments Crises," *Journal of Money, Credit and Banking* 11, 311-25.

[32] Kyotaki, N. and J. Moore (1997), "Credit Cycles," *Journal of Political Economy 105*, 211-248.

[33] McKinnon, R.I. (1993), *The Order of Economic Liberalization*, The Johns Hopkins University Press.

[34] McKinnon, R.I. and H. Pill (1997), "Credible Economic Liberalizations and Overborrowing," *American Economic Review* (Papers and Proceedings) 87, 189-193.

[35] de Melo, J., R. Pascale, and J. Tybout (1985), "Microeconomic Adjustments in Uruguay during 1973-81: The Interplay of Real and Financial Shocks," *World Development* 13, 995-1015.

[36] Mishkin, F.S. (1996), "Understanding Financial Crises: A Developing Country Perspective," *Annual World Bank Conference on Development Economics,* 29-62.

[37] Obstfeld, M. (1986), " Capital Flows, the Current Account, and the Real Exchange Rate: The Consequences of Liberalization and Stabilization," in S. Edwards and L. Ahamed (eds.), Economic Adjustment and Exchange Rates in Developing Countries, University of Chicago Press.

[38] Petrei, A.H. and J. Tybout (1985), "Microeconomic Adjustments in Argentina during 1976-81: The Importance of Changing Levels of Financial Subsidies," *World Development* 13, 949-968.

[39] Razin, A., E. Sadka, and C.-W. Yuen (1998), "A Pecking Order of Capital Inflows and International Tax Principles," *Journal of International Economics* 44, 45-68.

[40] Tornell, A. and F. Westermann (2002), "Boom-Bust Cycles in Middle Income Countries: Facts and Explanation," NBER WP No. 9219.

[41] Woodford, M. (1989), "Imperfect Financial Intermediation and Complex Dynamics," in W. Barnett et al. (eds), *Economic Complexity: Chaos, Sunspot, Bubbles and Nonlinearity.*

[42] World Bank (1997), *Private Capital Flows to Developing Countries,* Policy Research Report, Oxford University Press.

EMERGING MARKET BOND SPREADS AND SOVEREIGN CREDIT RATINGS

Reconciling Market Views with Economic Fundamentals

Amadou N. R. Sy[1]

Source: *IMF Working Paper* 01/165, 2001.

Abstract

This paper uses a panel data estimation of a simple univariate model of sovereign spreads on ratings to analyze statistically significant deviations from the estimated relationship. We find evidence of an asymmetric adjustment of spreads and ratings when such deviations are significant. In addition, the paper illustrates how significant disagreements between market and rating agencies' views can be used as a signal that further technical and sovereign analysis is warranted. For instance, we find that spreads were "excessively low" for most emerging markets before the Asian crisis. More recently, spreads were "excessively high" for a number of emerging markets.

I. INTRODUCTION

Emerging market bond spreads over U.S. Treasuries are often used as an indicator of sovereign risk. In fact, sovereign spreads are a function of credit risk and are often used to gauge market assessment of a country's economic and political fundamentals and as a proxy for capital market access. In addition, sovereign spreads depend on interest rate and currency risk as well as technical factors such as liquidity conditions and changes in the investor base for a particular country's bonds.

Similarly, sovereign ratings convey analysts' views of a country's economic and political risk variables. Rating agencies view ratings as providing a forward-looking indication of the relative risk that a debt issuer will have the ability—and willingness—to make full and timely payments of principal and interest over the life of a particular rated instruments. The agencies, however, do not regard their ratings as providing either a prediction of the timing of default or an indication of the absolute level of risk associated with a particular financial obligation.

Empirical studies find that sovereign ratings are generally consistent with economic fundamentals. For instance, Cantor and Packer (1996), using ratings from Moody's and S&P's on 49 countries as of September 1995 find that high ratings were associated with high per capita income, low inflation, more rapid growth, a low ratio of foreign currency external debt to exports, the absence of a history of default on foreign currency debt since 1970, and a high level of economic development (as measured by the IMF's classification as an industrial country). In a follow-up study, Juttner and McCarthy (1998) find that the factors identified by Cantor and Packer continued to adequately explain ratings in 1996 and 1997, but that this relationship broke down in 1998, in the wake of the Asian crisis. For 1998, additional variables appeared to have come into play—notably, problematic bank assets as a percent of GDP and the interest rate differential.

There is also evidence that sovereign ratings are key determinants of the pricing of sovereign bonds and that sovereign spreads incorporate market participants' views of expected credit rating changes (see Erb, Harvey, and Viskanta (2000)). In particular, trading strategies based on anticipations of the rating cycle are commonly used by market participants seeking to exploit profit opportunities. Furthermore, since investment restrictions are often based on credit ratings especially for institutional investors, portfolio managers monitor credit rating changes closely.

The relationship between sovereign ratings and spreads can help compare sovereign spreads on a rating-adjusted basis. It can also be used to contrast market views of a country's economic and political fundamentals with rating agencies' assessment of the same variables. This paper studies the relationship between emerging market sovereign spreads and ratings on their long-term foreign currency denominated debt in order to develop a simple framework for the monitoring of market and rating agencies' views on emerging markets. Unlike most studies which use cross-section analysis, this paper uses panel data estimation to exploit the cross-sectional and time series dimensions of sovereign spreads and ratings.

Using J.P. Morgan EMBI+ country spreads and an average of Moody's and S&P's long-term foreign currency debt for 17 emerging market countries (Argentina, Brazil, Bulgaria, Colombia, Ecuador, Korea, Mexico, Morocco, Panama, Peru, the Philippines, Poland, Qatar, Russia, South Africa, Turkey, and Venezuela), from January 1994 to April 2001, we document a few stylized facts and illustrate how the relationship between sovereign spreads and ratings can be used as a first stage in the analysis of market and rating agencies' views of emerging markets.

We find, not surprisingly, that there is a negative association—as measured by the Spearman rank correlation—between sovereign spreads and ratings, with higher ratings being associated with lower spreads. Furthermore, we find that this relationship has strengthened over the years. In addition, we find that the dispersion of spreads—as measured by the coefficient of variation—for similarly rated countries increased during the 1998 crisis, indicating that there was increased discrimination between countries during a crisis, but that this greater differentiation was not based on credit ratings. This result suggests, again not surprisingly, that market participants rely on factors other than ratings to differentiate between countries during episodes of market turbulence.

Using an unbalanced panel data estimation, we fit a simple univariate model of log spreads on ratings. The residuals of this estimation are used to analyze statistically significant deviations from the calculated relationship between market views and fundamentals. We find that sovereign spreads and ratings adjust differently depending on whether spreads are "excessively high"—defined as deviations above the 95 percent confidence interval—or "excessively low"— that is for observations below the 95 percent confidence interval. Indeed, our results indicate that periods with "excessively high" spreads are on average followed by episodes of spread tightening one month later rather than credit downgrades. In contrast, observations with "excessively low" spreads are on average followed by rating upgrades 3 months later rather than episodes of spread widening. These results suggest an asymmetric adjustment when actual spreads are significantly different from fitted spreads which are spreads justified by economic and political fundamentals, as measured by rating agencies. These findings suggest the existence of a predictability pattern in emerging market spreads, which could be exploited by investors.

Finally, as an illustration of the use of the relationship between sovereign spreads and ratings for the monitoring of market and rating agencies' views of emerging markets, an analysis of the panel estimation results finds that most emerging market spreads were "excessively low" before the Asian crisis. In contrast, in April 2001, Argentina, Turkey, and the Philippines had "excessively high" rating-based spreads while Brazil had rating-based spreads very close to the "excessively high" levels. The paper argues that such significant deviations from the levels predicted by ratings alone should indicate that increased scrutiny of a country's fundamentals and market technicals are warranted. The suggested framework is flexible enough to accommodate refinements such as a multivariate model of spreads or the use of "corrected" sovereign ratings obtained through in-house models.

The rest of the paper is organized as follows. Section II briefly reviews the literature on the relationship between sovereign spreads and ratings while section III documents a few stylized facts and studies in more details such a relationship. Section IV suggests a simple framework for the monitoring of market and rating agencies' views of emerging markets, and finally section V concludes.

II. Review of the literature

Our paper is closest in spirit to market analysis which compares sovereign or corporate bond spreads on a rating-adjusted basis. For instance, a study by Deutsche

Bank (2000) finds that a combination of technical factors and credit fundamentals could explain the observation that, on a rating-adjusted basis, Asian bonds were trading at between 150bp to 175bp tighter than Non-Asian (ex-Russia) bonds in 1999–2000.

The technical factors cited were mostly liquidity conditions and a broadening investor base that increased the demand for Asian bonds hence leading to tighter spreads. Indeed, in 1999-2000 the demand for Asian fixed-income instruments was said to have increased temporarily thanks to a combination of surging current account surpluses, financial sector recapitalization, improved liquidity in the interbank market, corporate deleveraging, and the entry of investor grade investors attracted by Asian investment grade such as Korea. In addition, the study describes an approach which consists in "correcting" ratings provided by agencies and compare these forward looking fitted ratings with market spreads in order to uncover profitable trading strategies.

Similarly, Erb, Harvey, and Viskanta (2000) show the importance of country risk in the pricing and returns of emerging market bonds. They sort every month the countries in the EMBI Global into two portfolios depending on the prior month's ICRG composite rating (Political Risk Services' International Country Risk Guide Composite Rating). They find that the riskier portfolio outperforms the less risky portfolio and the benchmark, but at substantially higher volatility and beta. As a result, they conclude that country risk discriminates between high and low expected return countries and that we should not be surprised to see that perceptions of country risk are reflected in sovereign yields and county bond returns.

Erb, Harvey, and Viskanta (2000) also show that commonly used country risk ratings do an impressive job in explaining the cross-section of real yields in a sample of developing market bonds. They examine the relation between Institutional Investor's country credit ratings and the spread over US Treasuries for the EMBI Global universe of countries. For each country, they estimate the spread for a 4-year spread duration on September 30, 1999. One of their main recommendation is that analysts need to concern themselves with the reasons behind the deviations from the calculated relationship between spreads and risk ratings in order to add value above and beyond a given benchmark. They suggest that, in the case of outliers, deciding whether the market is improperly estimating country risk or mispricing certain bonds is the key to active emerging market bond selection and that part of the issue may be that the market is already anticipating credit risk adjustments. As a result, forecasting future risk profiles adds another dimension to the analyst's job in active bond management.

All the previously described studies use secondary market data and cross-sectional analysis. In contrast, Eichengreen and Mody (1998) and Kamin and Kleist (1997) use a time series of primary market spreads for a sample of emerging market bonds. Kamin and Kleist (1997) analyze issue spreads on bonds and use country credit ratings, industrial country interest rates, time trends, and Mexican dummies to find that Latin American spreads are on average 39 percent higher than Asian spreads for a comparable credit rating. Eichengreen and Mody (1998) refine this analysis by controlling for the likelihood of new issues by different classes of borrowers (sovereign, public, private, and by region).

Unlike the rest of the literature, this paper studies the relationship between secondary market spreads on the EMBI+ country indices and sovereign ratings by using an unbalanced panel data estimation rather than a cross-sectional analysis. We choose secondary rather than primary market spreads as they are more likely to incorporate current market assessment of a country's economic and political fundamentals. In addition, they are less likely to depend on supply factors at the time of issuance. For instance, Eichengreen and Mody (1998) document that in poor market conditions, primary market spreads do not rise proportionately and even fall at times, when secondary market spreads rise. They attribute this observation to the tendency for the number of issues to fall and for only the less risky borrowers to remain in the market during such turbulent times.

III. The Relationship between Emerging Market Spreads and Ratings

A. Spreads and Ratings: Stylized Facts

Data Description

We use sovereign stripped spreads from January 1994 to April 2001, for 17 rated countries which have been included or are still part of the J.P. Morgan EMBI+. These countries are Argentina, Brazil, Bulgaria, Colombia, Ecuador, Korea, Mexico, Morocco, Panama, Peru, the Philippines, Poland, Qatar, Russia, South Africa, Turkey, and Venezuela. Since December 31, 1993, the Emerging Market Bond Index Plus tracks most traded external-currency-denominated debt instruments in the emerging markets and offers one of the longest and most comprehensive emerging market spreads series.

We use EMBI+ sovereign spreads as calculated by J.P. Morgan rather than traditional spreads over U.S. Treasuries as they control for floating coupons, unusual features, and principal collateral and rolling interest guarantees. Although the EMBI+ country indices are weighted averages of all external-currency-denominated individual bonds issued by a particular country, we find them useful because they are readily available and because we are interested in the monitoring of market and rating agencies' views of emerging markets and not in the relative valuation of one particular bond versus another.

Although the EMBI+ index is heavily biased toward Latin American debt and Brady bonds, it has several features that are useful for our analysis. Indeed, since we are interested in market and rating agencies' views of a member country, we can directly use the EMBI+ country indices and avoid the nontrivial task of using the spreads on individual debt instrument to form portfolios for each country. Furthermore, the fact that Bradys as well as most bonds in the index are U.S.

dollar denominated, makes the issue of controlling for foreign exchange risk irrelevant as there is little or no currency risk premium in the spreads.

Furthermore, since all instruments included in the index must satisfy certain liquidity criteria, the spreads used in our analysis have little or similar liquidity risk premia. In fact, instruments in the EMBI+ must have a minimum $500 million of face value and must be available and liquid. J.P. Morgan's liquidity ratings are based on a bond's face amount outstanding, its average bid-ask spreads, and the number of designated brokers quoting it. Furthermore, market participants agree that most benchmark emerging market bonds are highly liquid, even more than U.S. high yield bonds.

Although we do not use data on duration to control for interest rate risk, all bonds included in the index have a remaining maturity greater than 2.5 years. Furthermore, since the average maturity of most country indices are comparable, we find it reasonable to assume that duration considerations would not change our results substantially.

We also use the average of monthly Moody's and S&P's Long Term Foreign Currency ratings form January 1994 to April 2001[2]. Since a bond can only be added to the EMBI+ index as long as the country from which it is issued receives a rating of BBB+/Baal or lower from either S&P or Moody's, all the ratings used satisfy this requirement. Rating agencies claim that sovereign ratings combine a number of political and economic variables. For instance, Standard & Poor's (1998) report that such economic factors include a country's income and economic structure, economic growth prospects, fiscal flexibility, public debt burden, price stability, balance of payment flexibility, and external debt and liquidity. In addition, political variables include a country's form of government and adaptability of political institutions, the extent of popular participation, the orderliness of leadership succession, the degree of consensus on economic policy objectives, its integration into global trade and financial system, and its internal and external security risks.

Although credit ratings represent analysts' view of a particular country's economic and political fundamentals, a number of studies (Cantor and Packer (1996), Ul Haque, Kumar, Mark, and Mathieson (1996), Juttner and McCarthy (1998), Monfort and Mulder (2000), and Mulder (2001)), have found a close association between credit ratings and a reduced number of macroeconomic variables. Nonetheless, the framework suggested in this paper is flexible enough to incorporate additional variables as well as disagreements with observed ratings. In addition, more forward looking information such as the rating outlook on a particular country could be easily included.

Stylized Facts

Although sovereign spreads are more volatile than ratings, a graph of average sovereign spreads and ratings from 1994 to 2001 (Figure 1) shows a striking progression in the relationship between spreads and ratings. Since the early days of

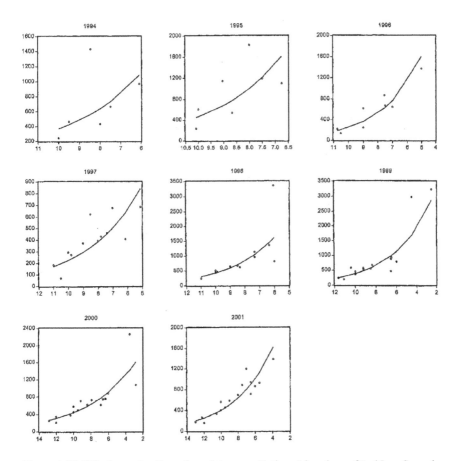

Figure 1 EMBI+ Sovereign Spreads and Average Ratings Line shows fitted Log Spreads

emerging market debt trading in 1994, there seems to be a stronger relationship between the two variables or in other words, credit ratings seem to explain sovereign spreads better. To document this observation, we study the Spearman rank correlation between spreads and ratings for the 17 emerging market countries in the sample. We also document whether there is evidence of increased differentiation during the 1998 market turbulences.

RANK CORRELATIONS

We compute Spearman rank correlations[3] between J.P. Morgan EMBI+ sovereign spreads and the average of Moody's and S&P's ratings for each year since 1994 to 2001 and for the whole sample (1994–2001). The rank correlation between sovereign spreads and ratings has always been negative and has

41

Table 1 Emerging Market Spreads and Ratings: Spearman Rank Correlations from 1994 to 2001

	1994–2001	*2001*	*2000*	*1999*	*1998*	*1997*	*1996*	*1995*	*1994*
Spearman Rank Correlation	-0.74	-0.93	-0.90	-0.85	-0.74	-0.73	-0.78	-0.64	-0.35
Number of obs	915	64	185	173	148	120	88	79	58
p-value	0.0000	0.00	0.0000	0.0000	0.0000	0.0000	0.0000	0.0000	0.0063

* up to April 2001

increased (in absolute value) from -0.35 in 1994 to -0.93 in 2001 (see Table 1 and Figure 2). Furthermore, this relationship has increased every year since 1994, with the exception of 1997 and 1998, illustrating a negative association between sovereign spreads and ratings (higher ratings corresponding to lower spreads).

SPREADS COEFFICIENT OF VARIATION BY RATING

As a measure of dispersion of spreads by rating, we compute the coefficient of variation of spreads. Figure 3 shows that the coefficient of variation increased in 1998 for most ratings, indicating that spreads for similarly rated countries are more dispersed during a crisis. Indeed, there is less discrimination in the 1998 crisis year as compared to the year before the crisis (for those rating categories with available data for both years). However, the increased differentiation between countries was not based on credit ratings. This suggests that during episodes of great market stress, market participants discriminate more among countries with the same ratings.

CROSS-SECTION REGRESSIONS

A simple regression of log spreads on ratings for each year shows that there is a negative relationship between spreads and ratings with higher rated sovereign debt being associated with lower spreads. Furthermore, the strength of the relationship increases over time as indicated by the increasing R^2. Table 2 shows that the explanatory power of the regression has increased from .15 in 1994 to 81 in 2001. This could be due to the fact that there were very few rated countries in the EMBI+ index in 1994 and that this number has increased gradually with time. Over the whole sample however, the R^2 is 0.56 and the obtained results are statistically significant. Interestingly, the R^2 coefficient has declined during periods of market turbulence, such as in 1997 and 1998 indicating that the relationship between spreads and ratings is less significant during period of crises.

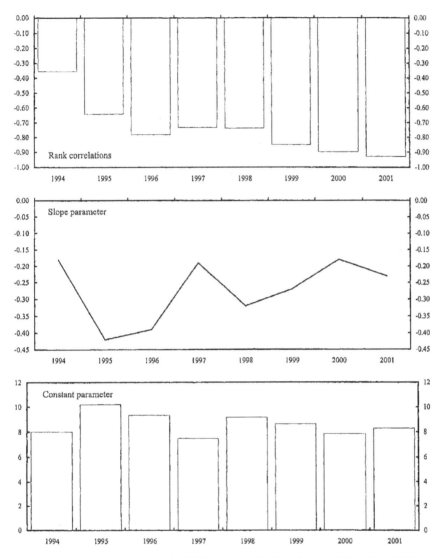

1/ Spearman correlation between spreads of EMBI+ country subindices and average of Moody's and S&P's ratings on sovereign foreign currency long-term debt.
2/ Parameters of a unbalanced panel data regression of log spreads on ratings using monthly data.

Figure 2 Emerging Markets: Spread and Ratings (1994–2001)

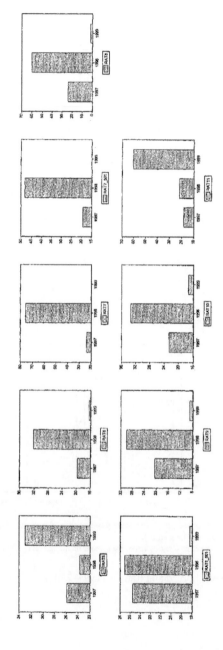

Figure 3 EMBI+ Spreads: Coefficient of Variation by Rating Category

Table 2 Emerging Market Spreads and Rating: Cross-section Regressions

	1994–2001	2001*	2000	1999	1998	1997	1996	1995	1994
R square 1/	0.56	0.87	0.76	0.79	0.63	0.53	0.69	0.51	0.15
Constant 1/	8.33	8.27	7.83	8.63	9.16	7.48	9.33	10.2	8
Slope 2/	-0.24	-0.23	-0.18	-0.27	-0.32	-0.19	-0.39	-0.42	-0.18

* up to April 2001.
1/ Cross-section regression of monthly log spreads on ratings
2/ Intermarket quality spreads (risk appetite).

RISK APPETITE

The regression estimates indicate that both the slope and the intercept coefficients are time-varying (see Table 2 and Figure 2). The slope can be interpreted as the intermarket quality spread as it measures investors[3] perception of default risk and the relative cost of financing for low rated countries compared to higher rated sovereigns. It indicates how much the market would charge a low rated borrower as compared with a high rated borrower. As such this measure can be seen as an indicator of market sentiment. Similarly, the intercept of the regression can be interpreted as the market overall attitude toward risk (see Eichengreen and Mody (1998) for a similar interpretation of both variables). Both measures indicate that there was higher risk appetite in 1994 and 1997, the periods before the Peso and Asian crises. In 2000, these measures were also at relatively high levels. In contrast, these measures indicate very reduced appetite for risk in 1995–1996 and 1998.

B. A Univariate Model of Bond Spreads

We use a univariate model of sovereign bond spreads in order to determine significant differences between market and rating agencies' views of a country's fundamentals. To fully exploit both the cross-sectional and time series nature of the data set, we use unbalanced panel data estimation of log spreads on a numerical transformation of average credit ratings. The relationship between spreads and ratings can be expressed as follows,

$$y_{it} = \alpha_i + \beta_i' x_{it} + \varepsilon_{it} \qquad (1)$$

for $i = 1, 2, \ldots 17$ cross-section units and periods $t = 1, 2, \ldots 88$ giving a total unbalanced panel of 915 observations as they were very few emerging market countries with rated foreign-currency external debt in 1994. The dependent variable is the log of sovereign spreads for a particular country's external debt in the EMBI+ and the independent variable is the average of Moody's and S&P's long-term country sovereign external debt ratings.

We first estimate a model with a common intercept $\alpha_i = \alpha$ where all coefficients are restricted to be the same across all countries thereby ignoring all cross-sectional information. The results show (see Table 3) a R^2 coefficient of 0.56. The

Table 3 A Univariate Model of Emerging Market Bond Spreads (Common Effects)

Unbalanced panel data estimation of $Y(i,t) = a(i) + b(i)X(i,t) + e(i,t)$

for i = 1, 2,..., 17 cross-section units and periods t = 1, 2, ...88 from january 1994 to April 2001, giving a total unbalanced panel of 915 observations, The dependent variable is the log of sovereign spreads for a particular country's external debt in the EMBI+ and the independent variables are numerical equivalents of the average of Moody's and S&P's long-term country sovereign external debt rating.

The model is estimated with a common intercept where all coefficients are restricted to be the same across all countries thereby ignoring all cross-sectional information.

Variable	Coefficient	Std. Error	p-Value
constant	8.330	0.060	0.000
Ratings	-0.238	0.007	0.000
R-squared	0.561		
Adj. R-Squared	0.561		
F-Statistic	1168.224		
p-value	0.000		

constant term which can be interpreted as an indicator for overall market sentiment for risk is statistically significant and comparable to levels reached in 1999 and 2001. Similarly, the slope of the regression, which indicates the spread differential paid by riskier borrowers is significant and comparable to the 1999 and 2001 levels.

We then use the same general specification as above, but with fixed effects for the intercept specification, $\alpha_{it} = \alpha_i$, $E(\alpha_i\varepsilon_{it}) \neq 0$, (see Table 4). The R^2 coefficient increases to 0.68 but with a less steeper slope of -0.15 indicating a reduction in the overall relative cost of financing (slope coefficient) and an overall indicator of market sentiment (intercept) smaller than the 1995 and 1998 crisis levels. Among the countries in the sample, Ecuador and Russia have the highest constant terms which is not surprising since they are the only countries that have defaulted in the sample. This result indicates that the market penalizes countries it regards as having defaulted by requiring an overall risk premium higher than that of other countries. In contrast, South Africa and Korea have the lowest constant terms indicating a lower overall risk premium. Interestingly enough, these countries have consistently been among the highest rated credits in the sample.

We also regress log spreads on ratings and on spreads of the Merrill Lynch U.S. high yield bond index to control for the time series variation in the overall price of risk. In particular, we estimate the following relationship:

$$y_{it} = \alpha_i + \beta_i'x_{it} + \gamma z_t + \varepsilon_i \qquad (2)$$

where all the variables are defined as before except z_t which denotes the monthly spreads over U.S. Treasuries for the Merrill Lynch U.S. high yield index. This

Table 4 A Univariate Model of Emerging Market Bond Spreads (Fixed Effects)

Unbalanced panel data estimation of $Y(i,t) = a(i) + b(i)X(i,t) + e(i,t)$

for $i = 1, 2, ., 17$ cross-section units and periods $t = 1, 2, ..., 88$ from January 1994 to April 2001, giving a total unbalanced panel of 915 observations. The dependent variable is the log of sovereign spreads for a particular country's external debt in the EMBI+ and the independent variables are numerical equivalents of the average of Moody's and S&P's long-term country sovereign external debt rating.

The model uses the same general spefication as in Table 3, but with fixed effects for the intercept specification.

Variable	Coefficient	Std. Error	p-value
Ratings	-0.146	0.017	0.000
R-squared	0.683		
Adj. R-Squared	0.677		
Fixed Effects			
Argentina	7.670		
Bulgaria	7.494		
Brazil	7.653		
Colombia	7.846		
Ecuador	8.112		
Korea	7.127		
Mexico	7.628		
Morocco	7.665		
Panama	7.447		
Peru	7.452		
Philippines	7.331		
Poland	7.143		
Qatar	7.503		
Russia	8.034		
South Africa	6.649		
Turkey	7.348		
Venezuela	7.912		

index is often used as an indicator of overall riskiness for both the emerging market and U.S. high yield asset classes. The results are approximately the same as before (see Table 5). The coefficient of the U.S. high yield bond spreads is not economically significant and the fixed effects coefficients barely change which suggests that the time-series variation of the previously obtained residuals are not just a reflection of changes in the overall price of risk.

C. Analysis of Outliers

Deviations from Rating-based Value

The fitted spreads obtained through the panel data estimation of the relationship between sovereign spreads and ratings can be seen as the average spreads warranted

Table 5 A Bivariate Model of Bonds Spreads

Unbalanced panel data estimation of $Y(i,t) = a(i) + b(i)X(i,t) + cZ(t) + e(i,t)$

for $i = 1, 2,...,17$ cross-section units and periods $t = 1, 2, ...88$ from january 1994 to April 2001, giving a total unbalanced panel of 915 observations. The dependent variable is the log of sovereign spreads for a particular country's external debt in the EMBI+ and the independent variables are numerical equivalents of the average of Moody's and S&P's long-term country sovereign external debt rating and spreads of the Merrill Lynch U.S. High Yield bond index.

Variable	Coefficient	Std. Error	p-value
Ratings	-0.146	0.017	0.000
Spreads on U.S. High Yield/Bonds	0.001	0.000	0.000
R-squared	0.695		
Adj. R-Squared	0.689		
Fixed Effects			
Argentina	7.465		
Bulgaria	7.266		
Brazil	7.446		
Colombia	7.558		
Ecuador	7.865		
Korea	6.864		
Mexico	7.424		
Morocco	7.398		
Panama	7.215		
Peru	7.218		
Philippines	7.132		
Poland	6.929		
Qatar	7.138		
Russia	7.787		
South Africa	6.484		
Turkey	7.054		
Venezuela	7.707		

by current ratings. More loosely, they can be interpreted as the spreads warranted by credit rating agencies' view of a particular country's economic and political fundamentals. When actual market spreads for a sovereign are significantly different from fitted spreads, or in other words when the regression's outliers are significantly different from zero, it is reasonable to assume the following two explanations:

1. Either actual ratings can be justified by economic and political fundamentals, in which case, market participants are mispricing the sovereign's bonds or;
2. Market participants are anticipating future credit rating adjustments and actual ratings are not justified by fundamentals.

Figure 4 offers a simple illustration of the dynamic relationship between spreads and ratings. In this example, Country Y has actual spreads that are higher than

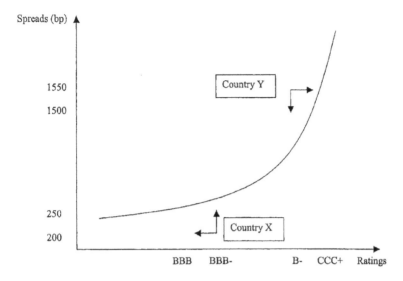

Figure 4 Spreads vs. Ratings Adjustment

fitted spreads which lie on the curve. These "excessively high" spreads could result in subsequent spread tightening if market participants judge that economic and political fundamentals do not warrant the current level of spreads. Another possibility is that markets are anticipating a rating downgrade and rating agencies could subsequently downgrade the sovereign's ratings thereby confirming the market's negative view on the country's fundamentals.

In contrast, Country X has "excessively low" spreads which lie below the fitted curve. These spreads could be justified by market expectations of an upgrade. Another possibility would be a mispricing of the country's bonds which would result in a future spread widening.

Of course in reality, the relationship between spreads and ratings could be more complicated as spreads are a function of both credit fundamentals and technical factors. As a result, Country X's "excessively low" spreads could also be justified by technical factors. For instance, Deutsche Bank (2000) suggests that in 1999–2000, technical factors such as liquidity conditions and a broadening investor base increased the demand for Asian bonds hence leading to tighter spreads. The reasons for the increased liquidity included a temporary combination of surging C/A surpluses, financial sector recapitalization, easing monetary policy (increased liquidity in the interbank market), corporate deleveraging, and the entry of investor grade investors attracted by Asian investment grade such as Korea. Similarly, a particular country's spreads could be "too low" because market participants are willing to pay a scarcity premium in order to hold its bonds.

In contrast, technical factors such as rumors, investors' trading strategies, or large capital movements by certain players could lead to "excessively high" spreads. For instance, traders may take short positions during a sell off triggered by bad news in a particular country, thereby pushing spreads well above the levels warranted by the initial bad news. Subsequently, spreads can swing in the other direction as traders begin to cover their shorts and this "pendulum effect" can occur until an equilibrium is found (see Vine (1995) for an illustration of technical analysis of emerging market debt).

How do Ratings and Spreads Adjust Following "Excessively High or Low" Spreads?

Do "high" spreads reflect market anticipation of deteriorating economic fundamentals (as measured by ratings), thereby implying an expected rating downgrade or do they reflect a temporary market underpricing implying a future spread tightening (price increase)? Similarly, do "low" spreads reflect market anticipation of improving economic fundamentals (as measured by ratings), implying market expectations of a rating upgrade or do they reflect a temporary market overpricing implying a future spread widening (price decrease)? We address these questions by defining countries with "excessively high (low)" spreads as those countries for which the outliers of the panel estimation of log spreads on credit ratings are above (below) the 95 percent confidence bands, in a particular month (see Figure 5–6). By identifying these outliers and differentiating between "excessively high and low" spreads, we find evidence that spreads adjust in an asymmetric fashion, when there are significant deviations from the estimated relationship between sovereign spreads and ratings. Our results indicate—not surprisingly—that ratings do not change frequently following "excessively high and low" spreads. However, when they do change, rating adjustments have the expected sign. In contrast, spreads are very volatile but do not necessarily adjust in the expected direction.

We find that, when spreads are "excessively low," the rating upgrade effect dominates the spread widening effect which suggests that spreads incorporate market participants' expectations of a rating upgrade. In contrast, when spreads are "excessively high," the spread tightening effect is more important than the downgrade effect which could indicate that bonds were mispriced.

In particular, when spreads are "too low," we find that there is a 50 percent likelihood of a widening or a tightening over the next month (see Table 6). However, when ratings change, there is an expected rating upgrade 3 months later in 13 percent of the cases and an unexpected downgrade in only 3 percent of the cases. In contrast, there is evidence of market mispricing when actual spreads are "too high" relative to fitted spreads. In fact, spreads tighten over the following month in 70 percent of the cases while ratings barely change. When they do change, however, ratings are downgraded in 10 percent of the cases compared to 2 percent cases of rating downgrades.

Table 6 Ratings and Spreads Adjustments

For each country, residuals outside the 95 percent confidence interval from a panel data estimation of log spreads on ratings are collected. Next, the average number of rating changes across countries, over the next 3 and 6 months and the average number of spread changes across countries, over the next month are calculated and expressed in percentage.

"Excessively Low" Spreads

Average Number of Changes	Expected Upgrade	Unexpected Downgrade	No Change	Total
3 months later	13.4	2.5	84.1	100
6 months later	21.2	3.3	75.5	100
	Expected Widening	Unexpected Tightening	No Change	Total
1 month later	49.6	50.4	-	100

"Excessively High" Spreads

Average Number of Changes	Expected Downgrade	Unexpected Upgrade	No Change	Total
3 months later	9.7	2.3	87.9	100
6 months later	16.1	4.3	79.6	100
	Expected Tightening	Unexpected Widening	No Change	Total
1 month later	70.4	29.6	-	100

We do not find enough evidence of rating adjustments for a one month horizon. In contrast, both rating and spread changes have the expected sign in an increased number of cases over longer horizons (6 and 3 months, respectively).

In the next section, we illustrate how the relationship between spreads and ratings could be used for the monitoring of market and rating agencies' views of emerging markets. The goal is to compare sovereign spreads on a rating-adjusted basis and identify countries that warrant increased scrutiny and further analysis because market participants are in disagreement with rating agencies (and more loosely with economic and political fundamentals).

IV. A Simple Tool for Monitoring Market and Rating Agencies' Views

When sovereign spreads and ratings are in disagreement, it may prove useful to examine in more detail the causes of the discrepancy between market views and economic fundamentals. As described above, we use statistically significant deviations from a panel data estimation of a univariate model of log spreads on ratings as a measure of such a disagreement. In this section, we relax the previously used definition of "excessively large" spreads and focus instead on outliers below or above the standard deviation of the regression.

Figure 5 illustrates deviations from rating-based spreads for the period[4] from January 1994 to June 1997. This period ends just before the July 1997 Thai devaluation and the estimation uses only the data available just before the Asian crisis. It is clear that most emerging market spreads—for which we have data—were "excessively low" indicating that either rating agencies found economic and political fundamentals not to be reflected in overoptimistic market spreads or market participants expected a rating upgrade in the near future. In any case, for the purpose of monitoring market and rating agencies' views of a member country, the model would have indicated that increased analysis of economic fundamentals and market technicals was warranted for Argentina, Bulgaria, Brazil, Mexico, the Philippines, Venezuela, and South Africa. In addition, Poland had spreads relatively close to the "excessively low" boundary.

More recently, when we use the whole sample from January 1994 to June 2001 to estimate the model, we find that emerging market spreads were either "excessively high" or relatively high. Figure 6 and Table 7 show the difference between actual spreads and fitted spreads in April 2001 for the set of countries in the J.P. Morgan EMBI+. Three countries, namely Argentina, Turkey, and the Philippines had "excessively high" spreads. In addition, Brazilian spreads were very close to being "excessively high." Our previous results suggest that more detailed analysis would have been warranted for these countries. For instance, were ratings justified by economic and political fundamentals? Were there other economic, financial, and political variables that were deteriorating for these particular countries?

In contrast, although there were no countries below the confidence intervals, residuals for Ecuador, Russia, Venezuela, Mexico, and Qatar were very close to the lower band. Were such low spreads justified? Did markets expect an upgrade? Were there technical factors that warranted such low spreads? Figure 7 illustrates the same relationship graphically and shows the difference between actual and fitted spreads. Again, Argentina, Turkey, and the Philippines clearly stand out.

A number of methods could be used to help answer these questions. One possibility would be to regress the residuals of the estimated relationship between log spreads and ratings on a number of candidate explanatory variables. For instance, bid-ask spreads and trading volume (when available) could be used as a proxy for liquidity. Another possibility, as described by Deutsche Bank (2000) is to assign "corrected" ratings to particular countries and estimate the relationship using these new ratings. These "corrected" ratings would presumably incorporate variables that have been overlooked by rating agencies.

In addition, it is equally important to analyze technical factors that could lead to substantial differences between rating-based and market spreads. For instance, knowledge of the investor base for a country's bonds and of market participants' trading strategies and positions can help explain the levels and movements of

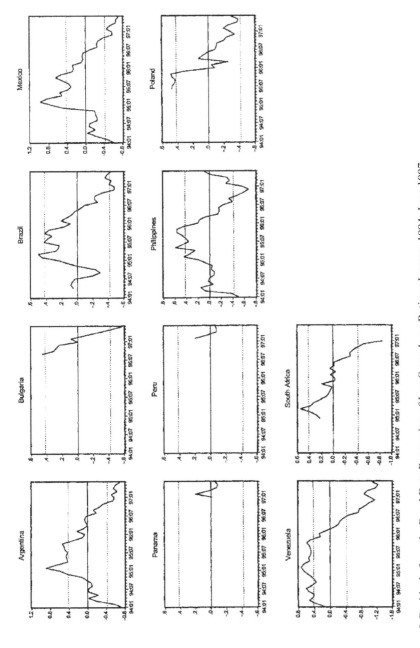

Figure 5 Residuals from the Panel Data Regression of Log Spreads on Ratings January 1994–June 1997

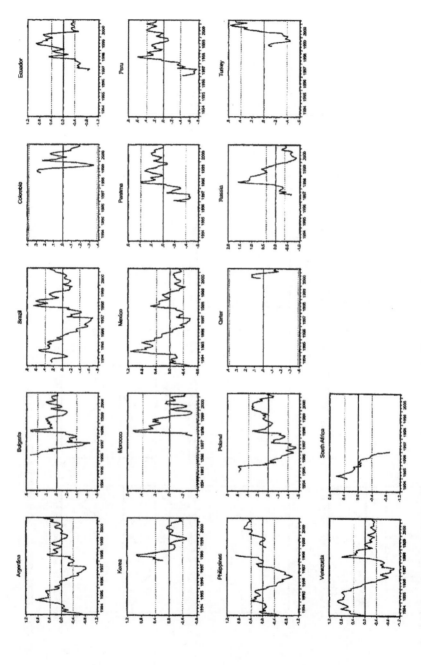

Figure 6 Residuals from the panel data regression of log spreads on ratings January 1994–June 2001

54

Table 7 Countries with "Excessively High/Low" Spreads on April 2001

Fitted spreads are obtained from a panel data estimation of log spreads on ratings.
Bands refer to the plus/minus one standard deviation interval.

	Rating	Actual Spread	Fitted Spread	Spread Differential	Status
Ecuador	3.5	1424	2002	-578	Close to lower band
Russia	5.5	922	1384	-462	Close to lower band
Turkey	**6**	**1058**	**648**	**410**	**Excessively High**
Venezuela	6	903	1139	-236	Close to lower band
Argentina	6.5	1552	831	721	**Excessively High**
Bulgaria	6.5	687	697	-10	
Brazil	7.5	948	707	241	Close to upper band
Peru	8	636	538	98	
Colombia	9	578	689	-111	
Morocco	9.5	422	535	-113	
Panama	10	401	400	1	
Philippines	**10**	**580**	**356**	**224**	**Excessively High**
Mexico	10.5	343	445	-102	Close to lower band
Korea	12	152	217	-65	
Qatar	12.5	255	294	-39	Close to lower band
Poland	13	197	191	6	

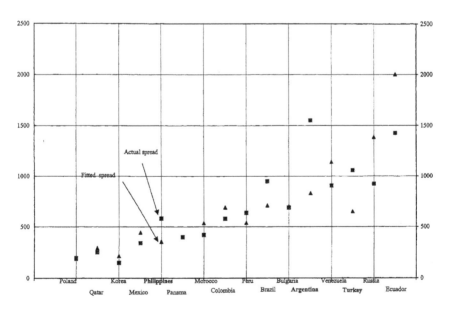

Figure 7 Actual Vs. Rating-based Spreads (April 2001)

spreads. The nature of these technical factors suggests that a qualitative analysis of capital markets is necessary to complement any quantitative assessment of market participants' views.

V. Conclusion

This paper uses data on sovereign spreads and ratings for 17 emerging market countries to suggest a simple framework for the monitoring of market and rating agencies' views of emerging markets. The cross-sectional and time series nature of the data is used to present stylized facts on the relationship between sovereign spreads and ratings, and to estimate a simple univariate model of log spreads on average credit ratings.

Sovereign spreads and ratings are sometimes judged to be of little value because both did not fare well as crisis predictors in 1997. Indeed, prior to the Asian crisis, both spreads and ratings were very low (see IMF (1999)). This paper argues that disagreements between market and rating agencies' assessment of a country's economic and political fundamentals are useful. Significant differences could be used as a signal that further analysis of a country's fundamentals and of its market technicals is warranted. As an illustration, we find that sovereign spreads were "excessively low" prior to the Asian crisis. More recently, we are able to identify Argentina, the Philippines, and Turkey as having "excessively high" spreads in April 2001.

The framework developed in this paper is flexible enough to control for technical factors or disagreements with rating agencies by correcting actual ratings. For instance, one could adjust ratings on a forward-looking basis, calculate fitted spreads, and analyze outliers. One could also control for independent variables to improve the explanatory power of the univariate model. Another direction for further analysis would be to use data on individual instruments and control for variables such as maturity, duration, rating outlook, recovery value, liquidity, and the presence of covenants such as collective action clauses, collateral, callable, and putable features. Although useful, the benefits of these improvements will have to be weighed against their costs in achieving the goal of assessing emerging markets' vulnerabilities.

Notes

1 The author wishes to thank Tobjom Becker, Jorge Chan Lau, Piti Disyatat, Donald Mathieson, Laura Papi, and Anthony Richards for valuable comments, and J.P. Morgan Chase, Silvia Iorgova and Peter Tran for their assistance with the data.
2 We convert S&P's and Moody's ratings to numerical values using a linear scale from 0 to 20 with SD and CC/Ca ratings corresponding to values of zero and 1 respectively, and AAA/Aaa ratings being assigned a value of 20.
3 See Scholtens (1999) for a similar approach using Institutional Investor's ratings.
4 We do not fit the model for the period before the Peso crisis because of too short an horizon.

References

Cantor, R., and F. Packer, 1996, "Determinants and Impact of Sovereign Credit Ratings," *Economic Policy Review*, Federal Reserve Bank of New York, Vol. 2 (October), pp. 37–53.

Deutsche Bank, 2000, "Focus on Asian Bond Markets: Exploring the "Asia Premium," *Asiamoney.*

Eichengreen B., and A. Mody, 1998, "What Explains Changing Spreads on Emerging Market Debt: Fundamentals or Market Sentiment?" *NBER Working Paper* 6408.

Erb, C., C. R. Harvey, and T. Viskanta, 2000, "Understanding Emerging Market Bonds," Emerging Markets Quarterly, Spring 2000, pp.7–23.

International Monetary Fund, 1999, *international Capital Markets: Developments, Prospects, and Key Policy Issues*, World Economic and Financial Surveys (Washington, September), pp. 180–99.

Juttner, J. D., and J. McCarthy, 1998, "Modeling a Ratings Crisis," (unpublished; Sydney, Australia: Macquarie University).

Kamin, S., and K. von Kleist, 1999, "The Evolution and Determinants of Emerging Market Credit Spreads in the 1990s," *Bank for International Settlements*, Working Paper 68.

Monfort, B., and C. Mulder, 2000, "Using Credit Ratings for Capital Requirements on Lending to Emerging Market Economies: Possible Impact of a New Basel Accord," *IMF Working Paper* WP/00/69 (Washington: International Monetary Fund).

Mulder, C., and R. Perrelli, 2001, "Foreign Currency Credit Ratings for Emerging Market Economies," *IMF Working Paper* (forthcoming; Washington: International Monetary Fund).

Scholtens, B., 1999, "On the Comovement of Bond Yield Spreads and Country Risk Ratings," *Journal of Fixed Income*, March, pp.99–103.

Ul Haque, N., M. Kumar, N. Mark, and D. J. Mathieson, 1996, "The Economic Content of Indicators of Developing Country Creditworthiness," *IMF Staff Papers*, Vol. 43, No 4, December, pp.688–723.

Vine, A. A., 1995, "High Yield Analysis of Emerging Markets Debt," Merrill Lynch.

17

DETERMINANTS AND IMPACT OF SOVEREIGN CREDIT RATINGS

Richard Cantor and Frank Packer

Source: *Federal Reserve Bank of New York Economic Policy Review,* October 1996, 37–54.

In recent years, the demand for sovereign credit ratings—the risk assessments assigned by the credit rating agencies to the obligations of central governments—has increased dramatically. More governments with greater default risk and more companies domiciled in riskier host countries are borrowing in international bond markets. Although foreign government officials generally cooperate with the agencies, rating assignments that are lower than anticipated often prompt issuers to question the consistency and rationale of sovereign ratings. How clear are the criteria underlying sovereign ratings? Moreover, how much of an impact do ratings have on borrowing costs for sovereigns?

To explore these questions, we present the first systematic analysis of the determinants and impact of the sovereign credit ratings assigned by the two leading U.S. agencies, Moody's Investors Service and Standard and Poor's.[1] Such an analysis has only recently become possible as a result of the rapid growth in sovereign rating assignments. The wealth of data now available allows us to estimate which quantitative indicators are weighed most heavily in the determination of ratings, to evaluate the predictive power of ratings in explaining a cross-section of sovereign bond yields, and to measure whether rating announcements directly affect market yields on the day of the announcement.

Our investigation suggests that, to a large extent, Moody's and Standard and Poor's rating assignments can be explained by a small number of well-defined criteria, which the two agencies appear to weigh similarly. We also find that the market—as gauged by sovereign debt yields—broadly shares the relative rankings of sovereign credit risks made by the two rating agencies. In addition, credit ratings appear to have some independent influence on yields over and above their correlation with other publicly available information. In particular, we find that rating announcements have immediate effects on market pricing for non-investment-grade issues.

What Are Sovereign Ratings?

Like other credit ratings, sovereign ratings are assessments of the relative likelihood that a borrower will default on its obligations.[2] Governments generally seek credit ratings to ease their own access (and the access of other issuers domiciled within their borders) to international capital markets, where many investors, particularly U.S. investors, prefer rated securities over unrated securities of apparently similar credit risk.

In the past, governments tended to seek ratings on their foreign currency obligations exclusively, because foreign currency bonds were more likely than domestic currency offerings to be placed with international investors. In recent years, however, international investors have increased their demand for bonds issued in currencies other than traditional global currencies, leading more sovereigns to obtain domestic currency bond ratings as well. To date, however, foreign currency ratings—the focus of this article—remain the more prevalent and influential in the international bond markets.

Sovereign ratings are important not only because some of the largest issuers in the international capital markets are national governments, but also because these assessments affect the ratings assigned to borrowers of the same nationality. For example, agencies seldom, if ever, assign a credit rating to a local municipality, provincial government, or private company that is higher than that of the issuer s home country.

Table 1 Rating Symbols for Long-Term Debt

Interpretation	Moody's	Standard and Poor's
INVESTMENT-GRADE RATINGS		
Highest quality	Aaa	AAA
High quality	Aa1	AA+
	Aa2	AA
	Aa3	AA-
Strong payment capacity	A1	A+
	A2	A
	A3	A-
Adequate payment capacity	Baa1	BBB+
	Baa2	BBB
	Baa3	BBB-
SPECULATIVE-GRADE RATINGS		
Likely to fulfill obligations, ongoing uncertainty	Ba1	BB+
	Ba2	BB
	Ba3	BB-
High-risk obligations	B1	B+
	B2	B
	B3	B-

Note: To date, the agencies have not assigned sovereign ratings below B3/B-.

Moody's and Standard and Poor's each currently rate more than fifty sovereigns. Although the agencies use different symbols in assessing credit risk, every Moody's symbol has its counterpart in Standard and Poor's rating scale (Table 1). This correspondence allows us to compare the sovereign ratings assigned by the two agencies. Of the forty-nine countries rated by both Moody's and Standard and Poor's in September 1995, twenty-eight received the same rating from the two agencies, twelve were rated higher by Standard and Poor's, and nine were rated higher by Moody's (Table 2). When the agencies disagreed, their ratings in most cases differed by one notch on the scale, although for seven countries their ratings differed by two notches. (A rating notch is a one-level difference on a rating scale, such as the difference between A1 and A2 for Moody's or between A+ and A for Standard and Poor's.)

Determinants of Sovereign Ratings

In their statements on rating criteria, Moody's and Standard and Poor's list numerous economic, social, and political factors that underlie their sovereign credit ratings (Moody's 1991; Moody's 1995; Standard and Poor's 1994). identifying the relationship between their criteria and actual ratings, however, is difficult, in part because some of the criteria are not quantifiable. Moreover, the agencies provide little guidance as to the relative weights they assign each factor. Even for quantifiable factors, determining the relative weights assigned by Moody's and Standard and Poor's is difficult because the agencies rely on such a large number of criteria.

In the article's next section, we use regression analysis to measure the relative significance of eight variables that are repeatedly cited in rating agency reports as determinants of sovereign ratings.[3] As a first step, however, we describe these variables and identify the measures we use to represent them in our quantitative analysis (Table 3). We explain below the relationship between each variable and a country's ability and willingness to service its debt:

- *Per capita income.* The greater the potential tax base of the borrowing country, the greater the ability of a government to repay debt. This variable can also serve as a proxy for the level of political stability and other important factors.
- *GDP growth.* A relatively high rate of economic growth suggests that a country's existing debt burden will become easier to service over time.
- *Inflation.* A high rate of inflation points to structural problems in the government's finances. When a government appears unable or unwilling to pay for current budgetary expenses through taxes or debt issuance, it must resort to inflationary money finance. Public dissatisfaction with inflation may in turn lead to political instability.
- *Fiscal balance.* A large federal deficit absorbs private domestic savings and suggests that a government lacks the ability or will to tax its citizenry to cover current expenses or to service its debt.[4]

Table 2 Sovereign Credit Ratings. As of September 29, 1995

Country	Moody's Rating	Standard and Poor's Rating
Argentina	B1	BB-
Australia	Aa2	AA
Austria	Aaa	AAA
Belgium	Aa1	AA+
Bermuda	Aa1	AA
Brazil	B1	B+
Canada	Aa2	AA+
Chile	Baa1	A-
China	A3	BBB
Colombia	Baa3	BBB-
Czech Republic	Baa1	BBB+
Denmark	Aa1	AA+
Finland	Aa2	AA-
France	Aaa	AAA
Germany	Aaa	AAA
Greece	Baa3	BBB-
Hong Kong	A3	A
Hungary	Ba1	BB+
Iceland	A2	A
India	Baa3	BB+
Indonesia	Baa3	BBB
Ireland	Aa2	AA
Italy	A1	AA
Japan	Aaa	AAA
Korea	A1	AA-
Luxembourg	Aaa	AAA
Malaysia	A1	A+
Malta	A2	A
Mexico	Ba2	BB
Netherlands	Aaa	AAA
New Zealand	Aa2	AA
Norway	Aa1	AAA
Pakistan	B1	B+
Philippines	Ba2	BB
Poland	Baa3	BB
Portugal	A1	AA-
Singapore	Aa2	AAA
Slovak Republic	Baa3	BB+
South Africa	Baa3	BB
Spain	Aa2	AA
Sweden	Aa3	AA+
Switzerland	Aaa	AAA
Taiwan	Aa3	AA+
Thailand	A2	A
Turkey	Ba3	B+
United Kingdom	Aaa	AAA
United States	Aaa	AAA
Uruguay	Ba1	BB+
Venezuela	Ba2	B+

Sources: Moody's; Standard and Poor's.

Table 3 Description of Variables

Variable Name	Definition	Unit of Measurement[a]	Data Sources
Determinants of Sovereign Ratings			
Per capita income	GNP per capita in 1994	Thousands of dollars	World Bank, Moody's, FRBNY estimates
GDP growth	Average annual real GDP growth on a year-over-year basis, 1991–94	Percent	World Bank, Moody's, FRBNY estimates
Inflation	Average annual consumer price inflation rate, 1992–94	Percent	World Bank, Moody's, FRBNY estimates
Fiscal balance	Average annual central government budget surplus relative to GDP, 1992–94	Percent	World Bank, Moody's, IMF, FRBNY estimates
External balance	Average annual current account surplus relative to GDP, 1992–94	Percent	World Bank, Moody's, FRBNY estimates
External debt	Foreign currency debt relative to exports, 1994	Percent	World Bank, Moody's, FRBNY estimates
Indicator for economic development	IMF classification as an industrialized country as of September 1995	Indicator variable: 1 = industrialized; 0 = not industrialized	IMF
Indicator for default history	Default on foreign currency debt since 1970	Indicator variable: 1 = default; 0 = no default	S&P
Other Variables			
Moody's, S&P, or average ratings	Ratings assigned as of September 29, 1995, by Moody's or S&P, or the average of the two agencies' ratings	B1(B+)=3; Ba3(BB-)=4; Ba2(BB)=5;... Aaa(AAA)=16	Moody's, S&P
Spreads	Sovereign bond spreads over Treasuries, adjusted to five-year maturities[b]	Basis points	Bloomberg L.P., Salomon Brothers, J.P Morgan, FRBNY estimates

Note: S&P= Standard and Poor's; FRBNY= Federal Reserve Bank of New York; IMF= International Monetary Fund.

[a] In the regression analysis, per capita income, inflation, and spreads are transformed to natural logarithms.

[b] For example, the spread on a three-year maturity Baa/BBB sovereign bond is adjusted to a five-year maturity by subtracting the difference between the average spreads on three-year and five-year Baa/BBB corporate bonds as reported by Bloomberg L.P. on September 29, 1995.

- *External balance.* A large current account deficit indicates that the public and private sectors together rely heavily on funds from abroad. Current account deficits that persist result in growth in foreign indebtedness, which may become unsustainable over time.

- *External debt.* A higher debt burden should correspond to a higher risk of default. The weight of the burden increases as a country's foreign currency debt rises relative to its foreign currency earnings (exports).[5]

- *Economic development.* Although level of development is already measured by our per capita income variable, the rating agencies appear to factor a threshold effect into the relationship between economic development and risk. That is, once countries reach a certain income or level of development, they may be less likely to default.[6] We proxy for this minimum income or development level with a simple indicator variable noting whether or not a country is classified as industrialized by the international Monetary Fund.

- *Default history.* Other things being equal, a country that has defaulted on debt in the recent past is widely perceived as a high credit risk. Both theoretical considerations of the role of reputation in sovereign debt (Eaton 1996) and related empirical evidence indicate that defaulting sovereigns suffer a severe decline in their standing with creditors (Ozler 1991). We factor in credit reputation by using an indicator variable that notes whether or not a country has defaulted on its international bank debt since 1970.

Quantifying the Relationship between Ratings and Their Determinants

In this section, we assess the individual and collective significance of our eight variables in determining the September 29, 1995, ratings of the forty-nine countries listed in Table 2. The sample statistics, broken out by broad letter category, show that five of the eight variables are directly correlated with the ratings assigned by Moody's and Standard and Poor's (Table 4). In particular, a high per capita income appears to be closely related to high ratings: among the nine countries assigned top ratings by Moody's and the eleven given Standard and Poor's highest ratings, median per capita income is just under $24,000. Lower inflation and lower external debt are also consistently related to higher ratings. A high level of economic development, as measured by the indicator for industrialization, greatly increases the likelihood of a rating of Aa/AA. As a negative factor, any history of default limits a sovereign's ratings to Baa/BBB or below.

Three factors—GDP growth, fiscal balance, and external balance—lack a clear bivariate relation to ratings. Ratings may lack a simple relation to GDP growth because many developing economies tend to grow faster than mature economies. More surprising, however, is the lack of a clear correlation between ratings and fiscal and external balances. This finding may reflect endogeneity in both fiscal policy and international capital flows: countries trying to improve their credit

Table 4 Sample Statistics by Broad Letter Rating Categories

	Agency	Aaa/AAA	Aa/AA	A/A	Baa/BBB	Ba/BB	B/B
MEDIANS							
Per capita income	Moody's	23.56	19.96	8.22	2.47	3.30	3.37
	S&P	23.56	18.40	5.77	1.62	3.01	2.61
GDP growth	Moody's	1.27	2.47	5.87	4.07	2.28	4.30
	S&P	1.52	2.33	6.49	5.07	2.31	2.84
Inflation	Moody's	2.86	2.29	4.56	13.73	32.44	13.23
	S&P	2.74	2.64	4.18	14.3	13.23	62.13
Fiscal balance	Moody's	-2.67	-2.28	-1.03	-3.50	-2.50	-1.75
	S&P	-2.29	-3.17	1.37	0.15	-3.50	-4.03
External balance	Moody's	0.90	2.10	-2.48	-2.10	-2.74	-3.35
	S&P	3.10	-0.73	-3.68	-2.10	-3.35	-1.05
External debt	Moody's	76.5	102.5	70.4	157.2	220.2	291.6
	S&P	76.5	97.2	61.7	157.2	189.7	231.6
Spread	Moody's	0.32	0.34	0.61	1.58	3.40	4.45
	S&P	0.29	0.40	0.59	1.14	2.58	3.68
FREQUENCIES							
Number rated	Moody's	9	13	9	9	6	3
	S&P	11	14	6	5	9	4
Indicator for economic development	Moody's	9	10	3	1	0	0
	S&P	10	11	1	1	0	0
Indicator for default history	Moody's	0	0	0	2	5	2
	S&P	0	0	0	0	6	3

Sources: Moody's; Standard and Poor's; World Bank; International Monetary Fund; Bloomberg L.P.; J.P. Morgan; Federal Reserve Bank of New York estimates.

64

standings may opt for more conservative fiscal policies, and the supply of international capital may be restricted for some low-rated countries.

Because some of the eight variables are mutually correlated, we estimate a multiple regression to quantify their combined explanatory power and to sort out their individual contributions to the determination of ratings. Like most analysts who transform bond ratings into data for regression analysis (beginning with Horrigan 1966 and continuing through Billet 1996), we assign numerical values to the Moody's and Standard and Poor's ratings as follows: B3/B-= 1, B2/B = 2, and so on through Aaa/AAA = 16. When we need a measure of a country's average rating, we take the mean of the two numerical values representing Moody's and Standard and Poor's ratings for that country. Our regressions relate the numerical equivalents of Moody's and Standard and Poor's ratings to the eight explanatory variables through ordinary least squares.[7]

The model's ability to predict large differences in ratings is impressive. The first column of Table 5 shows that a regression of the average of Moody's and Standard and Poor's ratings against our set of eight variables explains more than 90 percent of the sample variation and yields a residual standard error of about 1.2 rating notches. Note that although the model's explanatory power is impressive, the regression achieves its high R-squared through its ability to predict large rating differences. For example, the specification predicts that Germany's rating (Aaa/AAA) will be much higher than Uruguay's (Ba1/BB+). The model naturally has little to say about small rating differences—for example, why Mexico is rated Ba2/BB and South Africa is rated Baa3/BB. These differences, while modest, can cause great controversy in financial markets.

The regression does not yield any prediction errors that exceed three notches, and errors that exceed two notches occur in the case of only four countries. Another way of measuring the accuracy of this specification is to compare predicted ratings rounded off to the nearest broad letter rating with actual broad letter ratings. The average rating regression predicts these broad letter ratings with about 70 percent accuracy, a slightly higher accuracy rate than that found in the literature quantifying the determinants of corporate ratings (see, for example, Ederington [1985]).

Of the individual coefficients, per capita income, GDP growth, inflation, external debt, and the indicator variables for economic development and default history all have the anticipated signs and are statistically significant. The coefficients on both the fiscal and external balances are statistically insignificant and of the unexpected sign. As mentioned earlier, in many cases the market forces poor credit risks into apparently strong fiscal and external balance positions, diminishing the significance of fiscal and external balances as explanatory variables. Therefore, although the agencies may assign substantial weight to these variables in determining specific rating assignments, no systematic relationship between these variables and ratings is evident in our sample.

Quantitative models cannot explain all variations in ratings across countries: as the agencies often state, qualitative social and political considerations are also

Table 5 Determinants of Sovereign Credit Ratings

Explanatory Variable	Dependent Variable			
	Average Ratings	Moody's Ratings	Standard and Poor's Ratings	Moody's/Standard and Poor's Rating Differences[a]
Intercept	1.442	3.408	-0.524	3.932**
	(0.633)	(1.379)	(0.223)	(2.521)
Per capita income	1.242***	1.027***	1.458***	-0.431***
	(5.302)	(4.041)	(6.048)	(2.688)
GDP growth	0.151*	0.130	0.171**	-0.040
	(1.935)	(1.545)	(2.132)	(0.756)
Inflation	-0.611***	-0.630***	-0.591***	-0.039
	(2.839)	(2.701)	(2.671)	(0.265)
Fiscal balance	0.073	0.049	0.097*	-0.048
	(1.324)	(0.818)	(1.71)	(1.274)
External balance	0.003	0.006	0.001	0.006
	(0.314)	(0.535)	(0.046)	(0.779)
External debt	-0.013***	-0.015***	-0.011***	-0.004**
	(5.088)	(5.365)	(4.236)	(2.133)
Indicator for economic development	2.776***	2.957***	2.595***	0.362
	(4.25)	(4.175)	(3.861)	(0.81)
Indicator for default history	-2.042***	-1.463**	-2.622***	1.159***
	(3.175)	(2.097)	(3.962)	(2.632)
Adjusted R-squared	0.924	0.905	0.926	0.251
Standard error	1.222	1.325	1.257	0.836

Sources: Moody's; Standard and Poor's; World Bank; International Monetary Fund; Bloomberg L.P.; Salomon Brothers; J.P Morgan; Federal Reserve Bank of New York estimates.
Notes: The sample size is forty-nine. Absolute t-statistics are in parentheses.
[a]The number of rating notches by which Moody's ratings exceed Standard and Poor's.
* Significant at the 10 percent level.
** Significant at the 5 percent level.
*** Significant at the 1 percent level.

important determinants. For example, the average rating regression predicts Hong Kong's rating to be almost three notches higher than its actual rating. Of course, Hong Kong's actual rating reflects the risks inherent in its 1997 incorporation into China. If the regression had failed to identify Hong Kong as an outlier, we would suspect it was misspecified and/or overfitted.

Our statistical results suggest that Moody's and Standard and Poor's broadly share the same rating criteria, although they weight some variables differently (Table 5, columns 2 and 3). The general similarity in criteria should not be surprising given that the agencies agree on individual ratings more than half the time and most of their disagreements are small in magnitude. The fourth column of Table 5 reports a regression of rating differences (Moody's less Standard and Poor's ratings) against these variables. Focusing only on the statistically significant coefficients, we find that Moody's appears to place more weight on external debt and less weight on default history as negative factors than does Standard and Poor's. Moreover, Moody's places less weight on per capita income as a positive factor.[8]

In addition to the relationship between a country's economic indicators and its sovereign ratings, the effect of ratings on yields is of interest to market practitioners. Although ratings are clearly *correlated* with yields, it is far from obvious that ratings actually *influence* yields. The observed correlation could be coincidental if investors and rating agencies share the same interpretation of a body of public information pertaining to sovereign risks. In the next section, we investigate the degree to which ratings explain yields. After examining a cross-section of yields, ratings, and other potential explanatory factors at one point in time, we examine the movement of yields when rating announcements occur.

The Cross-Sectional Relationship between Ratings and Yields

In the fall of 1995, thirty-five countries rated by both Moody's and Standard and Poor's had actively traded Eurodollar bonds. For each country, we identified its most liquid Eurodollar bond and obtained its spread over U.S. Treasuries as reported by Bloomberg L.P. on September 29, 1995. A regression of the log of these countries' bond spreads against their average ratings shows that ratings have considerable power to explain sovereign yields (Table 6, column 1).[9] The single rating variable explains 92 percent of the variation in spreads, with a standard error of 20 basis points. We also tried a number of alternative regressions based on Moody's and Standard and Poor's ratings, but none significantly improved the fit.[10]

Sovereign yields tend to rise as ratings decline. This pattern is evident in Chart 1, which plots the observed sovereign bond spreads as well as the predicted values from the average rating specification. An additional plot of average corporate spreads at each rating shows that sovereign bonds rated below A tend to be associated with higher spreads than comparably rated U.S. corporate securities. One interpretation of this finding is that although financial markets generally agree with the agencies' relative ranking of sovereign credits, they are more pessimistic than Moody's and Standard and Poor's about sovereign credit risks below the A level.

Our findings suggest that the ability of ratings to explain relative spreads cannot be wholly attributed to a mutual correlation with standard sovereign risk indicators. A regression of spreads against the eight variables used to predict credit ratings explains 86 percent of the sample variation (Table 6, column 2). Because ratings alone explain 92 percent of the variation, ratings appear to provide additional information beyond that contained in the standard macroeconomic country statistics incorporated in market yields.

In addition, ratings effectively summarize the information contained in macroeconomic indicators.[11] The third column in Table 6 presents a regression of

Table 6 Do Ratings Add to Public Information?

	Dependent Variable: Log (Spreads)		
	(1)	*(2)*	*(3)*
Intercept	2.105***	0.466	0.074
	(16.148)	(0.345)	(0.071)
Average ratings	-0.221***		-0.218***
	(19.715)		(4.276)
Per capita income		-0.144	0.226
		(0.927)	(1.523)
GDP growth		-0.004	0.029
		(0.142)	(1.227)
Inflation		0.108	-0.004
		(1.393)	(0.068)
Fiscal balance		-0.037	-0.02
		(1.557)	(1.045)
External balance		-0.038	-0.023
		(1.29)	(1.008)
External debt		0.003***	0.000
		(2.651)	(0.095)
Indicator for economic development		-0.723**	-0.38
		(2.059)	(1.341)
Indicator for default history		0.612***	0.085
		(2.577)	(0.385)
Adjusted R-squared	0.919	0.857	0.914
Standard error	0.294	0.392	0.304

Sources: Moody's; Standard and Poor's; World Bank; International Monetary Fund; Bloomberg L.P.; Salomon Brothers; J.P. Morgan; Federal Reserve Bank of New York estimates.
Notes: The sample size is thirty-five. Absolute t-statistics are in parentheses.
* Significant at the 10 percent level.
** Significant at the 5 percent level.
*** Significant at the 1 percent level.

spreads against average ratings and all the determinants of average ratings collectively. In this specification, the average rating coefficient is virtually unchanged from its coefficient in the first column of Table 6, and the other variables are collectively and individually insignificant. Moreover, the adjusted R-squared in the third specification is lower than in the first, implying that the macroeconomic indicators do not add any statistically significant explanatory power to the average rating model.

The results of our cross-sectional tests agree in part with those obtained from similar tests of the information content of corporate bond ratings (Ederington, Yawitz, and Roberts 1987) and municipal bond ratings (Moon and Stotsky 1993). Like the authors of these studies, we conclude that ratings may contain information not available in other public sources. Unlike these authors, however, we find that standard indicators of default risk provide no useful information for predicting yields over and above their correlations with ratings.

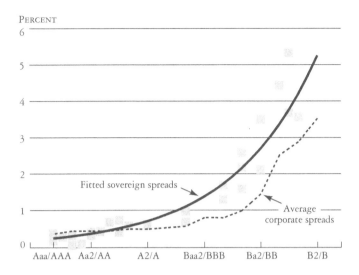

Chart 1 SOVEREIGN BOND SPREADS BY CREDIT RATING. As of September 29, 1995. Sources: Bloomberg L.P.; J.P. Morgan; Moody's; Salomon Brothers. Notes: The fitted curve is obtained by regressing the log (spreads) against the sovereigns' average. Average corporate spreads on five-year bonds are reported by Bloomberg L.P.

The Impact of Rating Announcements on Dollar Bond Spreads

We next investigate how dollar bond spreads respond to the agencies' announcements of changes in their sovereign risk assessments. certainly, many market participants are aware of specific instances in which rating announcements led to a change in existing spreads. Table 7 presents four recent examples of large moves in spread that occurred around the time of widely reported rating changes.

Of course, we do not expect the market impact of rating changes to be this large on average, in part because many rating changes are anticipated by the market. To move beyond anecdotal evidence of the impact of rating announcements, we conduct an event study to measure the effects of a large sample of rating announcements on yield spreads. Similar event studies have been undertaken to measure the impact of rating announcements on U.S. corporate bond and stock returns. In the most recent and most thorough of these studies, Hand, Holthausen, and Leftwich (1992) show that rating announcements directly affect corporate securities prices, although market anticipation often mutes the average effects.[12]

To construct our sample, we attempt to identify every announcement made by Moody's or Standard and Poor's between 1987 and 1994 that indicated a change in sovereign risk assessment for countries with dollar bonds that traded publicly during that period. Altogether, we gather a sample of seventy-nine such

Table 7 Large Movements in Sovereign Bond Spreads at the Time of Rating Announcements

Country	Date	Agency	Old Rating => New Rating	Old Spread => New Spread (In Basis Points)
DOWNGRADES				
Canada	June 2, 1994	Moody's	Aaa=>Aa1	13=>22
Turkey	March 22, 1994	Standard and Poor's	BBB-=>BB	371=>408
UPGRADES				
Brazil	November 30, 1994	Moody's	B2=>B1	410=>326
Venezuela	August 7, 1991	Moody's	Ba3=>Ba1	274=>237

Sources: Moody's; Standard and Poor's; Bloomberg L.P.; J.P. Morgan.
Note: The old (new) spread is measured at the end of the trading day before (after) the announcement day.

announcements in eighteen countries.[13] Thirty-nine of the announcements report actual rating changes—fourteen upgrades and twenty-five downgrades. The other forty announcements are "outlook" (Standard and Poor's term) or "watchlist" (Moody's term) changes:[14] twenty-three ratings were put on review for possible upgrade and seventeen for possible downgrade.

We then examine the average movement in credit spreads around the time of negative and positive announcements. Chart 2 shows the movements in relative yield spreads—yield spreads divided by the appropriate U.S. Treasury rate—thirty days before and twenty days after rating announcements. We focus on relative spreads because studies such as Lamy and Thompson (1988) suggest that they are more stable than absolute spreads and fluctuate less with the general level of interest rates.

Agency announcements of a change in sovereign risk assessments appear to be preceded by a similar change in the market's assessment of sovereign risk. During the twenty-nine days preceding negative rating announcements, relative spreads rise 3.3 percentage points on an average cumulative basis. Similarly, relative spreads fall about 2.0 percentage points during the twenty-nine days preceding positive rating announcements. The trend movement in spreads disappears approximately six days before negative announcements and flattens shortly before positive announcements. Following the announcements, a small drift in spread is still discernible for both upgrades and downgrades.

Do rating announcements themselves have an impact on the market's perception of sovereign risk? To capture the immediate effect of announcements, we look at a two-day window—the day of and the day after the announcement—because we do not know if the announcements occurred before or after the daily close of the bond market. Within this window, relative spreads rose 0.9 percentage points for

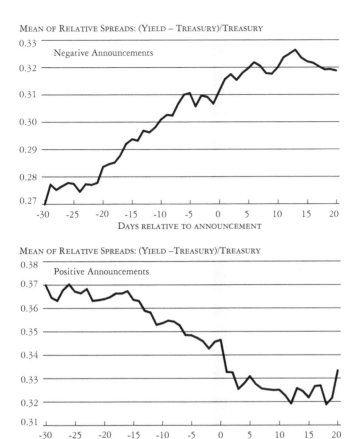

MEAN OF RELATIVE SPREADS: (YIELD – TREASURY)/TREASURY

MEAN OF RELATIVE SPREADS: (YIELD –TREASURY)/TREASURY

Chart 2 TRENDS IN SOVEREIGN BOND SPREADS BEFORE AND AFTER RATING ANNOUNCEMENTS. Sources: Bloomberg L.P.; J.P. Morgan; Federal Reserve Bank of New York estimates. Notes: The shaded areas in each panel highlight the period during which announcements occur. Spreads are calculated as the yield to maturity of the benchmark dollar bond for each sovereign minus the yield of the U.S. Treasury of comparable maturity. The charts are based on forty-eight negative and thirty-one positive announcements.

negative announcements and fell 1.3 percentage points for positive announcements. Although these movements are smaller in absolute terms than the cumulative movements over the preceding twenty-nine days, they represent a considerably larger change on a daily basis.[15] These results suggest that rating announcements themselves may cause a change in the market's assessment of sovereign risk.

Statistical analysis confirms that for the full sample of seventy-nine events, the impact of rating announcements on dollar bond spreads is highly significant.[16] Table 8 reports the mean and median changes in the log of the relative spreads during the announcement window for the full sample as well as for four pairs of rating announcement categories: positive versus negative announcements, rating change versus outlook/watchlist change announcements, Moody's versus Standard and Poor's announcements, and announcements concerning investment-grade sovereigns versus announcements concerning speculative-grade sovereigns.[17] Because positive rating announcements should be associated with negative changes in spread, we multiply the changes in the log of the relative spread by -1 when rating announcements are positive. This adjustment allows us to interpret all positive changes in spread, regardless of the announcement, as being *in the direction expected given the announcement.*

Roughly 63 percent of the full sample of rating announcements are associated with changes in spread in the expected direction during the announcement period, with a mean change in the log of relative spreads of about 2.5 percent. This finding is consistent with the announcement effect for U.S. corporate bonds documented by Hand, Holthausen, and Leftwich (1992). In fact, the share of responses in the expected direction is consistently above 50 percent regardless of the category of rating announcement. Moreover, the mean changes are always positive regardless of category.

Table 8 Do Dollar Bond Spreads Respond to Rating Announcements? Changes in Relative Spreads at the Time of Rating Announcements

	Number of Observations	Mean Change	Z-Statistic	Median change	Percent Positive
All announcements	79	0.025	2.38***	0.020	63.3***
Positive announcements	31	0.027	2.37***	0.024	64.5**
Negative announcements	48	0.023	1.15	0.017	62.5**
Rating changes	39	0.035	2.49***	0.026	61.5**
Outlook/watchlist changes	40	0.015	0.88	0.014	65.0**
Moody's announcements	29	0.048	2.86***	0.022	69.0**
Standard and Poor's announcements	50	0.011	0.81	0.016	60.0**
Investment grade	52	0.018	0.42	0.015	53.9
Speculative grade	27	0.038	3.49***	0.026	81.5***

Notes: Relative spreads are measured in logs, that is, ln [(yield - Treasury)/Treasury)]. Changes in the logs of relative spreads are multiplied by -1 in the case of positive announcements. Significance for the percent positive statistic is based on a binomial test of the hypothesis that the underlying probability is greater than 50 percent.
* Significant at the 10 percent level.
** Significant at the 5 percent level.
*** Significant at the 1 percent level.

Tests of statistical significance do suggest some differences between categories, however. Most strikingly, by both the mean change and percent positive measures, rating announcements have a highly significant impact on speculative-grade sovereigns but a statistically insignificant effect on investment-grade sovereigns. (By contrast, Hand, Holthausen, and Leftwich find that rating announcements have a significant impact on both investment-grade and speculative-grade corporate bonds.) Table 8 also reveals that the mean change statistics are not significant for negative announcements,[18] outlook/watchlist announcements, and Standard and Poor's announcements, although the percent positive statistics are significant for those categories. Because the statistical inferences for certain categories are ambiguous, and because the various categories overlap, we employ a multiple regression to sort out which categories of rating announcements imply meaningfully different effects on spreads.

We run a regression of the change in relative spreads against four indicator variables that take on the value 1 (or 0) depending on whether (or not) the rating announcements involve actual rating changes, positive events, Moody's decisions, or speculative-grade sovereigns (Table 9, column 1). As might be expected

Table 9 What Determines Reactions to Rating Announcements? Weighted Regressions of Changes in Relative Spreads on Explanatory Factors

	(1)	(2)	(3)	(4)	(5)
Constant	-0.02	-0.01	-0.03*	-0.02	-0.02
	(0.97)	(0.39)	(1.73)	(1.11)	(1.4)
Positive announcements	0.01	0.01	0.00	0.01	0.01
	(0.72)	(0.53)	(0.11)	(1.02)	(0.34)
Rating changes	0.02	0.01	0.01	0.00	-0.01
	(1.04)	(0.81)	(0.58)	(0.13)	(0.37)
Moody's announcements	0.03*	0.03	0.03*	0.02	0.02
	(1.8)	(1.61)	(1.92)	(1.53)	(1.51)
Speculative grade	0.03**	0.03**	0.03**	0.03*	0.03**
	(1.98)	(2.25)	(2.24)	(1.67)	(2.33)
Change in relative spreads from day -60 to day -1					
	-	-0.05	-	-	-0.06
		(0.98)			(1.1)
Rating gap indicator	-	-	0.04**	-	0.03*
			(2.34)		(1.7)
Other rating announcements from day -60 to day -1					
	-	-	-	0.05**	0.05**
				(2.42)	(2.15)
Adjusted R-squared	0.05	0.03	0.10	0.11	0.12

Notes: Absolute t-statistics are in parentheses. Relative spreads are measured in logs, that is, ln [(yield - Treasury)/Treasury]. Changes in the logs of relative spreads are multiplied by -1 in the case of positive announcements. Variables are weighted in the regressions by the inverse of the standard deviation of daily change in the log of relative spreads from day -100 to day -10.
* Significant at the 10 percent level.
** Significant at the 5 percent level.

from Table 8, the estimated coefficients are all positive. Only the coefficients on the Moody's and speculative-grade indicator variables, however, are statistically significant.[19] Thus, the multiple regression indicates that the immediate impact of an announcement on yield spreads is greater if the announcement is made by Moody's or if it is related to speculative-grade credit. By contrast, the impact of announcements does not appear to rely on the distinction between rating changes and outlook/watchlist changes or the distinction between positive and negative announcements.

We have established the impact of certain rating announcements on dollar bond spreads, but a second question arises: to what extent does anticipation by the market dilute the impact of these announcements? The presence of many well-anticipated events in our dataset could obscure highly significant responses to unanticipated announcements—including, perhaps, announcements by Standard and Poor's or announcements concerning investment-grade sovereigns.[20]

To pursue this issue, we construct three proxies for anticipation—changes in relative spreads, rating gaps between the agencies, and other rating announcements— all of which measure conditions before the announcement. The first proxy measures the change in relative spread (in the direction of the anticipated change) over the sixty days preceding the event. Prior movements in the relative spread may reflect the market's incorporation of information used by the agency in making the announcement. The second proxy indicates the sign of the gap between the rating of the agency making the announcement and the other agency's rating. An announcement that brings one agency's rating into line with the other's may be expected by market participants. In our regressions, the rating gap equals 1 (0) if the announcement moves the two agencies' risk assessments closer together (further apart). The third proxy is an indicator variable that equals 1 if another rating announcement of the same sign had occurred during the previous sixty days. This proxy is motivated by considerable evidence that rating announcements tend to be positively correlated—that is, positive announcements are more likely to be followed by positive announcements than by negative announcements and vice versa.[21]

We use each of the anticipation proxies in turn as a fifth explanatory variable in a multiple regression that includes the four indicator variables for actual rating changes, positive events, Moody's decisions, or speculative-grade sovereigns. A final regression adds all three anticipation proxy variables simultaneously to the basic regression (Table 9, columns 2–5).

Our earlier results are robust to the addition of the proxy variables. Announcements by Moody's and announcements pertaining to speculative-grade sovereigns continue to have a larger impact than announcements by Standard and Poor's or announcements pertaining to investmentgrade sovereigns. (Note, however, that the statistical significance of the differences between the effects of the different rating agencies declines below the 10 percent level in three of the four new specifications.)

Contrary to our expectations, however, the results reported in Table 9 suggest that market anticipation does not reduce significantly, if at all, the impact of a sovereign rating announcement. The estimated coefficient on the change in the relative spreads variable has the expected negative sign, but it is not statistically significant. Moreover, the estimated coefficients on both the rating gap and the other rating announcement indicators are unexpectedly positive and highly significant. According to these two measures, the impact of one agency's announcement is greater if the announcement confirms the other agency's rating or a previous rating announcement.

Conclusion

Sovereign credit ratings receive considerable attention in financial markets and the press. We find that the ordering of risks they imply is broadly consistent with macroeconomic fundamentals. Of the large number of criteria used by Moody's and Standard and Poor's in their assignment of sovereign ratings, six factors appear to play an important role in determining a country's rating: per capita income, GDP growth, inflation, external debt, level of economic development, and default history. We do not find any systematic relationship between ratings and either fiscal or current deficits, perhaps because of the endogeneity of fiscal policy and international capital flows.

Our analysis also shows that sovereign ratings effectively summarize and supplement the information contained in macroeconomic indicators and are therefore strongly correlated with market-determined credit spreads. Most of the correlation appears to reflect similar interpretations of publicly available information by the rating agencies and by market participants. Nevertheless, we find evidence that the rating agencies' opinions independently affect market spreads. Event study analysis broadly confirms this qualitative conclusion: it shows that the announcements of changes in the agencies' sovereign risk opinions are followed by bond yield movements in the expected direction that are statistically significant.

Although our event study results largely corroborate the findings of corporate sector studies, a few of our observations are surprising and invite further investigation. Our finding that the impact of rating announcements on spreads is much stronger for below-investment-grade than for investment-grade sovereigns is one puzzle. Another surprising result is that rating announcements that are more fully anticipated, at least by our proxy measures, have, if anything, a larger impact than those that are less anticipated.

In sum, although the agencies' ratings have a largely predictable component, they also appear to provide the market with information about non-investment-grade sovereigns that goes beyond that available in public data. The difficulty in measuring sovereign risk, especially for below-investment-grade borrowers, is well known. Despite this difficulty—and perhaps because of it—sovereign credit ratings appear to be valued by the market in pricing issues.

Notes

1 Although many studies have attempted to quantify the determinants of corporate and municipal bond ratings (see, for example, Ederington and Yawitz 1987; Moon and Stotsky 1993), our study is the first to quantify the determinants of the sovereign ratings assigned by Moody's and Standard and Poor's. Earlier researchers in the area of sovereign risk evaluated other measures of risk or presented a qualitative assessment of sovereign credit ratings. For example, Feder and Uy (1985) and Lee (1993) analyzed ordinal rankings of sovereign risk based on a poll of international bankers reported semiannually in *Institutional Investor*. Taylor (1995) discussed the importance of some of the same variables we examine, but he did not attempt to measure their individual and collective explanatory power.

2 Cantor and Packer (1995) provide a broad overview of the history and uses of sovereign ratings and the frequency of disagreement between Moody's and Standard and Poor's.

3 These variables also correspond closely to the determinants of default cited in the large academic literature on sovereign credit risk. See, for example, Saini and Bates (1984) and McFadden et al. (1985). This literature, focused largely on developing countries, estimates the importance of select variables in determining the probability that sovereign bank loans will default within one year. We do not, of course, analyze every variable considered in this literature. International reserves, a good indicator of short-term distress for developing economies, are unlikely to be helpful in explaining sovereign ratings, which measure default risk over a multiyear horizon for both developed and developing economies. We therefore do not consider this variable in our analysis.

4 Because of data limitations, we use central government debt as our measure of fiscal balance, although a more satisfactory measure would be the consolidated deficits of the federal, state, local, and quasi-public sectors.

5 Debtors undoubtedly care about a country's total debt burden, not just its foreign currency debts. Nonetheless, Moody's stresses that foreign currency obligations are generally given greater weight than total external liabilities in their sovereign ratings (Moody's 1991, p. 168).

Other measures of debt burden are also likely to be important, but they are not available for both developed and developing countries. Two such variables are net foreign assets and debt-servicing costs, both of which can be measured in domestic and foreign currencies. Although we do not measure these two factors directly, they are correlated with variables we do measure—net foreign assets represent the accumulation of past current account surpluses, and foreign currency debt service is roughly proportional to foreign currency debt. The maturity of external liabilities is another important debt-related variable of interest, but it is not generally available for most countries.

6 Countries with higher levels of development may also be less inclined to default on their foreign obligations because their economies are often substantially integrated with the world economy. As a result, developed economies are particularly vulnerable to the legal rights of creditors to disrupt trade or seize assets abroad. According to one strand of the theoretical literature on sovereign debt, the possibility of recourse to direct sanctions is a necessary condition for sovereign lending (Bulow and Rogoff 1989).

7 Although this estimation technique suffers from the limitation that ratings are treated as cardinal variables, it is the only feasible approach given that we have just forty-nine jointly rated sovereigns and sixteen potential rating categories. We found that the simple linear specification of the rating variable worked considerably better than nonlinear alternatives such as logarithmic or exponential functions. We also tried unsuccessfully to estimate the relationships with ordered probit techniques, relying only on the ordinal properties of credit ratings. Because of the large number of rating categories and the

relatively few sovereign rating assignments, our attempts to implement this approach were hindered by a failure of the maximum likelihood estimates to converge. In a similar study of corporate ratings, Ederington (1985) suggests that with larger sample sizes, inferences drawn from ordered probits are likely to be similar to, and perhaps slightly more accurate than, those drawn from least squares regressions. In contrast, in their study of corporate bond ratings, Kaplan and Urwitz (1979) argue that linear least squares estimators perform better out of sample than those estimators derived from ordered probits.

8 These results were confirmed by ordered-probit regressions for rating differences. Although not reported here, the results of the probit regressions are available from the authors on request.

9 The relationship between ratings and yields is nonlinear; hence, we report our preferred specification of the natural logarithm of yields against ratings. This specification eliminates heteroskedasticity in the residuals as measured against rating levels.

10 Specifically, we included ratings from one agency at a time or selected either the higher or the lower of the two ratings for each country. We also tried adding two dummy variables to the average rating regressor: one that indicated whether or not the two agencies disagreed and, separately, one that indicated the identity of the agency with the higher rating.

11 This conclusion holds whether or not the sovereign is investment grade: separate regressions for investment-grade and speculative-grade subsamples look very similar to the full-sample regressions.

12 Because bond data are less readily available, event studies on stock prices dominate the corporate rating literature. The event studies using bond data that precede Hand, Holthausen, and Leftwich (1992) focus solely on monthly observations and conclude that bond prices are not affected by rating changes (Weinstein 1977; Pinches and Singleton 1978; Wakeman 1984; Ederington and Yawitz 1987). A more recent study by Hite and Warga (1996) also uses monthly bond price data, but finds a significant announcement effect for downgraded firms.

13 We obtained the bond yield data by searching the daily time series data on Euro, Yankee, Global, and Brady bonds reported by Bloomberg L.P. and J.P. Morgan and made available to us by J.P. Morgan. For our event study, we used Bloomberg data for fifteen countries (Argentina, Australia, Belgium, Brazil, Canada, Colombia, Denmark, Finland, Ireland, Italy, Malaysia, New Zealand, Sweden, Thailand, and Turkey) and fifty-seven rating announcements. We use J.P. Morgan data for seven countries (Argentina, Brazil, Colombia, Hungary, the Philippines, Turkey, and Venezuela) and twenty-three rating announcements.

14 Standard and Poor's always indicates whether a sovereign has a positive, negative, or stable outlook, and many of its rating announcements report a change in this outlook alone. The agency also occasionally places a sovereign on review for probable upgrade or downgrade. Moody's does not indicate an outlook per se; however, it frequently places sovereigns on its watchlist for upgrades and downgrades.

15 Compare a 0.5 daily percentage point change during the announcement window for negative announcements with an average daily change of 0.1 for the preceding twenty-nine days. Similarly, compare a 0.7 daily percentage point change during the announcement window for positive announcements with an average daily change of 0.1 for the preceding period.

16 In the calculation of statistical significance, we control for potential heteroskedasticity with a procedure used by Mikkelson and Partch (1986) and Billet, Garfinkel, and O'Neal (1995). For each group of announcements, we calculate weighted (standardized) means in which the weights equal the inverse of the standard deviation of the relevant daily changes in the logged relative bond spread calculated during the ninety-day

period ending ten days before the announcement day. The Z-statistic for significance is the standardized mean times the square root of the number of announcements.

17 To be consistent with the log-linear relationship between ratings and spreads depicted in Chart 1, we report mean and median changes to the log of the relative spread, although the results are not particularly sensitive to this aspect of the specification.

18 By contrast, most studies using stock market data find a significant price reaction to downgrades but not to upgrades (Goh and Ederington 1993).

19 Because the average absolute errors of the regression are larger when ratings are lower, we employ weighted least squares to control for this source of heteroskedasticity.

20 Hand, Holthausen, and Leftwich (1992) find that Standard and Poor's announcements that corporate ratings are under review have significant market impact only when announcements classified by the authors as "expected" are excluded from the sample.

21 Of the 109 sovereign rating announcements between 1987 and 1994 that were followed by a rating change, 86 were followed by a change in the same direction. (Similarly, Altman and Kao [1991] have shown that corporate rating changes are often followed by further changes in the same direction.) Of the 79 rating announcements in our sample, 36 were preceded by a rating gap in the implied direction of the announcement. In 20 cases, other rating announcements in the same direction had been made in the preceding sixty days.

References

Altman, Edward, and Duen Li Kao. 1991. "Corporate Bond Rating Drift: An Examination of Rating Agency Credit Quality Changes Over Time." New York University-Salomon Brothers Working Paper S-91-40.

Billet, Matthew. 1996. "Targeting Capital Structure: The Relationship Between Risky Debt and the Firm's Likelihood of Being Acquired." JOURNAL OF BUSINESS. Forthcoming.

Billet, Matthew, Jon Garfinkel, and Edward O'Neal. 1995. "Insured Deposits, Market Discipline, and the Price of Risk in Banking." Federal Deposit Insurance Corporation, manuscript.

Bulow, Jeremy, and Kenneth Rogoff. 1989. "Sovereign Debt: Is to Forgive to Forget?" AMERICAN ECONOMIC REVIEW 79, no. 1: 43–50.

Cantor, Richard, and Frank Packer. 1994. "The Credit Rating Industry." Federal Reserve Bank of New York QUARTERLY REVIEW 19, no. 2 (winter): 1–26.

_____. 1995. "Sovereign Credit Ratings." Federal Reserve Bank of New York CURRENT ISSUES IN ECONOMICS AND FINANCE 1, no. 3 (June).

Eaton, Jonathan. 1996. "Sovereign Debt, Repudiation, and Credit Terms." INTERNATIONAL JOURNAL OF FINANCE AND ECONOMICS 1, no. 1 (January): 25–36.

Ederington, Louis. 1985. "Classification Models and Bond Ratings." FINANCIAL REVIEW 4, no. 20 (November): 237–62.

Ederington, Louis, and Jess Yawitz. 1987. "The Bond Rating Process." In Edward Altman, ed., HANDBOOK OF FINANCIAL MARKETS. New York: John Wiley & Sons: 23–57.

Ederington, Louis, Jess Yawitz, and Brian Roberts. 1987. "The Information Content of Bond Ratings." JOURNAL OF FINANCIAL RESEARCH 10, no. 3 (fall): 211–26.

Feder, G., and L. Uy. 1985. "The Determinants of International Creditworthiness and Their Implications." JOURNAL OF POLICY MODELING 7, no. 1: 133–56.

Goh, Jeremy, and Louis Ederington. 1993. "Is a Bond Rating Downgrade Bad News, Good News, or No News for Stockholders?" JOURNAL OF FINANCE 48, no. 5: 2001–8.

Hand, John, Robert Holthausen, and Richard Leftwich. 1992. "The Effect of Bond Rating Agency Announcements on Bond and Stock Prices." JOURNAL OF FINANCE 47, no. 2: 733–52.

Hite, Gailen, and Arthur Warga. 1996. "The Effect of Bond Rating Changes on Bond Price Performance." Unpublished paper.

Horrigan, J. 1966. "The Determination of Long-Term Credit Standing with Financial Ratios." EMPIRICAL RESEARCH IN ACCOUNTING 1966, JOURNAL OF ACCOUNTING RESEARCH 4 (supplement): 44–62.

Kaplan, Robert, and Gabriel Urwitz. 1979. "Statistical Models of Bond Ratings: A Methodological Inquiry." JOURNAL OF BUSINESS 52, no. 2: 231–61.

Lamy, Robert, and G. Rodney Thompson. 1988. "Risk Premia and the Pricing of Primary Issue Bonds." JOURNAL OF BANKING AND FINANCE 12, no. 4: 585–601.

Lee, Suk Hun. 1993. "Are the Credit Ratings Assigned by Bankers Based on the Willingness of LDC Borrowers to Repay?" JOURNAL OF DEVELOPMENT ECONOMICS 40: 349–59.

McFadden, Daniel, Richard Eckaus, Gershon Feder, Vassilis Hajivassiliou, and Stephen O'Connell. 1985. "Is There Life After Debt? An Econometric Analysis of the Creditworthiness of Developing Countries." In Gordon Smith and John Cuddington, eds., INTERNATIONAL DEBT AND THE DEVELOPING COUNTRIES. Washington, D.C.: World Bank.

Mikkelson, W, and M. Partch. 1986. "Valuation Effects of Security Offerings and the Issuance Process." JOURNAL OF FINANCIAL ECONOMICS 15, no. 1/2: 31–60.

Moody's Investors Service. 1991. GLOBAL ANALYSIS. London: IFR Publishing.

————. 1995. SOVEREIGN SUPRANATIONALS CREDIT OPINIONS, September.

Moon, C.G., and J.G. Stotsky. 1993. "Testing the Differences between the Determinants of Moody's and Standard and Poor's Ratings." JOURNAL OF APPLIED ECONOMETRICS 8, no. 1: 51–69.

Ozler, Sule. 1991. "Evolution of Credit Terms: An Empirical Examination of Commercial Bank Lending to Developing Countries." JOURNAL OF DEVELOPMENT ECONOMICS 38: 79–97.

Pinches, G., and J. Singleton. 1978. "The Adjustment of Stock Prices to Bond Rating Changes." JOURNAL OF FINANCE 33, no. 1: 29–44.

Saini, K, and P. Bates. 1984. "A Survey of the Quantitative Approaches to Country Risk Analysis." JOURNAL OF BANKING AND FINANCE 8, no. 2: 341–56.

Standard and Poor's. 1994. "Sovereign Rating Criteria." EMERGING MARKETS, October: 124–7.

Taylor, Joseph. 1995. "Analyzing the Credit and Sovereign Risks of Non-U.S. Bonds." In Ashwinpaul C. Sondhi, ed., CREDIT ANALYSIS OF NONTRADITIONAL DEBT SECURITIES. New York: Association for Investment Research, pp. 72–82.

Wakeman, L. 1984. "The Real Function of Bond Rating Agencies." In Michael Jensen and Clifford Smith, eds., THE MODERN THEORY OF CORPORATE FINANCE. New York: McGraw-Hill.

Weinstein, M. 1977. "The Effect of a Rating Change Announcement on Bond Price." JOURNAL OF FINANCIAL ECONOMICS 5, no. 3: 329–50.

18

EMPIRICAL DETERMINANTS OF EMERGING MARKET ECONOMIES' SOVEREIGN BOND SPREADS

Gianluigi Ferrucci

Source: *Working Paper No. 205*, Bank of England, London, 2003.

Abstract

This paper investigates the empirical determinants of emerging market sovereign bond spreads, using a ragged-edge panel of JP Morgan EMBI and EMBI Global secondary market spreads and a set of common macro-prudential indicators. The panel is estimated using the pooled mean group technique due to Pesaran, Shin and Smith (1999). This is essentially a dynamic error correction model where cross-sectional coefficients are allowed to vary in the short run but are required to be homogeneous in the long run. This allows a separation of short-run dynamics and adjustment towards the equilibrium. The model is used to benchmark market spreads and assess whether sovereign risk was 'overpriced' or 'underpriced' during different periods over the past decade. The results suggest that a debtor country's fundamentals and external liquidity conditions are important determinants of market spreads. However, the diagnostic statistics also indicate that the market assessment of a country's creditworthiness is more broad based than that provided by the set of fundamentals included in the model. We also find that the generalised fall in sovereign spreads seen between 1995 and 1997 cannot be entirely explained in terms of improved fundamentals.

1 Introduction

With the rise in the value of bond financing by emerging market economies (EMEs) over the course of the 1990s, secondary market yield spreads have become important indicators of financial fragility for surveillance purposes. The Bank of England for example uses EME bond spreads as a measure of the market's perception of the risk that a country might default and to assess EME external financing

80

conditions. But yield spreads are influenced by a variety of factors and inferring their exact information content may not always be straightforward.

Yield spreads measure the premium required by investors to hold securities issued by EME borrowers, which are perceived to be more likely to default on their obligations than a developed economy. This premium is measured as the difference between the yield on an EME bond and the yield on a bond of similar characteristics, but considered to be virtually free of default risk (typically a US Treasury security). Essentially, this premium serves to compensate bondholders for the risks to which they are exposed when holding EME debt securities: credit risk, market risk and liquidity risk (eg Cunningham, Dixon and Hayes (2001)).

Credit risk is the possibility that the debtor will not fulfil its obligations in full and on time. This risk of default depends on the fundamental characteristics of the issuer and on the ability of the lender to enforce the contract.[1] Market risk is the possibility that secondary market bond prices may move against the bondholder. Clearly, because changes in credit risk are one factor affecting secondary market prices, these two risks are related. But other factors may also give rise to market risk, such as changes in the willingness of investors to hold risky assets (risk appetite), and changes in other asset prices, which affect the opportunity cost of holding the security. Finally, liquidity risk is the risk that investors will not be able to liquidate their portfolios without depressing secondary market prices. Changes in market spreads thus reflect changes in the underlying macro fundamentals, leading investors to reassess their evaluation of a country's creditworthiness, and also the effect of external shocks (eg a change in US interest rates), changes in investors' risk appetite, and liquidity risk.[2] Disentangling the individual contribution of these factors may not always be easy.

The bond pricing literature suggests that EME credit spreads are a function of the market's perception of the risk of default and the expected recovery in the event of default. Models can normally be classified in two categories: structural and reduced form. Structural models of default risky assets posit a given stochastic process for assets and liabilities in the borrower's balance sheet and assume that default occurs if the asset value falls below a certain threshold, normally some proportion of liabilities. The default probability thus arises endogenously and depends on the average maturity of the debt, on the level of the risk-free interest rate, on the country's leverage ratio, and on the volatility of the underlying assets. These government-owned assets include official reserves and other fiscal assets, which in turn mainly consist of the net present value of the expected future fiscal primary surpluses.[3] The loss given default is normally also endogenous in this class of models and depends on how much the asset value after liquidation falls short of the face value of outstanding liabilities.[4] Reduced-form models in contrast obtain the value of a bond from a standard calculation of expected present value of the bond's contracted payment profile, where both the default probability and the recovery rate are exogenous. The default probabilities in turn are calibrated in a number of ways, for example using credit ratings or positing a relationship with a given set of macro-prudential indicators which are likely to affect the borrower's creditworthiness.

This paper develops a reduced-form model relating market spreads to a set of country-specific fundamental variables, controlling for investors' risk appetite and bonds' liquidity factors. The theoretical underpinning for the selection of the determinants of credit spreads is given by a simplified model of sovereign borrowing that formalises the consumption choices of an indebted small open economy. This model points to a set of variables that are important components of the internal and external constraints on government debt obligations. In our empirical estimation we also experiment with a number of additional factors that might be important determinants of credit spreads, though these are not discussed in the simplified theoretical model. The data set for the estimation is a ragged-edge panel of JP Morgan's EMBI and EMBI Global secondary market spreads and a number of country-specific macro-prudential indicators obtained from a variety of sources. Estimates are obtained using the pooled mean group technique due to Pesaran, Shin and Smith (1999). This is essentially a dynamic error correction model with heterogeneous cross-sectional coefficients in the short-run equations and homogeneous coefficients in the long-run relationship, which allows separating short-run dynamics and adjustment towards the equilibrium. The objective of the paper is to explain the long-run determinants of EME bond spreads, together with some short-run dynamic behaviours.

We use this model to address three main issues. First, we intend to assess what proportion of the change in market spreads is explained by changes in the underlying fundamentals, controlling for external factors, liquidity risk and market risk. Clearly, an important side benefit of this analysis is to improve our understanding of the empirical relationship between fundamentals and the determinants of EME financing costs.

Second, we aim to provide a benchmark measure of sovereign risk against which actual market spreads can be meaningfully compared. However, because the model is reduced form and is non-structural, it gives an econometrically fitted level of spreads based on the selected set of fundamental variables included in the estimating equation, rather than a theoretically justified measure that a structural model would imply. The benefits of this exercise are twofold. First, because the model relates credit risk to a set of common country-specific fundamentals and external shocks, it may be used to assess whether a certain level of market spreads is broadly consistent with the level implied by the selected fundamentals. Second, we may contrast from an *ex ante* perspective the model's assessment of the relative creditworthiness of two countries with that of market participants. In other words, we ask the question 'based on an assessment of fundamentals, is country X more creditworthy than country Y?' and if so, 'are markets pricing sovereign risk in the two countries accordingly?' In the paper we illustrate this application by looking at the relative pricing of Brazil and Colombia.

Third, we intend to use the model to explain patterns in spreads, from an *ex post* perspective. As a case study we analyse the generalised fall in secondary market EME bond spreads experienced between 1995 and 1997. The literature explains this fall in several ways, and ultimately the question of who is right has to be addressed empirically. For example, efficient market proponents point out that the trend was the consequence of the policies implemented in the early 1990s (economic and financial liberalisation, structural reforms), which led to a generalised improvement of macro and financial fundamentals in most developing countries. Others question whether fundamentals improved sufficiently to justify a decline of the magnitude experienced over the period. They suggest that the fall may simply reflect capital market imperfections, especially moral hazard following the bailout of Mexico by the IMF at the beginning of 1995, or higher risk appetite following the stimulative effect of more liberal credit conditions in the main financial centres (Eichengreen and Mody (1998a)).

Data limitations highlighted in the paper mean that the results have to be interpreted with caution. Nevertheless, the model is informative and allows us to reach interesting conclusions. Our main finding is that market spreads broadly reflect fundamentals, but that non-fundamental factors play perhaps a more important role. Comparing market-based spreads against their fundamental-based counterparts we find that recent market spreads mainly traded at a fair level, that is sufficiently close to a theoretical equilibrium level based on the selected set of macro-prudential indicators.

In the few cases where we observe large absolute misalignments we identify whether the divergence is due to unmeasured fundamentals or whether it is likely to depend on markets' mispricing of risk. Alternatively, it is possible that the model breaks down during crisis periods. In addition, the model suggests that based on fundamentals, Brazil's *ex-ante* creditworthiness is lower than Colombia's, consistent with the evaluation provided by the markets. Finally, we find that the fall in spreads between 1995 and 1997 cannot be explained solely in terms of improved fundamentals.

The paper is organised as follows. Section 2 places the model in the context of the previous literature. Section 3 discusses a simple theoretical framework that we use as a guide to select the relevant macro-prudential indicators to include in the empirical estimation. Section 4 presents the data set and discusses some data limitations. Section 5 discusses the selected estimation framework – pooled mean group (PMG). Section 6 presents the results, and Section 7 discusses the main implications. The final section concludes.

2 Previous literature

A seminal work in the literature on lending behaviour in international markets is Edwards (1984), which provides a simple valuation framework for the determination of the sovereign risk premium conventionally used in most subsequent investigations. This framework is derived from a model that views EMEs as small borrowers in perfectly competitive financial markets. Under this assumption, a country's fair value spread is a function of the probability that it will default on its external obligations. In turn, this probability depends on a set of macroeconomic fundamentals and external shocks affecting the country's solvency and liquidity. Using this framework Edwards estimates the determinants of primary yields on bank lending to EMEs.

Edwards (1986) extends this analysis running separate estimates of default risk premia in the international bank loan and bond markets. From a theoretical point of view there are a number of economic, legal and institutional reasons why one would expect risk premia on the two instruments to be priced differently. These have been widely explored in the literature, which has concluded that bond lending involves greater risks than loan lending, an intuition that is supported by the empirical findings in Edwards (1986).[5] More recently, Min (1998) adopted the same framework to investigate the determinants of launch yield spreads on sovereign bonds issued in the early 1990s.

Kamin and Kleist (1999) relate sovereign primary yields in bond and loan markets to borrowers' creditworthiness as summarised by the credit ratings issued by the major rating agencies, controlling for instrument characteristics. The main feature of this study is that macroeconomic, liquidity and solvency indicators are not included in the estimating equation. This reflects the well-established result (eg Cantor and Packer (1996)) that ratings are highly correlated to a small set of macroeconomic fundamentals and so adding both sets of variables would lead to multicollinearity.[6] In line with previous research, this study shows that EME spreads have strong and well-defined relationships with credit ratings and thus with borrower creditworthiness. It also finds that borrowers in Latin America and Eastern Europe are systematically charged higher spreads than borrowers in Asia and the Middle East. However, contradicting earlier findings, it shows that while spreads on bonds are systematically higher than spreads on bank loans, the elasticities to changes in the underlying determinants (ratings, maturity etc) are very similar for both instruments. Moreover, the model explores the relationship between EME launch bond spreads and industrial country interest rates. Though in principle there are a number of reasons why one would expect the two to be linked, the model cannot identify any robust, statistically significant relationship between the two variables.[7]

A common characteristic of all these studies is that they use primary yields as a measure of credit risk, a feature that may lead to sample selection biases. As observed in Eichengreen and Mody (1998a, 1998b) in poor market conditions, when secondary spreads rise, primary spreads do not rise proportionately, and in some cases they fall. Factors that increase the perceived risk of EME debt, while raising secondary market spreads, may have the opposite effect on launch spreads in so far as riskier borrowers are rationed out of the market, leaving only low-risk borrowers to launch new issues. As a consequence, a sample of primary yields may not be entirely random and estimates based on it may be biased.

One way to correct for this bias is to model primary yields simultaneously with a binary decision to issue or not to issue (Eichengreen and Mody (1998a, 1998b)). In practice, this method involves defining a Heckman correction model that accounts for the joint determination of the issue and pricing decisions, controlling for selectivity. This amounts to jointly estimating a two-equation model, including a 'traditional' linear relationship between launch spreads and a set of fundamentals, and a probit equation to account for the fact that spreads will only be observed when positive decisions to borrow and lend are made. The cost of this modelling strategy is that the database has to be supplemented with information on non-issuing countries, to allow estimation of the probit equation. The model provides clear evidence that bond issuance is not a random event and that selectivity biases can be significant when estimating a model of primary issues. For example, once these factors are taken into account, Eichengreen and Mody find that interest rates in developed countries become an important determinant of capital flows to EMEs – contradicting the findings in Kamin and Kleist (1999).

Another way to correct for sample selectivity is to use secondary market spreads, which do not suffer from this type of bias. A few recent papers have done this. Goldman Sachs (2000) estimate a long-run equilibrium model of EME sovereign spreads using monthly data from quotes of benchmark, long-maturity, sovereign bonds, which increase the length of the time series but raise issues about which bond to choose and how representative it is. To estimate their model, Goldman Sachs (2000) adopt the pooled mean group technique developed by Pesaran, Shin and Smith (1999), which involves defining a dynamic, error correction panel where short-run parameters are allowed to vary by cross-sections, while long-run elasticities are restricted to be identical across groups. Dell'Ariccia, Goedde and Zettelmeyer (2000) use EMBI Global spreads to assess the presence of moral hazard in international lending following the Russian crisis in 1998. The benefit of using EMBI Global spreads is that these are a balanced panel of readily available secondary market spreads, and that they are more broad-based than benchmark bonds. But there is a disadvantage in that time series are shorter (the EMBIG series starts in 1997). Estimates are obtained using a conventional, static, fixed-effect model. But for a robustness check, the model is also run on a database of launch spreads which has broader country coverage than the EMBIG, correcting for the selectivity bias using a Heckman correction algorithm, as in Eichengreen and Mody (1998a, 1998b).

Both Goldman Sachs (2000) and Dell'Ariccia et al (2000) need to interpolate their macro fundamental databases to obtain a sufficiently high number of observations, raising the issue of the appropriateness of doing so. Clearly, interpolation increases the sample size at the cost of imposing a given (in most cases, linear) model on the data generating process of the missing observations.

This paper uses the same database as Dell'Ariccia et al (2000), thus getting around the sample selection problems encountered in earlier literature, and the pooled mean group estimation technique used in Goldman Sachs (2000). However, we are careful in considering the implications of merging the EMBI and EMBI Global data sets, which raises quite separate selectivity issues than the previous literature on primary yields. We also attempt to minimise the need to interpolate macroeconomic series by using information from individual central banks and Ministries of Finance – thus building as high a frequency data set of macro fundamentals as possible.

3 Theoretical framework and variable selection

A conventional approach to modelling equilibrium sovereign yields is to assume that the spread over a risk-free interest rate is a function of the probability of default of a country and of the loss given default. In reduced-form models, this probability of default is exogenously determined and is tied to the sustainability of a given level of external debt through liquidity or solvency indicators, and hence to a set of macroeconomic fundamentals. For example, assuming risk neutral lenders and competitive financial markets, and following the standard model of risk premia, Edwards (1984) obtains a simple log-linear relationship of spread determinants:

$$\log s_{it} = \alpha + \sum_{j=1}^{J} \beta_{jit} x_{jit} + \varepsilon_{it} \tag{1}$$

where s_{it} is the yield spread of country i at time t, α is an intercept coefficient, the β_js are slope coefficients, the x_js are a set of J macro fundamentals, and ε are i.i.d. error terms. In the context of more complex theoretical frameworks, Feder and Just (1977), Eaton and Gersovitz (1980) and Sachs (1981) derive similar relationships.

The theoretical underpinning for the selection of the set of variables x_js in equation (1) is provided by a model of sovereign borrowing that formalises the consumption choices of an indebted small open economy (SOE). The SOE typically tries to smooth its consumption path over time by borrowing from abroad when domestic resources are scarce and paying back its debts when resources are abundant. In this setting, foreign lenders focus on two issues. The first is the ability of the SOE to generate enough foreign exchange resources to service its external obligations. The second is the SOE government's ability to generate enough domestic resources to purchase the foreign exchange required for servicing its external obligations.

This discussion can be formalised by introducing a simple dynamic programming problem:

$$
\begin{aligned}
Max \quad & U_0 = \sum_{t=0}^{\infty} \beta^t u(C_t), \\
\text{s.t.} \quad & G_t + rD_t \leq T_t + D_{t+1} - D_t, \\
& Y_t = C_t + G_t, \\
& T_t = f(Y_t), \\
& Y_t = (1+g)Y_{i-1}
\end{aligned}
\tag{2}
$$

where U_0 is an intertemporal welfare function depending on consumption (C_t), and β is the discount factor. This function is maximised subject to two constraints. The first is the government budget constraint, where primary public spending (G_t) and interest payments on the existing stock of external debt (rD_t) are financed through taxation (T_t) and debt issuance ($D_{t+1} - D_t$). For simplicity we assume that all external debt is public. The second constraint is the usual accounting identity, equating total domestic output (Y_t) to the sum of private and government consumption. Rearranging this identity using the government budget constraint we get:

$$D_{t+1} - D_t \geq Y_t - C_t - T_t + rD_t \tag{3}$$

In our simple setting, equation **(3)** represents the country's current account and hence the external constraint. This is defined as the change in total external debt between t and $t+1$ and has to be greater than or equal to the sum of private saving ($Y_t - C_t - T_t$) plus interest payments on the stock of external debt. The last two equations in problem **(2)** are required to close the model and define respectively tax revenues as a function of output and the evolution of output over time (which for simplicity is assumed to be exogenous).

In flow terms, the government budget constraint and the external constraint (given by equation **(3)**) motivate the importance of liquidity indicators, as borrowers need not only to be solvent in the long run, but also to fulfil their obligations at each point in time. These indicators are the fiscal budget balance, external debt amortisation, interest payments on external debt, and the amount of short-term debts (which define the country's gross external financing needs). As financing sources the model highlights the role of the current account balance. Official reserves (which are not discussed in our simple setting) are also important as they provide a buffer of foreign liquidity to insure against a temporary inability to roll over debts on the market.

It is easy to show that the two constraints can be rearranged in NPV terms in the following form:

$$(1+r)D_t \leq \sum_{i=0}^{\infty} \frac{PS_{t+i}}{(1+r)^i} \tag{4}$$

$$(1+r)D_t \leq \sum_{i=0}^{\infty} \frac{(C_{t+i} + T_{t+i} - Y_{t+i})}{(1+r)^i} \tag{5}$$

where $PS_t = T_t - G_t$, is the government primary fiscal surplus. Equation **(4)** gives the condition for the long-term sustainability of fiscal policy, and shows that for a borrower to be solvent the stock of external debt must be no greater than the net present value of future fiscal primary surpluses discounted by the cost of capital.

Equation **(5)** provides the condition for the sustainability of external debt – ie that the stock of external debt must be no greater than the present value of future private saving.

In stock terms, these constraints motivate the selection of a number of solvency indicators. For example, the sustainability of fiscal policy suggests the relevance of a low stock of public debt, low cost of capital, and high output growth rate, as tax collection varies proportionally with the level of economy activity. On the other hand, external solvency suggests the importance of low external indebtedness and, though not highlighted in this simple setting, high trade openness. Trade openness is key to external solvency. A low degree of openness may indicate that the required expected trade surpluses to meet future foreign debt repayments may not materialise. Additionally, incentives to repay debts are lower if the economy is relatively closed, because the losses from sanctions following debt repudiation are a smaller fraction of output. High rates of output growth and low interest rates are also important for external solvency as, *ceteris paribus,* they imply that lower trade surpluses would be compatible with sustainable external debts.

More complex models would highlight the role of external competitiveness indicators, such as the nominal or real exchange rate overvaluation, and the terms of trade, because these variables affect the allocation of resources between the tradable (which generates foreign exchange reserves) and the non-tradable sector. Additionally, a less competitive exchange rate can affect a sovereign's creditworthiness because it may lead to capital flight on the expectation of future realignment. Alternatively, currency devaluation may exacerbate fiscal problems when the economy has an open capital account but a relatively small tradable sector. This is because when exports are low and public debts are mainly foreign-currency denominated, currency devaluation provides a limited boost to economic activity and government revenues, while the domestic currency value of external debt service rises in tandem with the devaluation.

Oil prices are another important indicator that may affect the creditworthiness of an indebted SOE through several channels. The first and most obvious is through the consequences on world growth. For example, Hamilton (1983) finds that all but one post-war US recession was preceded by oil price increases. Slow world growth may tighten international capital availability and may lead to lower export growth in EMEs. Additionally, high oil prices may lower a country's external competitiveness and cause a deterioration of the trade balance. This may lead to an increased demand for foreign capital in oil importing countries, and possibly cause a balance of payment crisis. Clearly, the story is different for oil exporter countries, whose creditworthiness may be worsened by low oil prices, if for example government revenues are dependent on oil. However, with a few notable exceptions (eg Venezuela and Russia) oil exporter countries tend to have low levels of external debts, and in most cases are net exporters of capital.

More generally, many indebted EMEs are commodity exporters – and hence the relevance of an index of commodity prices. Domestic inflation is also an important factor. Min (1998) argues that sovereign risk depends on macroeconomic policy discipline, and that inflation can be broadly regarded as a proxy for the quality of economic and monetary management (eg, because high inflation may reflect accommodation of fiscal imbalances). McDonald (1982) estimates that high inflation is typically associated with a larger probability of a balance of payment crisis, and consequently with a higher probability of default. A history of debt crises can also be reflected in the cost of capital for EMEs, because sovereign borrowers face costs when they default in terms of rationed access to capital.

4 The data set

There are two issues related to the construction of a panel for our empirical investigation: the selection of an appropriate source for sovereign spreads and the choice of a set of explanatory variables.

For the choice of the dependent variable we look at secondary market spreads, to limit the selectivity biases associated with launch yields (as discussed earlier). To avoid the disadvantages of using specific instruments (as in Goldman Sachs (2000)), we draw the data from JP Morgan's indices of EME sovereign spreads (as in Dell'Ariccia et al (2000)). These include US$-denominated sovereign and quasi-sovereign (ie guaranteed by a sovereign) instruments that satisfy certain criteria, to ensure sufficient liquidity of the bonds. The spread of a bond is calculated as the premium paid by the EME over a US government bond with comparable features. A country's spread is then calculated as the average of the spreads of all the bonds that satisfy the inclusion criteria, weighted by the market capitalisation of the instruments. This measure of spreads brings a number of potential benefits, such as that it is readily available, that spreads are calculated as averages over portfolios of bonds and thus time series are continuous, without breaks as bonds mature, and that it only includes liquid instruments.

JP Morgan publish two variants of their EME sovereign spread indices (Cunningham (1999)). The broadest measure, the EMBI Global, comprises mainly Eurobonds and Brady bonds with minimum face value of US$500 million and maturity of at least 2½ years, and covers a wide cross-section of 27 countries, from 1998 onwards. A narrower measure including only Brady bonds and other restructured sovereign instruments, the EMBI, is available from 1991 but covers only 5 EMEs from 1992, and 11 from 1995. A choice between the two indices poses a trade-off between a longer time series (EMBI) and a wider cross-section (EMBIG). To by-pass this problem, we construct a ragged-edge, unbalanced panel of spreads using the broadest cross-section available at each point in time. This data set has a break at the point in time when we switch from one index to the other, a feature that may potentially affect estimation results in two ways. First, it may lead to sample selectivity bias, though of a different type from that highlighted in the literature on launch yields. Here the bias arises because observations may not be random as good debtors would be systematically excluded from the ragged-edge panel during the period covered by the EMBI, since this index only tracks returns on Brady and restructured bonds. Second, the measures of credit risk embedded in the EMBI and EMBIG may differ systematically because of the composition of the underlying portfolios in the two indices. Typically, we may expect EMBI country spreads to be higher than their EMBIG counterpart because they refer to restructured bonds.

The former problem can be corrected using a Heckman correction model (as in the early literature on primary yields) – an issue that we leave for further extensions of this research. In order to assess how important the latter issue is we have tried a number of experiments. Chart 1 compares the EMBI and EMBI Global spreads at different points in time, for the countries that are included in both indices. It shows that observations tend to cluster around the 45-degree line, but EMBI spreads tend to be slightly higher than the corresponding EMBIG spreads.

A more formal test is to measure the correlation coefficients between the individual EMBI and EMBIG country series and perform a t-test for the equality of sample means and variances. The basic idea of this test is that if the two series have the same first and second moments, they would differ by a random component (ignoring differences in higher moments). The results are reported in Table 1 and indicate that the hypothesis of equality of the sample means in the two country series is rejected in seven out of eleven countries, while equality of sample variances is rejected in six cases. However, the correlation coefficients are high, ranging between 92% and 99%. The Jarque-Bera statistics suggest that spread series have non-normal distributions.

Table 2 summarises the estimation output of the following simple model:

$$EMBIG_{it} = a_i + b_i EMBI_{it} + u_{it},$$

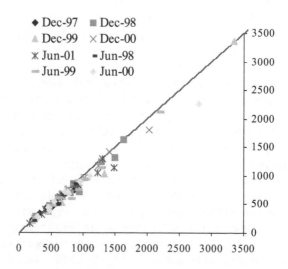

Chart 1 EMBI versus EMBIG spreads

Table 1 EMBI and EMBIG country series: tests for equality of means and variances[a]

	t-test for equality of sample means			F-test for equality of sample variances		Jarque-Bera statistic		Correl
	Obs	Statistic	Prob	Statistic	Prob	Statistic	Prob	
Argentina	1115	6.57	0.00	3.41	0.00	1750.5	0.00	0.98
Brazil	1115	3.01	0.00	1.11	0.07	817.0	0.00	0.99
Bulgaria	1115	0.00	0.99	1.00	0.99	103.1	0.00	1.00
Ecuador	1115	0.02	0.98	1.00	0.95	189.0	0.00	1.00
Mexico	1115	11.84	0.00	1.99	0.00	1312.9	0.00	0.98
Nigeria	824	15.67	0.00	1.19	0.01	114.8	0.00	0.92
Panama	1115	5.34	0.00	1.29	0.00	809.5	0.00	0.97
Peru	1115	0.16	0.87	1.01	0.85	188.8	0.00	0.99
Poland	1115	0.04	0.96	1.11	0.08	468.0	0.00	0.99
Russia	865	7.99	0.00	2.31	0.00	130.3	0.00	0.99
Venezuela	1115	6.55	0.00	1.75	0.00	116.5	0.00	0.99

Notes: (a) Observations are daily. Sample includes the subset of EMEs for which the EMBI and EMBIG spreads are simultaneously available and covers the period when the two indices overlap. The sample period is 31 December 1997 to 16 June 2002. For Nigeria the sample excludes the period from 31 March 1998 to 27 May 1999, when EMBI spreads are not available. For Russia the sample starts in December 1998.

91

Table 2 Test for equivalence of EMBIG and EMBI spreads[a]

	α	β	R-sq	DW	Obs	Test of H_0: $\alpha=0$, $\beta=1$	
						F-stat	Prob
Argentina	297.86	0.53	0.97	0.17	1115	16504.6	0.00
Brazil	17.76	0.95	0.99	0.13	1115	2204.97	0.00
Bulgaria	0.09	0.99	0.99	1.84	1115	0.03	0.97
Ecuador	2.95	0.99	0.99	1.57	1115	4.40	0.01
Mexico	63.01	0.70	0.98	0.08	1115	15125.10	0.00
Nigeria	-58.66	0.88	0.87	0.10	824	1095.36	0.00
Panama	45.36	0.86	0.95	0.10	1115	914.35	0.00
Peru	-3.70	1.00	0.99	0.92	1115	30.41	0.00
Poland	-9.31	1.04	0.97	0.13	1115	30.28	0.00
Russia	381.20	0.54	0.89	0.03	865	3887.97	0.00
Venezuela	161.96	0.75	0.99	0.15	1115	15950.01	0.00

Notes: (a) Observations are daily. Sample includes the subset of EMEs for which the EMBI and EMBIG spreads are simultaneously available and covers the period when the two indices overlap. The sample period is 31 December 1997 to 16 June 2002. For Nigeria the sample excludes the period from 31 March 1998 to 27 May 1999 (EMBI spreads not available). For Russia the sample starts in December 1998 (EMBI spreads not available earlier).

which we use to run a Wald test of the joint hypothesis: H_0: $a_i = 0$; $b_i = 1$. The rationale for this test is that under H_0 the EMBI and EMBIG would differ only by a random component. As shown in the table, at conventional significance level this hypothesis can be accepted only in the case of Bulgaria, and in 10 out of 11 countries there appear to be systematic differences between the two indices. However, in most cases the slope coefficients are close to unity (despite the statistical hypothesis of $b_i = 1$ not being accepted) and the R-squared of the regressions are always very high, ranging between 87% and 99%, which implies a high correlation between the two indices.

Overall this suggests that the two indices differ somewhat, but that they are sufficiently strongly correlated not to rule out the use of a ragged-edge panel of sovereign spreads. The analysis does however suggest some caution when interpreting the results. Moreover, the costs of using a ragged-edge panel should be weighted against the benefits. Clearly an important benefit is to increase dramatically the sample size, from 1,472 monthly observations using the EMBIG alone to 2,005 merging the two databases. Obviously, a wider sample size increases the degrees of freedom and puts fewer constraints on model selection and estimation technique.

The right-hand side variables of the model are a set of country-specific macro-fundamentals and external indicators chosen using the results from the section on the variable selection, but also keeping in mind the limited degrees of freedom due to the low sample size and high number of estimation parameters. This explains why for example we do not collect data on commodity and oil prices, and a number of other factors that are likely to affect the creditworthiness of some but not all the countries in our panel. Also, in assembling the database we face a number of data issues, such as that EME data are not always published and/or are not timely, that sources are not entirely consistent, and data are frequently revised.

To compile our database we use a number of different sources. Data on external debt are drawn mainly from the World Bank's Global Development Finance. Other macro-prudential indicators are drawn from the IMF's *International Financial Statistics,* the IIF, and from local economy ministry and central bank web sites. Using these sources, we assemble an unbalanced panel of 2,005 monthly observations, covering 5 countries from 1992 to 1995, 11 countries from 1996 to 1997, and 23 countries from 1998 onwards. For each cross-section, the complete database consists of 24 variables (the dependent variable, 16 country-specific macro fundamentals, five common external indicators, and two debt-specific dummies).

In most cases macro data are only available on a yearly or quarterly basis. Coupled with the short time series of spreads this implies a low size of our estimation sample, a feature that would limit the selection of appropriate estimation technique (pooled mean group for example cannot be employed on short samples). To increase the sample size we opt for a panel of monthly observations and generate missing observations by linear interpolation. Interpolation has been extensively used in previous studies (Goldman Sachs (2000); Dell'Ariccia *et al* (2000)). Clearly, it comes at the cost of imposing a (linear) model on the data generating process of the relevant indicators. However, it is possible to argue that this cost is not high in some cases, for example for stock variables (such as external debt and official reserves) which presumably do not change suddenly over time. Moreover, the cost of any alternative might be potentially higher. For example, we could drop all low frequency (eg yearly) indicators, but this might lead to omitted-variable bias and heteroscedasticity. Alternatively, we could drop single observations and work with a database of low-frequency (eg yearly or quarterly) data, but this would imply the loss of potentially relevant information and lower degrees of freedom, and thus would restrict model selection and estimation techniques.[8]

Table 3 summarises some simple descriptive statistics of the data. Panel A contains the statistics for the whole sample; panels B and C refer to the two subsamples of Latin American and non-Latin American countries. Confirming earlier findings (eg Min (1998)) the table shows that on average Latin American countries pay higher spreads than non-Latin countries (932 basis points versus 692 basis points). The external debt-to-GDP ratio of Latin American countries is lower than in non-Latin countries, but in the former trade openness as measured by the sum of imports and exports over GDP is lower (35% against 68%), inflation is higher (97.8% against 68.2% per annum) and the current account deficit is higher (2.3% of GDP versus 0.8%). Moreover, reserves are lower in Latin America (10% of GDP compared with 17% in non-Latin countries) and the ratio of external debt amortisation to reserves (a liquidity indicator) is higher (60% against 42%).

Table 3.a Descriptive statistics: all sample[a]

	Mean	Median	Max	Min	St dev	Skewness	Kurtosis	Jarque-Bera (p-value)
Spread	792	581	7078	66	795.30	3.57	21.14	0.0
Ext debt/ GDP	56.80	51.75	451.62	13.38	30.87	3.57	32.57	0.0
Budget/ GDP	-2.79	-1.96	5.37	-23.42	4.01	-1.88	7.58	0.0
Openness[b]	54.46	47.93	409.41	12.06	36.94	2.85	16.01	0.0
Trade bal/ GDP	-0.30	0.43	29.23	-40.70	11.67	-0.61	3.91	0.0
Inflation	56.43	7.07	4922.46	-4.30	300.26	9.68	114.28	0.0
Interest/ Ext debt	6.10	5.91	13.04	1.85	1.79	0.85	4.50	0.0
Amort/ Reserves	49.38	38.46	394.61	4.92	39.15	2.20	11.61	0.0
Curr account/ GDP	-1.40	-1.97	26.70	-38.67	8.06	-1.49	9.35	0.0
Arrears/ Ext debt	1.07	0.00	15.82	0.00	2.52	3.44	15.83	0.0
Reserves/ GDP	13.68	11.84	57.66	1.60	8.70	1.23	4.56	0.0
RER change[c]	41.77	0.64	4821.97	-80.12	289.09	9.97	120.85	0.0

Notes: (a) Spreads are in basis points, all other data are percentages. Spreads are annual. Flow data are 12-month moving averages. Percentage rate of changes are year-on-year changes. Panel covers 2,005 monthly observations over the period December 1991 to March 2003 and includes 23 unbalanced cross-sections: Argentina, Brazil, Bulgaria, China, Colombia, Côte d'Ivoire, Croatia, Ecuador, Korea, Lebanon, Malaysia, Mexico, Morocco, Nigeria, Panama, Peru, the Philippines, Poland, Russia, South Africa, Thailand, Turkey and Venezuela. (b) Defined as (Exports + Imports)/ GDP. (c) Plus sign is appreciation.

Table 3.b Descriptive statistics: Latin America[a]

	Mean	Median	Max	Min	St dev	Skewness	Kurtosis	Jarque-Bera (p-value)
Spread	932	698	7078	243	887.61	4.13	23.48	0.0
Ext debt/ GDP	52.18	48.00	182.72	22.55	23.81	1.77	8.31	0.0
Budget/ GDP	-2.01	-1.48	5.37	-7.94	2.32	-0.29	3.08	0.0
Openness[b]	35.02	32.40	66.43	12.06	15.53	0.16	1.75	0.0
Trade bal/ GDP	0.14	-0.11	22.29	-25.46	8.97	-0.74	4.88	0.0
Inflation	97.83	9.64	4922.46	-1.79	437.54	6.93	57.46	0.0
Interest/ Ext debt	6.63	6.66	9.81	2.92	1.39	-0.33	2.54	0.0
Amort/ Reserves	60.51	48.55	202.21	15.52	37.82	1.24	3.81	0.0
Curr account/ GDP	-2.28	-3.02	14.43	-14.40	4.79	0.84	4.48	0.0
Arrears/ Ext debt	0.61	0.00	11.14	0.00	1.43	3.56	17.94	0.0
Reserves/ GDP	9.60	8.32	21.61	1.98	4.32	0.83	2.76	0.0
RER change[c]	79.13	0.64	4821.97	-59.64	423.15	7.10	60.05	0.0

Notes: (a) Spreads are in basis points, all other data are percentages. Spreads are annual. Flow data are 12-month moving averages. Percentage rate of changes are year-on-year changes. Panel covers 831 monthly observations over the period December 1991 to March 2003 and includes 8 unbalanced cross-sections: Argentina, Brazil, Colombia, Ecuador, Mexico, Panama, Peru, and Venezuela. (b) Defined as (Exports + Imports)/ GDP. (c) Plus sign is appreciation.

95

Table 3.c Descriptive statistics: all sample excluding Latin America[a]

	Mean	Median	Max	Min	St dev	Skewness	Kurtosis	Jarque-Bera (p-value)
Spread	692	464.5	5783	66	706.56	2.66	13.15	0.0
Ext debt/ GDP	60.08	56.80	451.62	13.38	34.65	3.76	32.44	0.0
Budget/ GDP[b]	-3.35	-2.22	5.28	-23.42	4.79	-1.60	5.42	0.0
Openness[b]	68.23	57.84	409.41	14.07	41.26	2.66	13.16	0.0
Trade bal/ GDP	-0.61	2.20	29.23	-40.70	13.25	-0.51	3.26	0.0
Inflation	27.12	5.59	1722.36	-4.30	128.40	10.14	113.54	0.0
Interest/ Ext debt	5.72	5.25	13.04	1.85	1.94	1.50	5.97	0.0
Amort/ Reserves	41.51	33.06	394.61	4.92	38.17	3.22	20.41	0.0
Curr account/ GDP	-0.78	-0.59	26.70	-38.67	9.68	-1.68	7.90	0.0
Arrears/ Ext debt	1.39	0.00	15.82	0.00	3.03	2.88	11.23	0.0
Reserves/ GDP	16.57	15.00	57.66	1.60	9.80	0.74	3.29	0.0
RER change[c]	15.32	0.63	1629.11	-80.12	119.95	10.37	118.23	0.0

Notes: (a) Spreads are in basis points, all other data are percentages. Spreads are annual. Flow data are 12-month moving averages. Percentage rate of changes are year-on-year changes. Panel covers 1,174 monthly observations over the period December 1991 to March 2003 and includes 15 unbalanced cross-sections: Bulgaria, China, Côte d'Ivoire, Croatia, Korea, Lebanon, Malaysia, Morocco, Nigeria, the Philippines, Poland, Russia, South Africa, Thailand, and Turkey. (b) Defined as (Exports + Imports)/ GDP. (c) Plus sign is appreciation.

5 Estimation issues

We run the empirical estimations using the pooled mean group estimator (PMG) due to Pesaran, Shin and Smith (1999). This is essentially a dynamic error correction model that allows the short-run parameters to vary across individual groups, while restricting long-run elasticities to be identical across groups. Thus PMG is applicable to panels with cross-sectional variation in the short-run dynamics but long-run commonality in the equilibrium relationship.

Since Edwards (1984), it has been conventional to test models which use log-spreads (rather than their level). We follow this convention here, but unlike Edwards we allow for a cross-sectional specific intercept term, α_i. Under these hypotheses, a general long-run model of (log)-spread determinants for country i at time t is given by the following equation:

$$\log s_{it} = \alpha_i + \sum_{j=1}^{J} \beta_{ji} x_{jit} + \varepsilon_{it}, \quad i = 1, 2, \ldots N, \quad t = 1, 2, \ldots T \tag{6}$$

If we assume that all the variables are $I(1)$ and cointegrated, then the error term ε_{it} is $I(0)$ for all i. Assuming a fixed lag of one for the dependent and the independent variables, the resulting ARDL specification is:[9]

$$\log s_{it} = \mu_i + \lambda_i \log s_{it-1} + \sum_{j=1}^{J} \gamma_{1ji} x_{jit} + \sum_{j=1}^{J} \gamma_{2ji} x_{jit-1} + u_{it} \tag{7}$$

This can be rearranged to give the error correction equation:

$$\Delta \log s_{it} - \phi_i \left[\log s_{it-1} - \alpha_i - \sum_{j=1}^{J} \beta_{ji} x_{jit} \right] - \sum_{j=1}^{J} \gamma_{2ji} \Delta x_{jit} + u_{it} \tag{8}$$

where:

$$\phi_i = -(1 - \lambda_i), \, \alpha_i - \frac{\mu_i}{(1 - \lambda_i)}, \, \beta_{ji} - \frac{\gamma_{1ji} + \gamma_{2ji}}{(1 - \lambda_i)}$$

The term in square brackets in equation (8) is the long-run relationship and the β_{ji} are the long-run elasticities. The assumption of long-run commonalities in the equilibrium relationship (pooled model) requires the following restriction in equation (8): $\beta_{ji} = \beta_j$ for all cross-sections i, that is constant long-run slope coefficients for all cross-sections. The error correction coefficient ϕ_i and the short-term elasticities (γ_{2ji}) are unrestricted and are allowed to vary in each cross-section. Thus the estimating model becomes:

$$\Delta \log s_{it} = \phi_i \left[\log s_{it-1} - \alpha_i - \sum_{j=1}^{J} \beta_j x_{jit} \right] - \sum_{j=1}^{J} \gamma_{2ji} \Delta x_{jit} + u_{it} \tag{9}$$

Three main reasons underpin our choice of PMG rather than alternative procedures commonly used for panel data (such as pooled OLS, static fixed effects, mean group estimates). First, PMG assumes a dynamic model, which is more likely to capture the nature of the data. Second, PMG imposes homogeneity of long-run coefficients, which leads to more stable and economically plausible estimates. Baltagi and Griffin (1997) and Boyd and Smith (2000) show that pooled estimators have desirable properties and typically outperform their heterogeneous counterparts. For example, they find that pooled models tend to produce more plausible estimates even for panels with relatively long time series and that they offer overall superior forecast performance.[10] By contrast, heterogeneous estimators are normally unstable (individual country estimates vary within wide ranges) and unreliable, though they have the desirable property of allowing for differences among countries. PMG, which assumes long-run commonalities but permits short-term elasticities to vary across groups, combine the benefits of both classes of estimators. Third, PMG allows separating short-term dynamics and the adjustment towards the long-run equilibrium. This is important because, as shown by Haque, Pesaran and Sharma (2000), neglecting cross-country heterogeneity in short-run responses can lead to misleading inferences about the key determinants of the dependent variable in the regression. If differences across countries are ignored, one can overestimate the relative importance of specific explanatory variables and at the same time obtain significant, but spurious, non-linear effects for some of the potential determinants.

6 Results

We estimate equation **(9)** using maximum likelihood, as in Pesaran, Shin and Smith (1999). The estimates are computed with the Newton-Raphson algorithm, which uses both the first and the second derivatives of the likelihood function. These maximum likelihood estimators are referred to as PMG, to highlight both the pooling implied by the homogeneity restriction on the long-run coefficients, and the averaging across countries used to obtain means of the estimated error-correction coefficients and other short-run parameters. For a long-run relationship to exist the error correction coefficient has to be different from zero ($\phi_i \neq 0$, for all i in equation **(9)**).

The model allows alternative lag specifications. In general, we obtain most estimates from restricted ARDL models, imposing a common fixed lag of one for all cross-sections. But we also test more complex lag structures adopting a selection criterion through a two-step approach, as suggested by Pesaran, Shin and Smith (1999). This method involves stacking equation **(8)** by cross-section and running unrestricted ARDL with common lag structures for each country separately (we have tried maximum common lags of one and two). These estimates are then used to choose the appropriate lag order for each variable, using the Schwartz Bayesian Criterion (SBC) subject to a pre-specified maximum lag. Then, using these SBC determined lag orders we impose homogeneity and compute the maximum likelihood estimators of the long-run coefficients.

To choose a preferred model, we try a number of alternative specifications and select the model that best fits the data using a general-to-specific approach. But because we have to take into account the limited degrees of freedom and the high number of estimation parameters implied by the PMG technique, we are only able to test parsimonious models. Imposing homogeneity of long-run parameters, Table 4 reports PMG estimates for three alternative model specifications. Because the dependent variable is the log of sovereign spreads, all the parameters in the table represent semi-elasticities. The results are quite satisfactory, both from the viewpoint of the explanatory power of the regressions, and from the viewpoint of the sign and level of significance of the coefficients. In particular, all regression coefficients are statistically significant at conventional significance levels, with the exception of the coefficient on the current account balance-to-GDP ratio in one of the specifications and the coefficients on the fiscal budget-to-GDP ratio. Additionally, coefficients are broadly signed according to expectations, with few exceptions: the coefficients on the current account-to-GDP ratio and on US corporate yield spreads in Model (A) (where however the former is not significant); the coefficients on the fiscal budget-to-GDP in Models (B) and (C) (also insignificant), and that on the ratio of short-term external debt to total external debt in Model (C).[11] Moreover, estimates look generally robust across all models in the table (and indeed across most other models that we have tried).

Interestingly, the models point towards strong relationships between EME spreads and external factors. These are always highly significant, and have a strong economic impact on EME spreads in all the models under consideration. In particular, higher short-term US interest rates raise borrowing costs for EMEs, as indicated by the positive elasticity on 30-day US T-bill yields.

This is consistent with the main theoretical literature and earlier empirical findings. For example, Kamin and Kleist (1999) discuss reasons why industrial country interest rates are expected to be positively correlated with EME credit spreads. And Eichengreen and Mody (1998b) provide supporting empirical evidence (but contra, see Min (1998), and Kamin and Kleist (1999)). By contrast, higher long-term US interest rates – measured by the yield of a benchmark 10-year US government bond – have a strong negative impact on EME spreads. Taken together, short and long-term US interest rates suggest that the slope of the US yield curve is probably more important than the two independent levels, and that when the US yield curve becomes steeper EME spreads fall. One possible explanation for this effect is the behaviour of leveraged investors who may increase the demand for EME assets (pushing prices up and spreads down) when global credit conditions allow cheap borrowing.

Table 4 PMG estimates of long-run coefficients[a]

	Model (A)[b]	Model (B)[b]	Model (C)[c]
External debt/ GDP	0.25	0.70	0.73
	(0.12)**	(0.13)*	(0.12)*
Fiscal budget/ GDP	-0.72	0.27	0.47
	(0.58)	(0.47)	(0.37)
Openness	-0.37	-0.35	-0.24
	(0.11)*	(0.13)*	(0.11)**
Amortisation/ Reserves	0.19	0.23	-0.10
	(0.06)*	(0.04)*	(0.05)**
Interest payments/ External debt	-	5.69	-
		(1.32)*	
Current account/ GDP	0.14	-1.25	-1.34
	(0.35)	(0.29)*	(0.29)*
Short-term external debt/ External debt	-	-	-2.32
			(0.33)*
Yield of 30-day US T-bill	8.88	6.68	7.21
	(1.39)*	(0.85)*	(0.71)*
Yield of 10-year US government bond	-8.00	-8.55	-4.67
	(2.13)*	(1.40)*	(1.33)*
Log of yield spread between low and high-rating US corporate bonds	-0.44 (0.18)*	-	-
Log of US S&P 500 equity index	-0.60	-0.38	-0.24
	(0.12)*	(0.12)*	(0.06)*
Constant[d]	0.78	0.65	1.04
	(0.12)*	(0.12)*	(0.26)*
Error correction coefficient[d]	-0.15	-0.19	-0.39
	(0.02)*	(0.04)*	(0.09)*
Observations	1982	1982	1838
Cross sections	23	23	21
R-Squared[e]	0.40	0.40	0.27
RBAR-Squared[e]	0.21	0.21	0.10
Standard deviation of regressions[e]	0.065	0.065	0.069
Maximised Log likelihood	2891.51	2895.51	2623.26
No. of model parameters	262	262	146
Chi-sq test for:[f]			
Serial correlation	8	7	4
Functional form misspecification	17	16	17
Normality	16	18	18
Heteroscedasticity	20	22	15
LR test for equal long-run parameters:			
Chi-square stat	427.41	497.89	812.07
Degrees of freedom	198	198	180
p-value	0.00	0.00	0.00

Notes: (a) Dependent variable is log of spreads. Figures in parenthesis are standard errors. Sample period is December 1991 to March 2003. Observations are monthly. (b) A fixed lag of one has been selected for all groups. All 23 cross-sections have been included. (c) The Schwarz-Bayesian criterion has been used to select the appropriate lag orders for each group, conditional on a maximum lag of two. Two groups (Côte d'Ivoire and Croatia) have been excluded from estimations. (d) Average of group-specific coefficients. (e) Average of group-specific statistics. (f) Tests of estimation residuals from cross-section equations based on 5% significance level. Statistics shown indicate number of cross-sections where the null hypothesis cannot be rejected. * Significant at 1% s.l. ** Significant at 5% s.l.

One feature of our modelling strategy is that it controls for changes in liquidity and market premia. The need to control for liquidity risk arises because the bonds in the EME indices, while probably the most liquid available, may still likely be affected by some illiquidity problems. For US corporate bonds, for example, the current view is that the liquidity premium accounts for a larger proportion of the credit spread than do credit premia.[12] To control for this, and for lack of better data, we include the yield spreads between low and high-rating US corporate bonds as an explanatory variable of Model (A). The sign of the coefficient suggests that when this yield spreads rises EME spreads fall. Additionally, the models include the S&P 500 equity index to control for market risk. The sign of the coefficient suggests some complementarities between EME bonds and developed economies equity assets in investors' portfolios.

One advantage of PMG over traditional fixed effect panel models is that it allows the short-run dynamic specifications to be different in each cross-section. Table 4 reports two of these short-term elasticities, calculated as averages of the cross-section specific coefficients. One of them is the error correction coefficient, which is statistically significant in all regressions, suggesting that we can accept the hypothesis of a long-run relationship. The coefficient is also negative, implying that spreads tend to return back to equilibrium following a shock, and takes values between −0.15 and −0.39 across the three models. These values mean that between 15% and 39% of the gap between the equilibrium and the observed level of spreads is closed in each period, or that the half-life of the gap – the time required for the gap to halve – is between 3.8 and 1.5 months.

PMG imposes homogeneity of the long-run slope coefficients, but this is a hypothesis that can be tested using a likelihood ratio test, since PMG is a restricted version of the set of individual group estimates. Though it is common practice to use pooled estimators without testing the implied restrictions, in cross-country studies the likelihood ratio tests normally reject equality of error variances and slope coefficients at conventional significance levels. This is clearly the case in our models (bottom of Table 4). We will return on this point later, but one possible explanation is that the group-specific estimates may be biased because of omitted variables or measurement errors that are correlated with the regressors. If the bias is non-systematic and averages to zero over groups, pooled estimation would still be appropriate despite the homogeneity assumption being rejected. Unfortunately there is no obvious way to determine from the data whether this is the case (Pesaran, Shin and Smith (1999)).

Comparing the diagnostic tests for the three models (Table 4) we see that on balance Model (A) shows a relatively better performance. While Model (C) minimises issues of error term heteroscedasticity and serial correlation in the country-specific regressions, and Model (B) is the least affected by functional form misspecification, Model (A) maximises the sum of the corrected R-squared. Moreover, this model has low standard deviation of error terms and minimises issues of error term non-normality. For this preferred model (A), Table 5 reports some cross-section specific diagnostic statistics. The adjusted

Table 5 Model (A): diagnostic statistics

	Obs	RBAR- Sq[a]	Sigma[b]	Ch-SC[c]	Ch-FF[d]	Ch-NO[e]	Ch-HET[f]	LL[g]
Argentina	119	0.15	0.08	0.22	14.39	56.85	28.45	147.77
Brazil	135	0.24	0.07	0.71	11.92	69.97	11.84	185.67
Bulgaria	100	0.26	0.06	2.08	17.89	71.70	43.71	149.97
China	63	0.19	0.06	6.96	7.09	35.46	34.33	97.00
Colombia	63	0.28	0.06	0.02	4.03	1.76	7.27	99.91
Côte d'Ivoire	60	-0.10	0.09	24.80	21.18	140.28	31.31	71.17
Croatia	63	-0.25	0.08	1.00	9.11	2.16	7.48	83.19
Ecuador	93	0.27	0.07	0.72	2.29	2.71	43.52	124.49
Korea	63	0.27	0.07	11.72	1.76	5.72	1.68	92.66
Lebanon	60	0.04	0.06	4.10	0.11	0.02	2.11	98.31
Malaysia	63	0.29	0.06	0.01	1.41	2.35	5.99	103.37
Mexico	135	0.35	0.06	1.13	14.89	7.76	43.44	211.55
Morocco	63	0.12	0.09	11.85	17.21	123.60	36.50	74.52
Nigeria	135	0.21	0.07	2.29	18.84	19.63	22.61	185.60
Panama	73	0.36	0.05	4.46	8.58	2.39	18.01	134.25
Peru	70	0.13	0.06	1.07	7.22	4.06	5.89	104.87
Philippines	135	0.18	0.06	0.62	3.24	51.64	17.96	197.51
Poland	100	0.23	0.06	5.87	3.90	38.38	23.18	153.85
Russia	63	0.56	0.06	2.27	35.03	60.78	50.96	96.38
South Africa	63	0.30	0.05	2.64	5.35	2.62	5.01	112.63
Thailand	65	0.08	0.08	1.64	1.60	111.61	0.77	81.50
Turkey	63	0.31	0.06	20.26	11.27	8.84	5.97	102.64
Venezuela	135	0.25	0.07	1.43	26.78	78.97	67.98	182.72

Notes: (a) Corrected R-squared. (b) Standard deviation of regressions. (c) Chi-square test of residual serial correlation. (d) Chi-square test of functional form misspecification. (e) Chi-square test of normality of residuals. (f) Chi-square test of heteroscedasticity. (g) Maximised Log-likelihood.

R-squared is negative in two cases (Côte d'Ivoire and Croatia), and the weighted average of this statistic is 0.22. Individual country statistics are generally not high, but as observed in Goldman Sachs (2000) the model is intended to provide a predicted value of equilibrium spreads in the long term and thus a certain degree of misalignment in the short run must be expected. The standard deviation of the restricted model error terms varies between 5% in Panama and South Africa and 11% in Cote d'Ivoire and Morocco. At the 5% significance level, the restricted model error terms show problems of serial correlation in 8 out of 23 cross-sections, non-normality in 16, functional form misspecification in 17, and heteroscedasticity in 20.[13]

Reassuringly, the lagged dependent variable bias (which causes the estimates of ϕ_i to underestimate the true values for small T) is not a problem here, for two reasons. First, T is relatively large in our sample, ranging between 60 and 135 months. Second, even if estimates suffer a downward lagged dependent variable bias this may be offset by the upward heterogeneity bias discussed in Pesaran and Smith (1995).[14]

As we have discussed earlier, the lag structure that best fits the data is first chosen testing a number of unrestricted ARDL models, that is models where the long-run coefficients are not required to be the same across countries. To shed more light on the quality of the estimation output, Table 6 reports the output for these group-specific, unrestricted models. The cross-sectional averages of these coefficients (and the associated t-statistics) are also included at the bottom of the table. These are the mean group estimates (MGE). The picture is broadly similar to that presented for the restricted models. It is comforting that the long-run relationship is statistically significant in the majority of the countries (the hypothesis of no long-run relationship (H_0: $\phi_i = 0$) is rejected in 21 of the 23 cross-sections in the panel). The error correction coefficient varies from -0.09 in Brazil (half-life of the gap of around 6 months) to -0.77 in China (half-life of a fraction of a month). The long-run individual slope coefficients are more dispersed than the restricted estimates reported in Table 4. For example, the individual estimates of the external debt-to-GDP ratio vary from -15.3 in Croatia (which however is not statistically significant at conventional significance levels) to 8.84 in South Africa, which compare oddly with a long-run estimate of 0.25 in the restricted model. Additionally, these individual estimates are mostly insignificant – only 66 of the 230 coefficients reported in the table are statistically different from zero.

Boyd and Smith (2000) consider a number of explanations for this wide dispersion of cross-country estimates. First, they suggest that the dispersion may be the product of poor data – and indeed this may be plausible in our analysis, given the data limitation highlighted in previous sections. Second, it may be the result of simultaneity bias. One example of simultaneity bias is endogenous capital flows, but these would have to be highly speculative to create such large effects. Moreover, the covariances would have to be economically implausible to give, for example, a negative effect of the external debt-to-GDP ratio on spreads. Third, it may be the result of spurious regressions. The variables are not cointegrated and

Table 6 Model (A): group-specific estimates of error correction and long-run coefficients[a,b]

	Phi	DGDP	BDGT	OPN	AMRS	CABG	TBY	USLY	LUCS	LEQ
Argentina	-0.18 (0.08)†	2.28 (1.62)	14.34 (10.82)	-5.49 (4.53)	1.14 (0.46)‡	-6.02 (7.14)	7.54 (10.50)	-7.01 (12.48)	-0.79 (116)	-1.30 (0.96)
Brazil	-0.09 (0.06)	5.97 (4.62)	9.66 (10.55)	-10.09 (9.69)	-1.07 (0.96)	-16.49 (16.80)	17.40 (19.97)	-8.26 (16.66)	1.00 (1.35)	0.91 (2.30)
Bulgaria	-0.31 (0.07)‡	0.84 (0.50)†	-0.32 (1.50)	-0.97 (0.46)†	0.34 (0.26)	-0.81 (1.16)	10.63 (3.89)‡	-5.12 (5.85)	-0.29 (0.46)	-0.47 (0.56)
China	-0.77	-2.58 (8.87)	-10.71 (17.11)	-3.67 (1.45)‡	-10.73 (8.08)	-15.83 (8.01)	16.42 (5.79)‡	-10.84 (4.66)†	0.30 (0.32)	-0.28 (0.63)
Colombia	-0.30 (0.14)‡	6.61 (4.62)	-5.71 (7.35)	-8.60 (6.80)	-0.15 (2.47)	-6.93 (6.42)	23.11 (11.56)†	-3.47 (16.78)	0.81 (0.73)	-0.86 (1.48)
Côte d'Ivoire	-0.67 (0.16)†	-1.98 (0.84)†	-5.47 (8.61)	0.24 (1.91)	0.03 (0.08)	4.35 (11.45)	6.35 (11.34)	6.81 (9.16)	-0.72 (0.55)	-0.94 (1.09)
Croatia	-0.13 (0.15)‡	-15.30 (13.51)	3.78 (10.29)	-16.34 (12.09)	5.33 (8.34)	24.87 (24.30)	-7.42 (16.44)	-92.69 (82.40)	2.28 (2.71)	-5.20 (6.55)
Ecuador	-0.25 (0.11)	3.33 (0.90)‡	6.40 (5.35)	-6.15 (2.98)†	-0.04 (0.22)	-1.99 (1.86)	6.16 (6.80)	-16.76 (10.70)	0.45 (0.80)	-0.27 (0.68)
Korea	-0.57 (0.09)‡	1.21 (1.19)	5.69 (3.95)	-0.20 (0.86)	0.15 (0.38)	0.80 (3.54)	7.26 (5.93)	-11.25 (9.30)	-0.92 (0.54)†	-0.51 (1.49)
Lebanon	-0.57 (0.20)†	4.56 (3.12)	-2.48 (1.42)†	-0.31 (2.18)	2.54 (0.97)‡	-1.16 (1.97)	4.29 (4.75)	-1.59 (5.94)	1.31 (0.44)‡	-1.50 (0.90)†
Malaysia	-0.37 (0.15)‡	-3.58 (1.57)†	0.61 (3.87)	-2.19 (0.83)‡	1.22 (2.12)	-0.32 (1.90)	10.99 (5.08)†	9.16 (10.54)	-0.43 (0.58)	-1.46 (1.24)
Mexico	-0.27 (0.10)‡	2.01 (0.62)‡	7.00 (3.39)†	0.24 (0.74)	-0.02 (0.15)	-5.51 (1.47)‡	-2.71 (3.83)	-7.41 (4.79)	-0.26 (0.35)	0.54 (0.49)
Morocco	-0.57 (0.14)‡	1.08 (1.78)	-0.09 (1.72)	-0.95 (1.08)	-0.47 (1.01)	3.39 (3.34)	10.40 (7.96)	-16.27 (11.89)	0.05 (0.65)	-0.63 (1.08)
Nigeria	-0.29 (0.07)‡	1.25 (0.65)‡	2.40 (1.35)†	-0.61 (0.67)	0.25 (0.11)†	-2.59 (0.83)‡	7.66 (4.82)	-8.93 (5.45)	0.21 (0.44)	-0.06 (0.39)

104

	(1)	(2)	(3)	(4)	(5)	(6)	(7)	(8)	(9)	(10)
Panama	-0.48 (0.12)‡	0.32 (2.28)	0.10 (0.93)	-0.29 (2.44)	0.23 (0.17)	-1.97 (1.43)	2.38 (4.03)	-5.75 (6.35)	-0.02 (0.27)	-0.30 (0.49)
Peru	-0.61 (0.13)‡	-0.74 (1.45)	-7.23 (5.22)	-1.74 (5.54)	3.87 (1.85)†	-2.26 (3.77)	8.39 (3.32)‡	-9.45 (6.25)	-0.02 (0.30)	-1.92 (0.68)‡
Philippines	-0.30 (0.06)‡	1.30 (0.79)	10.05 (4.65)†	0.06 (0.58)	0.02 (0.23)	4.72 (1.15)‡	-4.36 (4.67)	-0.25 (4.38)	-0.40 (0.39)	-1.57 (0.37)‡
Poland	-0.27 (0.07)‡	4.05 (149)‡	8.77 (4.31)†	1.97 (1.81)	-2.18 (0.79)‡	6.88 (5.33)	2.14 (5.48)	0.07 (5.77)	0.55 (0.56)	-0.42 (0.90)
Russia	-0.41 (0.14)‡	1.71 (1.53)	6.18 (3.92)	2.57 (1.95)	0.51 (0.53)	-5.89 (1.64)‡	13.96 (4.84)‡	-4.56 (10.34)	-0.35 (0.60)	-3.01 (1.57)†
South Africa	-0.36 (0.11)‡	8.84 (2.82)‡	-3.51 (7.07)	-2.93 (1.04)‡	0.85 (0.77)	-4.75 (10.08)	9.65 (4.62)†	-11.60 (7.15)	0.59 (0.62)	-0.51 (0.87)
Thailand	-0.56 (0.14)‡	0.73 (0.43)†	3.75 (4.96)	0.22 (0.36)	0.88 (1.39)	2.71 (1.43)†	4.07 (5.37)	-3.97 (7.74)	-0.67 (0.45)	-1.40 (1.01)
Turkey	-0.52 (0.17)‡	0.42 (0.97)	2.11 (1.73)	-2.46 (0.88)‡	0.63 (0.35)†	-3.39 (2.15)	6.39 (8.00)	-2.57 (8.91)	-0.26 (0.37)	-1.22 (0.90)
Venezuela	-0.18 (0.06)‡	1.17 (1.69)	-4.55 (2.85)	-0.94 (1.59)	0.55 (0.60)	1.96 (1.51)	4.62 (8.22)	-5.36 (9.94)	-0.78 (0.86)	0.16 (1.60)
Min	-0.77	-15.3	-10.71	-16.34	-10.73	-16.49	-7.42	-92.69	-0.92	-5.2
Max	-0.09	8.84	14.34	2.57	5.33	24.87	23.11	9.16	2.28	0.91
Avg. (MGE)	-0.39 (0.04)‡	1.02 (0.95)	1.77 (1.31)	-2.55 (0.90)‡	0.17 (0.59)	-1.14 (1.68)	7.19 (144)‡	-9.44 (4.00)‡	0.07 (0.16)	-0.97 (0.26)‡
Std Error										
t-ratio	10.16	1.07	1.35	2.83	0.28	0.70	4.98	2.36	0.44	3.69

Notes: (a) Dependent variable is log of spreads. Figures in brackets are standard errors. Estimates based on ARDL specification with a fixed lag of one for all cross-sections. Sample period is December 1991 to March 2003. Observations are monthly. (b) Key to column headings: Phi: Error correction coefficient. DGDP: External Debt/ GDP. BDGT: Fiscal budget/ GDP. OPN: Trade openness, defined as (Exports + Imports)/ GDP. AMRS: Amortisation/ Reserves. CABG: Current account balance/ GDP. TBY: Yield of 30-day US T-bill. USLY: Yield of 10-year US government bond. LUCS: Log of yield spread between low and high-rating US corporate bonds. LEQ: Log of US S&P 500 equity index. † Significant at 5% s.l. ‡ Significant at 1% s.l.

the error term is I(1). Thus the coefficient estimates converge to non-degenerate random variables, accounting for the dispersion. But stationarity of the regressors is not strictly required in PMG, and we have tried modelling the first difference of spreads, with broadly similar dispersions.

Clearly, it is possible that countries are really different. While this may be true in the case under consideration, it cannot explain the size of the measured differences, which are so large as to be implausible. As we have mentioned before, a more plausible explanation may be that country-specific shocks and measurement errors associated with unobservable variables act like omitted variables correlated with the regressors. If these are structural factors, operating in all time periods and countries, they would cause a systematic bias in the average estimate of the long-run parameters. But if they are not structural, but just happen to be correlated in a particular sample, they would average to zero and would cancel out across countries or over time. Such correlated shocks would cause structural instability (because the biases are not constant overt time), heterogeneity (because the biases are not constant over countries) and forecasting failure.

If we estimate an equation for each individual group we might experiment with different specifications until plausible estimates are obtained ('Tender, Loving Care' discussed in Boyd and Smith (2000)). But in models with large groups this in not possible and a statistical solution is robust estimators which reduce the effect of outliers. A simple version of this involves using pooled estimators.

For the unrestricted ARDL models discussed so far, Table 7 reports diagnostic tests and other tests of goodness of fit. These tests show that the overall explanatory power of the equations is satisfactory. In 15 of the 23 countries considered the model explains over 50% of the change in the log of spreads, and in all but 6 countries (Argentina, Croatia, Morocco, the Philippines, Thailand and Venezuela) the corrected R-squared is higher than 30%. The standard error of the regressions varies from 4% in Panama to 8% in Morocco. Unsurprisingly, the equality of error variances across countries does not seem to be an appropriate assumption, a result born out by formal statistical tests: at the 5% confidence level, there is evidence of heteroscedastic error terms in 21 of 23 equations. Serial correlation is a problem in 7 countries, functional form misspecification in 18, and non-normal errors in 15.

To summarise, the restricted model provides overall satisfactory results in terms of sign and level of significance of coefficients, and in terms of explanatory power of the regressions, though because some variables may be missing the goodness of fit measures presented are probably lower bounds. Additionally, the specification tests suggest that the choice of a pooled model is probably more appropriate than mean group or other common unrestricted estimators. But the diagnostic statistics also suggest that there is a systematic pattern of the cross-sectional error terms, which we take as evidence that the market assessment of a country's creditworthiness may be more broad-based than that provided by the model. In other words, if spreads react to common external shocks, creditor factors, risk appetite, moral hazard and so on and these factors are not explicitly

Table 7 Model (A): diagnostic statistics of group-specific estimates

	Obs	RBAR-Sq[a]	Sigma[b]	Ch-SC[c]	Ch-FF[d]	Ch-NO[e]	Ch-HET[f]	LL[g]
Argentina	119	0.21	0.074	0.02	5.78	65.36	39.02	152.11
Brazil	135	0.30	0.064	0.18	16.96	58.71	14.91	190.49
Bulgaria	100	0.38	0.055	7.57	20.73	63.63	45.75	158.96
China	63	0.49	0.050	1.97	5.02	67.12	17.82	111.56
Colombia	63	0.40	0.055	0.11	8.37	0.51	8.32	105.46
Côte d'Ivoire	60	0.33	0.071	9.93	23.87	281.55	20.66	85.97
Croatia	63	0.15	0.064	0.65	2.73	0.18	4.65	95.47
Ecuador	93	0.41	0.064	0.15	2.63	1.19	50.77	134.46
Korea	63	0.40	0.061	15.16	0.11	2.86	10.65	98.86
Lebanon	60	0.39	0.046	0.49	0.07	0.36	0.42	111.77
Malaysia	63	0.50	0.048	0.19	0.88	0.59	1.77	114.46
Mexico	135	0.47	0.049	0.36	7.48	5.81	22.22	225.54
Morocco	63	0.28	0.081	5.94	13.35	193.8	19.92	80.74
Nigeria	135	0.32	0.062	1.63	10.48	35.07	23.02	195.69
Panama	73	0.50	0.040	2.99	8.47	6.66	19.12	143.44
Peru	70	0.35	0.055	0.45	13.24	3.60	12.69	115.03
Philippines	135	0.29	0.056	2.23	6.11	22.22	23.17	207.20
Poland	100	0.42	0.051	13.52	4.66	19.28	37.59	167.76
Russia	63	0.69	0.053	7.71	29.65	37.17	46.91	107.21
South Africa	63	0.44	0.044	2.21	5.47	2.51	8.30	119.92
Thailand	65	0.27	0.074	3.44	5.05	31.29	15.88	89.21
Turkey	63	0.43	0.052	8.93	9.5	4.80	3.97	108.71
Venezuela	135	0.28	0.066	1.38	27.19	82.44	61.38	185.19

Notes: (a) Corrected R-squared. (b) Standard deviation of regressions. (c) Chi-square test of residual serial correlation. (d) Chi-square test of functional form misspecification. (e) Chi-square test of normality of residuals. (f) Chi-square test of heteroscedasticity. (g) Maximised Log-likelihood.

modelled, they will affect the regression residuals, generating a certain degree of error persistence and non-normality.[15]

7 Implications

This section discusses the main implications of the model, comparing our estimation output with actual market spreads. Given the set of estimated coefficients for the preferred Model (A) in Table 4, we calculate for each country the fitted (predicted) spreads using the actual values of the explanatory variables (the macro fundamentals) at end-March 2003, and compare these with the corresponding market spreads. The results are reported in Table 8, together with the estimated misalignment expressed as the difference in basis points between the actual and predicted spreads. Similarly to Goldman Sachs (2000), the last column of Table 8 indicates whether bonds are trading at 'fair' value, are 'high' or 'low', using an evaluation criterion based on the 95% confidence interval around the (log of) fitted spreads. In particular, we define market spreads as 'fair' if they trade within the 95% confidence interval, 'high' if they rise above the upper bound of the confidence interval, and 'low' if they fall below the lower bound. Based on this criterion, Table 8 suggests that in March 2003 spreads were mainly trading at a fair level, that is sufficiently close to a theoretical equilibrium level based on fundamentals, and that spreads were too high or low in 5 of the 23 countries included in the sample. The table also shows that the largest absolute misalignments are for Argentina (which the model under-prices by more than 4500 basis points), and Côte d'Ivoire (under-priced by 1131 basis points). Large absolute misalignments are also reported for few countries where the evaluation is 'fair' (more than 600 basis points in Venezuela and Nigeria, and around 300 basis points in Brazil), but in these cases the volatility of the fitted values is also high.

The occurrence of large misalignments raises a general issue of interpretation: what do we make of spreads that are very different from those predicted by the model? Clearly, one possibility is that markets might be mispricing sovereign risk, but equally plausibly markets might be pricing risk correctly but have more information than the model. Unfortunately, there is no obvious way to address this problem, and the issue has to be resolved on a case by case basis. To this end, it is helpful to distinguish between measured fundamentals, which are included in the model, and unmeasured fundamentals. This should allow a more qualified assessment about whether the divergence is due to mispricing or unmeasured fundamentals.

On one hand, unmeasured fundamentals can probably help to explain the divergence in the pricing of sovereign debt in Nigeria, where markets likely supplement their country risk assessment with additional factors such as political risk, quality of institutions, and 'willingness to pay', which are not included in the model. Similarly, in Côte d'Ivoire the market price of sovereign risk may reflect political instability and the dependence of the macroeconomic outlook on a single commodity, cocoa. Oddly, the model also provides a poor prediction of Argentine

Table 8 Actual and fitted spreads[a]

Country	EMBIG spreads (1)	Fitted spreads (2)	Misalignment, (1)-(2)	St deviation of Fitted	Evaluation[b]
Argentina	6096	1558	4538	247	High
Brazil	1050	748	302	279	Fair
Bulgaria	253	458	-205	455	Fair
China	68	88	-20	41	Fair
Colombia	595	509	86	156	Fair
Cote d'Ivoire	2703	517	2186	1131	High
Croatia[c]	118	306	-188	87	Low
Ecuador	1372	1160	212	662	Fair
Korea	175	149	26	95	Fair
Lebanon[c]	592	321	271	114	High
Malaysia	200	192	8	51	Fair
Mexico	289	271	18	234	Fair
Morocco	372	454	-82	193	Fair
Nigeria	1292	664	628	674	Fair
Panama	399	367	32	84	Fair
Peru	477	435	42	149	Fair
Philippines	536	364	172	198	Fair
Poland	176	199	-23	93	Fair
Russia	365	559	-194	347	Fair
South Africa	187	252	-65	106	Fair
Thailand	120	116	4	78	Fair
Turkey	970	593	377	125	High
Venezuela	1406	781	625	412	Fair

Notes: (a) Data are for end-March 2003. (b) Based on the 95% confidence interval of (log) fitted spreads. By definition market spreads are 'fair' if $| EMBIG_i -Fitted_i | <1.96*\sigma(Fitted_i)$. They are 'high' if $(EMBIG_i - Fitted_i)>1.96*\sigma (Fitted_i)$. They are 'low' if $(EMBIG_i -Fitted_i) <-1.96\sigma CT(Fitted_i)$. (c) For Croatia and Lebanon the country-specific error correction coefficients and intercept terms are statistically insignificant and, for the purpose of the forecasts, they have been replaced with the coefficients from the pooled model, which are unbiased estimators of the country-specific coefficients for large number of cross-sections.

spreads (1500 basis points, against market spreads four times as high), and again we believe that is due to unmeasured fundamentals, as the model does not explain the debt default announced by the government at the end of 2001.[16] Unmeasured fundamentals in this case may be a by-product of the regression format, which contains only contemporaneous or backward-looking variables, while the market may be forward-looking. A misalignment of around 270 basis points is also reported for Lebanon where the bias is likely to be caused by poor data quality.

On the other hand, based on the selected set of fundamentals, the model predicts that sovereign risk in Bulgaria should be around 450 basis points, roughly the same level as in Peru (Table 8). By contrast, market spreads in the former are around 220 basis points lower than in the latter.

But there is no clear-cut reason to view Bulgaria as more creditworthy than Peru. Both countries (which have roughly similar per capita income) have recorded similarly low inflation rates and a relatively stable exchange rate in recent years. They have sustained restrained fiscal policy under IMF led economic programmes, and the fiscal deficit has been steadily declining. On the plus side, Bulgaria is more open to foreign trade and has higher foreign reserves relative to GDP than Peru. But Peru's external indebtedness is lower than Bulgaria's and on average its external debt is of longer duration. Moreover, Peru's external financing needs and current account deficit are also lower. The same line of argument may be applied to Morocco and the Philippines. Interestingly, the model prices Colombia's sovereign spreads at around 500 basis points, and Brazil's at around 750 basis points, which on itself would suggest a significant difference in the creditworthiness of the two countries. This is consistent with the views prevailing in the market (though in both countries market spreads are somewhat higher than the level consistent with the selected set of fundamentals) and with a comparative assessment of creditworthiness based on broad vulnerabilities to shocks. In particular, Colombia's external financing needs are lower than Brazil's and public sector debt is smaller. But unlike in Brazil, Colombia's debt dynamics are unstable on the basis of the prevailing macro financial variables without further fiscal consolidation.

Importantly, when interpreting these results we have to bear in mind that the largest misalignments are reported for countries that face or have recently faced a financial crisis. This raises two issues. First, the model may break down during crisis periods and it may not be able to pick up and price accordingly a sharp deterioration of macro conditions. Clearly, if the purpose of the investigation is to generate accurate predictions of sovereign spreads for each country we would probably need to focus on a country-specific model, and test a wide range of relevant macro fundamentals and non-fundamental variables, until we obtain plausible estimates. Second, the term structure of interest rates in crisis countries normally inverts before the actual default, reflecting market concerns over sovereign liquidity. So while market spreads may be driven up by these short-term concerns, spreads based on fundamentals (which measure mainly solvency – as opposed to liquidity – and are thus related primarily to the long end of the yield curve) may actually remain unchanged.

Table 8 compares fitted and actual spreads for all the countries in the panel at a specific point in time. To add some perspective, Chart 2 provides the same statistics over the whole length of the sample, allowing us to make the following points. First, the model tracks actual spreads fairly well in most countries. This is reassuring given the relatively short time series for some of the countries under consideration, the parsimony constraint, and the focus on macro fundamentals and external factors as explanatory variables. Second, market spreads normally exhibit higher volatility than fitted spreads. This pattern might have been easily anticipated and can be explained essentially in terms of sluggish macroprudential indicators, unmeasured fundamentals, and/or noisy market spreads. Third, for some countries (Argentina, Brazil, Ecuador, Nigeria, the Philippines and Venezuela) the misalignments rose significantly in the months between mid-1995 and 1998, as market spreads fell suddenly, while fundamental-based

110

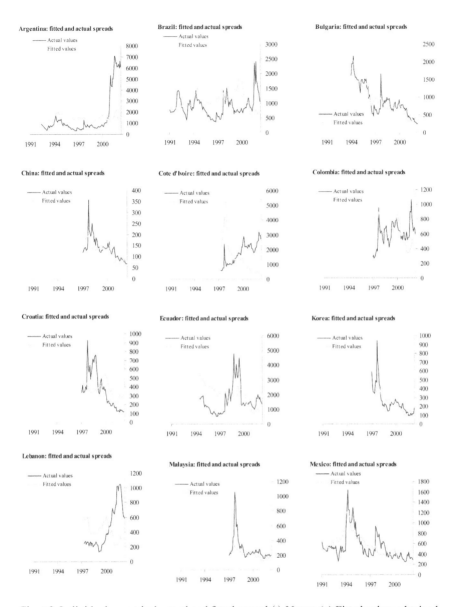

Chart 2 Individual countries' actual and fitted spreads[a]. Notes: (a) Fitted values obtained using the estimates of the common long-run parameters from Model (A) in Table 4 and country-specific intercept terms. For Croatia and Lebanon the country-specific error correction coefficients and the intercept terms are statistically insignificant and, for the purpose of these forecasts, they have been replaced by the coefficients from the pooled model, which are unbiased estimators of the country-specific coefficients for large number of cross-sections.

Morocco: fitted and actual spreads

Nigeria: fitted and actual spreads

Panama: fitted and actual spreads

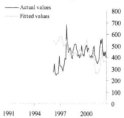

Peru: fitted and actual spreads

Philippines: fitted and actual spreads

Poland: fitted and actual spreads

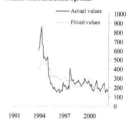

Russia: fitted and actual spreads

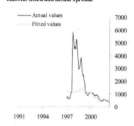

South Africa: fitted and actual spreads

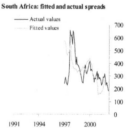

Thailand: fitted and actual spreads

Turkey: fitted and actual spreads

Venezuela: fitted and actual spreads

Chart 2 Continued.

spreads remained largely unchanged. This may be due to market mispricing of sovereign risk, a point on which we will return later. Fourth, the chart reports large and persistent misalignments between fitted and market spreads in the cases of Côte d'Ivoire and Lebanon, which we think are mainly explained by poor data quality.

To summarise the points made so far, Chart 3 reports a composite market index obtained as an average of the country-specific EMBI and EMBIG spreads, weighted using their relative weights in the EMBIG index, together with the average (calculated using the same weights) of the fitted country-specific spreads. The chart shows that the misalignment between the two indices was high and volatile between end-1991 and 1995. However during this period the panel covers only 5 countries and the overall pattern of the two indices seems to be driven by the behaviour of the individual country series in Brazil and especially Nigeria. Interestingly, the chart also confirms our earlier finding that markets on average underpriced sovereign risk between 1995 and 1997, when market spreads fell well below their fundamental-based levels. If we believe that the model gives a true picture of fundamental-based sovereign credit risk, we might conclude that the misalignment is mainly due to market imperfections. For example, the fall may be the result of investor moral hazard (eg following the IMF rescue package during the Mexican crisis at the beginnings of 1995) or higher investor risk appetite following the stimulative effect of more liberal credit conditions in the main financial centres. The possibility of some form of

Chart 3 Average market and fitted spreads[a]. Notes: (a) Calculated as averages of country-specific fitted and EMBI/EMBIG market spreads, weighted using the rolling end-of-month country weights in the EMBIG index.

Proportion of market value

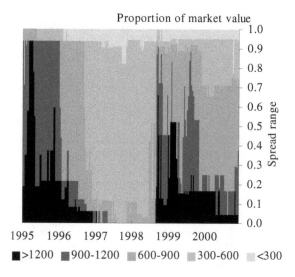

■>1200 ■900-1200 ■600-900 ■300-600 ■<300

Chart 4 Dispersion of EMBI spreads 1995-2001.

mispricing would be consistent with the finding of a more compressed dispersion of EMBI credit spreads during the same period (Chart 4). Chart 3 also
shows that misalignments have persisted in more recent times and that despite
the recent fall, on average market spreads have remained still somewhat higher
than their fundamental-based level.

8 Conclusions

This study investigates the empirical relationship between EME sovereign spreads
and a set of common macroeconomic fundamentals, using a ragged-edge panel of
JP Morgan EMBI and EMBIG secondary market spreads and a set of macro-prudential indicators. To underpin our choice of macro fundamentals, we introduce a
simple model of an indebted SOE. The estimation technique is PMG, which posits
a dynamic error correction model that allows short-run parameters to vary across
individual groups, while restricting long-run elasticities to be identical across
groups. This seems a sensible choice in a model of sovereign spreads because
restricted (pooled) models are shown to perform better than their heterogeneous
counterparts on a number of grounds. A number of specification tests performed
on the data corroborate this, suggesting that a pooled model is more appropriate
than a mean group estimator or unrestricted estimator.

The model provides overall satisfactory results in terms of the sign and significance of coefficients and in terms of explanatory power of the regressions.
The regression results suggest a strong empirical relationship between sovereign

spreads and external factors such as global liquidity conditions and US equity prices. But the diagnostic statistics also suggest that error terms in some country equations follow a systematic (non-random) pattern, which we take as evidence that the market assessment of a country's creditworthiness may be more broad based than that provided by the model. We use the estimated model to generate a time series of fitted (fundamental-based) country spreads, and compare these with actual market spreads. The purpose is threefold. First, we want to assess what proportion of the change in spreads is explained by changes in the underlying fundamentals. Second, we compare from an *ex-ante* perspective our assessment of a country's creditworthiness with that of market participants. Third, we explain the pattern in spreads, from an *ex-post* perspective. As a case study, we analyse the generalised fall in secondary market EME bond spreads experienced between 1995 and 1997.

We conclude that markets do take into account macro fundamentals when pricing sovereign risk (market spreads broadly reflect macro fundamentals) but non-fundamental factors also play an important role. Comparing market-based spreads against their model-based counterparts we find that spreads mainly trade at a level that is close to a theoretical equilibrium level based on our choice of fundamentals. Spreads are too high or low compared with the model-based benchmark in only 5 of the 23 countries included in the sample. In particular, we report large absolute misalignments in the case of Argentina and Côte d'Ivoire, and for a few countries where the market price is within the confidence interval around the fitted spreads (Venezuela, Nigeria, and Brazil among others) but where the volatility of the fitted values is also high. We suggest that unmeasured fundamentals can help to explain the divergence in the pricing of sovereign debt in some cases. And we quote the example of those countries where markets are likely to supplement their country risk assessment with additional information on political risk, quality of institutions, commodity dependence and 'willingness to pay', which are all excluded from the model. But we also suggest that mispricing may be at play in other cases. It is also possible that the model may break down during periods of crisis, possibly reflecting the occurrence of a structural break in estimation parameters, or yield curve effects.

The model suggests that markets on average underpriced sovereign risk between 1995 and 1997, when market spreads fell well below their fundamental-based levels. Assuming that the model provides a fair picture of fundamental-based sovereign credit risk, the misalignment must be due to capital market imperfections, such as investor exuberance due to moral hazard following the IMF bail-out of Mexico or higher investor risk appetite following the stimulative effect of more liberal credit conditions in the main financial centres. Moreover, these results corroborate the argument that the fall in market spreads cannot be explained entirely in terms of improved fundamentals. Finally, misalignments have persisted in more recent times. Despite the generalised fall in market prices, spreads have remained on average still somewhat higher than their fundamental-based level.

The views expressed are those of the author and do not necessarily reflect those of the Bank of England. I am indebted to Alastair Cunningham, Andrew Haldane, Victoria Saporta, Ron Smith and participants at the Emerging Market Group and Money Macro and Finance Research Group workshop on 'Emerging Capital Markets' at Cass Business School in November 2002, especially Mike Bowe, for helpful comments.

Notes

1 In other words, in the case of a sovereign borrower, willingness to pay may be as much a binding constraint as ability to pay. Eaton and Gersovitz (1981).

2 The link between spreads and fundamentals is particularly emphasised by the proponents of the efficient market hypothesis. According to this view, investors are rational and have powerful incentives to exploit all the available information and to discriminate among borrowers. As a result, asset prices always reflect the information publicly available, as evidenced by the yield differential on bonds issued by sovereign borrowers with different credit ratings and macro characteristics (Edwards (1984)). However, other observers, more sceptical about market efficiency, emphasise that market failures and imperfect information may cause distortions in the way assets are priced. They point out that the information necessary to forecast returns on EME debt is costly to acquire and process, and that asset prices are often determined on the basis of incomplete knowledge of a country's economic and financial position. This practice may generate herding and market volatility. Calvo and Mendoza (1995) for example develop a model where the incentive to gather costly information is a declining function of opportunities for portfolio diversification (because gathering information on a country implies a fixed cost, which is independent of the investment size). Under this hypothesis, investors may fail to raise the risk premium to reflect deteriorating macro conditions. News about this trend can then disproportionately impact the prices of particular bonds and can affect the allocation of funds across countries, and new information about a particular country may lead investors to revise their expectations about the prospects for other countries with superficially similar characteristics. Chari and Kehoe (1997) argue that herding behaviour may result from informational frictions about countries on the margin, ie countries whose fundamentals are not obviously attractive or bleak.

3 See for example Draghi, Giavazzi and Merton (2003).

4 This strand of literature follows the contingent claims approach developed by Merton (1974) for corporate debt. Applications to sovereign borrowers are still in an early stage and their value has been criticised on several grounds. In particular, some question the assumption that a simple stochastic process can capture the variation of a country's worth. Enforcement problems of sovereign debt contracts also mean that it is difficult to define a default trigger. Moreover, in a sovereign context insolvency does not normally result in the liquidation of the borrower's assets and partial repayment of the debt stock, but rather in a write-down of the stock of debt. And the process of sovereign debt restructuring is likely to be highly unclear until the crisis unfolds, so that investors may not have precise recovery scenarios to use when pricing a country's debt. For these reasons some questions that credit risk models designed for corporate debt – which have liquidation as the ultimate sanction – are also applicable to sovereign debt.

5 Edwards (1986) surveys the theoretical literature on the differences between the bond and loan markets.

6 Eichengreen and Mody (1998a, 1998b) and Dell'Ariccia, Goedde and Zettelmeyer (2000) consider both macro fundamentals and rating information, on the grounds that ratings often incorporate a broader assessment of sovereign risk than that based on mere macro fundamentals. However, to address the potential multicollinearity problem, these studies do not include the rating themselves, but rather a residual from the regression of the ratings on all included fundamentals.

7 See Kamin and Kleist (1999) and Eichengreen and Mody (1998b) for a discussion of the links between industrial country interest rates and EME spreads.

8 Generally in the literature a longer span of data is considered better than more high-frequency observations. However, Hansen and Hodrick (1980) show that there is information in higher-frequency data at a given span.

9 The presence of lagged variables in the estimating equation is not necessarily inconsistent with the efficient market hypothesis. Significant lags may be due to publication lags and data problems, and do not necessarily imply that markets are only slowly incorporating public information.

10 Boyd and Smith's (2000) explanation of why pooled models outperform their heterogeneous counterparts centres on the relative variability of the data between the individual time series and panels. They find that in most cases the efficiency gains from pooling appear to more than offset the biases due to cross-sectional heterogeneity.

11 It is possible that the odd sign of these coefficients stems from neglected non-linearities in model parameters, a hypothesis that we could not test owing to the parsimony constraint imposed by the selected modelling strategy.

12 I owe this point to an anonymous referee.

13 PMG corrects for cross-sectional heteroscedasticity as it allows the variances of the error terms to differ across groups. However, despite this correction embedded in the model, heteroscedasticity may still affect the results because of the nature of the time series. In particular three potential sources of heteroscedasticity may affect pooled models: *i)* aggregation over cross-sections of different size (unbalanced panel); *ii)* cross-sectional variances may differ across countries; iii) cross-sectional variances may differ across time. While PMG corrects for the first two types of heteroscedasticity, it does not correct for the third. The tests are described in Pesaran and Pesaran (1997).

14 Two further caveats relate with the use of a ragged-edge, unbalanced panel of spreads. First, because spreads for a given country may be systematically different under the EMBI and EMBIG there may be a structural break in the panel when switching from one index to the other. In theory, this is a hypothesis that may be tested formally. The test requires that we isolate two sub-samples based on the alleged breakpoint, and assumes that the error terms in the two sub-samples have the same variance. But because the latter hypothesis does not hold in this case (as we have discussed in the text) the test cannot be carried out. However, we look at this problem in Section 4 using alternative tools and conclude that our investigation supports a ragged-edge panel. Second, the spread panel may be affected by sample selection biases (as discussed in Section 4). On this problem future research might try to use a Heckman procedure, as per primary yields.

15 To define the likelihood function, PMG requires that the disturbances are normally distributed but this assumption is not strictly required for the asymptotic results on consistency, relative rates of convergence, and asymptotic distribution of the maximum likelihood estimators.

16 However, the model picks up somewhat the deterioration in Argentine fundamentals that followed the announcement of the debt moratorium in December 2001. For example, Chart 2 shows that predicted spreads rose significantly following the eruption of the crisis, peaking at 2200 basis points in September 2002 from around 1000 basis points immediately prior to the announcement of the default.

References

Baltagi, H B and Griffin, J M (1997), ' Pooled estimators vs. their heterogeneous counterparts in the context of dynamic demand for gasoline', *Journal of Econometrics,* No. 77, pages 303-27.

Boyd, D and Smith, R (2000), 'Some econometric issues in measuring the monetary transmission mechanism, with an application to developing countries', *Birkbeck College Discussion Paper in Economics,* No. 15/2000.

Calvo, G and Mendoza, E G (1995), ' Reflections on Mexico's balance of payment crisis: a chronical of a death foretold', unpublished manuscript, University of Maryland.

Cantor, R and Packer, F (1996), 'Determinants and impact of sovereign credit ratings', *Economic Policy Review,* Federal Reserve Bank of New York.

Chari, V V and Kehoe, P (1997), ' Hot money', Research Department, Federal Reserve Bank of Minneapolis.

Cunningham, A (1999), 'Emerging economy spread indices and financial stability', *Bank of England Financial Stability Review,* Issue 7, pages 115-27.

Cunningham, A, Dixon, L and Hayes, S (2001), 'Analysing yield spreads on emerging market sovereign bonds', *Bank of England Financial Stability Review,* Issue 11, pages 175-86.

Dell'Ariccia, G, Goedde, I and Zettelmeyer, J (2000), 'Moral hazard in international crisis lending: a test', *IMF Working Paper.*

Draghi, M, Giavazzi, F and Merton, R C (2003), 'Transparency, risk management and international financial fragility', *NBER Working Paper,* No. 9806.

Eaton, J and Gersovitz, M (1980), 'LDC participation in international financial markets: debt and reserves', *Journal of Development Economics,* No. 7, pages 3-21.

Eaton, J and Gersovitz, M (1981), 'Debt with potential repudiation: theoretical and empirical analysis', *Review of Economic Studies,* No. 48, pages 289-309.

Edwards, S (1984), ' LDC foreign borrowing and default risk: an empirical investigation, 1976-80', *American Economic Review,* Vol. 74, No. 4, pages 726-34.

Edwards, S (1986), ' The pricing of bonds and bank loans in international markets', *European Economic Review,* No. 30, pages 565-89.

Eichengreen, B and Mody, A (1998a), 'What explains changing spreads on EM debt: fundamentals or market sentiment?', *NBER Working Paper,* No. 6408.

Eichengreen, B and Mody, A (1998b), 'Interest rates in the north and capital flows to the south: is there a missing link?', *International Finance Discussion Papers,* pages 35-57.

Feder, G and Just, R E (1977), 'A study of debt servicing capacity applying logit analysis', *Journal of Development Economics,* No. 4, pages 25-38.

Goldman Sachs (2000), 'A new framework for assessing fair value in EMs hard currency debt', *Global Economics Paper,* No. 45.

Hamilton, J D (1983), ' Oil price and macroeconomy since World War II', *Journal of Political Economy,* Vol. 91, pages 228-48.

Hansen, P L and Hodrick, R J (1980), 'Forward exchange rates as optimal predictors of future spot rates: an econometric analysis', *Journal of Political Economy,* Vol. 88, pages 829-53.

Haque, N U, Pesaran, M H and Sharma, S (2000), 'Neglected heterogeneity and dynamics in cross-country savings regressions', in Krishnakumar, J and Ronchetti, E (eds), *Panel data econometrics – future direction: papers in honour of Professor Pietro*

Balestra, in the series, 'Contributions to economic analysis', Elsevier Science, (2000), Chapter 3, pages 53-82.

Kamin, S B and Kleist, K (1999), ' The evolution and determinants of EM credit spreads in the 1990s', *International Finance Discussion Papers,* No. 653.

McDonald, D C (1982), ' Debt capacity and developing country borrowing', *IMF Staff Papers,* No. 29, pages 603-46.

Merton, R C (1974), ' On the pricing of corporate debt: the risk structure of interest rates', *Journal of Finance,* No. 25, pages 1,921-39.

Min, H G (1998), ' Determinants of EM bond spread: do economic fundamentals matter?', *World Bank Working Paper in International Economics, Trade, Capital Flows,* No. 1899.

Pesaran, M H and Pesaran, B (1997), Microfit 4.0: Interactive econometric analysis, Oxford: Oxford University Press.

Pesaran, M H, Shin, Y and Smith, R P (1999), 'Pooled mean group estimation of dynamic heterogeneous panels', unpublished manuscript.

Pesaran, M H and Smith, R P (1995), 'Estimating long-run relationships from dynamic heterogeneous panels', *Journal of Econometrics,* No. 68, pages 79-113.

Sachs, J D (1981), ' The current account and macroeconomic adjustment in the 1970s', *Brooking Papers on Economic Activity,* No. 1, pages 201-68.

19

THE GREEK FINANCIAL CRISIS
Growing Imbalances and Sovereign Spreads

Heather D. Gibson, Stephen G. Hall, and George S. Tavlas

Source: *Journal of International Money and Finance* 31, 2012, 498–516.

ABSTRACT

We discuss the origins of the Greek financial crisis as manifested in the growing fiscal and current-account deficits since euro-area entry in 2001. We then extend a model typically used to explain risk premia to assess the extent to which credit ratings captured these premia. Next, we estimate a cointegrating relationship between spreads and their long-term fundamental determinants and compare the spreads predicted by this estimated relationship with actual spreads. We find that spreads were significantly below what would be predicted by fundamentals from end-2004 up to the middle of 2005; by contrast, since May 2010, actual spreads have exceeded predicted spreads by some 400 basis points.

1. Introduction

The entry of Greece into the euro area in 2001 provided that country's economy with a huge dividend in terms of sharply reduced interest rates. The nominal interest rate on 10-year Greek government bonds declined from about 20 per cent in 1994, the time that the then-government announced a goal of bringing Greece into the euro area in 2001, to less than $3^{1}/_{2}$ per cent in early 2005. With the eruption of the Greek financial crisis in late 2009, however, interest rates have shot upward, with the 10-year government bond yield increasing to almost 12 per cent at the end of 2010. To what extent have the wide swings in yields reflected economic fundamentals? This paper addresses that issue.

We use the interest-rate spread between 10-year Greek and German government bonds to estimate a cointegrating relationship between those spreads and their long-term fundamental determinants. Recent work on the determinants of spreads uses panel cointegration techniques on high frequency data where spreads are hypothesised to be driven by various financial market variables representing credit, liquidity and market risks (Dotz and Fischer, 2010; Fontana and Scheider,

2010; Gerlach et al., 2010). By contrast, we focus on one country alone and the macroeconomic determinants of spreads. We argue that during the period 2001–2009 the Greek economy was marked by growing, unsustainable fiscal and external imbalances. We posit that the sharp reduction in interest-rate spreads that occurred during much of this period did not adequately reflect these imbalances. Our empirical results provide some evidence for this view. We also provide evidence that the sharp, upward reversal of spreads following the outbreak of the Greek financial crisis also did not fully reflect fundamental factors. Thus, both undershooting and overshooting of spreads have occurred.

The remainder of this paper consists of six sections. Section 2 describes the origins of the Greek financial crisis, highlighting the crucial role of growing fiscal and external imbalances. Section 3 decomposes the risk premia on Greek sovereign debt into a part which can be explained by the rating given by the standard rating agencies and a part which seems to be idiosyncratic to the markets. Section 4 begins with a brief overview of the recent literature on the determinants of spreads. It then presents results of a fundamental modelling approach to the determination of spreads. Specifically, we use the methodology proposed by Johansen (1995) and Pesaran and Shin (2002) to assess the cointegrating rank of a VAR system, and then proceed to identify the structural relationship determining Greek spreads. As fundamental determinants, we include a measure of the fiscal situation, the competitiveness of the Greek economy, economic activity and oil prices (reflecting the high dependence of the Greek economy on imported energy). Section 5 presents the results. We compare the spreads predicted by the estimated relationship with actual spreads. Our findings suggest that spreads were significantly below what would be predicted by fundamentals from end-2004 up to the middle of 2005; by contrast, since May 2010, actual spreads have exceeded predicted spreads by some 400 basis points. Section 6 concludes.

2. The Greek financial crisis: origins

2.1 The years of growing imbalances: 2001–2008/09

On January 1, 2001, Greece became the twelfth member of the euro area.[1] The motivation for joining the euro area reflected an assessment that the benefits of joining would outweigh the costs. In what follows, we discuss these benefits and costs.

The adoption of the euro conferred several benefits on its members. These benefits were especially important for countries, such as Greece, with histories of high inflation and inflation variability.[2] The benefits include the following. (1) High and variable inflation increases the costs of acquiring information and performing efficient calculations on the prices of goods, services, and assets, creating uncertainty and leading to an inefficient allocation of resources. The euro – underpinned by the monetary policy of the European Central Bank – lowered inflation and inflation expectations in countries with histories of high inflation, reducing the uncertainty produced by inflation distortion. (2) The low inflation environment, and associated declines in inflation expectations and nominal interest rates, contributed to a lengthening of economic horizons, encouraging borrowing and lending at longer maturities, thereby stimulating private investment and economic growth. (3) The euro eliminated exchange-rate fluctuations and the possibility of competitive devaluations among participating countries, reducing exchange-rate uncertainty and risk premia.[3] (4) The reductions in risk premia and nominal interest rates lowered the costs of servicing the public-sector debt, facilitating fiscal adjustment and freeing resources for other uses.[4]

In the case of Greece, interest-rate spreads between 10-year Greek and German government bonds came down sharply in the years running up to, and the years following, entry into the euro area. These spreads are shown in Fig. 1 for the period 1998–2010 using monthly data.[5] As shown in the figure, spreads fell steadily, from over 1100 basis points in early 1998, to about 100 basis points one year prior to euro-area entry. Upon entry into the euro area in 2001, spreads had fallen to around 50 basis points and continued to narrow subsequently, declining to a range between 10 and 30 basis points from late 2002 until the end of 2007. During the latter period, the absolute levels of nominal interest rates on

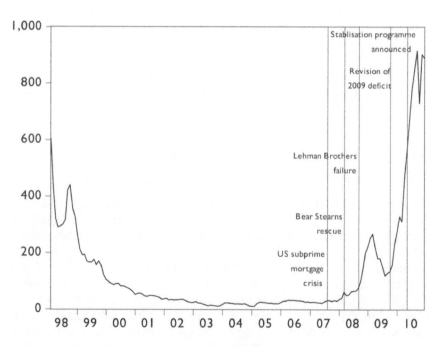

Figure 1 Greek spreads: yields on Greek over German 10-year benchmark bonds (basis points). Source: ECB Statistical Data Warehouse.

the 10-year instrument fluctuated in a range of 3.5–4.5 per cent, compared with a range of 5.0–6.5 per cent in the year prior to euro-area entry.

The low-interest-rate environment contributed to robust real growth rates. From 2001 through 2008, real GDP rose by an average of 3.9 per cent per year – the second-highest growth rate (after Ireland) in the euro area – underpinned by household spending for consumption, housing investment, and business investment. Inflation, which averaged almost ten per cent in the decade prior to euro-area entry, averaged only 3.4 per cent over the period 2001–2008.

Although entry into the euro area contributed to a period of prolonged and robust growth, and low (by Greece's historical standards) inflation, two deep-seated problems remained unaddressed; the country continued to run large fiscal imbalances and the country's competitiveness – already a problem upon euro-area entry – continued to deteriorate.

2.1.1 Fiscal policy

Fig. 2 reports data on fiscal deficits and government expenditure and revenue as percentages GDP, beginning with 2001. As indicated in the figure, fiscal policy was pro-cyclical throughout the period 2001–2009, with deficits consistently exceeding the Stability and Growth Pact's limit of 3 per cent of GDP by wide margins.[6] Expansionary fiscal policy was mainly expenditure-driven, leading to a rise in the share of government spending (to over 50 per cent of GDP in 2009, from about 45 per cent in 2001). The government debt-to-GDP ratio remained near 100 per cent throughout the period 2001–2009.

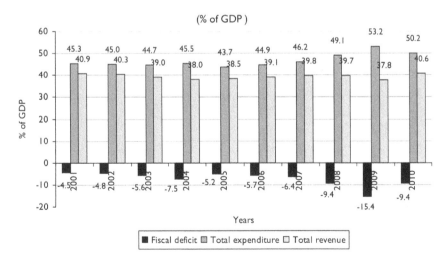

Figure 2 The fiscal deficit, total expenditure and total revenue (% of GDP). Source: European Commission, Excessive Debt Procedure Notification.

2.1.2 Competitiveness

Although inflation in Greece during 2001–2009 was low by the country's historical standards, inflation was relatively high by euro-area standards. Inflation was,
on average, more than one percentage point higher per year than in the rest of
the euro area (Fig. 3).[7] Wage increases, adjusted for productivity changes, also
exceeded the average increases in the rest of the euro area. With both prices and
wages growing at relatively high rates, competitiveness declined (Fig. 4). In the
period 2001–2009, competitiveness, as measured by consumer prices, declined
by around twenty per cent; as measured by unit labour costs, competitiveness
declined by about 25 per cent. With relatively high real growth rates and declining competitiveness, the current-account deficit, which had already topped 7 per
cent of GDP in 2001, rose to about 14.8 per cent of GDP in both 2007 and 2008
(Fig. 5).

The large and growing fiscal imbalances were clearly not sustainable. Upon
entry into the euro area, Greece gave up the ability to use two key tools to adjust
its economy in the case of a country-specific shock. First, it lost the ability to
set its own monetary policy. Second, it lost the ability to change the nominal
exchange rate of its own currency. To compensate for the loss of these tools, the
country needed to have the following: (i) relatively low fiscal imbalances, so that
fiscal policy could be used counter-cyclically in case of a country-specific shock,
and (ii) flexible labour and product markets so that the country could be competitive without having to rely on changes in the exchange rate of a domestic currency
to achieve and/or maintain competitiveness. As mentioned above, however, competitiveness declined substantially during 2001–2009, despite the already large

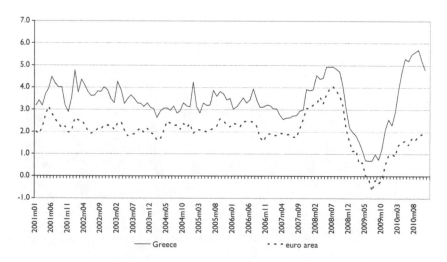

Figure 3 Greece and euro-area inflation 2001–2010 (based on annual percentage changes
in over all harmonized index of consumer prices). Source: EL.STAT.

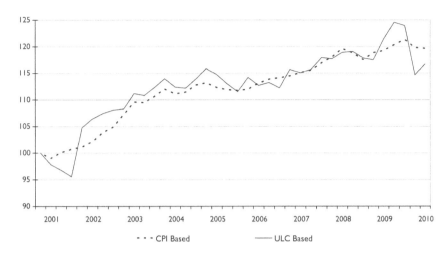

Figure 4 Real effective exchange-rate index (2001Q1=100). Source: Bank of Greece.

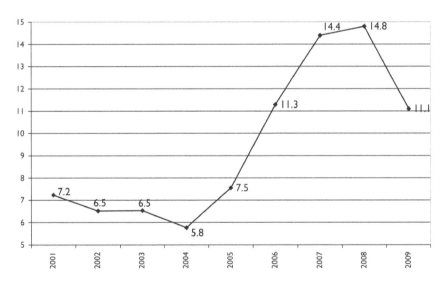

Figure 5 Greece: current-account deficit. Source: Bank of Greece.

current-account deficits at the time of entry into the union. Moreover, instead of providing the role of an automatic stabilizer, the pro-cyclical stance of fiscal policy acted as a major *source* of shocks.[8] Nevertheless, the low levels of interest-rate spreads during 2001–2008 suggest that financial markets paid little attention to the unsustainability of the fiscal and external imbalances during that period.[9]

2.2 The wake up call

The global financial crisis that erupted in August 2007, following the collapse of the US subprime mortgage market, initially had little impact on Greek financial markets; spreads on the 10-year instrument, which were in a range of 20–30 basis points during January-July of 2007, remained in the vicinity of 30 basis points for the remainder of 2007 and the first few months of 2008 (Fig. 1). With the collapse (and sale) of Bear Stearns in March 2008, spreads widened to about 60 basis points, where they remained until the collapse of Lehman Brothers in September. The latter event brought spreads up to around 250 basis points during the first few months of 2009, but they gradually came back down to about 120 basis points in August and September of 2009.

Then came a double shock in the autumn of 2009. Two developments combined to disrupt the relative tranquility of Greek financial markets. First, in October the newly elected Greek government announced that the 2009 fiscal deficit would be 12.7 per cent of GDP, more than double the previous government's projection of 6.0 per cent.[10] In turn, the 12.7 per cent figure would undergo further upward revisions, bringing it up to 15.4 per cent of GDP.[11] Second, in November 2009 Dubai World, the conglomerate owned by the government of the Gulf emirate, asked creditors for a six-month debt moratorium. That news rattled financial markets around the world and led to a sharp increase in risk aversion.

In light of the rapid worsening of the fiscal situation in Greece, financial markets and rating agencies turned their attention to the sustainability of Greece's fiscal and external imbalances. The previously held notion that membership of the euro area would provide an impenetrable barrier against risk was shaken. It became clear that, while such membership provides protection against exchange-rate risk, it cannot provide protection against credit risk.

The two shocks set-off a sharp and prolonged rise in spreads, which, by-and-large, continued throughout the course of 2010. As shown in Fig. 1, spreads on 10-year sovereigns widened from about 130 basis points in October 2009 to around 900 basis points one year later. The widening took place despite an agreement in early May 2010 between the Greek government and the International Monetary Fund, the European Central Bank, and the European Commission, for a three-year, €110 billion adjustment loan under which the Greek government committed to lower its fiscal deficit to 8.1 per cent of GDP in 2010 and to below 3.0 per cent in 2014.[12] Also, the widening occurred amid news that the European Central Bank had embarked on a programme to purchase those government bonds the spreads of which were seen as having risen for reasons unrelated to the fundamentals. To what extent did the rise in Greek spreads during 2010 relate to factors other than the fundamentals? We address this issue in what follows.

3. Spreads and the risk premium

In the 2010 report on *Financial Integration in Europe* (April 2011) from the European Central Bank (2011), a simple model of risk premia for sovereign debt yields is explored. In this section, we extend this model in terms of its specification and estimation methodology, applying the model to the case of Greek sovereign debt. In general, we may think of the relationship between a country's debt yields and that of a risk-free country (say, Germany) as being simply that of equality plus a risk premium, that is:

$$R_t^{gr} = R_t^{ge} + \rho_t + \varepsilon_t$$

where R_t^{gr} is the yield on Greek 10-year bonds, R_t^{ge} is the yield on German government bonds, ρ_t is a time-varying risk premium and ε_t is an error term. The risk premium may vary with a number of factors, including the fundamentals of the economy in question. In the ECB report mentioned above, the focus is on the ratings given to a country by the credit rating agencies and we focus on these ratings in this section. (We turn to the fundamental factors in the next section.)

We decompose the risk premium into two components, one of which can be justified on the basis of market information ρ_t^1 and one which is essentially irrational ρ_t^2. Then, parameterising the model slightly differently, we may restate the relationship as:

$$R_t^{gr} = \left(1 + \rho_t^2\right) R_t^{ge} + \rho_t^1 + \varepsilon_t \tag{1}$$

We focus on credit rating revisions on Greek sovereign debt during the period and include them in this relationship as dummy variables.[13] These revisions are:

D1	1/1/2000–4/11/2002	Moody's upgraded Greek debt from A2 to A1
D2	4/11/2002–16/12/2004	Fitch downgraded Greek debt from A+ to A
D3	14/1/2009–8/12/2009	Standard and Poor's downgraded Greek bonds from A+ to A
D4	8/12/2009–end-period	Standard and Poor's downgraded Greek bonds from A to BBB+

Hence, we may restate the relationship as:

$$R_t^{gr} = \left(1 + \rho_t^2\right) R_t^{ge} + D1 + D2 + D3 + D4 + \varepsilon_t \tag{2}$$

In the ECB study, this relationship is estimated in first differences, using OLS for a rolling window of data. We would argue that the first difference specification is inappropriate for a number of reasons. (1) Differencing the above equation would produce a non-invertible moving average error process which would present estimation problems. (2) The credit rating dummies were not differenced and, hence, the ECB study confuses the relationship between the risk premium and the spread.[14] (3) In addition, with high frequency data, the changes in yields may not be very closely linked and much of the relationship may be lost if sufficient lags are not included. We also argue that the use of OLS as an estimation technique is inherently inappropriate as the underlying assumption of OLS is that the parameters of the model are constant while the risk premium is clearly meant to be time varying. OLS is not therefore a consistent estimator of a true time-varying parameter and will yield biased results.

We, therefore, propose to estimate the following model using the Kalman Filter. The measurement equation is:

$$R_t^{gr} = \beta_t R_t^{ge} + \alpha_1 D1 + \alpha_2 D2 + \alpha_3 D3 + \alpha_4 D4 + \varepsilon_t \tag{3}$$

and the state equation is:

$$\beta_t = \beta_{t-1} + \varpi_t, \quad \omega \sim N\left(0, e^\gamma\right) \tag{4}$$

We estimate this model by maximum likelihood using daily data on 10-year benchmark yields for both Greek and German government bonds.[15] The results are presented in Table 1. The two initial changes in rating are not particularly significant while the latter are important in terms of generating a sizable risk premium. The variance of the state equation is also quite large indicating an important degree of time variation in the total risk premium.

The unexplained risk premium is given by the state variable β_t. This is shown in Fig. 6, where values above unity show the excess risk premium. The unexplained risk premium began to rise in late 2008 in advance of the first downgrade of Greek government bonds in early 2009. When this occurred, the unexplained risk premium fell back to normal levels. However, after this, and despite further downgrading in late 2009, the unexplained risk premium continued to rise through 2010, indicating that the spread on Greek bonds became considerably larger than can be explained by the downgrading alone. There are, of course, a range of other factors which may have been influencing the markets that are not

Table 1 Unexplained risk premium (estimating equations (3) and (4)).

	Coefficient	Std. error	z-Statistic	Prob.
α_1	0.114225	42.61476	0.002680	0.9979
α_2	0.096184	5.617794	0.017121	0.9863
α_3	0.980321	0.892404	1.098517	0.2720
α_4	2.016643	0.653974	3.083673	0.0020
Γ	−7.619053	0.180898	−42.11795	0.0000
	Final state	Root MSE	z-Statistic	Prob.
SV1	3.456468	0.089492	38.62305	0.0000
Log likelihood	−2887.520	Akaike info criterion		2.025574
Parameters	5	Schwarz criterion		2.036004
Diffuse priors	1	Hannan-Quinn criter.		2.029335

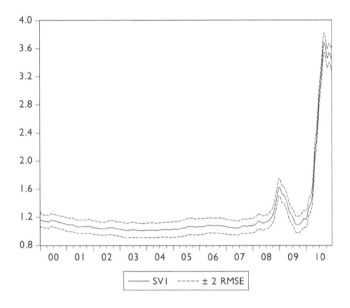

Figure 6 Risk premium left unexplained after accounting for rating changes, β_t (SV1).

captured by the credit rating schemes alone, although the credit ratings aim at capturing the effects of a country's main fundamental variables. Clearly, in the case of Greece, the credit ratings did not capture all of the factors that impacted on spreads. In what follows, we investigate a more structural approach to the risk premium to see if this can offer a better explanation of the unexplained premium.

4. The determinants of spreads

4.1 Previous literature

Previous empirical work on the determinants of spreads has, by-and-large, dealt with spreads in emerging market economies, *(e.g.,* Min, 1998; Ferucci, 2003; Grandes, 2007; Baldacci et al., 2008; Alexopoulou et al., 2009), although, as discussed below, some recent work has also investigated the determinants of spreads in euro-area economies (Attinasi et al., 2009; Codogno et al., 2003; Favero et al., 1997; Geyer et al., 2004). Typically, panel datasets have been used so that both similarities and differences among the countries can be identified.

The work dealing with emerging market economies often relates the spread to a set of determinants that can be classified into four broad categories: (1) liquidity/solvency risks, (2) external shocks, (3) market risks, and (4) other fundamentals. Effectively, each of the foregoing categories has been defined by authors to include, at least in part, various economic fundamental factors. *Liquidity and solvency risks* have been interpreted to include factors relating to fiscal and external sustainability, including export growth, the ratio of international reserves to GDP, and the debt-servicing ratio. *External shocks* typically have included oil prices and a measure of global interest rates *(e.g.,* often a U.S. dollar-denominated rate to account for the large stock of dollar-denominated debt held by emerging market economies). In assessing the impact of *market conditions* on spreads, authors of previous empirical studies[16] typically relate the spread in the economy under consideration to a global measure of market conditions (*e.g.,* the interest-rate spread between a low-risk sovereign and an average rate of a group of emerging market economies). Under the category, *other fundamentals,* authors of earlier work usually focus explicitly on macroeconomic determinants of spreads, including inflation, the real exchange rate, the terms of trade, and real economic growth. Going beyond economic fundamentals, they also address issues of political and country risk.[17]

Recent work on the determinants of spreads in euro-area economies has followed the general approach used in the literature dealing with emerging market economies. In this connection, Dotz and Fischer (2010) explained euro-area spreads by movements in macroeconomic fundamentals *(e.g.,* a country's real exchange rate) and financial variables (corporate bond spreads and the relative performance of equity prices). The authors found evidence of a structural break in the performance of spreads beginning with the rescue of Bear Stearns in March 2008. Gerlach et al. (2010) found evidence that spreads were affected by both financial variables (*e.g.,* the size of a country's banking sector) and macroeconomic fundamentals (*e.g.,* the ratio of government debt to GDP, measures of fiscal imbalances). Georgoutsos and Migiakis (2010) explained euro-area spreads by the slope of the yield curve – which the authors interpreted as providing information on both expected economic growth and expected inflation – relative equity returns, inflation differentials, and the differential between the interbank interest rate and the ECB's main refinancing rate.

4.2 Data and methodology

In contrast to much of the earlier literature, which largely focuses on panels, this paper focuses on the determinants of spreads in a single country, Greece, using time series cointegration techniques. The data sample is monthly and runs from January 2000 to September 2010. We seek to identify the fundamental long-run determinants of spreads for the 10-year benchmark Greek bond relative to the German 10-year bond. We then use these determinants to assess whether there is any evidence of market overshooting or undershooting. Thus, we purposely omit financial market data in explaining movements in spreads.[18] The variables used are as follows.

First, we include a measure of the fiscal situation. Potential explanatory variables are the ratio of government debt-to-GDP and the deficit-to-GDP ratio. Since Greece's entry to the euro area in 2001, Greek fiscal data have been subjected to a number of revisions, sometimes several years after the initial (real-time) release of the data. These revisions have often involved upward revisions of the fiscal imbalances, generating negative surprises. In order to capture the news (or surprise) element that has figured strongly in the Greek experience, we also construct some real-time fiscal data. To the best of our knowledge, this is the first time such a variable has been constructed and its impact on spreads investigated. In particular, using the European Commission Spring and Autumn forecasts,[19] we create a series of forecast revisions. For example, the revision in the Spring 2001 forecasts is the 2001 deficit/GDP ratio in the Spring compared to the forecast for 2001 made in the Autumn of 2000. This procedure allows us to generate a series of revisions (see Fig. 7), which, when cumulated over time, provides a cumulative fiscal news variable (see Fig. 8). The variable underestimates the extent of fiscal news which actually emerged during the period. For example, when the newly elected government revised the fiscal data in Autumn 2004, upward revisions of the deficit occurred not only for 2004 (captured in our variable), but also for the years 2000–2003.

Another example is given by the revisions to the deficit in 2009. In the Autumn 2009 forecasts, the deficit for 2009 was revised upwards to 12.7 per cent of GDP from the 5.7 per cent forecast in the Spring. This revision, however, does not account for subsequent revisions to the 2009 deficit which occurred in 2010 and brought the figure to 15.4 per cent. To help account for these subsequent revisions, we also include a series of the latest estimate of the fiscal deficit (as a percentage) of GDP in our empirical work.

Second, we seek to capture the decline in competitiveness experienced by the Greek economy since entering monetary union. With the exchange rate fixed, the

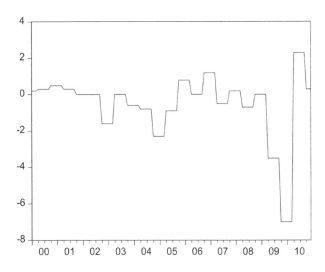

Figure 7 Greek general government balance: revisions to Commission Spring and Autumn forecasts (percentage points of GDP). Source: *European Economy*, various volumes.

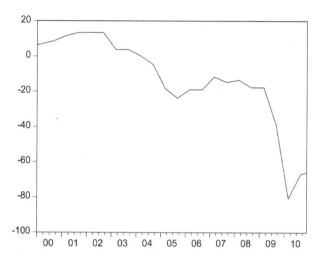

Figure 8 Cumulative fiscal news variable. Source: own calculations (see text)

Greek price level relative to that of Germany provides a measure of real apprecia-tion. We also examine the impact of the trade and current accounts (as percent-ages of GDP).

Third, economic activity has been found to be an important determinant of the ability of a country to meet its obligations. Given that GDP data are available only on a quarterly basis, we use the rate of change of a monthly coincident indicator of economic activity constructed by the Bank of Greece to provide a measure of growth (Hall and Zonzilos, 2003).

Finally, we assess the effects of several external factors, in particular, the price of oil. The Greek economy is the most oil-dependent economy in the euro area, and macroeconomic aggregates are sensitive to changes in the price of oil. Unlike much of the literature, we do not test for the significance of foreign interest rates given that almost 99 per cent of Greek government debt is denominated in its domestic currency, the euro.

We initially estimate a cointegrated VAR treating all variables, except for oil prices, as endogenous. This procedure generates a long-run relationship between spreads and the variables discussed above. Along the lines of Ferucci (2003), we use the long-run relationship to generate a series of spreads predicted by the mac-roeconomic fundamentals. A comparison of predicted with actual spreads allows us to comment on the degree to which the actual spread appears to overshoot and/or undershoot both in the pre-crisis and crisis periods.

The primary objective here is to identify the structural relationship which determines the long-run behaviour of the Greek spread. We therefore need to consider the issue of the formal identification of a cointegrated VAR (Johansen,

1988; Phillips, 1991). The identification problem for non-stationary models can be stated using the structural and reduced form vector equilibrium correction model VEqCM,[20] which are as follows.

$$A_0 \Delta \mathbf{z_t} = \sum_{j=1}^{p-1} A_j \Delta \mathbf{z_{t-j}} + \alpha^s \beta^{s'} \mathbf{z_{t-1}} + \delta + \varepsilon_t \tag{5}$$

$$\Delta \mathbf{z_t} = \sum_{j=1}^{p-1} \Gamma_j \Delta \mathbf{z_{t-j}} + A_0^{-1} \alpha \beta' \mathbf{z_{t-1}} + A_0^{-1} \delta + A_0^{-1} \varepsilon_t \tag{6}$$

Here $\mathbf{z}$ is a vector of N variables (as described above), A and Γ are matrices of suitably dimensioned parameters where $\Gamma_j = A_0^{-1} A_j, \delta$ is a vector of deterministic components, α^s, β^s are the structural loading weights and cointegrating vectors respectively and have the dimensions $N \times r$ to reflect the reduced rank nature of the system. The term ε_t is a vector of white noise error terms. Using (5) and (6) we can state the identification problem as simply one of being able to uniquely determine the parameters in the structural model (5) from the estimated reduced form model (6). In this sense the problem is formally identical to the Cowles-Commission identification problem. However, the identification problem for the model represented by equations (5) and (6) is different in a fundamental way to the Cowles-Commission (or standard) identification problem. This is because it now consists of two distinct parts. The first part is the problem of uniquely determining A_0 in (1). Since $\beta' z$ are a set of stationary variables (as they are the cointegrating combinations of the non-stationary variables), in this sense every term in equation (6) is stationary and this leads to the standard identification problem, which is that of uniquely determining A_0. This problem gives rise to the standard rank and order conditions. However, even if this first identification problem is dealt with, this still leaves a second part of the problem unresolved. This second problem arises because even if A_0 is known, we cannot uniquely determine the structural cointegrating vectors from the reduced form estimates.

The problem of identifying the structural cointegrating vectors is well known. Thus it is easily seen that α and β are not identified in general since $\alpha\beta' = \alpha^+ \beta^{+'} = \alpha \mathbf{P} \mathbf{P}^{-1} \beta'$ for any non-singular (r×r) matrix $\mathbf{P}$ (rotation). Hence in the reduced rank case the long-run part of the model is not identified. This is true even if A_0 is known, and it is this that leads to the second part of the identification problem. To resolve it, it is necessary to determine r, and identify β with a completely separate procedure. To determine the cointegrating rank, r, we can use standard tests. The next step is more difficult. To achieve full identification of the entire model, both the contemporaneous coefficients $\mathbf{A}_0$ *and* the long-run coefficients β need to be identified. These are logically separate issues, as there are no mathematical links between restrictions on $\mathbf{A}_0$ and those on β. It follows that restrictions are required to identify β *even if* $\mathbf{A}_0$ were known. Conversely, restrictions on β have no mathematical implication for the restrictions on $\mathbf{A}_0$.[21]

The derivation of formal identification criteria of the long-run in a VEqCM is the main subject of Johansen and Juselius (1990) and Pesaran and Shin (2002), where it is demonstrated that a necessary order condition for exact identification is that there are $k = r^2$ restrictions on the β vectors. Johansen (1995) and Pesaran and Shin (2002) also give a necessary and sufficient rank condition for exact identification, which, for example, rules out dependence amongst the r^2 restrictions. In general, if the number of available restrictions $k < r^2$ the β system is under-identified, if $k = r^2$ the β system is exactly identified, and when $k > r^2$ the β system is over-identified and, subject to the rank condition being satisfied, the over-identifying restrictions are testable.

The methodology employed in what follows is to begin by assessing the cointegrating rank of our VAR system and then to proceed to identify the structural relationship that determines the Greek spread. We will then present the impulse responses of the VEqCM for completeness, but our main focus will be on the long-run cointegrating vector which determines the spread, as this will allow us to identify the departures from the equilibrium spread.

5. Results

We begin by estimating a standard VAR of order 3 based on the Schwartz/Akaike information criterion, with the objective to minimise the VAR length subject to passing a selection of LM tests for serial correlation. The results of the chosen VAR are presented in Table 2. As usual, the VAR coefficients have very little economic interest as the individual coefficients are not interpretable. All that is important at this stage is that the VAR residuals are generally well behaved; in this case, the VAR residuals pass a range of LM tests for serial correlation and seem well behaved. Table 3 presents the results for the standard Trace and Maximum Eigenvalue tests for cointegration. Both tests reject the hypothesis of no cointegration, implying there is at least one cointegrating vector. The hypothesis that there is only one vector cannot be rejected at conventional levels of statistical significance. This implies that we have one cointegrating vector. In line with the existing literature, the results provide support for the significance of relative prices, economic activity and oil prices. In addition, our measure of fiscal news is also important in explaining movements in Greek spreads. Other variables – the final (latest) estimates of the fiscal-deficit-to-GDP ratio, the debt-to-GDP ratio, and measures of the trade or current accounts of the balance of payments – were found to be insignificant because their effects were captured by other (significant) variables. Thus, movements in relative prices best capture the effect of changes in external competitiveness on spreads, whereas real-time news about the fiscal aggregates, as measured by revisions to the Commission's forecasts, best captures the government's fiscal situation.

Table 2 VAR output.

	Fiscal news	Relative prices	Economic activity	Spread
Fiscal news (−1)	2.131542	0.000155	0.011867	3.396499
	(0.11306)	(0.00054)	(0.01137)	(2.19872)
	[18.8535]	[0.28634]	[1.04347]	[1.54476]
Fiscal news (−2)	−1.599330	−0.000765	−0.003501	−10.07221
	(0.21850)	(0.00105)	(0.02198)	(4.24929)
	[−7.31965]	[−0.72965]	[−0.15927]	[−2.37033]
Fiscal news (−3)	0.438646	0.000584	−0.009580	6.269450
	(0.11905)	(0.00057)	(0.01198)	(2.31534)
	[3.68441]	[1.02319]	[−0.79994]	[2.70779]
Relative prices (−1)	−1.181327	0.472012	1.223908	489.9511
	(19.4452)	(0.09329)	(1.95600)	(378.165)
	[−0.06075]	[5.05949]	[0.62572]	[1.29560]
Relative prices (−2)	24.34149	0.318379	−1.308089	127.3640
	(21.2828)	(0.10211)	(2.14085)	(413.902)
	[1.14371]	[3.11804]	[−0.61101]	[0.30772]
Relative prices (−3)	−18.58019	0.070298	3.276060	−285.0586
	(19.8023)	(0.09501)	(1.99192)	(385.109)
	[−0.93828]	[0.73993]	[1.64468]	[−0.74020]
Economic activity (−1)	1.429588	−0.000963	1.769862	0.771444
	(0.94130)	(0.00452)	(0.09469)	(18.3061)
	[1.51874]	[−0.21334]	[18.6920]	[0.04214]
Economic activity (−2)	−3.049898	0.005808	−0.749079	−6.573628
	(1.79107)	(0.00859)	(0.18016)	(34.8321)
	[−1.70284]	[0.67588]	[−4.15776]	[−0.18872]
Economic activity (−3)	1.858720	−0.004653	−0.056057	5.347972
	(0.94733)	(0.00454)	(0.09529)	(18.4233)
	[1.96207]	[−1.02370]	[−0.58826]	[0.29028]
Spread (−1)	−0.029655	9.15E−06	−0.000252	1.092140
	(0.00604)	(2.9E−05)	(0.00061)	(0.11739)
	[−4.91263]	[0.31585]	[−0.41495]	[9.30318]
Spread (−2)	0.052703	2.90E−05	−0.000824	0.281340
	(0.01049)	(5.0E−05)	(0.00105)	(0.20396)
	[5.02527]	[0.57714]	[−0.78146]	[1.37939]
Spread (−3)	−0.019748	−3.85E−05	0.000720	−0.345149
	(0.00644)	(3.1E−05)	(0.00065)	(0.12531)
	[−3.06473]	[−1.24422]	[1.11021]	[−2.75430]
Constant	0.855250	−0.022153	0.853438	78.40085
	(2.90124)	(0.01392)	(0.29184)	(56.4225)
	[0.29479]	[−1.59152]	[2.92437]	[1.38953]

(*Continued*)

Table 2 Continued

	Fiscal news	Relative prices	Economic activity	Spread
Oil price (−4)	0.018570	−1.78E−05	−0.001210	0.341134
	(0.00587)	(2.8E−05)	(0.00059)	(0.11406)
	[3.16625]	[−0.63414]	[−2.05128]	[2.99077]
TIME	−0.024947	0.000183	−0.005073	−0.768225
	(0.02139)	(0.00010)	(0.00215)	(0.41599)
	[−1.16626]	[1.78506]	[−2.35794]	[−1.84673]
R-squared	0.998845	0.994490	0.999206	0.990592
Adj. R-squared	0.998703	0.993813	0.999109	0.989437
Sum sq. Resids	76.53309	0.001762	0.774392	28945.80
S.E. equation	0.819355	0.003931	0.082419	15.93457
F-statistic	7039.891	1469.682	10251.13	857.3905
Log likelihood	−149.3683	539.4425	146.9060	−532.2053
Akaike AIC	2.548346	−8.130892	−2.045054	8.483803
Schwarz SC	2.880882	−7.798355	−1.712517	8.816340
Mean dependent	−11.29302	−0.007634	2.729329	90.66958
S.D. dependent	22.74915	0.049978	2.760866	155.0391

LM test for autocorrelation

Lags	LM-Stat	Prob
1	21.89358	0.1467
2	26.24410	0.0507
3	22.16579	0.1379
4	16.51045	0.4179

Table 3 Cointegration tests.

Hypothesised No. of CE(s)	Eigenvalue	Trace statistic	0.05 Critical Value	Prob.**
Unrestricted cointegration rank test (trace)				
None *	0.217116	55.81448	47.85613	0.0075
At most 1	0.127939	24.23897	29.79707	0.1905
At most 2	0.043489	6.579412	15.49471	0.6270
At most 3	0.006519	0.843711	3.841466	0.3583
Max-eigen statistic				
Unrestricted cointegration rank test (maximum eigenvalue)				
None*	0.217116	31.57551	27.58434	0.0145
At most 1	0.127939	17.65956	21.13162	0.1431
At most 2	0.043489	5.735701	14.26460	0.6473
At most 3	0.006519	0.843711	3.841466	0.3583

Trace test indicates 1 cointegrating eqn(s) at the 0.05 level. Max-eigenvalue test indicates 1 cointegrating eqn(s) at the 0.05 level. *Denotes rejection of the hypothesis at the 0.05 level. **MacKinnon-Haug-Michelis (1999) p-values.

We then construct a cointegrated VAR, imposing the restriction of one coin-tegrating vector and given that $\mathbf{r} = 1$ we need only one restriction to identify the relationship as a structural one determining the spread (this is to normalise the coefficient on the spread to be -1). The loading weight (the α^s) from the equation for the Greek spread is correctly signed and the cointegrated VAR is stable. In Fig. 9, we present the impulse responses of the Greek spread using the standard Cholesky decomposition for the shocks[22] to the other endogenous variables. With the exception of the response of the spread to cumulative fiscal news, the other impulse responses are as expected. Initially, the spread reacts incorrectly to an innovation to fiscal news – that is, good news initially causes the spread to rise, but after some months it falls to negative values, as expected.

In order to assess deviations of spreads from their long-run equilibrium values, we proceed to estimate a simple OLS model of the cointegrating vector. Moving to a simple OLS estimation is consistent with the existence of only one coin-tegrating vector in the model. The results are presented in Table 4. As is clear from that Table, explanatory variables enter the long-run equilibrium regression with the correct sign. The results suggest that an increase in economic activity or

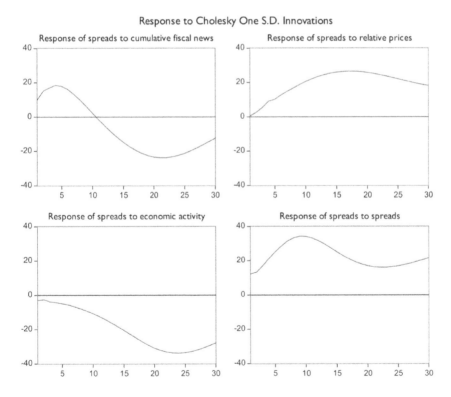

Response to Cholesky One S.D. Innovations

Figure 9 Impulse response functions.

Table 4 The long-run equilibrium relationship.

Dependent variable: Greek spreads

Variable	Coefficient	Std. Error	t-Statistic	Prob.
C	1227.195	209.2463	5.864832	0.0000
Economic activity	−49.58121	5.818096	−8.521897	0.0000
Relative prices	4496.757	1112.390	4.042429	0.0001
Fiscal news (cumulated)	−2.361796	0.858002	−2.752669	0.0068
TIME	−8.212937	1.586209	−5.177715	0.0000
Oil prices (−4)	0.666298	0.509717	1.307194	0.1936
R-squared	0.716565			
Adjusted R-squared	0.705044			
S.E. of regression	84.20158			
Prob (F-statistic)	0.000000	Second-stage SSR		872058.5

cumulative good fiscal news reduce the spread; by contrast, a rise in Greek prices relative to German or a rise in oil prices cause the spread to increase.

The relative economic importance of the variables can be derived by calculating the impact on spreads of a one standard deviation increase in each of the explanatory variables (based on the rationale that a one standard deviation change is actually observed in the data itself). The largest effect comes from relative prices: a one standard deviation increase in Greek prices relative to German prices causes spreads to rise by 225 basis points. This result highlights the importance of the deterioration in competitiveness for the terms on which the government can borrow. By contrast, economic activity has an important beneficial effect. A one standard deviation increase in economic activity causes spreads to fall by 138 basis points. The impact of cumulative fiscal news is smaller, but nonetheless significant – a one standard deviation increase in our cumulative fiscal news variable (defined as good news) causes spreads to fall by 54 basis points. It should be recalled, however, that although our fiscal variable aims to capture the effect of fiscal surprises, by construction, it likely understates the magnitude of those surprises. Finally, the effect of oil prices is, not surprisingly, relatively small, with a one standard deviation increase in the price of oil causing spreads to rise by only 17 basis points.

Fig. 10 graphs the actual spread along with that predicted by the long-run equilibrium equation in Table 4, allowing us to identify periods of undershooting and overshooting of actual spreads. We define undershooting and overshooting as cases where the difference between actual and predicted spreads lie outside the standard error bands around the residuals plotted in Fig. 10.

The first period in which the actual spread deviates significantly from the predicted spread runs from the end of 2004 until the beginning of 2005. This period

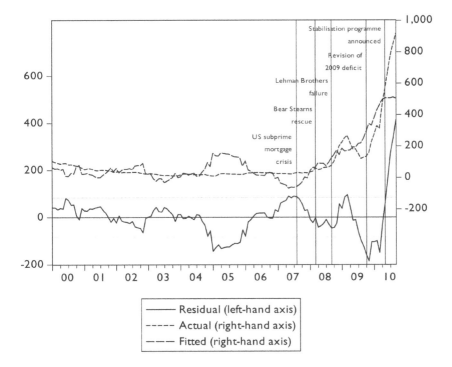

Figure 10 Actual spreads compared to long-run equilibrium spreads (basis points).

corresponds to the time (in late 2004) that a newly elected Greek government revised the fiscal deficits, leading to real larger deficits for the period 2000–2004. It appears, however, that spreads did not respond to these revisions – spreads were significantly lower than predicted. During that period, spreads were in a range of 10–25 basis points; on average, they were some 120 basis points below what is predicted by our model.

The second period during which actual spreads significantly deviated from those predicted by the model occurs at the end of our data sample. From mid-2009, predicted spreads rose sharply, mainly in response to the succession of fiscal surprises; from late 2009 through the first quarter of 2010, predicted spreads exceeded actual spreads by significant amounts (usually by over 100 basis points). Subsequently, actual spreads rose sharply and, beginning in May 2010, actual spreads exceeded predicted spreads; the difference became significant in June and remained significant through the end of our sample period (in September 2010). For example, whereas predicted spreads were just over 500 basis points in September 2010, the actual spread, at around 900 basis points, was about 400 basis points higher. Thus, our results suggest that there have been episodes of both significant undershooting and significant overshooting during the period since Greece joined the euro area.

6. Conclusions

Entry into the euro area provided Greece with the opportunity to benefit from the credibility of the monetary policy of the European Central Bank and the resulting environment of relatively low inflation rates and low nominal interest rates. In turn, the low interest rates reduced the cost of servicing the public-sector debt, facilitating fiscal adjustment and freeing resources for other uses. Instead of taking advantage of this environment to adjust the economy, during the period 2001–2009 successive Greek governments ran fiscal deficits that averaged over 6 per cent of GDP and they increased the share of government spending in the economy.

In this paper, we first presented evidence on that part of the risk premium unexplained by the credit rating of the Greek sovereign. After rising in late 2008, it returned to normal levels following a downgrade in early 2009. However, thereafter, despite further downgrades, the unexplained risk premium continued to rise.

To understand these results further, we moved on to model spreads as a function of economic fundamentals. The results suggest that, to some extent, the markets may have helped lull the Greek governments into believing that the low interest rate environment would be a permanent feature of the Greek economy. Our findings strongly support the view that the low levels of interest-rate spreads reached in the mid-2000s were not justified by the economic fundamentals. In turn, after the crisis erupted in 2009, interest-rate spreads appear to have strongly overshot in an upward direction.

Why were interest rates so low (relative to the fundamentals) in the mid-2000s and then so high after the crisis erupted? One explanation is that Greek interest rates, operating within the framework of a new regime created by the euro, were subject to a "peso problem".[23] When Greece became a member of the euro area, investors formed persistently biased expectations. Joining the euro area appeared to solve Greece's economic problems so that economic agents ignored data that were pointing towards the unsustainability of the macroeconomic imbalances. Similarly, after the crisis erupted, economic agents were not convinced that, after May 2010 – the time during which an adjustment programme was agreed between the Greek government and the IMF, the European Commission and the ECB – a regime change, involving sustainable, disciplined fiscal policy and structural reforms, had really taken place. Consequently, despite a substantial improvement in Greece's economic fundamentals during the course of 2010, interest-rate spreads remained above what was predicted by the fundamentals. This widening of spreads resulted in a self-fulfilling crisis, so that the successive increases in spreads made it increasingly difficult to bring the economy back to a sustainable growth path, undermining the goals of the adjustment programme. Although the markets' verdict of Greece's fiscal and external imbalances may have come late in the day, when it came, it came with a vengeance.

Acknowledgements

We are grateful to a referee for very constructive comments on an earlier draft of this paper. We would also like to thank the following colleagues at the Bank of Greece for assistance with data collection: Elena Argiri, Eleni Gazopoulou, Dora Kosma, Katerina Kotsoni and Angeliki Momtsia. The views expressed do not necessarily reflect those of the Bank of Greece.

Appendix. Data sources

Spread: 10-year benchmark German government bond minus 10-year benchmark Greek government bond – ECB Statistical Data Warehouse – monthly average.

Fiscal data: from Commission forecasts published in *European Economy* and Government Fiscal Statistics published by Eurostat. The forecasts are semi-annual; the actual data, quarterly. All series are interpolated.

Trade and current-account data: taken both from Bank of Greece and EL.STAT. Quarterly series were interpolated.

Relative prices: log difference of the monthly seasonally adjusted harmonised index of consumer prices (HICP) between Greece and Germany – Thomson-Reuters DataStream.

Economic activity: rate of change of coincident indicator of economic activity constructed by Bank of Greece (Hall and Zonzilos, 2003).

Oil prices: US dollars per barrel of Brent crude oil (FOB) – Thomson-Reuters Datastream.

Notes

1 At its inception on January 1,1999, the euro area consisted of eleven countries. Five countries have joined the euro area after Greece's entry, bringing the total number of members in 2011 to seventeen. For a detailed assessment of the euro area, see De Grauwe (2007).

2 Garganas and Tavlas (2001) provide data on inflation and inflation variability in Greece during the period 1975–2000.

3 During the 1980s and 1990s, the Greek economy experienced a series of exchange rate crises. See Garganas and Tavlas (2001).

4 These advantages of a common currency exist so long as the central bank of the monetary union delivers price stability and is credible. In the case of the euro, the European Central Bank quickly established its anti-inflation credentials and became credible.

5 In 1994, the then-Greek government set a goal to enter the euro area on January 1, 2001. The convergence of Greek economic indicators to those of other European Union countries contributed after 1994 to the narrowing of spreads prior to euro-area entry. For an analysis of the Greek economy before euro-area entry, see Garganas and Tavlas (2001).

6 The European Union's Stability and Growth Pact aims to keep members' fiscal deficits below 3 per cent of GDP and their debt-to-GDP ratios below 60 per cent of GDP. Entry into the euro area is, in part, contingent on the satisfaction of these fiscal criteria. In the case of the debt-to-GDP criterion, countries can be allowed to join if the debt ratio is

seen to be approaching the 60 per cent critical value at a satisfactory pace. The latter circumstance applied to Greece. In the year 2000, Greece was allowed entry into the euro area with a debt-to-GDP ratio near 100 per cent of GDP (because the ratio was on a declining path) and a fiscal deficit initially reported at 3.0 per cent of GDP; the latter figure was subsequently revised to 3.7 per cent of GDP after Greece became a member of Europe's monetary union.

7 An issue that arises is the extent to which Greece's systematically high inflation may have been due to a Harrod–Balassa–Samuelson (HBS) effect, under which the high inflation rate was part of an equilibrating mechanism. In this connection, an empirical study by Gibson and Malley (2008) found that while the HBS effect in Greece was substantial in the 1990s, after Greece entered the euro area the HBS effect contributed at best only about one-fifth of the country's inflation differential.

8 Given that inflation in Greece during 2001–2009 was higher than the average inflation rate in the rest of the euro area, the ECB's single nominal interest rate meant that real interest rates in Greece were relatively low. Wickens (2010) argues that this situation warranted tighter fiscal policy.

9 As mentioned in Section 3, however, real-time fiscal data understated the severity of the fiscal situation. The real-time data typically indicated that the fiscal imbalances were declining. Subsequent revisions of the data showed that the imbalances were, in fact, increasing.

10 On its website, the Bank of Greece publishes monthly cash data on the central-government (as opposed to the general government) fiscal accounts. These data are available with a two-week lag relative to the month for which they apply. The data pointed to a sharp, worsening trend in the central-government fiscal deficit during the course of 2009. In this connection, in early September 2009 (ahead of the general election in October) Bank of Greece Governor, George Provopoulos, alerted the leaders of the two main political parties of the deteriorating fiscal situation and the need of strong corrective actions. See Ziras (2009).

11 Part of the subsequent increase was due to a reclassification of some public enterprises. The enterprises in question, which had previously been excluded from the general government accounts, were brought into those accounts.

12 The loan also commits the government to undertake wide-ranging structural reforms aimed at making the economy more competitive. The 8.1 per cent deficit target for 2010 does not include the reclassification of public enterprises, mentioned above, which leads to an increase in the 2010 and 2011 fiscal deficits.

13 We do not use all downgrades since some downgrades are simply repeats of what other rating agencies have effectively done.

14 The ECB (2011) first differenced the interest-rate data, but kept the dummies in levels. Effectively, this procedure leads to the result that a permanent change in ratings leads to a permanently growing spread.

15 See the Appendix for detailed data sources.

16 See Ferucci (2003), Baek et al. (2005) and Grandes (2007).

17 See Baldacci et al. (2008) who attempt to include ideas of willingness to pay (Eaton and Gersovitz, 1981).

18 Measures of risk or risk appetite based on financial market data may help in tracking actual spreads, since financial market conditions across countries tend to be highly correlated, but they do not explain the fundamental determinants of spreads at the national level.

19 The European Commission publishes forecasts only twice a year.

20 See Davidson and Hall (1991), Canova (1995) and Pesaran and Smith (1998).

21 It remains possible though that the economic interpretation of a restricted set of cointegrating vectors $\beta'\mathbf{z}_t$ may have implications for the nature of restrictions on $\mathbf{A}_0$ that will be economically interesting, particularly when $\mathbf{A}^*$ is restricted via a. Mathematical,

and possibly economic, linkages then do exist between restrictions on the adjustment coefficients α and those required to identify β – see Hendry and Doornik (1997).

22 Note that since oil prices are assumed to be exogenous, they do not appear in the impulse response functions.

23 An early account of the peso problem was provided by Friedman and Schwartz (1963, pp. 186–188), who contrasted the declining prices in the United States during the period 1882–1892 with the persistently rising prices during the period 1903–1913, despite similarities of the other underlying fundamentals during the two periods. Friedman and Schwartz attributed the difference in price behaviour to differences in market expectations about exchange rates between the two periods.

References

Alexopoulou, I., Bunda, I., Ferrando, A., 2009. Determinants of government bond spreads in new EU countries. ECB Working Paper, no. 1093.

Attinasi, M., Chercherita, C., Nickel, C., 2009. What explains the surge in euro area sovereign spreads during the financial crisis of 2007–2009?. ECB Working Paper, no. 1131.

Baek, I., Bandopadhyaya, A., Du, C., 2005. Determinants of market-assessed sovereign risk: economic fundamentals or market risk appetite? Journal of International Money and Finance 24, 533–548.

Baldacci, E., Gupta, S., Mati, A., 2008. Is it (still) mostly fiscal? Determinants of sovereign spreads in emerging markets. IMF Working Paper, no. 259.

Canova, F., 1995. The economics of VAR models. In: Hoover, Kevin D (Ed.), Macroeconometrics: Developments, Tensions, and Prospects. Kluwer, Dordrecht.

Codogno, L., Missale, A., Favero, C., 2003. Yield spreads on EMU government bonds. Economic Policy 18 (37).

Davidson, J., Hall, S.G., 1991. Cointegration in recursive systems. Economic Journal 101 (405) March.

De Grauwe, P., 2007. Economics of Monetary Union, seventh ed. Oxford University Press.

Dotz, N., Fischer, C., 2010. What can EMU countries' sovereign bond spreads tell us about market perceptions of default probabilities during the recent financial crisis? Deutsche Bundesbank, Discussion Paper Series 1, Economic Studies, no. 11.

Eaton, J., Gersovitz, M., 1981. Debt with potential repudiation: theoretical and empirical analysis. Review of Economic Studies 48, 289–309.

European Central Bank, 2011. Financial Integration in Europe, Frankfurt (April).

Favero, C.A., Giavazzi, F., Spaventa, L., 1997. High yields: the spread on German interest rates. Economic Journal 107, 956–985.

Ferucci, G., 2003. Empirical determinants of emerging market economies' sovereign bond spreads. Bank of England Working Paper, no. 205.

Fontana, A., Scheider, M., 2010. An analysis of euro area sovereign CDS and their relation with government bonds. ECB Working Paper, no. 1271.

Friedman, M., Schwartz, A., 1963. A Monetary History of the United States, 1867–1960. Princeton University Press.

Garganas, N.C., Tavlas, G.S., 2001. Monetary regimes and inflation performance: the case of Greece. In: Bryant, R.C., Garganas, N. C., Tavlas, G.S. (Eds.), Greece's Economic Performance and Prospects. Bank of Greece – The Brookings Institution.

Georgoutsos, D.A., Migiakis, P.M., 2010. European sovereign bond spreads: monetary unification, market conditions and financial integration. Bank of Greece Working Paper, no. 115.

Gerlach, S., Schulz, A., Wolff, G.B., 2010. Banking and sovereign risk in the euro area. Deutsche Bundesbank, Discussion Paper Series 1, Economic Studies, no. 9.

Geyer, A., Kossmeier, S., Pichler, S., 2004. Measuring systematic risk in EMU government yield spreads. Review of Finance 8, 171–197.

Gibson, H.D., Malley, J., 2008. The contribution of sectoral productivity differentials to inflation in Greece. Open Economies Review 19, 629–650.

Grandes, M., 2007. The determinants of sovereign bond spreads: theory and facts from Latin America. Cuadernos de Economia 44, 151–181.

Hall, S.G., Zonzilos, N.G., 2003. An indicator measuring underlying economic activity in Greece. Bank of Greece Working Papers, no. 4, August.

Hendry, D.F., Doornik, J.A., 1997. The implications for econometric modeling of forecast failure. Scottish Journal of Political Economy 44, 437–461.

Johansen, S., 1988. Statistical analysis of cointegration vectors. Journal of Economic Dynamics and Control 12, 231–254.

Johansen, S., 1995. Identifying restrictions of linear equations with applications to simultaneous equations and cointegration. Journal of Econometrics 69, 111–132.

Johansen, S., Juselius, K., 1990. Maximal likelihood estimation and inference on cointegration – with applications to the demand for money. Oxford Bulletin of Economics and Statistics 52 (2), 169–210.

Min, H.G., 1998. Determinants of emerging market bond spread: do economic fundamentals matter?, Policy Research Working Paper, World Bank, no. 1899.

Pesaran, M.H., Shin, Y., 2002. Long run structural modelling. Econometric Reviews 21, 49–87.

Pesaran, M.H., Smith, R.P., 1998. Structural analysis of cointegrating VARs. Journal of Economic Surveys 12, 471–506.

Phillips, P.C.B., 1991. Optimal inference in cointegrated systems. Econometrica 59, 283–306.

Wickens, M., 2010. Fiscal flexibility is best for eurozone. Letter to the Financial Times Tuesday, 28 December.

Ziras, V., 2009. Interview with Governor George Provopoulos. Kathimerini (Greek edition), November 1.

20

EXPECTATIONS AND EXCHANGE
RATE DYNAMICS

Rudiger Dornbusch

Source: *Journal of Political Economy* 84, 6, 1976, 1161–1176.

The paper develops a theory of exchange rate movements under perfect capital mobility, a slow adjustment of goods markets relative to asset markets, and consistent expectations. The perfect foresight path is derived and it is shown that along that path a monetary expansion causes the exchange rate to depreciate. An initial overshooting of exchange rates is shown to derive from the differential adjustment speed of markets. The magnitude and persistence of the overshooting is developed in terms of the structural parameters of the model. To the extent that output responds to a monetary expansion in the short run, this acts as a dampening effect on exchange depreciation and may, in fact, lead to an increase in interest rates.

I. Introduction

The paper develops a simple macroeconomic framework for the study of exchange rate movements. The purpose is to develop a theory that is suggestive of the observed large fluctuations in exchange rates while at the same time establishing that such exchange rate movements are consistent with rational expectations formation. In developing a formal model we draw on the role of asset markets, capital mobility, and expectations that have been emphasized in recent literature.[1] We draw, too, on the fact of differential adjustment speeds in goods and asset markets. In fact, the dynamic aspects of exchange rate determination in this model arise from the assumption that exchange rates and asset markets adjust fast relative to goods markets.

The adjustment process to a monetary expansion in this framework serves to identify several features that are suggestive of recent currency experience. In the short run, a monetary expansion is shown to induce an immediate depreciation in the exchange rate and accounts therefore for fluctuations in the exchange rate and the terms of trade. Second, during the adjustment process, rising prices may be accompanied by an appreciating exchange rate so that the trend behavior of exchange rates stands potentially in strong contrast with the cyclical behavior of exchange rates and prices. The third aspect of the adjustment process is a direct effect of the exchange rate on domestic inflation. In this context the exchange rate is identified as a critical channel for the transmission of monetary policy to aggregate demand for domestic output.

The effect of monetary policy on interest rates and exchange rates is significantly affected by the behavior of real output. If real output is fixed, a monetary expansion will, in the short run, lower interest rates and cause the exchange rate to overshoot its long-run depreciation. If output, on the contrary, responds to aggregrate demand, the exchange rate and interest rate changes will be dampened. While the exchange rate will still depreciate, it may no longer overshoot, and interest rates may actually rise.

In Part II we develop a formal model in terms of explicit functional forms. That development allows us to derive an analytical solution for the time path of variables and, in Part III, for the expectations that generate the perfect foresight path. In Part IV, the model is used to investigate the effects of a monetary disturbance. While the major part of the analysis is developed for the case of fixed output, an extension to variable output is introduced in Part V.

II. The Model

We will assume a country that is small in the world capital market so that it faces a given interest rate. Capital mobility will ensure the equalization of expected net yields so that the domestic interest rate, less the expected rate of depreciation, will equal the world rate. In the goods market we will assume that the world price of imports is given. Domestic output is an imperfect substitute for imports, and aggregate demand for domestic goods, therefore, will determine their absolute and relative price.

A. Capital Mobility and Expectations

Assets denominated in terms of domestic and foreign currency are assumed to be perfect substitutes given a proper premium to offset anticipated exchange rate changes. Accordingly, if the domestic currency is expected to depreciate, interest rates on assets denominated in terms of domestic currency will exceed those abroad by the expected rate of depreciation. That relationship is expressed in (1) where r is the domestic interest rate, r^* is the given world rate of interest, and x is the expected rate of depreciation of the domestic currency, or the expected rate of increase of the domestic currency price of foreign exchange:

$$r = r^* + x. \tag{1}$$

Equation (1) is a representation of perfect capital mobility, and it is assumed that incipient capital flows will ensure that (1) holds at all times.

Consider next expectations formation. Here we distinguish between the long-run exchange rate, to which the economy will ultimately converge, and the current exchange rate. Denoting the logarithms of the current and long-run rate by e and $\bar{e}$, respectively, we assume that

$$x = \theta\left(\bar{e} - e\right). \tag{2}$$

Equation (2) states that the expected rate of depreciation of the spot rate is proportional to the discrepancy between the long-run rate and the current spot rate. The coefficient of adjustment θ is for the present taken as a parameter. The long-run exchange rate is assumed known, and an expression for it will be developed below. We note further that, while expectations formation according to (2) may appear ad hoc, it will actually be consistent with perfect foresight, as shown in Part III.

B. The Money Market

The domestic interest rate is determined by the condition of equilibrium in the domestic money market. The demand for real money balances is assumed to depend on the domestic interest rate and real income and will, in equilibrium, equal the real money supply. Assuming a conventional demand for money, the log of which is linear in the log of real income and in interest rates, we have[2]

$$-\lambda r + \phi y = m - p, \tag{3}$$

where m, p, and y denote the logs of the nominal quantity of money, the price level, and real income. For the remainder of this part we will take the nominal quantity of money and the level of real income as given.

Combining (1), (2), and (3) will give us a relationship between the spot exchange rate, the price level, and the long-run exchange rate, *given* that the money market clears and net asset yields are equalized:

$$p - m = -\phi y + \lambda r^{*} + \lambda\theta\left(\bar{e} - e\right). \tag{4}$$

Equation (4) can be simplified by noting that with a stationary money supply long-run equilibrium will imply equality between interest rates, because current and expected exchange rates are equal. This implies that the long-run equilibrium price level, $\bar{p}$, will equal

$$\bar{p} = m + \left(\lambda r^{*} - \phi y\right). \tag{5}$$

Substituting (5) in (4) gives us a relationship between the exchange rate and the price level:[3]

$$e = \bar{e} - (1/\lambda\theta)(p - \bar{p}). \tag{6}$$

Equation (6) is one of the key equations of the model. For given long-run values of exchange rates and prices, it serves to determine the current spot price of foreign exchange as a function of the current level of prices. Given the level of prices, we have a domestic interest rate and an interest differential. Given the long-run exchange rate, there is a unique level of the spot rate such that the expected appreciation, or depreciation, matches the interest differential. An increase in the price level, because it raises interest rates, gives rise to an incipient capital inflow that will appreciate the spot rate to the point where the anticipated depreciation exactly offsets the increase in domestic interest rates.

C. The Goods Market

The demand for domestic output depends on the relative price of domestic goods, $e - p$, interest rates, and real income. The demand function is assumed to have the form

$$\ln D = u + \delta(e - p) + \gamma y - \sigma r, \tag{7}$$

where D denotes the demand for domestic output and where u is a shift parameter.[4] From (7) we note that a decrease in the relative price of domestic goods raises demand, as does an increase in income or a reduction in interest rates. The rate of increase in the price of domestic goods, $\dot{p}$, is described in (8) as proportional to an excess demand measure:

$$\dot{p} = \pi \ln(D/Y) = \pi \left[u + \delta(e - p) + (\gamma - 1)y - \sigma r \right]. \tag{8}$$

We note that the long-run equilibrium exchange rate implied by (8) is[5]

$$\bar{e} = \bar{p} + (1/\delta) \left[\sigma r^* + (1 - \gamma)y - u \right], \tag{9}$$

where $\bar{p}$ is defined in (5). From (9) it is apparent that the long-run exchange rate depends with the conventional homogeneity properties on monetary variables, but obviously on real variables, too.

The price equation in (8) can be simplified by using the definition of the long-run rate in (9) and the fact that interest differences equal expected depreciation, $r - r^* = \theta(\bar{e} - e)$, to become[6]

$$\dot{p} = -\pi \left[(\delta + \sigma\theta)/\theta\lambda + \delta \right](p - \bar{p}) = -v(p - \bar{p}), \tag{10}$$

where

$$v \equiv \pi\left[(\delta + \sigma\theta)/\theta\lambda + \delta\right].$$ (11)

The price adjustment equation in (10) can be solved to yield

$$p(t) = \bar{p} + (p_0 - \bar{p})\exp(-vt),$$ (12)

which shows that the price of domestic output will converge to its long-run level at a rate determined by (11). Substitution of (12) in (6) gives the time path of the exchange rate

$$e(t) = \bar{e} - (1/\lambda\theta)(p_0 - \bar{p})\exp(-vt)$$
$$= \bar{e} + (e_0 - \bar{e})\exp(-vt).$$ (13)

From (13) the exchange rate will likewise converge to its long-run level. The rate will appreciate if prices are initially below their long-run level and, conversely, if prices initially exceed their long-run level.

D. Equilibrium Exchange Rates

The adjustment process of the economy can be described with the help of figure 1. At every point in time the money market clears and expected yields are arbitraged. This implies a relationship between prices and the spot exchange rate shown in (6) and reflected in the QQ schedule in figure 1. The positively sloped schedule $\dot{p}=0$ shows combinations of price levels and exchange rates for which the goods market and money market are in equilibrium.[7] Points above and to the left of that schedule correspond to an excess supply of goods and falling prices. Conversely, points to the right and below the schedule correspond to an excess demand. The $\dot{p}=0$ schedule is positively sloped and flatter than a 45° line for the following reason.[8] An increase in the exchange rate creates an excess demand for domestic goods by lowering their relative price. To restore equilibrium, domestic prices will have to increase, though proportionately less, since an increase in domestic prices affects aggregate demand, both via the relative price effect and via higher interest rates.

For any given price level the exchange rate adjusts instantaneously to clear the asset market. Accordingly, we are continuously on the QQ schedule with money-market equilibrium and international arbitrage of net expected yields. Goods-market equilibrium, to the contrary, is only achieved in the long run. Conditions in the goods market, however, are critical in moving the economy to the long-run equilibrium by inducing rising or falling prices. Specifically, an initial position such as point B, with a price level below the long-run level and, correspondingly,

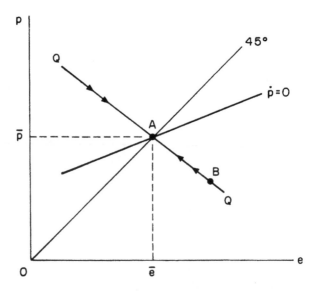

Figure 1

an exchange rate in excess of the long-run equilibrium, implies an excess demand for goods because domestic output commands a low relative price and because the interest rate is low. Accordingly, prices will be rising, thereby inducing over time a reduction in excess demand. The path of rising prices is accompanied by an appreciation of the exchange rate. As interest rates rise, as a consequence of declining real balances, the spot rate will approach the long-run rate. Once the long-run equilibrium at point A is attained, interest rates are equal internationally, the goods market clear, prices are constant, and expected exchange rate changes are zero.

III. Consistent Expectations

So far we have placed no restrictions on the formation of expectations other than the assumption that the expected rate of depreciation, as shown in (2) is proportional to the discrepancy between the long-run and the current exchange rate. From (12) and (13) we note that the rate at which prices and the exchange rate converge to equilibrium is given by v. From (11) it is apparent that the rate of convergence is a function of the expectations coefficient, θ.

Clearly, for the expectations formation process in (2) to correctly predict the actual path of exchange rates it must be true that $\theta = v$. Accordingly, the expectations coefficient, θ, that corresponds to perfect foresight, or, equivalently, that is consistent with the model is given by the solution to the equation

$$\theta = v \equiv \pi\left[(\delta + \sigma\theta)/\theta\lambda + \delta\right]. \tag{14}$$

The consistent expectations coefficient, $\tilde{\theta}$, obtained as the solution to (14), is a function of the structural parameters of the economy[9]

$$\tilde{\theta}(\lambda,\delta,\sigma,\pi) = \pi(\sigma/\lambda+\delta)/2 + \left[\pi^2(\sigma/\lambda+\delta)^2/4+\pi\delta/\lambda\right]^{1/2}. \qquad (15)$$

Equation (15) gives the rate at which the economy will converge to long-run equilibrium along the perfect foresight path. If expectations are formed according to (2) and (15), exchange rate predictions will actually be borne out.[10] The characteristics of the perfect foresight path are that the economy will converge faster the lower the interest response of money demand and the higher the interest response of goods demand and the price elasticity of demand for domestic output. The reason is simply that with a low interest response a given change in real balances will give rise to a large change in interest rates which, in combination with a high interest response of goods demand, will give rise to a large excess demand and therefore inflationary impact. Similarly, a large price elasticity serves to translate an exchange rate change into a large excess demand and, therefore, serves to speed up the adjustment process.

IV. The Effects of a Monetary Expansion

In this part we will study the adjustment process to a monetary expansion. The analysis serves to derive substantive results but also to highlight the manner in which expectations about the future path of the economy affect the current level of the exchange rate. This link is embodied in consistent expectations and makes the impact effect of a monetary disturbance depend on the entire structure of the economy.

In figure 2 we show the economy in initial full equilibrium at point A, with a long-run price level $\bar{p}$ and a corresponding long-run exchange rate $\bar{e}$ where the level of prices is determined, according to (5), by the nominal quantity of money, real income, and the interest rate. The long-run exchange rate by (9) will depend on the level of domestic prices and characteristics of the demand for domestic goods. The asset-market equilibrium schedule QQ that combines monetary equilibrium and arbitrage of net expected yields is drawn for the initial nominal quantity of money.

An increase in the nominal quantity of money that is expected to persist will cause a goods and asset market disequilibrium at the initial exchange rate and price. To maintain asset-market equilibrium, the increased quantity of money would have to be matched by higher prices and/or a depreciation in the exchange rate. The asset-market equilibrium schedule will shift out to $Q'Q'$, a shift that is (proportionately) equal to the increase in the nominal quantity of money.

It is immediately obvious that the new long-run equilibrium is at point C, where both goods and asset markets clear and exchange rate and price changes exactly reflect the increase in money.[11] This long-run homogeneity result is not surprising, since there is no source of money illusion or long-run price rigidity in the system.

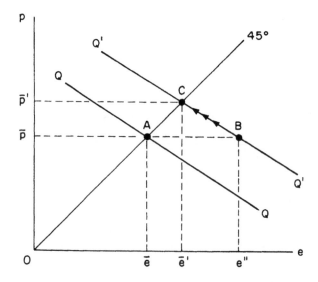

Figure 2

Consider next the adjustment process. At the initial level of prices, the monetary expansion reduces interest rates and leads to the anticipation of a depreciation in the long run and, therefore, at the current exchange rate, to the expectation of a depreciating exchange rate. Both factors serve to reduce the attractiveness of domestic assets, lead to an incipient capital outflow, and thus cause the spot rate to depreciate. The extent of that depreciation has to be sufficient to give rise to the anticipation of appreciation at just sufficient a rate to offset the reduced domestic interest rate. The impact effect of a monetary expansion is, therefore, to induce an immediate depreciation in the spot rate and one that exceeds the long-run depreciation, since only under these circumstances will the public anticipate an appreciating exchange rate and thus be compensated for the reduced interest on domestic assets. This is shown in figure 2 by the move from point A to the short-run equilibrium at point B.

From (4), noting that $d\bar{e} = dm = d\bar{p}$, we obtain a formal expression for the impact effect of a monetary expansion on the spot exchange rate:

$$de / dm = 1 + 1 / \lambda\theta. \tag{16}$$

Equation (16) confirms that in the short run the exchange rate will overshoot. The extent of the overshooting will depend on the interest response of money demand and the expectations coefficient.

A high interest response of money demand will serve to dampen the overshooting because it implies that a given expansion in the (real) quantity of money will only induce a small reduction in the interest rate. A small reduction in the interest rate in turn requires only a small expectation of appreciation to offset it and therefore, given the coefficient of expectations and the long-run rate, only a small depreciation of the spot rate (in excess of the long-run rate) to generate that expectation. A similar interpretation applies to the coefficient of expectations in (16).

It is quite obvious from the preceding explanation that the short-term effects of a monetary expansion, in this model, are entirely dominated by asset markets and, more specifically, by capital mobility and expectations. This feature places in sharp relief the assumption that asset markets and exchange rates adjust fast relative to the goods market and the price of domestic output. It is under these circumstances that a change in the nominal quantity of money is, in fact, a change in the real quantity of money, and the spot rate adjustment serves to achieve equilibrium in the asset markets by creating the expectation of appreciation of just sufficient an extent to balance the reduced interest rate on domestic assets.

The interpretation of (16) has not so far used the restriction that expectations be rational. That restriction is introduced by substituting (15) in (16) to obtain

$$de/dm = 1 + 1/\lambda\tilde{\theta} = 1 + \cfrac{1}{\pi(\sigma+\delta\lambda)/2 + \left[\pi^2(\sigma+\delta\lambda)^2/4 + \pi\delta\lambda\right]^{\frac{1}{2}}} \cdot \tag{17}$$

Equation (17) has two implications that cannot be derived from (16). The first is that with an interest response of money demand that approaches zero the initial depreciation remains finite and, in fact, approaches $de/dm = 1 + 1/\pi\sigma$. This result reflects the fact that, for the large interest rate changes that would result in these circumstances, the subsequent path of prices and the exchange rate is governed by the effect of interest rates on aggregate demand.

A second implication of (17) is the fact that the short-run overshooting of the exchange rate is inversely related to the speed of adjustment of the system, $\tilde{\theta}$. That fact is particularly obvious for the case where the speed of adjustment of prices, π, becomes infinite and where, accordingly, the economy jumps instantaneously to the new long-run equilibrium at point C.[12] More generally, those factors that serve to speed up the adjustment process, in particular high interest rate responsiveness of money demand, or aggregate spending, or high price elasticities, will therefore serve to dampen the impact effect of a monetary expansion on the exchange rate. This effect relies entirely on expectations about the subsequent path of the economy, rather than on *current* interaction between goods and asset markets.

Consider next the adjustment process from the short-run market equilibrium at point B to long-run equilibrium at point C. We note from figure 2 that at point B there is an excess demand for goods. That excess demand arises both from the decline in domestic interest rates and from the depreciation in the exchange rate that lowers the *relative* price of domestic goods. Each factor by itself is sufficient to account for this excess demand and, in fact, they constitute independent channels through which monetary changes affect demand for domestic output.

The exchange rate channel has been identified by Fleming and Mundell as an important avenue for monetary policy to act on aggregate demand.[13] In the present context the depreciation of the spot rate that is induced by the conditions of asset-market equilibrium serves to reduce the relative price of domestic goods and thereby to raise aggregate demand and give rise to inflationary pressure as opposed to an increase in output. The importance of this channel is larger, the higher the price elasticity of demand relative to the interest response of aggregate spending.

The lower interest rates and a lower relative price of domestic goods, that are characteristics of the impact effect, will cause domestic prices to rise and therefore be reflected in falling real money balances, rising interest rates, and an appreciating exchange rate. The adjustment process of rising prices over time restores the economy to the initial real equilibrium. An important feature of that adjustment process is the fact that rising prices are accompanied by an appreciating exchange rate. In terms of figure 2, this is described by the move along $Q'Q'$ from B to C. This result is due to the fact that rising prices cause the real money supply to be falling and interest rates to be rising. The rising interest rate, in turn, gives rise to an incipient capital inflow that appreciates the exchange rate at the same rate as interest rates are rising and thus maintains expected net yields in line. The model therefore confirms the link between interest rates and exchange rates that is emphasized in popular interpretations of foreign exchange events. The observation is correct, in the present circumstances, because rising interest rates are accompanied by the expectation of an appreciating exchange rate.

In summarizing this part we note that the ultimate effect of a monetary expansion is an equiproportionate increase in prices and the exchange rate. In the short run, however, the monetary expansion does exert real effects on interest rates, the terms of trade, and aggregate demand. The details of the adjustment process will depend on the economic structure. In particular, terms of trade changes will be both larger and more persistent the lower the speed of adjustment, $\tilde{\theta}$.

A key role in this analysis is played by the sluggish adjustment of prices as compared with asset markets. There is no very persuasive theoretical support for the slow adjustment of goods markets, but the facts clearly point in this direction. While the differential adjustment speed lacks theoretical backing, it implies, nevertheless, a behavior of exchange rates that is suggestive of recent experience.[14]

V. Short-Run Adjustment in Output

So far we have assumed that output is fixed at the full-employment level, $\bar{y}$. In the present part, the analysis is extended to allow for short-run adjustments in output in response to changes in aggregate demand.

Therefore, we replace equation (8) by an equilibrium condition in the domestic goods market,

$$y = \ln D \equiv u + \delta(e-p) + \gamma y - \sigma r, \tag{18}$$

where y is the log of the actual level of output that in the short run is demand determined. In addition to (18), we require a price adjustment equation which is shown in (19):

$$\dot{p} = \pi(y - \bar{y}). \tag{19}$$

According to (19) the rate of inflation is proportional to the discrepancy between actual and full employment, or "potential" output, $\bar{y}$. This price adjustment equation is a combination of a relationship between wage and price inflation, a relation between wage inflation and unemployment as in a Phillips curve, and a relation between unemployment and the departure from potential output, $y - \bar{y}$, as described by Okun's law.

It is shown in the Appendix below that the extension that incorporates (18) and (19) in place of (8) leaves most of the analysis of adjustments to a monetary increase unchanged. In particular, the price adjustment will continue to be exponential although the speed of adjustment will depend now also on the income elasticities of demand for domestic goods and real balances, γ and ϕ.

In the present framework it continues to be true that in the short run an increase in the nominal quantity of money is an increase in the real quantity of money. Accordingly, a monetary expansion has the conventional effect of increasing in the short run the level of output and inducing inflation. Since the inflation that is induced by the expansion in real output serves to raise over time the price level, real balances will decline back to their initial level until in the long run the expansion in money is fully matched by increased prices and output has returned to the full-employment level.

The impact effect of a monetary expansion on exchange rates and interest rates may, however, differ significantly from the analysis in Part IV. The new possibility that arises from the expansion in output in the short run is that the exchange rate depreciation will fall short of the monetary expansion rather than exceed it as in (16). That possibility arises because, in the short run, the income expansion raises money demand and may do so sufficiently to actually increase interest rates. If the output expansion were sufficiently strong to raise interest rates, equalization of net yields internationally would require the expectation of a depreciation and therefore a spot rate that falls short of the long-run equilibrium rate. Since the long-run equilibrium rate increases in the same proportion as the nominal quantity of money, it follows that the spot rate would increase less than the quantity of money. The condition that gives rise to this case is

$$1 - \phi\delta / (1 - \gamma) < 0. \tag{20}$$

The term $\delta/(1-\gamma)$ is the elasticity of equilibrium output with respect to the exchange rate. That term multiplied by the income elasticity of demand gives the increase in money demand due to a depreciation in the spot rate. Accordingly, (20) tells us whether at constant interest rates, and allowing the exchange rate to depreciate in the same proportion as the increase in money, we have an excess demand or supply of money and, accordingly, an increase or decrease in interest rates. The possibility of an excess demand and therefore an increase in interest rates is associated with a high income elasticity of money demand, high price elasticity, and a high income elasticity of demand for domestic goods.

The time path of exchange rates and the interest rate therefore depends on income and price elasticities, and the short-run overshooting of exchange rates is no longer a necessary feature of the adjustment process. In fact, if in the short run the interest rate rises and the exchange rate therefore depreciates less than proportionately to the increase in money, the adjustment process will be one of rising prices and a depreciating exchange rate. In this event, therefore, terms of trade fluctuations will be dampened as compared with the case described earlier where the exchange rate overshooting introduces large terms of trade variations in the adjustment process.

The analysis of a monetary expansion in this part confirms once more the Mundell-Fleming result that under conditions of capital mobility and flexible rates a small country can conduct, in the short run, an effective monetary policy. More important, the exchange rate proves a critical channel for the transmission of monetary changes to an increase in aggregate demand and output. That channel may, in fact, prove to be the only channel since, as was shown above, the interest rate may actually rise in the transition. Unlike in the Mundell-Fleming world, extension of the analysis to the long run shows that the effects of a monetary expansion are only transitory, since the inflation that is induced by the output expansion serves to reduce real balances and thereby return interest rates, relative prices, and real income to their initial level.

The possibility of short-run output adjustment has been shown to dampen exchange rate movements and possibly reverse the interest rate effects of a monetary expansion. It is appropriate, therefore, to ask which of the assumption, fixed or variable output, is a more relevant characteristic of the adjustment process. The answer no doubt is that the fixed output adjustment is a suitable characterization of the very short run. In the very short run we would not expect output to adjust instantaneously to meet an increase in aggregate demand and, accordingly, the adjustment will be primarily confined to the asset markets and will be characterized by a decline in interest rates and overshooting of exchange rates. In the intermediate run, on the contrary, the present analysis gains relevance, since here we would expect an adjustment of both output and prices in response to increased aggregate demand. On balance, therefore, the fixed output case retains relevance, and particularly so if output adjusts sluggishly to changes in aggregate demand.

Appendix

This Appendix extends the model to include short-run supply responses. For that purpose we replace the price adjustment equation in (8) by a goods-market equilibrium condition (A1) and a price equation (A2):

$$y = \mu\left[u + \delta(e - p) - \sigma r\right]; \quad \mu \equiv 1/(1-\gamma) > 0, \tag{A1}$$

$$\dot{p} = \pi(y - \bar{y}), \tag{A2}$$

where $\bar{y}$ denotes the full-employment level of output and where the price adjustment equation can be thought of as arising from a Phillips-curve relation between wage inflation and unemployment combined with an Okun's-law relation between the deviation from potential output, $y - \bar{y}$, and unemployment.[15]

The specification of the money market and exchange rate expectations remains unchanged, and equation (4) that represents these relations is repeated here for convenience:

$$p - m + \phi y = \lambda r^* + \theta\lambda(\bar{e} - e). \tag{A3}$$

Noting that in long-run equilibrium we have $y = \bar{y}$ and $r = r^*$, we obtain from (A1) the long-run goods-market relationship

$$\bar{y} = \mu\left[u + \delta(\bar{e} - \bar{p}) - \sigma r^*\right], \tag{A4}$$

and subtracting (A4) from (A1) we obtain the goods-market equilibrium condition expressed in terms of deviations from long-run equilibrium,

$$y - \bar{y} = \mu(\delta + \sigma\theta)(e - \bar{e}) + \mu\delta(\bar{p} - p), \tag{A5}$$

where we have used the fact that $r^* - r = \theta(e - \bar{e})$.

Next we proceed in a similar manner for the money market and rewrite the equilibrium condition as

$$\phi(y - \bar{y}) + (p - \bar{p}) = \lambda\theta(\bar{e} - e). \tag{A6}$$

Equations (A5) and (A6) can be simultaneously solved to yield the spot exchange rate and the level of output as a function of the existing price level. These solutions are, respectively,

$$y - \bar{y} = -w(p - \bar{p}), \tag{A7}$$

where

$$w \equiv \left[\mu(\delta + \theta\sigma) + \mu\delta\theta\lambda\right]/\Delta; \quad \Delta \equiv \phi\mu(\delta + \theta\sigma) + \theta\lambda,$$

and

$$e - \bar{e} = -\left[(1 - \phi\mu\delta)/\Delta\right](p - \bar{p}). \tag{A8}$$

Substitution of (A7) in (A2) yields the equilibrium rate of inflation as a function of the price level:

$$\dot{p} = -\pi w(p - \bar{p}). \tag{A9}$$

Following the procedure in Part III, rational expectations require that the expectations coefficient, θ, equal the rate at which exchange rates actually adjust, πw:

$$\theta = \pi w, \tag{A10}$$

which can be solved for the rational expectations coefficient of adjustment, $\tilde{\theta}$.

Consider next the impact effect of a monetary expansion. Remembering that in the long run an increase in money causes an equiproportionate increase in prices and the exchange rate, we have $d\bar{e} = d\bar{p} = dm$. Therefore, from (A8) we obtain the impact effect of a monetary expansion on the exchange rate as

$$de/dm = 1 + (1 - \phi\mu\delta)/\Delta > 0. \tag{A11}$$

Whether the exchange rate increases more or less proportionately than the nominal quantity of money depends on the condition

$$1 - \phi\mu\delta \gtrless 0, \tag{A12}$$

which determines, too, whether the interest rate declines or increases.

By (A7) the impact effect on real output is unambiguously positive and equal to $dy/dm = w$. The increase in the rate of inflation is given by $d\dot{p}/dm = \pi w$.

Since from (A9) the inflation rate converges monotonically to the long-run level, we know that output declines monotonically back toward the level of full employment. The exchange rate, following the impact effect, will appreciate, or depreciate, depending on (A12).

I am indebted to Stanley Black, Franco Modigliani, and Edward Tower who provided the stimulus for this paper. In revising various drafts I have had the benefit of many comments. I wish, in particular, to acknowledge the helpful suggestions I have received rom Wilfred Ethier, Stanley Fischer, Jacob Frenkel, and the thoughtful remarks of two anonymous referees. Financial support was provided by a grant from the Ford Foundation.

Notes

1 For recent work on flexible exchange rates that shares some of the present emphasis, see Black (1973, 1975), Henderson (1975), Niehans (1975), Dornbusch (1976a, 1976b), Frenkel (1976), Kouri (1976), and Mussa (1976). The classics remain Fleming (1962) and Mundell (1964, 1968).

2 Equation (3) is obtained by taking the logarithm of the money market equilibrium condition $M / P = Y^\phi \exp(-\lambda r)$.

3 In (3) we assumed that the appropriate deflator for money balance is the price of domestic output. An alternative is provided by a deflator that is a weighted average of domestic and import prices. In such a formulation the "price level," q, could be written as $q = \alpha p + (1 - \alpha) e$, where α and $(1 - \alpha)$ are the expenditure shares of domestic goods and imports. With such a formulation (6) would be amended to the following equation: $e = \bar{e} - \beta (p - \bar{p})$, where $\beta \equiv \alpha / [\lambda \theta + (1 - \alpha)]$. None of the qualitative results described below would be affected by this extension.

4 The complete relative price argument in (7) is $(e + p^* - p)$ where p^* is the logarithm of the foreign price level. Setting the foreign price level equal to unity implies that $p^* = 0$.

5 Equation (9) is obtained by setting $\dot{p} = 0$ and $r = r^*$ as is appropriate for the long run where markets clear and exchange rates are constant.

6 In (8) aggregate demand depends on the nominal interest rate. An alternative formulation allows aggregate demand to depend on the real interest rate, $r - \dot{p}$. Such a formulation requires that we substitute $\rho \equiv \pi / (1 - \sigma\pi) > 0$ in place of π in (11) and the equations below. The restriction that $\rho > 0$ is required for stability.

7 The $\dot{p} = 0$ schedule represents combined goods- and money-market equilibrium. Setting $\dot{p} = 0$ in (8) and substituting for the domestic interest rate from (3) yields the equation of the goods-market equilibrium schedule:

$$p = \left[\delta\lambda / (\delta\lambda + \sigma) \right] e + \left[\sigma / (\delta\lambda + \sigma) \right] m + \left[\lambda / (\delta\lambda + \sigma) \right] \left[u + (1 - \gamma) y - \phi\sigma y / \lambda \right].$$

8 The 45° line in fig. 1 is drawn through the origin on the assumption that, by appropriate choice of units, the prices of both goods are initially equal.

9 In (16) we have taken the positive and therefore stable root of the quadratic equation implied by (14).

10 Perhaps a remark about the perfect foresight path is in order here. Why should that path command our interest rather than being a mere *curiosum*? The reason is that it is the only expectational assumption that is not arbitrary (given the model) and that does not involve persistent prediction errors. The perfect foresight path is, obviously, the deterministic equivalent of rational expectations.

11 We have not drawn in fig. 2, the $\dot{p} = 0$ schedule. It is apparent, however, from the homogeneity properties of the model that the $\dot{p} = 0$ schedule will pass through point C.

12 The slope of the QQ schedule is $dp / de = -\tilde{\theta}\lambda$, and the schedule becomes vertical as $\tilde{\theta}$ approaches infinity.

13 In the Mundell-Fleming model with prices and interest rates fixed, the depreciation by worsening the terms of trade creates the necessary increase in aggregate demand to support the higher level of income required by monetary equilibrium (for a further discussion see Niehans [1975] and Dornbusch [1976]).

14 An extension of this paper would draw in an explicit manner on stochastic elements to provide a rationale for the short-run stickiness of prices. At the same time, such an extension would have interesting implications for the manner in which expectations are formed. Exchange rate determination in a stochastic setting has been studied by Black (1973), Kouri (1975), and Mussa (1976). Fischer (1976) has used a stochastic framework to evaluate fixed versus flexible exchange rate systems.

15 To deal with steady-state inflation we would have to add in (A2) the long-run rate of inflation which is given by the rate of monetary growth, which in the present treatment is assumed equal to zero.

References

Black, S. *International Money Markets and Flexible Exchange Rates.* Princeton Studies in International Finance, no. 32. Princeton, N.J.: Princeton Univ. Press, 1973.

_____. "Exchange Rate Policies for Less Developed Countries in a World of Floating Rates." Mimeographed. Vanderbilt Univ., 1975.

Dornbusch, R. "Exchange Rate Expectations and Monetary Policy." *J. Internat. Econ.* (1976), forthcoming, (*a*)

_____. "The Theory of Flexible Exchange Rate Regimes and Macroeconomic Policy." *Scandinavian J. Econ.* 2 (May 1976): 255-75. (*b*)

Fischer, S. "Stability and Exchange Rate Systems in a Monetarist Model of the Balance of Payments." In *The Political Economy of Monetary Reform,* edited by R. Aliber. London: Macmillan, 1976.

Fleming, M. "Domestic Financial Policies under Fixed and Floating Exchange Rates." *I.M.F. Staff Papers* 9 (November 1962): 369-79.

Frenkel, J. A. "A Monetary Approach to the Exchange Rate." *Scandinavian J. Econ.* 2 (May 1976): 200-221.

Henderson, D. "Monetary, Fiscal and Exchange Rate Policy in a Two-Country, Short-Run Macroeconomic Model." Mimeographed. Board of Governors, Federal Res., 1975.

Kouri, P. *Essays on the Theory of Flexible Exchange Rates.* Ph.D. dissertation, Massachusetts Inst. Tech., 1975.

_____. "The Exchange Rate and the Balance of Payments in the Short Run and in the Long Run." *Scandinavian J. Econ.* 2 (May 1976): 280-304.

Mundell, R. A. "Exchange Rate Margins and Economic Policy." In *Money in the International Order,* edited by C. Murphy. Dallas: Southern Methodist Univ. Press, 1964.

_____. *International Economics.* New York: Macmillan, 1968.

Mussa, M. "The Exchange Rate, the Balance of Payments and Monetary and Fiscal Policy under a Regime of Controlled Floating." *Scandinavian J. Econ.* 2 (May 1976): 229-48.

Niehans, J. "Some Doubts about the Efficacy of Monetary Policy under Flexible Exchange Rates." *J. Internat. Econ.* 5 (August 1975): 275-81.

21

FEAR OF FLOATING

Guillermo A. Calvo and Carmen M. Reinhart

Source: *Quarterly Journal of Economics* 117, 2, 2002, 379-408.

Many emerging market countries have suffered financial crises. One view blames soft pegs for these crises. Adherents of this view suggest that countries move to corner solutions—hard pegs or floating exchange rates. We analyze the behavior of exchange rates, reserves, and interest rates to assess whether there is evidence that country practice is moving toward corner solutions. We focus on whether countries that claim they are floating are indeed doing so. We find that countries that say they allow their exchange rate to float mostly do not—there seems to be an epidemic case of "fear of floating."

I. Introduction

After the Asian financial crisis and the subsequent crises in Russia, Brazil, and Turkey, many observers have suggested that intermediate exchange rate regimes are vanishing and that countries around the world are being driven toward corner solutions. The bipolar solutions are either hard pegs—such as currency boards, dollarization, or currency unions—or freely floating exchange rate regimes.[1] On the surface, at least, this statement accords with recent trends. Twelve countries in Europe chose to give up their national currencies, while Ecuador was the first of what may be several countries in Latin America to adopt the United States dollar as its official national tender. More recently, El Salvador has also moved in that direction. At the other end of the spectrum, South Korea, Thailand, Brazil, Russia, Chile, Colombia, Poland, and, more recently, Turkey have announced their intentions to allow their currencies to float. Hence, on the basis of labels, at least, it would appear that currency arrangements are increasingly bipolar.

In this paper we investigate whether countries are, indeed, moving as far to the corners as official labels suggest. Since verifying the existence of a hard peg is trivial, our focus is on the other end of the flexibility spectrum. Specifically, we examine whether countries that claim they are floating their currency are, indeed, doing so. We analyze the behavior of exchange rates, foreign exchange reserves, and interest rates across the spectrum of exchange rate arrangements to assess whether the official labels provide an adequate representation of actual country practice. The data span monthly observations for 39 countries during the January 1970–November 1999 period. One-hundred-and-fifty-five exchange rate arrangements are covered in this sample.

The paper proceeds as follows. In Section II we provide descriptive statistics for exchange rates, foreign exchange reserves, and money market interest rates. We then compare the behavior of these variables across different exchange rate arrangements. In Section III we present a simple model that replicates several of the key stylized facts in these data; this framework explains why a country might prefer a smooth exchange rate as a result of the combined roles of inflation targeting and low credibility. In Section IV we introduce an exchange rate flexibility index motivated by the model. This index is meant to provide a multivariate summary measure of the degree of exchange rate flexibility in each episode—hence, it enables us to compare each episode with the benchmark of some of the more committed floaters to see whether the actual country practices match official labels. The concluding section touches on some of the implications of our findings.

II. Fear of Floating: The Stylized Evidence

Our data are monthly and span January 1970–November 1999. Thirty-nine countries in Africa, Asia, Europe, and the Western Hemisphere constitute our sample. The countries are Argentina, Australia, Bolivia, Brazil, Bulgaria, Canada, Chile, Colombia, Cote D'Ivoire, Egypt, Estonia, France, Germany, Greece, India, Indonesia, Israel, Japan, Kenya, Korea, Lithuania, Malaysia, Mexico, New Zealand, Nigeria, Norway, Pakistan, Peru, Philippines, Singapore, South Africa, Spain, Sweden, Thailand, Turkey, Uganda, Uruguay, the United States, and Venezuela. One-hundred-and-fifty-five exchange rate arrangements are covered in this sample. Our analysis, however, does not give equal attention to all regimes. In the earlier part of the sample, there were pervasive capital controls that make these episodes less relevant for the purposes of comparison to the present environment of high capital mobility. Also, a few of the floating exchange rate episodes occur during hyperinflations, which also complicate comparisons. Our choice of countries was, in part, constrained by the need to be able to parallel official exchange arrangements as reported by the International Monetary Fund, and by data limitations, particularly as regards market-determined interest rates.[2] However, most regions have adequate coverage, and both developed and developing countries are well represented in the sample.[3]

In addition to bilateral exchange rates and foreign exchange reserves, we also focus on the time series properties of nominal and real ex post interest rates. The bilateral exchange rate is end-of-period. Whenever possible, the interest rate used is that most closely identified with monetary policy; if that is not available, a treasury bill rate is used. The Data Appendix provides the details on a country-by-country basis. Our desire for a long sample covering many countries precludes using higher frequency data. Relatively few countries report foreign exchange reserve data on a daily or weekly basis, and for many of those that do it is a relatively recent phenomenon. Interest rates are included in the analysis because many countries, particularly in recent years, routinely use interest rate policy to smooth exchange fluctuations—the use of interest rate policy to smooth exchange rate fluctuations in the context of an inflation target is an issue we take up in the next section. We focus on the behavior of monthly percent changes (unless otherwise noted) of each variable, one at a time, and compare these across regimes.[4]

II.1 Methodology Issues

It is widely accepted that a "pure float" is an artifact of economics textbooks. Yet, despite occasional instances of foreign exchange market intervention, sometimes even in a coordinated fashion, the United States dollar (US$) floated about as freely against the German deutsche mark (DM) (and now the euro), and the Japanese Yen (¥), as any currency has ever been allowed to float. Thus, if the only criterion was the extent of commitment to float their currencies, the G-3 are the best candidates to serve as a benchmark for comparing whether countries that claim they float are indeed doing so. However, the wealthy G-3 countries all share the common feature that (in varying degrees) their currencies are the world's reserve currencies, which somewhat reduces their value as benchmarks for smaller industrial nations and, especially, for emerging market economies. However, another comparator is also available: Australia, with a credible commitment to floating, shares some features of the other smaller industrial nations and developing countries that make up the lion's share of our sample. For example, the Australian dollar is not a world reserve currency, and Australia continues to rely heavily on primary commodity exports, like many of the developing countries in our sample. As a consequence of the latter, its terms of trade exhibit a higher volatility than those of the G-3, and it is more representative of the characteristics of many of the non-G-3 countries in our study. Giving weight to both criteria (commitment to floating and shared characteristics), we opted to use both Australia and the G-3 as benchmarks.

Our strategy is to compare what countries say and what they do. What they say is reported to the IMF, which classifies countries into four types of exchange rate arrangements: peg, limited flexibility, managed floating, and freely floating. Limited flexibility has been used, almost exclusively, to classify European countries (prior to the monetary union) with exchange rate arrangements vis-à-vis one another (i.e., the Snake, the Exchange Rate Mechanism, etc.).

What countries do can be described by the movement in their asset prices. Unless otherwise noted, the bilateral exchange rates are reported with respect to the DM for European countries and with respect to the United States dollar for everyone else. The choice of the DM owes to the fact that this was the most prominent reserve currency in Europe and, because Germany was the low inflation country for many years, the anchor for currencies in that region. For the remaining countries, the dollar is the usual anchor currency of choice. Indeed, the largest share of emerging market's external debt is denominated in US dollars, and world trade is predominantly invoiced in US dollars.

We denote the absolute value of the percent change in the exchange rate and foreign exchange reserves by ϵ, $\Delta F / F$, respectively. The absolute value of the change in the interest rate, $i_t - i_{t-1}$, is given by Δi. Letting x^c denote some critical threshold, we can estimate the probability that the variable x (where x can be ϵ, $\Delta F / F$, and Δi), falls within some prespecified bounds, conditional on a particular type of exchange rate arrangement. For example, if x^c is arbitrarily set at 2.5 percent, then the probability that the monthly exchange rate change falls within the 2.5 percent band should be greatest for the fixed exchange regimes and lowest for the freely floating arrangements, with the other two types of currency regimes positioned in the middle. In our notation, for $x = \epsilon$, we should observe

$$ P\left(x < x^c \middle| \text{Peg}\right) > P\left(x < x^c \middle| \text{Float}\right) \text{ for } x = \epsilon. $$

Because shocks to money demand and expectations when the exchange rate is fixed are accommodated through purchases and sales of foreign exchange reserves, the opposite pattern should prevail for changes in foreign exchange reserves. Hence, for $x = \Delta F / F$,

$$ P\left(x < x^c \middle| \text{Peg}\right) < P\left(x < x^2 \middle| \text{Float}\right). $$

Thus, the probability that changes in reserves fall within a relatively narrow band is a decreasing function of the degree of exchange rate rigidity, as money demand shocks and changes in expectations are accommodated to prevent a change in the exchange rate.

Theory provides less clear-cut predictions as to how the volatility of interest rates could covary with the extent of exchange rate flexibility. Interest rates could fluctuate considerably if the monetary authorities actively use interest rate policy as a means of stabilizing the exchange rate—an issue that we will explore more formally in a simple setting in the next section. But policy is only a partial source of interest rate volatility. Interest rates are bound to be volatile if expectations about future inflation or exchange rate changes are unanchored, as is the case when the authorities lack credibility. Hence, the likelihood of observing relatively large fluctuations in interest rates would depend on both the degree of credibility and on the policymakers' reaction function.

While we also consider other statistical exercises in Section IV, examining the probabilities that the variable of interest stays within a prespecified band has some definite advantages over alternative descriptive statistics. First, it avoids the problem of outliers that can distort variances. For example, it is not uncommon in this sample (particularly for countries with capital controls or in the earlier part of the sample) to have a crawling peg exchange rate for an extended period of time (hence, some degree of exchange rate flexibility), with some periodic large devaluations (upward of 100 percent is not unusual) and return to a crawl. Brazil in the 1970s is a good example of this type of policy.[5] Short-lived inflationary spikes create similar problems for interest rates. Second, the probabilistic nature of the statistic conveys information about the underlying frequency distribution that is not apparent from the variance.

II.2 Measuring Volatility: Exchange Rates and Reserves

Tables I and II present evidence on the frequency distribution of monthly percent changes in the exchange rate, foreign exchange reserves, and nominal money-market interest rates for recent or current exchange rate regimes that are classified as freely floating regimes and managed floaters; Appendix 1 presents the comparable statistics for limited flexibility arrangements and peg episodes. The first column lists the country, the second the dates of the particular exchange arrangement, and the remaining columns the relevant probability for changes in the exchange rate, international reserves, and interest rates, in that order. For exchange rates and foreign exchange reserves, our chosen threshold value is x^c = 2.5 percent, which is a comparatively narrow band. For instance, following the Exchange Rate Mechanism crisis, many European countries adopted a ± 15 percent band for the exchange rate. Chile, until recently, had comparable bands. Other examples include Mexico (prior to December 1994) which had in place an "ever-widening" band, as the lower end (appreciation) of the band was fixed and the upper ceiling (depreciation) was crawling; Israel and Colombia (during 1994–1998) also had fairly wide bands.[6]

For the United States, for example, as shown in column (3) of Table I, there is about a 59 percent probability that the monthly US\$/DM exchange rate change would fall within a relatively narrow plus/minus $2\frac{1}{2}$ percent band. For the US\$/¥ exchange rate, that probability is slightly higher, at 61 percent. By contrast, for Bolivia, Canada, and India (all declared floaters during that period), the probability of staying within the band is around 95 percent—significantly above the benchmark of Australia, where the comparable probability is about 70 percent.[5] Put in another way, there is only about a 5 percent probability in those three countries that the exchange rate will change more than $2\frac{1}{2}$ percent in any given month. On average, for this group of floaters, the probability that the exchange rate change is contained in this moderate plus/minus $2\frac{1}{2}$-percent band is over 79 percent—significantly above that for Australia, Japan, and the United States. The t-statistic for the difference in means test is 3.38 with a probability value of (0.00) under the null hypothesis of no difference. By this metric, post-crisis Mexico approximates a float more closely than any of the other cases—including Canada.[7]

Moderate-to-large monthly fluctuations in the exchange rate are even rarer among the so-called "managed float" episodes (Table II). For Egypt and Bolivia the probability of a monthly exchange rate change greater than 2.5 percent is

Table I Volatility of Selected Indicators in Recent or Current "Floating" Exchange Rate Regimes

| | | Probability that the monthly change is | | |
| | | Within a ±2.5 percent band: | | Greater than ±4 percent (400 basis points): |
Country (1)	Period (2)	Exchange rate (3)	Reserves (4)	Nominal interest rate (5)
Australia	January 1984–November 1999	70.3	50.0	0.0
Bolivia	September 1985–December 1997	93.9	19.6	14.8
Canada	June 1970–November 1999	93.6	36.6	2.8
India	March 1993–November 1999	93.4	50.0	23.8
Kenya	October 1993–December 1997	72.2	27.4	15.7
Japan	February 1973–November 1999	61.2	74.3	0.0
Mexico	December 1994–November 1999	63.5	28.3	37.7
New Zealand	March 1985–November 1999	72.2	31.4	1.8
Nigeria	October 1986–March 1993	74.5	12.8	1.4
Norway	December 1992–December 1994	95.8	51.9	4.1
Peru	August 1990–November 1999	71.4	48.1	31.4
Philippines	January 1988–November 1999	74.9	26.1	1.5
South Africa	January 1983–November 1999	66.2	17.4	0.5
Spain	January 1984–May 1989	93.8	40.1	4.1
Sweden	November 1992–November 1999	75.5	33.3	1.3
Uganda	January 1992–November 1999	77.9	32.9	3.6
United States$/DM	February 1973–November 1999	58.7	62.2	0.3

Source: International Financial Statistics, International Monetary-Fund.

nil—as was the case for Indonesia and Korea up to the 1997 crisis. Even for self-proclaimed flexible-rate advocates, such as Chile and Singapore, the frequency distribution of their monthly exchange rate fluctuations relative to the US dollar do not vaguely resemble that of Australia, let alone the US$/DM or US$/¥. Even a casual inspection reveals that a significantly higher proportion of observations

Table II Volatility of Selected Indicators in "Managed Floating" Exchange Rate Regimes

		Probability that the monthly change is		
		Within a ±2.5 percent band:		Greater than ±4 percent:
Country (1)	Period (2)	Exchange rate (3)	Reserves (4)	Nominal interest rate (5)
Bolivia	January 1998–November 1999	100.0	12.5	0.0
Brazil	July 1994–December 1998	94.3	51.8	25.9
Chile	October 1982–November 1999	83.8	48.2	51.2
Colombia	January 1979–November 1999	86.8	54.2	2.9
Egypt	February 1991–December 1998	98.9	69.4	0.0
Greece	January 1977–December 1997	85.3	28.9	0.7
India	February 1979–November 1993	84.5	36.7	11.2
Indonesia	November 1978–June 1997	99.1	41.5	5.2
Israel	December 1991–November 1999	90.9	43.8	1.1
Kenya	January 1998–November 1999	70.6	14.3	1.1
Korea	March 1980–October 1997	97.6	37.7	0.0
Malaysia	December 1992–September 1998	81.2	55.7	2.9
Mexico	January 1989–November 1994	95.7	31.9	13.9
Norway	January 1995–November 1999	90.2	42.3	0.0
Pakistan	January 1982–November 1999	92.8	12.1	14.1
Singapore	January 1988–November 1999	88.9	74.8	0
Turkey	January 1980–November 1999	36.8	23.3	61.4
Uruguay	January 1993–November 1999	92.0	36.5	60.1
Venezuela	April 1996–November 1999	93.9	29.4	n.a.

Source: International Financial Statistics, International Monetary Fund.

falls within the 2½ percent band. On average, there is an 88 percent probability that managed floaters' monthly changes in the exchange rate are confined to this narrow band. This exchange rate stability versus the US dollar (or DM if it is a European country) is surprising in light of the fact that for many emerging market countries during these episodes, inflation rates were well above U. S. or German levels, terms-of-trade shocks were frequent and large, and macroeconomic fundamentals were markedly more volatile than in any of the benchmark countries. Not surprisingly, the evidence presented in Appendix 1 shows that for limited flexibility arrangements and for pegs the probabilities that exchange rate changes are confined to this band are even greater, at 92 and 95 percent, respectively. Hence, the observed behavior accords with the priors that exchange rate variability is least for pegs and greatest for floaters. For the Float-Peg difference, the probability value from the means test is (0.00); for the Float-Managed, it is (0.04); for the Managed-Limited flexibility, the means test of the probability value is (0.32) while for the Limited flexibility-Peg it is (0.44).

Yet, we cannot glean from exchange rates alone what would have been the extent of exchange rate fluctuations in the absence of policy interventions; that is, we do not observe the counterfactual. To assess the extent of policy intervention to smooth out exchange rate fluctuations, we next examine the behavior of foreign exchange reserves. In principle, the variance of reserves should be zero in a pure float. In reality, however, it is not that simple, as reserves may change because of fluctuations in valuation and the accrual of interest earnings.[8] However, even absent these, there are other factors that influence changes in reserves. First, there are "hidden" foreign exchange reserves transactions. Credit lines may be used to defend the exchange rate during periods of speculative pressures. Indeed, several European countries made ample use of their lines of credit during the Exchange Rate Mechanism (ERM) crisis of 1992–1993. Central banks may engage in derivative transactions, much along the lines of Thailand in 1997, which borrowed dollars in the futures market, or issue debt denominated in a foreign currency, such as Brazil among others. These transactions hide the true level and variation in reserves. Second, even in the absence of any "hidden" reserve transactions, countries may rely more heavily on domestic open market operations and interest rate changes to limit exchange rate.

Column (4) of Tables I and II summarizes the frequency distribution of monthly foreign exchange reserve changes (in US dollars). With the exception of the United States and the few European countries in the sample, most countries represented in Tables I and II hold most of their foreign exchange reserve holdings in dollar-denominated assets—hence, for this group valuation changes are not much of an issue.[9] As Table I shows, there is about a 74 percent probability that Japan's monthly changes in foreign exchange reserves fall in a plus/minus 2.5 percent band, while for Australia the comparable probability is 50 percent. Yet, in the case of Mexico, there is only a 28 percent probability that changes in foreign exchange reserves are that small, while in the case of Bolivia that probability

168

is even lower; note that for postcrisis Thailand there is only a 6 percent probability that reserves changes are inside the band.[10] Indeed, for all other countries, large swings in foreign exchange reserves appear to be commonplace, consistent with a higher extent of intervention in the foreign exchange market—relative to what is to be expected a priori from a freely floating exchange rate regime. Nor is this exclusively an emerging market phenomenon—Canada's reserve changes are about seven times as volatile as those of the United States. For the group of "floaters" the average probability (shown in the right-hand panel of Figure I) is about 34 percent—about one-half the Japan-United States average and significantly below the Australian benchmark. The difference is statistically significant. Indeed, the observed behavior of international reserves runs counter to our priors—$P(\Delta F/F, < x^c|\text{Peg}) < P(\Delta F/F, <x^c|\text{Float})$. We find that reserve variability is highest for the "floaters" and least for the limited flexibility arrangements. This point is made starkly in the top panel of Figure I, which plots the probability that the monthly exchange rate change lies within a 2½ percent band (along the horizontal axis) and the probability that foreign exchange reserves change more that 2½ percent (along the vertical axis) for the four currency regimes and our three comparators. Two points are evident. First, the range of observed exchange rate variation is quite narrow, with all four regimes associated with a higher chance of changing in a narrow band than any of the three benchmarks. Second, the smoothness in the exchange rate seems to be the result of explicit policy choice: international reserves move more from month to month for those countries with the more stable exchange rates.

II.3 Interest Rate Volatility, Lack of Credibility, and Monetary Policy

As discussed earlier, policy intervention to dampen exchange rate fluctuations is not limited to purchases and sales of foreign exchange. Interest rates in the United States, Japan, Australia, and other developed economies are usually set with domestic considerations in mind. Yet, in many of the other countries in our sample, the authorities who set domestic interest rates accord a much higher weight to the stabilization of the exchange rate—particularly when there are credibility problems or a high passthrough from exchange rates to prices. This is also the case for countries which have inflation targets and have a high passthrough from exchange rates to prices, which is the case we model in Section III. For evidence that pass-through tends to be higher for emerging markets, see Calvo and Reinhart [2001]. This policy, coupled with credibility problems, may help explain the high relative volatility of interest rates in these countries. As shown in Table I, while the probability that interest rates change by 400 basis points (4 percent) or more on any given month is about zero for Australia, Japan, and the United States, that probability is close to 40 percent for Mexico and about 30 percent for Peru and India (among the floaters). Nominal and real interest rates in India are about four times as variable as in the United States; for Mexico, interest rates are about

Exchange rates and international reserves

Averaged across exchange rate regimes

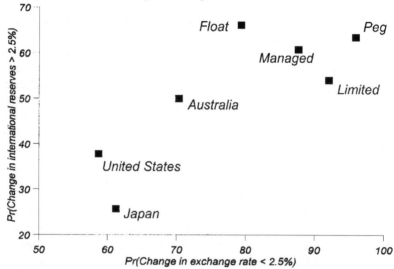

Exchange rates and interest rates

Averaged across exchange rate regimes

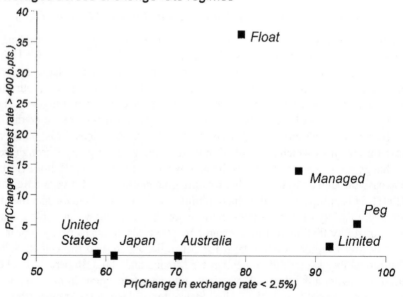

Figure I Source: Tables I and II and Appendix 1.

twenty times as variable—Peru holds the record.[11] A recent example of Chile and Mexico's use of high interest rates as a means to limit exchange rate pressures (despite a markedly slowing economy and an adverse terms-of-trade shock) comes from the aftermath of the Russian crisis in August 1998. At the time of this writing, Brazil's central bank hiked interest rates in the midst of a recession and an energy crisis to halt the slide of its currency, the real.

These examples, however, are not unique in emerging markets. Among the managed floaters (Table II), other emerging markets, including Brazil, Turkey, and Uruguay have an equally high or higher incidence of large fluctuations in interest rates. While in the case of Turkey and Uruguay, it is at least partially due to their comparatively high inflation rates, this is not the case for the others. The picture painted by the volatility of real ex post interest rates is quite similar.[12]

When comparing the four types of exchange rate regimes, interest rates are the most stable for the limited flexibility group—which is almost exclusively made up of European developed countries—and least stable for the managed floating group, which is comprised predominantly of developing countries.[13] Indeed, Calvo and Reinhart [2001] show that the variance of interest rates in low inflation in emerging markets is about four times that of developed economies, and that gap is far greater for countries with a history of inflation.

Moreover, such interest volatility is not the result of adhering to strict monetary targets in the face of large and frequent money demand shocks. In reality, most of these countries do not have explicit or implicit money supply rules. Interest rate volatility would appear to be the byproduct of a combination of trying to stabilize the exchange rate through domestic open market operations and lack of credibility. These findings are summarized in the lower panel of Figure I, which plots the relative probabilities of small changes in the exchange rate (again, along the horizontal axis) and large changes in the nominal interest rate (the vertical axis). As is evident, the countries that move their interest rates the most are those that, by self-identification, would seem to have to move them the least—those that follow a float or a managed float.

II.4 General Observations about the Findings

In this section we have presented evidence that the variability in international reserves and interest rates is high relative to the variations in the exchange rate. Taken together, these findings would suggest that in many cases the authorities are attempting to stabilize the exchange rate through both direct intervention in the foreign exchange market and open market operations. Furthermore, "fear of floating" does not appear to be limited to a particular region. Indeed, it would appear that in emerging markets floating has been largely confined to brief periods following currency crises or chaotic episodes of high inflation—an issue we examine in greater detail in Section IV. In the next section we develop a simple framework that replicates these stylized facts and provides a rationale for fear of floating.

III. Inflation Targeting, Lack of Credibility, and Fear of Floating

There are multiple reasons why countries may be reluctant to tolerate much variation in their exchange rates.[14] Liability dollarization, which is pervasive in emerging markets, may produce a fear of floating. In Lahiri and Végh's [2001] model, fear of floating arises because there is an output cost associated with exchange rate fluctuations; in the Caballero and Krishnamurthy [2001] setting, an inelastic supply of external funds at times of crises explains exchange rate overshooting and fear of floating. Calvo and Reinhart [2001] stress concerns about lack of credibility and loss of access to international capital markets.

In this paper we present a simple model where fear of floating arises from the combination of lack of credibility (as manifested in large and frequent risk-premiums shocks), a high passthrough from exchange rates to prices, and inflation targeting. It is worth pointing out that lack of credibility in this setting is not manifested in first moments. Lack of credibility is associated with the (higher) variance of the risk premiums shocks. This setting is motivated by the recent trend in emerging markets to couple floating with explicit inflation targets. Indeed, at present, this combination appears to have become the most popular alternative to fixing the exchange rate.[15]

Explanations of a central bank's choice of the expansion of nominal magnitudes have often been framed as some variant of Barro and Gordon's [1983] rules-versus-discretion model, whether allowing for uncertainty (as in Canzoneri [1985]), heterogeneity among potential central bankers (as in Rogoff [1985]), or even electoral choice among central bankers (as in Alesina and Grilli [1992]). Policy is cast as attempting to reconcile the long-run benefits of low inflation with the temptation to get extra output in the near term by generating an inflation surprise that works through a Phillips curve.

It could be argued that a formulation that describes discretionary monetary policy as attempting to exploit a Phillips curve is of little practical relevance for most emerging markets. A history of high and variable inflation in many emerging markets has eroded any meaningful trade-off between unemployment and inflation surprises. Furthermore, even in the absence of a notorious inflation history, the evidence suggests that monetary policy is often procyclical—as central banks raise interest rates in bad states of nature to restore investor confidence and stem capital outflows. Yet, this does not imply that the central bank is indifferent to inflation surprises. Indeed, in many emerging markets there has been a tendency to use inflation surprises to improve the government's fiscal position. Overreliance on the inflation tax (and other easy-to-implement taxes, such as tariffs) may be due to the fact that in many emerging markets tax collection is inefficient and evasion is rampant. That is, the benefits to the monetary authority are that surprise inflation generates additional revenue from money creation and erodes the real value of nominal government debt and public sector wages.

It could also be argued that the focus on a closed economy controlling the domestic inflation rate limits the seeming relevance of Barro-Gordon models for many developed and emerging market countries alike. In fact, central bankers in emerging market economies appear to be extremely mindful of external factors in general and the foreign exchange value of their currency, in particular. In what follows, the policy choice explicitly considers the problem of a small open economy setting its nominal interest rate.

Consider one period of an infinitely lived sequence.[16] Households make two sets of decisions at the start of the period based on incomplete information; that is, before shocks are realized. As workers, they bargain for nominal wages that will prevail over the period in anticipation that goods and service price inflation will equal π^e. As investors, they place part of their assets at banks in deposits that do not bear interest, implying an opportunity cost that is expected to be i^e, the market-based return on domestic government debt.

Foreign investors also hold domestic debt, with the home interest rate linked to the foreign interest rate i^*, by uncovered interest parity. Defining s to be the price of foreign currency in terms of domestic currency so that when s rises (falls), the home currency depreciates (appreciates). If ϵ is the expected rate of change in the exchange rate, then the uncovered interest parity condition holds up to a risk premium ρ:

$$i = i^* + \epsilon + \rho. \tag{1}$$

The risk premium is assumed to be a random shock, drawn from a distribution with mean $\mu_\rho = 0$ and variance $\sigma_{\rho^2}^2$. To keep notational clutter to a minimum, we will assume that the mean to the risk premium shock equals zero.

From the government's perspective, the public's willingness to hold money balances must be supported by noninterest-bearing domestic reserves, issued in the amount R. Because a central bank's balance sheet must balance, these domestic reserves can also be expressed in terms of their asset counterparts, foreign exchange reserves, and domestic credit. Since the central bank can issue R, this implies that it can issue less interest-bearing obligations. This interest saving is one measure of the seigniorage from money creation,

$$i(R/p), \tag{2}$$

where p is the domestic price level.[17] Our simplification of a fractional banking system is to assume a constant money multiplier k, so that

$$M = kR. \tag{3}$$

The demand for domestic real balances is written as a linear approximation,

$$\frac{M}{p} = c - \eta i^e + \zeta, \tag{4}$$

where ζ represents a random shock with mean zero and variance σ_ζ^2. As before, the assumption is that households place their balances at banks before the outcome of financial market clearing is known. Thus, the opportunity cost of holding money must be forecasted rather than known with certainty.

As a consequence of this specification of the financial sector, seigniorage can be written as

$$i\frac{c - \eta i^e + \zeta}{k}. \tag{5}$$

Notice the key wedge between anticipations and actions opened up in this product: seigniorage depends on both the expected interest rate (which determines the real stock of reserves) and the actual interest rate (which determines the earning rate of those reserves).

We also assume that foreign and domestic goods, prices at p^* and p, respectively, are perfect substitutes:

$$p = sp^*, \tag{6}$$

so that purchasing power parity prevails, which completes the description of economic behavior that the central bank takes as given. This, of course, implies a pass-through of unity from exchange rate to prices. This assumption can be relaxed without altering the qualitative results of the model. Here we assume that purchasing power of parity holds for "the" relevant country in the region; if there were more currencies, the analysis could also be extended to include less-than-unit pass-through.

Each period, the central bank is assumed to maximize its welfare, which is increasing in its seigniorage and decreasing in the deviation of the inflation rate from its target, with the target taken to be zero to save on notation. This welfare function can be written as

$$W = i\frac{R}{p} - \frac{b}{2}\pi^2, \tag{7}$$

where b is a coefficient representing the welfare loss (relative to one unit more of seigniorage) from inflation deviating from its target in either direction.

The two parity conditions combine to explain domestic inflation in terms of domestic nominal interest rates and variables from the external sector. As a result,

$$\pi = i - i^* - \rho + \pi^*. \tag{8}$$

Assuming that the foreign nominal interest rate and inflation rate equal zero, the objective function of the central bank can be written as

$$W = i \frac{c - \eta i^e + \zeta}{k} - \frac{b}{2}(i - \rho)^2. \tag{9}$$

First, we find the welfare-maximizing interest rate taking expectations as given. From the first-order condition we get,

$$i = \rho + \left(c - \eta i^e + \zeta\right)/bk. \tag{10}$$

As is evident, in setting the nominal interest rate, the central bank responds one for one to risk premium shocks but proportionally to money demand shocks. The key tension that produces time inconsistency is that the central bank's desired setting of the ex post nominal interest rate depends negatively on interest rate expectations, which are formed earlier in the period.

Second, on average, those expectations should be correct. This places the condition on the model that

$$i^e = c / \left(bk + \eta\right). \tag{11}$$

Even though both the real interest rate and the inflation target are zero, households will expect a positive nominal interest rate, implying that they expect some inflation. This is due to the presence of seigniorage in the objective function. The greater the weight on the inflation target, the smaller will be this inflation premium (as $b \to \infty$, then $i^e \to 0$).

It is important to note that there are two elements to this premium due to the importance of seigniorage itself in the objective function and the temptation to generate surprise inflation to get extra seigniorage because money demand depends on the expected interest rate. If money demand were to depend on the actual interest rate, that second element would be eliminated, although the first alone would still produce inflation in the long run. It can be shown in that circumstance that the expected nominal interest rate would equal

$$c / \left(2\eta + bk\right), \tag{12}$$

which is smaller than that in the baseline model. The difference between the two represents, in Rogoff's [1985] term, the premium paid to investors because the central bank succumbs to the temptation to cheat systematically. The irony, of course, in all these models is that systematic cheating yields no return.

The representation for interest rate expectations in the baseline model can be substituted into the interest rate equation. This yields an expression for the optimal setting of the nominal interest rate in the presence of shocks to asset holding—namely the risk premium and money demand,

$$i = \rho + \frac{\zeta}{bk} + \frac{c}{bk + \eta}. \tag{13}$$

Given our assumption that the shocks are uncorrelated, the variance of the domestic nominal interest rate is given by

$$\sigma_i^2 = \sigma_\rho^2 + \sigma_\zeta^2 / b^2 k^2 . \tag{14}$$

Note that the variance of the nominal interest rate declines as the commitment to the inflation target rises (b is larger) but increases when credibility is low; that is, when the variance of risk premium shocks are large. Emerging markets are routinely buffeted by large swings in risk premiums. This is evident, for example, in the volatility of emerging market sovereign credit ratings (see Reinhart [2001]). But still, even under an extreme commitment to an inflation target, nominal interest rates will vary as the central bank finds it optimal to offset risk premium shocks.

The other variables of interest follow directly. The expected change in the exchange rate will be, $i-\rho$, or

$$\epsilon = \frac{\zeta}{bk} + \frac{c}{bk+\eta} . \tag{15}$$

That is, in setting its nominal interest rate, the central bank will completely offset the effects on the exchange rate of foreign risk premium shocks and partially offset money demand shocks. The greater the importance of the inflation target, the greater will be the offset of money demand shocks.

As a result, the variance of the change in the exchange rate can be written as

$$\sigma_\varepsilon^2 = \sigma_\zeta^2 / b^2 k^2 . \tag{16}$$

Because risk premium shocks are offset completely, the variance of the exchange rate is independent of the variance of the risk premium. Moreover, the greater the commitment to an inflation target, the smaller will be the variance of the change in the exchange rate. Hence, in this setting inflation targeting can explain fear of floating.

The real domestic monetary base will equal

$$\frac{R}{p} = \frac{cb}{bk+\eta} + \frac{\zeta}{k} . \tag{17}$$

The level of real balances increases directly with the weight on inflation, in that a stronger commitment to low inflation generates a greater willingness to hold real balances. Real reserves also vary one for one with the money demand shock but are invariant to the risk premium shock. The reason, of course, that real reserves are invariant to the risk premium shock is that the decision by domestic investors to hold money balances depends on the expected, not actual, domestic interest rate.

Given this, the variance of the real monetary base will equal

$$\sigma_{R/p}^2 = \sigma_\zeta^2 / k^2. \tag{18}$$

As Calvo and Guidotti [1993] point out, the cost of discretionary policy is due to its effect on expectations, which induce households to change their behavior regarding real magnitudes. The cost of a policy that alters expectations has to be weighed against the possibility of reducing the variance of real magnitudes by offsetting shocks realized after expectations are formed. In our framework, smoothing the exchange rate reduces the variation in real outcomes. Offsetting risk premium shocks and thereby damping fluctuations in the exchange rate limits unnecessary variations in domestic inflation. For an inflation targeter, this may be an end that appears particularly attractive.

It is useful to define a variance ratio that captures the variation in the exchange rate relative to policy instruments—the domestic nominal interest rate and reserves—a form of exchange rate flexibility index. In particular,

$$\lambda = \sigma_\varepsilon^2 / \left(\sigma_i^2 + \sigma_{R/p}^2 \right). \tag{19}$$

In this model, this term reduces to

$$\lambda = \frac{\sigma_\zeta^2}{\left(1+b^2\right)\sigma_\zeta^2 + b^2 k^2 \sigma_\rho^2} < 1. \tag{20}$$

Note that this variance ratio goes to one as the weight on the inflation target declines. Conversely, as the weight on the inflation target increases, the variance ratio tends to zero. In the next section we examine the empirical relevance of this issue by contrasting the readings of the variance ratio given by equation (19) with the actual inflation performance for the various exchange rate arrangement episodes in our sample.

IV. An Exchange Rate Flexibility Index: Basic Tests and Comparisons

We begin this section by conducting some basic tests to assess the extent of foreign exchange market intervention (as measured by variability in foreign exchange reserves) in the 155 episodes that make up our study. We then proceed to construct an exchange rate flexibility index, along the lines suggested by the model in Section III. In both of these exercises, we compare those cases classified as floaters and managed floaters to the benchmark of the committed floaters (here taken to be Australia, Japan, and the United States).

IV.1. F-tests

As noted in Section II, with regard to exchange rates, interest rates, and other nominal variables in the local currency, outliers can significantly distort the variances of some of these variables. In the case of international reserves, which are reported in dollars and are less affected by periodic mega-devaluations or inflationary spikes, the outlier problem is somewhat less severe. Hence, in what follows, our emphasis will be on the variability of international reserves—although in the next subsection we construct a flotation index that is multivariate, as it includes the variances of the exchange rate and an interest rate.

As to the F-tests, the null hypothesis being tested is the equality of variances between the committed floaters and the particular country/episode in question; the alternative hypothesis is that, if there is fear of floating, the variance of reserves for the episode in question will exceed that of the more committed floaters serving as a benchmark. Hence, it is a one-tailed test. The results of the F-tests are summarized in Table III.[18] If the Australian benchmark is used, in those episodes classified as floaters, the null hypothesis of the equality of variances in favor of the alternative hypothesis (consistent with the fear of floating phenomenon) is rejected in 73 percent of the cases. If, instead, Japan is used as a benchmark, the null hypothesis can be rejected for 97 percent of the cases. For the managed floaters, there is a similarly high incidence of rejection of the null hypothesis. In effect, in the majority of cases, the variance of foreign exchange reserves is several orders of magnitude greater than for Australia, Japan, or the United States. It is also noteworthy that the results of these tests reveal that rejection of the null hypothesis is not appreciably different for the floaters than for those with fixed exchange rates or more limited flexibility arrangements. While on the surface this result seems paradoxical, it is consistent with both a high incidence of fear of floating among the group classified as floaters and a

Table III Proportion of Cases Where the Volatility of Reserves Significantly Exceeds that of the Benchmark Country: Summary of the F-tests

Regime according to IMF classification	Number of cases	Australia	Benchmark is Japan	United States
Peg	70	81.4	95.7	92.9
Limited flexibility	11	72.7	100	90.9
Managed floating	43	76.2	88.4	88.4
Floating	31	73.3	97.3	87.1
All	155	77.8	93.5	90.9

The alternative hypothesis, if fear of floating is present, is that the variance in reserves for country and episode I is greater than that for the benchmark country, b. Denoting the variance of reserves by σ_R^2, the alternative hypothesis is thus, $\sigma_{Ri}^2 > \sigma_{Rb}^2$. The individual case-by-case esults of the F-tests are available from the authors upon request.

higher incidence of capital controls among the fixers. If binding, the controls can help stabilize the exchange rate without the need for large fluctuations in international reserves.

IV.2. An Exchange Rate Flexibility Index

As discussed above, there is no single all-encompassing indicator that provides an adequate measure of the extent of exchange rate flexibility allowed by the monetary authorities. Yet from the model developed in Section III, we can motivate the construction of a multivariate index that captures different manifestations of the extent of exchange rate variability relative to the variability of the instruments that are at the disposal of the monetary authorities to stabilize the exchange rate.

As noted earlier, domestic reserves R can also be expressed in terms of their asset counterparts, which includes foreign exchange reserves F. As the results of the F-tests attest, reserve variability is significantly higher for the less committed floaters than for the benchmark countries. Furthermore, it is well-known that foreign exchange market intervention is commonplace in many of the cases studied here. For this reason, in the empirical application of the model, we focus on a variance ratio that looks at the central bank balance sheet from the asset side, implying that equation (19) should be modified to

$$\lambda = \sigma_\epsilon^2 / \left(\sigma_i^2 + \sigma_F^2 \right). \tag{21}$$

The values λ can range from zero, when there is a peg or a very high degree of commitment to inflation targeting, to one when seignorage has a high weight in the policymaker's objective function. As shown in Table IV, in about 83 percent of the cases the index of exchange rate flexibility is below that of Australia—for Japan and the United States the share of cases below these two benchmarks is 95 and 90, respectively. When we disaggregate the advanced economies from the emerging market countries, no obvious differences emerge on the proportion of cases that lie below and above the three benchmarks. Separating the two groups does shed light on the "causes" behind the high readings. For the advanced economies, there is no obvious link between a high flexibility index reading and high inflation or rising inflation, as is usually the case following a currency crisis. For emerging markets, however, between 66 and 93 percent of the cases (depending on whether the Australia or Japan benchmark is used) recording a "higher degree of variability" either had inflation rates above 30 percent per annum or the period in question is immediately following a currency crisis. This finding is broadly consistent with the model's predictions that the higher the weight placed on seignorage relative to the inflation target, the more variable the exchange rate relative to the instruments of policy, as the shocks to the risk premiums will not be offset to the same degree if the commitment to an inflation target is not binding.

179

Table IV Probabilities of "Floating" in Comparison to the Benchmark Country: A Composite Index of Exchange Rate Flexibility

	Benchmark is		
Proportion of total cases where	*Australia*	*Japan*	*United States*
All countries			
Index is below benchmark	83.0	95.0	90.0
Index is above benchmark	17.0	5.0	10.0
Advanced economies			
Index is below benchmark	78.0	100.0	90.0
Index is above benchmark	22.0	0.0	10.0
Of which: high inflation: 30 percent cutoff	0.0	0.0	0.0
Of which: post-crisis	0.0	0.0	0.0
Emerging market economies			
Index is below benchmark	85.7	91.4	90.0
Index is above benchmark	14.3	8.6	10.0
Of which: high inflation	33.0	42.9	42.9
Of which: post-crisis	30.0	50.0	42.9

Source: The authors. The indices for the individual country episodes are not reported here to economize on space but are available at www.puaf.umd.edu/papers/reinhart.htm.
The high inflation cutoff is 30 percent or higher during the episode in question; this is in keeping with the threshold used by Easterly [1998] and others.
For, the United States, the index uses the US$/DM (subsequently euro) exchange rate; very similar results obtain if the US dollar/yen exchange rate is used.
a. Another 22 percent of the cases above the Australian benchmark were accounted for by the G-3 countries.

Furthermore, the mode index level for emerging markets is well below the mode for the advanced economies group. This is also in line with the predictions of the model. The variance of nominal interest rates is determined on a one-to-one basis by the variance of risk premium shocks, σ_p^2 (equation (14))—as discussed earlier, risk premiums are far more volatile in emerging markets than in developed economies.

V. Concluding Remarks

Announcements of intentions to float, to be sure, are not new. The Philippines announced it would float on January 1988, yet less than ten years later, following its 1997 currency crises, its exchange rate policy would be lumped together with the rest of the affected Asian countries, under the commonly used (but ill-defined) label of a "soft peg." Bolivia announced it would float on September 1985, because of its hyperinflation—despite this announcement its exchange rate so closely tracked the United States dollar that the regime was reclassified as a managed float on January 1998. Korea and Thailand, despite their relatively new floating status, seem to amass reserves at every possible opportunity.[19]

While these episodes provide anecdotal evidence that countries may be reluctant to allow their currencies to float, the systematic evidence presented in this paper suggests that the fear of floating phenomenon is, indeed, widespread and cuts across regions and levels of development. Fear of floating—or more generally, fear of large currency swings—is pervasive for a variety of reasons, particularly among emerging market countries. The supposedly disappearing middle account makes up the predominant share of country practices. Indeed, one of the hardest challenges trying to draw lessons from the experiences of countries that are at the corners is that there are so few to study. The experiences of some of the floaters like the United States and Japan may not be particularly relevant for developing countries. Similarly, the number of countries with hard pegs is so small (excluding small islands) that it is difficult to generalize.

We have presented evidence in this paper that, when it comes to exchange rate policy, the middle has not disappeared. Yet, there is an apparent change in the conduct of monetary-exchange rate policy in many emerging markets—interest rate policy is (at least partially) replacing foreign exchange intervention as the preferred means of smoothing exchange rate fluctuations. This is evident in the high variability of interest rates in developing economies and in the practices of countries like Mexico and Peru. The use of interest rate policy to smooth exchange rate fluctuations has received considerable attention in recent years; see, for example, Lahiri and Végh (2000) and references therein.

Our finding that so many of the episodes that come under the heading of floating exchange rates look similar to many of the explicit less flexible exchange rate arrangements may help explain why earlier studies, which relied on the official classifications of regimes, failed to detect important differences in GDP growth rates and inflation, across peg and the floating regimes.[20]

In sum, economic theory provides us with well-defined distinctions between fixed and flexible exchange rate regimes, but we are not aware of any criteria that allow us to discriminate as to when a managed float starts to look like a soft peg. Indeed, the evidence presented in this paper suggests that it is often quite difficult to distinguish between the two. On the basis of the empirical evidence, perhaps, all that we can say is that, when it comes to exchange rate policy, discretion rules the day.

Data Appendix: Definitions and Sources

This appendix describes the data used in this study and their sources. IFS refers to the International Monetary Fund's *International Financial Statistics.*

1. Exchange rates. Monthly end-of-period bilateral exchange rates are used. For the European countries it is bilateral exchange rates versus the deutsche mark, except pre-1973, where it is bilateral rates versus the US dollar. For selected African countries (as noted) bilateral exchange rates versus the French franc are used, while for the remaining countries, which constitute

the majority, it is bilateral rates versus the US dollar. We focus on monthly percent changes. Source: IFS line ae.

2. Reserves. Gross foreign exchange reserves minus gold. As with exchange rates, we use monthly percent changes. Source: IFS line 1L.d.

3. Nominal interest rates. Where possible, policy interest rates were used. As these vary by country, the table below summarizes for each country which interest rate series is used and its source.

4. Real ex post interest rates. The nominal interest rates listed above, deflated using consumer prices (IFS line 64), expressed in percentage points. The real interest rate is given by $100 \times [((1 + i_t)p/P_{t+1-t}}$, where I is the nominal interest rate and p are consumer prices.

Country	Interest rate series used	IMF/IFS code
Argentina	Interbank	60B
Australia	Interbank	60B
Bolivia	Deposit	60L
Brazil	Interbank	60B
Canada	Interbank	60B
Chile	Deposit	60L
Colombia	Discount	60
Egypt	Discount	60
France	Interbank	60B
Germany	Interbank	60B
Greece	T-bill	60C
India	Interbank	60B
Indonesia	Interbank	60B
Israel	T-bill	60C
Ivory Coast	Discount	60
Japan	Interbank	60B
Kenya	T-bill	60C
Malaysia	Interbank	60B
Mexico	Interbank	60B
New Zealand	Interbank	60B
Nigeria	T-bill	60C
Norway	Interbank	60B
Pakistan	Interbank	60B
Peru	Discount	60
Philippines	T-bill	60C
Singapore	Interbank	60B
South Africa	Interbank	60B
South Korea	Interbank	60B
Spain	Interbank	60B
Sweden	Interbank	60B
Thailand	Interbank	60B
Uganda	T-bill	60C
United States	Federal funds	60B
Uruguay	Discount	60
Venezuela	Discount	60

Appendix 1: Volatility of Selected Indicators in "Limited Flexibility and Fixed" Exchange Rate Regimes

		Probability that the monthly percent change is		
		Within a ±2.5 percent band:		Greater than ±4 percent:
Country	Period	Exchange rate	Reserves	Nominal interest rate
"Limited flexibility"				
France	March 1979–November 1999	97.5	54.9	0.8
Greece	January 1998–November 1999	80.0	31.3	0.0
Malaysia	January 1986–February 1990	98.1	35.9	3.9
Spain	June 1989–November 1999	92.4	64.7	0.0
Sweden	June 1985–October 1992	92.1	39.3	3.4
"Fixed"				
Argentina	March 1991–November 1999	100.0	36.7	18.4
Bulgaria	June 1997–November 1999	93.1	48.2	3.57
Cote D'Ivoire	January 1970–November 1999	99.4	8.7	0.0
Estonia	June 1992–November 1999	100.0	32.6	5.7
Kenya	January 1970–September 1993	85.6	20.8	1.5
Lithuania	April 1994–November 1999	100.0	37.3	19.4
Malaysia	March 1990–November 1992	96.9	39.4	0.0
Nigeria	April 1993–November 1999	98.6	8.9	1.4
Norway	December 1978–November 1992	86.8	35.1	6.5
Singapore	January 1983–December 1987	96.6	83.3	0.0
Thailand	January 1970–June 1997	98.5	50.2	2.4

Recent pegs episodes with few monthly observations are Malaysia in September 1998 and Egypt in January 1999.

Source: International Financial Statistics, International Monetary Fund.

The authors wish to thank Alberto Alesina, Enrique Mendoza, Vincent Reinhart, Juan Trevino, Carlos Vegh, seminar participants at the Hoover Institution conference on "Currency Unions," Stanford, California, Summer Camp, Paracas, Peru, International Monetary Fund, and the NBER's Summer Institute 2000 in International Finance and Macroeconomics, and two anonymous referees for very useful suggestions, and Facundo Martin, Ioannis Tokatlidis, and Juan Trevino for superb research assistance. This paper was written while the authors were professors at the University of Maryland. The paper represents the views of the authors and not necessarily those of the institutions with which they are affiliated.

Notes

1 For recent interesting discussions of the corner solution hypothesis, see Frankel, Schmukler, and Servén [2001] and Fischer [2001]. Obstfeld and Rogoff [1995], who stress the increased difficulty of maintaining a peg in the face of rising capital mobility, also anticipate many of these issues.

2 While data on exchange rates and reserves are readily available for a much larger set of developing countries, data on interest rates pose a problem in many cases, as they are riddled with large gaps and discontinuities.

3 Many small countries in Africa and the Western Hemisphere with a long history of fixed exchange rates (for instance, the CFA Franc Zone) are not well represented in our sample. As we are primarily interested in verifying whether countries that are currently (or previously) classified as floaters or managed floaters behave like the truly committed floaters, this does not seem like a serious omission.

4 In a longer working paper version of this paper, we also studied the behavior of the monetary aggregates, real ex post interest rates, and primary commodity prices (see Calvo and Reinhart [2001]).

5 As another example, the variance of the monthly exchange rate change over Pakistan's pegged episode, which ended in December 1981, was 119.42; excluding a single monthly observation (the devaluation of May 1972), the variance plummets to 0.85. Some of the problems with the alternative exchange rate classification proposed by Levy Yeyati and Sturzenegger [1999] rest on their heavy reliance on second moments distorted by outliers.

6 In a longer working paper version, we also report comparable statistics for a ±1 percent band.

7 The variance of the monthly changes Mexican peso/US$ is about twice as large as the variance of the monthly changes in the ¥/US$ exchange rate (see Calvo and Reinhart [2001]).
   For a study of Peru's fear of floating, see Morón, Goñi, and Ormeño [1999], who estimate an implicit intervention band. For a discussion on East Asia's Dollar Standard, see McKinnon [2001].

8 For instance, in the case of New Zealand, reserves fluctuate due to the Treasury's management of its overseas currency debt rather than foreign exchange market intervention. We thank Governor Brash (in personal correspondence) for pointing this out.

9 One may also want to construct an estimate of interest earned by the reserve holdings and adjust the reported stocks accordingly. This is work in progress.

10 So while monthly changes in the Mexican peso/US$ exchange rate are almost twice as variable as monthly changes in the ¥/US$ rate—changes in Mexico's reserves are 18 times as volatile as changes in U. S. reserves and 25 times as variable as changes in Japan's reserves and more than four times as volatile as Argentina's reserves.

11 See Calvo and Reinhart [2000] for details.

12 See the working paper version of this paper.

13 It is important to note that some countries with a highly regulated financial sector and limited capital mobility simultaneously show exchange rate and interest rate stability; examples include Egypt, India (in the earlier managed floating period), Kenya, and Nigeria.

14 See also Hausmann, Panizza, and Stein [2001].

15 Inflation targeters include Australia (September 1994), Brazil (June 1999), Canada (February 1991), Colombia (September 1999), Czech Republic (January 1998), Finland (February 1993–June 1998), Israel (January 1992), South Korea (January 1998), Switzerland (January 2000), Mexico (January 1999), New Zealand (March 1990), Peru (January 1994), Poland (October 1998), South Africa (February 2000), Spain (November 1994–June 1998), Sweden (January 1993), Thailand (April 2000), and United Kingdom (October 1992). The dates in parentheses, which indicate when inflation targeting was introduced, highlight that for most of the emerging markets the policy change is relatively recent.

16 We will suppress time subscripts where possible.

17 In a growing economy, seigniorage would also include the increase in real balances induced as income expands.

18 The individual country and episode (there are 155 of these) results are available in the background material to this paper at www.puaf.umd.edu/papers/reinhart.htm.

19 Of course, one interpretation of these developments is that, burned by the liquidity shortage faced during the 1997–1998 crisis, these countries are seeking to build a "war chest" of international reserves in order to avoid having similar problems in the future.

20 See, for instance, Baxter and Stockman [1989], Ghosh, Gulde, Ostry, and Wolf [1997], and Edwards and Savastano [2000] for a review of this literature.

References

Alesina, Alberto, and Vittorio Grilli, "The European Central Bank: Reshaping Monetary Politics in Europe," in *Establishing a Central Bank: Issues in Europe and Lessons from the U. S.,* M. Canzoneri, V. Grilli, and P. Masson, eds. (Cambridge, UK: Cambridge University Press, 1992), pp. 49–77.

Barro, Robert J., and David Gordon, "Rules, Discretion and Reputation in a Model of Monetary Policy," *Journal of Monetary Economics,* XII (1983), 101–122.

Baxter, Marianne, and Alan C. Stockman, "Business Cycles and the ExchangeRate Regime: Some International Evidence," *Journal of Monetary Economics,* XXIII (1989), 377–400.

Caballero, Ricardo, and Arvind Krishnamurthy, "A "Vertical" Analysis of Crises and Intervention: Fear of Floating and Ex-Ante Problems," mimeograph, Massachusetts Institute of Technology, 2001.

Calvo, Guillermo A., and Pablo E. Guidotti, "On the Flexibility of Monetary Policy: The Case of the Optimal Inflation Tax," *Review of Economic Studies,* LX (1993), 667–687.

Calvo, Guillermo A., and Carmen M. Reinhart, "Fear of Floating," NBER Working Paper No. 7993, 2000.

Calvo, Guillermo A., and Carmen M. Reinhart, "Fixing for Your Life," in *Brookings Trade Forum 2000. Policy Challenges in the Next Millennium,* S. Collins and D. Rodrik, eds. (Washington, DC: Brookings Institution, 2001), pp. 1–39.

Canzoneri, Matthew B., "Monetary Policy Games and the Role of Private Information," *American Economic Review,* LXXV (1985), 1056–1070.

Edwards, Sebastian, and Miguel Savastano, "Exchange Rates in Emerging Economies: What Do We Know? What Do We Need to Know?" in *Economic Policy Reform: The Second Stage,* A. Krueger, ed. (Chicago: University of Chicago Press, 2000), pp. 453–510.

Fischer, Stanley, "Exchange Rate Regimes: Is the Bipolar View Correct?" *Journal of Economic Perspectives,* XV (2001), 3–24.

Frankel, Jeffrey A., Sergio Schmukler, and Luis Servén, "Verifiability and the Vanishing Exchange Rate Regime," in *Policy Challenges in the Next Millennium,* S. Collins and D. Rodrik, eds. (Washington, DC: Brookings Institution, 2001), pp. 59–109.

Ghosh, Atish, Anne-Marie Gulde, Jonathan Ostry, and Holger Wolf, "Does the Nominal Exchange Rate Regime Matter?" NBER Working Paper No. 5874, 1997.

Hausmann, Ricardo, Ugo Panizza, and Ernesto Stein, "Why Do Countries Float the Way They Float?" *Journal of Development Economics,* LXVI (2001), 387–417.

Lahiri, Amartya, and Carlos A. Végh, "Living with the Fear of Floating: An Optimal Policy Perspective," in *Preventing Currency Crises in Emerging Markets,* S. Edwards and J. Frankel, eds. (Chicago: University of Chicago Press for the National Bureau of Economic Research, 2001).

Levy Yeyati, Eduardo, and Federico Sturzenegger, "Classifying Exchange Rate Regimes: Deeds versus Words," mimeograph, Universidad Torcuato Di Tella, 1999.

McKinnon, Ronald I., "After the Crisis, the East Asian Dollar Standard Resurrected," in *Rethinking the East Asian Miracle,* J. Stiglitz and S. Yusuf, eds. (Washington, DC: World Bank and Oxford University Press, 2001), pp. 197–246.

Morón, Eduardo, Edwin Goñi, and Arturo Ormeño, "Central Bankers' Fear of Floating: The Peruvian Evidence," mimeograph, Universidad del Pacifico, 1999.

Obstfeld, Maurice, and Kenneth Rogoff, "The Mirage of Fixed Exchange Rates," *Journal of Economic Perspectives,* IX (1995), 73–96.

Reinhart, Carmen M., "Sovereign Credit Ratings Before and After Financial Crises," mimeograph, University of Maryland, College Park, 2001.

Rogoff, Kenneth, "The Optimal Degree of Commitment to an Intermediate Monetary Target," *Quarterly Journal of Economics,* C (1985), 1169–1190.

22

EXCHANGE RATE REGIMES

Is the Bipolar View Correct?

Stanley Fischer

Source: *Journal of Economic Perspectives* 15, 2, 2001, 3–24.

Each of the major international capital market-related crises since 1994—
Mexico, in 1994, Thailand, Indonesia and Korea in 1997, Russia and Brazil in
1998, and Argentina and Turkey in 2000—has in some way involved a fixed
or pegged exchange rate regime. At the same time, countries that did not have
pegged rates—among them South Africa, Israel in 1998, Mexico in 1998, and
Turkey in 1998—avoided crises of the type that afflicted emerging market countries with pegged rates.

Little wonder, then, that policymakers involved in dealing with these crises
have warned strongly against the use of adjustable peg and other soft peg exchange
rate regimes for countries open to international capital flows. That warning has
tended to take the form of the bipolar, or corner solution, view, which is that
countries need to choose either to peg their currencies hard (for instance, as in a
currency board), or to allow their currencies to float, but that intermediate policy
regimes between hard pegs and floating are not sustainable.[1]

Figure 1 shows the change in the distribution of exchange rate arrangements of
the IMF's member countries between 1991 and 1999. The three categories shown
are derived from a more detailed classification of de facto exchange regimes that
is presented in the *Annual Report 2000* of the International Monetary Fund (pp.
141–143).[2] The arrangements described as "hard pegs" in Figure 1 include currency boards and situations where countries have no national currency, either
because they are in a currency union or because they have dollarized by formally adopting the currency of some other country. The floating group contains
economies whose systems are described either as independently floating, or as
a "managed float," which means that while the central bank may intervene in
the exchange market, it has not committed itself to trying to bring about a particular exchange rate or exchange rate range. The "intermediate" group consists
of economies with a variety of soft peg currency arrangements: these include a
conventional fixed exchange rate peg; a crawling peg, in which the peg is allowed
to shift gradually over time; an exchange rate band, in which the central bank is

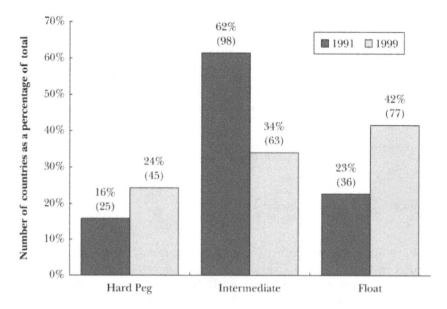

Figure 1 All Countries: Exchange Rate Regimes, 1991 and 1999. *Source:* IMF. *Note:* The number of countries is in parenthesis.

committed to keeping the exchange rate within a specified range; and a crawling band, which allows the exchange rate band itself to move over time.[3]

As Figure 1 shows, there has since 1991 been a thinning out of the middle or intermediate range, and increases in the percentage of countries having either hard pegs or floating.[4] The percentage of countries with hard pegs increased from 16 to 24 percent; the percentage with floating rate regimes increased from 23 to 42 percent. Correspondingly, whereas 62 percent of economies had intermediate regimes in 1991, only 34 percent did in 1999. Thus, it does appear that during the 1990s, countries were moving away from the intermediate arrangements and toward either hard pegs or floating exchange rate regimes. But the significance of this movement and the specific conditions under which it makes economic sense need to be spelled out and refined.

In seeking to refine the analysis, I will argue that proponents of what is now known as the bipolar view—myself included—probably have exaggerated their point for dramatic effect. The right statement is that *for countries open to international capital flows*: (i) soft exchange rate pegs are not sustainable; but (ii) a wide variety of flexible rate arrangements remain possible; and (iii) it is to be expected that policy in most countries will not be indifferent to exchange rate movements. To put the point graphically, if exchange rate arrangements lie along a line connecting hard pegs like currency unions, currency boards, and dollarization on the left, with free floating on the right, the intent of the bipolar view is not to rule out everything but the two corners, but rather to pronounce as unsustainable a segment of that line representing a variety of soft pegging exchange rate arrangements.[5]

This version of the bipolar argument accepts that countries are likely to be concerned about the level of their exchange rate. In particular, countries will often have what Calvo and Reinhart (2000) term a "fear of floating," because they are not willing to accept the extent of exchange rate fluctuations generated by a totally free float of the exchange rate. In this case, monetary policy and possibly foreign exchange intervention policy will respond to exchange market pressures.[6] The formulation also leaves open a variety of exchange rate arrangements. For countries open to international capital flows, it includes as sustainable regimes both very hard pegs and a variety of floating rate arrangements, including managed floats. For countries not as yet open to international capital flows, it includes the full gamut of exchange rate arrangements.

The question that then arises is what exchange rate arrangements are excluded by the bipolar view. The answer is: for countries open to international capital flows, exchange rate systems in which the government is viewed as being committed to defending a particular value of the exchange rate, or a narrow range of exchange rates, but has not made the institutional commitments that both constrain and enable monetary policy to be devoted to the sole goal of defending the parity. In essence, the excluded arrangements are fixed exchange rate pegs, adjustable exchange rate pegs, and narrow band exchange rate systems.

I will start this paper by focusing on the critical point that for developed and emerging market countries, adjustable peg exchange rate systems have not proved to be viable for the long term, and should not be expected to be viable. I will then take up a set of other issues: the "fear of floating" argument, and monetary policy under floating rate regimes; the nature of the hard peg arrangements that may be expected to be viable; the use of the exchange rate as a nominal anchor in disinflation; the behavior of exchange rates among the United States, Europe, and Japan; and what can be said about exchange rate arrangements for developing countries that are not open to international capital flows.

Exchange Rate Regimes for Developed and Emerging Market Countries

The fresh thinking about exchange rate regimes that has followed the crises of the last seven years centers on exchange rate systems for countries integrated or integrating into global capital markets.

Two groups of countries can be considered as integrated or integrating into international capital markets: the advanced countries, and emerging market countries. For the advanced countries, I draw on the list of "developed market" economies produced by Morgan Stanley Capital International (MSCI). This contains 22 economies, listed in Table 1. The emerging market group is defined as the 33 economies contained in the union of the 27 economies that are in the MSCI emerging markets index and the 17 economies that are in the Emerging Markets Bond Index Plus (EMBI+), which is from J.P. Morgan. These are listed in Table 2. Tables 1 and 2 also list exchange rate arrangements in place at the end of 1999.[7]

Figure 2 shows the development of exchange rate regimes among the developed and emerging market countries listed in Tables 1 and 2. In these cases, too,

Table 1 Developed Market Economies *(as of December 31, 1999)*

Euro Area		Other	
	Exchange Arrangement		*Exchange Arrangement*
Austria	No separate legal tender	Australia	Independent float
Belgium	No separate legal tender	Canada	Independent float
Finland	No separate legal tender	Denmark	Pegged rate in horizontal band
France	No separate legal tender	Hong Kong SAR	Currency board
Germany	No separate legal tender	Japan	Independent float
Ireland	No separate legal tender	New Zealand	Independent float
Italy	No separate legal tender	Norway	Managed float
Netherlands	No separate legal tender	Singapore	Managed float
Portugal	No separate legal tender	Sweden	Independent float
Spain	No separate legal tender	Switzerland	Independent float
		United Kingdom	Independent float
		United States	Independent float

Source: IMF, Annual Report 2000.
Note: Economies listed in the MSCI Developed Markets index.

Table 2 Emerging Market Countries Grouped by Exchange Rate Arrangement *(as of December 31, 1999)*

Exchange Rate Regime (Number of Countries)	Countries
No separate legal tender/ Currency board (3) (*3)	*Argentina, *Bulgaria, *Panama
Other fixed pegs (7) (*2)	*China, Egypt, Jordan, *Malaysia, Morocco, Pakistan, Qatar
Pegged rate in horizontal band (1) (*1)	*Greece
Crawling peg (1)	Turkey
Rates within crawling bands (5) (*2)	Hungary, *Israel, Poland, Sri Lanka, *Venezuela
Managed float (3) (*1)	Czech Republic, Nigeria, *Taiwan POC
Independent float (13) (*7)	*Brazil, *Chile, Colombia, Ecuador, *India, Indonesia, *Korea, *Mexico, Peru, *Philippines, Russia, *South Africa, Thailand

Source: IMF, Annual Report 2000.
Note: *indicates country whose weight in either the EMBI+ or MSCI index is 2% or greater. Numbers in parenthesis indicate number of countries in each group; asterisked numbers are self-explanatory.

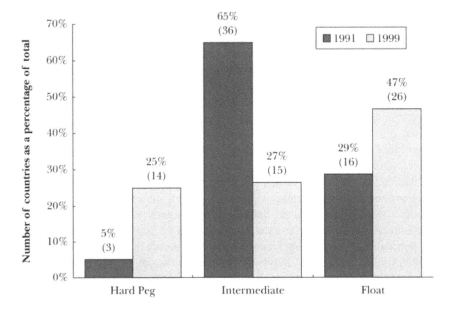

Figure 2 Developed and Emerging Market Countries: Exchange Rate Regimes, 1991 and 1999. *Source:* IMF. *Note:* The number of countries is in parenthesis.

there has been a shift in the bipolar direction, away from the soft peg center, towards harder pegs on one side, and floating arrangements on the other.

Of the 22 developed market economies in Table 1, all of which have complete or nearly complete capital mobility, 10 are in the euro area and are listed as having no separate legal tender.[8] Another 10 countries are listed as having floating rates, either independently floating or managed floating. The other two countries are Hong Kong SAR, with a currency board arrangement, and Denmark, which has not agreed to join the euro zone but is officially still pegging its exchange rate within a band to the other European currencies. *Thus, among the developed economies listed in Table 1, and depending on how the euro zone countries are regarded, half the economies have established very hard pegs, and nearly half the countries float.*

A decade ago, Table 1 would have looked quite similar for the non-euro area countries. However, the European countries were at that time operating under the European Monetary System (EMS), a set of adjustable exchange rate pegs operating within horizontal bands. Part of the belief in the nonrobustness of adjustable pegs derives from the manner in which EMS currencies were attacked in 1992 and 1993. It proved impossible to hold the adjustable pegs within the EMS after the rise in German interest rates necessitated by Germany's unification had imposed a domestically inappropriate monetary policy on the other EMS members. This example is particularly telling since the attack on the EMS was successful despite the political commitment to it by the system's members, who saw the adjustable peg system within the EMS as a stepping-stone towards the goal of monetary union. Part of the empirical support for the view that countries will move away from soft peg exchange rate mechanisms to hard pegs or fixed exchange rate mechanisms is based on the creation of the euro as a single currency for Europe.

The 33 emerging market economies are grouped by exchange rate arrangement in Table 2. The largest group of countries (13) consists of those described as independently floating. Six of those countries (Indonesia, Korea, Thailand, Russia, Brazil and Mexico) became floaters after the major crises of the last decade, while Colombia joined the group in 1999. This is the set of transitions that has most influenced the view that soft pegs are not viable for sustained periods—and it includes many of the largest emerging market economies. Three economies are described as having managed floats. Thus, half the emerging market group of countries has some form of floating rate arrangement. While there is room for judgment over whether these countries should be listed in the "managed" or "independent" floating group, there should be no dispute that all 16 belong in one or other of those categories. Furthermore, there has during the last decade been a significant shift among these emerging market economies from various forms of pegged arrangements towards floating.

Of the remaining 17 countries listed in Table 2, at the end of 1999 three either had currency boards or no independent legal tender. Ecuador and Greece have subsequently joined this group: Ecuador (an independent floater in December 1999) by dollarizing and Greece by joining the European Monetary Union. Eight countries had fixed or adjustable pegs at the end of 1999. Turkey had just instituted a crawling peg regime, which has now given way to a float. Five countries—Hungary, Israel, Poland, Sri Lanka and Venezuela—had crawling bands, which in the cases of both Israel and Poland have been widening over the years, to the point of considerable flexibility.

The pattern is similar if one looks at the 16 larger emerging market economies, which are identified with asterisks in Table 2. Half of these larger emerging market economies are floaters. Three have hard pegs, a number that by now has risen to four. Two have crawling bands. Only two of the countries in this group of larger emerging market economies have soft pegs: China and Malaysia.

Within the emerging market economies, the number of intermediate exchange rate arrangements declined in the 1990s and the number of floating and fixed regimes has increased.[9] This shift appears likely to continue. Looking ahead from the end of 1999, Greece has joined the euro zone, and Hungary and Poland are likely to. Israel is likely to move to an independently floating rate regime; Turkey is scheduled to move in that direction too, with possible membership in the euro zone a more distant prospect.

It is thus reasonable to say that economies open to international capital flows have been and are in the process of moving away from adjustable peg exchange rate systems, some towards harder pegs and more fixed exchange rates (especially in the creation of the euro zone), more towards systems with greater exchange rate flexibility. But why? *The reason is that soft peg systems have not proved viable over any lengthy period, especially for countries integrated or integrating into the international capital markets.* The fact that pegged exchange rates have a short life expectancy whether the economy is open to international capital flows or not was emphasized by Obstfeld and Rogoff (1995). But the collapse of the Bretton Woods system in the late 1960s and early 1970s, the repeated crises of the European Monetary System in the 1980s and the successful attacks on currencies within the system in 1992 and 1993, and the emerging market crises of 1994–2000 all drive home the lesson that this problem is especially intense for countries that are more open to international flows of capital.[10]

In several countries, extensive economic damage has been caused by the collapses of pegged rate regimes that had lasted for a few years. After a few years of exchange rate stability under a pegged regime, a belief gradually arises that the exchange rate will never change, which reduces perceptions of the risk of borrowing in foreign currencies and removes the need to hedge. Then, when an exchange rate crisis does strike, it is exceptionally damaging in its effects on banking systems, corporations, and government finances. In principle, it should be possible to reduce the potential damage through prudential regulations that limit the open foreign exchange positions of banks. But it is harder to control corporate sector international financing through such regulations. Moreover, it is in any case probably unwise to rely too heavily on regulatory supervision to prevent transactions that would otherwise be highly profitable.[11]

The concept of the "impossible trinity" points out that no economy can simultaneously have a fixed exchange rate, capital mobility, and a monetary policy dedicated to domestic goals. The major explanation for the nonviability of soft pegs is that they are an attempt by a country open to international capital flows to have both a fixed exchange rate and a monetary policy directed at domestic goals—and sooner or later, an irreconcilable conflict arises between these goals. But this insight leaves open three questions. First, if the impossible trinity is correct, why did soft peg arrangements survive for so long, and why did their vulnerability become so much more apparent only in the 1990s? The second question is one of political economy: Why can't domestic monetary policy be directed credibly solely towards maintenance of the soft peg exchange rate? The third question is whether to seek to combine a fixed exchange rate and a domestically-oriented monetary policy by using capital controls to limit the mobility of foreign capital.

The evidence shown in Figures 1 and 2 raises the question of what happened in the 1990s to cause exchange rate arrangements to shift in a bipolar direction. The beginnings of that move can be dated much earlier, to the breakup of the Bretton Woods system in the early 1970s. In the 1990s, the creation of the European Monetary Union accounts for much of the shift towards hard pegs. Among emerging market countries, the growing openness of capital accounts, combined with the associated development of private sector capital flows towards the emerging markets, made the force of the inconsistency expressed in the impossible trinity much more apparent and led to the collapse of several important soft pegged exchange rate arrangements in major crises.

The answer to the second question, the political economy question of why it is difficult for macroeconomic policy to protect a soft peg, must be that if the option of changing the exchange rate is open to the political system, then at a time when the short-run benefits of doing so appear to outweigh the costs, that option is likely to be chosen. Both foreign and domestic economic shocks (including policy actions) may move the equilibrium nominal exchange rate away from the official rate. If the official or pegged exchange rate is overvalued, then a government that wishes to prevent a devaluation typically has to raise interest rates. As long as the extent of the disequilibrium is small, and the requisite policy actions are taken in time, they can be expected to stabilize the situation. But if the disequilibrium has become large, either because policy was slow to react or because the country has been hit by a strong and long-lasting shock, the required high interest rates may not be viable—either for political reasons or because of the damage they will inflict on the banking system or aggregate demand. Under those circumstances, speculators can be expected to attack the currency, selling it in the anticipation that the government will be forced to devalue. If the disequilibrium is large, such a speculative attack on the exchange rate is likely to succeed.

Third, why not impose capital controls to protect the exchange rate from the effects of unwanted capital flows?[12] Among the 16 larger emerging market economies identified in Table 2, China successfully maintained its pegged exchange rate through the Asian crisis with the assistance of long-standing capital controls, providing an important element of stability in the regional and global economies. Malaysia's imposition of capital controls and pegging of the exchange rate in September 1998 has attracted more attention. However, evaluation of the effects of the Malaysian controls has been difficult since they were imposed after most of the turbulence of the first part of the Asian crisis was over—that is, after most of the capital that wanted to leave had done so—and when regional exchange rates were beginning to appreciate.[13]

In discussing capital controls, I shall assume that countries will in the course of their development want to liberalize the capital account and integrate into global capital markets. This view is based in part on the fact that the most advanced economies all have open capital accounts, which suggests that this is an appropriate goal for emerging market economies. It is also based on the view that the potential benefits of integration into the global capital markets—importantly including the benefits obtained by allowing foreign competition in the financial sector— outweigh the costs.[14]

It is necessary to distinguish between capital controls on outflows and on inflows. For controls on capital outflows to succeed, they need to be quite extensive, to cover potential loopholes. Even so, experience shows that controls on capital outflows cannot prevent a devaluation of the currency if domestic policies are fundamentally inconsistent with maintenance of the pegged exchange rate. Some countries have attempted to impose controls on outflows once a foreign exchange crisis is already underway. It is generally believed that this use of controls has been ineffective (Ariyoshi et al., 2000, pp. 18–29; Edwards, 1999, pp. 68–71). In addition, the imposition of controls on capital outflows is likely to have an effect on capital inflows to the country, since investors who are concerned about not being able to withdraw their capital from a country may respond by not sending it there in the first place.

Moreover, as an economy develops and experiences a growing range of contacts with foreign economies, controls on capital outflows are likely to become both more distorting and less effective. At some point the controls will need to be removed. Where controls on capital outflows are reasonably effective, they would need to be removed gradually, at a time when the exchange rate is not under pressure. The removal of controls on outflows sometimes results in a capital inflow, a result of either foreigners and/or domestic residents bringing capital into the country in light of the greater assurance it can be removed when desired. If the country is moving from a fixed exchange rate regime with controls on capital outflows to floating exchange rates, it is desirable to begin allowing some flexibility of exchange rates as the controls are gradually eased. Moreover, prudential controls that should be put in place for the efficient operation of the financial system often have a similar effect to some capital controls—for instance, limits on foreign exchange positions taken by domestic institutions. More generally, to reduce the economy's vulnerability to crises, a strong domestic financial system should be in place when capital controls are removed.

The IMF has supported the use of market-based capital inflow controls: for example, those that impose a tax on capital inflows. The typical instance occurs when a country is trying to reduce inflation using an exchange rate anchor. For anti-inflationary purposes, the country needs interest rates higher than those implied by the sum of foreign interest rates and the expected rate of currency depreciation. In such circumstances, the high interest rate will attract an inflow of foreign capital, which will tend to cause an exchange rate appreciation; alternatively, the country can permit the inflows and try to sterilize their monetary impact, but this typically becomes costly. A tax on capital inflows can in principle help a country maintain a high domestic interest rate without experiencing a substantial inflow of capital. In addition, by taxing short-term capital inflows more than longer-term inflows, capital inflow controls can also in principle influence the composition of inflows.

Evidence from the Chilean experience with controls on capital inflows suggests that controls on capital inflows were for a time successful in allowing some monetary policy independence, and also in shifting the composition of capital inflows towards longer-term investment. However, the Chilean controls eventually seemed to lose their effectiveness (Edwards, 2000), and they have recently been removed.

Direct controls on inflows are also used by some countries. These may be aimed at specific types of inflows, for instance, short-term (hot money) flows, or sometimes foreign direct investment. Direct investment inflows are typically quite stable, and indeed at the aggregate level continued rising even during the Asian crisis; they also bring advantages in the form of new technology. Most countries that seek to control inflows prefer long-term direct investment to short-term inflows. Nonetheless, some countries have liberalized short-term flows, while seeking to keep long-term flows out, thereby exacerbating the volatility of short-term capital flows as market uncertainties increased.

There is little question that capital controls—whether on outflows or inflows—can for some time help a country sustain a soft peg exchange rate regime. Nonetheless, such controls tend to lose their effectiveness over time. Moreover, as countries develop, they are likely to want to integrate further into global capital markets. Countries in these circumstances would be well advised to move away from a soft peg exchange rate, typically towards a more flexible exchange rate regime.

Fear of Floating

Many countries that claim to have floating exchange rates do not allow the exchange rate to float freely, but rather deploy interest rates and intervention policy to affect its behavior. As long as such interventions are not undertaken to defend a particular exchange rate, or narrow range of exchange rates, this paper has categorized such behavior as a managed float. But such fear of floating behavior has been described as demonstrating that many—particularly emerging market— countries are not willing to allow their exchange rates to float.

It is hardly a surprise that most policymakers in most countries are concerned with the behavior of the nominal and the real exchange rates. Changes in the nominal exchange rate are likely to affect the inflation rate. Changes in the real exchange rate may have a powerful effect on the wealth of domestic citizens, and on the allocation of resources, which may have not only economic but also political effects—especially in the case of currency appreciations, in countries where exporters matter.

Thus in most countries, even those with floating exchange rate regimes, monetary policy is likely to respond to some extent to movements of the exchange rate. The United States is one of the few examples of a country that largely ignores its exchange rate in the conduct of monetary policy. But most of the other G-7 countries (Canada, France, Germany, Italy, Japan, and the United Kingdom) and emerging market economies do pay attention to exchange rates in the conduct of monetary policy. Canada, for example, until recently used a monetary conditions index to guide monetary policy, which was based on movements in both the exchange rate and the interest rate.

Many of the recent converts to floating exchange rates (several of whom were forcibly converted) have opted for inflation targeting, and that system seems to be working well and has much to commend it. With the inflation targeting approach to monetary policy, movements in the exchange rate will be taken into account indirectly in setting monetary policy, because the exchange rate affects price behavior. This will generally produce a pattern of monetary tightening when the exchange rate depreciates, a response similar, but not necessarily of the same magnitude, to that which would be undertaken if the exchange rate were being targeted directly.

Why should monetary policy not target both the nominal exchange rate and the inflation rate? Central banks may face this issue with particular force in a situation with an appreciated real exchange rate and the current account in large deficit. The first answer must be that monetary policy fundamentally affects the nominal exchange rate and not the real exchange rate, and that if any part of macroeconomic policy should take care of the current account balance by redressing an imbalance between domestic savings and investment, it is fiscal policy.

However, there is an unresolved issue about whether monetary policy in a floating rate system should be used in the short run to affect the real exchange rate. If the nominal exchange rate moves faster than the real exchange rate, then monetary policy can influence the real exchange rate in the short run. In many respects, this issue is similar to that of how monetary policy in an inflation-targeting framework should respond to movements in output and unemployment. There is almost certainly a short-run tradeoff between the real exchange rate and inflation, analogous to the Phillips curve, although it has not received much empirical attention.[15] This is not the place to pursue the issue, but just as answers have been developed to how to deal with the short-run Phillips curve in an inflation-targeting framework, so that a central bank can take into account the short-run impact of its actions on output and unemployment while recognizing that the long-run effects are negligible, it remains necessary to answer the question of how to deal with the short-run tradeoff between the real exchange rate and inflation, recognizing that in the long run greater inflation will not affect the real exchange rate.

Beyond the use of interest rates, some countries intervene directly from time to time in the foreign exchange markets to try to stabilize the exchange rate. So long as they are not perceived as trying to defend a particular rate, such interventions can be useful in reducing the degree of volatility in exchange rate markets. This is one of the remaining areas in which central bankers place considerable emphasis on the touch and feel of the market, and where systematic policy rules are not yet common. There is of course controversy over whether exchange rate intervention works at all—and even if it does, whether it is wise to use it. The Banco de Mexico has developed a method of more-or-less automatic intervention designed to reduce day-to-day movements in exchange rates, which could provide lessons in this area.

Recognizing the difficulty for an emerging market country of defending a narrow range of exchange rates, John Williamson (2000) proposes alternative regimes. He calls these BBC arrangements: basket (that is, a peg to a basket of currencies rather than a single currency), band, and crawl. He also recommends that countries if necessary allow the exchange rate to move temporarily outside the band, so that speculators cannot predict with certainty when the central bank is going to intervene. In these circumstances, a moving and elastic band would be serving as a weak nominal anchor for the exchange rate, but it is not at all clear why such a system is preferable to an inflation-targeting framework. Possibly the exchange rate band could be thought of as a supplement to an inflation-targeting framework, but it would need to be demonstrated what benefits that brings, if any. One possibility—which is not very plausible—is that by committing weakly to some range of exchange rates, the authorities make it more likely that fiscal policy will be brought into play if the real exchange rate moves too far from equilibrium.

Viable Hard Pegs

At the end of 1999, 45 of the IMF's then-182 members had hard peg exchange rate systems, either with no independent legal tender, or a currency board. Except for the 11 countries in Europe, all of the 37 economies with no independent legal tender were small. But the exception of the European single currency, the euro, is a very big one. Argentina and Hong Kong SAR are the biggest economies with currency boards. Since the end of 1999, Ecuador and El Salvador have dollarized, so that over a quarter of the IMF's 183 members have very hard pegs; the proportion in terms of GDP is similar.

At the end of 1990, plans for a single European currency did not yet exist, and there were only three currency board economies. The appraisal of the performance of currency boards, once regarded as a historical curiosity, has undoubtedly changed, as a result of several factors: the tireless proselytizing by Steve Hanke and others (for instance, Hanke and Schuler, 1994); examination of their historical record; and their performance in a number of economies, including Hong Kong SAR, Argentina, and the transition economies of Estonia, Lithuania, Bulgaria, and Bosnia-Herzegovina. Ghosh, Gulde and Wolf (2000, p. 270) provide a balanced summary:

> First, the historical track record of currency boards is sterling . . . Countries that did exit . . . did so mainly for political, rather than economic reasons, and such exits were usually uneventful. . . . Second, modern currency boards have often been instituted to gain credibility following a period of high or hyperinflation, and in this regard have been remarkably successful. Countries with currency boards experienced lower inflation and higher (if more volatile) GDP growth compared to both floating regimes and simple pegs. . . . The GDP growth effect is significant, but may simply reflect a rebound from depressed levels. Third, . . . the successful introduction of a currency board . . . [is] far from trivial . . . Moreover, there are thorny issues, as yet untested, regarding possible exits from a currency board . . .

The great strength of the currency board arrangement, the virtual removal of the nominal exchange rate as a means of adjustment, is also its principal weakness. In the case of an internal or external macroeconomic shock, the economy can adjust via a change either in exchange rates or domestic prices and wages. The nominal exchange rate adjustment is typically much quicker, and that via wages and prices more prolonged and, certainly in the case of the need for a decline in the real exchange rate, more difficult. In late 2000, this difficulty was evident in Argentina, where a currency board arrangement prevents the nominal exchange rate from moving, but even in Argentina, the adjustment *is* taking place as domestic prices and costs decline relative to foreign prices and costs.

It is difficult to make a general evaluation of the benefits and costs of the constraints imposed by the commitment to a currency board. For a country with a history of extreme monetary disorder, a currency board appears to be a means of obtaining credibility for a low-inflation monetary policy more rapidly and at lower cost than appears possible any other way. For a country like Argentina, with a long and unhappy inflationary history, the society may be willing to accept the occasional short-run costs of doing without the exchange rate as a means of adjustment in exchange for lower inflation, just as the memory of the German hyperinflation in the 1920s has colored German attitudes to inflation ever since.

The extensive discussion leading up to the European single currency emphasized how member countries, when deprived of exchange rate flexibility, would need to adjust to shocks with wage and price flexibility, the mobility of labor and capital, and fiscal compensation. A currency board country is unlikely to have access to fiscal compensatory measures from abroad, and nor is its labor likely to be as mobile internationally as that in the European Union will be—but we should not exaggerate the role of geographical labor mobility as a means of short-run adjustment to shocks even in large national economies. For such a country, the emphasis has to be on wage and price flexibility as well as internal labor market mobility. Domestic fiscal policy can play a countercyclical role in a currency board economy, provided the fiscal situation is strong enough in normal times for fiscal easing during a recession not to raise any questions about long-term fiscal sustainability.

Policies to this end—to encourage internal factor mobility, wage and price flexibility, and fiscal prudence in normal times—are entirely possible, and can help ensure the sustainability of a currency board over time. Such policies are of course generally desirable in *any* economy, but the need for them is greater if the exchange rate is not available as a tool of adjustment.

Another disadvantage sometimes cited for a currency board arrangement is that since the central bank cannot create money, it may not be able to act as lender of last resort. However, the circumstance envisaged by the classic argument for lender of last resort—a pure panic-based run on banks into currency—is rare. Most often financial crises have a real basis, and take real resources to resolve, as Goodhart and Schoenmaker (1995) have shown. One way or another, these resources come from the fiscal authority. The absence of a central bank capable of acting as lender of last resort can be compensated for in various ways: by the creation, typically with fiscal resources, of a banking sector stabilization fund (as has been done in Bulgaria); by setting up a deposit insurance scheme, financed by the banks and if necessary in the final resort by the treasury; by strengthening financial sector supervision and prudential controls; by allowing foreign banks to operate in the economy; and by lining up contingency credits for the banking system.

The discussion so far has implicitly centered on how the goods and factor market and the current account would adjust in world of floating or fixed exchange rates. Those who strongly favor hard pegs, such as Calvo and Reinhart (2000) or Eichengreen and Hausmann (2000), tend to focus on international flows of capital and on asset markets. Their argument is that with respect to asset markets, a country obtains essentially no benefit—seigniorage aside—from exchange rate flexibility. For example, emerging market economies cannot borrow abroad in their own currencies, and so the exchange rate creates a source of additional risk and higher interest rates for all foreign borrowing. Given this, they argue for going beyond currency boards to dollarization and perhaps in the longer run to wider currency unions.

If a country intends never to use the exchange rate as a mechanism of adjustment, then retaining exchange rate flexibility is clearly counterproductive. Hence the argument for dollarization relative to a currency board must turn on an appraisal of the gains from dollarization that would be obtained in the capital markets, for example in the reduction of spreads between domestic and foreign interest rates and by the strengthening of the financial system, versus the losses implied by forgoing both seigniorage and the option of changing the exchange rate in extremis by giving up a national currency. The balance of the argument would be tilted if a politically acceptable means could be found of transferring seigniorage to dollarizing countries; the Mack bill in the previous Congress would have done that, suggesting that, at least in the case of the dollar, some means of transferring seigniorage from the use of the dollar could eventually become politically feasible.

Both Ecuador and El Salvador dollarized in 2000, but under very different circumstances. Ecuador's decision was essentially one of desperation (Fischer, 2000); El Salvador's was based on careful consideration. The Ecuadorian case provides much food for thought about what it takes for dollarization to succeed. It was implemented without many of what were thought of as the prerequisites for success, such as a strong banking system, being in place. Much work remains to be done, particularly in the banking sector, to ensure the long-term success of Ecuador's dollarization. But at least in its first year, it has worked reasonably well.

Hard peg exchange rate systems have become more attractive than had been thought some years ago. For a small economy, heavily dependent in its trade and capital account transactions on a particular large economy, it *may* make sense to adopt the currency of that country, particularly if provision can be made for the transfer of seigniorage. While the requirements for the effective operation of such a system are demanding, in terms of the strength of the financial system and fiscal soundness, meeting those requirements is good for the economy in any case. To be sure, careful consideration needs to be given to the nature of the shocks affecting the economy. For example, even though the Canadian economy is closely connected to the U.S. economy, Canadian policymakers regard their country as benefiting from the shock-absorber role of the floating exchange rate with the U.S. dollar. But there is clearly a trend, which can be expected to accelerate if the euro zone succeeds, in the direction of hard pegged exchange rate regimes. This trend is already reducing the number of currencies in existence, and further reductions should be expected in future.

The Exchange Rate as a Nominal Anchor for Disinflation

The benefits and risks of using the exchange rate as a nominal anchor to disinflate from triple-digit inflation, as well as the real dynamics associated with such stabilizations, have been extensively studied (for a summary, see Mussa et al., 2000, Appendix III, pp. 44–47; Calvo and Végh, 1999). There are few instances in which a successful disinflation from triple-digit inflation has taken place without the use of an exchange rate anchor, particularly in countries that have suffered from chronic monetary instability. The exchange rate anchor in such disinflations sometimes takes the form of a very hard peg, for instance a currency board, but is more often a softer peg, often a crawling peg regime.

Of the eleven major exchange rate-based stabilizations since the late 1980s studied in Mussa et al. (2000), four of them—Argentina in 1991, Estonia in 1992, Lithuania in 1994 and Bulgaria in 1997—entered currency boards and disinflated successfully. The other seven countries (and Israel in 1985 could be added to this sample) generally either undertook exchange rate devaluations a step at a time, or introduced crawling exchange rate bands, which in many cases have widened over time. The disinflations of three countries—Mexico in 1994, Russia in 1998 and Brazil in 1999—ended in a currency crash, though in each case low inflation was preserved or rapidly regained following the crisis.

Countries which disinflate using a soft peg exchange rate strategy must consider their exit strategy from the pegged arrangement. An IMF study of exit strategies in this case showed that exit is best undertaken when the currency is strong, something which is quite likely to happen as the stabilization gains credibility and capital inflows expand (Eichengreen et al., 1998). This was the pattern for instance in Poland and Israel, where the band was widened as pressure for appreciation mounted. However, the political economy of moving away from a peg is complicated, even in this case. When the currency is strong, the authorities generally see no reason to move off the peg; when it is weak, they argue that devaluation or a widening of the band under pressure would be counterproductive. But the longer the peg continues, the more the dangers associated with soft pegs grow. In some cases in which the currencies of disinflating countries crashed, the IMF had been pushing unsuccessfully for greater exchange rate flexibility.

The need to move away from a soft peg is one of the reasons an exit mechanism was built into the Turkish stabilization and reform program that began in December 1999. Nonetheless, as a result of unresolved banking sector problems, the failure to undertake corrective fiscal actions when the current account widened, and political difficulties, the crawling peg failed to hold and in February 2001, Turkey was forced to float its exchange rate.

Big Three Exchange Rates

The remarkable instability of exchange rates among the major currencies is a perennial topic of concern and discussion. Movements in exchange rates among the big three—the United States, Europe, and Japan—can create difficulties for other countries, particularly for those that peg to one of those currencies. Thus the exports of east Asian countries were adversely affected by the appreciation of the dollar that began in 1995, and the strengthening of the dollar was also a factor in the difficulties faced by Argentina and Turkey in 2000.

There have been frequent proposals for target exchange rate zones among the dollar, the euro and the yen. If the target zones were to be narrow, monetary policy in each currency area would have to be dedicated to maintenance of the exchange rate commitment. There is no political support for a commitment to narrow target zones; it is not clear that monetary policy could maintain the desired exchange rate commitment; and there is not a persuasive case that the gains from maintaining a narrow commitment would be large. But given the extent of exchange rate movements among the major currencies, even wide target zones could be stabilizing.

In practice, something akin to such a system appears to operate, informally and loosely. When exchange rates get far out of line with fundamentals, two or three countries of the big three agree to intervene in the currency markets. This happened in mid-1995 when the yen-dollar exchange rate reached 80, implying a yen that was significantly appreciated relative to estimates of its equilibrium value, and in the fall of 2000, when the euro was significantly depreciated relative to its estimated equilibrium value.[16]

This informal system differs from a formal target zone system in three important ways. First, there are no preannounced target zones, and so no commitment to intervene at any particular level of exchange rates. This removes the possibility of one-way bets for speculators, but of course also removes the certainty about future exchange rates that a credible target zone system would provide—if such a system were possible. Second, the informal system operates more through coordinated interventions in the foreign exchange market than through coordinated monetary policy actions. While exchange rate movements may influence interest rates in the big three, both through their implications for inflation, and probably more directly in the cases of the Bank of Japan and the European Central Bank, coordinated interest rate changes with the sole purpose of affecting exchange rates do not appear to be on the current agenda. Third, such interventions are rare.

All of which is to say that the system is indeed informal and loose. Nonetheless it provides some bounds on the extent to which exchange rates among the United States, Europe and Japan are likely to diverge from equilibrium.

Exchange Rate Regimes for Other Countries

I have focused so far on exchange rate regimes for 55 developed and emerging market economies, which account for the bulk of global GDP, trade, and international capital flows. Figure 3 shows the distribution of exchange rate arrangements among the other members of the IMF as of end-1999 and end-1991, respectively. Table 3 groups these countries by their exchange rate regime at the end of 1999. The pattern is a familiar one: There has been a mild shift towards hard pegs on one side and a stronger shift to more flexible exchange rate regimes on the other.

These countries represented in Figure 3 are developing economies that are not classified as emerging market, which means that they typically have low per capita incomes. Many of them are also small economies and not very well integrated into the world economy. Such countries will display a wide range of situations and experiences, which makes it hard to make any definite recommendations on what exchange rate regimes would work best for countries in this group. In a review of exchange rate arrangements in these economies, Mussa et al. (2000, p. 31) state:

> Reflecting wide differences in levels of economic and financial development and in other aspects of their economic situations, no single exchange rate regime is most appropriate for all such countries, and the regime that is appropriate for a particular country may change over time.[17] Because of their limited involvement with modern global financial markets, some

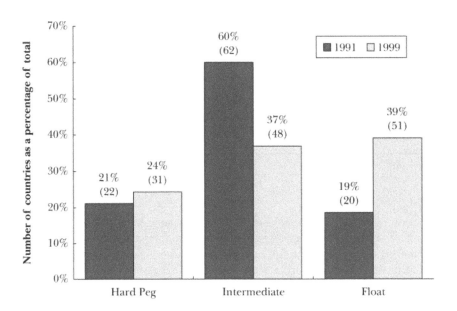

Figure 3 All Other Countries: Exchange Rate Regimes, 1991 and 1999. *Source:* IMF.
Note: The number of countries is in parenthesis.

Table 3 All Other Countries Grouped by Exchange Rate Arrangements *(as of December 31, 1999)*

Exchange Rate Regime (Number of countries)	Countries
No separate legal tender/Currency board (31)	Antigua and Barbuda, Benin, Bosnia and Herzegovina, Brunei Darussalam, Burkina Faso, Cameroon, Central African Rep., Chad, Congo (Rep. of), Côte d'Ivoire, Djibouti, Dominica, Equatorial Guinea, Estonia, Gabon, Grenada, Guinea-Bissau, Kiribati, Lithuania, Luxembourg, Mali, Marshall Islands, Micronesia, Niger, Palau, San Marino, Senegal, St. Kitts and Nevis, St. Lucia, St. Vincent and the Grenadines, Togo
Other fixed pegs (38)	Aruba, Bahamas, Bahrain, Bangladesh, Barbados, Belize, Bhutan, Botswana, Cape Verde, Comoros, El Salvador, Fiji, Iran, Iraq, Kuwait, Latvia, Lebanon, Lesotho, Macedonia FYR, Maldives, Malta, Myanmar, Namibia, Nepal, Netherlands Antilles, Oman, Samoa, Saudi Arabia, Seychelles, Solomon Islands, Swaziland, Syrian Arab Republic, Tonga, Trinidad and Tobago, Turkmenistan, United Arab Emirates, Vanuatu, Zimbabwe
Pegged rate in horizontal band (4)	Cyprus, Iceland, Libya, Vietnam
Crawling peg (4)	Bolivia, Costa Rica, Nicaragua, Tunisia
Rates within crawling bands (2)	Honduras, Uruguay
Managed float (23)	Algeria, Azerbaijan, Belarus, Burundi, Cambodia, Croatia, Dominican Rep., Ethiopia, Guatemala, Jamaica, Kenya, Kyrgyz Republic, Lao PDR, Malawi, Mauritania, Paraguay, Romania, Slovak Rep., Slovenia, Suriname, Tajikistan, Ukraine, Uzbekistan
Independent float (29)	Afghanistan, Albania, Angola, Armenia, Congo (Dem. Rep.), Eritrea, Gambia, Georgia, Ghana, Guinea, Guyana, Haiti, Kazakhstan, Liberia, Madagascar, Mauritius, Moldova, Mongolia, Mozambique, Papua New Guinea, Rwanda, São Tome and Príncipe, Sierra Leone, Somalia, Sudan, Tanzania, Uganda, Yemen, Zambia

Source: IMF, Annual Report 2000.

form of exchange rate peg or band or highly managed float is generally more viable and more appropriate for them than for most of the emerging market countries. Even this conclusion, however, leaves a wide range of possible regimes—for a diverse range of developing and transition countries.

They add: "IMF advice to members . . . reflects this ambiguity and diversity. Consistent with the Articles of Agreement, the IMF generally respects the member's choice of exchange rate regime and advises on policies needed to support that choice."

There is room for further research on the characteristics of exchange rate systems and accompanying financial sector structural policies most suited to particular types of countries that are not yet integrated into the global financial system, taking into account the likelihood that as the country develops, it will want to open up its capital account.

Summary and Conclusions

In the last decade, there has been a hollowing out of the middle of the distribution of exchange rate regimes in a bipolar direction, with the share of both hard pegs and floating gaining at the expense of soft pegs. This is true not only for economies active in international capital markets, but among all countries. A look ahead suggests this trend will continue, certainly among the emerging market countries. The main reason for this change, among countries with open capital accounts, is that soft pegs are crisis-prone and not viable over long periods.

A country's choice between a hard peg and floating depends in part on the characteristics of the economy, and in part on its inflationary history. The choice of a hard peg makes sense for countries with a long history of monetary instability, and/or for a country closely integrated in both its capital and current account transactions with another or a group of other economies. However, countries with a historical tradition of monetary stability, or no obvious subset of other countries with which to form a monetary union, or a belief that a flexible exchange rate helps their economy adjust to the sorts of macroeconomic shocks that it experiences, may be better off with a floating exchange rate.

As more countries adopt very hard exchange rate pegs of one sort or another, including dollarization and currency unions, there will in the future be fewer independent national currencies. Exchange rates among the remaining independent currencies will mostly be floating, and for all but the biggest countries, monetary policy—and occasionally exchange market intervention—will react to and sometimes seek to affect the nominal exchange rate.

In the medium term, as in recent years, as the center of the distribution of exchange rate regimes hollows out, the shift will likely be more towards the floating than the hard peg end of the spectrum. However, over the longer term, and depending on how well the euro area and dollarized economies operate, the trend could well be to move from the floating to the hard peg ends of the spectrum.

■ *This paper is an edited version of a lecture delivered to a joint session of the Society of Government Economists and the American Economic Association at the meetings of the Allied Social Science Associations in New Orleans, Louisiana, on January 6, 2001. I would like to thank Timothy Taylor for his excellent editing. I am grateful to my colleagues at the IMF for continuing discussion of these issues, and, in the preparation of this paper, particularly to Ratna Sahay and*

Grace Juhn for their assistance, Shogo Ishii, Barry Johnson, Nadia Malikyar, and Inci Otker for their work in classifying exchange rate regimes, and many other colleagues for further information regarding those classifications. Thanks, too, to Stanley Black, Olivier Blanchard, Robert Chote, Dan Citrin, Stijn Claessens, Brad De Long, David Goldsbrough, Taka Ito, Mohsin Khan, Louis Kuijs, Jaewoo Lee, Eduardo Levy-Yeyati, Paul Masson, Paolo Mauro, Sandy McKenzie, Jacques Polak, Dani Rodrik, Federico Sturzenegger, Gyorgy Szapary, Teresa Ter-Minassian, Michael Waldman, John Williamson, and Holger Wolf for their comments. Views expressed are those of the author, not necessarily of the International Monetary Fund.

Notes

1 Exchange rate regimes will be defined more precisely below: soft pegs are exchange rates that are currently fixed in value (or a narrow range of values) to some other currency or basket of currencies, with some commitment by the authorities to defend the peg, but with the value likely to change if the exchange rate comes under significant pressure. The adjustable peg exchange rates of the Bretton Woods regime were typically soft pegs.

2 Until recently the IMF's categorization of exchange rate regimes was based on self-descriptions by member countries, which are presented in the IMF's *Exchange Arrangements and Exchange Restrictions* (EAER) publication. The categorization used in this paper, taken from the *Annual Report 2000,* is based on the IMF staffs evaluation of the de facto arrangements actually in place, rather than what the authorities say the regime is. Several authors, including Ghosh et al. (1997) and Levy-Yeyati and Sturzenegger (2000), have wrestled with the difficulty that the authorities' own description of exchange rate regimes in *EAER* is patently inaccurate for some countries, and Levy-Yeyati and Sturzenegger have developed their own categorization, based on aspects of exchange rate and reserve variability. The staff of the IMF is currently developing data for earlier years on de facto exchange rate regimes corresponding to the information provided in the *Annual Report 2000.*

3 Classification of the exchange rate regime may be difficult in marginal cases; for instance, whether a very broad exchange rate band should be classified as a soft peg or a managed float.

4 The exchange rate classifications for 1991 used in Figure 1 were provided by the staff of the IMF, on the same basis as those for 1999—that is, using their judgment of the de facto exchange rate arrangements actually in place in member countries.

5 For analyses of exchange rate systems, see Mussa et al. (2000), Calvo and Reinhart (2000), Edwards (2000), Frankel (1999), Summers (2000), and Velasco (2000).

6 Several colleagues who commented on the first draft of this paper emphasized that monetary and exchange rate policy should not be regarded as separate, and that the key issue in choosing an exchange rate policy is the consistency of the overall macroeconomic policy framework. This perspective is of course correct, but for expositional reasons I focus more narrowly on the choice of exchange rate regime, taking it for granted that no exchange rate regime can be sustained if it is inconsistent with overall macroeconomic policy.

7 For further information on indexes from Morgan Stanley Capital International, see (http://www.msci.com). For a general discussion of EMBI+, which tracks total returns for traded external debt instruments in the emerging markets, see (http://www.jpmorgan.com/MarketDataInd/EMBI/embi.html). The MSCI list of developed market econ-

omies excludes six that are included in the IMF listing of "Advanced Economies": Greece, Iceland, Israel, Korea, Luxembourg, and Taiwan POC. Except for Iceland and Luxembourg, these are included in the emerging market economies listed in Table 1. The description of the exchange rate regime for Taiwan POC, which is not listed in the original source, is provided by the author.

8 Technically, the national currencies for the euro area countries are scheduled to continue as legal tender within each country until the first half of 2002.

9 Fischer and Sahay (2000) document a very similar pattern over time among the transition economies in the 1990s.

10 John Williamson (2000) offers an alternate argument for the movement away from soft pegs, suggesting that it is because of pressure from the IMF and U.S. Treasury.

11 I return to a closely related point below in discussing the potential use of capital controls.

12 This question is examined by Edwards (2000), Mussa et al. (2000) and Williamson (2000). For more detailed discussion of experience with capital controls, see Ariyoshi et al. (2000).

13 See Kaplan and Rodrik (2000) for a relatively positive appraisal of the Malaysian controls.

14 The argument is developed at greater length in Fischer (1998). The point has been much disputed, including by Jagdish Bhagwati (1998).

15 Cushman and Zha (1997) contain vector autoregressions from which the implied trade-off can be calculated in the Canadian case. See also Calvo, Reinhart and Végh (1995).

16 For the IMF's methodology for estimating equilibrium exchange rates, see Isard and Faruqee (1998). These estimates come with a wide confidence interval, but from time to time discrepancies between actual and estimated equilibrium exchange rates can be clearly identified. Several private sector financial institutions also estimate equilibrium exchange rates; see Edwards (2000) for discussion of the methodologies and the range of estimates provided by different sources.

17 At this point the authors note that this is the conclusion reached by Frankel (1999).

References

Ariyoshi, Akira, Karl Habermeier, Bernard Laurens, Inci Ötker-Robe, Jorge Iván Canales-Kriljenko and Andrei Kirilenko. 2000. *Capital Controls: Country Experiences with Their Use and Liberalization*, IMF Occasional Paper 190.

Bhagwati, Jagdish. 1998. "The Capital Myth." *Foreign Affairs.* May/June, 77:3, 7–12.

Broda, Christian. 2000. "Coping with Terms of Trade Shocks: Pegs vs. Floats," in Alberto Alesina and Robert Barro, eds. *Currency Unions*, forthcoming. Stanford: Hoover Institution Press.

Calvo, Guillermo A. 2000. "Capital Markets and the Exchange Rate, With Special Reference to the Dollarization Debate in Latin America," University of Maryland, April.

Calvo, Guillermo A. and Carmen M. Reinhart. 2000. "Fear of Floating," NBER Working Paper 7993, November.

Calvo, Guillermo A. and Carmen M. Reinhart. 2000. "Reflections on Dollarization," in Alberto Alesina and Robert Barro, eds. *Currency Unions*, forthcoming. Stanford: Hoover Institution Press.

Calvo, Guillermo A., Carmen M. Reinhart, and Carlos A. Végh. 1995. "Targeting the Real Exchange Rate: Theory and Evidence." *Journal of Development Economics*, 47, pp. 97–133.

Calvo, Guillermo A. and Carlos Végh. 1999. "Inflation Stabilization and BOP Crises in Developing Countries," NBER Working Paper 6925.

Chang, Roberto and Andres Velasco. 2000. "Exchange Rate Policy for Developing Countries." *American Economic Review, Papers and Proceedings.* May, 90:2, pp. 71–75.

Cushman, David O. and Tao Zha. 1997. "Identifying Monetary Policy in a Small Open Economy under Flexible Exchange Rates." *Journal of Monetary Economics.* 39, pp. 433–48.

Edwards, Sebastian. 1999. "How Effective are Capital Controls?" *Journal of Economic Perspectives.* Fall, 13:4, pp. 65–84.

Edwards, Sebastian. 2000. "Exchange Rate Regimes, Capital Flows and Crisis Prevention," NBER, December.

Eichengreen, Barry and Ricardo Hausmann. 1999. "Exchange Rates and Financial Fragility," NBER Working Paper 7418, November. 1998. *Exit Strategies: Policy Options for Countries Seeking Greater Exchange Rate Flexibility,* IMF Occasional Paper 168.

Fischer, Stanley. 1998. "Capital-Account Liberalization and the Role of the IMF," in *Should the IMF Pursue Capital-Account Convertibility?* Princeton University, International Finance Section, Essays in International Finance, May, 207, pp. 1–10.

Fischer, Stanley. 2000. "Ecuador and the IMF," in Alberto Alesina and Robert Barro, eds. *Currency Unions,* forthcoming. Stanford: Hoover Institution Press.

Fischer, Stanley and Ratna Sahay. 2000. "The Transition Economies After Ten Years," IMF Working Paper, WP/00/30, International Monetary Fund, Washington D.C., February.

Frankel, Jeffrey A. 1999. No Single Currency Regime is Right for All Countries or At All Times. Princeton University, International Finance Section, Essays in International Finance, August, 215.

Ghosh, Atish R., Anne-Marie Gulde, Jonathan D. Ostry and Holger C. Wolf. 1997. "Does the Nominal Exchange Rate Regime Matter?" NBER Working Paper 5874, January.

Ghosh, Atish R., Anne-Marie Gulde and Holger C. Wolf. 2000. "Currency Boards: More than a Quick Fix?" *Economic Policy.* October, 31, pp. 270–335.

Goodhart, Charles and Dirk Schoenmaker. 1995. "Should the Functions of Monetary Policy and Bank Supervisor be Separated?" *Oxford Economic Papers.* 47, pp. 539–60.

Hanke, Steve H. and Kurt Schuler. 1994. *Currency Boards for Developing Countries.* International Center for Economic Growth. San Francisco: ICS Press.

Hausmann, Ricardo, Michael Gavin, Carmen Pages-Serra and Ernesto Stein. 1999. "Financial Turmoil and the Choice of Exchange Rate Regime." Inter-American Development Bank, Working Paper 400.

International Monetary Stability Act of 2000. 106th Congress, 2nd Session, S. 2101.

Isard, Peter and Hamid Faruqee, eds. 1998. Exchange Rate Assessment: Extensions of the Macroeconomic Balance Approach, IMF Occasional Paper 167.

Kaplan, Ethan and Dani Rodrik. 2000. "Did the Malaysian Capital Controls Work?" Kennedy School of Government, December.

Kenen, Peter. 2000. "Currency Areas, Policy Domains, and the Institutionalization of Fixed Exchange Rates." Princeton University, April.

Levy-Yeyati, Eduardo and Federico Sturzenegger. 2000. "Exchange Rate Regimes and Economic Performance," paper presented at IMF First Annual Research Conference, November.

Mussa, Michael, Paul Masson, Alexander Swo-boda, Esteban Jadresic, Paolo Mauro and Andrew Berg. 2000. *Exchange Rate Regimes in an Increasingly Integrated World Economy*, IMF Occasional Paper 193.

Obstfeld, Maurice and Kenneth Rogoff. 1995. "The Mirage of Fixed Exchange Rates." *Journal of Economic Perspectives.* Fall, 9:4, pp. 73–96.

Summers, Lawrence H. 2000. "International Financial Crises: Causes, Prevention, and Cures." *American Economic Review, Papers and Proceedings.* May, 90:2, pp. 1–16.

Velasco, Andres. 2000. "Exchange Rates in Emerging Markets: Floating Toward the Future," Egyptian Center for Economic Studies, Cairo, Working Paper 46, November.

Williamson, John. 2000. Exchange Rate Regimes for Emerging Markets: Reviving the Intermediate Option. Washington, D.C.: Institute for International Economics, September.

23

FINANCING vs. FORGIVING A DEBT OVERHANG

Paul Krugman

Source: *Journal of Development Economics* 29, 3, 1998, 253–268.

This paper examines the tradeoffs facing creditors of a country whose debt is large enough that the country cannot attract voluntary new lending. If the country is unable to meet its debt service requirements out of current income, the creditors have two choices. They can *finance* the country, lending at an expected loss in the hope that the country will eventually be able to repay its debt after all; or they can *forgive,* reducing the debt level to one that the country can repay. The post-1983 debt strategy of the IMF and the US has relied on financing, but many current calls for debt reform call for forgiveness instead. The paper shows that the choice between financing and forgiveness represents a tradeoff. Financing gives the creditors an option value: if the country turns out to do relatively well, creditors will not have written down their claims unnecessarily. However, the burden of debt distorts the country's incentives, since the benefits of good performance go largely to creditors rather than itself. The paper also shows that the tradeoff itself can be improved if both financing and forgiveness are made contingent on states of nature that the country cannot affect, such as oil prices, world interest rates, etc.

1 Introduction

Discussion of new approaches to the developing country debt problem is more intense now than at any time since 1983. Some proposals, such as the Baker initiative, involve revitalization and continuation of the 1983 strategy of financing without either debt forgiveness or change in the nature of claims. Other proposals, such as the Bradley Plan, call for major debt forgiveness in an effort to clear the books and restore normal conditions. In between are a variety of proposals for changing the character of the relations between debtors and creditors, including interest capitalization, lending or debt relief contingent on world prices, conversion of debt into equity or equity-like claims, and so on.

Somewhat surprisingly, this practical discussion is taking place with little parallel analytical discussion among economists. While there is a fairly substantial theoretical literature on the problem of sovereign risk [surveyed by Eaton et al. (1986)], the bulk of this literature has focussed either on the case of creditor rationing of a country that is borrowing with no existing debt, or the choice by a country whether to repay or default. The position in the real world, however, is one of both repayment and new borrowing; countries have arrived in the current situation with a stock of 'inherited' debt, which they cannot fully service without new borrowing. If the countries' future repayment were not in doubt, they would have no difficulty in borrowing to service existing debt, but for a group of large debtors doubt about future repayment is sufficient that only through extraordinary measures have creditors been induced to provide new money.

Now there does exist a small theoretical literature that bears on the actual debt problem fairly closely. This is the literature on the problems posed by a debt *overhang*. By a debt overhang I mean the presence of an existing, 'inherited' debt sufficiently large that creditors do not expect with confidence to be fully repaid. The effects of such a debt overhang have been analyzed in only a few papers, including Sachs (1984, 1986) and Krugman (1985a,b). These papers have shown that the presence of a debt overhang may give creditors an incentive to lend at an expected loss to protect their existing claims [Sachs (1984), Krugman (1985a,b)]. It also shows that there may be a conflict between creditors' individual and collective interest, and that free rider problems may compromise the ability to achieve desirable new lending. On the other hand, the incentives of a debtor may be distorted by the presence of a debt overhang, and the distortion will be reduced if creditors provide immediate debt forgiveness rather than providing new money and hoping for more favorable future conditions [Sachs (1986)]. The debt overhang approach is highly suggestive of the desirability of innovative approaches to the provision of funds, and perhaps of changes in the nature of bank claims on developing countries.

The purpose of this paper is to provide a synthetic presentation of the debt overhang analysis that, although abstract, may help clarify ideas for practical discussion. Section 2 sketches out three examples that are intended to convey some of the key issues. Section 3 presents a more formal model that focusses on the tradeoff between new lending and debt forgiveness as ways of coping with a debt overhang. Section 4 then examines how changing the nature of claims might help resolution of a debt overhang.

2 The debt overhang problem: Some illustrative examples

A debtor country is something like a debtor firm, although the parallel is not exact. At any given time, the creditors of a firm view that firm as having a probability distribution over streams of future earnings, out of which debt service can be paid. If the present value of the stream of earnings is expected to be less than the firm's debt, then creditors will not expect to be fully repaid – although they may prefer to wait and see rather than force the firm immediately into bankruptcy proceedings.

A country, like a firm, has an expected stream of earnings, but not all of this stream is potentially available to service debt. Instead, some fraction of national income represents the maximum resource transfer that the country can be induced to make. Loosely, we can think of the expected stream of potential resource transfers from a country to its creditors as analogous to the expected stream of earnings of a firm.

Now the analogy is less than exact, because the potential resource transfer from a country to its creditors is not really a fixed number. Instead, the maximum level of resource transfer is determined ultimately by the country's willingness to pay, which in turn reflects both rational calculations of the cost of default and internal political considerations. There is a bargaining problem between creditors, who would like to get the most possible out of a country, and the country, which would like to minimize resource transfer. Some progress has been made on the bargaining issue, for example by Bulow and Rogoff (1986). However, it is useful for analytical purposes to put this bargaining issue aside, and imagine that the rate of resource transfer that is possible at any point in time is a well-defined number (although perhaps uncertain ex ante).

If we grant ourselves the enormous simplification of taking maximum resource transfer as given, we are left with a straightforward definition of the problem of debt overhang. *A country has a debt overhang problem when the expected present value of potential future resource transfers is less than its debt.*

To illustrate the implications of debt overhang, I will consider three highly stylized examples of the problems that such overhang can cause. The three examples share a common structure, in which the action takes two periods. In the first period a country starts with an inherited debt, all of which (for simplicity) is due during that period. The country attempts to pay that debt with resource transfer plus new borrowing. The new borrowing, in turn, must be repaid with resource transfer in the second period.

What happens if a country is unable to repay fully at the end? For the moment, I will ignore the problem of costs of default and assume that creditors simply share the maximum resource transfer the country can make. Thus if the country is unable to repay fully in the second period, the result is effectively that part of the debt is forgiven. This shifts the emphasis to the first period. The key question is whether the country will experience a liquidity crisis. Will the country be able to attract new borrowing in order to service its inherited debt? This depends on the behavior of lenders. I will assume that lenders are risk neutral, and face a given opportunity cost of funds on world markets. An important question is whether creditors are purely competitive or can operate collusively in their joint interest. We will consider both cases.

2.1 Debt overhang without uncertainty

Consider first the situation where there is no uncertainty, i.e., the potential resource transfers in periods 1 and 2 are known from the beginning. We assume that all of the debt comes due in period 1, with required debt repayment D; the resource transfer possible in each period is x_1, x_2. We let i be the opportunity cost of funds to lenders.

Does this country have a liquidity problem? The country can make repayment of debt equal to x_1 out of current resources; if current debt service exceeds this amount, it must engage in new borrowing equal to $D - x_1$. Lenders will supply this voluntarily at their opportunity cost i if they believe that they will be fully repaid, as they indeed they will provided that $(1+i)(D-x)_1 < x_2$, or, equivalently, if $x_1 + x_2 / (1+i) > D$. Not surprisingly, there will be no problem of liquidity if the present value of potential resource transfer exceeds the inherited debt.

Suppose on the other hand that $x_1 + x_2 / (1+i) < D$. Then the country will not be able to meet its debt service. It certainly cannot borrow the needed resources $D - x_1$ at the safe rate, since it will be seen to be unable to repay its loans in full. Nor can it attract additional lending by offering an interest rate above the safe rate. The total resources available for debt repayment in period 2 are x_2, with a present value of $x_2 / (1+i)$. Regardless of the interest rate on period 1 loans, that is what creditors will get, and it is less than the value of the necessary loans.

Thus the best that the initial creditors can do is reach a settlement with the country that immediately reduces the country's obligations. The mechanics of the settlement are, at this level of abstraction, arbitrary. Any combination of rescheduling, forgiveness of principal, forgiveness of interest, and new lending at concessional rates will do as long as it brings the actual resource transfer in line with what is possible.

In the absence of uncertainty, then, the problem of what to do about debt overhang would be straightforward. If the country can pay, there will be no liquidity problem. If it cannot, the debt must be written down at the outset.

2.2 Debt overhang with uncertainty

Now consider a country that similarly has inherited a debt D, but faces an uncertain future. Either because the world economic environment is uncertain, or because the country's own economic performance cannot be predicted, the potential resource transfer in period 2 is a random variable. To keep things simple, we suppose that first-period resource transfer is a known value x_1, while in the second period the maximum transfer will take on only one of two values, x_G (good case) or x_B (bad case). In the bad case, the present value of potential resource transfer will be less than the initial debt, while in the good case it may be possible that the debt can be repaid.

Is this country solvent? This is not a well-defined question. Unless the present value of resource transfer is less than the debt in both states, it is simply unknown whether the country can earn enough to repay its debt. However, we can ask whether the country will have a liquidity problem, and here there is a straightforward answer: it will be able to borrow to service its debt if and only if the *expected* present value of the resource transfer is at least as great as the debt.

To see this, let p be the probability of a good outcome, $1 - p$ be the probability of a bad outcome. What we want to ask is whether there is an interest rate that the country can offer that will induce lenders to supply the resources $L = D - x_1$ that are necessary to allow debt service. Suppose that the country offers an interest rate r on its new borrowing such that $L(1+r) = x_G$. This is the highest interest rate that makes sense, since the country cannot even in the best case pay more than this. Then lenders will receive all of the potential resource transfer in either state. The expected present value of their receipts will be $[px_G + (1-p)x_B]/(1+i)$. They will be induced to lend if this exceeds the necessary lending $D - x_1$. But the condition $[px_G + (1-p)x_B]/(1+i) > D - x_1$ is simply the condition that the expected present value of resource transfer exceed the value of the inherited debt.

As long as this criterion is satisfied, the country will be able to borrow enough to service its debt simply by paying a sufficiently high interest premium. If it is not satisfied, the country will not be able to attract voluntary borrowing, and will thus be unable to service its debt.

Now if that were that, we would simply see a default whenever financial markets view a country as having less future ability to pay than its existing debt. However, it is in the interest of existing creditors to prevent this. Even without any explicit modelling of how a liquidity crisis is played out, it seems obvious that the creditors are not likely to collect the full potential resource transfer from the country if there is a disorderly default. Let Z be the present value of what creditors expect to be able to collect from a country if there is a liquidity crisis in period 1; it seems safe to assume that $Z < x_1 + [px_G + (1-p)x_B]/(1+i) < D$. Yet it is not necessary that creditors accept the certainty of loss. Suppose that they are able to relend enough to the debtor to avert default in period 1, and postpone the reckoning until period 2. Then, if they are lucky, they may receive full repayment after all; while if they are unlucky, they will still be better off than if they had allowed a default to take place immediately.

We can easily construct a strategy that will achieve this aim. Let the existing creditors relend the country $L = D - x_1$ at an interest rate such that $L(1+r) = x_G$. Then the creditors will receive all of the potential second-period resource transfer in either state. Viewed in isolation, this will still be a losing proposition: the expected present value of their receipts will be $[px_G + (1-p)x_B]/(1+i) < L$. Thus no lender would voluntarily enter the package if she had no stake in the repayment of the original debt. From the point of view of the initial creditors, however, a lending package insures that they receive the full present value of the country's potential resource transfer, which is more than they would get without the lending. Thus lending that would be unprofitable viewed in isolation is worth doing as a way of defending the value of existing debt.

There are several points worth noting about this kind of defensive lending scenario, since even this simple an example is enough to show that several commonly held beliefs about debt problems are incorrect.

First, much discussion about the debt problem tries to make a clear distinction between liquidity and solvency, with the argument being that new lending to cover debt service is appropriate for liquidity but not for solvency problems. Even this simple schematic approach makes clear, however, that the distinction is not useful. If we knew that the country could repay the full present value of its debt – or even if the expected value of potential payments were large enough – the country could attract voluntary lending by offering a sufficiently high interest premium. The inability to attract funds comes because the expected ability to pay is too low; a liquidity crisis must occur because of doubts about solvency. As we have just seen, however, the expectation of insolvency does not prevent new lending from being in the interest of existing creditors.

Second, some commentators have pointed to the large discounts at which developing country debt sells on secondary markets as evidence that further lending is inappropriate. Clearly in this model new lending to the debtor would immediately sell at a discount, since it has an expected present value less than the value of the lending. The discount is just another aspect of the fact that the new lending is unprofitable viewed in isolation. The point is, however, that it is still worth doing because it does not take place in isolation; it is essential to the repayment of existing debt.

Third, we have seen that it is in the interests of existing creditors to relend enough to avoid an immediate default on the part of the country. However, it is only in their *collective* interest. Any *individual* creditor would be better off if it could opt out of the new lending and let other creditors carry the burden. Thus we have the free rider problem emphasized by Cline (1983) and many others. This free rider problem could lead to a liquidity crisis even though this is not in anyone's interest.

Fourth, we often ask whether or not the new lending that takes place to debtors is at concessionary terms or not. The standard usually used is a comparison with market interest rates. However, the example makes it clear that the market rate comparison is essentially irrelevant. From the point of view of the lenders, the loans yield an expected return less than the market rate, whatever the face interest rate; thus they will view this as lending at concessional terms. Whether the interest rate on the loan is more or less than their opportunity cost of funds depends on how favorable the good state is. The interest they charge is defined by the relationship $L(1+r)=x_G$. The rate r will exceed i if $x_G/(1+i)>D-x_1$, be less than i if $x_G/(1+i)<D-x_1$, that is, on whether even in the good state the present value of resource transfer exceeds the opportunity cost of funds.

This last observation raises a puzzle. The example suggests that if there is *any* state in which the present value of resource transfer exceeds the value of existing debt, the interest rate charged by creditors on new lending should exceed their opportunity cost of funds. Presumably for most debtors there is at least the possibility of such a favorable state; even Bolivia might discover a valuable, unsuspected natural resource. Yet this description of creditor behavior seems both wrong in practice and disturbing; isn't there any circumstance under which new lending (or rescheduling of existing debt) will take place at concessional rates? To develop any motivation for debt forgiveness, we need to have an example in which creditors have to be concerned about the incentives they give the debtor.

2.3 Incentive effects

In the last example, creditors have an incentive to lend to the debtor, even at an expected loss, as a way to defend the value of their existing claims. However, their incentive is to lend at the highest interest rate that could be paid, even in the most favorable state of nature; only in this way can they ensure that they collect the maximum resource transfer from the country. In effect, while the creditors are taking an expected loss, they will have an incentive to provide financial relief to the country entirely through new money rather than through interest rate reduction. Indeed, as long as there is any state of nature in which the present value of resource transfer exceeds the value of inherited debt, the creditors will charge an interest rate that is higher than their opportunity cost of funds.

In order to soften this result, we need to take into consideration the effect of the debt burden on the incentives facing the debtor. In the real world there are a variety of actions that debtors can take which affect their future ability to make resource transfers: exchange rate adjustment, investment, budget policies, and so on. Let us summarize these policies under the vague heading of 'adjustment effort'. Then creditors will want a country to make as much adjustment effort as possible, certainly more than the country would like to undertake. Now suppose that the debt burden on a country is as large as the maximum that the country could possibly pay, even with maximum adjustment effort. Then there is in fact no reason for the country to make the adjustment effort, since the reward goes only to its creditors. It makes sense, therefore, for the creditors to demand less than this maximum, in order to provide the creditor with some incentive to adjust.

For our third example, we consider the extreme case where the potential resource transfer depends only on the action of the debtor, and not at all on the state of nature [this is the case considered by Sachs (1986)]. In period 1, as always, there is a debt service requirement D and a known maximum resource transfer x_1. Creditors thus must lend $D-x_1$ to prevent a liquidity crisis. In the second period, however, the potential resource transfer depends on the adjustment effort. If the adjustment effort is high, maximum resource transfer is x_H; if it is low, x_L. Other things equal, the debtor would prefer to make the lower adjustment effort.

The maximum interest rate that could conceivably be paid is defined by $L(1+r)=x_H$. If the creditors charge this interest rate, however, the debtor will have no incentive to make the high adjustment effort. It may thus be in the interest of creditors to charge an interest rate sufficiently low that the debtor make the higher adjustment effort. If there is a liquidity problem, and no uncertainty, the optimal interest rate in the absence of uncertainty must be one that is below the market rate i.

Several observations follow from this example. First, we note that charging an interest rate that is below the maximum resource transfer and below the market rate is actually in the interest of the creditors. If we compare the value of their claims with the optimal interest rate with the value with a higher interest rate, we will find that reducing the face value of loans actually raises their market value.

Second, this example suggests both the motivation for conditionality and the problems of enforcing it. The creditors would like to impose a requirement for high adjustment as a condition for the loan – in which case the interest rate could be higher. On the other hand, the threat not to lend if the country fails to act correctly may be hard to establish credibly, since it remains in the interest of the creditors to avoid provoking a liquidity crisis.

Third, while debt forgiveness may be desirable from the point of view of creditors as a way of creating incentives, it is clearly a blunt instrument for this purpose. The example immediately suggests that loans are the wrong form of claim; some form of contingent claim would be preferable. (The specification of the optimal claim is left to the more elaborate discussion below.)

We have now gone about as far as we can with simple examples. In order to integrate the insights from these examples, we now turn to a formal model.

3 A formal model of debt overhang

As in the simplified examples, we consider a country that has inherited a stock of debt D, all of it due in the first of two periods. In period 1 the country can make a known maximum resource transfer x_1. In period 2 the country's resource transfer potential is unknown, so that

$$x_2 = s + z, \tag{1}$$

where s is a random variable that ranges from $\underline{s}$ to $\bar{s}$ and z is a choice variable capturing the concept of 'adjustment effort' by the debtor country.

The country is assumed to care about two things: the level of resources left to it in the second period, and the size of the adjustment effort it is required to make. Let C_2 be the difference between the country's potential resource transfer x_2 and the actual payment it must make to creditors:

$$C_z = x_2 - P. \tag{2}$$

For simplicity, and to avoid mixing insurance issues into our analysis, the country's objective function will be assumed linear in C:

$$U = C_2 - v(z), \quad v' > 0, \quad v'' > 0, \tag{3}$$

where the function $v(z)$ captures the dislike of the country for making adjustments that enlarge its future ability to pay creditors.

Suppose that the creditors are able to overcome the free rider problems we mentioned in the previous section and lend enough to avert default in the first period. Then it follows that first-period lending will be equal to the difference between maximum potential debt service and the value of the debt,

$$L = D - x_1. \tag{4}$$

Suppose that the creditors have charged an interest rate r on their new lending. If potential resource transfer exceeds $L(1+r)$, the loan will be repaid in full. If it does not, we assume that the creditors will receive the maximum possible, so that

$$
\begin{aligned}
P &= x_2 && \text{if} \quad x_2 < L(1+r) \\
&= L(1+r) && \text{if} \quad x_2 > L(1+r).
\end{aligned} \tag{5}
$$

We can now think of this as a game in which the creditors first choose the interest rate, then the debtor chooses the level of adjustment effort. To solve this game, we first solve the debtor's problem conditional on the interest rate. From (3) and (5) we derive the expected utility of the country:

$$\text{EU} = \int_{L(1+r)-Z}^{\bar{s}} \left[(s+z) - L(1+r)\right] f(s)\,ds - v(z), \tag{6}$$

An increase in the adjustment effort z raises the resources of the country in favorable states when it does not have to pay all of its potential resource transfer to the creditors, but is costly in and of itself:

$$\frac{\partial EU}{\partial z} = \int_{L(1+r)-z}^{\bar{s}} f(s)\,ds - v'(z). \tag{7}$$

If the effort level has an interior maximum. we must have $\partial EU / \partial z = 0$ and $\partial^2 EU / \partial z^2 < 0$, where

$$\partial^2 EU / \partial z^2 = f\left[L(1+r) - z\right] - v''(z). \tag{8}$$

We now want to calculate the response of adjustment effort to the interest rate charged by creditors. To do this we first calculate the cross-derivative

$$\partial^2 EU / \partial z \partial r = -L\left[L(1+r) - z\right] < 0. \tag{9}$$

Then we use the implicit function theorem to derive the response

$$dz/dr = Lf\left[L(1+r) - z\right] / \left(\partial^2 EU / \partial z^2\right) < 0. \tag{10}$$

Thus the higher the interest rate, the lower the country's adjustment effort.

The objective of the creditors is to maximize the expected value of their new lending. From (5)

$$ER = \int_{\underline{s}}^{L(1+r)-z} (s+z)f(s)\,ds + L(1+r) = \int_{L(1+r)-z}^{\bar{s}} f(s)\,ds \qquad (11)$$

The creditors' first-order condition is therefore

$$\partial ER/\partial r = L \int_{L(1+r)-z}^{\bar{s}} f(s)\,ds + (dz/dr) \int_{\underline{s}}^{L(1+r)-z} f(s)\,ds = 0 \qquad (12)$$

This condition clearly indicates the two motives facing the creditors. The first term, which is always positive, is the 'new-money' bias imparted by the presence of uncertainty. Since something may always turn up that allows the debtor to pay more than you expected, creditors have an incentive to roll over debt at as high an interest rate as possible in order to be able to benefit from good news. The second term, which is always negative, represents the 'debt forgiveness' bias imparted by the problem of incentives for the debtor. Creditors do not want to make the country's situation too hopeless, or it will have no incentive to improve its ability to repay.

If the situation were dominated only by one or the other consideration, the choice between new money and debt forgiveness would be clear. If uncertainty were the only issue, it would always be best for creditors to finance but not forgive, so as to preserve the option of cashing in on unexpected good fortune. If incentives were the only issue, it would on the contrary be best for creditors to take their loss up front so that it does not act as a prohibitive tax on debtors' effort. Unfortunately, in reality both issues are present, so that the choice of the right strategy is not an easy one.

The dilemma presented by this tradeoff, however, is not inescapable. It is due to the fact that both new money and debt forgiveness are rather blunt instruments for dealing with the problem of debt overhang. Can an innovative repayment scheme, one that effectively changes the nature of claims, do better? In principle, at least, it can.

4 Changing the nature of claims

A number of proposals have been advanced for converting debt into some other kind of claim. The proposals range from piecemeal debt-equity conversions, to Bailey's (1982) proposal to convert debt to proportional claims on exports, to proposals that either interest rates or new lending be indexed automatically to prices of exports. The approach taken in this paper cannot do justice to the details of such schemes, since it treats the real economy as a 'black box' out of which resources are somehow extracted. Nonetheless, it is possible to capture some of the spirit of innovative proposals by considering schemes in which the required repayment depends on the size of the potential resource transfer.

We may divide proposals to change the nature of claims into two broad classes. First are schemes that link repayment to some general measure of ability to repay. The best-known examples are proposals that debt repayment be proportional to export revenues. The key point about these schemes is that they make no distinction between favorable results due to national effort and those due to factors outside the nation's control. On the other side are proposals to link repayment to some measure of the shocks experienced by a country, such as the level of world interest rates or the price of the country's principal export good. These two kinds of proposal are quite different at least in principle.

There is a further distinction within these proposals between debt postponement and debt forgiveness. Most proposals that link repayment either to ability to pay or to the state of nature do not, at least on paper, reduce the *eventual* obligation of a country to pay: the obligation is simply rescheduled, at market interest rates, into the future. However, it will be easier analytically to imagine that what is at stake is immediate debt forgiveness. We can then ask whether debt postponement is similar in its implications.

4.1 Repayment linked to ability to repay

Suppose that we have a country exactly like that described in the previous section, but that its creditors take an innovative approach to its problem. Instead of lending it the money needed to service its debt, they establish a claim that varies with the ability to repay. We can approximate such a scheme by supposing that repayment is a function of second-period potential resource transfer:

$$P = A + Bx_2, \quad 0 < B < 1. \tag{13}$$

Does such a scheme resolve creditors' conflict between taking advantage of good news and providing debtors with an incentive to adjust? Unfortunately, it does not. Consider the first-order condition of the debtor. Given the repayment schedule, the difference between potential and actual resource transfer will be

$$C_2 = -A + (1 - B)x_2. \tag{14}$$

Thus the debtor will maximize

$$EU = \int_{\underline{s}}^{\bar{s}} \left[-A + (1 - B)(s + z) \right] f(s)\, ds - v(z) \tag{15}$$

with the first-order condition

$$\partial EU/\partial z = (1-B) - v'(z) = 0. \tag{16}$$

This condition may be interpreted as follows: the country receives only a fraction $(1 - B)$ of the benefit from any improvement in its resource transfer capacity. There is a tradeoff in substituting a claim contingent on ability to repay for a simple loan: it is no longer the case that in bad states of nature extra adjustment effort provides no benefit to the debtor, but the benefit it receives in good states is diluted. It is unclear without a detailed model of the economy which will distort incentives more.

This analysis shows that proposals to link repayment to exports or other measures of capacity to repay do not eliminate the problem of incentives, and therefore do not eliminate the tradeoff between new money and debt forgiveness. Notice, however, that while this is the only issue that can be addressed in the stylized framework presented here, in practice exchange participation notes or other schemes might still be valuable for other reasons, for example as a way to allow debt service to rise over time in line with economic growth and inflation.

4.2 Payment linked to the state of nature

The alternative class of proposal would link repayment to some measure of the state of nature. An ideal measure would separate perfectly between the consequences of the country's effort and events outside its control; it is easiest to concentrate our formal analysis on this case, then discuss how the imperfection of real measures affects the argument.

In the context of our formal model, the form of an optimal scheme is obvious: it would appropriate all of the gains that result from the state of nature s, but none of the consequences of the effort level z:

$$P = A + s. \tag{17}$$

The resulting first-order condition will be

$$\partial EU/\partial z = 1 - v'(z) = 0. \tag{18}$$

Thus the distortion in the country's incentive to adjust is completely eliminated.

For the creditors, the degree of freedom in the scheme would be in setting the constant term A. At first glance, it might seem that the creditors could set A equal to the optimal z, so that they would provide the debtor with a marginal incentive to adjust yet in the end capture all of the debtor's potential resource transfer by the debtor. This may look too clever to be real, and it is. In addition to satisfying the *marginal* condition (18), the debtor's choice of adjustment effort must be *globally* optimal. If there is no gain from adjusting, the debtor will be better off choosing its own preferred level of effort and simply defaulting on the payment scheme (17). Thus the expected resource transfer that can be extracted from the country will be limited by the need to provide enough incentive for the country to participate in the debt initiative. This constraint is not, however, unique to state-contingent schemes. The only unique feature is that a perfect state-contingent scheme would extract from the country less than its maximum resource transfer in *all* states of nature, even the least favorable.

It is clear from the analysis that an ideal state-contingent scheme should be able to do better than either a simple loan that will probably not be repaid in full or a claim linked to broad ability to repay. In reality, of course, a scheme will be less than ideal, if only because the state of nature cannot be fully specified. For example, repayment might be linked to the price of the country's principal export, but shocks arising from weather fluctuations might not be included. What this imperfection will do is to blur the effectiveness of the state-contingency in eliminating incentive problems. There will be some states of nature in which the country will be unable to meet its obligations, even though these will in principle be indexed to the state of nature. At the margin, an improvement in the country's ability to pay will in these states of nature benefit only the creditors, not the country; thus the country's incentive to adjust will be diluted. Clearly, however, the dilution will be less if the obligations at least somewhat reflect the state of nature than if they do not. So an imperfect state-contingent claim is still better than a claim that is not state-contingent at all.

4.3 Debt postponement

So far we have discussed only schemes that link debt forgiveness to either ability to pay or the state of nature. However, the more immediate issue is one of proposals to link new money to export revenues or export prices. Is this something completely different, or is the analysis similar?

The essential point here is that once we are in a situation of defensive lending by existing creditors, the creditors do not expect to be fully repaid – nor do the debtors expect to pay fully. Thus new money contains a concessional element, even if it does not do so on paper. As a result, the same considerations that apply to eventual forgiveness also apply to new money.

Consider an extension of our basic model to *three* periods. In period 1 the country makes a decision about adjustment effort, which affects maximum resource transfer in period 2; ability to repay in period 3 is also uncertain. Then any relief from the burden of resource transfer in period 2 will not be fully offset by an increase in the expected burden in period 3. It follows that the incentive to adjust initially will depend on the conditions attached to new money in period 2. If creditors will demand the maximum possible resource transfer regardless of the state of nature, there will be no incentive to adjust. If, on the contrary, new lending is linked to the state of nature, so that adjustment effort at the margin benefits the country rather than the creditors, the incentive to adjust will be greater.

Although the analysis is highly abstract, then, we seem to be left with a clear conclusion: linking either eventual repayment or new money to measures of the state of nature is a good idea.

5 Concluding remarks

This paper has presented a highly abstract analysis of the issues involved in dealing with the developing country debt problem. I have argued that the best way to think about that problem is as one of *debt overhang:* the 'inherited debt' of some countries is larger than the present value of the resource transfer that their creditors expect them to make in the future.

Much popular discussion seems to presume that the appropriate handling of a debt problem is simply contingent on the distinction between liquidity and solvency. If it is a liquidity problem, financing should be provided until the country has worked its way out; if it is a solvency problem, some kind of bankruptcy procedure is called for. What even a highly abstract analysis of the debt overhang problem shows is that this is a misleading way to view the issue. There is no such thing as a pure liquidity problem; it must arise because of doubts about solvency. Even if there is a significant possibility that debt will not be repaid in full, however, it may still be in creditors' interest to provide enough financing to avert an immediate default. As is fairly widely appreciated, however, there is a conflict between the collective interest of creditors in providing financing and the individual interest of each creditor in getting out.

The choice between financing and debt forgiveness should not, according to the analysis presented here, hinge on some attempt to settle the liquidity vs. solvency question. Instead, it represents a tradeoff between the option value of a large nominal debt and the incentive effects of a debt that is unlikely to be repaid. Since good news is always possible, creditors would like to keep their claims high, so that if by some chance a country should turn out to be able to repay, they will not turn out to have forgiven debt unnecessarily. On the other hand, if a country is not going to be able to repay except in exceptional circumstances, it will have little incentive to try to adjust. Thus creditors may wish to forgive part of a country's debt to increase the likelihood that it will repay what remains. It is because of the tension between these two objectives that the issue of how much to rely on debt forgiveness and how much to rely on financing is a difficult one.

There seems to be a compelling case that the tradeoff between forgiveness and financing can be improved by indexing repayment to the state of nature. If payment is linked to some measure of conditions outside the country's control, the probability for any given expected payment that adjustment effort will at the margin benefit the country, not its creditors, will be increased. Thus the analysis in this paper, abstract though it is, does suggest that linking new money and possibly debt relief to measures of economic conditions could be to the mutual benefit of debtors and their creditors.

References

Bailey, N., 1983, A safety net for foreign lending, Business Week, January 10.

Bulow, J. and K. Rogoff, 1986, A constant recontracting model of sovereign debt, Mimeo (Stanford University, Stanford, CA).

Cline, W, 1983, International debt and the stability of the world economy (Institute for International Economics, Washington, DC).

Eaton, J., M. Gersovitz and J. Stiglitz, 1986, The pure theory of country risk, European Economic Review 30, no. 3, 481–513.

Krugman, P., 1985a, International debt strategies in an uncertain world, in: J. Cuddington and G. Smith, eds., International debt and the developing countries (World Bank, Washington, DC).

Krugman, P., 1985b, Prospects for international debt reform, in: UNCTAD, International monetary and financial issues for the developing countries (UNCTAD, Geneva).

Sachs, J., 1984, Theoretical issues in international borrowing, Princeton Studies in International Finance 54.

Sachs, J., 1986, The debt overhang problem of developing countries, Paper presented at the conference in memorial to Carlos Diaz-Alejandro, Helsinki, August 1986.

24

SEQUENCING OF ECONOMIC REFORMS IN THE PRESENCE OF POLITICAL CONSTRAINTS

César Martinelli and Mariano Tommasi

Source: *Economics and Politics* 9, 2, 1997, 115–131.

This paper presents a model portraying a country in a political deadlock about economic reform proposals in which certain measures hurt strongly organized interests. We show that when governments are unable to precommit and interest groups have veto power, only far-reaching reforms (even if quite costly) have hope of success. The model intends to explain why in recent years several Latin American countries have opted for radical reform.

1 Introduction

Several economists[1] have argued for sequencing market-oriented reforms, such as macroeconomic stabilization and trade liberalization, in a particular order. Several countries, mostly in Latin America, have apparently ignored this advice and implemented all types of reform simultaneously. As a result, these countries have endured high unemployment as well as balance of payment problems.[2]

An explanation for the apparent failure to follow the prevailing economic advice could be that policymakers doubted its accuracy and therefore felt little obligation to follow it. In this paper we explore an alternative explanation: policymakers may have faced political constraints that made big-bang reforms the best (and in some cases the only) *feasible* strategy.[3]

The argument is based on the distributive consequences of reform. By widening the scope of efficiency improving reforms, the government is more likely to gain the support of larger segments of the population if the losers of each particular measure benefit from other measures. If the government needs to pass a threshold of popular support at each step, a gradual process risks being stopped at each stage by the group being hurt at that point. Hence, the government may need to implement all reforms simultaneously even if this entails some aggregate costs. That is, the gradual introduction of reforms in some specific order can be

225

time-inconsistent even if it is optimal from an economic point of view. Notice that we assume that there is an economic case for gradual sequencing. This is far from obvious, although it has been part of the conventional wisdom in policy circles in Latin America for some time. The reader who is skeptical about the economic case for gradualism should read our paper as a further argument for comprehensiveness of reform, on top of economic ones like those in Mussa (1982).

Our paper provides a counterpoint to recent contributions that have argued for sequencing reforms on the basis of other assumed payoff structures and rules of the political game. Moreover, our paper also undermines some of the economic arguments for gradualism which rely on lack of credibility, which in turn must be a consequence of political infeasibility (see e.g. Calvo 1989). In other words, if the political constraints are overcome by means of big-bang reform, a part of the economic case for gradualism may disappear as well. We discuss this literature in Section 2.

We develop the argument in Section 3, using a simple game-theoretic model. The model portrays a country in a political deadlock about reform proposals that hurt strongly organized interest groups. The government is represented as an agenda-setter interested in carrying out economic reforms. Under democratic conditions, and without precommitment, only far reaching reforms, even if quite costly, have hope for success. The more general message is that, once we incorporate political sustainability restrictions into the analysis, the optimal course of action for a government interested in reform may be different from the one we would infer from an unconstrained economic perspective.

In Section 4 we illustrate the argument with an economic example, which has the following characteristics. Public sector restructuring results in a large number of workers looking for new jobs. Simultaneous trade liberalization calls for further reallocation of resources, thus leading to more unemployment. The resulting rate of unemployment is excessively high due to congestion externalities in labor markets. This suggests a gradual sequencing of economic reforms. We identify political-economic constraints that preclude an agenda-setting government from following such a path, rendering a big-bang as the best feasible strategy. Section 5 offers concluding remarks.

2 An Overview of Related Literature

2.1 Economic Literature on Sequencing of Reforms

It is instructive to review briefly the arguments in favor of gradualism given by economists advising reforming countries. The early literature on timing and sequencing of economic reforms was spurred by the experience of the Southern Cone of Latin America in the late 1970s and early 1980s. The attempted liberalizations under military rule in Chile, Argentina, and Uruguay led to a series of bank panics and financial collapses. These difficulties were soon interpreted as due to mistakes in the order of liberalization (Diaz Alejandro, 1985; Corbo and de

Melo, 1985; Edwards and Cox-Edwards, 1987). The need to balance the central government finances before undertaking other reforms was commonly empha- sized. The debate centered on the order of liberalization of the trade and capital accounts, with the majority of authors favoring the opening of the former before the liberalization of the latter in order to avoid undesirable capital flows (see, e.g. McKinnon, 1991). Most of the early literature was informal; the emphasis was in giving policy advice to avoid the difficulties that plagued efforts at economic reform in Latin America. Edwards (1992b) summarizes these views.

Subsequent research has been more precise in making statements about welfare gains or losses associated with different sequences. It is important to make the dis- tinction between economic reform and economic restructuring. In economies that have been highly distorted, economic restructuring is bound to take a long time, even if economic reform (a collection of policy decisions) occurs all of a sudden. The question here is whether transition costs are minimized by a particular policy sequence. Clearly, under frictionless competitive equilibrium assumptions, wel- fare maximization is obtained by removing all distortions simultaneously. As long as the perceived private costs and benefits correspond to the true social costs and benefits, private economic agents will choose the socially correct pace of adjust- ment following a full scale liberalization. "Radical reform" is the first-best reform strategy, argued Mussa (1982) early on in the debate. Hence, arguments for gradu- alism must rely on the presence of distortions during the adjustment process.

One possibility is the presence of preexisting distortions in one or several mar- kets that cannot be removed at the time the reform plan is announced. Potential candidates are labor market interventions, domestic capital market imperfections, and limits to foreign indebtedness that are not perceived as binding by individual agents (see for instance Edwards and Van Wijnberger, 1986; Edwards, 1992). In all of these cases, one can imagine circumstances in which the second-best reform strategy will involve some degree of gradualism, for instance in the sequencing of trade and capital account opening.

A related argument by Calvo (1989) emphasizes the equivalence of imper- fect credibility to an intertemporal distortion. If the public wrongly believes that a trade liberalization will be reverted in the future, quantitative control of the capital account may be called for. The problem with this type of argument is that it assumes the credibility problem arises because the government "knows better" than the public what is going to happen in the future. A closer look at the source of the credibility problem is necessary to assess the right policy response. For instance, if imperfect credibility arises because the public is unsure about the "true preferences" of the government, overshooting can act as a signalling device (Rodrik, 1989b). Or, as argued in the next section, if credibility problems are related to political sustainability of the reforms, a big bang can be the only way of cutting through the Gordian knot of implicit rents generated by government interventions.

Other authors such as Murrell (1992) argue in favor of gradualism on the basis of an evolutionary approach: rapid reforms that disrupt existing relationships also destroy existing information stocks. Murrell also emphasizes the benefits of flexibility when undertaking policy measures under imperfect information. (A similar argument is presented in Dewatripont and Roland, 1995, which we discuss below.)

More recently, Gavin (1993) has focused on inefficiencies inherent to the adjustment process itself. The private sector response to reform may be suboptimal (too fast) if there is a congestion externality due to limited capacity of absorption in the labor market. A related problem is the lack of an adequate safety net to buffer the effects of massive labor displacement during the process of economic transformation. Latin American and Eastern European countries have had fragmentary and rudimentary systems for income maintenance and welfare delivery (Przeworski, 1991). Our example in Section 4 introduces a congestion externality of this type to make gradualism optimal from the point of view of economic efficiency.

2.2 The Political Economic Literature

It is instructive to compare our results with other papers in the literature, which have argued for sequencing of reforms on the basis of other assumed payoff structures and rules of the game.

Dewatripont and Roland (1992a,b) discuss the merits of gradualism versus fast reform in the context of a model of industrial restructuring in which a reform-minded government faces a sector requiring massive layoffs. In the case they present, fast reform may be too costly because it entails paying the same exit bonuses to all laid-off workers, even though they have different (privately-known) outside opportunities. As a solution, the government may be able to use agenda-setting powers to pass a gradual series of measures that, if proposed as a package, would be rejected by workers because it would given them a negative expected payoff.

Wei (1993) advances a related argument in favor of the gradual sequencing of reforms, based on an insight originally posited by Fernandez and Rodrik (1991). Wei explains that, due to individual uncertainty about the distribution of gains and losses from the reform, an economically efficient reform may not obtain the approval of the majority ex-ante even if it could do so ex-post. If this is the case with the full set of economic reforms, then the reforms can be achieved if one designs a sequence of specific measures, each of which enjoys a majority of support ex-ante.

Dewatripont and Roland (1995) offer a different argument in favor of sequencing reforms based on aggregate uncertainty about the outcomes of reforms. If reversing the reform process is costly, the authors note, gradualism makes reforms easier to initiate because it keeps open the possibility of early reversal. Furthermore, strong economic complementarity can help ingrain the (gradual) reform process once it has begun. If initial reforms prove successful, but cannot be sustained without some others that are less popular, in the next stage people will be confronted with a choice between costly reversal or acceptance of further reforms. Correct sequencing thus can strengthen popular support for reform.

In terms of the underlying payoff structure, we deviate from these contributions by assuming (1) that the reform package as a whole has a positive net outcome for the relevant political players, although some specific reforms have a negative effect on some of these politically organized groups, and (2) that this is known to the actors. On the one hand, it is hard to believe that market- oriented economic reform as a whole could have a negative expected outcome. On the other, individual and aggregate uncertainties about the outcomes of reform are probably more problematic in transitions from former communist to market economies than in economic reforms in developing countries that have had a long experience with the market. Both Wei (1993) and Dewatripont and Roland (1995) focus on the process of transition to the market, while we focus on the process of reform in developing economies.[4] Also, one could add uncertainty to our model, without necessarily altering the main conclusions.

Another major difference between the approach of Dewatripont and Roland (1995) and ours is that we assume that economic complementarity of reforms is not strong enough to deter interest groups from attempting to halt the process midway. Strong complementarities are more plausible when the basis of a market economy are completely absent, which is the case for former communist economies but not for developing economies. For instance, the assets of firms to be privatized cannot be properly valued if prices are not freed. On the other hand, it is likely that macroeconomic stabilization or public sector reform can be carried out successfully even in the absence of trade liberalization.[5]

In terms of the political game, while previous contributions assume majority rule, we assume that policy decisions are subject to the veto power of politically organized groups.[6] The choice of veto power over majority rule is motivated by the structure of political decision making in many developing countries, particularly in Latin America, where a broad consensus is needed for any reform involving substantial gains and losses for different groups (see, e.g., the conclusions of Burgess and Stern (1993)). In many of these countries dissatisfaction among certain groups is enough to bring down the government (Ames, 1987). Our results are consistent with majority rule if the benefits of each particular reform are concentrated and the costs are diffuse. However, we believe that in many cases reform is precisely about *suppressing* distortions that benefit a minority at the expense of the majority.

Under our assumptions, simultaneous introduction of reforms permits the government to overcome potential veto threats because losses due to one specific measure are compensated by other reforms such that all politically organized groups are net beneficiaries of the package. In contrast, if the government were to attempt a gradual sequencing of reforms, and approval had to be obtained at each step of the process, some groups could benefit from derailing the process at some point.

If the government and the interest groups were able to make credible commitments to implement the complete optimal sequence, that would be the recommended course of action. In other words, "constitutional" agreements such as social pacts, or agreements with international institutions with very high costs of reneging, might enable the implementation of reforms with lower transition costs.

While we do not think that there is a right set of assumptions about the payoff structure and the political game valid for all reform episodes, we believe that the assumptions necessary for our argument have been satisfied in a number of cases, particularly in Latin America. We turn now to a formal presentation of the argument.

3 The Political-Economy Case for Radical Reform

In this section, we use a simple game in extensive form to show the logic of the following argument: by widening the scope of efficiency-improving reforms initiated simultaneously, a government can gain the support of larger segments of the population. For many agents, losses from one reform can be more than compensated by gains from the others. Hence, linking the fate of the reforms can be a way of weakening the opposition to them. If the government is not able to commit to a certain course of action, it may need to implement all reforms simultaneously, even if economic reasoning would call for a gradual sequencing of reforms.[7]

Consider a government trying to implement reforms F and T. We could think of them as a fiscal reform and a trade reform. There are two interest groups, f and t. Reform F, if carried out alone, will hurt group f and will benefit group t. The opposite is true for reform T. It is assumed that, on optimality grounds, reform T should be carried out after F is in place. This could be the case because, for instance, fiscal reform provides macroeconomic stability needed to minimize transition costs associated with trade reform.

If the optimal sequencing of reforms is pursued – that is, if T is undertaken after F is completed – both f and t end up being better off than in the initial situation. However, group t would prefer that the reform process be truncated after reform F is accomplished.

Alternatively, the government can start both reforms simultaneously. The payoffs of following this approach are higher for f and t than those from the initial situation, but lower than those obtained after the optimal sequence of reforms.

The government is modeled as an agenda-setter who holds the initiative to propose reforms at several points in time. We assume, that the government is interested in maximizing the sum of the utilities of the groups. The same results can be obtained from a number of specifications of the government's objective. For example, a predator government that takes a percentage of the total pie, and a government which is a perfect agent for one group, are also consistent with the payoff specification. We also assume that pressure groups can veto any reform plan. In deciding a sequence of proposals, the government must take into account not only economic considerations (the payoffs associated with the final result) but also the possibility of successfully installing the entire reform package. Neither the government nor the different interest groups have the capacity to commit to their actions.

Figure 1 shows schematically the extended form of this game.[8]

Payoffs have been chosen for illustration purposes and reflect the following assumptions: (i) there is a need for reform (low payoff of status quo); (ii) if feasible, a gradual sequencing of reforms is preferable to a simultaneous introduction of all reforms; and (iii) a partial or truncated implementation of reforms will favor one group and hurt the other.

The government has three choices at the initial node: propose a gradual sequence of reforms (starting by reforming sector F), do nothing, or propose a comprehensive attempt at reform. If the government makes a proposal, the groups can accept it or reject it. The opposition of any group is enough to paralyze the government's proposal.

It is easy to see that comprehensive reform is the unique subgame perfect equilibrium of this game (a subgame perfect equilibrium requires rational choice by every decision maker at every possible node of the game, whether or not it is reached in equilibrium). Suppose the government attempts to follow a gradual reform and proposes F. Group f will veto this proposal because, if T is proposed at the next stage, group t will veto it, and group f will end up being worse off than in the status quo. Hence, even though a gradual sequence is preferred to comprehensive reform by the interest groups and the government, it is not going to be proposed.

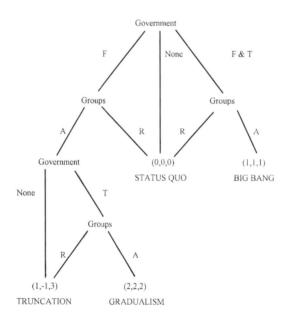

Figure 1 Payoffs: (Government. Group f, Group t)

Notice that if group t could commit to accepting the government proposal in the second stage, both interest groups and the government would be better off. In this sense, there is a time-consistency problem similar to the well known time-consistency problem in games between the government and the general public. The absence of any commitment device in the case of sequenced reforms is crucial for the results.

Our results are also consistent with some alternative assumptions about the payoff structure and the political game. For instance, the payoff corresponding to the status quo could be -2 for both interest groups and the government. The interpretation would be that F is beneficial for both interest groups so that nobody stands to lose from truncated reform. In that case, truncated reform would be feasible. However, a big-bang would still be the best reform path from the point of view of the government. That is, we do not require that *each* reform hurts somebody, only that some reforms along the optimal gradual sequence hurt enough people to risk that the process of reforms be halted. In terms of the political game, we do not require that *everybody* in the economy have veto power nor that the government cares about the utility of *everybody* in the economy. What is required is that a blocking coalition be able to stop the optimal gradual sequence at some point, and that all potential blocking coalitions expect to be better off after the comprehensive introduction of reforms.

Finally, our results are not inconsistent with majority voting. To see this, suppose there is a third group that suffers losses from each reform. Payoffs to the government would not change if the third group's losses are relatively minor. If each of the three groups represents a third of the population, bunching the two reforms together would still be the only way to gather enough political support to install all of the reforms successfully. Note, however, that this majority voting scenario relies on the benefits of each reform being concentrated and its costs diffuse, which we consider contradictory to actual reform experiences in the Third World. The reality of concentrated costs and diffuse benefits in recent reform processes, therefore, fuels our preference for the veto power assumption over that of majority voting. Concentrated costs have prevailed because various sectors of society have had to renounce their apportionment of special privileges.

4 A General Equilibrium Model with Transitional Unemployment

This section is intended to demonstrate that payoffs that are strategically equivalent to those in Figure 1 can be obtained from a fully specified economic model.

4.1 The Economy

Consider an economy with two sectors, one producing exports (X) and the other producing importables (Y). Both sectors use labor (L) as a factor of production. There are three different types of agents in this economy: workers (who supply all the labor), owners of the export firms, and owners of the firms that produce importables. Agents in this economy only consume importables. The exchange rate and the international prices of exports and importables are equal to one. In the initial situation, there is a tariff, τ, on imports and a fraction of the labor force, L_b, is absorbed by a useless bureaucracy. This extreme assumption captures the reality of overemployment and low productivity in the public sector. Agents live for three periods. Time is indexed by $t = 0, 1, 2$. There is no discounting.

The technology for producing exports and the technology for producing importables are given by:

$$X_t = L_{x,t}^{1/2}$$
$$Y_t = L_{y,t}^{1/2}$$

(4.1)

where X_t and Y_t are, respectively, the production of exports and the production of importables at time t, and $L_{x,t}$ and $L_{y,r}$ are, respectively, employment in the export and importable sectors at time t. It will be assumed that firms are restricted in their decisions to increase their use of labor, in such a way that

$$L_{j,t} \in \left[0, L_{j,t-1} + K_{j,t}\right]; \quad j = X, Y$$

(4.2)

Where $K_{j,t}$ is the capacity of labor absorption of sector j in period t.[9]

Time 0 is taken to be the pre-existing (distorted) situation, with salaries being identical across sectors, $w_{x,0} = w_{y,0} = w_{b,0}$, and no unemployment. The action transpires over periods 1 and 2. At the beginning of each period, each worker has to decide whether to stay at his current job or to quit and search for employment elsewhere. It is not possible to look for employment in more than one sector, and once a worker quits, he cannot work in the same firm in that period. Public employment (L_b) is treated as a policy variable. Let $S_{j,t}$ be the number of workers looking for a job in sector j at the beginning of period t. If the number of workers searching for employment in sector j exceeds the capacity of absorption of that sector ($S_{j,t} > K_{j,t}$), then some of those workers will remain unemployed. The probability of finding a job in sector j at time t equals $\min\{K_{j,t} / S_{j,t}, 1\}$.

Production takes place after (some of) the searching workers and firms are matched. Firms are assumed to pay wages equal to the value of the marginal product of labor in the sector. That is,

$$w_{x,t} = \frac{1}{2} L_{x,t}^{-1/2}$$
$$w_{y,t} = \left(1 + \tau_t\right) \frac{1}{2} L_{y,t}^{-1/2}$$

(4.3)

where τ_t is the level of tariffs at time t.

Labor is supplied inelastically by employed workers. The quantity of labor available in the economy is normalized to one. At the beginning of each period we have:

$$\bar{L}_{x,t} + \bar{L}_{y,t} + L_{b,t} + S_{x,t} + S_{y,t} = 1 \qquad (4.4)$$

where $\bar{L}_{x,t}$ and $\bar{L}_{y,t}$ are workers who remain employed in each sector from the previous period, $L_{b,t}$ are workers who remain employed in the bureaucracy, and $S_{x,t}$ and $S_{y,t}$ are workers searching for a job in each of the two productive sectors. After matching takes place, workers will either be employed in one of the two productive sectors, employed in the bureaucracy, or unemployed, such that

$$L_{x,t} + L_{y,t} + L_{b,t} + U_s = 1. \qquad (4.5)$$

We now proceed to specify the value functions on the basis of which workers will make their search choices. At $t=2$ (the final period), the value of searching for a job in section j, $V_{j,2}$, will be given by the probability of getting a job in sector j multiplied by the wage expected in that sector (since the value of being unemployed during the final period is equal to zero):

$$V_{x,2} = \min\left\{\frac{K_{x,2}}{S_{x,2}}, 1\right\} w_{x,2}$$

$$V_{y,2} = \min\left\{\frac{K_{y,2}}{S_{y,2}}, 1\right\} w_{y,2}. \qquad (4.6)$$

Notice that the wage that will result each period is supposed to be correctly anticipated, even though the decision to look for a job in a given sector is made at the beginning of the period.

The values of search at $t=1$ are:

$$V_{x,1} = \min\left\{\frac{K_{x,1}}{S_{x,1}}, 1\right\}\left(w_{x,1} + \max\{w_{x,2}, V_{y,2}\} + \left(1 - \min\left\{\frac{K_{x,1}}{S_{x,1}}, 1\right\}\right)\right)$$

$$\max\{V_{x,2}, V_{y,2}\}$$

$$V_{y,1} = \min\left\{\frac{K_{y,1}}{S_{y,1}}, 1\right\}\left(w_{y,1} + \max\{w_{y,2}, V_{x,2}\} + \left(1 - \min\left\{\frac{K_{y,1}}{S_{y,1}}, 1\right\}\right)\right)$$

$$\max\{V_{x,2}, V_{y,2}\} \qquad (4.7)$$

They include the probability of finding a job multiplied by the value of the job (wage at $t=1$ plus value of optimal choice at $t=2$ for an employed worker), plus the probability of unemployment multiplied by the value of unemployment (the value of the optimal choice at $t=2$ for an unemployed worker).

In equilibrium,

$$V_{x,2} = V_{y,2}$$
$$V_{x,1} = V_{y,1}.$$

(4.8)

Given a set of policy parameters (τ_1, $L_{b,1}$, τ_2 and $L_{b,2}$), we can obtain equilibrium search decisions, wages, employment, production, and profits in each sector in each period, as well as expected payoffs for the different types of agents. We now proceed to provide one example in which a sequential reform (paring the bureaucracy first and lowering tariffs later) is the most desirable policy from the point of view of the government, but in which the political environment makes that sequence infeasible, leaving comprehensive reform as the best feasible option.

4.2 The Political Environment

Suppose that a reformist government intends to pass trade reform and fiscal reforms, that would take tariffs and the level of superfluous employment in the public sector to zero. In the initial situation, distortions in the economy are given by $\tau_0 = 0.30$ and $L_{b,0} = 0.20$, and there is no unemployment. The initial capacity of absorption of new labor in the export sector, $K_{x,1}$, is set at 0.07. As we will see, this implies that gradualism does not lead to unemployment, but big bang reform does. There are no other constraints to the capacity of absorption of new labor (that is, $K_{x,2} = K_{y,1} = K_{y,2} = \infty$).

The following are the institutional rules:

(i) The government is the agenda-setter. During period 1, it can propose contemporaneous changes in τ_1 and $L_{b,1}$. During period 2, it can propose contemporaneous changes in τ_2 and $L_{b,2}$. We assume that $\tau_t \in \{0, 0.30\}$ and $L_{b,t} \in \{0, 0.20\}$ to concentrate on the question of sequencing, ignoring issues of speed.

(ii) Each group of agents (workers, producers of importables, and exporters) has the power to veto any policy initiative. In case of veto, the resulting outcome is the status quo. As political agents, producers of importables and exporters seek to maximize profits in their respective sectors, and workers seek to maximize aggregate payments to labor.

(iii) The budget is balanced via proportional income taxes or subsidies.

(iv) The objective of the government is to maximize aggregate income.

(v) There are no side payments.

4.3 Solution to the Game

Aggregate real income of workers (I_l), of exporters (I_x), and of owners of the importable firms (I_y) are given, respectively, by the total payroll, profits in the exports sector, and profits in the importables sector, deflated by the price of importables ($1+\tau$):

$$I_{l,t} = \frac{w_{x,t}L_{x,t} + w_{y,t}L_{y,t} + w_{b,t}L_{b,t}}{1+\tau_t}$$

$$I_{x,t} = \frac{X_t - w_{x,t}L_{x,t}}{1+\tau_t} \tag{4.9}$$

$$I_{y,t} = \frac{(1+\tau_t)Y_t - w_{y,ts}L_{y,t}}{1+\tau_t}.$$

Equations above represent pre-tax income. Let T represent taxes needed to close the budget. T is equal to payments to public sector employees minus tariff revenues. We ignore inter temporal balance of payment issues and assume that imports equal exports in every period. Hence,

$$T_t = \frac{w_{b,t}L_{b,t}}{1+\tau_t} - \frac{\tau_t}{1+\tau_t}X_1. \tag{4.10}$$

It is easily verified that:

$$I_{l,t} + I_{x,t} + I_{y,t} - T_t = X_t + Y_t \tag{4.11}$$

Let $I_t \equiv I_{l,t} + I_{x,t} + I_{y,t} - T_t$ represent the total consumption of importables by the economy (equal to total production evaluated at international prices). Stage payoffs (payoffs per period) to workers, owners of X, owners of Y, and the government are, respectively, $(1-t)I_l, (1-t)I_x, (1-t)I_y$, and I, where $t = T/(I+T)$ is the tax rate. Given that there is no discounting, each group tries to maximize the sum of payoffs over periods 1 and 2. The extensive form of the game is depicted in Figure 2. The appendix shows how to compute payoffs.

There are two possible paths from the initial situation to an undistorted economy. One possibility is to eliminate in the first period the distortion caused by bureaucratic employment and in the second period the distortion created by the tariff. That is, $L_{b,1} = 0, \tau_1 = 0.3$, and $L_{b,2} = \tau_2 = 0$. We call this path gradualism. The other possibility is to remove all distortions in period 1. That is, $L_{b,1} = \tau_1 = L_{b,2} = \tau_2 = 0$. We call this other path big-bang.[10]

As we show in the appendix, unemployment under a big-bang is larger than under gradualism. Gradualism is preferable to a big bang not only from an efficiency perspective, but also from the point of view of income distribution, since

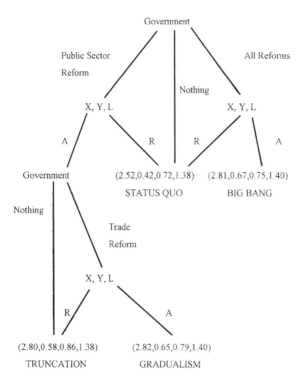

Figure 2 Payoffs: (Government, X, Y, L).

unemployed workers are the least favored social group in the model. The feasibility problem with gradualism is the following: Suppose that everybody agrees with the prescribed decisions in period 1. When period 2 arrives, producers of importable goods will not find it convenient to support a move towards free trade. Therefore, gradualism is not a credible path to free trade because it is not politically sustainable.

A big-bang entails a lower aggregate payoff than gradualism during period 1, and it implies that some workers will be unemployed (more generally, it implies more unemployment than is strictly necessary). However, unlike gradualism, it is a politically sustainable path to an undistorted economy.

5. Final Remarks

An understanding of the conditions under which political considerations induce biases toward radical reform is important both to evaluate recent experiences in developing countries and to help in the design of new reform programs.

In this paper, we offer a possible explanation for why a number of Latin American countries, some of which failed to complete gradual reforms in the early 1980s, have undertaken comprehensive reform programs in recent years. These attempts were somewhat surprising to outside economic analysts given their increased economic and administrative costs in relation to gradual reform processes. A key motivation seems to have been that a more extensive package of reform permitted a wider accumulation of political support. Thus, reform has usually been accompanied by political realignment. Since no sector of society wants to be first in renouncing its apportionment of special privileges, reformist governments felt it was necessary to cut through the Gordian knot of government-created rents.

From a normative point of view, our main insight is that political considerations can make reforms "complementary", even in circumstances in which economic reasoning would indicate that reforms should be made sequentially. Policy-makers may need to be well aware of those considerations in implementing reform programs. Our result stands in contrast to Rodrik's (1989) recommendation of undertaking deep reforms with a narrow scope. As a former finance minister of New Zealand put it, "large packages provide the flexibility to ensure that losses suffered by any one group are offset by gains by the same group in other areas" (Douglas, 1989). Our result also highlights the need for international agencies to assess the political restrictions while assisting countries undertaking liberalization processes. Ideally, these institutions, as well as international treaties, might play a role as commitment devices to allow for the implementation of reforms with lower transition costs.

Appendix: Computing Payoffs for Figure 2

Table A shows *stage* payoffs (that is, payoffs per period) to the different groups under different scenarios.

TABLE A: STAGE PAYOFFS			
	I	II	III	IV
τ	0.3	0.3	0.0	0.0
L_b	0.2	0.0	0.0	0.0
NI_x	0.21	0.29	0.31	0.36
NI_y	0.36	0.43	0.39	0.36
NI_l	0.69	0.69	0.69	0.71
I	1.26	1.40	1.39	1.42

The initial situation is represented by column I. Since there is no initial unemployment, $L_{x,0} + L_{y,0} = 0.8$. from (4.3) and $w_{x,0} = w_{y,0}$ we obtain $L_{y,0} = (1.3)^2 L_{x,0}$. This implies $L_{x,0} = 0.3, L_{y,0} = 0.5$, and $w_0 = 0.91$. From there we can obtain $I_0 = X_0 + Y_0 = 1.26$. Using equations (4.9) and (4.10) we obtain the other elements of column I.

Column IV shows a steady state in which all distortions have been removed and there is no unemployment. Again, wages are equalized. The derivation is identical to that of column I. That column shows the maximum possible value of the level of aggregate income.

We consider two possible paths from I to IV. The first one is a gradualist process given by setting $L_{b,1} = 0, \tau_1 = 0.3$, and $L_{b,2} = \tau_2 = 0$. Column II represents transition during a gradualist process. No unemployment arises during a gradualist process: If we let $L_{x,1} + L_{y,1} = 1$, using (4.3) we obtain $L_{x,1} = 0.37$ (which is consistent with $L_{x,0} = 0.3$ and $K_{x,0} = 0.07$). From there we can obtain $I_1 = X_1 + Y_1 = 1.40$. Using equations (4.3), (4.9), and (4.10) we obtain the other elements of column II.

The other path from I to IV is a big-bang given by setting $L_{b,1} = \tau_1 = L_{b,2} = \tau_2 = 0$. Column III represents transition during a big-bang. In this case, the constraint on labor absorption by sector X is binding in the first period. Hence, $L_{x,1} = L_{x,0} + K_{x,1} = 0.37$. There is no unemployment in the final period, so that equations (4.7) and (4.8) imply $(K_{x,1} / S_{x,1}) w_{x,1} = w_{y,1}$. Using equation (4.3) and $S_{x,1} = 1 - L_{x,0} - L_{y,1}$ we obtain $(0.7 / S_{x,1}) \times 0.82 = \frac{1}{2}(0.7 - S_{x,1})^{-1/2}$. From the last expression we obtain $S_{x,1} = 0.09$ and then $L_{y,1} = 0.61$. From there we can obtain $I_1 = X_1 + Y_1 = 1.39$. Using equations (4.3), (4.9), and (4.10) we obtain the other elements of column III.

The Status Quo payoffs in Figure 2 correspond to twice the payoffs of column I. The Truncated Reform payoffs correspond to twice the payoffs in column II. The Gradualist Reform payoffs correspond to the payoffs in column II plus the payoffs in column IV. Finally, the Radical Reform payoffs correspond to the payoffs of column III plus the payoffs of column IV.

We thank Christopher Clague, Anne Krueger, Gian Maria Milesi-Ferretti, Martin McGuire, Dani Rodrik, Seonghwan Oh, Mancur Olson, Adam Shapiro, Rich Sicotte, Peter Rosendorff, Gordon Tullock, Michael Wallerstein, an anonymous referee, and seminar participants at UCLA, Georgetown, Maryland, IMF, Columbia, Chicago, MIT, and the WEA meetings for helpful comments. This paper was written while the first author was a student and the second author a faculty member at UCLA, and revised while the second author was a fellow at the Harvard/MIT RTG in Positive Political Economy. We thank the financial support of the UCLA Academic Senate, of the Project on "Institutional Reform and the Informal Sector" (IRIS) at the University of Maryland under Cooperative Agreement DHR-0015-A-00-0031-00 with the Center of Economic Growth of the US Agency for International Development, and of the Spanish CICYT (grant SEC 93–0839).

Notes

1 E.g., Calvo (1989), Corbo and De Melo (1985), Corbo and Fischer (1990), Edwards (1992a, b), Fischer (1986), Frenkel (1982), Harberger (1986), Krueger (1981), McKinnon (1984, 1991).

2 These countries include Bolivia, Ghana, Mexico, and Poland (World Bank, 1991, p. 117), Argentina (Dornbusch, 1992), and Peru (Paredes, 1991). For comprehensive analysis of reform episodes, we refer the reader to the volumes edited by Bates and Krueger (1993) and Haggard and Kaufman (1992).

3 This paper is concerned with the introduction of measures in different fronts (such as macroeconomic stabilization or trade liberalization), not with the speed of reform in each particular front. We (and many previous authors) are guilty of using *speed* terminology ("gradual", "radical", "big-bang") to talk about *sequencing* issues. See Tommasi and Velasco (1996) for a more detailed discussion of this distinction.

4 It is interesting to note the contrast between the assumptions in Dewatripont and Roland (1992a, b) and those in Fernandez and Rodrik (1991) and Wei (1993). Workers know their chances of getting a job in the growing sectors all too well in Dewatripont-Roland, while they have no clue in Fernandez-Rodrik-Wei.

5 Also, Martinelli and Tommasi (1995) show that even under the conditions necessary for gradualism to have lower experimentation costs (in Dewatripont and Roland, 1995), the distributional implications of the different reforms can lead to the gradual path being time- inconsistent in a political game.

6 Veto power by interest groups is a common assumption in the literature on the *delay* of reforms (Alesina and Drazen, 1991; Drazen and Grilli, 1993). The assumption of veto players is also implicit in Dewatripont and Roland (1992a, b). In their model of industrial restructuring, they assume that the government cannot fire workers from the inefficient sectors, but has to bribe them to exit.

7 A similar idea underlies the discussion about economic reform in Buchanan (1991). In a similar vein, Rodrik (1994) argues that a government may be able to sneak in a reform with distributive consequences alongside one with across-the-board benefits by packaging the two together.

8 In order to simplify Figures 1 and 2, we have used single nodes to represent the simultaneous moves of groups. A means acceptance by *all* groups, while R means rejection by *any* group.

9 The sector-level behavior we describe can be obtained by having n firms with technology $q_{i,t} = (l_{i,t} / n)^{1/2}$, with $l_{i,t} \in [0, l_{i,t-1} + K_{i,t}/n]$. This stark but simple way of capturing convex costs of training new workers is inspired by Gavin (1993).

10 Another path, which we are ignoring, would consist of lowering tariffs in period 1 and reducing the bureaucracy in period 2. We could call this path "gradualism with the wrong sequence" because it would entail suppressing the most important distortion in the second period. We ignore this path because it would lead to lower payoffs for the government that any of the other two.

References

Alesina, Alberto and Allan Drazen, 1991, Why are Stabilizations Delayed? *American Economic Review* 81, 1170–1188.

Ames, Barry, 1987, Political Survival: Politicians and Public Policy in Latin America (University of California Press).

Bates, Robert and Anne Krueger, 1993, Political and Economic Interactions in Economic Policy Reform: Evidence from Eight Countries (Basil Blackwell).

Buchanan, James, 1991, Achieving Economic Reform, chapter 9 in J. Buchanan, *The Economics and the Ethics of Constitutional Order*. Michigan.

Burgess, Robin and Nicholas Stern, 1993, Taxation and Development. *Journal of Economic Literature* 31, 762–830.

Calvo, Guillermo, 1989, Incredible Reforms, in: G. Calvo et al., eds., *Debt, Stabilization and Development: Essays in Memory of Carlos Diaz Alejandro* (Basil Blackwell).

Corbo, Vittorio and Jaime de Melo, 1985, Liberalization with Stabilization in the Southern Cone of Latin America: Overview and Summary. *World Development* 13, 515 August.

Corbo, Vittorio and Stanley Fischer, 1990, Adjustment Programs and Bank Support: Rationale and Main Results, in Corbo, Fischer and Webb (eds), *Adjustment Lending Revisited: Policies to Restore Growth.* The World Bank.

Dewatripont, Mathias and Gerard Roland, 1992a, Economic Reform and Dynamic Political Constraints. *Review of Economic Studies* 59, 703–730.

Dewatripont, Mathias and Gerard Roland, 1992b, The Virtues of Gradualism and Legitimacy in the Transition to a Market Economy. *Economic Journal* 102, 291–300.

Dewatripont, Mathias and Gerard Roland, 1995, The Design of Reform Packages under Uncertainty. *American Economic Review* 85, 1207-1223.

Diaz Alejandro, Carlos, 1985, Good Bye Financial Repression, Hello Financial Crash. *Journal of Development Economics* 19, 1–24.

Dornbusch, Rudiger, 1992, Progress Report on Argentina, Working Paper. December.

Douglas, Roger, 1990, The Politics of Successful Structural Reform. *The Wall Street Journal*, January 17.

Drazen, Allan and Vittorio Grilli, 1993, The Benefits of Crises for Economic Reforms. *American Economic Review* 83, 598–607.

Edwards, Sebastian, 1992, Sequencing and Welfare: Labor Markets and Agriculture. NBER WP No. 4095.

Edwards, Sebastian, 1992b, The Sequencing of Structural Adjustment and Stabilization. ICEG Occasional Paper No. 34.

Edwards, Sebastian and Alejandra Cox-Edwards, 1987, *Monetarism and Liberalization: The Chilean Experiment,* Ballinger Publishing Co.

Edwards, Sebastian and Sweder van Wijnbergen, 1986, Welfare Effects of Trade and Capital Market Liberalization: Consequences of Different Sequencing Scenarios. *International Economic Review*, February.

Fernandez, Raquel and Dani Rodrik, 1991, Resistance to Reform: Status Quo Bias in the Presence of Individual-Specific Uncertainty. *American Economic Review* 81, 1146–1155. Fischer, Stanley, 1986, Issues in Medium-Term Macroeconomic Adjustment. *The World Bank Research Observer* 1, 163–182.

Frenkel, Jacob, 1982, The Order of Economic Liberalization: A Comment, in Brunner and Meltzer (Eds), *Economic Policy in a World of Change.* North Holland.

Gavin, Michael, 1993, Unemployment and the Economics of Gradualist Reform. Columbia University, Mimeo.

Haggard, Stephan and Robert Kaufman, 1992, *The Politics of Economic Adjustment.* Princeton University Press.

Harberger, Arnold, 1986, Welfare Consequences of Capital Inflows, in Choksi and Papageorgiou (Eds), *Economic Liberalization in Developing Countries.* Basil Blackwell.

Krueger, Anne, 1981, Interactions Between Inflation and Trade-Regime Objectives in Stabilization Programs, in Cline and Weintraub (Eds), *Economic Stabilization in Developing Countries.* Brookings Institution.

Martinelli, Cesar and Mariano Tommasi, 1995, Economic Reforms and Political Constraints: On the Time-Inconsistency of Gradual Sequencing, Mimeo, Universidad Carlos III, Madrid.

241

McKinnon, Ronald, 1984, The International Capital Market and Economic Liberalization in LDC's. *The Developing Economies* 22, December.

McKinnon, Ronald, 1991, The Order of Economic Liberalization: Financial Control in the Transition to a Market Economy. Johns Hopkins.

Murrell, Peter, 1992, Evolutionary and Radical Approaches to Economic Reform, IRIS Working Paper No 5. University of Maryland. Forthcoming in *The Economics of Planning.*

Mussa, Michael, 1982, Government Policy and the Adjustment Process, in J. Bhagwati (Ed.), *Import Competition and Response.* University of Chicago Press.

Paredes, Carlos, 1991, Epilogue: In the Aftermath of Hyperinflation, in C. Paredes and J. Sachs (Eds), *Peru's Path to Recovery: A Plan for Economic Stabilization and Growth.* Brookings Institution.

Rodrik, Dani, 1989, Credibility of Trade Reform: A Policymaker's Guide. *The World Economy* 12, 1–16.

Rodrik, Dani, 1994, The Rush to Free Trade in the Developing World: Why so Late? Why Now? Will it Last? in Haggard and Webb (Eds), *Voting for Reform: Democracy, Political Liberalization and Economic Adjustment.* Oxford University Press.

Tommasi, Mariano and Andres Velasco, 1996, Where Are We in the Political Economy of Reform? *Journal of Policy Reform* 1, 187–238.

Wei, Shang-Jin, 1993, Gradualism versus Big Bang: Speed and Sustainability of Reforms. Harvard University. Mimeo.

World Bank, 1991, World Development Report: The Challenge of Development. Oxford University Press.

25

CREDIBLE ECONOMIC LIBERALIZATIONS AND OVERBORROWING

Ronald I. McKinnon and Huw Pill

Source: *American Economic Review* 87, 2, 1997, 189–193.

When undertaking reform and stabilization programs, some countries are prone to excessive foreign borrowing that ultimately proves unsustainable. A sharp withdrawal of foreign funds, declines in asset values, and a painful economic downturn may follow.

The policy reforms favoring free trade, privatization, deregulation of domestic industry, and fiscal consolidation pursued by Chile in the mid-1970s led to massive capital inflows through 1981, followed by a financial crash and economic downturn during 1982–1983. In Mexico after 1988, similarly comprehensive real-side reforms attracted large capital inflows, which suddenly reversed during the December 1994 financial panic and steep 1995 downturn. Argentina currently faces the depressed aftermath of a reform program during which it borrowed too much and subsequently had to retrench.

This pattern is not confined to developing countries. After a dismal period of high inflation and public intervention in Britain in the 1970s, the Thatcher government undertook apparently successful industrial restructuring and fiscal consolidation in the early 1980s. Enthusiasm for Britain's changed economic prospects attracted capital inflows, increased consumption, and triggered a boom in residential and commercial real estate in the late 1980s that culminated in the bust of the early 1990s.

Nevertheless, not all liberalizing countries attracting large capital inflows need experience this boom-and-bust cycle. Indonesia, Malaysia, and Thailand have all had current-account deficits of 5–8 percent of GNP (similar to Mexico before the fall) for almost a decade, without a Mexico- or Chile-type debacle. These East Asian economies achieved virtual steady-state growth with high saving and very high investment, although doubts about its quality could yet provoke a cutback in foreign lending.

In contrast to the East Asian experience, this paper is more concerned with the *transition* from economic repression to liberalization (McKinnon, 1993; Pill,

1996; McKinnon and Pill, 1996). When does an economy undertaking apparently well conceived industrial and financial reforms suddenly become vulnerable to overborrowing? In particular, both Chile and Mexico showed sharp declines in private saving in the early stages of the reforms. Does this make sense in a "first-best" model of intertemporal optimization? Alternatively, does a fall in saving indicate something wrong with the capital market, or that the structural reforms lack credibility?

I. The Model

Initially, we believed that the problem was a matter of getting the exchange rate right. However, here we abstract from monetary variables (the money supply, exchange rate, and price level) altogether, as did J. P. Conley and W. F. Maloney (1995). To pursue the analysis one step further, we build a highly simplified Fisher two-period model of borrowing and investing to show how the capital market could malfunction when, in moving from repression to reform, uncertainty about payoffs to new investments greatly increases.

In Figure 1, the function $f(\cdot)$ portrays the pre-reform opportunity set, linking investments in period 1 to payoffs in period 2, open to a representative firm-household with an endowment (m_1, m_2). In the standard Fisherian mode, $f(\cdot)$ displays diminishing returns overall; and, because agents are identical, the capital market is redundant: point A represents the intertemporal consumption *and* production equilibrium (i.e., $c_1 = x_1$).

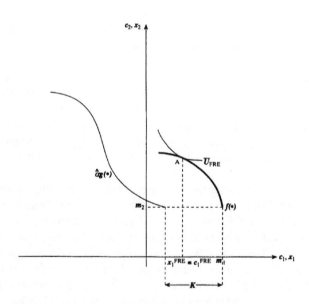

Figure 1 Equilibrium in the Financially Repressed Economy (FRE)

244

The potential economic gains from a real-side reform, such as a move to free trade, are portrayed by a new investment function $\hat{\alpha}g(\cdot)$, which shows a segment with much higher payoffs in period 2 from investments in period 1. Because $\hat{\alpha}g(\cdot)$ incorporates indivisibilities and increasing returns, the capital market is now critically important if the new export opportunities are to be exploited. Only after discrete setup costs (K in Fig. 1) are incurred does further investment in $\hat{\alpha}g(\cdot)$ show increasing yields. Then, at a much higher level of average productivity, diminishing returns (from the economy's fixed factors of labor, land, etc.) eventually set in at the margin.

Suppose, however, that the reforming economy remains financially repressed because of inflation and high-reserve requirements for financial intermediaries that are outside of our nonmonetary Fisherian model, and because agents cannot borrow abroad. In this financially repressed economy (FRE), the potentially superior investment opportunities represented by $\hat{\alpha}g(\cdot)$ have setup costs that are too large to be self-financed by individual firm-households. Thus, despite the trade reform, the economy remains mired close to A, which we shall call the FRE equilibrium.

Alternatively, when the real-side reform occurs, suppose that the domestic (bank-based) capital market, but not international capital flows, is open: our so-called domestically liberalized economy (DLE) shown in Figure 2. It assumes that investment payoffs in period 2 are known with certainty so that moral hazard in the banks remains latent and the domestic capital market works efficiently. In this risk-free DLE economy, some agents borrow to invest in the superior $\hat{\alpha}g(\cdot)$ technology (point A), while others are confined to the old $f(\cdot)$ technology (point B). The latter become net depositors in the banking system. This double tangency, where both the new and old investment technologies coexist in the DLE, reflects the high setup costs (indivisibilities) of jumping to the new technology. The active bidding for investment resources to exploit the new, more productive, investment technology drives up the rate of interest to induce some disinvestment in the old less efficient technology and to curb current consumption. Thus, without foreign-capital flows in our DLE, saving does not fall in period 1.

In this "first-best" (FB) equilibrium where future payoffs to investment are known, everybody's welfare increases regardless of whether they be borrowers or depositors. Because firm-households are identical, their now-higher utility (and, by implication, their consumption choices) must be the same, as shown by the tangency of $\bar{U}^{\text{DLE}}$ with the budget line in Figure 2. Borrowers investing in the new technology gain from output in period 2 exceeding the cost of repaying their loans, while lenders (who all stay with the old technology) gain from the higher yields on their deposits made with the banks.

However, this state of bliss need not hold once uncertainty is introduced. By subsuming monetary and exchange-rate risk into an ex ante probability distribution of returns on investment, we sidestep the complex details of how macroeconomic management of the reforms affects profitability. Let the random variable α modify the function $g(\cdot)$, so that $\alpha g(\cdot)$ is the actual investment payoff in period 2.

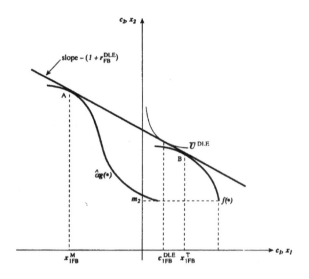

Figure 2 First-Best Solution in the Domestically Liberalized Economy (DLE)

Based on the best information available in period 1, the expected value of α is $\hat{\alpha}$. (In the deterministic cases portrayed in Figs. 1 and 2, investment outcomes were known exactly.)

Because α now varies stochastically, Figures 3, 4, and 5 represent possible investment equilibria in period 1 together with the corresponding *expected* payoffs in period 2. But how do nonbank firms decide what the returns to investment in the (radically) transformed economy likely will be? Here we posit a substantial informational asymmetry. Banks are special because (i) they are at the center of the flow of funds in the economy, and (ii) collectively they can price credit and determine its availability to liquidity-constrained enterprises.

The upshot is that, in period 1, the aggressiveness of the banks' lending behavior offers an implicit signal to the nonbank sector of the likely success of the reforms (i.e., of the mean realization of a). Domestic firm-households, perhaps naively, rely on these implicit signals from the "expert" banking system to generate their expectations of $\hat{\alpha}$. Besides enabling firms to finance their setup costs and so stimulate current economic activity, easy credit signals that new investments in the reform technology will have high payoffs, and so it increases peoples' estimates of their future income.

If accurate, having the banks implicitly signal how successful the reforms will be could be efficient. In Figure 3 portraying a DLE, $\hat{\alpha} g(\cdot)$ now gives the unbiased locus of expected investment outcomes in period 2 when banks are free from moral hazard. If firm-households are risk-neutral in this stochastic world, the double tangency of the borrowing-lending line with $f(\cdot)$ and $\hat{\alpha} g(\cdot)$ is the firstbest solution, where expected two-period income is maximized.

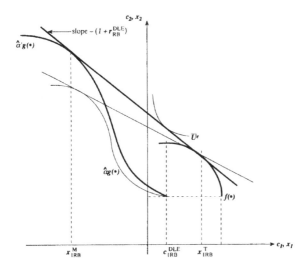

Figure 3 Rational-Beliefs Equilibrium in the DLE

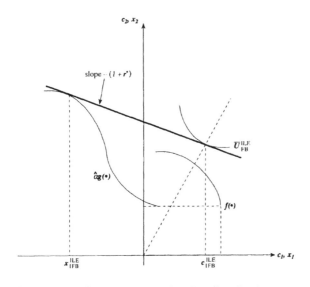

Figure 4 The First-Best Solution in the Internationally Liberalized Economy (ILE)

The problem comes when banks exploit the potential for moral hazard implied by the implicit or explicit government guarantee of bank deposits. If prudential supervision is insufficient, risk-neutral banks will truncate the true probability distribution of future investment returns by unduly discounting the possibility of bad outcomes. They and their depositors know that if the overall reform program fails

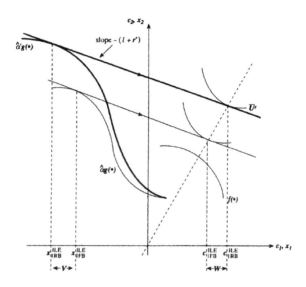

Figure 5 Rational-Beliefs Equilibrium in the ILE: The Overborrowing Syndrome

to deliver and leads to widespread bankruptcies and panic, the government will enter to bail out distressed institutions. Thus, ex ante, risk-neutral banks could run their loan programs overly optimistically as if the mean realization of α were $\hat{\alpha}'$, where $\hat{\alpha}' > \hat{\alpha}$. The result seen by nonbanks is the unduly inflated investment payoff function $\hat{\alpha}'g(\cdot)$ shown in Figure 3.

Unaware of the inadequacy of bank supervision, firm-households take this overly optimistic signal at face value and bid eagerly for funds to exploit the pseudo higher returns. The equilibrium interest rate, as shown by the double tangency of the domestic interest rate with $\hat{\alpha}'g(\cdot)$ and $f(\cdot)$ in Figure 3, is bid up higher than it would have been if the signal from the banks had been accurate. This corresponds to what Mordecai Kurz (1994) has called a *rational-beliefs* (RB) equilibrium. Unlike a full rational-expectations equilibrium, in our model nonbank agents with rational beliefs have insufficient information to reject a false signal from the banks. Under deposit insurance, loosely supervised banks prefer to gamble with the government's money.

Nevertheless, because the capital account of the balance of payments remains closed in the RB equilibrium shown for a DLE in Figure 3, the false optimism about the higher returns to investment does not lead the economy into serious overinvestment or overconsumption. Although firm-households see their future income to be too high, the sharp increase in the domestic interest rate above the first-best level (and probably far above international rates as well) restrains consumption and investment in period 1. Income and substitution effects offset each other so that current saving does not fall.

True, in period 2, when investments in the RB case turn out to yield less than anticipated, and high-cost bank loans must be repaid, bankruptcies could cause severe problems between debtors and creditors. But all of this is bottled up within the domestic economy. Moral hazard in the domestic banking system did not induce the nation as a whole to overborrow because, by definition, the capital account of the DLE remains closed, a crude fail-safe condition.

II. Opening the Model to International Capital Flows

Our analytical machinery also applies directly to an internationally liberalized economy (ILE), where the capital account is left open when credible real-side reforms are implemented. Now *all* our identical firm-households become net borrowers in period 1 in order to surmount the discrete setup costs of investing to exploit the structural reforms. The pace of technical advance quickens.

Suppose first that there is no moral hazard in the banking system; that is, a strong regulatory system prevents banks from discounting bad macroeconomic outcomes. Figure 4 shows that consumption rises (saving falls) in an ILE in period 1 because income and substitution effects now pull in the same direction. Not only does expected income rise into the indefinite future, but domestic interest rates fall to the world level r^*. (Remember, we are abstracting from currency risk and other monetary considerations.) The open international capital market allows people to borrow against their much higher incomes expected in the future in order to increase consumption today.

Although authorities in the ILE might get nervous about the large observed currentaccount deficit in period 1, it diminishes naturally in period 2 as loans are repaid. The fall in saving in period 1 (see Fig. 4), beyond that shown for a DLE (Fig. 2), is simply part and parcel of the first-best solution: the reforming economy's resources for investment and consumption are optimally distributed intertemporally. Welfare improves beyond what would prevail if the capital account had remained closed.

The potential for disaster arises when there is moral hazard in the capital market *and* international financial flows are unrestricted. Suppose now that the banks lend too exuberantly. They signal higher payoffs for investments than the reforms warrant. In the resulting RB equilibrium as shown by the tangency of the world interest rate with the investment function $\hat{\alpha}'g(\cdot)$ in Figure 5, saving declines further, and the corresponding current-account deficit mushrooms. Relative to the first-best equilibrium, first-period (over-) consumption increases by W, and (over-) investment increases by V.

Unless the economy experiences a lucky (upper-tail) payoff to today's investments, this RB equilibrium in Figure 5 is unsustainable. If the actual payoff is its true unbiased mean, $\hat{\alpha}g(\cdot)$, firms will have trouble repaying investment loans, and households debt burdens will escalate relative to their incomes. Widespread loan defaults could cause the domestic banking system to seize up and could require a bailout from foreign indebtedness.

III. Policy Conclusions

First, when real-side reforms are credible and expected to be permanent, private saving in period 1 could decline, with some domestic consumption financed by foreign-capital inflows in a first-best equilibrium, even if moral hazard in the banks is absent.

Second, the authorities still need be concerned that a decline in private saving, and a surge in investment, may result, at least in part, from a false euphoria regarding what the eventual payoffs from the credible reforms will be. The unavoidable presence of deposit insurance may lead banks to lend overly aggressively, which in turn sends a falsely optimistic signal to nonbank firms and households regarding the macroeconomic outcome of the reform process.

Third, the effectiveness of prudential banking regulations is particularly hard to assess at a time of great structural change in the economy. But if foreign capital inflows and domestic consumer credit are insufficiently restrained, the effect of moral hazard in the banks becomes much more damaging, as the Chilean and Mexican experiences attest.

References

Conley, J. P. and Maloney, W. F. "Optimum Sequencing of Credible Reforms with Uncertain Outcomes." *Journal of Development Economics*, October 1995, *48*(1), pp. 15166.

Kurz, Mordecai. "On the Structure and Diversity of Rational Beliefs." *Economic Theory,* October 1994, *4*(6), pp. 877–900.

McKinnon, Ronald I. *The order of economic liberalization: Financial control in the transition to a market economy,* 2nd Ed. Baltimore, MD: Johns Hopkins University Press, 1993.

McKinnon, Ronald and Pill, Huw. "Credible Liberalizations and International Capital Flows: The Overborrowing Syndrome," in T. Ito and A. Krueger, eds., *Financial deregulation and integration in East Asia.* Chicago: University of Chicago Press, 1996, pp. 7–42.

Pill, Huw. "A Simple Model of the OverBorrowing Syndrome." Working paper, Division of Research, Harvard Business School, 1996.

26

INSTITUTIONS RULE

The Primacy of Institutions Over Geography and Integration in Economic Development

Dani Rodrik, Arvind Subramanian, and Francesco Trebbi

Source: *Journal of Economic Growth* 9, 2, 2004, 131–165.

We estimate the respective contributions of institutions, geography, and trade in determining income levels around the world, using recently developed instrumental variables for institutions and trade. Our results indicate that the quality of institutions "trumps" everything else. Once institutions are controlled for, conventional measures of geography have at best weak direct effects on incomes, although they have a strong indirect effect by influencing the quality of institutions. Similarly, once institutions are controlled for, trade is almost always insignificant, and often enters the income equation with the "wrong" (i.e., negative) sign. We relate our results to recent literature, and where differences exist, trace their origins to choices on samples, specification, and instrumentation.

> Commerce and manufactures can seldom flourish long in any state which
> does not enjoy a regular administration of justice, in which the people do
> not feel themselves secure in the possession of their property, in which
> the faith of contracts is not supported by law, and in which the authority
> of the state is not supposed to be regularly employed in enforcing the
> payment of debts from all those who are able to pay. Commerce and
> manufactures, in short, can seldom flourish in any state in which there is
> not a certain degree of confidence in the justice of government.
>
> Adam Smith, *Wealth of Nations*

1. Introduction

Average income levels in the world's richest and poorest nations differ by a factor of more than 100. Sierra Leone, the poorest economy for which we have national income statistics, has a per capita GDP of $490, compared to Luxembourg's

$50,061.[1] What accounts for these differences, and what (if anything) can we do to reduce them? It is hard to think of any question in economics that is of greater intellectual significance, or of greater relevance to the vast majority of the world's population.

In the voluminous literature on this subject, three strands of thoughts stand out. First, there is a long and distinguished line of theorizing that places geography at the center of the story. Geography is a key determinant of climate, endowment of natural resources, disease burden, transport costs, and diffusion of knowledge and technology from more advanced areas. It exerts therefore a strong influence on agricultural productivity and the quality of human resources. Recent writings by Jared Diamond and Jeffrey Sachs are among the more notable works in this tradition (see Diamond, 1997; Gallup et al., 1998; Sachs, 2001).

A second camp emphasizes the role of international trade as a driver of productivity change. We call this the integration view, as it gives market integration, and impediments thereof, a starring role in fostering economic convergence between rich and poor regions of the world. Notable recent research in this camp includes Frankel and Romer (1999) and the pre-geography work of Sachs (Sachs and Warner, 1995).[2] It may be useful to distinguish between "moderate" and "maximal" versions of this view. Much of the economics profession would accept the hypothesis that trade can be an underlying source of growth once certain institutional pre-requisites have been fulfilled. But a more extreme perspective, and one that has received wide currency in public debates, is that trade/integration is the major determinant of whether poor countries grow or not. It is the latter perspective that characterizes such widely cited papers as Sachs and Warner (1995) and Dollar and Kraay (2004).

Finally, a third group of explanations centers on institutions, and in particular the role of property rights and the rule of law. In this view, what matters are the rules of the game in a society and their conduciveness to desirable economic behavior. This view is associated most strongly with Douglass North (1990). It has received careful econometric treatment recently in Hall and Jones (1999), who focus on what they call "social infrastructure," and in Acemoglu et al. (2001), who focus on the expropriation risk that current and potential investors face.

Growth theory has traditionally focussed on physical and human capital accumulation, and, in its endogenous growth variant, on technological change. But accumulation and technological change are at best proximate causes of economic growth. No sooner have we ascertained the impact of these two on growth—and with some luck their respective roles also—that we want to ask: But why did some societies manage to accumulate and innovate more rapidly than others? The three-fold classification offered above—geography, integration, and institutions—allows us to organize our thoughts on the "deeper" determinants of economic growth. These three are the factors that determine which societies will innovate and accumulate, and therefore develop, and which will not.

Since long-term economic development is a complex phenomenon, the idea that any one (or even all) of the above deep determinants can provide an adequate accounting of centuries of economic history is, on the face of it, preposterous. Historians and many social scientists prefer nuanced, layered explanations where these factors interact with human choices and many other not-so-simple twists and turns of fate. But economists like parsimony. We want to know how well these simple stories do, not only on their own or collectively, but more importantly, vis-à-vis each other. How much of the astounding variation in cross-national incomes around the world can geography, integration, and institutions explain? Do these factors operate additively, or do they interact? Are they all equally important? Does one of the explanations "trump" the other two?

The questions may be simple, but devising a reasonable empirical strategy for answering them is far from straightforward. This is not because we do not have good empirical proxies for each of these deep determinants. There are many reasonable measures of "geography," such as distance from the equator (our preferred measure), percentage land mass located in the tropics, or average temperature. The intensity of an economy's integration with the rest of the world can be measured by flows of trade or the height of trade barriers. The quality of institutions can be measured with a range of perceptions-based indicators of property rights and the rule of law. The difficulty lies instead in sorting out the complex web of causality that entangles these factors.

The extent to which an economy is integrated with the rest of the world and the quality of its institutions are both endogenous, shaped potentially not just by each other and by geography, but also by income levels. Problems of endogeneity and reverse causality plague any empirical researcher trying to make sense of the relationships among these causal factors. We illustrate this with the help of Figure 1,

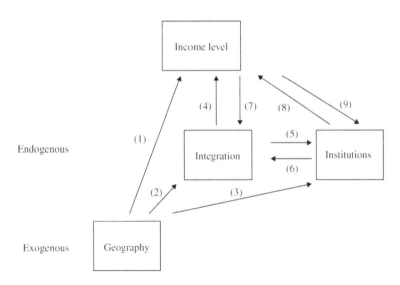

Figure 1 The "deep" determinants of income.

253

adapted from Rodrik (2003). The plethora of arrows in the figure, going in both directions at once in many cases, exemplifies the difficulty.

The task of demonstrating causality is perhaps easiest for the geographical determinists. Geography is as exogenous a determinant as an economist can ever hope to get, and the main burden here is to identify the main channel(s) through which geography influences economic performance. Geography may have a direct effect on incomes, through its effect on agricultural productivity and morbidity. This is shown with arrow (1) in Figure 1. It can also have an indirect effect through its impact on distance from markets and the extent of integration (arrow (2)) or its impact on the quality of domestic institutions (arrow (3)). With regard to the latter, economic historians have emphasized the disadvantageous consequences for institutional development of certain patterns of factor endowments, which engender extreme inequalities and enable the entrenchment of a small group of elites (e.g., Engerman and Sokoloff, 1994). A similar explanation, linking ample endowment of natural resources with stunted institutional development, also goes under the name of "resource curse" (Sala-i-Martin and Subramanian, 2003).

Trade fundamentalists and institutionalists have a considerably more difficult job to do, since they have to demonstrate causality for their preferred determinant, as well as identify the effective channel(s) through which it works. For the former, the task consists of showing that arrows (4) and (5)—capturing the direct impact of integration on income and the indirect impact through institutions, respectively—are the relevant ones, while arrows (6) and (7)—reverse feedbacks from incomes and institutions, respectively—are relatively insignificant. Reverse causality cannot be ruled out easily, since expanded trade and integration can be mainly the result of increased productivity in the economy and/or improved domestic institutions, rather than a cause thereof.

Institutionalists, meanwhile, have to worry about different kinds of reverse causality. They need to show that improvements in property rights, the rule of law and other aspects of the institutional environment are an independent determinant of incomes (arrow (8)), and are not simply the consequence of higher incomes (arrow (9)) or of greater integration (arrow (5)).

In econometric terms, what we need to sort all this out are good instruments for integration and institutions—sources of exogenous variation for the extent of integration and institutional quality, respectively, that are uncorrelated with other plausible (and excluded) determinants of income levels. Two recent papers help us make progress by providing plausible instruments. Frankel and Romer (1999) suggests that we can instrument for actual trade/GDP ratios by using trade/GDP shares constructed on the basis of a gravity equation for bilateral trade flows. The Frankel and Romer approach consists of first regressing bilateral trade flows (as a share of a country's GDP) on measures of country mass, distance between the trade partners, and a few other geographical variables, and then constructing a predicted aggregate trade share for each country on the basis of the coefficients estimated. This constructed trade share is then used as an instrument for actual trade shares in estimating the impact of trade on levels of income.

Acemoglu et al. (2001) use mortality rates of colonial settlers as an instrument for institutional quality. They argue that settler mortality had an important effect on the type of institutions that were built in lands that were colonized by the main European powers. Where the colonizers encountered relatively few health hazards to European settlement, they erected solid institutions that protected property rights and established the rule of law. In other areas, their interests were limited to extracting as much resources as quickly as possible, and they showed little interest in building high-quality institutions. Under the added assumption that institutions change only gradually over time, Acemoglu et al. argue that settler mortality rates are therefore a good instrument for institutional quality. Frankel and Romer (1999) and Acemoglu et al. (2001) use their respective instruments to demonstrate strong causal effects from trade (in the case of Frankel and Romer) and institutions (in the case of Acemoglu et al.) to incomes. But neither paper embeds their estimation in the broader framework laid out above. More specifically, Acemoglu et al. control for geographical determinants, but do not check for the effects of integration. Frankel and Romer do not control for institutions.

Our approach in this paper consists of using the Frankel and Romer and Acemoglu et al. instruments simultaneously to estimate the structure shown in Figure 1. The idea is that these two instruments, having passed what might be called the American Economic Review (AER)-test, are our best hope at the moment of unraveling the tangle of cause-and- effect relationships involved. So we systematically estimate a series of regressions in which incomes are related to measures of geography, integration, and institutions, with the latter two instrumented using the Frankel and Romer and Acemoglu et al. instruments, respectively. These regressions allow us to answer the question: what is the independent contribution of these three sets of deep determinants to the cross-national variation in income levels? The first stage of these regressions provides us in turn with information about the causal links among the determinants.

This exercise yields some sharp and striking results. Most importantly, we find that the quality of institutions trumps everything else. Once institutions are controlled for, integration has no direct effect on incomes, while geography has at best weak direct effects. Trade often enters the income regression with the "wrong" (i.e., negative) sign, as do many of the geographical indicators. By contrast, our measure of property rights and the rule of law always enters with the correct sign, and is statistically significant, often with t-statistics that are very large.

On the links among determinants, we find that institutional quality has a positive and significant effect on integration. Our results also tend to confirm the findings of Easterly and Levine (2003), namely that geography exerts a significant effect on the quality of institutions, and via this channel on incomes.[3]

Our preferred specification "accounts" for about half of the variance in incomes across the sample, with institutional quality (instrumented by settler mortality) doing most of the work. Our estimates indicate that an increase in institutional quality of one standard deviation, corresponding roughly to the difference between measured institutional quality in Bolivia and South Korea, produces a two log-points rise in per capita incomes, or a 6.4- fold difference—which, not coincidentally, is also roughly the income difference between the two countries. In our preferred specification, trade and distance from the equator both exert a negative, but insignificant effect on incomes (see Table 3, panel A, column (6)).

Much of our paper is devoted to checking the robustness of our central results. In particular, we estimate our model for three different samples: (a) the original 64-country sample used by Acemoglu et al.; (b) a 79-country sample which is the largest sample we can use while still retaining the Acemoglu et al. instrument; and (c) a 137-country sample that maximizes the number of countries at the cost of replacing the Acemoglu et al. instrument with two more widely available instruments (fractions of the population speaking English and Western European languages as the first language, from Hall and Jones, 1999.) We also use a large number of alternative indicators of geography and integration. In all cases, institutional quality emerges as the clear winner of the "horse race" among the three. Finally, we compare and contrast our results to those in some recent papers that have undertaken exercises of a similar sort. Where there are differences in results, we identify and discuss the source of the differences and explain why we believe our approach is superior on conceptual or empirical grounds.[4]

One final word about policy. As we shall emphasize at the end of the paper, identifying the deeper determinants of prosperity does not guarantee that we are left with clearcut policy implications. For example, finding that the "rule of law" is causally implicated in development does not mean that we actually know how to increase it under the specific conditions of individual countries. Nor would finding that "geography matters" necessarily imply geographic determinism—it may simply help reveal the roadblocks around which policy makers need to navigate. The research agenda to which this paper contributes is one that clarifies the priority of pursuing different objectives—improving the quality of domestic institutions, achieving integration into the world economy, or overcoming geographical adversity—but says very little about how each one of these is best achieved.

The plan of the paper is as follows. Section 2 presents the benchmark results and robustness tests. Section 3 provides a more in-depth interpretation of our results and lays out a research agenda.

2. Core Results and Robustness

2.1. Data and Descriptive Statistics

Table 1 provides descriptive statistics for the key variables of interest. The first column covers the sample of 79 countries for which data on settler mortality have been compiled by Acemoglu et al.[5] Given the demonstrated attractiveness of this variable as an instrument that can help illuminate causality, this will constitute our preferred sample. The second column contains summary statistics for a larger sample of 137 countries for which we have data on alternative instruments for institutions (fractions of the population speaking English and other European

Table 1 Descriptive statistics.

	Extended Acemoglu et al. Sample (79 countries)	Large Sample (137 countries)
Log GDP per capita (PPP) in 1995	8.03	8.41
(LCGDP95)	(1.05)	(1.14)
Rule of law (RULE)	−0.25	0.08
	(0.86)	(0.95)
Log openness (LCOPEN)	3.94	4.01
	(0.61)	(0.57)
Distance from equator in degrees (DISTEQ)	15.37	23.98
	(11.16)	(16.26)
Log European settler mortality (LOGEM4)	4.65	—
(deaths per annum per 1,000 population)	(1.22)	—
Log constructed openness	2.76	2.91
(LOGFRANKROM)	(0.76)	(0.79)
Fraction of population speaking other	0.30	0.24
European language (EURFRAC)	(0.41)	(0.39)
Fraction of population speaking English	0.11	0.08
(ENGFRAC)	(0.29)	(0.24)

Notes: Standard deviations are reported below the means. Rule of law ranges between −2.5 and + 2.5. Openness is measured as the ratio of trade to GDP. Constructed openness—the instrument for openness—is the predicted trade share and is from Frankel and Romer (1999). The Appendix describes in detail all the data and their sources.

languages). Data for the Frankel and Romer instrument on trade, on which we will rely heavily, are also available for this larger sample.

GDP per capita on a PPP basis for 1995 will be our measure of economic performance. For both samples, there is substantial variation in GDP per capita: for the 79-country sample, mean GDP in 1995 is $3,072, the standard deviation of log GDP is 1.05, with the poorest country's (Congo, DRC) GDP being $321 and that of the richest (Singapore) $28,039. For the larger sample, mean income is $4,492, the standard deviation is 1.14, with the richest country (Luxembourg) enjoying an income level of $34,698.

The institutional quality measure that we use is due to Kaufmann et al. (2002). This is a composite indicator of a number of elements that capture the protection afforded to property rights as well as the strength of the rule of law.[6] This is a standardized measure that varies between −2.5 (weakest institutions) and 2.5 (strongest institutions). In our sample of 79 countries, the mean score is −0.25, with Zaire (score of −2.09) having the weakest institutions and Singapore (score of 1.85) the strongest.

Integration, measured using the ratio of trade to GDP, also varies substantially in our sample. The average ratio is 51.4 percent, with the least "open" country (India) posting a ratio of 13 percent and the most "open" (Singapore) a ratio of 324 percent. Our preferred measure of geography is a country's distance from the equator (measured in degrees). The typical country is about 15.4 degrees away from the equator.

2.2. OLS and IV Results in the Core Specifications

Our paper represents an attempt to estimate the following equation:

$$\log y_i = \mu + \alpha \text{INS}_i + \beta \text{INT}_i + \gamma \text{GEO}_i + \varepsilon_i, \tag{1}$$

where y_i is income per capita in country i, INS_i, INT_i, and GEO_i are respectively measures for institutions, integration, and geography, and ε_i is the random error term. Throughout the paper, we will be interested in the size, sign, and significance of the three coefficients α, β, and γ. We will use standardized measures of INS_i, INT_i, and GEO_i in our core regressions, so that the estimated coefficients can be directly compared.

Before we discuss the benchmark results, it is useful to look at the simple, bivariate relationships between income and each of the "deep determinants." Figure 2 shows these scatter plots, with the three panels on the left hand side corresponding to the sample of 79 countries and the three panels on the right to the larger sample of 137 countries. All the plots show a clear and unambiguously positive relationship between income and its possible determinants. Thus, any or all of them have the potential to explain levels of income. This positive relationship is confirmed by the simple OLS regression of equation (1) reported in column (6) of Table 2. The signs of institution, openness, and geography are as expected and statistically significant or close to being so. Countries with stronger institutions, more open economies, and more distant from the equator are likely to have higher levels of income.

To get a sense of the magnitude of the potential impacts, we can compare two countries, say Nigeria and Mauritius, both in Africa. If the OLS relationship is indeed causal, the coefficients in column (6) of Table 2 would suggest that Mauritius's per capita GDP should be 10.3 times that of Nigeria, of which 77 percent would be due to better institutions, 9 percent due to greater openness, and 14 percent due to better location. In practice, Mauritius's income ($11,400) is 14.8 times that of Nigeria ($770).

Of course, for a number of reasons described extensively in the literature— reverse causality, omitted variables bias, and measurement error—the above relationship cannot be interpreted as causal or accurate. To address these problems, we employ a two-stage least squares estimation procedure. The identification strategy is to use the Acemoglu et al. settler mortality measure as an instrument for institutions and the Frankel and Romer measure of constructed trade shares as an instrument for integration. In the first-stage regressions, INS_i and INT_i are regressed on all the exogenous variables. Thus

$$\text{INS}_i = \lambda + \delta \text{SM}_i + \phi \text{CONST}_i + \psi \text{GEO}_i + \varepsilon_{\text{INS}_i}, \tag{2}$$

$$\text{INT}_i = \theta + \sigma \text{CONST}_i + \tau \text{SM}_i + \omega \text{GEO}_i + \varepsilon_{\text{INT}_i}, \tag{3}$$

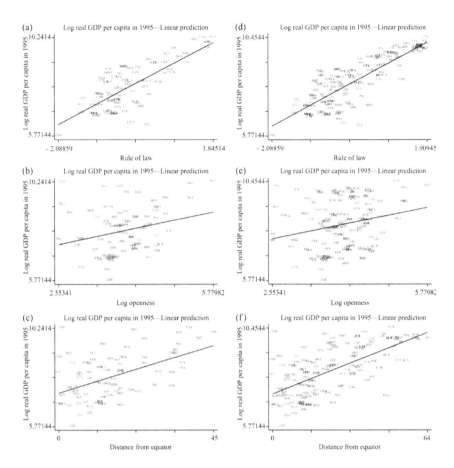

Figure 2 Simple correlations between income and its determinants (sample of 79 countries for (a)–(c); sample of 137 countries for (d)–(f)).

where SM_i refers to settler mortality and $CONST_i$ to the Frankel and Romer instrument for trade/GDP. The exclusion restrictions are that SM_i and $CONST_i$ do not appear in equation (1).

Equations (1)–(3) are our core specification. This specification represents, we believe, the most natural framework for estimating the respective impacts of our three deep determinants. It is general, yet simple, and treats each of the three deep determinants symmetrically, giving them all an equal chance. Our proxies for institutions, integration, and geography are the ones that the advocates of each approach have used. Our instruments for institutions and integration are sensible, and have already been demonstrated to "work" in the sense of producing strong second-stage results (albeit in estimations not embedded in our broader framework).

259

Table 2 Determinants of development: Core specifications, ordinary least squares estimates.

	Log GDP per capita								
	Acemoglu et al. Sample			Extended Acemoglu et al. Sample			Large Sample		
Dependent Variable	(1)	(2)	(3)	(4)	(5)	(6)	(7)	(8)	(9)
Geography (DISTEQ)	0.74	0.20	0.32	0.80	0.22	0.33	0.76	0.20	0.23
	(4.48)*	(1.34)	(1.85)**	(5.22)*	(1.63)	(2.11)**	(10.62)*	(2.48)**	(2.63)*
Institutions (RULE)		0.78	0.69		0.81	0.72		0.81	0.78
		(7.56)*	(6.07)*		(9.35)*	(6.98)*		(12.12)*	(10.49)*
Integration (LCOPEN)			0.16			0.15			0.08
			(1.48)			(1.53)			(1.24)
Observations	64	64	64	79	79	79	137	137	137
R-square	0.25	0.57	0.59	0.26	0.61	0.62	0.42	0.71	0.71

Notes: The dependent variable is per capita GDP in 1995, PPP basis. There are three samples for which the core regressions are run: (i) the first three columns correspond to the sample of 64 countries in Acemoglu et al. (2001); (ii) columns (4)–(6) use a sample of 79 countries for which data on settler mortality (LOGEM4) have been compiled by Acemoglu et al.; and (iii) columns (7)–(9) use a larger sample of 137 countries. The regressors are: (i) DISTEQ, the variable for geography, which is measured as the absolute value of latitude of a country; (ii) Rule of law (RULE), which is the measure for institutions; and (iii) LCOPEN, the variable for integration, which is measured as the ratio of nominal trade to nominal GDP. All regressors are scaled in the sense that they represent deviations from the mean divided by the standard deviation. All regressors, except DISTEQ and RULE, in the three panels are in logs. See the Appendix for more detailed variable definitions and sources. t-statistics are reported under coefficient estimates. Significance at the 1, 5, and 10 percent levels are denoted respectively by *, **, and ***.

260

Panel A of Table 3 reports the two-stage least squares estimates of the three coefficients of interest. The estimation is done for three samples of countries: (i) for the sample of 64 countries analyzed by Acemoglu et al.; (ii) for an extended sample of 79 countries for which Acemoglu et al. had compiled data on settler mortality; and (iii) for a larger sample of 137 countries that includes those that were not colonized. In Acemoglu et al., the quality of institutions was measured by an index of protection against expropriation. We use a rule of law index because it is available for a larger sample. The IV estimates of the coefficient on institutions in the first three columns of panel A are very similar to those in Acemoglu et al., confirming that these two indexes are capturing broadly similar aspects of institutions, and allowing us to use the larger sample for which data on settler mortality are available.

Columns (4)–(6) report our estimates for the extended Acemoglu et al. sample (which as we shall explain below will be our preferred sample in this paper). Columns (5) and (6) confirm the importance of institutions in explaining the cross-country variation in development. Once the institutional variable is added, geography and openness do not have any additional power in explaining development. Institutions trump geography and openness. In our preferred specification (column (6)), not only are institutions significant, their impact is large, and the estimated coefficients on geography and openness have the "wrong" sign! The coefficient on institutions in the IV estimation is nearly three times as large as in the corresponding OLS estimation (2 versus 0.7), suggesting that the attenuation bias from measurement error in the institution variables swamps the reverse causality bias that would tend to make the OLS estimates greater than the IV estimates.

The results are similar for the larger sample of countries (panel A, columns (6)–(9)). In this sample, we follow Hall and Jones (1999) in using the following two variables as instruments for institutional quality (in lieu of settler mortality): ENGFRAC, fraction of the population speaking English, and EURFRAC, fraction of the population speaking other European languages. Once again, institutions trump geography and openness, although the size of the estimated coefficient is smaller than that for the smaller sample. Figure 3 plots the conditional relationship between income and each of the three determinants for the 79- country (left panels) and 137-country (right panels) samples. In contrast to Figure 2, which showed a positive partial relationship between income and all its determinants, Figure 3 shows that only institutions have a significant and positive effect on income once the endogenous determinants are instrumented.[7]

The first-stage regressions (reported in panel B) are also interesting. In our preferred specification, settler mortality has a significant effect on integration: the coefficient is correctly signed and significant at the 1 percent level. This result holds for the range of specifications that we estimate as part of the robustness checks reported below. The geography variable has a significant impact in determining the quality of institutions as does integration, although its coefficient is significant only at the 5 percent level. The table also reports a number of diagnostic

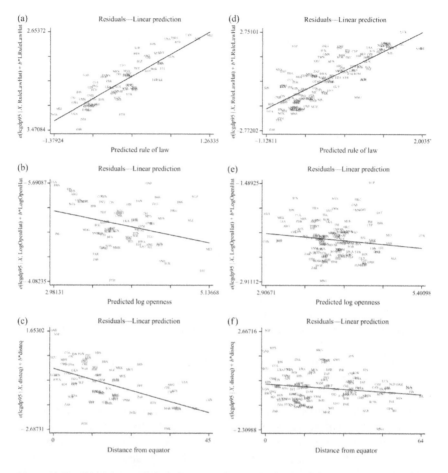

Figure 3 Conditional correlations between income and its determinants (sample of 79 countries for (a)–(c); sample of 137 countries for (d)–(f)).

statistics on weak instruments. These provide little evidence that our results suffer from the presence of weak instruments. The F-statistic for both firststage regressions is well above the threshold of 10 suggested by Staiger and Stock (1997);[8] the partial R-squares are reasonable; and the correlation between the fitted values of the endogenous variables appears to be sufficiently low.[9]

While all three samples provide qualitatively similar results, our preferred sample will be the 79-country sample: obviously this sample Pareto-dominates the 64-country sample. We also prefer this sample to the 137-country sample because settler mortality appears to be a superior instrument to those used in the 137-country sample (ENGFRAC and EURFRAC). Panel B shows that the instruments for the IV regressions in the 137-country sample fail to pass the over-identification tests despite the well-known problems of these tests having low power. Indeed, this turns out to be true not just for the core specifications in Table 3, but for many of the robustness tests that we discuss below. Thus, while it is reassuring that the main result regarding the primacy of institutions also holds in the larger sample, we will focus mainly on the 79-country sample in the rest of the paper (referring to results for the larger sample in passing).[10] We shall examine the robustness of our main results in the following section.

Table 4 illustrates the inter-relationships between integration and institutions in the 79- country sample. We regress trade and institutional quality separately on geography and on each other (instrumenting the endogenous variables in the manner discussed previously). While it is possible to envisage non-linear relationships among these determinants—trade may have sometimes positive and sometimes negative effects on the quality of institutions, for example,—we keep the specifications simple and linear as in all our core specifications. The IV regressions show that each of these exerts a positive impact on the other, with the larger quantitative and statistically significant impact being that of institutional quality on trade. A unit increase in institutional quality increases the trade share by 0.45 units, while a unit increase in trade increases institutional quality by 0.22 units.[11]

Taking these indirect effects into account, we can calculate the total impacts on incomes of these two determinants by combining the estimated parameters. Our estimates of α and β (the direct effects) in our preferred sample and specification are 1.98 and –0.31, respectively (column (6)). We can solve the system of equations implied by the additional results in columns (1) and (2) of Table 4 to calculate the total effects on log incomes of "shocks" to the error terms in the institution and trade equations.[12]

The results are as follows. If we consider the point estimates in column (6) of Table 3 and in columns (1) and (2) in Table 4 as our best estimate of the various effects, a unit (positive) shock to the institutional quality equation ultimately produces an increase in log incomes of 1.85; a unit (positive) shock to the trade equation ultimately produces an increase in log incomes of 0.09. This is a 22-fold difference. Alternatively, we could consider only those impacts that are statistically significant. Under this assumption, a unit shock to the institutional quality equation is the estimate from column (6), namely 1.98. The corresponding unit shock to the trade equation has no impact on income at all. Institutions overwhelmingly trump integration.

The much greater impact of institutions is the consequence of four factors: (i) the estimated direct effect of institutions on incomes is positive and large; (ii) the estimated direct effect of trade on incomes is negative (but statistically insignificant); (iii) the estimated indirect effect of trade on institutions is positive, but small and statistically insignificant; and (iv) the estimated indirect effect of institutions on trade is large and statistically significant but this has either a negative or no impact on incomes because of (ii).

Repeating this exercise, and taking into account only the statistically significant coefficients, we find that the total impact of a unit shock to geography on

Table 3 Determinants of development: Core specifications, instrumental variables estimates.

	Acemoglu et al. Sample			Extended Acemoglu et al. Sample			Large Sample		
	(1)	(2)	(3)	(4)	(5)	(6)	(7)	(8)	(9)
Panel A. Second-stage: Dependent variable = Log GDP per capita									
Geography (DISTEQ)	0.74	−0.42	−0.56	0.80	−0.45	−0.72	0.76	−0.06	−0.14
	(4.48)*	(−1.19)	(−1.23)	(5.22)*	(−1.26)	(−1.38)	(10.62)*	(−0.5)	(−0.93)
Institutions (RULE)		1.68	1.78		1.75	1.98		1.19	1.30
		(4.29)*	(3.78)*		(4.42)*	(3.56)*		(8.02)*	(7.09)*
Integration (LCOPEN)			−0.18			−0.31			−0.15
			(−0.71)			(−1.10)			(−1.09)
No. of observations	64	64	64	79	79	79	137	137	137
R-square	0.25	0.54	0.56	0.26	0.51	0.52	0.417	0.51	0.56
Test for over-identifying restrictions (*p*-value)								(0.0089)	(0.0354)
Panel B: First Stage for Endogenous Variables (Institutions (RULE) and Integration (LCOPEN))									
Dependent variable	RULE	RULE	LCOPEN	RULE	RULE	LCOPEN	RULE	RULE	LCOPEN
Geography (DISTEQ)	0.41	0.47	−0.25	0.47	0.54	−0.18	0.67	0.66	−0.05
	(2.8)*	(3.21)*	(−2.00)**	(3.34)*	(3.87)*	(−1.37)	(10.81)*	(11.23)*	(−0.84)
Settler mortality (LOGEM4)	−0.39	−0.40	−0.30	−0.34	−0.34	−0.27			
	(−3.87)*	(−4.1)*	(−3.51)*	(−3.69)*	(−3.82)*	(−3.22)*			
Population speaking English (ENGFRAC)							0.19	0.18	0.17
							(2.69)*	(2.69)*	(2.65)*
Population speaking other European langages (EURFRAC)							0.14	0.17	−0.11
							(1.94)**	(2.55)**	(−1.67)**

264

Constructed openness (LOGFRANKROM)	na	0.20 (1.95)**	0.90 (10.32)*	na	0.19 (2.16)**	0.80 (9.67)*	na	0.23 (3.99)*	0.70 (12.33)*
F-statistic	22.9	17.2	41.7	24	18.5	36.9	50.09	45.79	41.39
R-square	0.41	0.44	0.66	0.37	0.40	0.58	0.52	0.57	0.54
Partial R-square		0.16	0.58		0.12	0.51		0.18	0.52
corr(RULEFIT, LCOPENFIT)			0.14			0.21			0.27

Notes: The dependent variable in panel A is per capita GDP in 1995, PPP basis. There are three samples for which the core regressions are run: (i) the first three columns correspond to the sample of 64 countries in Acemoglu et al. (2001); (ii) columns (4)–(6) use a sample of 79 countries for which data on settler mortality (LOGEM4) have been compiled by Acemoglu et al.; and (iii) columns (7)–(9) use a larger sample of 137 countries for which the instrument for institutions is similar to that in Hall and Jones (1999). The regressors in panel A are: (i) DISTEQ, the variable for geography, which is measured as the absolute value of latitude of a country; (ii) Rule of law (RULE), which is the measure for institutions; and (iii) LCOPEN, the variable for integration, which is measured as the ratio of nominal trade to nominal GDP. All regressors are scaled in the sense that they represent deviations from the mean divided by the standard deviation. The dependent variables in panel B are measures of institutions (RULE) and/or integration (LCOPEN) depending on the specification. The regressors in panel B are: (i) DISTEQ described above; (ii) settler mortality (LOGEM4) in the first six columns; (iii) the proportion of the population of a country that speaks English (ENGFRAC) and the proportion of the population that speaks any European language (EURFRAC) in the last three columns; (iv) instrument for openness (LOGFRANKROM) obtained from Frankel and Romer (1999). All regressors, except DISTEQ and RULE, in the three panels are in logs. See the Appendix for more detailed variable definitions and sources. Standard errors are corrected, using the procedure described in Frankel and Romer (1999), to take into account the fact that the openness instrument is estimated. Significance at the 1, 5, and 10 percent levels are denoted respectively by *, **, and ***. t-statistics are reported under coefficient estimates.

Table 4 Inter-relations between integration and institutions.

Dependent Variable	Extended Acemoglu et al. Sample		Large Sample	
	RULE (1)	LCOPEN (2)	RULE (3)	LCOPEN (4)
Panel A. OLS Estimates				
Geography (DISTEQ)	0.79	−0.43	0.66	−0.2
	(5.79)*	(−3.48)*	(10.81)*	(−2.8)*
Institutions (RULE)		0.34		0.27
		(4.17)*		(3.8)*
Integration (LCOPEN)	0.32		0.27	
	(3.35)*		(3.55)*	
R-square	0.42	0.23	0.52	0.12
Panel B. Second Stage IV Estimates				
Geography (DISTEQ)	0.75	−0.51	0.66	−0.02
	(5.19)*	(−3.08)*	(10.88)*	(−0.16)
Institutions (RULE)		0.45		0.02
		(2.33)**		(0.09)
Integration (LCOPEN)	0.22		0.27	
	(1.02)		(1.34)	
No. of observations	79	79	137	137
R-square	0.31	0.09	0.49	0.02
Panel C. First Stage IV Estimates				
Dependent variable	LCOPEN	RULE	LCOPEN	RULE
Geography (DISTEQ)	0.02	0.47	−0.04	0.67
	(0.13)	(3.34)*	(−0.7)	(10.81) *
Settler mortality (LOGEM4)		−0.34		
		(−3.69)*		
Constructed openness	0.79		0.71	
(LOGFRANKROM)	(9.08)*		(12.35)*	
Population speaking English				0.19
(ENGFRAC)				(2.69)*
Population speaking other European				0.14
langages (EURFRAC)				(1.94)***
F-statistic	44.7	24.0	76.3	50.1
R-square	0.54	0.39	0.53	0.53

Notes: The dependent variable in panels A and B are per capita GDP in 1995, PPP basis. There are two samples for which the core regressions are run: (i) the first two columns correspond to the sample of 79 countries for which data on settler mortality (LOGEM4) have been compiled by Acemoglu et al.; and (ii) columns (3) and (4) use a larger sample of 137 countries for which the instrument for institutions is similar to that in Hall and Jones (1999). The regressors in panels A and B are: (i) DISTEQ, the variable for geography, which is measured as the absolute value of latitude of a country; (ii) Rule of law (RULE), which is the measure for institutions; and (iii) LCOPEN, the variable for integration, which is measured as the ratio of nominal trade to nominal GDP. All regressors are scaled in the sense that they represent deviations from the mean divided by the standard deviation. The dependent variables in panel C are measures of institutions (RULE) and/or integration (LCOPEN) depending on the specification. The regressors in panel C are: (i) DISTEQ described above; (ii) settler mortality (LOGEM4) in the first two columns; (iii) the proportion of the population of a country that speaks English (ENGFRAC) and the proportion of the population that speaks any European language (EURFRAC) in the last two columns; (iv) instrument for openness (LOGFRANKROM) obtained from Frankel and Romer (1999). All regressors, except DISTEQ and RULE, in the three panels are in logs. See the Appendix for more detailed variable definitions and sources. Standard errors are corrected, using the procedure described in Frankel and Romer (1999), to take into account the fact that the openness instrument is estimated. t-statistics are reported under coefficient estimates. Significance at the 1, 5, and 10 percent levels are denoted respectively by *, **, and ***.

income is about 1.49, only a quarter less than that of institutions. The large impact of geography stems from the sizable indirect impact that it has in determining institutional quality (coefficient of 0.75 in Panel B, column (1) of Table 4).[13]

We next analyze the channels through which the deep determinants influence incomes. The proximate determinants of economic growth are accumulation (physical and human) and productivity change. How do the deep determinants influence these channels? To answer this question, we regressed income per worker and its three proximate determinants, physical, human capital per worker, and total factor productivity (strictly speaking a labor-augmenting technological progress parameter) on the deep determinants. Data for the left hand side variables for these regressions that is, income, physical, and human capital per worker, and factor productivity are taken from Hall and Jones (1999). These results are reported in Table 5 for both the 79-country sample (columns (1)–(4)) and the 137-country sample (columns (5)–(8)).[14] Three features stand out.

First, the regression for income per worker is very similar to the regressions for per capita income reported in Tables 2–4, with institutions exerting a positive and significant effect on income, while integration and geography remain insignificant. Second, and interestingly, the same pattern holds broadly for the accumulation and productivity regressions; that is, institutions are an important determinant of both accumulation and productivity, while integration and geography are not influential in determining either accumulation or productivity.[15] Finally, it is interesting to note that institutions have a quantitatively larger impact on physical accumulation than on human capital accumulation or productivity; for example, in the 79-country sample the coefficient on physical capital accumulation is about six times greater than on human capital accumulation and about 3.2 times greater than on productivity. One possible interpretation is that these results emphasize the particularly important role that institutions play in preventing expropriability of property which serves as a powerful incentive to invest and accumulate physical capital.

2.3. Robustness Checks

Tables 6–8 present our robustness checks. In Table 6 we test whether our results are driven by certain influential observations or by the four neo-European countries in our sample (Australia, Canada, New Zealand, and Australia), which are arguably different from the rest of the countries included. We also check to see whether the inclusion of regional dummies affects the results.

In columns (1)* and (1)** of Table 6 we use the Belsey-Kuh-Welsch (1980) test to check whether individual observations exert unusual leverage on the coefficient estimates, discarding those which do so. In the specification without regional dummies ((1)*), two observations—Ethiopia and Singapore—are influential. Once these are dropped, the coefficient estimate for institutions not only remains statistically unaffected, but increases in magnitude. In the equation with regional dummies, the test requires the observation for Ethiopia to be omitted, and the

Table 5 Determinants of development: Channels of influence.

Dependent Variable	Extended Acemoglu et al. Sample				Larger Sample			
	Income per worker (1)	Capital per worker (2)	Human Capital per worker (3)	Total Factor productivity (4)	Income per worker (5)	Capital per worker (6)	Human Capital per worker (7)	Total Factor productivity (8)
Geography (DISTEQ)	-0.97	-1.72	-0.26	-0.33	-0.25	-0.38	-0.05	-0.13
	(-1.52)	(-1.63)	(-1.54)	(-1.02)	(-1.18)	(-1.14)	(-1.00)	(-0.85)
Institutions (RULE)	2.21	3.39*	0.56	1.06	1.32	1.90	0.34	0.69
	(3.30)	(3.03)*	(3.14)*	(3.08)*	(5.30)*	(4.72)*	(5.64)*	(3.74)*
Integration (LCOPEN)	-0.42	-0.70	-0.15	-0.13	-0.30	-0.46	-0.11	-0.11
	(-1.36)	(-1.30)	(-1.86)***	(-0.84)	(-1.79)**	(-2.10)**	(-3.00)*	(-0.84)
R-square	0.60	0.52	0.51	0.44	0.58	0.54	0.58	0.36
No. of observations	73	73	73	73	119	119	119	119

Notes: The four dependent variables—income per worker, capital per worker, human capital per worker, and the level of total factor productivity-are expressed in natural logarithms and are from Hall and Jones (1999). The IV estimates for the Acemoglu et al. sample use settler mortality (LOGEM4) as the instrument for institutions and EURFRAC and ENGFRAC as the instrument for the larger sample. All regressors, except RULE, are in logarithms and are scaled. Standard errors are corrected, using the procedure described in Frankel and Romer (1999), to take into account the fact that the openness instrument is estimated. *t*-statistics are reported under coefficient estimates. Significance at the 1, 5, and 10 percent levels are denoted respectively by *, **, and ***.

Table 6 Determinants of development: Robustness to "influential" observations, neoeuropes, legal systems, origin of colonizer, and religion.

	Baseline 1	(1)*	(1)**	(1)***	(1)****	Baseline 2	(2)*	(2)**	(2)***	(3)	(4)	(5)
Two-stage Least Squares: Dependent Variable is log GDP per Capita in 1995												
Geography (DISTEQ)	-0.72 (-1.38)	-1.37 (-1.71)***	-0.71 (-1.42)	-0.92 (-1.18)	-0.62 (-0.82)	-0.14 (-0.93)	-0.14 (-0.94)	0.02 (0.20)	-0.34 (-1.48)	-1.00 (-1.53)	-0.78 (-1.05)	-0.82 (-1.31)
Institutions (RULE)	1.98 (3.56)*	2.66 (3.06)*	1.86 (3.26)*	2.77 (2.45)**	1.99 (1.64)	1.30 (7.09)*	1.30 (7.14)*	0.90 (8.54)*	1.64 (5.15)*	2.43 (3.08)*	2.32 (2.46)**	2.09 (3.04)*
Integration (LCOPEN)	-0.31 (-1.10)	-0.45 (-1.12)	-0.33 (-1.26)	-0.74 (-1.31)	-0.44 (-0.80)	-0.15 (-1.09)	-0.15 (-1.02)	0.02 (0.18)	-0.31 (-1.92)**	-0.42 (-1.48)	-0.28 (-0.87)	-0.32 (-1.08)
Regional Dummies												
Latin America (LAAM)			0.42 (1.18)		0.15 (0.28)			0.25 (1.65)***				
East Asia (ASIAE)			0.22 (0.50)		0.05 (0.10)			0.13 (0.65)				
Legal origin										[0.135]		
Identity of colonizer											[0.080]***	
Religion												[0.021]**
R-square	0.52	0.56	0.65	0.44	0.63	0.56	0.59	0.68	0.55	0.54	0.55	0.59
No. of observations	79	77	78	75	75	137	136	134	133	79	79	79
Omitted observations	None	Singapore, Ethiopia	Ethiopia	Australia, Canada, NewZealand, USA	Australia, Canada, NewZealand, USA	None	Singapore	Cuba, Czech Rep., Germany	Australia, Canada, NewZealand, USA	None	None	None

Notes: The dependent variable is per capita GDP in 1995, PPP basis. Baseline 1 corresponds to the specification in column (6) of Table 3. Baseline 2 corresponds to the specification in column (9) of Table 3. In columns labeled with one and two asterisks, influential observations are defined according to the Belsey et al. (1980) DFITS statistic, which requires omitting those observations for which DFITS exceeds $2(k/n)^{(1/2)}$, where k is the number of regressors and n is the sample size. In columns labeled with three or four asterisks, observations for Australia, Canada, New Zealand, and Canada (Neoeuropes) are omitted. Standard errors are corrected, using the procedure described in Frankel and Romer (1999), to take into account the fact that the openness instrument is estimated, t-statistics are reported under coefficient estimates. For legal origin, identity of colonizer, and religion, p-values for joint significance of the underlying variables (LEGFR and LEGSO for legal origin, COLUK and COLFR for colonizer's identity, and CATH, PROT, and MUSE for religion) are reported. Significance at the 1, 5, and 10 percent levels are denoted respectively by *, **, and ***. All regressors are scaled as described in the notes to Tables 2–4.

revised specification (column (1)**) yields results very similar to the baseline specification, with the coefficient estimate on institutions remaining strong and significant. The inclusion of regional dummies for Latin America, sub-Saharan Africa, and Asia tends to lower somewhat the estimated coefficient on institutions, but its significance level remains unaffected. Note also that none of the regional dummies enters significantly, which is reassuring regarding the soundness of our parsimonious specification.

The tests for influential observations suggest that there is no statistical basis for discarding neo-European countries. Nevertheless to confirm that these countries are not driving the results, we re-estimated the baseline specification without these observations. As the column labeled (1)*** confirms, the coefficient estimates are unaffected; indeed, once again the size of the coefficient on institutions rises substantially, suggesting the greater importance of institutions for the non-neo-European colonized countries. The remaining columns (columns (2)* and (2)**) confirm that our results are robust also for the larger sample of countries.

We then check whether our results are robust to the inclusion of dummies for legal origin (column (3)), for the identity of colonizer (column (4)), and religion (column (5)). La Porta et al. (1998) argue that the type of legal system historically adopted in a country or imported through colonization has an important bearing on the development of institutions and hence on income levels. Similar claims are made on behalf of the other variables. In all cases, while these variables themselves tend to be individually and in some cases jointly significant, their inclusion does not affect the core results about the importance of institutions and the lack of any direct impact of geography and integration on incomes. Indeed, controlling for these other variables, the coefficient of the institutions variable increases: for example, in the 79-country sample, this coefficient increases from two in the baseline to 2.43 when the legal origin dummies are included.[16]

In Table 7 we check whether our particular choice of measure for geography (distance from the equator) influences our results. We successively substitute in our baseline specification a number of alternative measures of geography used in the literature. These include percent of a country's land area in the tropics (TROPICS), access to the sea (ACCESS), number of frost days per month in winter (FROSTDAYS), the area covered by frost (FROSTAREA), whether a country is an oil exporter (OIL), and mean temperature (MEAN TEMPERATURE). (Recall that we had already introduced regional dummies as part of our basic robustness check above.) The variables FROSTDAYS and FROSTAREA are taken from Masters and McMillan (2001), who argue that the key disadvantage faced by tropical countries is the absence of winter frost. (Frost kills pests, pathogens and parasites, thereby improving human health and agricultural productivity.) We find that none of these variables, with the exception of the oil dummy, is statistically significant in determining incomes. Equally importantly, they do not change qualitatively our estimates of the institution variable, which remains significant, nor of the integration variable, which remains insignificant and "wrongly" signed.[17]

Table / Determinants of development: Robustness to alternative measure of geography.

	Baseline	(1)	(2)	(3)	(4)	(5)	(6)	(7)	(8)	(9)	(10)	(11)
Two-stage Least Squares: Dependent Variable is log GDP per Capita in 1995												
Institutions (RULE)	1.98	1.47	1.99	1.48	1.45	1.97	1.89	1.81	0.65	0.94	0.91	1.04
	(3.56)*	(2.96)*	(3.57)*	(6.09)*	(7.03)*	(3.39)*	(3.03)*	(4.23)*	(2.34)*	(3.90)*	(1.67)***	(2.47)*
Integration (LCOPEN)	-0.31	-0.19	-0.35	-0.10	0.00	-0.42	0.00	-0.25	-0.02	-0.11	-0.08	-0.14
	(-1.10)	(-0.91)	(-1.00)	(-0.52)	(0.01)	(-1.10)	(0.01)	(-0.65)	(-0.01)	(-0.71)	(-0.46)	(-1.00)
Geography (DISTEQ)	-0.72	-0.41							-0.25	-0.34	-0.26	-0.28
	(-1.38)	(-0.97)							(-0.91)	(-1.35)	(-1.07)	(-1.11)
Regional dummies Latin America (LAAM)	0.43										0.25	0.29
	(1.57)										(0.61)	(0.74)
Sub-Saharan Africa (SAFRICA)	-0.31										-0.20	-0.06
	(-0.97)										(-0.60)	(0.10)
East Asia (ASIAE)	0.29										0.26	0.34
	(0.83)										(0.97)	(1.22)
Area under tropics (TROPICS)			0.63									
			(1.45)									
Access to sea (ACCESS)				0.06								
				(0.19)								
Major oil exporter (OIL)					0.23							
					(2.10)*							
Days under frost (FROSTDAYS)						-1.07						
						(-1.47)						
Area under frost (FROSTAREA)							-0.62					
							(-1.17)					
Temperature (MEANTEMP)								0.52				
								(1.27)				
Malaria proportion in population (MALFAL94)									-0.69		-0.36	
									(-5.26)*		(-0.67)	
Malaria proportion in population * proportion of fatal species (MALFAL)										-0.47		-0.30
										(-5.28)*		(-0.62)
R-square	0.52	0.63	0.54	0.52	0.54	0.53	0.51	0.64	0.52	0.52	0.63	0.63
No. of observations	79	79	76	76	67	76	66	69	75	75	75	75

Notes: The dependent variable is per capita GDP in 1995, PPP basis. Baseline corresponds to the specification in column (6) of Tables 2–4. Standard errors are corrected, using the procedure described in Frankel and Romer (1999), to take into account the fact that the openness instrument is estimated, t-statistics are reported under coefficient estimates. Significance at the 1, 5, and 10 percent levels are denoted respectively by *, **, and ***.

271

In response to the findings reported in an earlier version of this paper, Sachs (2003) has produced new empirical estimates which attribute a more significant causal role to geography. Arguing that distance from equator is a poor proxy for geographical advantage, Sachs uses two explanatory variables related to malaria incidence. The first of these is an estimate of the proportion of a country's population that lives with risk of malaria transmission (MAL94P), while the second multiplies MAL94P by an estimate of the proportion of malaria cases that involve the fatal species, *Plasmodium falciparum* (MALFAL). Since malaria incidence is an endogenous variable, Sachs instruments for both of these using an index of "malaria ecology" (ME) taken from Kiszewski et al. (2003). In columns (8) and (9) we add these variables to our core specification, instrumenting them in the same manner as in Sachs (2003). Our results are similar to Sachs', namely that malaria apears to have a strong, statistically significant, and negative effect on income. Note that the statistical significance of institutional quality is unaffected by the addition of the malaria variables, something that Sachs (2003) notes as well.

We are inclined to attach somewhat less importance to these results than Sachs does. First, it is difficult to believe that malaria, which is a debilitating rather than fatal disease, can by itself exert such a strong effect on income levels. If it is a proxy for something else, it would be good to know what that something else is and measure it more directly. Second, we are a bit concerned about the endogeneity of the instrument (ME). Sachs (2003, 7) asserts that ME is exogenous because it is "built upon climatological and vector conditions on a country-by-country basis," but he does not go into much further detail. The original source for the index (Kiszewski et al. 2003), written for a public health audience, has no discussion of exogeneity at all. Third, the malaria variables are very highly correlated with location in sub-Saharan Africa.[18] The practical import of this is that it is difficult to tell the effect of malaria variables apart from those of regional dummies. This is shown in columns (10) and (11) where we add regional dummies to the specifications reported earlier. Both malaria variables now drop very far below statistical significance, while institutional quality remains significant (albeit at the 90 percent level in one case).

Finally, we experimented with a series of specifications (not reported) that involved interacting the different geography variables with each other as well as introducing different functional forms (e.g., exponential) for them. These did not provide evidence in favor of additional significant direct effects of geography on income. Overall, we conclude that there seems to be some, albeit modest, support for the direct impact of geography on income, although one that is not as robust as that of institutional quality.[19] The first stage regressions, however, point clearly in favor of an important indirect role of geography via institutions.

In Table 8, we undertake a series of robustness checks on the side of trade. First, we check whether our results are sensitive to our omission of market size variables. Frankel and Romer (1999) argue that smaller countries tend to trade more, and that one should therefore control for country size when looking for the effect of trade on incomes. The column labeled (1) in Table 8 includes two

Table 8 Determinants of development: Robustness to alternative measures and instruments for integration.

	Baseline	(1)	(2)	(3)	(4)	(5)	(6)	(7)
Two-Stage Least Squares: Dependent Variable is log GDP per Capita in 1995								
Geography (DISTEQ)	-0.72	-0.56	-0.63	0.13	0.12	-1.16	-1.24	-0.86
	(-1.38)	(-0.83)	(-0.88)	(0.38)	(0.35)	(-1.25)	(-1.14)	(-1.17)
Institutions (RULE)	1.98	1.83	1.90	0.97	0.99	2.70	2.84	2.55
	(3.56)*	(2.64)**	(2.58)**	(2.39)**	(2.46)**	(2.14)**	(1.82)**	(2.11)**
Integration (LCOPEN)	-0.31	0.12	-0.01	-0.87	-0.85			
	(-1.38)	(0.10)	(-0.01)	(-0.90)	(-0.94)			
Land area (AREA)		0.27	0.24	-0.40	-0.39			
		(0.77)	(0.67)	(-0.97)	(-0.99)			
Population (POP)		0.11	0.39	-0.43	-0.42			
		(0.16)	(0.05)	(-0.63)	(-0.65)			
"Real openness" (LNOPEN)						-0.77	-0.94	
						(-0.83)	(-0.70)	
"Policy openness" (SW)								-2.04
								(-1.07)
R-square	0.52	0.61	0.61	0.60	0.60	0.55	0.55	0.61
No. of observations	79	79	79	136	136	71	71	69

Notes: The dependent variable is per capita GDP in 1995, PPP basis. All regressors, except DISTEQ, RULE, and SW, are expressed in logs. Baseline corresponds to the specification in column (6) of Table 3. In columns (1), (3) and (5) the instrument for openness (LOGFRANKROM) is from Frankel and Romer (1999). In columns (2), (4) and (6), the instrument for openness (LOGFRANKROMR) is derived by re-estimating the gravity equation in Frankel and Romer (1999) with the left-hand side variable defined as nominal bilateral trade to nominal GDP. In Frankel and Romer, the left hand side variable was defined as nominal trade divided by PPP GDP. Standard errors are corrected, using the procedure described in Frankel and Romer (1999), to take into account the fact that the openness instrument is estimated. *t*-statistics are reported under coefficient estimates. Significance at the 1, 5, and 10 percent levels are denoted respectively by * , ** , and *** . All regressors are scaled as described in the notes to Tables 2–4.

273

measures of country size—area and population. These variables do not have additional explanatory power in the income equation, which is different from the results in Frankel and Romer (1999). The size and significance of the coefficient on institutions are unaffected. The coefficient on openness becomes positive, but is highly insignificant. Column (3) replicates this exercise for the larger sample. The coefficient on institutions does not change qualitatively (but the standard error is sharply reduced as is the coefficient estimates), while the coefficient on openness is still negatively signed.

Alcalá and Cicconé (2004) have recently advocated the use of what they call "real openness", which is measured as the ratio of trade to PPP GDP. They argue that this is a better measure of integration than the simple ratio of trade to nominal GDP (that Frankel and Romer and we favor) in the presence of trade-driven productivity change. We have a number of conceptual and empirical problems with the Alcalá and Cicconé approach, which we discuss in Appendix A at the end of the paper and to which the interested reader can turn. Here we simply point out that our results are robust to the use of this alternative measure of openness. Column (5) presents the findings when we substitute the Alcalá and Cicconé measure of openness for ours. This integration measure is also "wrongly" signed and insignificant, while the coefficient on institutions increases in size and remains significant, albeit at the 5 percent level.[20]

Columns (2), (4), and (6) replicate the three robustness checks described above but with an instrument for openness that is slightly different from that in Frankel and Romer (1999). To obtain their instruments, Frankel and Romer estimated a gravity equation with the dependent variable defined as trade to PPP GDP. Strictly speaking therefore, theirs was an appropriate instrument for Alcalá and Cicconé's "real openness." We re-estimated the gravity equation on the original Frankel and Romer sample of 63 countries, with trade to GDP as the dependent variable. We then used the coefficients from this gravity equation to construct the instrument for openness for all the 137 countries in our larger sample. The results in columns (2), (4), and (6) are very similar to those using the original Frankel and Romer instruments. The choice of instruments thus does not affect our main results.

Finally, in column (7) we substitute a "policy" measure for the trade variable. For reasons explained later, we believe that it is not appropriate to use policy variables in level regressions. We nevertheless sought to test the robustness of our results to one of the most widely used measures in the trade and growth literature due to Sachs and Warner (1995), which has been endorsed recently by Krueger and Berg (2002).[21] The results show that the institutional variable remains significant at the 5 percent level and the Sachs-Warner measure is itself wrongly signed like the other openness measures.

3. What Does It All Mean?

The present paper represents in our view the most systematic attempt to date to estimate the relationship between integration, institutions, and geography, on the one hand, and income, on the other. In this section, we evaluate and interpret our results further. This also gives us an opportunity to make some additional comments on the related literature. We group the comments under three headings. First, we argue that an instrumentation strategy should not be confused with building and testing theories. Second, we relate our discussion on institutions to the discussion on "policies." Third, we discuss the operational implications of the results.

3.1. An Instrument Does Not a Theory Make

Insofar as our results emphasize the supremacy of institutions, they are very close to those in Acemoglu et al. Note that we have gone beyond Acemoglu et al. by using larger sample sizes, and by including measures of integration in our estimation. We now want to clarify a point regarding the interpretation of results. In particular, we want to stress the distinction between using an instrument to identify an exogenous source of variation in the independent variable of interest and laying out a full theory of cause and effect. In our view, this distinction is not made adequately clear in Acemoglu et al. and is arguably blurred by Easterly and Levine (2003).

One reading of the Acemoglu et al. paper, and the one strongly suggested by their title—"The Colonial Origins of Comparative Development"—is that they regard experience under the early period of colonization as a fundamental determinant of current income levels. While the Acemoglu et al. paper is certainly suggestive on this score, in our view this interpretation of the paper's central message would not be entirely correct. One problem is that Acemoglu et al. do not carry out a direct test of the impact of colonial policies and institutions. Furthermore, if colonial experience were the key determinant of income levels, how would we account for the variation in incomes among countries that had never been colonized by the Europeans?

To illustrate the second point, Figure 4 presents histograms of per capita incomes for 163 countries for which we have data on per capita GDP in 1995. The sample is split into two groups, a group of 103 countries that were colonized by one of the major Western European powers sometime before the twentieth century, and a group of 60 countries that were not colonized. The latter group includes some very high-income countries such as Finland and Luxembourg as well very poor countries such as Ethiopia,[22] Yemen, and Mongolia. (Afghanistan is another low-income non-colonized country, but we do not have income data for it.) As the figure reveals, the dispersion of incomes within the colonized sample is not hugely different than that in the non-colonized sample. The standard deviations of log income per capita are 1.01 and 0.89 for the colonized and non-colonized samples, respectively. The income gaps that separate Ethiopia from Turkey, or China from Luxembourg are huge, and can obviously not be explained by any of these countries' colonial experience.

While colonial history does not quite provide a satisfactory account of income differences around the world, it can still provide a valid instrument. And that,

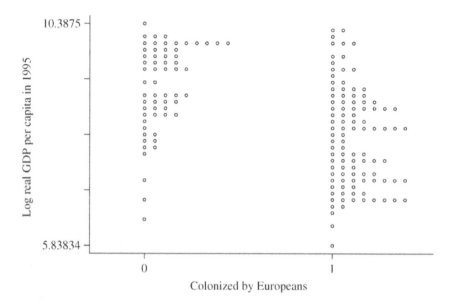

Figure 4 Distribution of incomes for colonized and non-colonized countries.

in our view, is where the Acemoglu et al. paper is successful. An instrument is something that simply has some desirable statistical properties. It need not be a large part of the causal story.[23] To illustrate the distinction between a theory and an instrument, here is an analogy that draws on a well-known paper by Angrist and Krueger (1991).

Angrist and Krueger (1991) use quarter of birth as an instrument for the level of educational attainment, to disentangle the effects of schooling on personal earnings from those of unobserved attributes (such as "ability"). The story is that compulsory schooling requirements, requiring schooling until age 16 or 17, interacting with school-entry requirements, imply variation in the level of schooling that is correlated with quarter of birth but not with other personal attributes. The authors show for example that students born in the first quarter of the year have a systematically lower level of average schooling in the population. This is a plausible strategy for identification, but it obviously does not imply a quarter-of-birth theory of earnings. Similarly, the Acemoglu et al. strategy does not amount to a direct test of a colonial-origins theory of development.[24]

Easterly and Levine (2003) also assign a causal role to the settler mortality instrument and interpret it as a geographical determinant of institutions such as "crops and germs," rather than viewing it as a device to capture the exogenous source of variation in institutions. Indeed, although they stress the role of institutions, they appear to come close to a geography theory of development. Our view is that we should not elevate settler mortality beyond its status as an instrument, and avoid favoring either a colonial view of development (as some readings of Acemoglu et al. would have it) or a geography-based theory of development (as some readings of Easterly and Levine would have it).

3.2. The Primacy of Institutional Quality Does Not Imply Policy Ineffectiveness

Easterly and Levine (2003) assert that (macroeconomic) policies do not have an effect on incomes, once institutions are controlled for. Our view on the effectiveness of policy is similar to that expressed in Acemoglu et al. (2001, 1395): there are "substantial economic gains from improving institutions, for example as in the case of Japan during the Meiji Restoration or South Korea during the 1960s" or, one may add, China since the late 1970s. The distinction between institutions and policies is murky, as these examples illustrate. The reforms that Japan, South Korea, and China undertook were policy innovations that eventually resulted in a fundamental change in the institutional underpinning of their economies.

We find it helpful to think of policy as a flow variable, in contrast to institutions, which is a stock variable. We can view institutions as the cumulative outcome of past policy actions. Letting p_i denote policy on dimension i (i = fiscal, trade, monetary, etc.), I institutional quality, and δ the rate at which institutional quality decays absent countervailing action, the evolution of institutional quality over time can be written as $\dot{I} = \Sigma \alpha_i p_i - \delta I$, where α_i denotes the impact of policy i on institutional quality.

This suggests that it is inappropriate to regress income levels on institutional quality and policies, as Easterly and Levine (2003) do. The problem is not just that incomes move slowly while policies can take sudden turns. In principle this could be addressed by taking long-term averages of policies. (Easterly and Levine average their policy measures over a number of decades.) It is that measures of institutional quality already contain all the relevant information about the impact of policies. If the appropriate specification for income is $\ln y = \beta I + u$, the effect of policies should be sought in a regression of the form $d \ln y/dt = \beta \dot{I} + v = \alpha_0 + \beta \Sigma \alpha_i p_i + v$. In other words, one should look for the effect of policies in a regression of growth of income on policies.

Moreover, a geography theory of institutions can understate the impact that policies can play in changing them over time. As an empirical matter, institutions have changed remarkably in the last three decades. For example, one indicator of institutional quality— the index measuring the constraint on the executive in the Gurr Polity IV dataset, which is available on a consistent basis for several decades—shows a marked improvement between the 1970s and 1990s. For 71 countries in our core sample, this index had a mean value of 3.21 in the 1970s, 3.52 in the 1980s, and 4.37 in the 1990s. A purely geographical theory of institutions would have difficulty in accounting for these changes. Indeed, if the first stage regressions reported in panel B of Table 3 are run over the last three decades, the coefficient on settler mortality, declines from −1.14 in the 1970s to −1.04

in the 1980s and 0.86 in the 1990s, illustrating the mutability of institutions, and the declining importance of history (on the Acemoglu et al. interpretation of settler mortality) or geography (on the Easterly and Levine interpretation of settler mortality) in explaining the cross-national variation in institutions.[25]

3.3 The Hard Work is Still Ahead

How much guidance do our results provide to policymakers who want to improve the performance of their economies? Not much at all. Sure, it is helpful to know that geography is not destiny, or that focussing on increasing the economy's links with world markets is unlikely to yield convergence. But the operational guidance that our central result on the primacy of institutional quality yields is extremely meager.

Our indicators of institutional quality are investors' and other observers' ratings of the institutional environment. They quantify these observers' views as to the likelihood that investors will retain the fruits of their investments, the chances that the state will expropriate them, or that the legal system will protect their property rights. While it is important to know that these ratings matter—and matter a great deal in fact—it remains unclear how the underlying evaluations and perceptions can be altered. In terms of the formulation developed above, what we have estimated is β, while what policy makers need to know are the α_i (policy impacts) for the policies at their disposal. In fact, since our identification strategies rely on exogenous sources of variation in these evaluations, they are doubly unhelpful from a policy perspective.

We illustrate the difficulty of extracting policy-relevant information from our findings using the example of property rights. Obviously, the presence of clear property rights for investors is a key, if not the key, element in the institutional environment that shapes economic performance. Our findings indicate that when investors believe their property rights are protected, the economy ends up richer. But nothing is implied about the actual form that property rights should take. We cannot even necessarily deduce that enacting a private property-rights regime would produce superior results compared to alternative forms of property rights.

If this seems stretching things too far, consider the experiences of China and Russia. China still retains a socialist legal system, while Russia has a regime of private property rights in place. Despite the absence of formal private property rights, Chinese entrepreneurs have felt sufficiently secure to make large investments, making that country the world's fastest growing economy over the last two decades. In Russia, by contrast, investors have felt insecure, and private investment has remained low. Our institutional quality indicators bear this out, with Russia scoring considerably lower than China despite a formal legal regime that is much more in line with European norms than China's. Credibly signaling that property rights will be protected is apparently more important than enacting them into law as a formal private property rights regime.

So our findings do not map into a determinate set of policy desiderata. Indeed, there is growing evidence that desirable institutional arrangements have a large element of context specificity, arising from differences in historical trajectories, geography, political economy, or other initial conditions. As argued in Mukand and Rodrik (2002), this could help explain why successful developing countries—China, South Korea, and Taiwan among others—have almost always combined unorthodox elements with orthodox policies. It could also account for why important institutional differences persist among the advanced countries of North America, Western Europe, and Japan—in the role of the public sector, the nature of the legal systems, corporate governance, financial markets, labor markets, and social insurance mechanisms, among others.

It is important to underscore that this does not mean economic principles work differently in different places. We need to make a distinction between economic principles and their institutional embodiment. Most first-order economic principles come institutionfree. Economic ideas such as incentives, competition, hard-budget constraints, sound money, fiscal sustainability, property rights do not map directly into institutional forms. Property rights can be implemented through common law, civil law, or, for that matter, Chinese-type socialism. Competition can be maintained through a combination of free entry and laissez-faire, or through a well-functioning regulatory authority. Macroeconomic stability can be achieved under a variety of fiscal institutions. Institutional solutions that perform well in one setting may be inappropriate in other setting without the supporting norms and complementary institutions. In the words of Douglass North

"economies that adopt the formal rules of another economy will have very different performance characteristics than the first economy because of different informal norms and enforcement. The implication is that transferring the formal political and economic rules of successful Western economies to third-world and Eastern European economies is not a sufficient condition for good economic performance." (North 1994, 366)

In addition, since policy makers always operate in second-best environments, optimal reform trajectories—even in apparently straightforward cases such as price reform— cannot be designed without regard to prevailing conditions and without weighting the consequences for multiple distorted margins.

Consequently, there is much to be learned still about what improving institutional quality means on the ground. This, we would like to suggest, is a wide open area of research. Crossnational studies of the present type are just a beginning that point us in the right direction.

Appendix A: Problems with the Use of the Alcalá and Cicconé Measure of "Real Openness"

Alcalá and Ciccone (2004) propose a different measure of integration, which they claim is superior to that used by Frankel and Romer and others. They argue that the conventional measure of openness—nominal trade divided by nominal

GDP—can yield an estimate of trade on incomes that is biased downwards. The logic is as follows. Suppose that an increase in trade raises productivity, but that it does so predominantly in the tradables sector. Unless non-tradables are inferior in demand, this will raise the relative price of nontradables. This will in turn tend to depress the ratio of trade to nominal GDP. The result is that the initial increase in the openness ratio will be attenuated. AC therefore prefer to use what they call "real openness," nominal trade divided by PPP GDP.

A First Pass

Alcalá and Ciccone (2004) find a relationship between "real openness" and income within their empirical framework that they claim is more robust than when the conventional measure of openness is used. This seems to be the case even when institutional quality is entered, which shows up significantly in their regressions as well. Since we were unable to obtain their data set, we could not replicate their results exactly. However, as we have already discussed, the use of "real openness" within our empirical specification does not alter the central results of our paper, namely the importance of institutions and the insignificance of openness (see columns (5) and (6) of Table 8). Here we discuss a number of misgivings we have with the Alcalá and Ciccone approach.

As a first step, it is useful to explain the mechanics of why "real openness" (Ropen) does much "better" than openness (Open) in Alcalá and Cicconé-type regressions. Ropen and Open are linked by the identity log Ropen = log Open + log P, where P is a country's price level. We know from the Balassa-Samuelson argument that P has a close relationship to a country's income/productivity level. This can be seen explicitly in the chart below, which shows the relationship between (log Ropen − log Open) and GDP per worker (The simple correlation coefficient between the two is 0.76).

Hence what Alcalá and Cicconé are doing is to augment the standard measure of openness (Open) with a component that is highly correlated with income/productivity. This procedure is virtually guaranteed to generate a high correlation between productivity and openness. (The correlation between log Open and log P is extremely weak, 0.05, while the correlation between log Ropen and log P is 0.66.) Even after instrumentation, what ends up doing the heavy lifting in their paper appears to be the strong correlation between price levels and labor productivity.[26]

Theoretical Issues

The Alcalá and Cicconé argument strikes us as being misleading on purely conceptual grounds. The use of "real openness" can yield in fact an opposite, and potentially more severe, bias. What Alcalá and Cicconé do not recognize is that the actual null hypothesis that is tested is that trade does not cause productivity. Under that null, Alcalá and Cicconé's real openness measure generates a positive correlation between income and openness that is entirely spurious. In effect, the Alcalá and Cicconé adjustment has the consequence that any and all increases in the productivity of tradables, regardless of source, can produce a rise in their measure of openness. Any increase in tradables productivity, whether driven by trade or not, will raise non-tradables prices at home and the price level of an economy relative to others. "Adjusting" for this by using PPP GDP as the denominator drives up measured openness. The conventional measure of openness does not suffer from that shortcoming, and hence is preferable. We explain and illustrate this point using a simple model.

Imagine a symmetric world populated with a large number of small endowment economies. Each economy i has a fixed endowment of non-traded and traded goods, denoted by N_i and T_i, respectively. Let each country produce a different traded good (the Armington assumption), but consume all the varieties of traded goods produced around the world. If there is a very large number of countries, each country's consumption of its own endowment of the traded good will be negligible: (almost) all of its traded good will be exported in exchange for imports of the traded goods produced elsewhere. Let PN_i stand for the price of non-traded goods in country i and let the prices of all traded goods be fixed at unity. Since the sum of exports and imports are given by $2T_i$, conventionally measured openness in a country i can then be expressed as $ON_i = 2Ti / (PN_i^* N_i + T_i)$.

Assume that preferences in each country take the Cobb-Douglas form, such that non- traded goods and traded goods (in aggregate) have fixed budget shares. Under this assumption, $2T_i / (PN_i^* N_i + T_i)$ will be constant and independent of a country's endowments of T and N. (This is because $dPN_i/PN_i = dT_i/T_i - dN_i/N_i$.) Cross-country differences in conventionally measured openness, ON_i, will arise solely from differences in Cobb-Douglas budget shares. Assume also that differences in the endowment of the traded good are the only source of cross-country differences in income. That is, all countries have identical N_i but varying T_i. Countries with larger T_i are richer.

Under the above assumptions, there is no causal relationship that goes from trade to incomes. Cross-country differences in income are due entirely to differences in endowments. And if we run a regression of income on openness, we will get nothing. Trade shares either do not vary across countries, or they vary "randomly" with the Cobb- Douglas parameter. They have no systematic relationship to levels of income. So the econometrics will provide a good guide to the underlying reality.

Now suppose that we follow Alcalá and Cicconé, and construct their real openness measure, OR_i. This adjustment consists of expressing the value of i's non-traded production at some benchmark country's prices, PB, instead of domestic prices, PN_i. The Alcalá and Cicconé measure of real openness is therefore $OR_i = 2T_i / (PB^* N_i + T_i)$. Note that OR_i is increasing in T_i. When we correlate OR_i with incomes across countries, we will get a positive relationship. This is a spurious relationship, since the only source of productivity differences in this model is differences in endowments.

Hence, in this benchmark model, the conventional measure of openness does exactly what we would like a measure of openness to do under the null hypothesis that trade does not cause productivity. The Alcalá and Cicconá variant, meanwhile, imparts a positive bias to the estimated trade-income relationship. A key feature of the model above is that the elasticity of substitution in demand between T and N is unity. This ensures that the rise in PN is just enough to keep (conventional) openness invariant to changes in the endowment (or productivity) of tradables. When the elasticity of substitution differs from one, conventional openness does not always deliver such a helpful result, but the bias is not unidirectional. So with an elasticity of substitution greater than one, a regression of income on conventional openness will yield (misleadingly) a positive coefficient, while with an elasticity less than one, the regression will yield (misleadingly) a negative coefficient. However, the AC real openness measure is invariant to the elasticity of substitution and hence is always positively biased.

Empirics

Another point relates to the choice between real openness and openness on econometric grounds. Recall that the authors' original argument on behalf of Ropen is based on the idea that there is reverse causality from productivity to Open, via the price level. If the Frankel- Romer constructed trade share is a valid instrument, in the sense of being uncorrelated with productivity through any channel other than trade, any type of reverse causality—positive or negative—is already taken care of. The reverse causality that Alcalá and Cicconé worry about should be handled by the instrument as well! For the authors' argument to be valid, instrumentation should fail when Open is used, but work when Ropen is used (even though the same instruments are used in both cases). The authors do not provide any justification for this, and it is unclear to us that any justification could be produced.

Moreover, it is possible that the Alcalá and Cicconé strategy does exactly the reverse and that it weakens the instrument. As we mentioned above, we were unable to obtain Alcalá and Cicconá's data and could not replicate their results exactly. But in our attempted replications of their baseline specification, we repeatedly found that the firststage F-statistics were lower, sometimes substantially so, when real openness was used in lieu of openness. In fact, the F-statistic was typically below 10 when real openness was used (and always above 10 when openness was used).[27] A more formal test for weak instruments with two endogenous regressors (which in our case are institutions and openness) is the G-statistic proposed by Stock and Yogo (2002). Our baseline specification with Open yielded a value for this statistic of 4.85 exceeding the critical value of 4.58, while the specification with Ropen yielded a value of 3.89.[28]

In sum, we do not find the case for "real openness" particularly compelling. We worry that the "more robust" results that Alcalá and Cicconé claim for it derive from the interaction of strong reverse causality with imperfections of the instrument.

Appendix B: Data and Sources

AFRICA = Dummy variable taking value 1 if a country belongs to Africa, 0 otherwise.

ASIA = Dummy variable taking value 1 if a country belongs to Asia, 0 otherwise.

ACCESS = Dummy variable taking value 1 for countries without access to the sea, 0 otherwise.

AREA = Land area (thousands sq. mt.) Source: Frankel and Romer (1999).

ASIAE = Dummy variable taking value 1 if a country belongs to South-East Asia, 0 otherwise.

CATH = Dummy variable taking value 1 if the country's population is predominantly catholic.

COLFR = Dummy variable taking value 1 if the colonizer was France.

COLUK = Dummy variable taking value 1 if the colonizer was England.

DISTEQ = Distance from Equator of capital city measured as abs(Latitude)/90.

ENGFRAC = Fraction of the population speaking English. Source: Hall and Jones (1999).

EURFRAC = Fraction of the population speaking one of the major languages of Western Europe: English, French, German, Portuguese, or Spanish. Source: Hall and Jones (1999).

FROSTAREA = Proportion of land with > 5 frost-days per month in winter. Source: Masters and McMillan (2001).

FROSTDAYS = Average number of frost-days per month in winter. Source: CID Harvard University (2002) from Masters and McMillan (2001).

LAAM = Dummy variable taking value 1 if a country belongs to Latin America or the Caribbean, 0 otherwise.

LCGDP95 = Natural logarithm of per capita GDP in Purchasing-Power-Parity US dollars (PPP GDP). Source: Penn World Tables, Mark 6, in 1995. For the following countries the 1996 CGDP value in the PWT was utilized: Bahrain; Kuwait; Mongolia; Oman; Qatar; Saudi Arabia; Swaziland. The 1995 value for CDGP95 in PWT, Mark 6, was obtained by dividing the 1996 observation by the corresponding percentage change in real GDP computed using International Financial Statistics (IFS, IMF 2002) nominal GDP and GDP deflator series.

LCOPEN = Natural logarithm of nominal openness. Nominal openness is given by the ratio of nominal imports plus exports relative to GDP (in exchange rate US dollars). Source: Penn World Tables (PWT), Mark 6. Average over-all 195098 available data. For the following countries the 1996 observation available in the PWT has been utilized: Bahrain; Bahamas; Bermuda; Bhutan; Djibouti; Eritrea; Georgia; Kuwait; Laos; Mongolia; Oman; Qatar; Saudi Arabia; Sudan; Swaziland; Tajikistan; Turkmenistan. For Myanmar and Suriname LCOPEN (Average over all 1950–95 available data) is constructed from IFS (IMF) using Exports and Imports in Goods and Services in national currencies and nominal GDP in national currencies for the available years.

LFR = Dummy variable taking a value of 1 if a country has a legal system deriving from that in France.

LNOPEN = Natural logarithm of "real" openness. Real openness is given by the ratio of nominal imports plus exports to GDP in Purchasing-Power-Parity US dollars (PPP GDP). Source: Penn World Tables, Mark 5.6 and World Bank (2002).

LOGA = Labor-augmenting technological progress parameter in 1998. Source: Hall and Jones (1999).

LOGEM4 = Natural logarithm of estimated European settlers' mortality rate. Source: Acemoglu et al. (2001).

LOGFRANKROM = Natural logarithm of predicted trade shares computed following Frankel and Romer (1999) from a bilateral trade equation with "pure geography'' variables. Source: Frankel and Romer (1999).

LOGFRANKROMR = Natural logarithm of predicted trade shares computed as for LOGFRANKROM except that the dependent variable in the bilateral trade (gravity) equation is nominal trade divided by nominal GDP (both in US dollars). Source: Authors' estimates.

LOGHL = Natural logarithm of human capital per worker in 1988. Source: Hall and Jones (1999).

LOGKL = Natural logarithm of physical capital per worker in 1988. Source: Hall and Jones (1999).

LOGYL = Natural logarithm of GDP in Purchasing-Power-Parity US dollars (PPP GDP) per worker in 1988. Source: Hall and Jones (1999).

LSO = Dummy variable taking a value of 1 if a country has a socialist legal system.

MALFAL94: Malaria index, year 1994. Source: Gallup and Sachs (1998).

MEANTEMP = Average temperature (Celsius). Source: CID Harvard University (2002).

MUSL = Dummy variable taking value 1 if the country's population is predominantly Muslim.

OIL = Dummy variable taking value 1 for a country being major oil exporter, 0 otherwise.

POP: Population.

PROT = Dummy variable taking value 1 if the country's population is predominantly protestant.

RULE = Rule of Law index. Refers to 2001 and approximates for 1990s institutions. Source: Kaufmann et al. (2002).

SAFRICA = Dummy variable taking value 1 if a country belongs to Sub-Saharan Africa, 0 otherwise.

SW = Dummy variable taking value 0 if the country had BMP = 1, MON = 1, SOC = 1, TAR > 0.4, or NTB > 0.4; 1 otherwise. Source: Sachs and Warner (1995).

TROPICS = Percentage of tropical land area. Source: Gallup and Sachs (1998).

XCONST1970 = Constraint on the executive in the 1970s. Source: Polity IV dataset.

Acknowledgments

We thank three referees, Chad Jones, James Robinson, Will Masters, and participants at the Harvard-MIT development seminar, joint IMF-World Bank Seminar, and the Harvard econometrics workshop for their comments, Daron Acemoglu for helpful conversations, and Simon Johnson for providing us with his data. Dani Rodrik gratefully acknowledges support from the Carnegie Corporation of New York.

The views expressed in this paper are the authors' own and not of the institutions with which they are affiliated.

Notes

1 These are figures for 2000, and they are expressed in current "international" dollars, adjusted for PPP differences. The source is the World Development Indicators CD-ROM of the World Bank.

2 One can question whether it is appropriate to treat trade as one of the ultimate determinants of economic prosperity, but here we are simply following a long literature that has attached central causal importance to it.

3 The Easterly and Levine approach is in some ways very similar to that in this paper. Easterly and Levine estimate regressions of the levels of income on various measures of endowments, institutions, and "policies." They find that institutions exert an important effect on development, while endowments do not, other than through their effect on institutions. Policies also do not exert any independent effect on development. The main differences between our paper and Easterly and Levine are the following. First, we use a larger sample of countries (79 and 137) to run the "horse" race between the three possible determinants. The Easterly and Levine sample is restricted to 72 countries. Second, Easterly and Levine do not test in any detail whether integration has an effect on development. For them, integration or open trade policy is part of a wider set of government policies that can affect development. Testing for the effect of policies in level regressions is, however, problematic as discussed in greater detail below. Policies pursued over a short time span, say 30-40 years, are like a flow variable, whereas development, the result of a much longer cumulative historical process, is more akin to a stock variable. Thus, level regressions that use policies as regressors conflate stocks and flows.

4 We note that many of the papers already cited as well as others have carried out similar robustness tests. For example, Acemoglu et al. (2001) document that geographic variables such as temperature, humidity, malaria risk exert no independent direct effects on income once institutions are controlled for. A followup paper by the same authors (Acemoglu et al., 2003) shows that macroeconomic policies have limited effects after institutions are controlled. Easterly and Levine (2003) produce similar robustness results on the geography front. Our contribution is to put these and other tests in a broader framework, including trade, and to provide an interpretation of the results which we think is more appropriate.

5 Acemoglu et al. actually compiled data on settler mortality for 81 countries, but data on our other variables are unavailable for Afghanistan (for per capita PPP GDP for 1995) and the Central African Republic (for rule of law).

6 Acemoglu et al. (2001) use an index of protection against expropriation compiled by Political Risk Services. The advantage of the rule of law measure used in this paper is that it is available for a larger sample of countries, and in principle captures more elements that go toward determining institutional quality. In any case, measures of

institutional quality are highly correlated: in our 79-country sample, the two measures have a simple correlation of 0.78.

7　The finding that trade enters with a negative (albeit insignificant) coefficient may be considered puzzling. In further results (available from the authors), we found that this is due largely to the adverse effects of trade in primary products. When total trade is broken into manufactures and non-manufactures components, it is only the latter that enters with a negative coefficient.

8　Although this threshold applies strictly to the case where there is a single endogenous regressor, it is nevertheless reassuring that our specifications yield F-statistics well above it.

9　In Appendix A, we explain that our core specification also passes a more formal test (suggested by Stock and Yogo, 2002) for weak instruments in the presence of two endogenous regressors.

10　We emphasize that we have not found an instance in which the use of one sample or another makes a qualitative difference to our results.

11　Breaking trade into manufactures and non-manufactures components as before, we find that it is only manufactures trade that has significant positive effect on institutional quality (results are available from the authors).

12　Note that these calculations omit the feedback effect from income to trade and institutions, since we are unable to estimate these. Our numbers can hence be viewed as impact effects, taking both direct and indirect channels into account, but ignoring the feedback from income.

13　In light of our quantitative estimates, our main difference with Sachs (2003) seems to relate to whether the sizable effects of geography are direct (the Sachs position) or indirect, operating via institutions (our position).

14　Actual sample sizes are smaller than for our core specifications because of the unavailability of data for some countries in the Hall and Jones (1999) data set.

15　In the larger sample, integration has a negative and significant effect on income and accumulation but this result is not robust to the inclusion of additional variables such as land and area.

16　We do not report the results for the larger sample but they are very similar. For the 79-country sample, interesting results are obtained for some of the individual legal origin and other variables. For example, as in Acemoglu et al. (2001), the French legal origin dummy has a positive total effect on incomes; the total impact of having been colonized by the United Kingdom is negative and statistically significant even though former UK-colonies have better quality of institutions on average. As for religion, suffice it to say that Weber is not vindicated!

17　In most of these regressions (columns (1)–(7)), the geography variable is a significant determinant of institutions in the first stage regressions.

18　Regressing MALFAL and MAL94P, respectively, on a sub-Saharan African dummy yields t-statistics of above 10 and R^2s above 0.40.

19　See also Acemoglu et al. (2002) who document that the regions of the world that were relatively rich around 1,500 underwent a "reversal of fortune" subsequently. They argue that this militates against a geographic determinist view of income difference.

20　An alternative, albeit imperfect, way of taking the Alcalá and Cicconé concern into account is to use a measure of trade openness that excludes services (the main source of non-tradables) from the measure of GDP in the denominator. When we use this measure of openness (trade as a share of "goods GDP") we get similar results to those reported above (these results are available from authors).

21　The shortcomings of the Sachs-Warner index as a measure of trade policy are discussed at length in Rodriguez and Rodrik (2001).

22　Ethiopia was included in the Acemoglu et al. sample of colonies, even though this country has never been colonized. (It was occupied for a period of several years by Italy during 1936-1941, but this neither counts as colonization, nor could have had much to do with the settler mortality rates from the 19th century). Excluding Ethiopia from the Acemoglu et al. sample makes no difference to the basic Acemoglu et al. results—and in fact it improves these results, as eyeballing Acemoglu et al.'s Figures 1 and 2 would indicate.

23 In Acemoglu et al. (2002), the authors provide a fuller account of comparative develop-ment, emphasizing the interaction between the quality of institutions, on the one hand, and the prevailing opportunities to industrialize, on the other.

24 Acemoglu et al. themselves are somewhat ambiguous about this. They motivate settler mortality as an instrument, but then their account gravitates towards a colonial origins theory of institutional development. And their title strongly suggests that they consider the contribution of their paper to have been a theory as opposed to an identification strategy. In personal communication, one of the authors has explained that the colonial experience allows them to exploit the exogenous source of variation in institutions and not all the variation. The fit of the first-stage regressions of about 25 percent leaves room for most of the variation to be explained by factors other than colonization.

25 The R-squares also decline over time for these first-stage regressions.

26 Indeed the Alcalá and Cicconé argument that the true relationship between trade and productivity can be ascertained only by holding the price level constant suggests estimating a more general framework of the kind: $\log y = \alpha + \beta_1 \log \text{Open} + \beta_2 \log P + v$. When we do so, using an instrument set close to that in Alcalá and Cicconé, we find that the coefficient on openness is negative and insignificant, and that on the price level positive and highly significant. The comparable equation estimated with real openness yields a coefficient that is positive and significant. Whatever effect Ropen has on productivity, it seems to be operating via P, not via Open. So this more general framework yields little evidence that there is a significant causal effect from openness to productivity, holding the price level constant. Indeed, if we are to interpret these results literally, they suggest that causality runs from the price level to productivity.

27 A little exploration reveals why the instruments work much better with openness than with real openness. The first stage regressions associated with estimating the equation described in the previous footnote, which is based on the decomposition of real open-ness into openness and price, show that the first-stage for the price level equation has an F-statistic of 1.92. Apparently, the instruments do much worse with real openness because of the very weak correlation between the instrument set and the price level. Another issue is why Alcalá and Cicconá use such an odd instrument list, entering the levels of population and land area, as well as their logs, whereas the second-stage equa-tion has only the logs. It is hard to defend the idea that the level of land area, say, can be safely excluded from the second stage when its log belongs in it.

28 The tabulated critical values for the weak instrument test for an exactly identified problem of two endogenous variables such as ours are, respectively, 7.03, 4.58, and 3.95 for desired maximal sizes of r in a 5 percent linear restrictions Wald test of 0.10, 0.15, and 0.20.

References

Acemoglu, D., S. Johnson, and J. A. Robinson. (2001). "The Colonial Origins of Comparative Development: An Empirical Investigation," *American Economic Review* 91, 1369–1401.

Acemoglu, D., S. Johnson, and J. A. Robinson. (2002). "Reversal of Fortune: Geography and Institutions in the Making of the Modern World Income Distribution," *Quarterly Journal of Economics* 117, 1231–1294.

Acemoglu, D., S. Johnson, J. Robinson, and Y. Thaicharoen. (2003). "Institutional Causes, Macroeconomic Symptoms: Volatility, Crises and Growth," *Journal of Monetary Economics* 50, 49–123.

Alcalá, F., and A. Cicconé. (2004). "Trade and Productivity," *Quarterly Journal of Economics* (forthcoming).

Angrist, J. D., and A. B. Krueger. (1991). "Does Compulsory School Attendance Affect Schooling and Earnings?" *Quarterly Journal of Economics* 106, 979–1014.

Belsey, D. A., E. Kuh, and R. E. Welsch. (1980). *Regression Diagnostics.* New York: John Wiley and Sons.

Diamond, J. (1997). *Guns, Germs, and Steel.* New York: W.W. Norton & Co.

Dollar, D., and A. Kraay. (2004). "Trade, Growth, and Poverty," *The Economic Journal* 114, 22–9.

Easterly, W., and R. Levine. (2003). "Tropics, Germs, and Crops: How Endowments Influence Economic Development," *Journal of Monetary Economics* 50, 3–0.

Engerman, S. L., and K. L. Sokoloff. (2004). "Factor Endowments, Institutions, and Differential Paths of Growth Among New World Economies: A View from Economic Historians of the United States," National Bureau of Economic Research Working Paper No. H0066.

Frankel, J., and D. Romer. (1999). "Does Trade Cause Growth?," *American Economic Review* 89, 379–399.

Gallup, J. L., and J. D. Sachs. (1998). *The Economic Burden of Malaria.* Center for International Development, Harvard University, mimeo.

Gallup, J. L., J. D. Sachs, and A. D. Mellinger. (1998). "Geography and Economic Development," National Bureau of Economic Research Working Paper No. w6849.

Hall, R., and C. I. Jones. (1999). "Why Do Some Countries Produce So Much More Output per Worker than Others?" *Quarterly Journal of Economics* 114, 83-116.

Kaufmann, D., A. Kraay, and P. Zoido-Lobatán. (2002). "Governance Matters II—Updated Indicators for 2000/ 01," World Bank Policy Research Department Working Paper No. 2772, Washington DC.

Kiszewski, A., A. Mellinger, A. Spielman, P. Malaney, S. E. Sachs, and J. Sachs (2003). *A Global Index Representing the Stability of Malaria Transmission.* Center for International Development, Harvard University, mimeo.

Krueger, A., and A. Berg. (2002). "Trade, Growth, and Poverty," Paper presented at the 2002 World Bank Annual Conference on Development Economics, Washington DC.

La Porta, R., F. Lopez-de-Silanes, A. Shleifer, and R. W. Vishny. (1998). "The Quality of Government," *Journal of Law, Economics, and Organization* 15, 1113–1155.

Masters, W. A., and M. S. McMillan. (2001). "Climate and Scale in Economic Growth," *Journal of Economic Growth* 6, 167–186.

Mukand, S., and D. Rodrik. (2002). In Search of the Holy Grail: Policy Convergence, Experimentation, and Economic Performance. Harvard University, mimeo.

North, D. C. (1990). Institutions, Institutional Change and Economic Performance. New York: Cambridge University Press.

North, D. C. (1994). "Economic Performance Through Time," *The American Economic Review* 84, 359–368.

Rodríguez, F., and D. Rodrik. (2001). "Trade Policy and Economic Growth: A Skeptic's Guide to the Cross National Evidence." In B. Bernanke and K. S. Rogoff (eds), *Macroeconomics Annual 2000.* Cambridge, MA: MIT Press.

Rodrik, D. (2003). "Institutions, Integration, and Geography: In Search of the Deep Determinants of Economic Growth." In D. Rodrik (ed.), *In Search of Prosperity: Analytic Country Studies on Growth.* Princeton, NJ: Princeton University Press.

Sachs, J. D. (2001). "Tropical Under development," National Bureau of Economic Research Working Paper No. w8119.

Sachs, J. (2003). "Institutions Don't Rule: Direct Effects of Geography on Per Capita Income," National Bureau of Economic Research Working Paper No. 9490.

Sachs, J., and A. Warner. (1995). "Economic Reform and the Process of Global Integration," *Brookings Papers on Economic Activity* 1, 1–118.

Sala-i-Martin, X., and A. Subramanian. (2003). "Addressing the Curse of Natural Resources: An Illustration from Nigeria," National Bureau of Economic Research Working Paper No. 9804.

Staiger, D., and J. H. Stock. (1997). "Instrumental Variables Regression with Weak Instruments," *Econometrica* 65, 557–586.

Stock, J. H., and M. Yogo. (2002). "Testing for Weak Instruments in Linear IV Regressions." In D. W. K. Andrews and J. H. Stock (eds), *Festschrift in Honor of Thomas Rothenberg.* Cambridge: Cambridge University Press, forthcoming.

27

FACTOR ENDOWMENTS, INSTITUTIONS, AND DIFFERENTIAL PATHS OF GROWTH AMONG NEW WORLD ECONOMIES

A View from Economic Historians of the United States

Stanley L. Engerman and Kenneth L. Sokoloff

Source: *NBER Working Paper* No. 10246 (December 1994), pp. 260–304.

ABSTRACT

Many scholars are concerned with why the United States and Canada have been so much more successful over time than other New World economies. Since all New World societies enjoyed high levels of product per capita early in their histories, the divergence in paths can be traced back to the achievement of sustained economic growth by the United States and Canada during the eighteenth and early-nineteenth centuries, while the others did not manage to attain this goal until the late-nineteenth or twentieth centuries. Although many explanations have been offered, this paper highlights the relevance of substantial differences in the degree of inequality in wealth, human capital, and political power in accounting for the variation in the records of growth. Moreover, we suggest that the roots of these disparities in the extent of inequality lay in differences in the initial factor endowments of the respective colonies. Of particular significance for generating extreme inequality were the suitability for the cultivation of sugar and other crops in which there were economies of production in the use of slaves, as well as the presence of large concentrations of Native Americans. Both of these conditions encouraged the evolution of societies where relatively small elites of European descent could hold highly disproportionate shares of the wealth, human capital, and political power - and establish economic and political dominance over the mass of the population. Conspicuously absent from the nearly all-inclusive list of New World colonies with these conditions were the British settlements in the northern part of the North American continent. After demonstrating the importance of the early factor endowments for generating major differences in inequality and in the structure of economies, we call attention to the tendencies of government policies to maintain the basic thrust of those initial conditions or the same general degree of inequality along the respective economy's path of development. Finally, we explore the effects of the degree of inequality on the evolution of institutions conducive to broad participation in the commercial economy, markets, and technological change during this specific era, and suggest that their greater equality in wealth, human capital, and political power may have predisposed the United States and Canada toward earlier realization of sustained economic growth. Overall, we argue that the role of factor endowments has been underestimated, and the independence of institutional developments from the factor endowments exaggerated, in theories of the differential paths of growth among New World economies.

I. INTRODUCTION

Economic historians of the United States, with their traditional reliance on Europe as the reference point, normally focus on factor endowments in accounting for the record of economic growth. They routinely attribute the country's long history of high and relatively equally distributed incomes, as well as impressive rates of advance, to an extraordinarily favorable resource endowment. This conventional framework, tracing back to Adam Smith, highlights how widespread knowledge of European technologies among a free citizenry, coupled with the relative abundance of land and other resources per capita, would be expected to, and did, yield a relatively high marginal productivity of labor or wage – and thus, a relatively egalitarian society with a high standard of living and excellent prospects for realizing sustained progress. Hence, treatments of the settlement of the New World that are organized about a comparison of the thirteen colonies with the economies the settlers left behind provide a welcome fit between the evidence and the theory.[1]

Puzzles arise, however, when scholars of the United States turn to the experiences of Latin American economies. These other New World societies also began with – by European standards of the time – vast supplies of land and natural resources per person, and were among the most prosperous and coveted of the colonies in the seventeenth and eighteenth centuries. Indeed, so promising were these other regions, that Europeans of the time generally regarded the thirteen British colonies on the North American mainland and Canada as of relatively marginal economic interest – an opinion evidently shared by Native Americans who had concentrated disproportionately in the areas the Spanish eventually developed.[2] Yet, despite their similar, if not less favorable, factor endowments, the U.S. and Canada ultimately proved to be far more successful than the other colonies in realizing sustained economic growth over time. This stark contrast in performance suggests that factor endowments alone cannot explain the diversity of outcomes, but in so doing, raises the question of what can.

Those seeking to account for the divergent paths of the United States and Latin America have usually made reference to differences in institutions, where the concept is interpreted broadly to encompass not only formal political and legal structures, but culture as well.[3] Many specific contrasts in institutions have been proposed to be potentially significant, including the degree of democracy, the extent of rent-seeking, security in property rights, the inclination to work hard or be entrepreneurial, as well as culture and religion. Where there is explicit discussion of sources of institutional differences, the norm has been to relate them to presumed exogenous differences between British, Spanish, Portuguese, and various Native American heritages. Although the possible influences of factor endowment on the path of economic and institutional development have been neither ignored nor excluded, few have attempted to identify or explore systematic patterns. It is as if the deviance of the Latin American economies from the United States model has in itself been viewed as evidence of the predominance of exogenous idiosyncratic factors. In reality, of course, it is the United States that proved to be the atypical case.

In this paper, we explore the possibility that the role of factor endowments has been underestimated, and the independence of institutional development from the factor endowments exaggerated. Our analysis is inspired by the observation that despite beginning with roughly the same legal and cultural background, as well as drawing immigrants from similar places and economic classes, the British colonies in the New World evolved quite distinct societies and sets of economic institutions. Only a few were ultimately able to realize sustained economic growth. The majority that failed shared certain salient features of their factor endowments with Latin American New World societies, and we suggest that although these conditions allowed for average standards of living that were high for that time, they were less well suited for the realization of sustained economic growth than were those prevailing in economies like the United States and Canada.[4]

In brief, we argue that a hemispheric perspective across the range of European colonies in the New World indicates that although there were many influences, the factor endowment and attitudes toward it reflected in policy had profound and enduring impacts on the structure of respective colonial economies, and ultimately on their long-run paths of institutional and economic development. While all began with an abundance of land and other resources relative to labor, at least after the initial depopulation, other aspects of their factor endowments varied – contributing to substantial differences across them in the distribution of landholdings, wealth, and political power. Some, like the colonies in the Caribbean, Brazil, or the southern colonies on the North American mainland, had climates and soil conditions well suited for growing crops like sugar, coffee, rice, tobacco, and cotton that were of high value on the market and much more efficiently produced on large plantations with slave labor. The substantial shares of the populations composed of slaves and the scale economies both served to generate a vastly unequal distribution of wealth and political power. The Spanish colonies in Mexico and Peru were likewise characterized early in their histories by extreme inequality, at least partially because of their factor endowments. In these cases, the extensive populations of natives and the Spanish practices of awarding

292

claims on land, native labor, and rich mineral resources to members of the elite encouraged the formation of highly concentrated landholdings and extreme inequality. In contrast, small family-size farms were the rule in the northern colonies of the North American mainland, where climatic conditions favored a regime of mixed farming centered on grains and livestock that exhibited no economies of scale in production. The circumstances in these latter regions encouraged the evolution of more equal distributions of wealth, more democratic political institutions, more extensive domestic markets, and the pursuit of more growth-oriented policies than did those in the former. We suggest further that there are reasons for expecting regions with more equal circumstances and rights to be more likely to realize sustained economic growth, and that the breadth of evidence provided by the experiences of New World colonies supports this view.[5]

Although we reject the simple determinism implied by the concept of "path dependence", by arguing for the long-run effects of factor endowment we are endorsing the idea that patterns of growth may be path-influenced. Given the large number of societies implicitly treated, our generalizations could well seem breathtaking, if not reckless. Such exercises in comparative history are nevertheless useful if, in specifying patterns of economic and institutional development, they help us to understand better the issues involved and how to direct our future studies of the underlying processes.[6]

II A BRIEF SKETCH OF THE GROWTH OF THE NEW WORLD ECONOMIES

The "discovery" and exploration of the Americas by the Europeans were part of a grand and long-term effort to exploit the economic opportunities in underpopulated or underdefended territories around the world. European nations competed for claims, and set about extracting material and other advantages through the pursuit of transitory enterprises like expeditions and the establishment of settlements. At the micro-level, individuals, elite and humble, invested their energy and other resources across a range of activities and projects that were rent seeking as well as more conventionally entrepreneurial. At both the levels of national governments and private agents, formidable problems of organization were raised by the radically novel environments, as well as by the difficulties of effecting the massive and historically unprecedented intercontinental flows of labor and capital. Surveying the histories of the New World colonies, enormous diversity in the specific types of ventures and or institutions is evident. The explanatory factors include differences across colonies in the backgrounds of the European and African immigrants, in the backgrounds of the native populations, in factor endowments (land, labor, climate, and other resources), as well as chance or idiosyncratic circumstances.

Common to all New World colonies was a high marginal product of labor, and especially of European labor. One indication of this return to labor is the extensive and unprecedented flow of migrants who traversed the Atlantic from Europe and

Africa to virtually all of the colonies (see Table 1) despite a high cost of transportation.[7] Moreover, that over 60 percent were Africans brought over involuntarily as slaves is a testament to the predominance of the economic motive of capturing the gains associated with a high productivity of labor. With their prices set in competitive international markets, slaves ultimately flowed to those locations where their productivity met the international standard. There were no serious national or cultural barriers to owning or using them; slaves were welcomed in the colonies of all the major European powers, with only Spanish and British settlements drawing less than two-thirds of their pre-1760 immigrants from Africa. In contrast, nearly 90 percent of all immigrants to the French and Dutch colonies through 1760 were slave, and the figure was over 70 percent for the Portuguese.

As the rate of movement to the New World accelerated over time, there were several salient changes in the composition and direction of the flow. First, the fraction of migrants who were slaves grew continuously over the four sub-periods specified, from roughly 20 percent prior to 1580 to nearly 75 percent between 1700 and 1760. Second, there was a marked shift in relative numbers away from the Spanish colonies, whose share of migrants declined continuously from 63.4 percent between 1500 and 1580 to 13.4 percent between 1700 and 1760. This precipitous fall in the relative prominence of the Spanish colonies was only partially due to the extraordinary rise of British America. The rate of flow to Spanish America peaked between 1580 and 1640 when 477,000 settled in the colonies of Spain, 291,000 in those of Portugal, and 3,000 in those of France. Between 1700 and 1760, however, the numbers of new settlers in Spanish America were stagnant at 464,000, while the numbers moving to the possessions of Portugal and France had grown to 1,038,000 and 445,000 respectively. During the interval of just over a century, the flow of migrants increased dramatically to the colonies of all major nations but Spain.

Another, and not unrelated, change suggested by these figures was the growing share of immigrants settling in colonies specialized in the production of sugar, tobacco, coffee, and a few other staple crops for world markets. This is evident from the increasing proportion over time going to the colonies of Portugal, France, and the Netherlands, as well as the continued quantitative dominance (over 90 percent – see Table 2) in the destinations of migrants to British America of colonies in the West Indies and on the southern mainland. Virtually all of these colonies were heavily oriented toward the production of such crops, and attracted such substantial inflows of labor (especially slaves) because their soils and climates made them extraordinarily well suited for producing these valuable commodities, and because of the substantial economies in producing crops like sugar, coffee, and rice on large slave plantations. Indeed, over the era of European colonization of the New World, there are few examples of significant colonies which were not so specialized: only the Spanish settlements on the mainlands of North and South America and the New England, Middle Atlantic, and Canadian settlements of Britain and France. It was not coincidental that these were also the colonies which relied least on slaves for their labor force.[8]

Table 1 European Directed Transatlantic Migration, 1500 to 1760 By European Nation and Continent of Origin

	(1) Africans Arriving In New World By Region Claimed		(2) Europeans Leaving Each Nation For New World (Net)		3) Total Flow of Migrants To New World (Col. 1 + Col. 2)		(4) Flow of Africans Relative To That of Europeans (Col. 1/Col. 2)
	(000)	(%)	(000)	(%)	(000)	(%)	
1500–1580							
Spain	45	78.0%	139	60.0%	184	63.4%	0.32
Portugal	13	22.0	93	40.0	106	36.6	0.14
Britain	**0**	-	0	-	0	**0.0**	0
TOTAL	58	100.0	232	100.0	290	100.0	0.25
1580–1640							
Spain	289	59.8	188	43.9	477	52.5	1.54
Portugal	181	37.5	110	25.7	291	31.9	1.15
France	1	0.2	2	0.5	3	0.3	0.50
Netherlands	8	1.7	2	0.5	10	1.1	4.00
Britain	4	0.2	126	29.4	130	14.3	0.03
TOTAL	483	100.0	428	100.0	911	100.0	1.13
1640–1700							
Spain	141	18.4	158	31.9	299	23.7	0.89
Portugal	225	29.3	50	10.1	275	21.8	4.50
France	75	9.8	27	5.4	102	8.1	2.78
Netherlands	49	6.4	13	2.6	62	4.9	3.77
Britain	277	36.1	248	50.0	525	41.6	1.12
TOTAL	767	100.0	496	100.0	1,263	100.0	1.55
1700–1760							
Spain	271	10.5	193	22.2	464	13.4	1.40
Portugal	768	29.7	270	31.0	1,038	30.0	2.84
France	414	16.0	31	3.6	445	12.9	13.35
Netherlands	123	4.8	5	0.6	128	3.7	24.60
Britain	1,013	39.1	372	42.7	1,385	40.0	2.72
TOTAL	2,589	100.0	871	100.0	3,460	100.0	2.97
1500–1760							
Spain	746	19.1	678	33.4	1,424	24.0	1.10
Portugal	1,187	30.5	523	25.8	1,710	28.9	2.27
France	490	12.6	60	3.0	550	9.3	8.17
Netherlands	180	4.6	20	1.0	200	3.4	9.00
Britain	1,249	33.2	746	36.8	2,040	34.4	1.73
TOTAL	3,897	100.0	2,027	100.0	5,924	100.0	1.92

Notes and Sources: These are based upon the yet unpublished estimates prepared by David Eltis. They draw upon a number of primary and secondary sources, and while some of the specific numbers will no doubt be revised with further research, the basic patterns will probably not be altered. We wish to thank Eltis for permission to use these numbers in this essay.

Table 2 Patterns of Net Migration To, And Wealtholding In, Categories of British Colonies

Net Migration (000) to	New England		Middle Atlantic		Southern		West Indies	
	#	row %	#	row %	#	row %	#	row %
Whites, 1630–1680	28	11.0	4	1.6	81	31.9	141	55.5
Whites, 1680–1730	-4	-1.8	45	19.9	111	49.1	74	32.7
Whites, 1730–1780	-27	-10.7	101	40.1	136	54.0	42	16.7
Overall Whites, 1630–1780	-3	-0.4	150	20.5	328	44.8	257	35.1
Blacks, 1650–1680	0	-	0	-	5	3.7	130	96.3
Blacks, 1680–1730	2	0.47	5	0.9	64	12.0	461	86.7
Blacks, 1730–1780	-6	-0.9	-1	-0.2	150	23.4	497	77.7
Overall Blacks, 1650–1780	-4	-0.3	4	0.3	219	16.8	1088	83.2
Total, 1630–1680	28	7.2	4	1.0	86	22.1	271	69.7
Total, 1680–1730	-2	-0.3	50	6.6	175	23.1	535	70.6
Total, 1730–1780	-33	-3.7	100	11.2	286	32.1	539	60.4
Overall Total, 1630–1780	-7	-0.3	154	7.6	547	26.8	1345	66.0

Wealtholding. c. 1774	New England	Middle Atlantic	Southern	West Indies
Total Wealth Per Capita (£)	36.6	41.9	54.7	84.1
Nonhuman Wealth Per Capita (£)	36.4	40.2	36.4	43.0
Total Wealth Per Free Capita (£)	38.2	45.8	92.7	1200.0
Nonhuman Wealth Per Free Capita (£)	38.0	44.1	61.6	754.3

Notes and Sources: David W. Galenson, "The Settlement and Growth of the Colonies: Population, Labor, and Economic Development," in Stanley L. Engerman and Robert E. Gallman, eds., *The Cambridge Economic History of the United States*, vol. I, *The Colonial Period* (Cambridge, U.K.: Cambridge University Press, 1995), forthcoming. The estimates for wealtholding in the West Indies pertain to Jamaica.

What stands out from the estimates presented in Table 3, is how small the percentages of the populations composed of those of European descent were among nearly all of the New World economies – well into the nineteenth century. The populations of those colonies suitable for cultivating sugar, like Barbados and Brazil, came to be quickly dominated by those of African descent who had been imported to work the large slave plantations.[9] The Spanish colonies were predominantly populated by Indians or mestizos, largely because they had generally been established and built up in those places where there had been substantial

Table 3 The Distribution and Composition of Population In New World Economies

Composition of Population		Panel A			
		White (%)	Black (%)	Indian (%)	Share In New World Population
Spanish America					
	1570	1.3%	2.5%	96.3%	83.5%
	1650	6.3	9.3	84.4	84.3
	1825	18.0	22.5	59.5	55.2
	1935	35.5	13.3	50.4	30.3
Brazil					
	1570	2.4	3.5	94.1	7.6
	1650	7.4	13.7	78.9	7.7
	1825	23.4	55.6	21.0	11.6
	1935	41.0	35.5	23.0	17.1
U.S. and Canada					
	1570	0.2	0.2	99.6	8.9
	1650	12.0	2.2	85.8	8.1
	1825	79.6	16.7	3.7	33.2
	1935	89.4	8.9	1.4	52.6
	Panel B				
1) Barbados	1690	25.0%	75.0%	-	
2) Barbados	1801	19.3	80.7	-	
3) Mexico	1793	18.0	10.0	72.0%	
4) Peru	1795	12.6	7.3	80.1	
5) C. Venezuela	1800–09	25.0	62.0	13.0	
6) Cuba	1792	49.0	51.0	-	
7) Brazil	1798	31.1	61.2	7.8	
8) Chile	1790	8.3	6.7	85.0	
9) U.S. - Nation	1860	84.9	14.0	1.1	
10) U.S. South	1860	61.7	37.7	0.7	
11) U.S. North	1860	96.2	2.6	1.3	
12) Canada	1881	97.0	0.5	2.5	
13) Argentina	1918	95.6	1.2	3.2	

Notes and Sources:

Panel A: The data for 1570, 1650, and 1825 are from Angel Rosenblat, *La Poblacion Indigena y El Mestizaje en America*, volume I: *La Populacion Indigena. 1492–1950* (Buenos Aires: Editorial Nova, 1954), pp. 88 (1570); 58 (1650); and 35–36 (1825); the data for 1935 are from Robert R. Kuczynski, *Population Movements* (Oxford: Clarendon Press, 1936), pp. 109–110. The Antilles have been included within Spanish America in all years. In 1825, the category "castas", which included "mestizajes, mulattos, etc.," and represented 18.17% of the total population in Spanish America, was divided two-thirds Indian, one-third black, except for the Antilles where all were considered to be blacks. In 1935, there were a number counted as "others" (generally Asian), so the distributions may not total to 100 percent.

Panel B:
Lines 1–2 – David Watts, *The West Indies: Patterns of Development. Culture, and Environmental Change Since 1492* (Cambridge: Cambridge University Press, 1987), p. 311.
Lines 3–6 – taken from James Lockhart and Stuart B. Schwartz, *Early Latin America: A History of Colonial Spanish America and Brazil* (Cambridge: Cambridge University Press, 1983), p. 342.
Line 7 – Thomas W. Merrick and Douglas H. Graham, *Population and Economic Development in Brazil: 1800 to the Present* (Baltimore: Johns Hopkins University Press, 1979), p. 29.
Line 8 – Markos J. Mamalakis, *Historical Statistics of Chile: Demography and Labor Force: Volume 2* (Westport: Greenwood Press, 1980), pp. 7–9.
Lines 9–11 – U.S. Census, Eighth (1860), *Population of the United States in 1860* (Washington: Government Printing Office, 1864), pp. 598–599, 605.
Line 12 – F.H. Leacy (ed.), *Historical Statistics of Canada: Second Edition* (Ottawa, Statistics Canada, 1983), Series A154–184.
Line 13 – Ernesto Tornquist & Co., Limited, *The Economic Development of the Argentine Republic in the Last Fifty Years* (Buenos Aires: Ernesto Tornquist & Co., Limited, 1919), p. 23. The Argentine figure for Indians is considerably lower than that for 1825 given in Kuczynski (67.9 percent, p. 106) and by Rosenblat (31.7 percent Indian, and possibly about one-third "castas", most being mestizaje), but is above that of Kuczynski for 1935, which is under one percent of the total population. Robert R. Kuczynski, *Population Movements* (Oxford: Clarendon Press, 1936), pp. 106, 110. As the estimate given by Lockhart and Schwartz, p. 342, indicates the share of Indians in the Buenos Aires population at the start of the 19th century was similar to that of all Argentina at the start of the twentieth century.

populations of Native Americans beforehand, and because of the restrictive immigration policies of Spain. As a result, less than 20 percent of the population in colonies like Mexico, Peru, and Chile were composed of whites as late as the turn of the nineteenth century. The Spanish Antilles, however, did have a relatively large white population, reflecting the limited number of Indians after depopulation, and the long lag between the beginnings of the settlement and the sugar boom which developed there only after the start of the nineteenth century.[10]

In contrast, because the territories that were to become the United States and Canada had only small numbers of Native Americans prior to the arrival of the Europeans, the composition of their populations soon came to be essentially determined by the groups who immigrated and their respective rates of natural increase. Since their endowments were generally more hospitable to the cultivation of grains than of sugar, these colonies absorbed relatively more Europeans than African slaves, as compared to other areas of high immigration in the New World, and their populations were accordingly disproportionately composed of whites. Even with substantial numbers of slaves in the U.S. South, roughly 80 percent of the population in the United States and Canada was white in 1825, while the shares in Brazil and in the remainder of the New World economies overall were below 25 and 20 percent respectively. It would not be until later in the nineteenth century that the populations of Latin American countries like Argentina and Chile would attain the predominantly European character that they have today – through major new inflows from Europe as well as increased death rates and low fertility among native Indians. This greater prevalence of whites in the United States and Canada may help to explain why there was less inequality and more potential for economic growth in these economies. Both the more equal distributions of human capital and other resources, as well as the relative abundance of the elite racial group would be expected to have encouraged the evolution of legal and political institutions that were more conducive to active participât ion in a compet itive market economy by broad segments of the population.

The estimates of the composition of population suggest that colonists of European descent could enjoy relatively elite status and rely on slaves and Indians to provide the bulk of the manual labor in most of the New World. It should not be surprising, therefore, that the principal areas of exception, the northern United States and Canada, were at first less attractive to Europeans. Reasons for their movement to the New World other than economic must have been of quite secondary importance in general. If they were not attracted primarily by the prospect of improvements in material welfare, and rights to the ownership of land, it is not easy to comprehend why so many of them would have voluntarily made multi-year commitments to serve as indentured servants, braved the discomfort and not insubstantial risks of death on their voyages, and located in the adverse disease environments characteristic of the places best suited for growing sugar and tobacco. The implications of the magnitude of the intercontinental migration are made all the more compelling by the awareness that the relative, if not absolute, stagnation of the flow to Spanish colonies was to a large degree effected by the tight control of the authorities over the number and composition of migrants.[11]

Although direct information on the productivity or incomes of individuals during the colonial period is fragmentary, the overall weight of the evidence seems clear. The patterns of migration, wage rates prevailing in free labor markets, anthropmetric measurements, as well as data on wealth holdings, all suggest that incomes and labor productivity for Europeans throughout the New World must have been high by Old World standards. The estimates of wealth holdings on the eve of the American Revolution for the English colonies presented in Table 2, for example, provide perhaps the most systematic comparative record of economic performance across colonies. The qualitative result is robust to whichever of four alternative definitions of wealth is employed. Jamaica, representative of the many colonies in the Caribbean specializing in sugar, generated as much nonhuman wealth per capita as any group of colonies on the North American mainland, and much much more per free individual. The stark contrast between the per capita and per free capita figures, reflects the larger shares of the population composed of slaves, the high returns to ownership of slaves, and the much greater inequality in the sugar colonies. Among those on the mainland, the record of the southern colonies (from the Chesapeake south) fell between that of Jamaica and those of their northern neighbors (New England and the Middle Atlantic) – with roughly equivalent performance on a per capita basis, but offering much more wealth to the average free individual.

Systematic estimates of the records of relative per capita income over time have not yet been constructed for many of the New World economies, but Table 4 conveys a sense of the current state of knowledge. The figures suggest that the advantage in per capita income enjoyed by the United States (and Canada) over Latin American economies materialized during the late-eighteenth and nineteenth centuries when the United States (as well as Canada) began to realize sustained economic growth well ahead of their neighbors in the hemisphere. Indeed, as Coatsworth has suggested, there was virtual parity (given the roughness of the estimates) in terms of per capita income at 1700 between Mexico and the British colonies on the mainland that were to become the United States. Moreover, product per capita appears to have been far greater in the sugar islands of the Caribbean, where Eltis finds that in Barbados the level was more than 50 percent higher.[12] If the current estimates are correct, then those of European descent in Mexico and Barbados were much better off than their other counterparts on the North American mainland, because they accounted for a much smaller share of the population and their incomes were far higher than those of the Native Americans or slaves (Table 3). Estimates of per capita income for other Latin American economies do not extend as far back, but it does seem apparent that they must have been closer to U.S. levels during this era than they have been since. Moreover, by the same logic as proposed for Mexico, incomes for populations of European descent must have been comparable or higher in South America and the Caribbean than in the northern parts of North America.

Table 4 The Record of Gross Domestic Product Per Capita in Selected New World Economies: 1700–1989

GDP per capita in 1985 U.S. $

	1700	1800	1850	1913	1989
Argentina	-	-	$874	$2,377	$3,880
Barbados	$736	-	-	-	5,353
Brazil	-	$738	901	700	4,241
Chile	-	-	484	1,685	5,355
Mexico	450	450	317	1,104	3,521
Peru	-	-	526	985	3,142
Canada	-	-	850	3,560	17,576
United States	490	807	1,394	4,854	18,317

Annual Rates of Growth in GDP Per Capita

	1700–1800	1800–1850	1850–1913	1913–1989
Argentina	0.0%	-	1.6%	0.6%
Barbados	-	-	-	-
Brazil	-	0.4%	-0.4	2.4
Chile	0.4	-	2.0	1.5
Mexico	0.0	-0.7	2.0	1.5
Peru	0.1	-	1.0	1.5
Canada	-	-	2.3	2.1
United States	0.5	1.1	2.0	1.8

Notes and Sources: The main sources are John H. Coatsworth, "Notes on the Comparative Economic History of Latin America and the United States," in Walther L. Bernecker and Hans Werner Tobler, eds., *Development and Underdevelopment in America: Contrasts of Economic Growth in North and Latin America in Historical Perspective* (New York: Walter de Gruyter, 1993); and Angus Maddison, *Dynamic Forces in Capitalist Development* (New York: Oxford University Press, 1991). The GDP per capita estimates for Barbados are from (for 1989) Central Intelligence Agency, *The World Factbook* (Washington, DC: Government Printing Office, 1992), pp. 30–31, and from (for 1700) David Eltis, "The Total Product of Barbados, 1664–1701," unpublished paper, 1994. The precise estimate was computed from Eltis's estimate that GDP per capita in Barbados was 40 percent higher than in England and Wales at 1700, and by employing the relative per capita income estimates for the U.S. and England and Wales in 1770 prepared by Alice Hanson Jones, *Wealth of a Nation To Be* (New York: Columbia University Press, 1980), p. 68 together with the estimated rates of GDP per capita growth drawn from Coatsworth. The growth rates reported for 1700 to 1800 were assumed to apply to the period 1700 to 1770. The Canadian GDP per capita figure for 1850 was computed by using the 1870–1913 rate of growth from Maddison to extrapolate back to 1850. The Peruvian estimates of GDP per capita were computed by assuming that the ratio of it to Mexican GDP per capita in 1989 was equal to the ratio between the respective GNP per capita income estimates for that year reported in the *World Development Report* (New York: The World Bank, 1991), pp. 204–205; and that GDP per capita in Peru grew at the same rate as in Mexico between 1900 and 1913.

Although all of the major New World colonies may have provided high living standards for Europeans, it is clear that they evolved dissimilar economic structures and institutions early in their histories. This divergence has long been noted, and explanations have often made reference to differences in the origins or backgrounds of the settlers. With the recent accumulation of evidence of wide disparities among colonies of the same European country, however, alternative sources of diversity deserve a reexamination. As economic historians of the United States, we are most impressed with the importance of factor endowments, broadly construed.

Economists traditionally emphasize the pervasive influence of factor endowment, and thus the qualitative thrust of our argument is not entirely novel. Indeed, our analysis has some antecedents in the work of Domar and Lewis, who were concerned with the problems that factor endowments can pose for underdeveloped economies and explored polar cases, with Domar focusing on labor scarcity and Lewis on labor surplus.[13] We interpret factor endowment more broadly, however, and argue that the United States and Canada were relatively unusual among New World colonies, because their factor endowments (including climates, soils, and the density of native populations) predisposed them toward paths with relatively equal distributions of wealth and income and corresponding institutions that favored the participation of a broad range of the population in commercial activity. This is significant, in our view, because the patterns of early industrialization in the United States suggest that such widespread involvement in commercial activity was quite important in realizing the onset of economic growth. In contrast, the factor endowments of the other New World colonies led to highly unequal distributions of wealth, income, human capital, and political power early in their histories, along with institutions which protected the elites. Together, these conditions inhibited the spread of commercial activity among the general population – lessening, in our view, the prospects for growth.

It is convenient for both our exposition and analysis to distinguish between three types of New World colonies. The usefulness of this abstraction from the uniqueness of each society, must be judged ultimately by how meaningful and coherent our stylized types are and by the explanatory power they help provide. Our first category encompasses those colonies that possessed climates and soils which were extremely well suited for the production of sugar and other highly valued crops characterized by extensive scale economies associated with the use of slaves. Most of these sugar colonies, including Barbados, Brazil, Cuba, and Jamaica, were in the West Indies, but there were also a number in South America. They specialized in the production of sugar and other such crops early in their histories, and through the persistent working of technological advantage, their economies came to be dominated by large slave plantations as were their populations by slaves of African descent. The greater efficiency of the very large plantations, and the overwhelming fraction of the populations that came to be black and slave, made their distributions of wealth and human capital typically extremely unequal.[14] Even among the free population, there was greater inequality in such economies than in those on the North American mainland.[15]

Although the basis for the predominance of an elite class in such colonies may have been the enormous advantages in sugar production available to those able to assemble a large company of slaves, as well as the extreme disparities in human capital between blacks and whites, the long-run success and stability of the members of this elite was also undoubtedly aided by their disproportionate political influence. Together with the legally codified inequality intrinsic to slavery, the greater inequality in wealth contributed to the evolution of institutions which commonly protected the privileges of the elites and restricted opportunities for the broad mass of the population to participate fully in the commercial economy even after the abolition of slavery. Progress in these post-emancipation economies was further slowed by the difficulties of adjusting to the loss of the productive technology on which they had long been based.[16]

A second category of New World colonies includes exclusively Spanish colonies like Mexico and Peru, which were characterized both by relatively substantial numbers of natives surviving contact with the European colonizers and by the distribution among a privileged few (encomenderos) of claims to often enormous blocs of land and native labor. The resulting large-scale estates, established by grant early in the histories of these colonies, were to some degree based upon preconquest social organizations whereby Indian elites extracted tribute the general population, and endured even where the principal production activities were lacking in economies of scale. Although small-scale agriculture was typical of grain agriculture during this era, their essentially non-tradeable property rights to tribute (in the form of labor and other resources) from rather sedentary groups of natives gave large landholders the means (a major competitive advantage) and the motive to continue to operate at a large scale. For different reasons, therefore, this category of colonies was rather like the first in generating an economic structure in which large-scale enterprises were predominant, as was a very unequal distribution of wealth. These latter colonies relied on the labor of natives with low levels of human capital, instead of slaves; in both cases, the elites were racially distinct from the bulk of the population. Instead of the existence of scale economies in slavery supporting the competitive success or persistence of the largest units of production, large-scale enterprises in this second class of colonial economies were sustained by the disinclination or difficulty of the natives in evading their obligations to the estate-owning families and in obtaining positions that allowed them to participate fully in the commercial economy. These estates were not unlike feudal manors, where lords held claims on the local population that could not be easily transferred, and where labor mobility was limited.[17]

To almost the same degree as in the colonial sugar economies, the economic structures that evolved in this second class of colonies were greatly influenced by the factor endowments, viewed in broad terms. Although the Spanish need not have treated the native population as a resource like land, to be allocated to a narrow elite, the abundance of low-human-capital labor was certainly a major contributor to the extremely unequal distributions of wealth and income that generally came to prevail in these economies. Moreover, without the rich supply of native labor, it is highly unlikely that Spain could have maintained its policies of restriction of European migration to its colonies and of generous awards of property and tribute to the earliest settlers. The early settlers in Spanish America endorsed having formidable requirements for obtaining permission to go to the New World – a policy which undoubtedly limited the flow of migrants and helped to preserve the political and economic advantages enjoyed by those who had earlier made the move. A larger number of Europeans vying for favors would have raised the cost of maintaining the same level of benefits to all comers, as well as increased the competition – political and otherwise – for the special privileges enjoyed by the early arrivals. Because of the differences in settlement patterns, the fights for control between creoles and peninsulares took a quite different form in Spanish America than did the colonial-metropolitan conflicts of British America.[18]

Paths of development similar to that observed in Mexico are repeated in virtually all of the Spanish colonies that retained substantial native populations. During the initial phase of conquest and settlement, the Spanish authorities allocated encomiendas, often involving vast areas along with claims on labor and tribute from natives, to relatively small numbers of individuals. The value of these grants were somewhat eroded over time by reassignment or expiration, new awards, and the precipitous decline of the native population over the sixteenth century that necessarily decreased the amount of tribute to be extracted. These encomiendas had powerful lingering effects, however, and ultimately gave way to large-scale estancias or haciendas, which obtained their labor services partially through obligations from natives, but increasingly through local labor markets. Although the processes of transition from encomienda to hacienda are not well understood, it is evident that large-scale agriculture remained dominant especially in districts with linkages to extensive markets. It is also clear that the distribution of wealth remained highly unequal, not only at points in time, but also over time because elite families were able to maintain their status over generations. These same families, of course, generally acted as corregidors and other local representatives of the Spanish government in the countryside – wielding considerable local political authority.[19]

The final category of New World colonies is best typified by the colonies on the North American mainland – chiefly those that became the United States, but inclusive of Canada as well. With the exception of the southern states of the U.S., these economies were not endowed with substantial populations of natives able to provide labor, nor with climates or soils that gave them a comparative advantage in the production of crops characterized by major economies of scale or of slave labor. For these reasons, their growth and development, especially north of the Chesapeake, were based on labor of European descent who had relatively high and similar levels of human capital. Correspondingly equal distributions of wealth were also encouraged by the limited advantages to large producers in the production of grains and hays predominant in regions like the Middle Atlantic and New England. With abundant land, and low capital requirements, the great majority of adult men were able to operate as independent proprietors. Conditions were somewhat different in the southern colonies, where crops like tobacco and rice did exhibit some limited scale economies. But even here, the size of the slave plantations, as well as the degree of inequality in these colonies, were quite modest by the standards of Brazil or the sugar islands.[20]

Spain had several colonies on the South American mainland that might also be placed in this category. Most notable among them is Argentina, although the Indian share of the population there remained high into the 1800s. Despite not being suited for growing sugar as a major crop, and ultimately flourishing as a producer of grains, the economy came to be characterized by substantial inequality in the distribution of land. Rooted in large grants to military leaders and favored families, this inequality may have persisted because of limited scale economies in raising cattle on the pampas.[21] Argentina failed to attract many immigrants until well into the nineteenth century, and remained a relative backwater, partially because of Spanish restrictions on European immigration and on trade, as well as the relative absence of lures like valuable mineral resources or stocks of readily available native labor who were concentrated in the southern part of the country). Despite such ambiguous cases, however, there appears to be no serious question that the structure of the economies in the northern colonies of the North American mainland was quite different from those of their counterparts elsewhere in the New World.

In our discussion of the first two categories of New World colonies, we raised the possibility that the relatively small fractions of their populations composed of whites as well as their highly unequal distributions of wealth may have contributed to the evolution of political, legal, and economic institutions that were less favorable toward full participation in the commercial economy by a broad spectrum of the population. The deviant case represented by the United States and Canada highlights this point. It seems unlikely to have been coincidental that those colonies with more homogenous populations, in terms of both human capital and other forms of wealth, evolved a set of institutions that were more oriented towards the economic aspirations of the bulk of the adult male population.

III THE ROLE OF INSTITUTIONS IN SHAPING FACTOR ENDOWMENT

We have suggested that various features of the factor endowments of three categories of New World economies, including soils, climates, and the size or density of the native population, may have predisposed them toward paths of development associated with different degrees of inequality in wealth, human capital, and political power, as well as with different potentials for economic growth. Although these conditions might reasonably be treated as exogenous at the beginning of European colonization, it is clear that such an assumption becomes increasingly tenuous as one moves later in time after settlement. Factor endowments may influence the directions in which institutions evolve, but these institutions in turn ultimately affect the evolution of factor endowments. It is our contention, however, that the initial conditions had long lingering effects, both because government policies and other institutions tended generally to reproduce the sorts of factor endowments that gave rise to them, and because certain fundamental characteristics of the New World economies and their factor endowments were difficult to change.

Crucial legislations influencing the evolution of the factor endowment, as well as the pace and pattern of economic development in the New World colonies, were those relevant to land policy, policy regarding immigration, and the regulation of trading arrangements between colonies, the metropolis, and the outside world. During the era of colonization, most European countries followed some variant of mercantilism. Although the specifics of national policy could vary with economic and other circumstances, the aim of colonies was to benefit the metropolis. Significant changes occurred in the late eighteenth century for the British, with the successful Revolution in the American colonies, and the full acquisition of Canada and various Caribbean islands from the French. In the first quarter of the nineteenth century most of the mainland North and South American colonies of Spain achieved their independence, as did Brazil from Portugal. Independent nations did not necessarily pursue the same sets of policies as when these areas were colonies; at the very least, even if variants of mercantilism were still being pursued, they were now aimed at benefiting the former colonies and not the metropolis.

During the colonial period, there were significant differences across the New World in immigration patterns and policies. The British emigration was to a large extent of indentured labor, an extension of its internal arrangements for agricultural labor (servants in husbandry).[22] Neither practice was to be seen among Iberian nations, where immigrants were more frequently missionaries or in the military. The distribution of Native Americans prior to European settlement meant that areas settled by the Spanish had much larger numbers than did those settled by the British, and the Spanish introduced more controls over Indians in order to better exploit this available resource and obtain labor from them. Since all New World economies were able to obtain slaves from Africa, the composition of the population in different regions reflected the numbers of whites and Native Americans only in part. More important, was the nature of the crops produced and traded in international markets – a condition influenced by natural factors as well as by governmental regulations.

Lands were frequently given as grants to military men, missionaries, and other settlers, as well as made available – often through sales – to other individuals in what could be smaller holdings. The more important were governmental land grants, as with the Spanish, the larger tended to be the holdings, and the more unequal the distributions of wealth and political power would become, relative to places where small holdings were made available. The size of holdings was often shaped by the nature of the crop to be produced and its technological requirements, but, as seen in the case of encomienda in Spanish America, the importance of renters in late-nineteenth-century Argentina, and the rise of sharecropping in the post-emancipation South of the U.S., the distribution of land ownership need not be the same as the distribution of operating farm sizes. Nevertheless, the initial policy of land distribution did have a profound influence on the distribution of wealth and political power, and thus on the future course of growth. Since the post-settlement policies for allocation of land were affected by the distribution of political power determined from the policies at the time of settlement, the long-term economic and political significance of these early policies is manifest.

In regard to immigration, the British, fearing overpopulation at home and responding to the perception in the colonies of an acute scarcity of labor, actively encouraged immigration to their colonies, first those in the Caribbean and then those on the mainland. Indeed, the right to migrate remained open for people from other European countries, generating a more diverse white population and a broader base of participation in the commercial economy than was to be found elsewhere. In stark contrast, Spanish immigration was tightly controlled, and even declined somewhat over time. Not only was Spain believed to be suffering from underpopulation rather than overpopulation, but the advantages which served as implicit subsidies provided to those who migrated led to a concern for limiting the flow as well. The authorities in Spain were motivated by a desire to keep costs down, while those who had already migrated sought to maintain their levels of support and privileged positions. A restrictive stance toward further immigration could not have been retained, however, if there had not already been a substantial supply of Indians to work the land and otherwise service the assets owned by the elites and the Spanish Crown; in this sense, at least, the policy must have been due to the factor endowment.[23] Overall, there were strict controls over who could settle in the Americas, with preference shown for relatives of those already there, with permission denied to citizens of other European countries as well as to those not Catholic – in the purported interest of achieving a more homogenous white society. Grants of permission to emigrate were initially restricted to single men, but were ultimately extended to married men accompanied by their families? single white women were never allowed.[24]

After the wave of independence movements early in the nineteenth century, most nations introduced or followed a relatively free immigration policy to attract new workers, mainly from Europe, with only a few restrictions on the racial or ethnic composition of the immigrants. Indeed, several countries advertised for migrants and attempted to induce, by subsidy (including land grants), or other measures, more permanent arrivals. Despite the marked easing of restrictions on immigration by Latin American countries, however, by far the dominant stream of European transatlantic migratory flows over the nineteenth century was directed to the United States, reflecting both the larger size of its economy as well as the hoped-for greater opportunities possible with the higher per capita income, the more equal distributions of wealth and political power, and the greater availability of small landholdings. It was not until late in the century that the Latin American economies received substantial new inflows of labor from Europe.[25]

African slaves were imported into some areas until the 1860s, with especially large flows into Brazil and Cuba during the 1830s and 1840s – partially due to the ending of the British and U.S. slave trades in 1808, and the emancipation of British slaves in the 1830s.[26] In the aftermath of slavery (and in the case of Cuba, while slavery still existed), extensive contract labor movements from India, China, and elsewhere in Asia took place to various parts of the Caribbean.[27] There was also some movement of contract workers from China, Japan, and, for a few years, Polynesia, to Peru for sugar production. Peru's principal export crop at midcentury, guano, was a government monopoly, using the labor of slaves, contract workers, convicts, and military deserters for production.[28] In general, however, while slaves and indentured servants dominated the eighteenth century, it was free white migration that accounted for the bulk of new immigrants to most parts of the Americas in the nineteenth century overall. There was, even here, another important difference in the nature of the immigrants to the United States, Canada, and to Latin America. The former two received migrants primarily from northwestern Europe, where economic growth was already under way and literacy was expanding. The major recipients in Latin America drew mainly from areas which had lagged, such as Argentina from Italy and Spain, and Brazil principally from Italy and Portugal. Thus, even after restrictions on European migration were lifted, it is probable that those going to the United States and Canada had generally higher levels of human capital than those moving to Latin America.[29]

All the New World colonies were settled at a time of relatively low population densities in the productive sectors, and thus confronted the problems of attracting sufficient labor while determining the rate at which (and by whom) new lands would be brought into production. In understanding the nature of policies toward land, it is useful to point to not only its expanse (which will also influence the ease of getting away from areas of high density), but also the soil type, climate, and disease environment, which will influence which crops can profitably be grown as well as the desirability of settlement by different groups. Policies concerning transportation development influenced the accessibility to markets, and the willingness of the government to construct, operate, and subsidize such activities affected the pace of settlement and the relative production of different crops.

These considerations, which determine which crops could be produced by settlers, given appropriate trade policies and the availability of labor, will thus dictate the technology to be used in profitable production and the optimum scale of production. The optimum scale will in turn affect the nature of landholdings and the form of the allocation of land, while the preferences of free workers for desired working conditions will influence the type of labor that could be used in production. It is therefore, not unexpected that among the British colonies, those in which sugar was the primary crop had a quite different racial composition of their labor force, and distribution of wealth and political power, than those in which grains were the principal crop grown.

Since the governments of each colony or nation were regarded as the owners of the land, they were able to set those policies which would influence the pace of settlement for effective production as well as the distribution of wealth, by controlling its availability, setting prices, establishing minimum or maximum acreages, granting of tax credits, and designing tax systems. Land policy could also be used to affect the labor force, either by encouraging immigration through making it readily available or by increasing the pool of wage labor through limiting availability. In most cases, although there were initial attempts at a slow, orderly process of settlement, this became more difficult to control over time. In the United States, where there were never major obstacles, the terms of land acquisition became easier over time and the course of nineteenth century.[30] Similar changes were sought around the mid-nineteenth-century in both Argentina and Brazil, as a means to encourage immigration, but these seem to have been less successful than in the U.S. and Canada in getting land to smallholders.[31] That the major crops produced in the expansion of the U.S. and Canada were grains, permitting relatively small farms given the technology of the times, may help explain why such a policy of smallholding was implemented and was effective.[32] But as the example of Argentina indicates, smallholder production of wheat was possible even with ownership of land in large units, maintaining a greater degree of overall inequality in wealth and political power.[33] Argentina, in the second half of the nineteenth century, was somewhat unusual in not having a national land policy, that being left to individual state governments. Unlike in the United States, however, where rivalry among the sub- federal governments seemed to spur investment in transportation infrastructure and banks, accelerating the pace of economic growth, no such beneficial effects were manifest in Argentina. Thus, the nature of factor endowments (inclusive of soils, climates, the composition and relative sizes of populations, and existing distributions of land and political power) as well as the particular crops grown did influence land policies, and the particular land policies pursued in different areas had significant impacts on future levels and distributions of income. While the ruling political coalitions may have gotten what they sought, that did not mean that the country would grow most rapidly.

It is rather difficult to design the counterfactual worlds necessary to demonstrate whether land policies in countries such as the United States, which generally encouraged rapid settlement, influenced economic growth relative to an alternative that would have meant slower settlement, permitting land to be sold only in larger, more expensive units. Arguments for a slower, more concentrated pattern were made by such contemporary observers as Henry Carey and Edward G. Wakefield, claiming economies of scale in production from higher density and cheaper workers who would be available to labor in nascent industrial establishments if there were no "open frontier" for potential labor to go to.[34] Whether this earlier application of the Nieboer-Domar hypothesis points to a higher national income or not, it does suggest a difference in economic structure, increasing manufacturing output relative to agriculture (or output in settled agricultural areas relative to frontier agriculture), as well as raising the returns to capital and land relative to those of labor. Greater access to land, on the other hand, promoted agriculture, led to higher rates of mobility, internal and external, and was important in attaining a greater degree of equality among whites in the antebellum United States than existed elsewhere in the world at that time.[35] Together with the high per capita income, this degree of equality, in turn, led to a broad participation in commercial activity, a large middle-class market permitting mass production of standardized goods – "the American System of Manufactures", and to conditions conducive to a sustained increase in the commitment to inventive activity with a corresponding acceleration of technical change.[36] In this way, the early achievement of economic growth in the United States can be related to its unusual, even for the New World, resource endowment.

The basic tripartite classification of New World colonies indicates that the United States (particularly the northern states) and Canada, with their reliance on grain agriculture and relative smallholdings, were unique both in their rates of long-term growth and the degree of equality. The basic influence of their factor endowments was reinforced by their policies of offering small units of land for disposal and maintaining open immigration, particularly by Europeans. Elsewhere there were large landholdings, greater inequality, as well as ultimately a later, if any, achievement of modern economic growth. In much of the Caribbean this reflected the importance of sugar plantations producing for world markets, and the large number of slaves in their populations. In areas such as Mexico (where corn was the principal crop), Peru, and Argentina, land and labor policies led to large landholdings and great inequality, whether on the basis of large numbers of Native Americans as in Mexico and Peru or with immigrant renters as in Argentina. The latter nations had relatively few Africans and only a small plantation sector, but their patterns of land distribution during the earlier stages of settlement meant that more substantial inequalities were generated than in the United States and Canada.

IV THE EXTENT OF INEQUALITY AND THE TIMING OF INDUSTRIALIZATION

We have argued above that despite the high living standards all New World colonies offered Europeans, fundamental differences in their factor endowments, which were perpetuated by government policies, may have predisposed them toward different long-term growth paths. Most of these economies developed extremely unequal distributions of wealth, human capital, and political power early in their histories as colonies, and maintained them after independence. The United States and Canada stand out as rather exceptional in being characterized right from the beginning by high material living standards among both elites and common people, as well as relative equality in other dimensions. It may, we suggest, not be coincidental that the economies in this latter group began to industrialize much earlier, and thus realized more growth over the long run.

The idea that the degree of equality or of democracy in a society might be associated with its potential for realizing economic growth is hardly new. On the contrary, controversy over the existence and nature of the relationship can be traced back a long way.[37] Those who favor the notion that more unequal distributions of wealth and or income have proved conducive to the onset of growth traditionally posit higher savings or investment rates by the well-to- do.[38] Their focus on the capability for mobilizing large amounts of capital stems from a belief that either major capital deepening or the introduction of a radically new generation of technologies and capital equipment was necessary for sustained growth, and skepticism that labor-intensive sectors or enterprises of small scale could have generated much in terms of technological progress.[39] Proponents of the opposite view have held that greater equality in circumstances has historically stimulated growth among early industrializers through encouraging the evolution of more extensive networks of markets, including that for labor, and commercialization in general. This provided impetus to self- sustaining processes whereby expanding markets induce, and in turn are induced by, more effective or intensified use of resources, the realization of scale economies, higher rates of inventive activity and other forms of human capital accumulation, as well as increased specialization by factors of production.[40] This perspective views the acceleration of economic growth as the cumulative impact of incremental advances made by individuals throughout the economy, rather than being driven by progress in a single industry or the actions of a narrow elite. By highlighting how the extension of markets elicits responses from broad segments of the population, this school of thought suggests a greater potential for economic growth where there are both high per capita incomes and relative equality in circumstances.[41]

Despite the complexity of the relationship between equality and the onset of growth, and the likelihood that it varies with context, we believe that recent work on the processes of early industrialization in the United States provides support to the hypothesis that those New World economies with more equality were better positioned to realize economic growth during the eighteenth and early- nineteenth centuries. The new evidence comes primarily from investigations of the sources and nature of productivity growth during that era when the United States pulled ahead. Studies of both agriculture and manufacturing have found that productivity increased substantially over these first stages of industrialization, but that the advances were indeed based largely on changes in organizations, methods, and designs which did not require much in the way of capital deepening or dramatically new capital equipment.[42] On the contrary, in the great majority of industries the progress appears largely a cumulation of incremental improvements, which did not require extraordinary technical knowledge to discover, over older basic technologies. The level of productivity generally, and the acceleration in the rate of advance which accompanied the initial phase of industrialization in particular, seems to have been closely related to the development of markets. The greater their access to broad markets, the more productive and innovative individuals and enterprises were. In agriculture, farms with easy access to the expanding markets became more specialized, used their labor and other resources more intensively, and were more apt to adopt new crops and products. Manufacturing firms in proximity to broad markets appear to have maintained higher levels of productivity for a variety of reasons including new organizations of labor based on the spread of standardized products, more invention and innovation generally, as well as economies of scale. The conclusion that technical progress was stimulated by market development is consistent with both the geographic patterns of productivity, as well as the incremental nature of the changes made in technique. Although their cumulative impact could have been major, it is conceivable, if not entirely natural, to think of individually marginal improvements as outcomes of efforts to respond creatively to technological problems raised by competition and opportunities in the marketplace.

Perhaps more directly, recent work with U.S. patent records has demonstrated that the growth of inventive activity was strongly and positively associated with the extension of markets as economic growth began to accelerate during the first half of the nineteenth century.[43] The independent effect of expanding markets was isolated by examining how the record of patenting across geographic areas – down to the county level – varied with proximity to navigable inland waterways, the cheapest form of transportation for all but short routes prior to the railroad. Not only was patenting higher in districts with such access to broad markets, but the construction of canals or other additions to the transportation infrastructure yielded immediate and large jumps in patenting activity. Also indicative of the importance of contact with the market was the widening range of occupations represented among patentees in those geographic areas where patenting per capita rose. A broad spectrum of the population appears to have become engaged in looking for better ways of carrying out production, spurring the rate at which improved methods diffused as well as boosting rates of invention and innovation. This association between patenting and access to broad markets held for ordinary patents, as well as for patents awarded to individuals credited with responsibility for technologically significant inventions. Moreover, the finding that manufacturing firms in districts with higher patenting rates, holding other factors constant, had higher total factor productivity provides further support to the interpretation that invention and technical change was genuinely induced by the expansion of markets.[44]

There are several reasons for believing that the association of markets with economic growth during the first half of the nineteenth century is relevant to the question of whether the condition of greater overall equality was an important contributor to the earlier onset of industrialization in the United States than elsewhere in the New World. First, the coincidence of high per capita incomes with equality would be expected to attract relatively more resources to the production and elaboration of standardized manufactures, because free whites of the middling sort would ultimately expend higher shares of their income on manufactures than would the poor (or than would be expended on in the case of slaves),[45] Moreover, although the wealthy might also devote large shares of income to manufactures, they generally consumed manufactures that were non-standard or customized. This is significant, both because markets were more likely to develop around goods or assets with uniform characteristics, and because many of the most fundamental advances in technology during the nineteenth century were concerned with the production of standardized manufacturing products.

Second, greater equality in wealth, human capital, and political power likely promoted the evolution of broad deep markets through the supply side as well. In some cases, the stimulus was associated with the existence of scale economies in activities such as transportation or financial intermediation with high fixed costs or capital intensity. Greater densities of potential users and beneficiaries raised the projected returns on investment in such projects and facilitated the mobilization of necessary political and financial backing. In the northeast region of the United States, for example, the great majority of banks and much of the transportation infrastructure (roads and canals) in place during the initial phase of growth, were organized locally and relied on broad public participation and use.[46] Without the substantial numbers of small businesses (including farms) and households seeking better access to product and capital markets, there would have been less potential for realizing the substantial scale economies characteristic of transportation and financial intermediation – and much less investment in these crucial areas.[47]

Greater equality in economic circumstances among the U.S. population not only encouraged investment in financial intermediaries and transportation directly through the structure of demand, but also through a legal framework that was conducive to private enterprise in both law and administration.[48] The right to charter corporations was reserved to state governments, and this authority was generously wielded in order to promote investments in transportation and financial institutions in particular, but ultimately manufacturing as well. Responding to widespread sentiment that there should be few obstacles to private initiatives as well as to opposition to privilege, many state governments had in effect routinized the process of forming a corporation with general laws of incorporation by the middle of the nineteenth century.[49] Another example is provided by the relationship between equality and rates of invention. Not only is it likely that the greater equality in human capital accounted partially for the high rates of invention in the U.S. overall, but the more general concern with the opportunities for extracting the returns from invention contributed to a patent system which was probably the most favorable in the world to common people at the time.[50] This pattern stands in stark contrast to that in Mexico and Brazil, where patents were restricted by costs and procedures to the wealthy or influential, and where the rights to organize corporations and financial institutions were granted sparingly, largely to protect the value of rights already held by powerful interests.[51] Differences in the degree of equality in circumstances between these economies and the United States seem likely to play an important role in explaining the divergence in experience. For a variety of reasons, therefore, a large degree of inequality might be expected to hamper the evolution of markets, and hence delay the realization of sustained economic growth.[52]

One might ask whether one can legitimately draw inferences about what the experiences of the New World economies in Latin America could have been like from the experience of the United States. Our implicit assumption is that there was a fundamental nature to the process of early economic growth during the eighteenth and nineteenth centuries, prior to the widespread introduction of mechanization and other heavily capital-intensive technologies, that was essentially the same across all economies. A complex and heroic counterfactual is obviously involved, but there are reasons to be encouraged. Of central importance here, is the observation that the region of the United States that was most like the other categories of New World societies, the South, had an economic structure that resembled in some dimensions those of its Latin American neighbors in the concentration on large-scale agriculture and in having a higher degree of overall inequality – at the same time that its processes of economic growth were much like those under way in the northern United States.

The South thrived in terms of growth of output per capita, but, both before and after the Civil War, lagged the North in evolving a set of political and economic institutions that were conducive to broad participation in the commercial econ-omy, as well as in the development of extensive capital and product markets.[53] The successes of the antebellum plantation meant that the southern population was more rural than the North's, with generally more production of manufactures as well as foodstuffs on the farm. Together with the greater inequality in income and human capital, this relative self-sufficiency of slave plantations reduced the extent of market development, both relative to the North and to what might other-wise have been in the South.[54] Moreover, the scale of labor requirements and the nature of differing seasonal patterns of production encouraged a greater degree of diversification on the part of southern slave planations than was the case in small-scale northern agriculture, and thus relatively few commercial cities and towns. Because manufacturing productivity was strongly associated with proximity to extensive markets, their more limited extent in the South likely contributed to that region's lower levels of manufacturing output per capita as well as productivity.[55] Inventive activity, at least as gauged by patenting, was also much lower than in the North.

The Civil War and the emancipation of the slaves led to dramatic changes in southern agriculture, with the disappearance of the plantation as a producing unit. While concentration of landholdings persisted, the dominant producing unit became the small farm, whether owner-operated or worked by tenants under vari-ous arrangements.[56] These tenants in the South, particularly the blacks, generally had limited incomes and wealth relative to farmers in the North, and they faced major obstacles to their accumulation of both physical and human capital.[57] It was several decades before the South began to develop a more urbanized economy with a larger manufacturing base, and the region continued to trail the rest of the nation for nearly a century.

Despite many parallels with other New World economies that relied on slav-ery early in their histories, however, the southern economy was an intermediate case, and ultimately realized a record of growth more like those of the northern U.S. or Canada. Within our analytical perspective, there are two features of the South that we would highlight in explaining why its economy performed better over the long run. First, its general unsuitability for sugar meant that the scale of slave plantations, and the shares of the population composed of slaves, were never as great in the South as in the Caribbean or Brazil. Inequality in income, human capital, and political power was accordingly never as extreme. Second, much of the political and economic institutional framework in the South was determined at the federal level, or through competition between states, and therefore had many features in common with the North. These circumstances help explain why the South evolved a more commercialized and competitive economy, with a broader range of its population participating fully, than other New World economies with a legacy of slavery. Nevertheless, when one notes the similarities between the records of the South and of these others, it is hard not to be impressed with the influence of factor endowment, and with the basis for employing evidence from the United States to assess, in general, how New World economies developed – or might have developed with a different factor endowment.[58]

V CONCLUSIONS

Many scholars have long been concerned with why the United States and Canada have been so much more successful over time than other New World economies since the era of European colonization. As we and others have noted, all of the New World societies enjoyed high levels of product per capita early in their histories. The divergence in paths can be traced back to the achievement of sustained economic growth by the United States and Canada during the eighteenth and early nineteenth centuries, while the others did not manage to attain this goal until late in the nineteenth or in the twentieth century, if ever. Although many explanations have been offered, in this paper we have highlighted the relevance of substantial differences in the degree of inequality in wealth, human capital, and political power in accounting for the divergence in the records of growth. Moreover, we have suggested that the roots of these disparities in the extent of inequality lay in differences in the initial factor endowments of the respective colonies. Of particular significance for generating extreme inequality were the suitability for the cultivation of sugar and other highly valued commodities in which there were economies of production in the use of slaves, as well as the presence of large concentrations of Native Americans. Both of these conditions encouraged the evolution of societies where relatively small elites of European descent could hold highly disproportionate shares of the wealth, human capital, and political power – and establish economic and political dominance over the mass of the population. Conspicuously absent from the nearly all-inclusive list of New World colonies with these conditions were the British settlements in the northern part of the North American continent.

We have also called attention to the tendencies of government policies toward maintaining the basic thrust of the initial factor endowment or the same general degree of inequality along their respective economy's path of development. The atypical immigration policies of Spanish America have been given special emphasis in this regard. While other European nations promoted and experienced mushrooming immigration to their New World colonies, Spain restricted the flows of Europeans, leading to a stagnant or declining number of migrants to its settlements during the late-seventeenth and eighteenth centuries. It was not until late in the nineteenth century that former Spanish colonies like Argentina began to recruit and attract Europeans in sufficiently large quantities to shift the composition of their populations, and erode the rather elite status and positions of the small communities of old families of European descent. The New World economies that had long histories of importing slaves to exploit the advantages of their soils and climates for the production of crops like sugar also continued to be characterized by much inequality and to be dominated by small, white segments of their populations. Why extreme inequality persisted for centuries in these classes of New World economies is unclear. Certainly large deficits in wealth, human capital, and political power, such as plagued Native Americans and slaves (and free blacks, after emancipation), are always difficult to overcome, especially in pre-industrial societies. Elites would be expected to (and did) use their political control to restrict competition they faced over resources, and large gaps in literacy, familiarity with technology or markets, and in other forms of human capital could take generations to close in even a free and seemingly evenhanded society. Indeed, these factors undoubtedly go far in explaining the persistence of inequality over the long run in the New World cases of concern here. The close correspondences between economic standing and race, however, may also have contributed to the maintenance of substantial inequality, either through natural, unconscious processes, or by increasing the efficacy of direct action by elites to retain their privileged positions and holdings.

Our discussion of why the United States and Canada led other New World economies in the realization of sustained economic growth during the eighteenth and nineteenth centuries raises another old controversy. Past treatments of the relationship between economic growth and inequality have tended to focus either on the effect of equality on rates of capital accumulation, or on the impact of growth on the extent of inequality. Our emphasis on the implications of greater equality for the evolution of markets, institutions conducive to widespread commercialization, and technological change, proposes a different direction for future research. This hypothesis is suggested by recent findings about the process of early industrialization in the United States. It is based on the idea, consistent with the evidence examined to date, that pre-industrial economies of this era had a large potential for sustained productivity growth derived from a cumulation of innumerable incremental improvements discovered and implemented throughout an economy by small-scale producers with rather ordinary sets of skills. These advances in practice were induced in the United States by alterations in incentives and opportunities associated with the spread of markets, and were made possible by a broad acquaintance with basic technological knowledge, as well as by broad access to full participation in the commercial economy.

Our conjecture that other New World economies might have been able to realize growth in much the same way as the United States, if not for their initial factor endowments and the government policies which upheld their influence, is obviously speculative and requires further study. Nevertheless, regardless of the outcome of such evaluations, the systematic patterns we have identified in the development of the New World economies should stand. Moreover, we hope that our attempt to outline a theory of how the paths of various New World economies diverged will stimulate more work on the subject, and ultimately lead to a better understanding of the interplay between factor endowments, institutions, and economic growth – in this context and more generally.

Notes

1 See, for example, the discussion of colonial economic growth in John J. McCusker and Russell R. Menard, *The Economy of British America. 1607–1789* (Chapel Hill: University of North Carolina Press, 1985).

2 See the regional breakdowns provide in the Epilogue to William M. Denevan, (ed.), *The Native Population in the Americas in 1492* (Madison: University of Wisconsin Press, 1976), pp. 289–292.

3 For general discussions of the role of institutions in worldwide economic growth, see Douglass C. North, *Structure and Change in Econoic History* (New York: W.W. Norton, 1981); and E. L. Jones, *Growth Recurring: Economic Change in World History* (Oxford: Clarendon Press, 1988). For a recent comparison of Argentina and Canada that discusses the role of institutions as well as makes reference to factor endowments, see Jeremy Adelman, *Frontier Development: Land Labour, and Capital on the Wheatlands of Argentina and Canada, 1890–1914* (Oxford: Clarendon Press, 1994).

4 For a general discussion of the diversity among British colonies in the New World, as well as of its sources, see Jack P. Greene, *Pursuits of Happiness* (Chapel Hill: University of North Carolina Press, 1988). For a fascinating account of radical divergence even among the Puritan colonies in the New World, see the recent Karen Ordahl Kupperman, *Providence Island. 1630–1641: The Other Puritan Colony* (Cambridge: Cambridge University Press, 1993), especially the discussions of the quite unusual patterns of land ownership and settlement.

5 This paragraph is based upon readings in numerous primary and secondary sources. For Latin America, particularly useful secondary works were: James Lockhart and Stuart B. Schwartz, *Early Latin America: A History of Colonial Spanish America and Brazil* (Cambridge: Cambridge University Press, 1983); Lyle N. McAlister, *Spain and Portugal in the New World. 1492–1700* (Minneapolis: University of Minnesota Press, 1984); Charles Gibson, *Spain in America* (New York: Harper & Row, 1966); Mark A. Burkholder and Lyman L. Johnson, *Colonial Latin America* (New York: Oxford University Press, 1994); and the first five volumes of the *Cambridge History of Latin America*, Leslie Bethell, (ed.), (Cambridge: Cambridge University Press, 1984). For the British colonies, see the work of McCusker and Menard, *The Economy of British America*, and the essays in Robert E. Galiman and John Joseph Wallis, (eds.), *American Economic Growth and Standards of Living Before the Civil War* (Chicago: University of Chicago Press, 1992).

6 For studies comparing records of growth in various New World economies, see Walther L. Bernecker and Hans Werner Tobler (eds.), *Development and Underdevelopment in America: Contrasts of Economic Growth in North and Latin America in Historical Perspective* (Berlin: Walter de Gruyter, 1993), particularly the essays by. John H. Coatsworth and Daniel D. Garcia. The editor's introduction provided several of the comparisons made earlier in this section. For a useful guide to an earlier debate, see Lewis Hanke (ed.), *Do the Americas Have a Common History: A Critique of the Bolton Theory* (New York: Alfred A. Knopf, 1964), particularly the essay by Sanford A. Mosk, first published as "Latin America versus the United States," *American Economic Review* 41 (May 1951): 367–383.

7 Table 1 is based upon the estimates of David Eltis. For estimates through 1830, see David Eltis, "Free and Coerced Transatlantic Migrations: Some Comparisons,"

American Historical Review 88 (April 1983): 251–280. For recent discussions and descriptions of migration flows in the period studied see, in particular, Ralph Davis, *The Rise of the Atlantic Economies* (Ithaca: Cornell University Press, 1973); Nicolas Sanchez-Albornoz, *The Population of Latin America: A History* (Berkeley: University of California Press, 1974); Philip D. Curtin, *The Atlantic Slave Trade: A Census* (Madison: University of Wisconsin Press, 1969); P.C. Emmer and M. Morner (eds.), *European Expansion and Migration: Essays on the Intercontinental Migration from Africa, Asia, and Europe* (New York: Bers, 1992); Ida Altman and James Horn (eds.), *To Make America: European Migration in the Early Modern Period* (Berkeley: University of California Press, 1991); and the essays by Woodrow Borah, Peter Boyd-Bowman, and Magnus Morner in Fredi (ed.), *First Images of America: The Impact of the New World on the Old* (Berkeley: University of California Press, 1976).

8 There is now a substantial literature documenting the existence of very substantial economies in the production of certain agricultural products on large slave plantations. The magnitude of these economies varied across crops, but appear to have been: most extensive in the cultivation of sugar, coffee, rice, and cotton; small, but present in tobacco; and absent in grains. Overall, there are two types of compelling evidence in support of this generalization. The first consists of comparisons of total factor productivity by size of the producing unit, as has been done for the United States South prior to the Civil War. The second is the consistent pattern across economies of dramatic and persistent differences in the sizes and types of farms producing different crops, or in the shares of output of those crops accounted for by different classes of farms. For example, virtually all sugar in the New World was produced by large slave plantations until the wave of slave emancipations during the nineteenth century. In contrast, the great bulk of wheat and other grains were produced on small-scale farms. For further discussions of the subject and evidence, see Robert William Fogel, *Without Consent or Contract* (New York: W.W. Norton, 1989); Stanley L. Engerman, "Contract Labor, Sugar, and Technology in the Nineteenth Century," *Journal of Economic History* 43 (September 1983): 635–659; and Noel Deerr, *The History of Sugar* (London: Chapman and Hall, 1949–50).

9 See, in particular, Richard S. Dunn, *Sugar and Slaves: The Rise of the Planter Class in the English West Indies. 1624–1713* (Chapel Hill: University of North Carolina Press, 1972), on the English colonies, and Stuart B. Schwartz, *Sugar Plantations in the Formation of Brazilian Society: Bahia, 1550–1835* (Cambridge: Cambridge University Press, 1985), on Brazil.

10 On the Caribbean in general, and for a discussion of the patterns of Cuban settlement, see Franklin W. Knight, *The Caribbean: The Genesis of a Fragmented Nationalism* (second edition), (New York: Oxford University Press, 1990). For an ethnic breakdown of Caribbean populations in 1750, 1830, and 1880, see Stanley L. Engerman and B.W. Higman, "The Demographic Structure of the Caribbean Slave Societies in the Eighteenth and Nineteenth Centuries," in Franklin W. Knight (ed.), *UNESCO General History of the Caribbean.* Volume III (forthcoming).

11 In addition to the works cited in footnote 4, see also the discussions of Spanish migration in Ida Altman, *Emigrants and Society: Extremadura and America in the Sixteenth Century* (Berkeley: University of California Press, 1989); Magnus Morner (with the collaboration of Harold Sims), *Adventurers and Proletarians: The Story of Migrants in Latin America* (Pittsburgh: University of Pittsburgh Press, 1985); Mary M. Kritz, "The British and Spanish Migration Systems in the Colonial Era: A Policy Framework," in International Union for the Scientific Study of Population, *The Peopling of the Americas*, vol. I (Vera Cruz: I.U.S.S.P., 1992), pp. 263–281; as well as several old classics, E.G. Bourne, *Spain in America. 1450–1580* (New York: Harper and Brothers, 1904); Bernard Moses, *The Establishment of Spanish Rule in America: An Introduction*

to the History and Politics of Spanish America (London: G.P. Putnam's Sons, 1898); and C. H. Haring, *The Spanish Empire in America* (New York: Oxford University Press, 1947). Spanish policies also reduced the numbers of slaves being imported, both through direct limitations as well as through decreasing demand by placing more restrictions on the use of slaves in its colonies (lessening their value to slaveholders) than other New World economies adhered to. These policies may help to account for why Spanish colonies like Mexico, Cuba, and Puerto Rico were relatively slow to turn to production of sugar on large-scale slave plantations. See Fogel, *Without Consent or Contract*, pp. 36–40 for discussion.

12 See the paper cited above by Coatsworth, "Notes on the Comparative Economic History of Latin America and the United States," in Bernecker and Tobler, *Development and Underdevelopment in America*, as well as David Eltis, "The Total Product of Barbados, 1664–1701," unpublished paper, 1994.

13 See Evsey D. Domar, "The Causes of Slavery or Serfdom: A Hypothesis," *Journal of Economic History* 30 (March 1970): 18–32. The problem of growth with "unlimited supplies of labor" occupied most of W. Arthur Lewis's work on economic development. Probably the first full presentation of this model can be seen in W.A. Lewis, "Economic Development With Unlimited Supplies of Labour," in *Manchester School of Economic and Social Studies* 23 (May 1955): 139–191.

14 On the early Caribbean sugar plantations, see Dunn, *Sugar and Slaves*: Richard Sheridan, *Sugar and Slavery: An Economic History of the West Indies. 1623–1775* (Aylesbury: Ginn and Company); and Manuel Moreno Fraginals, *The Sugarmill: The Socioeconomic Complex of Sugar in Cuba* (New York: Monthly Review Press, 1976).

15 For a detailed examination of how unequal the distribution of wealth among free household heads on a sugar island was, see the analysis of the census of 1680 for Barbados in Dunn, *Sugar and Slaves*, chpt. 3.

16 See Stanley L. Engerman, "Economic Adjustments to Emancipation in the United States and the British West Indies," *Journal of Interdisciplinary History* 12 (Autumn 1982): 191–220.

17 See the excellent and comprehensive overview of the encomienda, of the evolution of large-scale estates, and of their relation to preconquest forms of social organization in different parts of Spanish America, provided by Lockhart and Schwartz, *Early Latin America*. As they emphasize, the paths of institutional development varied somewhat across Spanish colonies, reflecting significant differences between Indian populations in "social capabilities" and other attributes. For example, the preconquest forms of social organization for Indians in highland areas were quite different from those of populations on the plains or in the jungle.

18 For a discussion of a more traditional form of conflict between the colonies and the metropolis in respect to the empire's trade policy, however, see Geoffrey J. Walker, *Spanish Politics and Imperial Trade. 1700–1789* (Bloomington: Indiana University Press, 1979).

19 In addition to Lockhart and Schwartz, *Early Latin America*, see treatments of Mexico and Peru in Eric Van Young, "Mexican Rural History Since Chevalier: The Historiography of the Colonial Hacienda," *Latin American Research Review* 18 (1983): 5–62; and Nils Jacobsen, *Mirages of Transition: The Peruvian Altiplano, 1780–1930* (Berkeley: University of California Press, 1993), chpts. 1–4.

20 For a dissenting analysis of the Brazilian slave distributions, based on early nineteenth-century data, see Schwartz, *Sugar Plantations*. Chapter 16, which is based on his article, "Patterns of Slaveholding in the Americas: New Evidence from Brazil," *American Historical Review* 87 (February 1982): 56–86.

21 On the late and never quite important Argentine sugar industry, see Donna J. Guy, *Argentine Sugar Politics: Tucuman and the Generation of Eighty* (Tempe: Arizona

State University Press, 1980). On the Argentine economy more generally, see Carlos F. Diaz Alejandro, *Essays on the Economic History of the Argentine Republic* (New Haven: Yale University Press, 1970).

22 See David W. Galenson, *White Servitude in Colonial America: An Economic Analysis* (Cambridge: Cambridge University Press); and Ann Kussmaul, *Servants in Husbandry in Early Modern England* (Cambridge: Cambridge University Press, 1981).

23 At first it seems somewhat puzzling, or contradictory to the idea that the factor endowment was the crucial determinant of policy, that Spanish authorities did not actively encourage immigration to colonies without a substantial supply of readily available Indian labor, like Argentina. On reflection, however, it seems likely that Spanish policy toward immigration to places like Argentina was simply incidental, with the overall policy as regards immigration to the New World based on the factor endowments and politics in all of Spanish America together. Hence, Spanish policy was probably driven by conditions in Mexico and Peru - the most populous and valued colonies. Since these centers of Spanish America had an abundance of Indian labor, the local elites and the authorities in Spain were able to maintain restrictive policies.

24 See the sources cited in footnote 9.

25 For the basic data on international migration during this period, see Imre Ferenczi and Walter F. Willcox, *International Migrations*. 2 vols., (New York: National Bureau of Economic Research, 1929, 1931).

26 See David Eltis, *Economic Growth and the Ending of the Transatlantic Slave Trade* (New York: Oxford University Press, 1987).

27 For data and references on contract labor movements, see Stanley L. Engerman, "Servants to Slaves to Servants: Contract Labour and European Expansion," in P.C. Emmer (ed.), *Colonialism and Migration: Indentured Labor Before and After Slavery* (Dordrecht: Martinus Nijhoff, 1986): 263–294.

28 See W.M. Mathew, "A Primitive Export Sector: Guano Production in Mid- Nineteenth-Century Peru," *Journal of Latin American Studies* 8 (May 1976): 35–57.

29 For a comparion of the streams of Italian migrations to North and to South America, pointing to a different pattern for this group, see Herbert S. Klein, "The Integration of Italian Immigrants into the United States and Argentina: A Comparative Analysis," *American Historical Review* 88 (April 1983): 306–329, and the discussion on the following page.

30 See the comprehensive overview of U.S. land policy in Paul W. Gates, *History of Public Land Law Development* (Washington, D.C.: Government Printing Office, 1968). There are discussions of Canadian land policy in Carl E. Solberg, *The Prairies and the Pampas: Agrarian Policy in Canada and Argentina 1880–1913* (Stanford: Stanford University Press, 1987); Richard Pomfret, *The Economic Development of Canada* (Toronto: Methuen, 1981), pp. 111–119; and Adelman, *Frontier Development*, chpt. 2.

31 See Warren Dean, "Latifundia and Land Policy in Nineteenth-Century Brazil," *Hispanic American Historical Review* 51 (November 1971): 606–625; Emilia Viotti da Costa, *The Brazilian Empire: Myths and Histories* (Chicago: University of Chicago Press, 1985), Chpt. 4; Solberg, *Prairies and Pampas*, and his earlier essay in D.C.M. Platt and Guido di Telia (eds.), *Argentina. Australia, and Canada: Studies in Comparative Development, 1870–1965* (London: Macmillan, 1985); as well as Adelman, *Frontier Development*, chpt. 3.

32 On northern U.S. agriculture, see Jeremy Atack and Fred Bateman, *To Their Own Soil: Agriculture in the Antebellum North* (Ames: Iowa State University Press, 1987); and Clarence H. Danhof, *Change in Agriculture: The Northern United States. 1820–1870* (Cambridge: Harvard University Press, 1969).

33 See Carl E. Solberg, *Immigration and Nationalism: Argentina and Chile. 1890- 1914* (Austin: University of Texas Press, 1970), as well as his *Prairies and Pampas*. In addi-

tion to grains, livestock production increased dramatically during the late-nineteenth century on the basis of large landholdings. Indeed, scale economies in the raising of livestock may have helped maintain the large estates.

34 The theme is developed by Henry Charles Carey in many of his works, such as *Principles of Social Science*. 3 vols., (Philadelphia: J.B. Lippincott, 1858- 1860). The clearest statement by Wakefield is found in Edward Gibbon Wakefield, *A View of the Art of Colonization* (London: John W. Parker, 1849).

35 For systematic information on the extent of U.S. income and wealth inequality, see Jeffrey G. Williamson and Peter N. Lindert, *American Inequality: A Macroeconomic History* (New York: Academic Press, 1980); and Lee Soltow, "Inequalities in the Standard of Living in the United States, 1798–1875," in Gallman and Wallis (eds.), *American Economic Growth*: 121–166.

36 See the discussion in Harold F. Williamson, "Mass Production, Mass Consumption, and American Industrial Development," in First International Conference of Economic History, *Contributions and Communications* (Paris: Mouton, 1960), pp. 137–147. Williamson draws upon Alfred Marshall, *Industry and Trade: A Study of Industrial Techniques and Business Organization; and of Their Influences on the Conditions of Various Classes and Nations* (London: Macmillan, 1919).

37 This point was made for the northern United States by Adam Smith, *The Wealth of Nations* (Oxford: Clarendon Press, 1979), vol. 2, pp. 571–575; and later became the central argument in the interpretation of the history of the United States by Frederick Jackson Turner. See, for example, the collected essays in Frederick Jackson Turner, *The Frontier in American History* (New York: H. Holt, 1948).

38 For a recent discussion of this long-debated idea, see Lance E. Davis and Robert E. Gallman, "Savings, Investment, and Economic Growth: The United States in the Nineteenth Century," in John A. James and Mark Thomas (eds.), *Capitalism in Context: Essays on Economic Development and Cultural Change in Honor of R.M. Hartwell* (Chicago: University of Chicago Press, 1994): 202–229.

39 See W.W. Rostow, *The Stages of Economic Growth* (Cambridge: Cambridge University Press, 1960); and W. Paul Strassman, "Economic Growth and Income Distribution," *Quarterly Journal of Economics* 70 (August 1956): 425–440. These points were at issue during the debates among development economists during the 1950s and 1960s concerning the relative importance of theorizing about balanced growth in contrast to an emphasis on so-called leading sectors. Robert Fogel's work on the railroads represented a basic criticism of the leading sector approach as applied to United States growth by Rostow. See Robert W. Fogel, *Railroads and American Economic Growth; Essays in Econometric History* (Baltimore: Johns Hopkins University Press, 1964).

40 For a classic discussion of how the extension of markets into agricultural areas radically alters the environment in which small farmers operate, the incentives they face, and thus the decisions they make about the allocation of resources, see Theodore W. Schultz, *Transforming Traditional Agriculture* (Chicago: University of Chicago Press, 1964).

41 See Strassman, "Economic Growth and Income Distribution"; and Kenneth L. Sokoloff, "Invention, Innovation, and Manufacturing Productivity Growth in the Antebellum Northeast," in Gallman and Wallis (eds.), *American Economic Growth*: 345–378.

42 See, for example, Winifred B. Rothenberg, "The Productivity Consequences of Market Integration: Agriculture in Massachusetts, 1771–1801," in Gallman and Wallis (eds.), *American Economic Growth*: 311–338; and Kenneth L. Sokoloff, "Productivity Growth in Manufacturing During Early Industrialization: Evidence from the American Northeast, 1820 to 1860," in Stanley L. Engerman and Robert E. Gallman (eds.), *Long-Term Factors in American Economic Growth* (Chicago: University of Chicago Press, 1986): 679–736.

43　See Kenneth L. Sokoloff, "Inventive Activity in Early Industrial America: Evidence from Patent Records, 1790–1846," *Journal of Economic History* 48 (December 1988): 813–850; Kenneth L. Sokoloff and B. Zorina Khan, "The Democratization of Invention During Early Industrialization: Evidence from the United States, 1790–1846," *Journal of Economic History* 50 (June 1990): 363–378; B. Zorina Khan and Kenneth L. Sokoloff, "'Schemes of Practical Utility': Entrepreneurship and Innovation Among 'Great Inventors' in the United States, 1790–1865," *Journal of Economic History* 53 (June 1993): 289–307.

44　Sokoloff, "Invention, Innovation, and Manufacturing Productivity Growth."

45　This idea is related to the well established relationship between per capita income and the proportion of expenditures devoted to non-agricultural products known as Engel's Law. The extension does not necessarily hold, however, because slaves were not able to choose their consumption bundles, as well as because Engel's Law itself makes no distinction between manufactures and other non- agricultural products. We are also relying, however, on the work of Viken Tchakerian, "Productivity, Extent of Markets, and Manufacturing in the Late Antebellum South and Midwest," *Journal of Economic History* 54 (September 1994):497–525; and Fred Bateman and Thomas Weiss, *A Deplorable Scarcity; The Failure of Industrialization in a Slave Economy* (Chapel Hill: University of North Carolina Press, 1981). These scholars find relatively little manufacturing output per capita in the South as compared to agricultural areas in the North, as well as a relative lack of firms producing standardized manufactures.

46　For an excellent overview of these developments, see George Rogers Taylor, *The Transportation Revolution. 1815–1860* (New York: Holt, Rinehart, and Winston, 1951); and John Majewski, "Commerce and Community: Economic Culture and Internal Improvements in Pennsylvania and Virginia, 1790–1860," (University of California, Los Angeles: Ph.D. Dissertation, 1994).

47　For discussions of the extensive scale economies in transportation and in financial intermediaries during this era, and of the importance of broad political support for investment in such enterprises, see Albert Fishlow, *American Railroads and the Transformation of the Ante-bellum Economy* (Cambridge: Harvard University Press, 1965); Carter Goodrich, *Government Promotion of American Canals and Railroads* (New York: Columbia University Press, 1960); Lance E. Davis and Robert E. Gallman, "Capital Formation in the United States During the Nineteenth Century," in Peter Mathias and M.M. Postan (eds.), *The Cambridge Economic History of Europe, Volume VII. The Industrial Economies: Part 2. The United States. Japan, and Russia* (Cambridge: Cambridge University Press, 1978): 1–68. Davis and Gallman, "Savings, Investment, and Economic Growth"; and Majewski, "Commerce and Community."

48　For similar interpretations of the role of the legal framework in promoting growth, but with different evaluations, compare the writings of J. Willard Hurst, *Law and the Conditions of Freedom in the Nineteenth-Century United States* (Madison: University of Wisconsin Press, 1956); with Morton J. Horowitz, *The Transformation of American Law, 1780–1860* (Cambridge: Harvard University Press, 1977).

49　On the changing means of forming corporations in the United States, see George Heberton Evans, Jr., *Business Incorporations in the United States. 1800- 1943* (New York: National Bureau of Economic Research, 1948). Also see Joseph Stancliffe Davis, *Essays in the Earlier History of American Corporations*. 2 vols., (Cambridge: Harvard University Press, 1917); and Shaw Livermore, "Unlimited Liability in Early American Corporations," *Journal of Political Economy* 43 (October 1935): 674–687.

50　The patent system in the United States was more favorable to common people in several dimensions. First, the cost of obtaining a patent was much less, especially relative to the annual wage, than in any other country with a functioning patent system. Second, the granting of patents operated according to prescribed rules which were independent of the social class of the applicant for the patent, and appear to have been adhered to. Third, the property rights in invention entailed in a patent appear to have been well enforced by the courts, making it much easier for a person of limited wealth to secure returns to his or her inventions. No other country had such favorable conditions for inventors from modest backgrounds. For international comparisons of patent systems, as well as a discussion of the concern with enforcement in the U.S., see H.I. Dutton, *The Patent System and Inventive Activity Purina the Industrial Revolution. 1750–1852* (Manchester: Manchester University Press, 1984); B. Zorina Khan, "Property Rights and Patent Litigation in Early Nineteenth Century America," *Journal of Economic History* 55 (March 1995): forthcoming; and Fritz Machlup, *An Economic Review of the Patent System.* Study of the Committee on the Judiciary, United States Senate (Washington, D.C.: Government Printing Office, 1958).

51 See Stephen H. Haber, "Industrial Concentration and the Capital Markets: A Comparative Study of Brazil, Mexico, and the United States, 1830–1930," *Journal of Economic History* 51 (September 1991): 559–580? Haber, *Industry and Underdevelopment: The Industrialization of Mexico. 1890–1940* (Stanford: Stanford University Press, 1989); and Ted Beatty, "Institution, Invention, and Innovation: The Evolution of a Patent System in Nineteenth-Century Mexico," unpublished manuscript, 1993.

52 As highly capital-intensive technologies became available, the need to involve broad segments of the population in the market economy in order to achieve sustained growth may have diminished. For a classic statement of a closely related idea, see Alexander Gerschenkron, *Economic Backwardness in Historical Perspective: A Book of Essays* (Cambridge: Harvard University Press, 1962), chpt. 1. For a discussion of different stages in technology and in the sources of productivity growth, see Sokoloff, "Invention, Innovation, and Manufacturing Productivity Growth."

53 Greene, *Pursuits of Happiness?* Majewski, "Commerce and Community"? C. Vann Woodward, *Origins of the New South. 1877–1913* (Baton Rouge: Louisiana State University Press, 1971); and J. Morgan Kousser, *The Shaping of Southern Politics: Suffrage Restriction and the Establishment of the One-Party South. 1880–1910* (New Haven: Yale University Press, 1974).

54 Robert E. Gallman and Ralph V. Anderson, "Slavery as Fixed Capital: Slave Labor and Southern Economic Development," *Journal of American History* 64 (1977): 24–46; William N. Parker, "Slavery and Southern Economic Development: An Hypothesis and Some Evidence," *Agricultural History* 44 (1970): 115–125? Fogel, *Without Consent or Contract*; and Eugene D. Genovese, *The Political Economy of Slavery: Studies in the Economy and Society of the Slave South* (New York: Pantheon, 1965).

55 Tchakerian, "Productivity, Extent of Markets, and Manufacturing."

56 Fogel, *Without Consent or Contract*; Ralph Shlomowitz, "Transition from Slave to Freedman: Labor Arrangements in Southern Agriculture, 1865–1870," (University of Chicago: Ph.D. Dissertation, 1979); and Nancy Lynn Virts, "Plantations, Land Tenure and Efficiency in the Postbellum South: The Effects of Emancipation on Southern Agriculture," (University of California, Los Angeles: Ph.D. Dissertation, 1985).

57 Robert Higgs, *Competition and Coercion: Blacks in the American Economy, 1865–1914* (Cambridge: Cambridge University Press, 1977); and Robert A. Margo, *Race and Schooling in the South. 1880–1950* (Chicago: University of Chicago Press, 1990).

58 For a different view, see Fogel, *Without Consent or Contract*.

28

CAPITAL ACCOUNT AND COUNTERCYCLICAL PRUDENTIAL REGULATIONS IN DEVELOPING COUNTRIES

José Antonio Ocampo

Source: From *Capital Surges to Drought: Seeking Stability for Emerging Markets* (Palgrave Macmillan, London, 2003), pp. 217–244.

The association between capital flows and economic activity has been a strong feature of the developing world, and particularly of emerging markets, for a quarter of a century. This highlights the central role played by the mechanisms that transmit externally generated boom-bust cycles in capital markets to the developing world, as well as the vulnerabilities they engender. The strength of business cycles in developing countries, and the high economic and social costs they generate, are thus related to the strong connections between domestic and international capital markets.

This implies that an essential objective of macroeconomic policy in developing countries is to reduce the intensity of capital account cycles and their effects on domestic economic and social variables. This chapter explores the role of two complementary policy tools in achieving these objectives: capital account regulations and countercyclical prudential regulation of domestic financial intermediation. After a brief look at the macroeconomics of boom-bust cycles, the chapter focuses on the possibility of directly affecting the source of the cycles through capital account regulations, and then considers the role of countercyclical regulations.

The macroeconomics of boom-bust cycles

Capital account cycles in developing countries are characterized by the twin phenomena of volatility and contagion. The first is associated with significant changes in risk evaluation during booms and crises of what international market agents consider to be risky assets, which involve a shift from an 'appetite for risk' (or more properly, an underestimation of risks) to a 'flight to quality' (risk aversion). The second implies that, due to information asymmetries, developing countries are pooled together in risk categories that are viewed by market agents as strongly correlated. Beyond any objective criteria that may underlie such views, this practice turns such correlations into a self-fulfilling prophecy.

Capital account volatility is reflected in variations in the availability of financing, in the procyclical pattern of spreads (narrowing during booms, widening during crises) and in the equally procyclical variation of maturities (reduced availability of long-term financing during crises). Such cycles involve both short-term movements – such as the very intense movements observed during the Asian and, particularly, the Russian crises – and, perhaps primarily, medium-term fluctuations, as the two cycles experienced over the last three decades indicate: The boom in the 1970s was followed by a debt crisis in a large part of the developing world, and another boom in the 1990s was followed by a sharp reduction in net flows after the Asian crisis. Due to contagion, such cycles tend to affect all developing countries, although with some discrimination by the market, reflecting the perceived level of risk of specific countries or groups of countries.

The main way in which the economic literature has explored the effects of external financial cycles on developing countries is by analyzing the mechanisms through which vulnerability is built up during capital-account booms. This may lead to the endogenous unstable dynamics analyzed by Minsky (1982) and Taylor (1998), among others, whereby the accumulation of risk leads to a sudden reversal of flows, and eventually to, a financial crisis. Alternatively the accumulated vulnerability is reflected in sensitivity to an exogenous shock, for example a contagion effect generated by a crisis in other developing countries or a downturn in financial markets in the industrialized world.

Thus in addition to the effects of traditional trade shocks, new sources of vulnerability have arisen. These are associated with the flow and balancesheet effects of capital account fluctuations on domestic financial and nonfinancial agents, and with the impact of such fluctuations on macroeconomic variables. Some of these effects are transmitted through public sector accounts, but the dominant feature of the 'new generation' of business cycles in developing countries is the sharp fluctuation in private spending and balance sheets. The macroeconomic effects are amplified if the stance of macroeconomic policy is procyclical, as market agents actually expected it to be. The credibility of macroeconomic authorities and domestic financial intermediaries plays a key role throughout this process.

If the fiscal policy stance is procyclical, temporary public sector revenues and readily accessible external and domestic financing induce an expansion of public sector spending, which is later followed by an adjustment when those conditions are no longer present. Furthermore, during the downswing interest payments follow an upward trend due to devaluation and to increased domestic interest rates and international spreads. This trend, together with downward pressure on public sector revenues, triggers a procyclical cut in primary spending, but this may be insufficient to avoid a sudden jump in public sector debt ratios.

The structure of public sector debt plays a crucial role in this dynamic. In particular, if most of the public sector debt is short term the necessary rollovers considerably increase the financing requirements during the crisis, thus undermining confidence in the capacity of the government to service the debt. If the short-term debt is external, risk premiums increase and the availability of financing may be curtailed. If it is domestic, there may be strong pressure on interest and exchange rates, as asset holders' high liquidity facilitates the substitution of foreign assets for public sector debt securities.

As in the past, exchange rate fluctuations also play an important part in the business cycle, but their flow effects are now mixed with, or even dominated by, the wealth effects they have in economies with large net external liabilities. The capital gains generated by appreciation during the upswing helps to fuel the private spending boom, whereas the capital losses generated by depreciation have the opposite effect in the downturn. Furthermore such gains induce additional net inflows when there are expectations of exchange rate appreciation, and the opposite effect if depreciation is expected, thus endogenously reinforcing the capital account cycle. The income effects may have similar signs, or at least in the short run, if the traditional conditions for the contractionary effects of devaluation (or the expansionary effects of appreciation) are met (Krugman and Taylor, 1978). Policy-induced overvaluation of the exchange rate, generated by antiinflationary policies that anchor the price level to a fixed exchange rate, accentuate these effects.

Domestic financial multipliers play an additional role through their effects on private spending and balance sheets. Indeed the domestic financial sector is both a protagonist and a potential victim of the macroeconomics of boom-bust cycles. The external lending boom facilitates domestic credit expansion and private sector spending during the upswing, but private sector debt overhangs accumulated during the boom subsequently trigger a deterioration in portfolios and a contraction in lending and spending during the downswing. At the same time banks and other financial intermediaries have inherent weaknesses that make them particularly vulnerable to changes in market conditions since they operate with high leverage ratios; they can be affected by maturity mismatches between deposits and lending (which are essential to their economic role of transforming maturities), and are subject to market failures that affect the assessment of credit risk.

Market failures are associated with information asymmetries, adverse selection and (possibly) moral hazard, all of which distort risk assessments and the allocation of funds to investment (Stiglitz, 1994; Mishkin, 2001). Buoyant expectations and their effects on the value of assets and liabilities may cause market agents to underestimate risks during booms. Overestimation of credit quality increases the speed of credit growth. In many cases, under the pressure of increased competition banks relax their standards of risk appraisal and make loans to borrowers with a lower credit quality. This strategy is more frequent in the case of new participants in the market, since the older and larger institutions tend to retain the best-quality borrowers. Overall a deterioration of banks' balance sheets results from the excessive risk taking that characterizes lending booms, but it only becomes evident after a lag. De Lis *et al.* (2001) refer to 'a strong positive impact of credit growth on problem loans with a lag of three years'.

Eventually the risks that have built up are revealed in a rise in nonperforming loans. In the absence of new capital, which is hard to raise when balances have deteriorated, banks are forced to cut lending even if borrowers are willing to pay higher interest rates. The protection provided by loan-loss provisions and capital may be insufficient to absorb the adverse shocks. The severity of the ensuing credit crunch depends on the magnitude of the credit boom and its effects on credit quality, and may be exacerbated by the fragility of the balance sheets of non-financial firms. Even the best- run banks may find it difficult to manage a shock that severely affects their clients.

The accumulation of currency and maturity mismatches on the balance sheets of both financial and non-financial agents is an additional source of vulnerability. Mismatches are associated with asymmetries in the financial development of industrialized and developing countries – that is, the considerable 'incompleteness' of markets in the latter (Ocampo, 2002a). In particular domestic financial sectors in developing countries have a short-term bias. Domestically financed firms thus have significant maturity mismatches on their balance sheets. Whereas small and medium-sized enterprises (SMEs) are unable to avoid such mismatches, large corporations may compensate for them by borrowing in external markets, but firms operating in non-tradable sectors then develop currency mismatches. A variable mix of maturity and currency mismatches is therefore a structural feature of non-financial firms' balance sheets in developing countries.

Domestic asset prices reinforce these cyclical dynamics. The rapid increase of asset prices during booms (particularly of stocks and real estate) stimulates credit growth. In turn, lending booms reinforce asset demand and thus asset price inflation. The resulting wealth effects intensify the spending boom. This process is further reinforced by the greater liquidity that characterizes assets during periods of financial euphoria. However this behaviour also increases the vulnerability of the financial system during the subsequent downswing, when debtors have difficulty serving their obligations and it becomes clear that the loans did not have adequate backing or that asset price deflation has reduced the value of collateral. Asset price deflation is reinforced as debtors strive to cover their financial obligations and creditors seek to liquidate the assets received in payment for outstanding debts under conditions of reduced asset liquidity. The negative wealth effect of decreasing asset prices contributes to the contraction of the economy and the credit crunch that follows in its wake.

Monetary policy has a limited degree of freedom to smooth out the dynamics of boom-bust cycles under all exchange rate regimes. In a fixed exchange rate regime, reserve accumulation during the boom fuels monetary expansion, which together with falling international spreads leads to a reduction in domestic interest rates. Under a floating exchange rate, both can be avoided, but only by inducing exchange rate appreciation, which also has expansionary wealth effects. Intermediate regimes (including dirty floating) generate variable mixes of these effects. A contractionary monetary policy will induce, in all cases, endogenous incentives that amplify the capital surge. The typical instrument of a contractionary monetary policy – that is, sterilized foreign-exchange reserve accumulation – also has large quasifiscal costs. The inducement to borrow abroad is also reflected in additional currency mismatches in the portfolios of either financial or non-financial intermediaries. The opposite types of pressure arise during a downswing, thereby exposing the accumulated financial vulnerabilities. Under a fixed exchange regime or a dirty float, the increase in interest rates and the reduction in financing generated by contractionary monetary policy aimed at containing speculative attacks on the currency exert strong pressure on weak balance sheets, particularly on agents with significant maturity mismatches. In a floating exchange rate regime, strong pressure is placed on agents with currency mismatches.

The frequency and intensity of financial crises is thus associated with the vulnerabilities generated by boom-bust cycles. In historical perspective, the frequency of 'twin' external and domestic financial crises is indeed a striking feature of the period that started with the breakdown of the Bretton Woods exchange rate arrangements in the early 1970s (IMF, 1998; Bordo et al., 2001). The most important policy implication of this is that developing- country authorities need to focus their attention on crisis prevention – that is, on managing booms – since in most cases crises are the inevitable result of poorly managed booms. Focusing attention on crisis prevention recognizes, moreover, an obvious fact: that the degree of freedom of the authorities is greater during booms than during crises. The way crises are managed is not irrelevant, however. In particular, different policy mixes may have quite different effects on economic activity and employment, as well as on the domestic financial system (see Chapter 13; see also ECLAC, 2002; Ocampo, 2002b).

Capital-account regulations

The dual role of capital-account regulations

As we have seen, the accumulation of risks during booms depends not only on the magnitude of private- and public-sector debts but also on maturity and currency mismatches on the balance sheets. Thus capital account regulations potentially have a dual role: as a macroeconomic policy tool to provide some room for countercyclical monetary policies that smooth out debt ratios and spending; and as a 'liability policy' to improve private sector external debt profiles. Complementary liability policies should also be adopted, particularly to improve public sector debt profiles. The emphasis on liability structures rather than on national balance sheets recognizes the fact that, together with liquid assets (particularly international reserves), they play an essential role when countries face liquidity constraints; other assets play a secondary role in this regard.

Viewed as a macroeconomic policy tool, capital account regulations aim at the direct source of boom-bust cycles: unstable capital flows. If they are successful, they provide some room to 'lean against the wind' during periods of financial euphoria through the adoption of a contractionary monetary policy and/or reduced appreciation pressures. If effective, they also reduce or eliminate the quasifiscal costs of sterilized foreign exchange accumulation. During crises they provide breathing space for expansionary monetary policies. In both cases, capital account regulations improve the authorities' ability to mix additional degrees of monetary independence with a more active exchange rate policy.

Viewed as a liability policy, capital account regulations recognize the fact that the market rewards sound external debt profiles (Rodrik and Velasco, 2000). This reflects the fact that, during times of uncertainty, the market responds to gross (and not merely net) financing requirements, which means that the rollover of short-term liabilities is not financially neutral. Under these circumstances a maturity profile that leans towards longer-term obligations will reduce domestic liquidity risks. This indicates that an essential component of economic policy management during booms should be measures to improve the maturity structures of both the private and the public sector's external and domestic liabilities. On the equity side, foreign direct investment (FDI) should be preferred to portfolio flows, as the former has proved to be less volatile than the latter. Both types of equity flow have the additional advantage that they allow all risks associated with the business cycle to be shared with foreign investors, and FDI may bring parallel benefits (access to technology and external markets). These benefits should be balanced against the generally higher costs of equity financing.

Innovations in capital account regulations in the 1990s

A great innovation in this sphere during the 1990s was unquestionably the establishment of an unremunerated reserve requirement (URR) for foreign- currency liabilities in Chile and Colombia. The advantage of this system was that it created a simple, non-discretionary and preventive (prudential) price-based incentive that penalized short-term foreign-currency liabilities more heavily. The corresponding levy was significantly higher than the level suggested for an international Tobin tax: about 3 per cent in the Chilean system for one-year loans, and an average of 13.6 per cent for one-year loans and 6.4 per cent for three-year loans in Colombia in 1994-98. As a result of the reduced supply of external financing after the Asian crisis, the system was phased out in both countries. Other capital account regulations complemented reserve requirements, particularly the one-year minimum-stay requirement for portfolio capital (lifted in May 2000) and approval (subject to minimum requirements) for the issuance of ADRs and similar instruments in Chile, as well as the direct regulation of portfolio flows in Colombia.

The effectiveness of reserve requirements has been the subject of a great deal of controversy.[1] There is broad agreement that they were effective in reducing short-term debt flows and thus in improving or maintaining good external debt profiles. However in contrast to this positive view of these regulations as a liability policy there has been widespread controversy about their effectiveness as a macroeconomic policy tool. This question has been made more complex by the fact that neither country was free from the strong pressures generated by the external financing cycle that emerging economies faced during the 1990s, or from the effects of procyclical macroeconomic policies (Ocampo, 2002b).

However, judging from the solid evidence that exists on the sensitivity of capital flows to interest rate spreads in both countries, it can be asserted that reserve requirements do influence the volume of capital flows at given interest rates.[2] This may reflect the fact that national firms' access to external funds is not independent from their maturities – that is, that the substitution effect between short- and long-term finance is imperfect on the supply side – and/or that the available mechanisms for evading or eluding regulations may be costly.[3] In any case, a significant part of the history of these regulations, particularly in Chile, was associated with the closing of regulatory loopholes.[4] Alternatively, the URR allows the authorities to maintain higher domestic interest rates at a given level of capital inflows, and thus of the money supply. Hence in broader terms the usefulness of reserve requirements as a macroeconomic policy tool depends on the ability to affect capital flows, domestic interest rates or both, with the particular combination being subject to policy choice.[5] To the extent that capital flows affect the supply of foreign exchange, exchange rates may also be affected. Given the numerous channels through which the URR can affect the economy, the effectiveness of these regulations can best be measured by a broad index of 'monetary pressures' that includes capital inflows, domestic interest rates and exchange rates. This is the procedure used below.

In Colombia, where these regulations were modified more extensively during the 1990s, there is strong evidence that increases in the reserve requirements reduced flows (Ocampo and Tovar 1998, 1999) or, alternatively, were effective in increasing domestic interest rates (Villar and Rincón, 2002). Similar evidence is available for Chile (see Larraín et al., 2000; Le Fort and Lehman, 2000; for interest rate spreads see De Gregorio et al., 2000). The evidence of effects on exchange rates is more mixed, though this may reflect the difficulties inherent in exchange rate modelling (Williamson, 2000: ch. 4).

Some problems in the management of these regulations were associated with changes in the relevant policy parameters. The difficulties experienced in this connection by the two countries differed. In Chile the basic problem was the variability of the rules pertaining to the exchange rate, since the lower limits of the exchange rate bands were changed on numerous occasions before the exchange rate was allowed to float in September 1999. During capital account booms, this gave rise to a 'safe bet' for agents bringing in capital, since when the exchange rate neared the floor of the band (in pesos per dollar) the probability that the floor would be adjusted downward was high. In Colombia the main problem was the frequency of the changes made to the reserve requirements. Changes foreseen by the market sparked speculation, thereby diminishing the effectiveness of such measures for some time after the modification. It is interesting to note that in both countries the reserve requirements were seen as complementary to, rather than a substitute for, other macroeconomic policies, which were certainly superior in Chile. In particular the expansionary and contractionary phases of monetary policy were much more marked in Colombia, and this country's fiscal position deteriorated throughout the decade.

Malaysia also made major innovations in its capital account regulations in the 1990s. In January 1994 it prohibited non-residents from buying a wide range of domestic short-term securities and established other limitations on short-term inflows; these restrictions were lifted later in the year. These measures also had a preventive focus, but were quantitative rather than price-based. They proved highly effective, indeed superior in terms of reducing capital flows and asset prices than the Chilean regulations (Palma, 2002). They also improved the country's debt profile (Rodrik and Velasco, 2000). However, after they were lifted a new wave of debt accumulation and asset price increases developed, though the debt profile was kept at more prudential levels than in other Asian countries hit by the crisis in 1997 (Kaplan and Rodrik, 2001; Palma, 2002).

An additional innovation came with the Asian crisis. In September 1998 Malaysia established strong restrictions on capital outflows. The main objective was to eliminate offshore trading of the local currency – that is, the segmentation of its demand – by restricting its use to domestic operations by residents. Ringgit deposits abroad were made illegal, and it was determined that those held abroad by nationals had to be repatriated. Trade transactions had to be settled in foreign currency. It was also decided that ringgit deposits held in the domestic financial system by non-residents could not be converted into a foreign currency for a year. In February 1999 this regulation was replaced by an exit levy on the principal, with a decreasing rate for investments held for a longer period and no tax on those held for more than a year. For new capital inflows, an exit tax on capital gains was established, with a higher rate for capital that stayed less than a year (30 per cent; 10 per cent otherwise). The exit tax was reduced to a flat 10 per cent in September 1999; in January 2001 it was decided that it would henceforth apply only to portfolio flows held for less than a year, and in May 2001 it was eliminated altogether.

Significant discussions have taken place on the effects of these controls. Kaplan and Rodrik (2001) provide the strongest argument on the effectiveness of the regulations.[6] Drawing on previous studies, they show that the regulations were highly effective in rapidly closing the offshore ringgit market and reversing financial market pressure, as reflected in the trends in foreign exchange reserves and exchange and interest rates. The removal of financial uncertainties, together with the additional scope for expansionary monetary and fiscal policies, led to a speedier recovery of economic activity, lower inflation and better employment and real wage performance than comparable IMF-type programmes during the Asian crisis. This is true even adjusting for the improved external environment when the Malaysian controls were imposed, and despite the fact that the country did not receive large injections of capital; indeed the initial reaction of external capital markets to the regulations was negative.

Figure 1 offers a simple way to view the effectiveness of capital account regulations in the three countries. Based on similar indicators used in the literature,

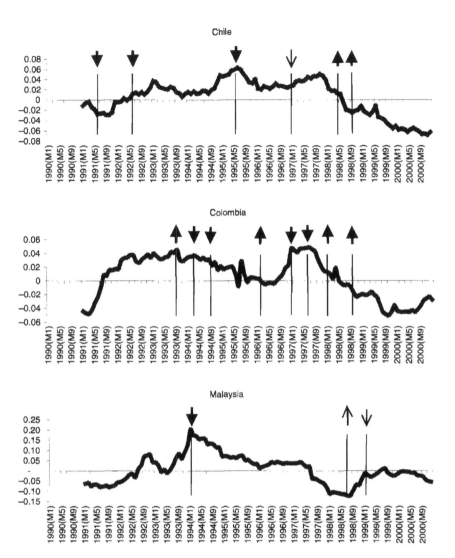

Figure 1 Index of expansion monetary pressures, 1990–2000. ▼ ▲ Imposition or relaxation of restrictions on capital inflows, respectively (the direction of the arrows indicates the expected effect on the index). ↑ ↓ Imposition or relaxation of restrictions on capital outflows, respectively. Index = $aR + be - ci$, where R = international reserves corrected by the log trend e = the twelve-month variation of the real exchange rate, i = the real deposit interest rate, and a, b, c are the standard deviations of R, e and i, respectively. *Source*: Estimates based on IMF data.

it calculates an index of expansionary monetary pressures. Since a capital surge generates expansionary effects through three different channels – the accumulation of international reserves, an appreciation of the exchange rate and a reduction in interest rates – the index weights the trends of these three indicators by their standard deviation during the period analyzed. A simple inspection of the graph indicates that the Malaysian controls were extremely effective, both in reversing the strong expansionary effect of capital surges in 1994 and in stopping the strong contractionary effects generated by capital outflows in 1998. The price-based capital account regulations in Chile and Colombia had weaker effects, particularly in the first case. Indeed the introduction of such regulations in Chile in June 1991 and their strengthening in May 1992 was not accompanied by a reversal of the expansionary trend;[7] those instituted in July 1995 had a more discernible effect. In Colombia, which used price-based regulations more aggressively, the effects were stronger. In particular the movement in the index of expansionary pressures was more closely tied to changes in capital account regulations in 1993-97. In both countries the capital account turned contractionary in 1998, with the reduction in the URR having only a negligible effect on this trend.

Overall the innovative capital account regulations in the 1990s served as useful instruments, both for improving debt profiles and for improving the exchange rate/monetary stance trade-off. However the macroeconomic effects depended on the strength of the regulations, which were only temporary and operated as 'speed bumps' rather than as permanent restrictions, to use Palma's (2002) expression. The basic advantages of the price-based instrument used by Chile and Colombia were its simplicity, its non-discretionary character and, as we shall see in the following section, its neutral effect on corporate borrowing decisions. The more quantitative-type Malaysian system had stronger short-term macroeconomic effects.

It must be emphasized that these systems were designed for countries that chose to be integrated into the international capital markets. In the case of Colombia the transition from the old type of exchange controls to price- based capital account regulations was, in effect, a liberalization of the capital account, as reflected in the increased sensitivity of capital flows to interest arbitrage incentives (Ocampo and Tovar, 1998).[8]

Traditional exchange controls and capital account regulations may therefore be superior if the policy objective is significantly to reduce domestic macroeconomic sensitivity to international capital flows. India provides an alternative successful example in this regard. Despite the slow and cautious liberalization that has taken place in India since the early 1990s, this country still largely relies on quantitative restrictions on flows: overall quantitative ceilings, minimum maturities for external borrowing and end-use restrictions (most of which have been liberalized in recent years), plus the prohibition of borrowing in foreign currencies by non-corporate residents; direct regulation (including, in some instances, explicit approval) of portfolio flows in the case of non-residents, as well as of ADRs and investment abroad by domestic corporations; some sectoral restrictions on FDI;

and minimum maturities and interest rate regulations on deposits by non-resident Indians (Habermeier, 2000; Reddy, 2001; Rajaraman, 2001; Nayyar, 2002). It must be emphasized that, despite the reduced sensitivity to the Asian crisis and the increased macroeconomic autonomy that this system has allowed, India has not been entirely detached from external financing cycles.

In contrast to the successful experiences previously analyzed, crisis-driven quantitative controls generate serious credibility issues and may be ineffective, as a strong administrative capacity is essential for any capital account regime to be effective. This implies that a tradition of regulation may be necessary, and that permanent regulatory regimes that are tightened or loosened through the cycle may be superior to the alternation of different (even opposite) capital account regimes. In broad terms this means that it is essential to maintain the autonomy to impose capital account regulations and thus the freedom to reimpose controls if necessary (Rajaraman, 2001; Reddy, 2001; Ocampo, 2002a, 2002b). This is indeed a corollary of the incomplete nature of international financial governance (Ocampo, 2002a) and a basic lesson from the Malaysian experience. Also, traditional quantitative capital account regulations and direct approval of sensitive flows (external portfolio flows, issuance of ADRs and investment abroad by residents) can make perfect sense if they are sufficiently well managed to avoid loopholes, high administrative costs and, in particular, corruption. Indeed simple quantitative restrictions that rule out certain forms of indebtedness (for example short-term foreign borrowing, except trade credit lines, or borrowing in foreign currency by residents operating in non-tradable sectors) are also preventive in character and easier to administer than price-based controls (Ariyoshi *et al.*, 2000). These restrictions are more attractive and effective when domestic financial development is limited, but they may become obstacles to financial development. Indeed this may, be viewed as one of the basic costs of capital account regulation. More broadly, there may be inherent trade-offs between domestic financial deepening and capital account volatility (due in part to the dismantling of capital controls). We shall explore some aspects of these trade-offs in the following section.

Certain regulations on current-account transactions (export surrender requirements or the obligation to channel trade transactions through certain approved intermediaries) and effective segmentation of the market for financial instruments denominated in the domestic currency may be essential to guarantee the effectiveness of regulations. This implies a need to avoid or strongly regulate the internationalization of the domestic currency, as well as to take a highly conservative approach to domestic financial dollarization (Reddy, 2001). These are in fact common features of the four case studies considered above; and in the case of Malaysia, achieving this objective involved dismantling the offshore market for the domestic currency.

It should be emphasized again that capital account regulations should always be seen as an instrument that, by providing an additional degree of freedom to the authorities, facilitates the adoption of sensible countercyclical macroeconomic policies. Hence it can never be a substitute for them.

Complementary liability policies

Prudential regulation and supervision can, in part, be substituted for capital account regulations. Indeed the distinction between capital controls and prudential regulations that affect cross-border flows is not clear cut. In particular, higher liquidity (or reserve) requirements for the financial system's foreign currency liabilities can be established, and domestic lending to firms operating in non-tradable sectors that have substantial foreign-currency liabilities can be discouraged by more stringent regulatory provisions.

The main problem with these options is that they only indirectly affect the foreign-currency liabilities of non-financial agents, and indeed may encourage them to borrow abroad. Accordingly they need to be supplemented with other regulations, including rules on the types of firm that can borrow abroad and the prudential ratios with which they must comply; restrictions on the terms of corporate debts that can be contracted abroad (minimum maturities and maximum spreads); public disclosure of the short-term external liabilities of firms; regulations requiring rating agencies to give special weight to this factor; and tax provisions for foreign-currency liabilities (for example no or only partial deductions for interest payments on international loans).[9] Some of the most important regulations of this type concern external borrowing by firms operating in non-tradable sectors. A simple rule that should be considered is the strict prohibition of foreign borrowing by non-financial firms without income in foreign currency or restrictions on the maturities (only long term) or end use (only investment) of such borrowing.

Price-based capital account regulations may thus be a superior alternative and may be simpler to administer than an equivalent system based on prudential regulations plus additional policies aimed at non-financial firms. Among their virtues, *vis-à-vis* prudential regulation and supervision, we should also include the fact that they are price-based (some prudential regulations, such as prohibitions on certain types of operation, are not), nondiscretionary (whereas prudential supervision tends to be discretionary in its operation) and neutral in terms of the choice made by corporations between foreign-currency-denominated borrowing in the domestic market versus the international market. Indeed equivalent practices are used by private agents, for example the selling fees imposed by mutual funds on investments held for a short period in order to discourage short-term holdings (JP Morgan, 1998: 23).

In the case of the public sector, specific legal limits and regulations are required. Direct approval of borrowing and the establishment of minimum maturities and maximum spreads by the Ministry of Finance or the central bank may be the best liability policy. Provisions of this sort should cover the central administration as well as autonomous public sector agencies and subnational governments (ECLAC, 1998: ch. 8). Such regulations should apply both to external and to domestic public-sector liabilities. The most straightforward reason for this is that residents who hold short-term public-sector securities have, in periods of external or domestic financial instability, other options besides rolling over the public sector debt, including capital flight. This is even more so if foreigners are allowed to purchase domestic public sector securities.

Thus when the gross borrowing requirements are high, the interest rate will have to increase to make debt rollovers attractive. Higher interest rates are immediately reflected in the budget deficit, thereby rapidly changing the trend in public sector debt, as happened in Brazil prior to the 1999 crisis. In addition rollovers may be viable only if the risk of devaluation or future interest rate hikes can be passed on to the government, which generates an additional source of destabilization. Mexico's widely publicized move in 1994 to replace peso-denominated securities (Treasury Certificates, or Cetes) with dollar-denominated bonds (Tesobonos), which was one of the crucial factors in the crisis that hit the country late that year, was no doubt facilitated by the short-term profile of Cetes (Sachs *et al.*, 1996; Ros, 2001). The short-term structure of Brazil's debt was also the reason why, after late 1997, fixed-interest bonds were swiftly replaced by variable-rate and dollar- denominated securities, which cancelled out the improvements that had been made in the public debt structure in previous years. It is important to emphasize that, despite its fiscal deterioration, no substitution of a similar magnitude was observed in Colombia during the 1998-99 crisis; this country's tradition of issuing public sector securities with a minimum one-year maturity is a significant part of the explanation (Figure 2).

Thus a sound maturity profile for domestic public sector debt is an essential complement to a sound public and private external debt profile when trying to reduce the degree of vulnerability to capital account shocks. Furthermore, on strictly prudential grounds, external borrowing by the public sector generates currency mismatches (except for public sector firms operating in tradable sectors) and should thus be avoided. However this principle should not be translated into simple prohibitions for two reasons.

The first reason is macroeconomic in character. To the extent that external private capital flows are procyclical, it is reasonable for the public sector to follow a countercyclical debt structure strategy. This means that, during capital account surges, it should reduce the borrowing requirements and adopt a liability policy aimed at substituting domestic for external liabilities. The opposite is true during periods of reduced private flows. Indeed in this case the public sector may be one of the best net suppliers of foreign exchange, thanks to its better access to external credit, including credit from multilateral financial institutions. Such external borrowing may also be helpful in maintaining a better external debt profile and avoiding private borrowing abroad at excessively high spreads during crises.

The second reason relates to the depth of domestic bond markets, which determines the ability to issue longer-term domestic debt securities. This attribute includes the existence of secondary markets and active agents (market makers) that provide liquidity for these securities. In the absence of these preconditions the government faces a serious trade-off between maturity and currency mismatches, a trade-off that is typical of all domestic agents that produce non-tradable goods and services. Indeed a domestic market for public sector debt securities with an

335

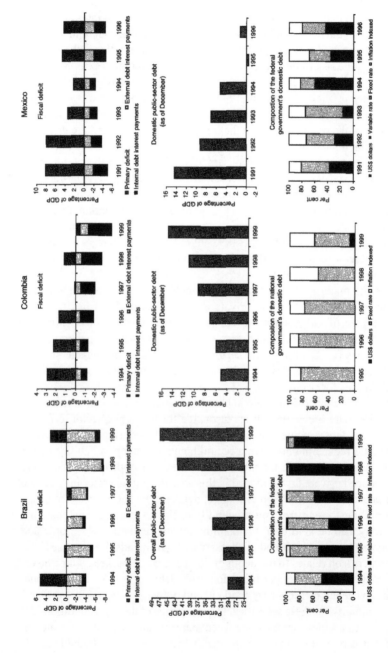

Figure 2 Fiscal deficit and public debt: Brazil (1994-99), Colombia (1994-99) and Mexico (1991-96). *Source:* Central Bank of Brazil; IDEA; Ministry of Finance of Colombia; Secretary of Finance and Public Credit of Mexico; Bank of Mexico.

excessive short-term bias can be extremely destabilizing during a crisis. It may therefore make sense to choose a debt mix that includes an important component of external liabilities, despite the associated currency mismatch. In the long term the objective of the authorities should be to deepen the domestic capital markets. Indeed, due to the lower risk levels and the greater homogeneity of the securities it issues, the central government has a vital function to perform in the development of longer-term primary and secondary markets for domestic securities, including the creation of benchmarks for private sector instruments.

The development of such markets will not eliminate the need for an active external liability policy, however, as deeper capital markets are also more likely to cause volatile portfolio flows. Unfortunately the trade-offs are not simple in this regard as international institutional investors may help to develop domestic capital markets. Thus the authorities must choose between less volatile external capital flows and the development of deeper, liquid domestic capital markets. Chile's decision to eliminate the one-year minimum maturity for portfolio flows in May 2000, as well as Colombia's decision in 1996 to allow foreign investment funds to participate in the domestic market for public sector securities, may be understood as a choice for the second of these options at the cost of additional capital account volatility. Similar trade-offs may be faced in relation to the development of deep domestic private-sector stock and bond markets.

The role of countercyclical prudential regulations

Micro- and macroeconomic dimensions of prudential policies

As we have seen, the origins of problems that erupt during financial crises are associated both with excessive risk taking during booms, as reflected in a rapid increase in lending, and with maturity and currency mismatches on financial and non-financial agents' balance sheets. In many countries these problems are related to inadequate risk analysis by financial agents, as well as weak prudential regulation and supervision of the domestic financial systems. The combination of these factors becomes explosive under conditions of financial liberalization in the midst of a boom in external financing. The underestimation of risks that characterizes environments of economic optimism is then combined with inadequate practices for evaluating risks, both by private agents and by supervisory agencies.

This underscores just how important the sequencing of financial liberalization processes is. This became evident during the first wave of financial crises that hit Latin America in the early 1980s (see for example Díaz-Alejandro, 1988: ch. 17) but was broadly ignored in later episodes of financial liberalization in the developing world. Since the Asian crisis it has finally become a mainstream idea. Indeed it is now widely recognized that financial liberalization should take place in a suitable institutional setting, which includes strong prudential regulation and supervision. Such regulation should ensure, first of all, the solvency of financial institutions by establishing appropriate capital adequacy ratios relative to the risk assumed by lending institutions, strict write-offs of questionable portfolios and appropriate standards of risk diversification. Properly regulated and supervised financial systems are structurally superior in terms of risk management since they create incentives for financial intermediaries to avoid assuming unmanageable risks.

To the extent that agents assume that the sources of financial risks have a macroeconomic origin, the traditional microeconomic focus of prudential regulation and supervision must be complemented with regulations that take account of such macroeconomic factors. This is particularly true in developing countries, where the dynamics associated with boom-bust cycles in external financing are particularly intense. Due attention should thus be paid to the links between domestic and external financing, the links among these factors and asset prices and economic activity, and the links between domestic financial risks and variations in interest and exchange rates.

The basic problem in this regard is the inability of individual financial intermediaries to internalize the collective risks assumed during boom periods, which are essentially of a macroeconomic character and therefore entail coordination problems that exceed the possibilities of any one agent. Moreover risk assessment and traditional regulatory tools, including Basel standards, have a procyclical bias in the way they operate. Indeed in a system in which loan-loss provisions are tied to loan delinquency, precautionary regulatory signals are ineffective during booms, and hence do not hamper credit growth. On the other hand the sharp increase in loan delinquency during crises does reduce financial institutions' capital, and hence their lending capacity. This, in conjunction with the greater subjectively perceived level of risk, triggers the credit squeeze that characterizes such periods, thereby reinforcing the downswing in economic activity and asset prices, and in turn the quality of the portfolios of financial intermediaries.[10]

Indeed the sudden introduction of strong regulatory standards during a crisis may worsen a credit squeeze, so although the authorities must adopt clearly defined rules to restore confidence during a financial crisis, the application of stronger standards should be gradual. In order to avoid moral hazard problems, the authorities must never bail out the owners of financial institutions by guaranteeing that their losses will be written off, up to their net worth, if regulators have to intervene in these institutions.

In order to take account of the macroeconomic factors that affect risks, instruments need to be designed that will introduce a countercyclical element into prudential regulation and supervision. In this regard the major instrument is undoubtedly forward-looking provisions. Such provisions should be estimated when loans are disbursed on the basis of expected or latent losses, taking into account the full business cycle, rather than on the basis of loan delinquency or short-term expectations of future loan losses, which are highly procyclical. This means, in fact, that provisioning should approach the criteria traditionally followed by the insurance industry (where provisions are made when the insurance policy is issued) rather than the banking industry. This practice could help to smooth out the cycle by increasing provisions or reserves during capital account surges, thus helping to reduce the credit crunch that takes place during busts.

It must be emphasized that all regulatory approaches have clear limits and costs that cannot be overlooked. Prudential regulation involves some nonprice signals, and prudential supervision is full of information problems and is a discretionary activity that is susceptible to abuse. Some classic objectives of prudential regulation, such as risk diversification, may be difficult to attain when macroeconomic issues are at the root of the difficulties. The experience of many industrialized countries indicates that even well-regulated systems are subject to periodic episodes of euphoria, when risks are underestimated. The recent crisis in Argentina is a specific case in which a system of prudential regulations that was considered to be one of the best in the developing world – working within the framework of a financial sector characterized by the large-scale presence of multinational banks – clearly failed to avert the effects of major macroeconomic shocks on the domestic financial system. Moreover, being able to separate cyclical from long-term trends is always a difficult task, as any process that involves learning will always generate path-dependent mechanisms in which short- and long-term dynamics are interconnected. Learning processes include those associated with the formation of expectations of future macroeconomic events, which is particularly difficult in developing economies facing substantial shocks (Heyman, 2000).

Moreover many regulatory practices aimed at correcting risky practices on the part of financial intermediaries shift the underlying risks to non-financial agents, thus generating indirect risks that are expressed in credit risks. The net effect of regulation on banks' vulnerabilities is therefore partial, as the literature on the migration of risks indicates. Thus regulatory standards that establish lower risk ratings for short-term credits and reduce mismatches between the maturities of bank deposits and lending will reduce direct banking risks, but will also reinforce the short-term bias in lending. Maturity mismatches are thereby displaced to non-financial agents. Indeed the net effect of this type of regulation may be an inadequate supply of long-term financing and reduced fixed capital investment. Also, prudential regulations that forbid banks to hold currency mismatches in their portfolios will reduce their direct risk, but may encourage non-financial agents to borrow abroad. The risks assumed by corporations, particularly those operating in non-tradable sectors, will eventually be translated into credit risk by domestic financial institutions that are also their creditors.

For the same reason, stronger regulation will result in higher spreads in domestic financial intermediation, particularly if it results in more stringent domestic *vis-à-vis* international regulatory practices, which is a likely outcome given the stronger volatility of developing countries. Higher spreads will generate incentives for corporations with direct access to international capital markets to borrow abroad, thus increasing the likelihood of currency mismatches in the portfolios of these agents. They may also result in a suboptimal supply of financing for SMEs, or an excessively short-term bias in the supply of credit for such firms. In all these cases the reduced vulnerability of the domestic financial sector will have as a corollary the maturity and currency mismatches of non-financial agents (as well as suboptimal fixed capital investment), which may become credit risks for domestic financial agents during the downturn.

The differentiation between systemic and non-systemic risks that is typical in portfolio risk analysis is particularly relevant in this regard. The former depends on the correlation of the price fluctuations of each particular asset with prices for the entire market and arises from exposure to common factors (for example economic policy or the business cycle) while non-systemic risks depend on the individual characteristics of each stock and may be reduced by diversification. Whereas the second type of risk can be reduced by adequate regulations aimed at improving microeconomic risk management, the first cannot, and in the face of systemic risks the use of common risk management techniques can actually result in greater macroeconomic volatility (Persaud, 2000). Thus to a large extent, macroeconomic risks that are systemic in character can only be shifted to other market agents within a specific economy and are only authentically diversified when external economic agents are willing to assume them. Nonetheless countercyclical prudential policies can help to reduce the collective risks that agents may assume during periods of euphoria. They can also help to generate improved incentives for financial agents that behave procyclically (those exposed to industries with high systemic risks).

In all cases, as in the case of capital controls, improved prudential regulation, including the introduction of strong countercyclical components that take into account the macroeconomics of boom-bust cycles, is a complement but not a substitute for appropriate countercyclical macroeconomic policies.

Instruments to protect against credit risk

Under generally accepted accounting principles, provisions should cover expected losses, though of an uncertain magnitude, and are thus registered as expenses, while reserves apply to unexpected losses and are part of capital. These principles also imply that banks should charge an interest premium for expected risk while stockholders should cover unexpected risks. Accounting practices also differentiate between general and specific provisions. In most countries the calculation of specific provisions is done on an individual basis for commercial loans and on a pooled basis for retail loans. General provisions are estimated on the basis of pools of loans, or the total portfolio. In some countries they are treated as reserves, and as such as capital, while in others they are subtracted from assets. With traditional accounting methods, specific provisions are made shortly before or even after a loan becomes delinquent. In this sense a system based wholly on this type of provision will not reflect the true credit risk of the loan portfolio and, as indicated above, will be inherently procyclical. The rules on general provisions and reserves are usually more flexible and allow for more forward-looking approaches in the appraisal of risk.

In some countries the authorities (the government or the central bank) take a restrictive approach and establish statutory rules that determine the level of provisions. In others the system varies from a strict formula to statistical approaches that use historical data, information on peer groups and more explicit internal risk models. Several OECD countries allow the constitution of forward-looking provisions based on past experience and the expectation of future events. However most of them are oriented towards the short term, using a one-year horizon to measure risk.

The best-known exception to this rule is Spain, which in December 1999 issued a regulation requiring countercyclical provisions calculated by statistical methods. The main feature of this approach is the estimation of 'latent risk' based on past experience over a period long enough to cover at least one business cycle. This generates a dynamic in which provisions build up during economic expansions and are drawn upon during downturns (Poveda, 2000; De Lis *et al.,* 2001). The major innovation of this system is its explicit recognition that risks are incurred when credits are approved and disbursed, not when they fall due.

More particularly, under this scheme statistical or actuarial provisions for latent risks must be estimated for homogeneous categories of credit according to the possible loss that a typical asset (loan, guarantee, interbank or fixed income portfolio investment) in each category is expected to involve, estimated on the basis of a full business cycle. Either the internal risk management model of the financial institution or the standard model proposed by the Banco de España can be used for that purpose. The latter establishes six categories, with annual provisioning ratios that range from 0 to 1.5 per cent. These statistical provisions must be accumulated in a fund, together with special provisions (traditional provisions for non-performing assets or the performing assets of borrowers in financial difficulties) and recovered non-performing assets.[11] The fund can be used to cover loan losses, thus in effect entirely substituting for special provisions if resources are available in adequate amounts. If this is so the provisions actually follow the credit cycle.

Although the accumulation and drawing down of the fund made up by statistical and specific provisions has a countercyclical dynamic, this only reflects the cyclical pattern of bank lending. In this regard the system is, strictly speaking, 'cycle-neutral' rather than countercyclical, but it is certainly superior to the traditional procyclical provisioning for loan losses or forward looking provisioning based on short time horizons.

Therefore a system such as this should be complemented by strictly countercyclical prudential provisions, decreed by the regulatory authority for the financial system a whole, or by the supervisory authority for special financial institutions, on the basis of objective criteria. These criteria could include the growth rate of credit, the bias in lending towards sectors characterized by systemic risks or the growth of foreign-currency-denominated loans to non-tradable sectors. Voluntary prudential provisions could also be encouraged. In both cases it is essential that tax deductibility be granted to the provisions. Indeed accounting and taxation rules contribute to failures in risk assessment because, in general, they make it necessary to register events that have already occurred.

The foregoing analysis indicates that an appropriate policy for managing the macroeconomic effects of boom-bust cycles in developing countries should involve a mixture of: (1) forward-looking provisions for latent risks, to be made when credit is granted so that financial intermediaries will have to take account of the risks they incur throughout the entire business cycle; and (2) more discrete countercyclical prudential provisions based on a series of objective criteria. Specific provisions should be managed together with forward-looking provisions, as in the Spanish system. As we shall see in the following sections, these provisions should be supplemented by regulations in other areas. Reserves or general provisions play a less clear role and in fact are not distinguishable from the role of capital in covering unexpected losses.

A system of provisions such as this would certainly be superior to the use of capital adequacy ratios to manage the effects of business cycles. Capital adequacy requirements should instead focus on long-term solvency criteria rather than on cyclical performance. Insofar as developing countries are likely to face more macroeconomic volatility, there may be an argument for requiring higher capital-asset ratios (see the additional arguments below), but there is none for requiring that capital adequacy requirements should be, as such, countercyclical.

It should also be remembered that the stricter standards in developing countries for the management of macroeconomic risks – in terms of provisions, capital or other variables – increase the costs of financial intermediation, thereby reducing international competitiveness and creating arbitrage incentives to use international financial intermediation as an alternative. Also, prudential policies are certainly not a solution for the risks that procyclical macroeconomic policies may generate.

Prudential treatment of currency and maturity risks, and volatile asset prices

Experience indicates that currency and maturity mismatches are essential aspects of financial crises in developing countries. Prudential regulation should thus establish strict rules to prevent currency mismatches (including those associated with hedging and related operations) and to reduce imbalances between the maturities of the assets and liabilities of financial intermediaries. In addition, liquidity regulations should be established to manage such imbalances.

The strict prohibition of currency mismatches in the portfolios of financial intermediaries is the best rule. The authorities should also closely monitor the intermediation of short-term external credits. As we have seen, the currency risks of non-financial firms, particularly those operating in nontradable sectors, may eventually turn into credit risks for banks.[12] This points to the need for better monitoring of the currency risks of these firms, and probably for specific regulations on lending to firms in non-tradable sectors with substantial liabilities in foreign currency. In particular, regulations could be used to establish more stringent provisions and/or risk weighting for those operations, or a strict prohibition on lending in foreign currencies to non-financial firms with no income in those currencies; capital account regulations would have to establish complementary norms for direct borrowing abroad by these firms (see above).

In addition, prudential regulation needs to ensure adequate levels of liquidity for financial intermediaries so that they can handle the mismatch between the average maturities of assets and liabilities that is inherent in the financial system's essential function of transforming maturities, which generates risks associated with volatility in deposits and/or interest rates. This underscores the fact that liquidity and solvency problems are far more closely interrelated than traditionally assumed, particularly in the face of macroeconomic shocks. Reserve requirements, which are strictly an instrument of monetary policy, provide liquidity in many countries, but their declining importance makes it necessary to find new tools. Moreover their traditional structure is not geared to the specific objective of ensuring financial intermediaries' liquidity in the face of the maturity mismatches they hold in their portfolios. An important innovation in this area was the system created in 1995 in Argentina, which set liquidity requirements based on the residual maturity of financial institutions' liabilities (that is, the number of days remaining before reaching maturity).[13] These liquidity requirements – or a system of reserve requirements with similar characteristics – have the additional advantage that they offer a direct incentive to the financial system to maintain an appropriate liability structure. The quality of the assets with which the liquidity requirements are met is obviously a crucial factor. In this regard it must be pointed out that allowing such assets to be invested in public sector bonds was an essential weakness of the Argentinean system, as it increased the vulnerability of the financial system to public sector debt restructuring, a risk that turned into reality in 2001.

The valuation of assets used as collateral for loans also presents problems when these assets exhibit price volatility, because in many cases *ex ante* assessments may be significantly higher than *ex post* prices. Limits on loan- to-value ratios and rules to adjust the value of collateral for cyclical price variations should be adopted. One approach in this regard is the 'mortgage lending value', a valuation procedure applied in some European countries that reflects long-term market trends in real estate prices based on experience (ECB, 2000).

The proposal for the new Basel Accord attempts to align risk weights with the evaluations of external credit rating agencies. Unfortunately this would introduce an additional procyclical bias, given the procyclical pattern of credit ratings (see Chapter 7). The high concentration of the rating industry is an additional argument against adopting this recommendation. Moreover it would be difficult to apply this practice in developing countries due to the absence of adequate credit ratings for most firms.

Conclusions

This chapter has explored the complementary use of two instruments to manage capital account volatility in developing countries: capital account regulations and the countercyclical prudential regulation of domestic financial intermediaries. These instruments should be seen as complementary to countercyclical macroeconomic policies, but neither of them can nullify the risks that procyclical macroeconomic policies can generate.

Overall the innovative capital account regulations of the 1990s can be seen as useful instruments in terms of improving debt profiles and facilitating the adoption of (possibly temporary) countercyclical macroeconomic policies. The main advantages of the price-based unremunerated reserve requirement pioneered by Chile and Colombia are its simplicity, nondiscretionary character and neutral effect on corporate borrowing decisions. The more quantitative Malaysian system has been shown to have stronger short-term macroeconomic effects. Traditional quantitative exchange controls may be superior if the objective of macroeconomic policy is significantly to reduce domestic macroeconomic sensitivity to international capital flows.

Prudential regulation and supervision can, in part, be substituted for these direct regulations on the capital account. The main problem with this option is that it has, at best, indirect effects on the foreign-currency liabilities of non-financial agents and may encourage them to borrow abroad. Accordingly they need to be supplemented with other disincentives for external borrowing by those firms. Unremunerated reserve requirements may be a superior alternative and may be simpler to administer. In the case of the public sector, direct regulation of external borrowing should be combined with a strategy aimed at the development of domestic bond markets.

Prudential regulation and supervision should take into account not only microeconomic risks but also the macroeconomic risks associated with boom-bust cycles. In particular, instruments need to be designed that will introduce a countercyclical element into prudential regulation and supervision. More specifically, we argue for a regulatory approach that involves a mixture of: (1) forward-looking provisions for latent risks, with provisions to be made when credit is granted on the basis of the credit risks that are expected throughout the full business cycle (this was the approach adopted by the Spanish authorities); and (2) more discrete countercyclical prudential provisions, to be applied by the regulatory authority to the financial system a whole, or by the supervisory authority for special financial institutions, on the basis of objective criteria (for example the growth rate of credit, or the growth of credit for specific risky activities). Capital adequacy requirements should focus on long-term solvency criteria and should not be countercyclical, but it may be advisable for countries facing strong cyclical fluctuations to establish higher capital-asset ratios.

The system of countercyclical prudential regulation and supervision should be complemented by regulations in other areas. In particular, prudential regulation should establish strict rules to prevent currency mismatches (including those incurred by firms operating in non-tradable sectors when borrowing in foreign currency), liquidity requirements and limits on loan to collateral value ratios or rules on the valuation of collateral designed to reflect long-term market trends in asset prices.

This chapter has benefited from joint work undertaken with Maria Luisa Chiappe for the Expert Group on Development Issues (EGDI), Ministry of Foreign Affairs of Sweden.

Notes

1 For documents that support the effectiveness of these regulations in Chile see Agosin (1998), Larraín *et al.* (2000), Le Fort and Lehmann (2000), Agosin and Ffrench-Davis (2001) and Palma (2002). For a more mixed view see Valdés-Prieto and Soto (1998) Ariyoshi *et al.* (2000), De Gregorio *et al.* (2000) and Laurens (2000). For strong views on their positive effects in Colombia see Ocampo and Tovar (1998, 1999) and Villar and Rincón (2002); for a more mixed view see Cárdenas and Barrera (1997) and Cárdenas and Steiner (2000).

2 Indeed evidence of the insensitivity of the volume of capital flows to capital account regulations comes from econometric analysis in which URR is not included as a determinant of interest rate spreads but rather as an additional factor affecting capital flows. This may be seen as an inadequate econometric specification.

3 Some of these mechanisms, such as the use of hedging, enable investors to cover some of the effects of these regulations, but in large part this is done by transferring risks (more specifically, the risk associated with longer-term financing) to other agents who would only be willing to assume them at an adequate reward. More generally, if there is no stable external demand for the domestic currency, hedging may be available only in limited quantities, a fact that affects the maturities and costs involved.

4 In Brazil some authors have argued that the capital account regulations, which included a mechanism similar to the URR (direct taxation of capital flows), were ineffective due to widespread loopholes associated with the existence of sophisticated domestic financial instruments (Ariyoshi *et al.,* 2000; García and Valpassos, 2000). However they provide no statistical evidence comparable to that available for Chile and Colombia.

5 This is the very apt interpretation provided by Williamson (2000: ch. 4). Indeed with this interpretation the conflicting evidence on the Chilean system largely disappears.

6 See Ariyoshi *et al.* (2000), Ötker-Robe (2000) and Rajaraman (2001) for additional evidence of the effectiveness of these regulations.

7 The level of the URR may account for this result. Valdés-Prieto and Soto (1998) find evidence of a 'threshold effect', which would explain why these regulations were only effective in reducing capital flows in 1995-96. It must be emphasized that this does not imply a better evaluation of the overall macroeconomic policy package of 1995-96 compared with that of 1991-92. Agosin and Ffrench-Davis (2001) argue that, on broader grounds, macroeconomic management in the earlier part of the 1990s was more appropriate.

8 This is captured in other studies (for example Cárdenas and Steiner, 2000) through the use of a dummy variable for the period during which the URR was in place, and has been interpreted (inaccurately, according to the alternative view presented in the text) as evidence against the effectiveness of regulations.

9 For an analysis of these issues see World Bank (1999: 151) and Stiglitz and Bhattacharya (2000).

10 For recent analyses of these issues and policy options for managing them, see BIS (2001: ch. 7), Borio *et al.* (2001), Clerc *et al.* (2001) and Turner (2002).

11 In addition, general provisions equivalent to 0 per cent, 0.5 per cent and 1.0 per cent of three classes of assets are required.

12 For an analysis of the risks associated with non-tradable sectors see Rojas-Suárez (2001).

13 Banco Central de la República Argentina (1995), 11-12.

References

Agosin, M. (1998) 'Capital Inflow and Investment Performance: Chile in the 1990s', in R. Ffrench-Davis and H. Reisen (eds), *Capital Inflows and Investment Performance: Lessons from Latin America,* Paris and Santiago: OECD Development Centre/ ECLAC.

_____ and R. French-Davis (2001) 'Managing Capital Inflows in Chile', in S. Griffith-Jones, M. F. Montes and A. Nasution (eds), *Short-term Capital Flows and Economic Crises,* New York and Oxford: Oxford University Press for UNU/WIDER.

Ariyoshi, A., K. Habermeier, B. Laurens, I. Ötker-Robe, J. I. Canales-Kriljenko and A. Kirilenko (2000) *Capital Controls: Country Experiences with Their Use and Liberalization,* Occasional Paper 190, Washington, DC: IMF.

Banco Central de la República Argentina (1995) *Informe Anual,* Buenos Aires, October.

Bank for International Settlements (BIS) (2001) *71st Annual Report,* Basel: BIS, June.

Bordo, M., B. Eichengreen, D. Klingebiel and M. S. Martinez-Peria (2001) 'Is the Crisis Problem Growing More Severe?', *Economic Policy,* 32 (April).

Borio, C., C. Furfine and P. Lowe (2001) 'Procyclicality of the Financial System and Financial Stability: Issues and Policy Options', in *Marrying the Macro- and MicroPrudential Dimensions of Financial Stability,* BIS Papers no. 1, Basel: BIS, March.

Cárdenas, M. and F. Barrera (1997) 'On the Effectiveness of Capital Controls: The Experience of Colombia During the 1990s', *Journal of Development Economics,* 54, 1 (October).

_____ and R. Steiner (2000) 'Private Capital Flows in Colombia', in F. Larraín (ed.), Capital Flows, Capital Controls, and Currency Crises: Latin America in the 1990s, *Ann Arbor, MI: University of Michigan Press.*

Clerc, L., F. Drumetz and O. Jaudoin (2001) 'To What Extent are Prudential and Accounting Arrangements Pro- or Countercyclical with Respect to Overall Financial Conditions?', in *Marrying the Macro- and Micro-Prudential Dimensions of Financial Stability,* BIS Papers no. 1, Basel: BIS, March.

De Gregorio, J., S. Edwards and R. Valdés (2000) 'Controls on Capital Inflows: Do They Work?', *Journal of Development Economics,* 63, 1 (October).

De Lis, F. S., J. Martínez and J. Saurina (2001) 'Credit Growth, Problem Loans and Credit Risk Provisioning in Spain', in *Marrying the Macro- and Micro-Prudential Dimensions of Financial Stability,* BIS Papers no. 1, Basel: BIS, March.

Díaz-Alejandro, C. F. (1988) Trade, Development and the World Economy. Selected Essays of Carlos F. Díaz-Alejandro, edited by Andrés Velasco, Oxford: Basil Blackwell.

ECLAC (1998) The Fiscal Covenant. Strengths, Weaknesses, Challenges, Santiago: ECLAC.

_____ (2002) 'Growth with Stability: Financing for Development in the New International Context', *Libros de la CEPAL,* 67 (March).

European Central Bank (ECB) (2000) Asset *Prices and Banking Stability,* Frankfurt am Main: ECB, April.

García, M. G. P. and M. V. F. Valpassos (2000) 'Capital Flows, Capital Controls, and Currency Crisis: The Case of Brazil in the 1990s', in F. Larraín (ed.), *Capital Flows, Capital Controls, and Currency Crises: Latin America in the 1990s,* Ann Arbor, MI: University of Michigan Press.

Habermeier, K. (2000) 'India's Experience with the Liberalization of Capital Flows Since 199T, in Ariyoshi *et al.* (2000).

Heyman, D. (2000) 'Major Macroeconomic Upsets, Expectations and Policy Responses', *CEPAL Review*, 70, (Santiago).

International Monetary Fund (IMF) (1998) World Economic Outlook, 1998 – Financial Crises: Characteristics and Indicators of Vulnerability, Washington, DC: IMF, May.

JP Morgan (1998) *World Financial Markets*, New York: JP Morgan, 7 October.

Kaplan, E. and D. Rodrik (2001) 'Did the Malaysian Capital Controls Work?', *NBER Working Paper* no. 8142, Cambridge, MA: NBER, February.

Krugman, P. and L. Taylor (1978) 'Contractionary Effects of Devaluations', *journal of International Economics*, 8.

Larraín, F., R. Labán and R. Chumacero (2000) 'What Determines Capital Inflows? An Empirical Analysis for Chile', in F. Larraín (ed.), *Capital Flows, Capital Controls, and Currency Crises: Latin America in the 1990s*, Ann Arbor, MI: University of Michigan Press.

Laurens, B. (2000) 'Chile's Experience with Controls on Capital Inflows in the 1990s', in Ariyoshi *et al.* (2000).

Le Fort, G. and S. Lehman (2000) 'El Encaje, los Flujos de Capitales y el Gasto: una Evaluación Empírica', *Documento de Trabajo* no. 64, Santiago: Central Bank of Chile, February.

Minsky, H. P. (1982) Can 'It' Happen Again?: Essays on Instability and Finance, Armonk, NY: M. E. Sharpe.

Mishkin, F. (2001) *The Economics of Money, Banking and Financial Markets*, 6th edn, Boston, MA: Addison Wesley Longman.

Nayyar, D. (2002) 'Capital Controls and the World Financial Authority – What Can we Learn from the Indian Experience?', in J. Eatwell and L. Taylor (eds), *International Capital Markets – Systems in Transition*, New York: Oxford University Press.

Ocampo, J. A. (2002a) 'International Asymmetries and the Design of the International Financial System', in A. Berry (ed.), *Critical Issues in Financial Reform: A View from the South*, New Brunswick, NJ: Transaction.

_____ (2002b) 'Developing Countries' Anti-Cyclical Policies in a Globalized World', in *A. Dutt and J. Ros (eds)*, Development Economics and Structuralist Macroeconomics: Essays in Honour of Lance Taylor, *Aldershot: Edward Elgar.*

_____ and Camilo Tovar (1998) 'Capital Flows, Savings and Investment in Colombia, 1990-96', in R. Ffrench-Davis and H. Reisen (eds), *Capital Flows and Investment Performance: Lessons from Latin America*, Paris and Santiago: OECD Development Centre and ECLAC.

_____ and_____ (1999) 'Price-Based Capital Account Regulations: The Colombian Experience', *Financiamiento del Desarrollo Series*, no. 87 (LC/L.1262-P), Santiago: ECLAC.

Ötker-Robe, I. (2000) 'Malaysia's Experience with the Use of Capital Controls', in Ariyoshi *et al.* (2000).

Palma, G. (2002), 'The Three Routes to Financial Crises: The Need for Capital Controls', in J. Eatwell and L. Taylor (eds), *International Capital Markets – Systems in Transition*, New York: Oxford University Press.

Persaud, A. (2000) Sending the Herd Off the Cliff Edge: The Disturbing Interaction between Herding and Market-sensitive Risk Management Practices, London: State Street.

Poveda, R. (2000) La Reforma del Sistema de Provisiones de Insolvencia, Madrid: Banco de España, January.

347

Rajaraman, I. (2001) 'Management of the Capital Account: A Study of India and Malaysia', mimeo, New Delhi, National Institute of Public Finance and Policy, March.

Reddy, Y. V. (2001) 'Operationalising Capital Account Liberalisation: The Indian Experience', *Development Policy Review* (Overseas Development Institute), 19, 1 (March).

Rodrik, D. and A. Velasco (2000) 'Short-Term Capital Flows', *Annual World Bank Conference on Development Economics 1999,* Washington, DC: World Bank.

Rojas-Suárez, L. (2001) 'Can International Capital Standards Strengthen Banks in Emerging Markets', mimeo, Washington, DC: Institute for International Economics, October.

Ros, J. (2001) 'From the Capital Surge to the Financial Crisis and Beyond: Mexico in the 1990s', in R. Ffrench-Davis (ed.), *Financial Crises in 'Successful' Emerging Economies,* Washington, DC: Brookings Institution/ECLAC.

Sachs, J., A. Tornell and A. Velasco (1996) 'The Mexican Peso Crisis: Sudden Death or Death Foretold?', *NBER Working Paper* no. 5563, Cambridge, MA: NBER, May.

Stiglitz, J. E. (1994) 'The Role of the State in Financial Markets', *Proceedings of the World Bank Annual Conference on Development Economics 1993,* Washington, DC: World Bank.

_____ and A. Bhattacharya (2000) 'The Underpinnings of a Stable and Equitable Global Financial System: From Old Debates to a New Paradigm', *Annual World Bank Conference on Development Economics 1999,* Washington, DC: World Bank.

Taylor, L. (1998) 'Capital Market Crises: Liberalisation, Fixed Exchange Rates and Market-Driven Destabilisation', *Cambridge Journal of Economics,* 22, 6 (November).

Turner, P. (2002) 'Procyclicality of Regulatory Ratios', in J. Eatwell and L. Taylor (eds), *International Capital Markets – Systems in Transition,* New York: Oxford University Press.

Valdés-Prieto, S. and M. Soto (1998) 'The Effectiveness of Capital Controls: Theory and Evidence from Chile', *Empirica,* 25 (Dordrecht: Kluwer).

Villar, L. and H. Rincón (2002) 'The Colombian Economy in the Nineties: Capital Flows and Foreign Exchange Regimes', in A. Berry (ed.), *Critical Issues in Financial Reform: A View from the South,* New Brunswick: Transaction.

Williamson, J. (2000) 'Exchange Rate Regimes for Emerging Markets: Reviving the Intermediate Option', *Policy Analyses in International Economics,* 60, Washington, DC: Institute for International Economics, September.

World Bank (1999) Global Economic Prospects and the Developing Countries, 1998-99 – Beyond Financial Crisis, Washington, DC: World Bank.

29

CAPITAL MARKET LIBERALIZATION, ECONOMIC GROWTH, AND INSTABILITY

Joseph E. Stiglitz

Source: *World Development* 28, 6, 2000, 1075–1086.

The world is just emerging from the worst financial and economic crisis since the great Depression. The World Bank estimated that in 1999 output of the 5 crisis countries of East Asia, two years after the onset, was still some 17% below what it would have been had the growth trend of the ten years before the crisis continued. In 2000 matters were only slightly better.[1] The fragile recoveries in Korea and Malaysia are being threatened by a global economic slowdown, originating in the U.S. Elsewhere, matters are even bleaker: Indonesia remains in depression, civil unrest affecting many of its far-flung islands. In Thailand, as the economy barely struggled to attain pre-crisis levels three years later, with between a quarter and 40% of loans still non-performing, voters gave a resounding defeat to a government that had followed the prescriptions of the IMF perhaps better than any other. While exchange rates have stabilized in East Asia, other financial variables, like stock prices, have not fared so well, and unemployment remains far higher than before the crisis, and real wages far lower.

Elsewhere, large parts of the world remain in a precarious economic position—with deep recession or depression facing several countries in Latin America, and output in many of the economies in transition still markedly below what it was a decade ago.

It has become increasingly clear that financial and capital market liberalization—done hurriedly, without first putting into place an effective regulatory framework—was at the core of the problem. It is no accident that the two large countries that survived the crisis—and continued with remarkably strong growth in spite of a difficult global economic environment—were India and China, both countries with strong controls on these capital flows.[2] In retrospect, it appears that Malaysia's capital controls, so roundly condemned at the time they were imposed—with political leaders like Secretary Rubin of the United States forecasting (and wishing) the most dire of outcomes—have not had the adverse effects predicted; and Malaysia recovered faster, with a far shallower downturn, and with a far smaller legacy of public debt.

The crisis in East Asia was not the only crisis of recent years. Indeed, there have been, by one reckoning, eighty to a hundred crises over the past quarter century.[3] Crises have become more frequent and more severe, suggesting a fundamental weakness in global economic arrangements. As I put it in one lecture, when there is a single accident on a highway, one suspects that the driver's attention may have lapsed. But when there are dozens of accidents at the same bend in the same highway, one needs to re-examine the design of the road.

I suggested that one might compare capital account liberalization to putting a race car engine into an old car and setting off without checking the tires or training the driver. Perhaps with appropriate tires and training, the car might perform better; but without such equipment and training, it is almost inevitable that an accident will occur. One might actually have done far better with the older, more reliable engine: performance would have been slower, but there would have been less potential for an accident. Similarly, the international economic architecture must be designed to "work" not just in the presence of perfect economic management, but with the kind of fallible governments and public officials that in fact occur in democratic societies.

As the crisis spread from East Asia to Russia, and then to Latin America, it became clear that even countries with good economic policies and relatively sound financial institutions (at least as conventionally defined) were adversely affected, and seriously so. (Indeed, this was consistent with earlier research which had shown that changes in capital flows, and even crises, were predominantly precipitated by events outside the country, such as changes in interest rates in the more developed countries.[4]) Thus, the rhetoric with which the crisis was begun— that globalization, liberalization, and the market economy delivered its fruits to virtuous countries and that problems were only visited upon countries that, in one way or another, had sinned—was re-examined, and a more cautionary approach was taken to the reforms that had been long advocated by the zealots. At the same time, the analytic arguments for—and against—capital market liberalization were subject to greater scrutiny. The case for capital market liberalization was found wanting—especially striking given the zeal with which the IMF had requested an extension of its mandate to include capital market liberalization a short two years earlier at the Annual Meetings in Hong Kong. It should have been clear then, and it is certainly clear now, that the position was maintained either as a matter of ideology or of special interests, and not on the basis of careful analysis of theory, historical experience or a wealth of econometric studies. Indeed, it has become increasingly clear that there is not only no case for capital market liberalization, but that there is a fairly compelling case *against* full liberalization. (The fact that the international financial community came so close to adopting a position which could not justified on the basis of theory or evidence should, in itself, provide an important cautionary note, especially in the context of the debate over reforming the international economic architecture. Clearly, before reforms of this magnitude are adopted, there needs to be more open debate, and all the affected parties—including workers who are threatened with unemployment and falling wages, and small businesses who are threatened with bankruptcy as interest rates soar to usurious levels—need to have a seat at the discussion table. Unfortunately, in some of the circles in which the pivotal issues are being discussed, not only are these groups not represented, but the developing countries do not even have a formal membership.)

In this paper, I want to review briefly the arguments for capital market liberalization, and identify their theoretical and empirical weaknesses. This will provide the foundations for the argument for intervention in short-term capital flows. I shall then briefly discuss the various ways in which such interventions may be implemented. Throughout much of the discussion, I shall talk about "interventions" in fairly general terms. It should be clear, however, that not all interventions are identical. Today for instance, while there is widespread acceptance of interventions that stabilize inflows, interventions on outflows remain highly controversial. Some—even many—forms of intervention may not bring benefits commensurate with their costs. The central argument in this paper is that there exists *some* forms of intervention that are likely to be welfare-enhancing.

Before beginning the discussion, I want to make it clear that I am focusing my attention on short-term speculative capital flows. The argument for foreign direct investment, for instance, is compelling. Such investment brings with it not only

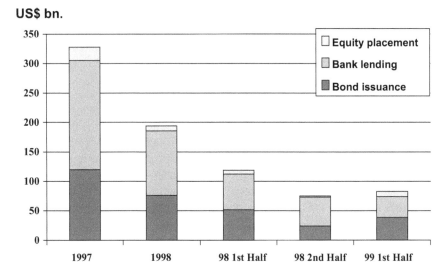

Figure 1 Capital Market Flows to Developing Countries. Source: Euromoney Loanware and Bondware.

resources, but technology, access to markets, and (hopefully) valuable training, an improvement in human capital. Foreign direct investment is also not as vola-tile—and therefore as disruptive—as the short-term flows which can rush into a country, and just as precipitously, rush out.[5] (The magnitude of these changes in flows can be enormous, as shown in Figure 1. In the case of Thailand, the change in flows amounted to 14 percent of the GDP and in the case of South Korea 9 percent of the GDP. In the case of East Asia as a whole, the turnaround in capi-tal flow between 1996 and 1997 amounted to $105 billion, more than 10 percent of the GDP of these combined economies. If the United States experienced the change in flow that Thailand did for example, this could be equivalent to a change in capital flows of over $1 trillion. Even with its strong financial and other institu-tions, it is not clear how well the U.S. would whether such a storm.)[6] Moreover, it is also clear that one can intervene in short-term flows, and still provide a hospi-table environment for foreign direct investment, as China, the largest recipient of foreign direct investment, amply demonstrates.

The Case for Capital Market Liberalization

The case for capital market liberalization is largely based on standard efficiency arguments, employing a conventional neoclassical model and ignoring the spe-cial ways in which financial and capital markets differ from markets for ordinary goods and services, like steel. The proponents focus on efficiency effects, ignoring the distributional consequences, presumably believing that if the gains are large enough, either the benefits will trickle down to the poor, or that the government will take active measures to ensure that the poor will not be harmed. While the evidence in support of either hypothesis may not be there, my concern here is to evaluate the more case *on its own terms*, that is, the case the capital market liber-alization leads to higher output and greater efficiency. There are five components to the argument:

a) Countries should be concerned with *maximizing GNP*—the incomes of their citizens—not GDP, the output of the country. Therefore, if the citizens of a country can find an outlet for their funds with a higher return than any invest-ment in their country, then GNP is maximized by allowing the funds to leave the country. (Moreover, the higher returns themselves might stimulate the citizens of the country to *save* more.) By the same token, if a foreign investor finds an investment opportunity within the country with a higher return than the opportunity cost of his funds, complementary factors within the country will benefit, as their marginal product is increased.

b) International *competition* for funds provides a needed spur for countries to create an economic environment attractive to business. It is behind closed doors that countries can engage in efficiency-decreasing practices, e.g., regu-lations for which the benefits are not commensurate with the costs.

352

c) Open capital markets help *stabilize* the economy through *diversification.* As a country faces a downturn, the lower wages will attract funds into the country, helping to stimulate it. This was a central argument for capital market liberalization in East Asia. After all, the governments had demonstrably worked hard to create an environment in which the economy, and the private sector in particular, had flourished; growth rates had been phenomenal for three decades or more. Savings rates were already very high; indeed, it was remarkable that the countries were able to absorb the high level of savings, investing them productively. Other countries with such high savings rates had not fared so well. One could hardly argue that, given the high savings rates, they needed to open their capital markets to obtain needed funds.

d) On the other hand, for much of the rest of the world, open capital markets were important as a *source of funding* for needed investment projects.

e) Finally, the case for opening capital markets was made by way of *analogy to free trade in goods and services.* A central tenet in economics—at least since Adam Smith—was that free trade was beneficial to a country. Indeed, it paid a country to eliminate trade barriers unilaterally—even if trading partners did not. "Capital," it was argued, was just like another good. The case for capital market liberalization was thus the same as the case for free trade in general. And that case was so well known, it hardly needed to be repeated.[7]

The Evidence

The predictions of the advocates of capital market liberalization are clear, but unfortunately, historical experience has not been supportive.

Growth. There is a wealth of cross country studies supporting the view that trade liberalization leads to faster economic growth,[8] though to be sure, there are a few studies providing suggestions to the contrary. In contrast, for the case of capital market liberalization, there are relatively few studies, but what evidence there is, is not supportive for liberalization. Figure 2, borrowed from Danny Rodrik's study, shows growth in different countries related to the openness of capital markets, *as measured by the IMF.* (This is particularly important, because it provides a metric which corresponds to the kinds of actions which the IMF might have taken in attempting to open up the capital markets.) Figure 3 provides some insights into why this might be the case—it plots investment in different countries related to the openness of capital markets.[9] Again, there is no relationship.

Stability. The global economic crisis has centered attention around another aspect of economic performance, stability. Stability is important for several reasons. Research has shown that instability has persistent effects on economic growth—growth is slowed down for several years after a crisis has occurred.[10] Indeed, the large unit root literature suggests that an economy that suffers a large

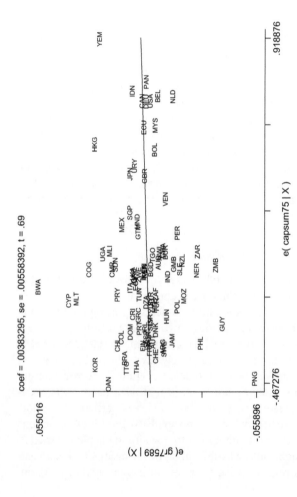

Figure 2 Economic Growth and Capital-account Liberalization, 1975–89. This scatter plot controls for per-capita income, secondary education, quality of governmental institutions, and regional dummies for East Asia, Latin America, and sub-Saharan Africa. Source: Rodrik [1998].

354

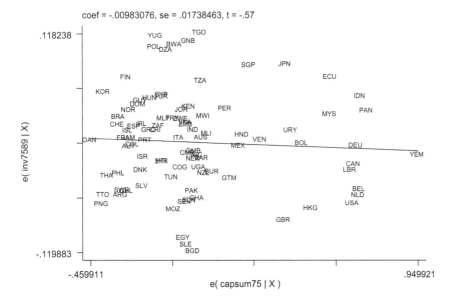

Figure 3 Investment/GDP and Capital-account Liberalization, 1975–89. This scatter plot
controls for per-capita income, secondary education, quality of governmental
institutions, and regional dummies for East Asia, Latin America, and sub-
Saharan Africa. Source: Rodrik [1998].

fall in output never fully recovers—output remains persistently below what it
would have been. Thus, the present discounted value of loss output associated
with magnitude of declines observed in East Asia or Ecuador are enormous.[11]
Moreover, instability often has marked distributional consequences, especially in
developing countries. Even in developed countries, like the U.S., the poor bear
a disproportionate burden in terms of increased unemployment.[12] But in most
developing countries, safety nets are inadequate or non-existent. The recent crises
have amply demonstrated this burden—with unemployment increasing 3 to 4 fold
in Korea and Thailand (and by more in Indonesia), and with real wages falling
10% in Korea, and by as much as a quarter in Thailand and Indonesia.

I already alluded to the increased frequency of financial and economic crises,
and suggested that this change is related to financial and capital market liberalization. Cross country studies have confirmed this.[13] In addition, cross country
econometric studies looking more broadly at the impact of capital market liberalization on the likelihood of an economy having a recession have again confirmed
the adverse effects.[14]

Thus, it is clear that not only is there no compelling empirical case *for* capital market liberalization—there is a compelling case *against* capital market liberalization, at least until countries have found ways of managing the adverse
consequences.

355

Why Capital Market Liberalization
Produces Instability, Not Growth

Given the seemingly compelling case for capital market liberalization, why does the evidence point so much in the opposite direction? Where did the theories go wrong?

The Fallacies in the Standard Arguments

We begin our discussion by identifying the fallacies in the standard arguments. The most fundamental is this: financial and capital markets are fundamentally different from markets for ordinary goods and services. The central function of capital and financial markets is information—in particular, assessing which projects and firms are most likely to yield the highest returns, and monitoring to ensure that the funds are used in the appropriate way. And markets for information are fundamentally different from "ordinary" markets. For instance, whenever information is imperfect, markets are essentially never constrained Pareto efficient—in marked contrast to standard results for competitive markets with perfect information.[15] Thus, the fifth argument—that the argument for capital liberalization is exactly the same as the argument for trade liberalization—is simply false.

Perhaps the most telling deficiency in the standard argument is in the third— the argument that opening capital markets allows for diversification and thereby enhances stability. As we have seen, capital market liberalization is systemically associated with greater instability, and for good reason: capital flows are markedly pro-cyclical, exacerbating economic fluctuations, when they do not actually cause them. The behavior is consistent with the popular adage about bankers being willing to lend when one does not need the money. When the bankers see economic weakness, they pull their money out of the country. In addition, capital market liberalization exposes countries to vicissitudes associated with changes in economic circumstances outside the country; a sudden change in lenders' perceptions concerning "emerging market risk" can lead to huge capital outflows, undermining the viability of the entire financial system. Moreover, there is mounting evidence that there is "excess volatility" in asset markets[16], perhaps related to herding behavior[17].

The argument that governments should be concerned with GNP—the income of their citizens—and therefore should be *unconcerned* about capital outflows, has some validity, but misses a central issue in development: there are a variety of reasons to believe that investors do not appropriate the full value of their contributions. Recent literature, for instance, has emphasized the importance of returns to scale, network externalities, and a variety of other spillovers.[18] These externalities may be particularly important in early stages of development, or in the early stages of transition to a market economy. This was seen most dramatically in Russia. The oligarchs, having obtained their wealth through privatizations widely viewed as highly illegitimate, had every reason to take their money out of their country where it would be safe against a later government re-examining what had gone on. But as each took his money out, as the economy sunk deeper into recession and depression, their incentives became even stronger: where would any reasonable person put his money, in the booming U.S. stock market or in the depression Russian economy, with its hostile business environment and insecure property rights? While if investors could not have taken their money out, there might have been a Nash equilibrium in which each had invested his money back into Russia, given the exit option provided by capital market liberalization, a new equilibrium emerged: each took his money out. In effect, capital market liberalization changes "the rules of the game," with adverse consequences for the country. (In addition, whenever there are taxes on capital, social benefits from investing at home may exceed private benefits, unless the government can impose commensurate taxes on investments abroad, which it often cannot.)

The issue of whether capital market liberalization provides additional sources of funding is also questionable: as the data above suggested, it does not lead to more investment. There are two related issues. First, does more short-term capital—unstable as it is—provide a basis for investment? The answer is clearly no. What country would sensibly build a factor using funds that could be pulled out on a moment's notice? The second is, do restrictions on short-term capital flows discourage foreign direct investment or other forms of longer term investment? Again, the answer appears to be no. We already noted that the country that has been the most successful in recruiting foreign direct investment—China—also imposes a high level of restrictions on short-term capital flows. However there is little evidence that countries that have imposed restrictions on short-term flows— Chile on inflows, Malaysia on outflows—have had their long term flows adversely affected.[19] Indeed, as I note below, there may even be reasons why foreign direct investment may be attracted: as we noted, capital market liberalization is associated with greater economic volatility, or at least a higher probability of a recession. Such uncertainty clearly makes investment less attractive.

But actually, in many cases, the argument that opening capital account is important for enhancing a flow of capital into the country is turned on its head: in many instances, the key issue is not capital flowing into the country, but flowing out. As we have already noted in the context of Russia, opening the capital account has facilitated capital flight, and thus contributed to the weakening of the economy.[20] Africa too has been plagued with capital flight.[21] And several of the recent crises (not only Indonesia, but Mexico[22]) if not caused by, have been amplified by capital flight.[23]

The argument with which I am most sympathetic is that opening the capital account imposes "discipline". Countries are "forced" to have good economic policies, less capital flow out of the country. But I have argued that far more relevant for the long run success of the economy is foreign direct investment; and the desire to acquire and sustain FDI provides strong discipline on the economy and the political process. The question is, does opening of the short-term capital account—making the country subject to short run oscillations in sentiment—provide significant *extra* external discipline? On the negative side, the openness to capital flight makes countries especially sensitive e.g. to corporate or capital tax rates or to changes in interest rates. Thus, openness may impose costly *constraints* on the ability of government to pursue legitimate objectives.

One of those objectives is economic stability. China was able to pursue active countercyclical macro-policies—staving off a recession and maintaining robust growth of close to 8%—because the capital account restrictions provided it some room to maneuver. It had no need to raise interest rates to levels that killed the economy, in order to "save" it from capital flight.

Why capital account liberalization has not contributed to growth.

The result cited earlier that capital account liberalization is not associated with faster investment—and therefore faster growth—should not come as a surprise. We have already noted that the case for *positive* effects is weak: firms are unlikely to engage in productive long term investments on the basis of short-term funds. But there are even reasons to expect that capital market liberalization can have negative effects on growth. We argued above that it leads to greater instability, and instability (especially financial market crises) has adverse effects on economic growth.

The channels through instability exercises its adverse effects on the average *level* of growth are several. First, given the limited ability to divest risk, especially in developing countries, instability increases the "risk premium," the returns that investors demand in order to be willing to invest. Second, crises lead to the destruction of firm net worth, reducing firm's willingness and ability to invest. In the more extreme cases, as in East Asia, crises lead to bankruptcy, and corporate bankruptcy leads to undermining financial institutions; in both cases, there is a loss of organizational and informational capital, a loss which cannot easily be reversed. There are important asymmetries and hysteresis effects: the booms do not make up for the losses, nor do the gains by some make up for the losses of others.[24]

Indeed, it is not only the downturn itself which has lasting effects, but the very presence of the risk of instability that is likely to have an adverse effect on growth. The greater risk limits the use of debt finance, and the rapid growth in Korea and other East Asian countries depended on debt finance. In the absence of debt finance, firms would have had to rely on self-finance, and this would have limited their rate of growth. Indeed, the experience in the recent crisis— including the huge increases in interest rates—will almost surely lead to less debt finance, and lower growth. To be sure, one could argue that the countries would have been better off had they made more use of equity rather than debt; but raising capital in the form of equity from large numbers of shareholders is difficult under the best of circumstances (for well known reasons having to do with informational imperfections[25]); a relatively small fraction of new investment is financed by new equity issues, even in the United States[26]. A legal structure which provides strong protection for shareholders, and especially minority shareholders, is required[27]; and only the U.K., U.S., and Japan seem to have the requisite legal structure. Reforms under way in the more advanced of the developing countries may change this in the future, but for the moment, the only way to channel funds from the household to the corporate sector is through debt.

There is an equally compelling argument for why capital market liberalization (at the short end) might be expected to have adverse effects on growth. Countries today are encouraged to maintain adequate reserves, to protect themselves against volatility in international financial markets. A key indicator is the ratio of reserves to foreign denominated short-term indebtedness. When that number falls below unity, investors and lenders become worried—and indeed recent econometric work has suggested that this variable provides the best explanation for which countries were adversely affected by the global financial crisis.[28] Of course, if all investors believe that all other investors are looking at that variable, to determine whether or when to pull out their money from a country, it can become a self-fulfilling prophecy.[29] Now consider a poor developing country. A company within the country borrows, say, a $100 million from a U.S. bank, which charges him 20%. If the country has been maintaining what it views as minimum prudential reserves—kit recognizes the high opportunity cost of reserves—then it will have to add $100 million to reserves. For simplicity, assume it holds those reserves in U.S. T-bills. Consider the implications from the perspective of the country's balance sheet and income flows: It has lent the U.S. $100 million and borrowed from the U.S. the same amount—it has no new net capital. But it pays to the U.S. every year $20 million in interest, while it receives from the U.S.$5 million, the interest on the T-bill. Clearly, this is a good deal for the U.S.—one might understand why the U.S. might be in favor of rules that encourage such transactions—but is hardly the basis for more rapid growth by the poor developing country. (The costs may even be higher than these calculations suggest, because the opportunity cost of the funds that the government has to use for reserves could even exceed 20%.)

To be sure, the adverse effects on economic performance may (especially going forward) be unnecessarily increased as a result of the particular policies that the IMF has customarily employed in response to the crises which may, as we have seen, be systemically associated with full capital account convertibility. Excessively restrictive monetary and fiscal policies[30] resulted in deep recessions or depressions. The "unit root literature" suggests that these negative effects are persistent.[31] Moreover, as we have noted, looking forward, businesses will view debt financing as highly risky; in the event of another crisis (and as we have noted, such crises have become increasingly frequent and deep, in spite of rhetoric that might suggest otherwise), a firm with even a moderate debt equity ratio could be put into distress. Firms will thus have to limit expansion to what they can largely self-finance—with strong adverse effects on long term economic growth.

Social disruption

The recessions and depressions that have been associated with the risks associated with capital market liberalization have had a direct, negative effect on growth and poverty. But there is an indirect channel that is no less important. They frequently give rise to social and political turmoil, especially when it is believed that the burdens are inequitably shared, as in the case of Indonesia. Persistent unemployment too leads to alienation of those who cannot find meaningful jobs, and this often leads to dysfunctional social behaviors—e.g. the urban violence which has marred Latin America or the civil strife so frequent in Africa. And such turmoil provides an inhospitable environment for investment.

The Case for Intervention

There is now a well developed theory of when governments should intervene in markets: when there are market failures, associated with externalities, incomplete markets giving rise to coordination failures, imperfections of information, and so forth. The analysis of interventions involves two steps: first, identifying the market failure, and secondly, showing that there are interventions which could in principle and are likely in practice to improve matters. We take up the second question in the next section.

First, we note that the fact that the central function of capital markets is the production, utilization, and dissemination of information means that the standard competitive model, with its assumptions of perfect, or at least fixed, information is simply irrelevant, as is the conclusion that is derived from that model, that markets are pareto efficient. When information is imperfect and markets are incomplete, markets are almost never (constrained) Pareto efficient, even taking into account the costs of information or marketing; the traditional presumption that government should not intervene in the market is turned on its head.[32]

That having been said, there are at least three major categories of market failure: externalities, coordination failures, and broader macro-economic failures. In each case, there are discrepancies between social and private returns, and because of these discrepancies, there is a case for collective action.

Externality of Private Behaviour on Overall Risk

Once one recognizes that short-term capital flows can give rise to economic instability, there is a compelling economic case for intervention: the instability associated with short-term capital movements results in there being a marked discrepancy between private and social returns and risks. The capital flows imposed a huge negative externality: Indeed, it should be obvious that the crisis which resulted from these volatile flows has affected many others besides the borrowers and lenders—workers who saw their incomes plummet and small businesses that were forced into bankruptcy as a result of the soaring interest rates. (Ironically, the design of the policy response probably increased the magnitude of the externality. The IMF explicitly argued for increasing interest rates, with huge adverse effects on firms not engaged in international speculation, in order to avoid the adverse effects on those who had uncovered foreign denominated borrowings.

At the same time, the very fact that the IMF has engaged in these bail-outs itself implies that there is a discrepancy between social and private returns, and exacerbates those differences, as firms have less an incentive to obtain cover for their foreign exchange exposures.)

The nature of this externality can be seen in a number of ways. Clearly, the borrowing countries—the workers and small businessmen—have paid a high price. Alternatively, we can see the externality exercised through the prudential reserve management policies described earlier. A $100 million capital inflow that has to be offset by a $100 million in increased reserves imposes huge costs on those who might have benefited from other uses of these funds. The $100 million could have been spent to build schools, health clinics, or roads to attract more investment. Clearly then, the private decision to borrow has imposed a high negative cost on society.[33]

Whenever there are such discrepancies, the economists' natural reaction is to impose a "tax" to correct the externality, in order to eliminate, or at least reduce, the difference between social and private returns. To be sure, such taxes might discourage some capital flows; but this criticism is like pointing out that a tax on air pollution discourages the production of goods, like steel, that contribute to air pollution. The point is that firms should be made to pay the full social cost of their activity; doing so will, and should, reduce the level of activities that create negative externalities.

The consequences of the externalities may depend on the circumstances of the country. More advanced industries economies typically have more built-in automatic stabilizers and strong safety nets, so they can absorb the shocks better. In poorer countries, not only may there not be automatic stabilizers, they may face constraints (e.g. on borrowing) that exacerbate fluctuations. For instance, while fiscal policy in developed countries is typically countercyclical, in developing countries, it is pro-cyclical.[34] And as we have already noted policies recommended to, and in some cases effectively forced on, developing countries may make matters worse.[35] Weak financial institutions may make a country particularly vulnerable to large and sudden changes in short-term flows.

The recognition of the importance of these externality effects associated with short-term flows has constituted perhaps the major shift in thinking in discussions over the international financial architecture during the past two years. During the World Bank and IMF Annual Meetings in Hong Kong in October 1997, shortly after the crisis began, there was a call for a change in the IMF charter to push through the agenda of capital account liberalization. This proposal was accompanied, appropriately, by several caveats. Proponents of the change recognized that liberalization required sufficiently strong and stable financial institutions, which in turn meant that a strong regulatory framework would have to be in place as a prerequisite.

Today, there is a greater recognition of the importance of those caveats. Even advanced industrialized countries have found it difficult to establish strong financial institutions and effective regulatory structures—as witnessed by the financial crises in Scandinavia and the United States. These examples show that crises can easily occur in countries with high degrees of transparency, and that one hardly needs crony capitalism to generate a crisis. If there had been any question about the increasing difficulties of good financial regulation posed by the growing role of derivatives, the matter was settled by the government-engineered, privately financed bailout of Long Term Capital Management (LTCM) in October 1998. This single hedge fund had an exposure estimated in excess of a trillion dollars that, according to those who defended the role of the government in the bailout (and who resisted allegations that underlying the publicly orchestrated privately financed bail-out was crony capitalism and corporate misgovernance, American, rather than East Asian, style), posed a threat to global financial stability. Much of the money for LTCM exposure came from supposedly well-regulated banks.

Clearly, even without exposing themselves to the volatility of short-term capital flows, developing countries face greater risks (for instance, because of their less diversified economies and the weaker role of automatic stabilizers) and typically have relatively lower regulatory capacity in the financial sector. Given these features of their economies, the caveat that developing countries should have strong financial institutions and regulatory structures in place before liberalizing their capital accounts suggests that the entire question is now moot. In the immediate future, few countries should be pressed to move far in the direction of liberalization.

Coordination Failures

A second market failure underlies the earlier discussion of capital flight, e.g. as in Russia. There might have been a Pareto dominant equilibrium in which all investors kept their funds in Russia, but given risk aversion, the equilibrium which naturally emerges entails capital flight.

The restrictions on capital outflows eliminates the "bad" equilibrium; in effect, it ensures the economy coordinates on the good equilibrium where everyone reinvests in the economy. The interesting aspect of this intervention is that (as modeled) it is costless to enforce. Given that everyone else is investing in the economy—and the economy is booming—it pays everyone to invest in the economy.

Unemployment

Market economies are not self-regulating; they do not necessarily quickly return to full employment after an adverse shock. That is why there is now general agreement on the need for government intervention through monetary and fiscal policy to maintain the economy at full employment. Capital market liberalization restricts the ability of the government to manage the macro-economy. In the extreme case, the country completely loses discretion over monetary policy—any deviation of interest rates from international rates results in a huge flow of capital in or out of the country—and accordingly must rely exclusively on fiscal policy. But fiscal policy often is not as flexible as monetary policy, and some might say in some circumstances (e.g. Japan in recent years) not very effective. Moreover the "costs" of relying on fiscal policy—and the loss in discretion over monetary policy-- may be high. The contrast between Malaysia and other East Asian countries is instructive. Because it imposed capital controls, Malaysia could keep its interest rates at lower levels than did the other countries. It's economic downturn was shallower and shorter than theirs; and equally important for the country's future, the legacy of public debt, and economic and social disruption was less. The direct effect is obvious: because it had to rely less on deficits to stimulate the economy, the cumulative debt is lower. But the indirect effect is probably even more important: it avoided the bankruptcy, and the knock-on effect on the financial institutions, arising from high interest rates, and thereby reduced the costs of restructuring the financial system. The financial and corporate distress that would have resulted from high interest rates would have shifted to the left the aggregate supply curve; output and employment would as a result been lower, even if government had used fiscal policy effectively, so that unemployment would have been higher, and the social distress—especially in a country with a history such as that of Malaysia—could have had disastrous long term economic effects.

The market failure analysis presented above (the discrepancy between social and private returns), the strong empirical evidence of the high risks associated with short-term capital flows, and the absence of convincing evidence of growth-enhancing benefits associated with capital account liberalization (in the short-term) — all these points lead one to question the fundamental premises underlying the drive for capital account liberalization.

Designing Effective Interventions

Hence, while 36 months ago there were calls for full capital account liberalization, today the debate has shifted. It is no longer whether some form of intervention might be desirable in principle, but whether there exists interventions which are effective, and which do not have adverse ancillary effects. The fact that China and India have managed to weather the storm and maintain strong growth; the fact, already alluded to several times, that China has managed to attract huge amounts of foreign direct investment while maintaining controls on short-term capital; the fact that countries that have capital market restrictions seem to have done as well as those that have not suggests that it is possible to impose such restrictions without significant adverse effects.

The purpose of the *stabilizing* interventions is to equate social and private costs and to stabilize the short-term flows. To understand what is at issue, an analogy may be useful. Dams do not stop the flow of water from the top of a mountain to the ocean. But without the dam, sudden powerful flows may cause death and destruction; with the dam in place, not only are lives saved and property protected, but the water itself can be channeled into constructive uses. And a dam can serve a useful role in averting a flood even if it is not perfect, i.e. even if some of the water spills over the top and makes its way down the mountainside, bypassing the dam. So too for interventions in capital markets: it is not a valid criticism to say that they are not perfect, that their will be leaks, or that there will be some circumvention of the regulations or taxes. The question is, do they nonetheless serve to stabilize the flows, and at not too great a cost to the economy? More recently, attention has focused on three sets of interventions, restrictions on capital inflows, restrictions on capital outflows, and restrictions imposed on the banking system.

Capital inflows

Chile has imposed what amounts to a tax on short-term inflows. In doing so, it has succeeded in stabilizing these flows, without adversely affecting the flow of long-term productive capital. (Incidentally, even a tax on capital inflows can serve to stabilize outflows. Those who seek quick returns by taking their money out for a brief time in the hopes of a devaluation, and then bringing it back, are made to pay a high price for this round trip.)

Some critics have interpreted Chile's actions in the recent crisis—where the tax rate was set at zero—as an abandonment by that country of this policy. But that is simply wrong. The point of the tax is to stabilize the flow—to discourage excess inflows when that appears to be the problem. But in the global financial crisis, no developing country faced excess inflows. Indeed, it might even be conceivable that, faced with a shortage of inflows, the country might have a negative tax. But the tax structure is in place: if global financial markets recover, as they almost surely will, and the country again faces an excess of capital inflows, then the tax rate could again be raised.

Today, the IMF endorses the idea that countries should consider such stabilizing interventions. But this is just one of many interventions that can help stabilize financial flows. I would argue that, given the potentially severe consequences of volatile flows, the international community should encourage experimentation with other interventions. One country, for instance, is discussing limiting the tax deductibility (for purposes of the corporation income tax) of interest on foreign-denominated, short-term debt. (This intervention has the further advantage of being largely "self-reporting."[36])

Capital outflows

Malaysia tried a quite different experiment: controls on the outflow of capital. Many within the international capital markets greeted this experiment with little enthusiasm or even explicit expressions of distaste. These rhetorical attacks typically failed to note the many subtleties of Malaysian policies, including the provisions designed to protect interests of long-term investors. Recently, the country moved to a more market-based exit tax. It is too soon to evaluate the experiment, but preliminary results suggest that it has been far from the disaster that the naysayers had predicted; the removal of the tax went smoothly, the country used the time provided to make significant progress in financial and corporate restructuring (far more progress than some of its neighbors), and foreign direct investment continued at a relatively strong pace. And as we noted, the country used the greater freedom that it afforded in the conduct of monetary and fiscal policy to reduce the magnitude and duration of the downturn and the legacy of public debt.

Regulating capital flows through the banking system

The East Asian crisis highlighted the importance of the financial system; weaknesses in the financial system—generated, for instance, between a mismatch between foreign denominated liabilities and domestically denominated assets—can give rise to systemic weaknesses in the entire economy. Observers of the crisis, however, noted that focusing on the financial system may not be enough; after all, two thirds of the foreign-denominated borrowing in Indonesia was by corporates. Indeed, the argument was put forward that limiting bank borrowing by itself would be like putting a finger into a dike. If foreign banks were offering highly favorable terms, the pressure for foreign borrowing would show up somewhere else in the system. Improved banking regulation might limit direct weaknesses in the banking system, but lead to more corporate exposure.

But this perspective ignores the central role that the financial system plays in the economy, and the ability of government to exercise pervasive effects through the regulation of the banking system. Governments can—and indeed should—insist that banks look at the uncovered exposure of firms to whom they have lent. For that (uncovered) exposure can affect greatly the likelihood that the firms to whom they have lent will not be able to repay their loans. Again, Malaysia provides a case in point: bank regulations succeeded in limiting exposure of Malaysian firms. (In principle, the bank regulations can be market based; that is, bank regulators could impose risk weights in the capital adequacy requirements so that loans to firms with high exposure received higher risk weights. Thus, banks would only make loans to such firms if they received an interest rate high enough to compensate them for the higher costs (and risks). But no government imposes the kind of sophisticated risk-based capital adequacy standards that this would imply; in the near term, emerging markets are probably better served by employing simple regulatory structures.)

Indeed, given the strictures against capital market interventions that have become fashionable—countries that experiment with even market based interventions run the risk of being treated as pariahs—there is much to be said for interventions mediated through the financial system. There is now general recognition of the need for regulations in the banking system that go well beyond capital adequacy requirements, and such regulations can go a long way towards modulating the instability of short term capital flows.

Tax policy

Tax policy can also be used to reduce foreign denominated short term capital inflows. Many countries have corporate income tax structures in which interest is tax deductible. Limiting interest deductibility for foreign denominated short term loans would serve to deter such borrowing.[37]

Which Intervention?

Stabilizing capital flows, and limiting short term exposure, may be easier than preventing long term capital flight, though several countries have shown that the task is not insurmountable, and need not be accompanied by high levels of corruption. In the case of a country like Russia, where much of the foreign exchange results from the sale of natural resources, in principle it may be even easier to address problems of evasion of the regulation than in economies where revenues are generated from the sale of exports (where underinvoicing may be a problem).

Concluding Remarks

In the aftermath of the global financial crisis and the recognition of the high costs that those in the developing world had had to pay, there emerged extensive discussion of a new global economic architecture. Everyone agreed that attention should be focused on preventing future crises, though upon further reflection, the goal became modified to making such crises less frequent and less deep. Early discussions focused on improving transparency—though most recognized that most of the relevant information (e.g. the high leverage of Korea's firms and the heavy investment in the highly cyclical chip industry) was already readily available. When it was further observed that the last major set of crises occurred in three of the most transparent countries (Norway, Sweden, and Finland), it became clear that transparency itself would hardly inoculate a country against a crisis. Deeper analysis further questioned the transparency explanation: the affected countries had experienced three decades of rapid and relatively stable growth; if anything, there had been an increase in transparency. Moreover, many countries that were less transparent did not have a crisis. More broadly, while improved information (transparency) might lead to better resource allocations, both theoretical and empirical analyses questioned its role in enhancing economic stability (See Furman and Stiglitz, 1999). Enthusiasm for the transparency agenda in some quarters was further eroded when it was pointed out that to be meaningful, transparency had to be comprehensive, including off-shore banking and hedge funds, and possibly even the actions of central bankers!

A second major strand of reforms focused on strengthening of financial institutions. Again, while desirable, the difficulties that even advanced industrial countries had in establishing strong financial institutions suggested that this would remain a long-term challenge in emerging markets. A host of other reforms—from collective action clauses in bonds, to systemic bankruptcy provisions, to improved corporate governance—were put on the table. Some, like the collective action clauses, received active opposition. Some, like systemic bankruptcy provisions, involved matters that were too technical to receive widespread discussion.

In some areas, like improved corporate governance progress seemed likely—though their role in the crisis may have been overblown (see Stiglitz, 1999).

The one area in which there is an emerging consensus—a major change in perspectives— is short-term capital flows. The risks are recognized to be greater, the benefits lower, the circumstances in which countries should engage in full liberalization more restrictive than was the case before the crisis. Given the growing body of theory, evidence, and experience against full capital account liberalization, the speech of the Managing Director of the IMF, Michel Camdessus, before the Annual Bank-Fund Meetings in Washington in September, 1999, raised fundamental questions. There he argued, "Freedom has its risks! Let's go then for an orderly liberalization of capital movements. . . . . the objective is to foster the smooth operation of international capital markets and encourage countries to remove controls in a way that supports the drive toward sustainable macroeconomic policies, strong monetary and financial sectors, and lasting liberalization."[38]

Are international policies in this area being designed on the basis of the best available economic theories and evidence, or is there another agenda—perhaps a special interest agenda— seemingly impervious to the effects of such policies, not only on growth, but on stability and poverty? If that is the case, is there a more fundamental problem in the international economic architecture, going beyond the details discussed above, to issues of accountability and representativeness. Do those making decisions which affect the lives and livelihoods of millions of people throughout the world reflect the interests and concerns, not just of financial markets, but of businesses, small and large, and of workers, and the economy more broadly? These are the deeper questions posed by the crisis through which the world is just emerging.

Notes

1 Although real GDP growth for the 5 countries (Indonesia, Korea, Malaysia, Thailand and the Phillippines) is estimated to be around 6.9% in 2000, the World Bank's projected long term slower annual growth of 5.5% between 2003 and 2010 (Table A1.1, World Bank 2001).

2 India grew at a rate of 5.2% and China at a rate of 7.8% in 1998. This contrasted with declines in much of the rest of the developing world. In particular, the East Asian crisis countries suffered a 8.2% decline that year.

3 See Lindgren, Garcia, and Saal (1996, p.20).

4 Calvo, Leiderman, and Reinhart [1993]. They documented the importance of external factors in explaining between thirty to sixty percent of the variance in their proxy for monthly capital flows to Latin American countries in the early 1990s. These external factors included U.S. interest rates, balance of payments developments, or growth; institutional innovations that lead to greater global integration; changes in sentiment toward different regions (or emerging markets as a whole) or reductions in the degree of "irrational" home bias in investment; as well as overall changes in the market "risk premium." See also Fernandez-Arias [1995].

5 See Figure 1 from *Global Economic Prospects 2000* which demonstrates how capital flows were almost halved in the space of a year. See World Bank [1999 Forthcoming].

6 Institute of International Finance[1998], as cited in Rodrik[1998].

7 Note that the standard argument for free trade assumed an economy at full employment, with perfect competition, and ignored distributional concerns.

8 See, e.g. Sachs and Warner [1995], Wacziarg [1998], and Vamvakidis [1999].

9 Figures taken with author permission from Rodrik [1998].

10 See Caprio [1997].

11 In Indonesia, output in 1998 was an estimated 14% below that of 1997, in Thailand, 10% below. In Ecuador, estimates are than 1999 output will be 8 to 12% below 1998. World Bank Development Prospects Group.

12 Furman and Stiglitz [1999b].

13 Demigurc-Kunt and Detragiache [1998].

14 Easterly et al [1999].

15 See, e.g. Greenwald and Stiglitz [1986].

16 See Shiller [1989].

17 See, e.g. Banerjee [1992], Shiller [1995].

18 See for example Hoff [1997].

19 See for example Lee [1996].

20 Capital flight played an important role in contributing to the Mexican crisis and in exacerbating the effects of the Indonesian crisis. (See Dooley [1998]). There is a growing consensus the capital outflows out of Russia have played a key role in that economy's dismal performance over the past eight years.

21 See Collier and Gunning [1999].

22 See Dooley [1996].

23 A recent IMF study by Rossi [1999] suggests that restrictions on capital outflows have a positive effect on economic growth. While his study corroborates earlier studies that restrictions on capital inflows contributed to economic stability, his results suggest that they may have adverse effects on economic growth. As the discussion below illustrates, the arguments for these effects are not convincing. As always,
one needs to treat cross country regressions with care, especially when inadequate account is taken of problems of simultaneity.

24 See Greenwald and Stiglitz [1993] and Greenwald [1998.]

25 See Greenwald, Stiglitz, and Weiss [1984] or Myers and Maljuf [1984].

26 See Mayer [1987].

27 See Dyck [1999].

28 See Rodrik and Velasco [1999] and Furman and Stiglitz [1999].

29 Earlier studies did not include the ratio of reserves to foreign denominated short-term debt, on the grounds that individuals within the country could, with full capital account convertibility in principle, convert domestic currency into foreign currency. Thus, disturbances can be caused not only by foreigners refusing to roll over loans, but also by domestic investors seeking to flee the country.

30 For a discussion of these responses, see Stiglitz [1998, 1999b], World Bank [1998a, 1998b] and Lane et al. [1999].

31 This literature argues, roughly, that if output today falls by 5%, output 100 years from now is 5% lower than it otherwise would have been. The economy never fully recovers. This stands in marked contrast to the "reversion" view which argues that the economy is like a spring: the more that it is pulled down in a particular year, the faster it grows in subsequent years. If there is a reversion effect, it appears to be very weak. Greenwald and Stiglitz [1993] present a theoretical model explaining why such persistence is to be expected.

32 See Greenwald and Stiglitz [1993].

33 One might have argued that the government would have been better off lending the $100 million directly to the firm. The country as a whole is worse off; it pays, say 18% to the United States, but receives only 4% on the reserves which it holds, say, in US T-bills. But the country may not have the "banking" capacity, i.e. screening and moni-

toring. The point, however, is not that the country should not use the foreign banking services, but that there is a cost to society arising from such short term borrowing.

34 See Easterly et al [1999] and Hausmann [1996].

35 In addition to the excessively contractionary monetary and fiscal policies noted above, policies directed at the problems of a weak financial sector may accentuate the downturn, e.g. the closing down of 16 banks in Indonesia, which led to a run on other banks, further restricted the flow of credit. More generally, in the event of systemic weaknesses in the financial system, the rigid enforcement of capital adequacy standards may give rise to an accelerator-like effect enhancing the magnitude of the contraction. See Stiglitz [1999].

36 Firms may, of course, commit fraud, by declaring short-term foreign denominated debt is not foreign denominated, or not short-term, but such fraud would be subject to the same kinds of penalties that other forms of income tax fraud is. Special attention would have to be paid to derivatives, and other actions designed to circumvent the intent of the provision. Again, it might be easy to design such regulations. For instance, firms would be required to report consolidated positions, include those of derivatives; any derivatives, or contracts embedding derivatives, not reported would have junior status in any bankruptcy proceedings, or could not be enforced in court.

37 Problems of avoidance through the use of derivatives present a technical problem, which can be addressed in a variety of ways, e.g. by requiring disclosure of such derivative positions if they are to be enforced in court or to have status in bankruptcy proceeding, and netting out such positions in determining whether the country is, in effect, borrowing short.

38 See Camdessus [1997].

References

Banerjee, Abhijit. 1992. "A Simple Model of Herd Behavior". *Quarterly Journal of Economics* v107 (3): 797–817.

Calvo, G., A., L. Leiderman and C. M. Reinhart. 1993. "Capital Inflows and Real Exchange Rate Appreciation in Latin America. The Role of External Factors." *International Monetary Fund Staff Papers* 40(1): 108–151.

Camdessus, M. 1997. Address to the Board of Governors of the International Monetary Fund. Hong Kong, China, September 23. Internet Address: http://www.imf.org/external/np/speeches/1997/MDS9711.HTM

Caprio, G. 1997. "Safe and Sound Banking in Developing Countries: We're Not in Kansas Anymore." Research in Financial Services: Private and Public Policy 9: 79–97.

Collier, Paul and J.W. Gunning. 1999. "Explaining African Economic Performance". *Journal of Economic Literature* v37, n1 (March 1999): 64–111.

Collin, Mayer. 1987. "New Issues in Corporate Finance". Centre for Economic Policy Research Discussion Paper: 181.

Demirgüç-Kunt, A., and E. Detragiache. 1998. "Financial Liberalization and Financial Fragility." *Proceedings of Annual Bank Conference on Development Economics.* Washington, D.C., April 20–21.

Dooley, M. 1996. "Capital Controls and Emerging Markets". *International Journal of Finance and Economics* v1(3): 197–205.

_____. 1998. "Indonesia: Is the Light at the End of the Tunnel Oncoming Traffic?" Deutsche Bank Research, Emerging Markets Research June.

Easterly, W., R. Islam, and J. E. Stiglitz. 1999. "Shaken and Stirred: Volatility and Macroeconomic Paradigms for Rich and Poor Countries." Given as Michael Bruno

Memorial Lecture, International Economics Association World Congress, Buenos Aires.

Fernández-Arias, E. 1995. "The New Wave of Private Capital Inflows: Push or Pull?" *Journal of Development Economics* (December).

Furman, J. and J. E. Stiglitz. 1999. Economic Crises: Evidence and Insights from East Asia. *Brookings Papers on Economic Activity.* Volume 2, Washington, D.C.

_____. 1999b. "Economic Consequences of Income Inequality. *Federal Reserve Bank* Review of Kansas City (Forthcoming).

Greenwald, Bruce. 1998. "International Adjustments in the Face of Imperfect Financial Markets". Paper prepared for the Annual World Bank Conference on Development Economics, Washington, D.C., April 20–21, 1998.

Greenwald, B. and J. E. Stiglitz. 1986. "Externalities in Economies with Imperfect Information and Incomplete Markets". *Quarterly Journal of Economics,* May 1986, pp. 229–264.

_____. 1993. "Financial Market Imperfections and Business Cycles". *Quarterly Journal of Economics,* 108(1), pp. 77–114. (Paper prepared for the Far-Eastern Meeting of the Econometric Society, Seoul, June 1991, NBER Working Paper 2494.)

Greenwald, B., J. E. Stiglitz and A. Weiss. 1984. "Informational Imperfections in the Capital Markets and Macroeconomic Fluctuations". *American Economic Review,* 74(2), pp. 194–199.

Hausmann, R, and M. Gavin. "Securing Stability and Growth in a Shock Prone Region: The Policy Challenge for Latin America." Inter-American Development Bank, Office of the Chief Economist. *Working Paper 315,* January.

Hoff, K. 1997. "A Bayesian Model of the Infant Industry Argument." *Journal of International Economics.* Vol. 43 (3/4): 400–436.

Institute of International Finance. 1998. *Capital Flows to Emerging Market Economies.* Washington DC. January 29.

Greenwald, B. and J.E. Stiglitz. 1986. "Externalities in Economics with Imperfect Information and Incomplete Markets." *Quarterly Journal of Economics,* pp. 229–264. May.

Lane, T., A. Ghosh, J. Hamann, S. Phillips, M. Schulze-Ghattas, and T. Tsikata. 1999. "IMF-Supported Programs in Indonesia, Korea, and Thailand. A Preliminary Assessment. " International Monetary Fund Occasional Paper 178.

Lee, J. 1997. "Implications of a Surge in Capital Inflows: Available Tools and Consequences for the Conduct of Monetary Policy." International Monetary Fund Working Paper 53. May.

Lindgren, C., G. Garcia, and M. Saal. 1996. *Banking Soundness and Macroeconomic Policy.* Washington: International Monetary Fund.

Myers, Stewart C. and N. Majluf. 1984. "Corporate Financing and Investment Decisions When Firms Have Information That Investors Do Not Have". NBER Working Paper: 1396.

Rodrik, D. 1998. "Who Needs Capital-Account Convertibility?" *Essays in International Finance* 207, International Finance Section, Department of Economics, Princeton University, (May): 55–65.

Rossi, M. 1999. "Financial Fragility and Economic Performance in Developing Economies: Do Capital Controls, Prudential Regulation, and Supervision Matter?" International Monetary Fund Working Paper 66. Washington, D.C.

Sachs, J. and A. Warner. 1995. "Economic Reform and the Process of Economic Integration." *Brooking Papers on Economic Activity.* Vol.1, pp. 1–118.

Shiller, Robert.1989. "An Unbiased Reexamination of Stock Market Volatility: Discussion". *Journal of Finance,* Vol. 40, No. 3, Papers and Proceedings of the Forty-Third Annual Meeting American Finance Association, Dallas, Texas, December 28–30, 1984. (Jul., 1985), pp. 688–689.

_____. 1995. " Conversation, Information, and Herd Behavior". The *American Economic Review,* Vol. 85, No. 2, Papers and Proceedings of the Hundredth and Seventh Annual Meeting of the American Economic Association Washington, DC, January 6–8, 1995. (May, 1995), pp. 181–185.

Stiglitz, J. E. 1998. "Responding to Economic Crises: Policy Alternatives for Equitable Recovery and Development". Paper presented to North-South Institute. Ottawa, Canada, September 29.

_____. 1999a. Forthcoming. "Principles Of Financial Regulation: A Dynamic, Portfolio *Approach."* World Bank Research Observer.

_____. 1999b. "Lessons from the Global Financial Crisis." Lecture given to Federal Reserve Bank of Chicago. September 30, 1999

Vamvakidia, A. 1999. "Regional Trade Agreements or Broad Liberalization: Which Path Leads to Faster Growth?" International Monetary Fund Staff Papers. Vol 46 No.1 March. pp. 42–68.

Wacziarg, R. 1998. "Measuring the Dynamic Gains From Trade." Working Paper. Harvard University, May.

World Bank. 1998a. Global Economic Prospects 1998/99: Beyond Financial Crisis. Washington, DC.

_____. 1998b. *East Asia: Road to Recovery.* Washington, DC: World Bank

_____. 1999 Forthcoming. Global Economic Prospects and the Developing Countries 1999/2000. Washington D.C.

_____. 2001 Forthcoming. Global Economic Prospects and the Developing Countries 2001. Washington D.C.

30

THE WASHINGTON CONSENSUS

Assessing a Damaged Brand

*Nancy Birdsall, Augusto de la Torre, and
Felipe Valencia Caicedo*

Source: *Center for Global Development Working Paper* 211 (May 2010).

Abstract

In this paper we analyze the Washington Consensus, which at its original formulation reflected views not only from Washington but also from Latin America.
We trace the life of the Consensus from a Latin American perspective in terms
of evolving economic development paradigms. We document the extensive
implementation of Consensus-style reforms in the region as well as the mismatch
between reformers' expectations and actual outcomes, in terms of growth, poverty reduction, and inequality. We then present an assessment of what went wrong
with the Washington Consensus-style reform agenda, using a taxonomy of views
that put the blame, alternatively, on (i) shortfalls in the implementation of reforms
combined with impatience regarding their expected effects; (ii) fundamental
flaws—in either the design, sequencing, or basic premises of the reform agenda;
and (iii) incompleteness of the agenda that left out crucial reform needs, such as
volatility, technological innovation, institutional change and inequality.

1. Introduction

It is hard to overemphasize the practical and ideological importance of the
Washington Consensus in Latin America. The Decalogue of Consensus policies
laid out by John Williamson in his 1989 landmark paper became in the minds
of advocates and pundits alike a manifesto for capitalist economic development.
In the words of Moisés Naím (2000) the term "soon acquired a life of its own,
becoming a brand name known worldwide and used independently of its original intent and even of its content." For its advocates, the Consensus reflected a
doctrine of economic freedom that was best suited for the political democracies
to which many Latin countries had returned after a long spell of military dictatorships (Williamson, 1993). For its opponents, as Williamson (2002) himself noted

later on, the Consensus was an unjust "set of neoliberal policies (...) imposed on hapless countries by the Washington-based international financial institutions." Regardless of the political stance, there is no denying that overall the Consensus became, in Moisés Naím's (2002) epigrammatic expression, a "damaged brand."

The social and economic philosophy implicit in the Consensus was not created by Williamson. It was, so to speak, "in the air"—a robust intellectual and ideological current of the times which emphasized the virtuous combination of political democracy and free markets. Williamson's article rode on a global wave that transformed the conventional wisdom in favor of free market economics, which included the rise of neoclassical economics and the rational expectations revolution among academic macroeconomists. It is not a coincidence then that the appearance in 1989 of the Washington Consensus coincided with fall of the Berlin Wall, which symbolically marked the burial of centrally planned economies.

This article analyzes the birth, evolution, implications, and controversy surrounding Williamson's Decalogue from a Latin American standpoint. It is structured as follows. Section 2 provides the intellectual and economic context that preceded and gave rise to Washington Consensus. Section 3 examines the Consensus itself, as formulated in Williamson's article, and distinguishes between its academic origins and subsequent incursion into the ideological sphere. Section 4 describes the extent of implementation of Consensus-style reforms during the 1990s and Section 5 analyzes their economic outcomes. Section 6 presents a typology views on what went wrong with the Washington Consensus and Section 7 concludes.

2. Economic and Intellectual Antecedents to the Consensus

Around the time when Williamson's article was first published, the intellectual effervescence had been sufficient to move the dominant economic development policy paradigm away from state dirigisme—which had prevailed in Latin America and the Caribbean (LAC) during the 1960s and 70s— towards a greater reliance on markets. This mutation started in the 1970s, gained momentum during the 1980s—when a corrosive and generalized debt crisis sunk the region into a "lost-decade" of economic slump—and reached its heights during the 1990s— arguably the glorious years for the Washington Consensus.

The mutation of the economic development paradigm that led to the Washington Consensus was neither easy nor smooth, or completely linear. But the general outlines of this transition are clear enough and worth sketching. Prior to this change, the policy views in the region had drawn heavily from the early development literature's emphasis on capital accumulation and the view that widespread market failures in developing countries would hinder accumulation. Markets were simply not expected to work properly in developing countries (Rosenstein-Rodin 1943, Gerschenkron, 1962; Hirschman, 1958; and Rostow, 1959).[1] It was less important to gain an adequate understanding of why private markets failed than to verify that they did fail, and badly. Economic development—the argument went—was too important to be left at the mercy of flawed market forces and the state had to play a major role in accelerating capital accumulation. The state was to control, directly or indirectly, the "Commanding Heights" of the economy and mobilize and allocate resources purposefully (often via multiyear planning).

Interestingly and in contrast with the experience in East Asia, the pre-Washington Consensus LAC model of state dirigisme promoted inward-oriented economic development. There was of course no necessity in the internal logic of government activism for it to be associated with inward orientation, but in LAC it was and in a major way. This link was promoted by important intellectual strands prevalent in the region. It was consistent with the structuralist vision heralded by the Economic Commission for Latin America and the Caribbean (ECLAC) and underpinned by the writings of Raul Prebisch (1950) and Hans Singer (1950). For this vision, a virtuous circle between manufacturing growth and the expansion of domestic demand would enable LAC countries to break free from the terms-of-trade-deterioration trap.[2] Prebisch (1950) thus famously declared that "industrialization has become the most important means of expansion." Inward orientation was also consistent with Hirschman's notion—popular then in LAC— that the formation of strong backward linkages was crucial for sustained growth and hinged mainly on domestic economy dynamics. It was also in line with the Marxist inspired Dependency Theory (Gunder Frank, 1967; Furtado, 1963; and Cardoso and Faletto, 1979), which interpreted the relation of the "periphery" (developing countries) to the "center" (rich countries) as one of debilitating dependency—i.e., a structural subordination of the periphery's economic activity to the interests of the center that stifled the former's technological dynamism and economic diversification.

Dependency theory thus joined ECLAC-style structuralism and Hirschmanian views in emphasizing that the cure for underdevelopment was a proactive state pursuing industrial policies to secure the expansion of production for the *domestic* market. This underpinned the import substituting industrialization (ISI) model that dominated the region in the 1960s and 1970s. Promoting domestic manufacturing to replace imports implied an intense, hands-on involvement of the state through a large set of interconnected interventions, including, state owned firms and banks, subsidization of infant industries, central planning, widespread price controls, high import tariffs and quotas, administered interest rates and directed credit.[3]

LAC did grow robustly during the height of the ISI period but so did the world; hence, its per capita income did not on average converge significantly towards that of the rich countries—a fact that often goes unnoticed (Figure 1). In any case, ISI showed signs of exhaustion around the late 1970s, as the initial growth dynamism of inward-looking industrialization subsided and associated macroeconomic imbalances mounted. While this was a heterogeneous process and with different timings across countries in the region,[4] it was the Debt Crisis of the 1980s that intensified and synchronized LAC countries' movement away from ISI to embrace the rising global wave of pro-market policies.[5] While triggered by

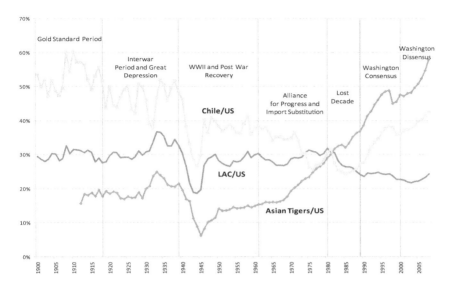

Figure 1 Latin America and East Asia: Relative GDP per capita (1900–2008) (Ratio to US GDP per capita, in constant 1990 USD). Note: GDP PPP figures, LAC is the weighted average of Argentina, Brazil, Chile, Colombia, Mexico, Peru, Uruguay and Venezuela. Last two years using WDI growth rates. *Source: Historical Statistics of the World Economy, Maddison (2006) and World Development Indicators (2010).*

an external shock—the sharp rise in dollar interest rates engineered by the U.S. Fed to fight inflation—the severity of the debt crisis reflected the magnification of that shock by the dangerous accumulation of domestic vulnerabilities, until then hidden under the mirage created of an unusually benign external environment (Kuczynski and Williamson, 2003). Global interest rates as well as high commodity prices had invited or at least allowed what in retrospect were unsustainable policies.

As the debt crisis deepened, the dark side of inward-looking industrialization and associated macro imbalances was manifested in a well-known catalog of maladies. These included internationally uncompetitive industries; severely distorted relative prices leading to inefficient allocation of resources; rent-seeking and corruption in the administered allocation or rationing of credit, fiscal, and foreign exchange resources; bottlenecks and economic overheating; large public deficits; excessive foreign borrowing by Latin sovereigns; rising and unstable inflation (and actual hyperinflation in several countries).[6]

The economic and social pain involved in the adjustment process of the 1980s was immense, so much so that the period became known as the Lost Decade. As capital inflows abruptly stopped and terms of trade deteriorated sharply, the region was forced to shift from an aggregate external current account deficit of almost U\$2 billion in 1981 to a surplus of more than U\$39 billion in 1984.[7] This was induced by major currency devaluations and severe restrictions on imports, including of vital capital and intermediate goods, which implied a dramatic erosion of real wages and living standards. To put the fiscal accounts in order, countries embarked on deep and highly disruptive expenditure cuts, which hit disproportionately social and infrastructure investment programs. Living standards collapsed—the regional average per capita income in 1985 barely exceeded that of 1975 and for some countries it fell to levels prevailing in the mid-1960s (Balassa et al., 1986). Unemployment rose to more than 15 percent in many countries while underemployment swelled. Inflation averaged 150 percent in the region, exploding into hyperinflation in Bolivia, Argentina and Brazil. Concerted debt rescheduling and roll-overs coupled with "new money" were engineered during the 1980s but they proved woefully insufficient as the problem was one of debt overhang.[8] It was solved belatedly, as the internationally community reluctantly accepted the need for debt reduction and restructuring, implemented during 1989–1995 by a number of LAC countries (including Mexico, Costa Rica, Venezuela, Argentina, Brazil, Dominican Republic, Ecuador, Peru) under the Brady Initiative.

Given the severity of the crisis, it is not surprising that by the end of the 1980s and the beginning of the 1990s the region was prepared for a major change. Economically, Sebastian Edwards (1995) summed up this paradigmatic change: "During the 1980s and early 1990s, there was a marked transformation in economic thinking in Latin America. The once-dominant view based on heavy state interventionism, inward orientation, and disregard for macroeconomic balance slowly gave way to a new paradigm based on competition, market orientation and openness." Politically, the economic hardships tested the recently restored democracies (which followed the military dictatorships of the 1960s and 1970s in Argentina, Brazil, Bolivia, Ecuador, Guatemala, Haiti, Honduras, Nicaragua, Panama, Paraguay and Uruguay). Against this background, by 1989 the shift away from "state-led industrialism" (as Ocampo and Ros, forthcoming 2010, aptly name it) or "import-substitution industrialization" (as it is more commonly known) towards a market-led model gained critical momentum.

3. The Washington Consensus

Williamson's article was thus published when the region was already on the road of change. What Williamson did was to summarize in a Decalogue of 10 policies (Table 1) the converging views that had clearly emerged among the participants (including many prominent Latin American scholars and policy makers) in an 1989 Institute of International Economics Conference organized in Washington, D.C. by John Williamson himself entitled *Latin American Adjustment: How Much Has Happened?* While reflecting his own views, Williamson's (1990) article constitutes a synthesis of policies already in vogue at the time—in Washington and the region as well. Indeed, Williamson is better portrayed as a recorder than

Table 1 The Decalogue of Washington Consensus Policies (1989)

1. Fiscal Discipline	Budget deficits—properly measured to include local governments, state enterprises, and the central bank—should be small enough to be financed without recourse to the inflation tax.
2. Public Expenditure Re-Prioritization	Public spending should move away from politically popular but economically unwarranted projects (bloated bureaucracies, indiscriminate subsidies, white elephants) and towards neglected fields with high economic returns and the potential to improve income distribution (primary health and education, infrastructure).
3. Tax Reform	To improve incentives and horizontal equity, the tax base should be broad and marginal tax rates moderate. Taxing interest on assets held abroad ("flight capital") should become a priority in the medium term.
4. Positive Real Interest Rates	Ultimately, interest rates should be market determined. As this could be destabilizing in an environment of weak confidence, policy should have more modest objectives for the transition, mainly to abolish preferential interest rates for privileged borrowers and achieve a moderately positive real interest rate.
5. Competitive Exchange Rates	Countries need a unified (at least for trade transactions) exchange rate set at a level sufficiently competitive to induce a rapid growth in non-traditional exports, and managed so as to assure exporters that this competitiveness will be maintained in the future.
6. Trade Liberalization	Quantitative trade restrictions should be replaced by tariffs, and these should be progressively reduced until a uniform low tariff in the range of 10 percent is achieved.
7. Foreign Direct Investment	Barriers impeding foreign direct investment and the entry of foreign firms should be abolished; foreign and domestic firms should be allowed to compete on equal terms.
8. Privatization	State enterprises should be privatized.
9. Deregulation	Governments should abolish regulations that impede the entry of new firms or restrict competition, and ensure that all regulations are justified by such criteria as safety, environmental protection, or prudential supervision of financial institutions.
10. Property Rights	The legal system should provide secure property rights without excessive costs, and make these available to the informal sector.

Sources: Williamson (1990) and Williamson (1993).

a creator of the new paradigm, and the real actors in the drama of the decade that ensued were the technocrats and political leaders in the region itself.[9]

These winds of change were reflected not just in Williamson's piece but in other visible—though less influential—writings of the time, who urged export-orientation, increased savings along with efficient investment, as well as a simplification and streamlining of a hitherto all too present role of government.

Williamson would later make repeated reference to *Toward Renewed Economic Growth in Latin America* (Balassa et al., 1986) in his own formulation. Even ECLAC—still viewed as the intellectual home of a more state-led approach to development—supplemented the shift away from inward orientation. For example, Bianchi, Devlin and Ramos (1987) argued that "the debt problem requires a structural transformation of the economy in at least two senses: the growth strategy needs to be outward oriented and largely based on an effort to raise savings and productivity." Similarly, Fajnzylber (1990), after examining the contrast with East Asia, saw the need for a major change in Latin America's economic policy direction in order to combine market-oriented reforms with policies targeted towards the poor.

The Washington Consensus was a Latin version of what had in fact become a worldwide consensus by the 1990s. It had in common with the international version the conviction that economic prosperity could only be obtained by *harnessing the power of markets.* This was associated with a view of government interventionism as a fountainhead of distortions that represses creativity and causes resources to be misallocated. The new paradigm called for allowing the free play of market forces to coordinate through price signals myriads of decentralized decisions of firms and individuals, thus enabling efficient resource allocation and fostering creative entrepreneurship. In sharp contrast with the old paradigm, the new one proclaimed that economic development was too important to be left in the hands of government planners and bureaucrats. Development policy, therefore, had to focus on freeing and enabling markets to "get prices right." Official World Bank and Inter-American Development Bank (IDB) documents that appeared during the 1980s heralded the coming of this new age for development thinking, clearly signaling that the view had left academic circles and was being mainstreamed into practical policy.[10]

But there were two other defining features in the Latin version of the new paradigm that were duly captured in the Washington Consensus. The first was the *quest for macroeconomic stabilization.* The second entailed a *marked shift towards an outward oriented growth strategy.* Given that chronic macroeconomic maladies had become a Latin trademark, it is not at all surprising that the need to introduce macroeconomic policy rectitude would be high in LAC's development agenda. The shift towards sound macro management was understood as a precondition for market-based development. The shift towards an outwardly orientated growth strategy was propelled by the exhaustion of import substitution and the success of East Asian export-led growth, which had put these economies on a frank path towards per capita income convergence with the industrialized countries.[11]

A careful review of Table 1 shows clearly that Williamson's actual formulation of the Consensus emphasized the technical dimensions of economic policy and is measured and balanced in its overall prescriptions. Its Latin American flavor comes through policy prescriptions geared to addressing Latin-specific maladies: macroeconomic stabilization (e.g., fiscal discipline to avoid high inflation, tax reform to broaden the tax base and positive real interest rates to overcome financial repression) and outward orientation (e.g., the elimination of import quotas and low and uniform import tariffs and a competitive exchange rate to induce nontraditional export growth and the removal of barriers to FDI). The pro-market agenda was embodied in policies aimed at: removing the entrepreneurial function of the state (e.g., privatization of state enterprises); freeing and enabling markets (via deregulation, the strengthening of property rights, moderate marginal tax rates, low and uniform import tariffs and a level playing field for foreign and domestic firms); and complementing markets (via the reorientation of public expenditures to primary education, health and infrastructure, both for growth and to improve the distribution of income).

In contrast to the popular perception, Williamson's Decalogue is a far cry from market fundamentalism. He does not even mention the liberalization of the (non-FDI) capital account— which became increasingly controversial in the policy debate as the 1990s unfolded. On the liberalization of domestic financial markets, Williamson is restrained calling only for gradually allowing interest rates to be market determined. Similarly, he steers away from the polar choices in exchange rate policy—a hard peg or a fully free floating rate—which are arguably most consistent with the unfettered play of market forces.[12] Instead, he advocates keeping a "competitive exchange rate" which in practice requires discretional intervention by the central bank. Paradoxically, as will be seen later, actual policy implementation in Latin America was much more aggressive precisely with respect to financial liberalization and exchange rate policy, the two areas where Williamson had been distinctively cautious.

Williamson's formulation is also a far cry from a radical view in favor of a minimalist state that is commonly attributed to the Consensus. There is no supply-side economics calling for a reduction in tax burdens or a major shrinking of the size of the state. To be sure, the privatization of state enterprises is a central policy in Williamson's Decalogue, but it is not justified as a means to reduce the size of the state but to achieve economic efficiency and *reorient* government spending in favor of health, education and infrastructure, much of this in order for the state to play a greater redistributive role. In this respect, Williamson subsumed some of the equity considerations that had appeared, for instance, in UNICEF's (1987) report on *Adjustment with a Human Face.*

Later on, Williamson (2000) characterized his ten policy items as summarizing the "lowest common denominator of policy advice being addressed by the Washington-based institutions to Latin American countries as of 1989." But this narrow characterization was a late and ultimately unsuccessful effort to keep it the Washington Consensus term from being dragged into an excessively ideological realm.[13] By then it was already seen as a synonym of market fundamentalism and neo-liberalism. The induction of the appealing "Washington Consensus" term into the ideological sphere is now a fact of history. And this helps explain why such renowned economists as Nobel Prize winner Joseph Stiglitz criticize the Consensus sharply even as they warn about the dangers of unrestrained financial liberalization and recommend measured trade liberalization, along the same lines of Williamson's initial formulation. It is therefore more appropriate to characterize the Consensus—as done in this chapter—as an expression of a broader change in economic development policy, a paradigmatic shift in favor of macroeconomic stabilization and market-based development.

In the next sections, we keep this broad understanding of the Washington Consensus but focus on its economic dimensions, staying away from the heavy ideological connotations that came to dominate the popular view. We start by inquiring how the Consensus, thus understood, fared in Latin America in terms of actual reform implementation and consequent outcomes.

4. Consensus-Style Reforms: Implementation

This section documents the intensity of reform implementation without assessing its effectiveness. The latter is a most relevant dimension of inquiry but lies outside of the scope of this chapter. The reader is referred to the numerous sources that assess implementation effectiveness more rigorously, often extensively, by type of reform.[14]

During the 1990s, most Latin American countries enthusiastically embraced Consensus-style reforms, with the strong support from international institutions, particularly in the context of IMF stabilization programs and policy-based lending programs of multilateral development banks. While the record is mixed and varied across countries,[15] the vigor of reform implementation in the region was higher than at any time in memory. Eduardo Lora (2001) detects a "great wave" of Consensus-style structural reforms during the 1990s, with particular intensity and concentration in the first half of the 1990s (Figure 2). His structural reform index—which is measured on a scale from 0 to 1 and combines policy actions in the areas of trade, foreign exchange, taxation, financial liberalization, privatization, labor and pensions—rose steeply from about 0.4 in 1989 to almost 0.6 in 1995.[16] As the structural reform process lost momentum around 2000, the 1990s can be considered as the "glorious years" of the Washington Consensus.

One key reform area concerned macroeconomic stabilization, where policy action was impressive. It was in the 1990s when Latin America finally conquered inflation—bringing it down from hyperinflation or chronically high levels to single digit rates in most countries (Figures 3a and 3b). Behind this achievement were important reforms to central banking that virtually eliminated the monetary financing of fiscal deficits. While progress on the fiscal front was less impressive than in the monetary area, things generally moved in the direction of greater viability, a process that, as noted, was aided in several countries by sovereign debt reduction agreements reached with external creditors under the Brady Initiative. The average public sector deficit in the region declined from minus 2.4 percent of GDP in 1980–1989 to almost zero during the mid-1990s, while public sector external debt fell on average from 60 percent to 40 percent of GDP during the

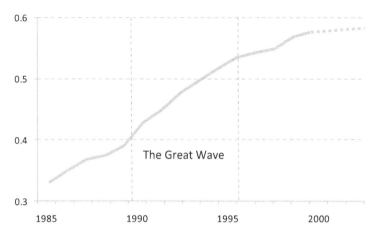

Figure 2 Latin American Structural Reform Index Average (1985–2002). Note: The advance of the reforms is measured as the margin for reform existing in 1985 that has been utilized in subsequent years. The index combines measures of trade, financial, tax and privatization policies. *Source: Lora (2001).*

1990s, even if the total (external and internal) public debt did not decrease much (Figures 4a and 4b).

Considering specific components of structural reform, action was concentrated in the area of liberalization, both in trade and finance. With respect to trade, the 1990s saw a confirmation of a liberalization trend that had started in the mid-1980s, involving mainly the removal of import quotas and the reduction of average import tariffs. The average tariff rate for the region, which had fallen from nearly 50 percent in the early 1980s to around 33 percent in 1990, declined further during the 1990s to around 10 percent by 1999 (Figure 5). The 1990s added to this trend a new feature—a significant reduction in the variance of import tariffs to only one fourth from 1990 to 1999.

But it was arguably in finance where—departing from Williamson's cautious formulation—Latin America's liberalization-oriented reforms were most aggressively implemented. While the region had lagged considerably behind the global wave of financial liberalization of the 1980s, it embraced it with vengeance during the 1990s. The financial liberalization index developed by Kaminsky and Schmukler (2003) shows that it took only the first half of the 1990s for the region to bring relatively closed and repressed financial systems to a level of liberalization comparable to that of developed countries (Figure 6). Financial liberalization was carried out on the domestic and external fronts. Direct credit controls were abandoned and interest rates deregulated. Restrictions on foreign investment were lifted, and other controls on foreign exchange and capital account transactions were dismantled. Foreign banks were allowed and encouraged to establish local presences.

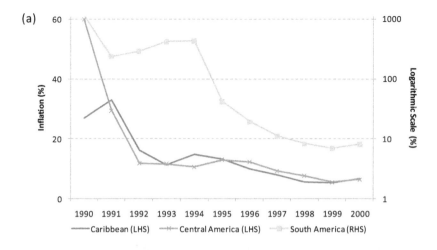

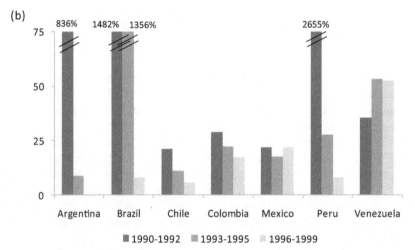

Figure 3 (a) Latin American Inflation (1990–2000). Note: Weighted regional averages. *Source: World Economic Outlook and IFS, IMF (2010).* (b) LAC Inflation, Selected Countries (1990–2000). (In Percentage). *Source: World Economic Outlook and International Financial Statistics, IMF (2010).*

Liberalization on the external front may have been attractive for many countries because of the region's low domestic savings, despite its potential effects on exchange rates and financial systems. (Fukuyama and Birdsall, (eds.), forthcoming 2010). Private domestic savings were low while public savings were constrained by high public debt service (see Figure 7, comparing Latin American and East Asian savings). Perhaps this is why Williamson included taxing "flight capital" as a priority in the medium term. The reliance on foreign capital inflows was in

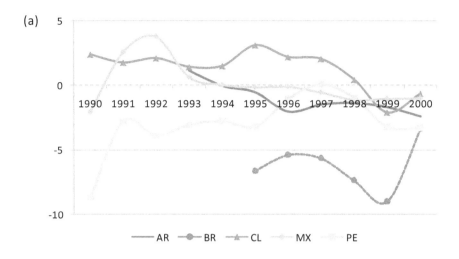

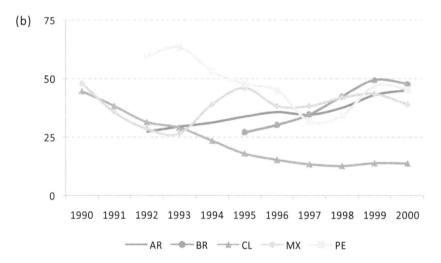

Figure 4 (a) LAC Budget Balance, Selected Countries (1990–2000). (Percent of GDP).
Note: Central government budget. *Source: Economist Intelligence Unit (2010).*
(b) LAC Public Debt, Selected Countries (1990–2000). (Percent of GDP). Note:
Central government debt. *Source: Economist Intelligence Unit (2010).*

turn associated with constant appreciation pressures on the exchange rates, which
undermined competitiveness in non-commodity exports. Again the comparison
with East Asia is apt. And while it is well known that the reform and moderniza-
tion of the regulatory and supervisory arrangements for financial markets lagged
their liberalization—which, as noted later on, constituted a source of systemic
vulnerability—the 1990s did see important, if insufficient, improvements in legal,

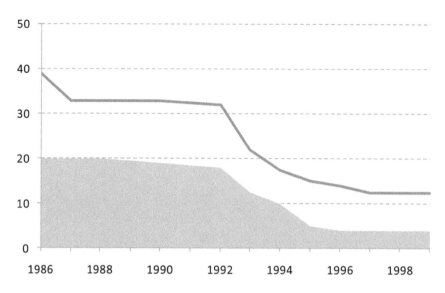

Figure 5 Latin American Import Tariff Liberalization (1985–1999). (Average and Deviations in Percentages). Note: The solid line represents the simple average tariff rate for Argentina, Bolivia, Brazil, Chile, Colombia, Costa Rica, Ecuador, Guatemala, Mexico, Peru, Uruguay and Venezuela. The area represents the average deviation of the tariff rate across countries. Costa Rica and Guatemala are excluded from the deviation calculations. *Source: Lora (2001).*

regulatory, trading and informational infrastructures that are germane to financial markets. These included the revamping or upgrading of banking and capital markets legislation (Figure 8).

The 1990s also registered a wave of privatizations (of public banks and enterprises) and significant, albeit one-dimensional, pension reforms. More than 800 public enterprises were privatized between 1988 and 1997 (Birdsall, de la Torre and Menezes, 2001) and the cumulative amount of funds raised through privatizations during the 1990s was on the order of US$200 billion (Figure 9).[17] In pensions, Chile's pioneering reform of 1981 had a major demonstration effect throughout the region. Similar systems were adopted during the 1990s by Argentina, Bolivia, Colombia, Costa Rica, El Salvador, Mexico, Peru and Uruguay.[18] These reforms consisted basically of a shift away from government-administered, pay-as-you-go, defined-benefit pension systems for private sector employees to systems that rely mainly on a so-called "second pillar" of mandatory, defined and privately administered pension funds. The market orientation herein is clear, as these pension reforms shifted from the state to the capital markets the dominant role in administering retirement-related savings.

Lastly, structural reform intensity was more modest in tax reform and virtually nonexistent in labor markets (Figure 10). Lora's index of labor market reforms

Figure 6 International Financial Liberalization Index (1973–2002). Note: The liberalization index is calculated as the simple average of three indices (liberalization of the capital account, domestic financial sector and stock market) that range between 1 and 3, where 1 means no liberalization and 3 means full liberalization. The regional averages are simple country averages. *Source: De la Torre and Schmukler (2007).*

barely rose during the 1990s (progress was actually negative by 1994 and only slightly positive by 1999). Williamson's inclusion of "public expenditure reprior-itization" has usually not been viewed by students of the Consensus as a structural reform and is not even included in the reform indices— which is itself a commentary on the tendency even in scholarly work to overlook aspects of the Consensus that are not associated with market liberalization.[19]

5. Consensus-Style Reforms: Outcomes

While Latin America championed the Washington Consensus in the 1990s, the observed outcomes were disheartening and puzzling. Disheartening because of what was arguably too meager a payoff relative to the intensity of the reform effort. Puzzling because of the lack of clarity on what went wrong. This section discusses the disheartening side of the equation. The next addresses the puzzles.

As noted before, inflation reduction and macroeconomic stabilization were an undeniable achievement of the 1990s. In addition, the optimism inspired by the convergence of views around Consensus-style reforms contributed to a major surge in net private capital inflows to the region. These inflows rose from US$14 billion in 1990 to $86 billion in 1997, before declining to US$47 billion in 1999 in

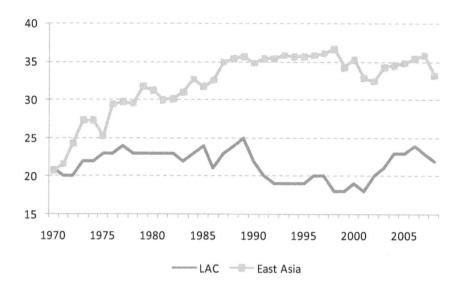

Figure 7 Latin America and East Asia: Gross Domestic Savings (1970–2008). (Percent of GDP). Note: East Asia is the un-weighted average of Hong Kong, Singapore, South Korea, Taiwan, Indonesia, Thailand and Malaysia, while LAC covers the whole Latin American and Caribbean region. *Source: World Development Indicators (2010).*

the wake of the Asian financial crisis (Birdsall, de la Torre and Menezes, 2001). Whether these inflows led to higher investment is a different question, and it seems that in general might have not (Ffrench-Davis and Reisen, 1998).

But when the attention is focused on the outcome variables that really matter for economic development—per capita income, poverty and income distribution—it appears that the Washington Consensus yielded little progress during the 1990s relative to expectations in most of Latin America with the notable exception of Chile (and even there excluding income distribution).[20]

5.1 Factual Overview

Consider first GDP growth and per capita income. Regional growth did recover modestly—from 1.1 percent per year in 1980–1990 to 3.6 percent in 1990–1997 and 3 percent average for the 1990s as a whole. But this hardly involved productivity growth and was not sufficient to reduce the convergence gap in per capita income between the region and the rich economies.[21] Instead, the ratio of per capita income in Latin America relative to the United States, which had already fallen precipitously during the "lost decade" of the 1980s, continued to decline, albeit marginally, throughout the 1990s (see again, Figure 1). This stands in sharp contrast with the experience of the East Asian Tigers, whose per capita income gap

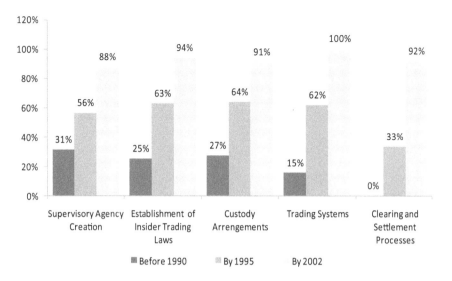

Figure 8 Latin American Capital Markets Reform Implementation (1990–2002). Note: Percentage of Latin American countries having implemented reforms. *Source: De la Torre and Schmukler (2007).*

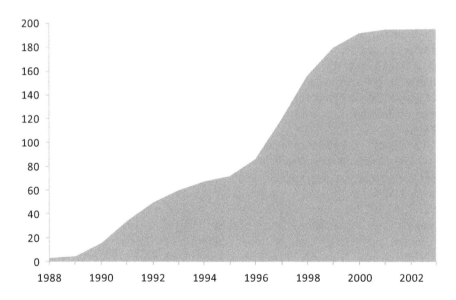

Figure 9 Latin American Cumulative Amount Raised by Privatizations (1988–2003). (In billion USD). *Source: De la Torre and Schmukler (2007).*

387

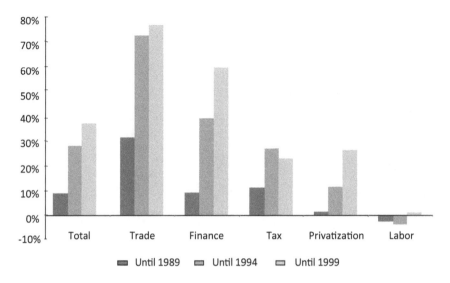

Figure 10 Latin American Advance of Reforms (1989–1999). Note: The advance of the reforms is measured as the margin for reform existing in 1985 that has been utilized by 1989, 1995 and 1999. *Source: Lora (2001).*

with the U.S. narrowed significantly, while countries pursued policies that were not framed in the Washington Consensus spirit of liberalization, privatization and macroeconomic stabilization. The exception in the disappointing growth picture for Latin America was Chile, which became the poster child of the Washington Consensus policy agenda. Real GDP growth in this country rose to an average of 6.4 percent per annum during the 1990s from 4.5 percent in the 1980s, so that the ratio of Chilean to U.S. per capita income increased significantly over the decade (Figure 1).

Outcomes in the social arena were even more disappointing. Consider first poverty. The expectation was that the pickup of growth in the 1990s, modest though it was, would lead to a proportional reduction in poverty.[22] That expectation was not realized. While the region's per capita GDP increased by a cumulative 12 percent from 1990 to 2000, poverty rate (measured at 4 dollars a day in PPP terms) did not decrease (Figure 11). Moreover, the absolute number of poor in the region (calculated on the basis of countries' own definitions of the poverty line) remained roughly constant, at around 200 million people throughout the 1990s (World Bank, 2009). Similar figures from ECLAC (2010) give a 1.5 percent yearly growth from 1990 to 2000 rate for Latin America and the Caribbean along with a slight decrease in poverty from 48.3 percent to 43.9 percent. Only in Chile did the poverty rate fall sharply, from 38.6 percent in 1990 to 20.2 percent in 2000.

The distributional outcomes were equally frustrating as income inequality remained stubbornly high throughout the 1990s (Figure 12). The non-weighted

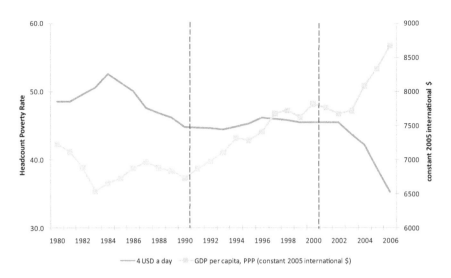

Figure 11 Latin American Poverty and GDP per capita (1980–2006). *Source: World Bank (2009b).*

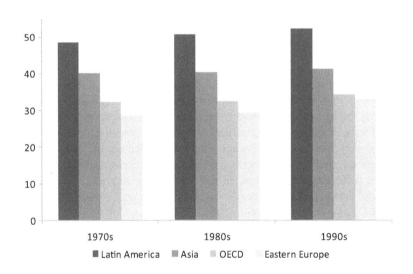

Figure 12 International Gini Coefficients (1970–1999). *Source: World Bank (2004).*

average Gini coefficient for income distribution in the region increased some-what, from 50.5 in the early 1990s to 51.4 in 2000, while the weighted average remained virtually unchanged (World Bank, 2004).[23] Even Chile's Gini coeffi-cient was stuck at around 55 during the 1990s. The fact is that income inequality is stickier than poverty everywhere and has remained stubbornly high in the region

389

for decades (declining later on for the first time, and only modestly, in Brazil and Mexico during the 2002–2007 period of faster growth).[24]

From a strictly technical point of view, the limited progress on social outcomes might have been foreseen. The Washington Consensus reforms, as will be seen later, were mainly meant to liberalize and stabilize the economies and allow for growth, not reduce inequality. But to the extent that the 1990s became in the public consciousness the decade of the Washington Consensus reforms, and those reforms became synonymous with expectations of social and economic growth outcomes, expectations were disappointed.

5.2 Counter-Factual Overview

There is little doubt that outcomes during the 1990s in terms of growth, poverty and inequality were disheartening relative to expectations. But would the assessment change if the focus is placed on reform impacts not relative to expectations but compared to the counterfactual—i.e., to what would have happened in the absence of Consensus-style policies? This line of inquiry—evidently of greater interest to academics than to the average citizen—has given rise to copious empirical research. When all is said and done, the preponderance of the econometric evidence arising from this research suggests that Latin America would have been worse off without the reforms. Per capita income and output in the 1990s would have been lower and poverty deeper. Moreover, the relatively strong performance of Latin America during the global crisis of 2008–2009 can be attributed to a significant extent to improvements in macroeconomic and financial fundamentals resulting in part from the reforms of the 1990s and early 2000s (more on this later).

The results from econometric studies have to be taken with a large grain of salt considering the numerous and thorny technical complications with the associated empirical tests. These include: small sample sizes; the potential presence of global trends that may affect both reforms and outcomes; difficulties in quantitatively isolating impacts; complications in establishing a causal relationships; problems with adequately measuring reforms, their degree of implementation and, even more, their quality; and the dependency of results on time periods under investigation. In any case, while studies differ in terms of evidence and methodology and their results are difficult to compare, a general pattern emerges: earlier research that focuses on the first half of the 1990s tends to produce results that are more favorable to Consensus-style reforms than later research focusing on the second half of the 1990s.

An important paper that sets the tone in the earlier wave of research is Lora and Barrera (1997). These authors compare 1987–1989 with 1993–1995 and find that structural reforms and their accompanying macro stabilization spurred growth by 2.2 percentage points relative to the growth rate that would have been obtained in the absence of reforms, of which 1.9 points are due to structural reforms and the remainder to stabilization policies. Other studies in this group went further to argue that actual growth performance in the region during the first part of the 1990s was better than that predicted by econometric models. In this sense, growth outcomes are considered to have exceeded expectations—if expectations are defined as those arising from econometric predictions. For example, Easterly, Loayza and Montiel (1997), using a panel from 1960 to 1993 with 70 countries, 16 of them Latin American, find that reforms allowed the region to return to a 2 percent per capita growth rate from 1991 to 1993, a rate that—given country characteristics and the relative depth of the reforms implemented—was higher than predicted by their model. Similarly, Fernández-Arias and Montiel (1997), using a panel from 1961 to 1995 with 69 countries, 18 of which were Latin American, find that the aggregate contribution of stabilization and structural reforms to long-run growth was 1.84 percentage points and argue that, despite a negative external environment, Latin American growth during the 1990s was greater than otherwise predicted.

While the generation of early research converges on the view that reforms boosted growth in the first half of the 1990s by about 2 percentage points,[25] later studies have a much less favorable assessment. For example, Lora and Panizza (2002) compare 1985–1987 with 1997–1999 and find that the reforms lifted growth in the latter period by only 0.6 percentage points. They conclude that the beneficial impact of reforms decreased as the 1990s unfolded and that their effects were largely transitory, raising the level of income but not the rate of growth. A series of studies spearheaded by ECLAC also yielded very modest results and Ffrench-Davis (2000) calls for the reforming of the reforms. Escaith and Morley (2001) find a minimal and non-robust effect of the reforms taken as a whole. Stallings and Peres (2000) conclude that a 10 percent increase in the overall reform index boosted growth by a meager 0.2 of a percentage point and that the effects of individual reforms were ambiguous. While import liberalization, privatization and capital account opening had a positive effect, the same is not true for the tax or the financial reforms. In a review article, Ocampo (2004) notes that the positive post-reform performance in the first part of the 1990s stands in contrast with the low growth of the "lost-half decade" of 1998–2002, stressing that growth during the decade was sluggish and volatile.

Studies on the effects of Consensus-style reforms on poverty and inequality, independent of their growth effects, are rarer, with the notable exceptions of Székely and Londoño (1998) Morley (2000), and Behrman, Birdsall and Székely (2007). Most studies conclude that financial sector liberalization was associated with an increase in income inequality, though with diminishing effects over time. Other reforms, including privatization, seem to have reduced inequality. The privatization of water and other services actually improved access for the poor and reduced the prices they paid (see studies in Nellis and Birdsall, 2005). But the overall effect of the reforms was at best neutral and at worst harmful in terms of income inequality outcomes.

5.3 Bottom Line

The conclusion is inescapable that, with the exception of Chile, outcomes during the 1990s generally fell significantly short of the reformers' expectations. Even if inequality is not considered, growth and poverty reduction outcomes were disheartening when compared to the intensity of the reform effort. There is reasonable support for the technical counterfactual argument that growth in the first part of the 1990s would have been lower and poverty higher in the absence of Consensus-type reforms. But even this view loses force when: the years beyond 1997 are taken into account, individual reforms are examined separately and growth volatility (not just the growth rate) is also considered. Moreover, the counterfactual reasoning—that without reforms things would have been worse—provides little consolation to the region's many poor and unemployed citizens.

The sense of disenchantment with the Washington Consensus deepened dramatically in the late-1990s and early-2000s when the region was hit by a wave of financial turbulence that pushed several countries into crippling twin (banking and currency) crises, including Ecuador (1999–2000), Argentina (2001–2002), Uruguay (2002) and the Dominican Republic (2003). Not surprisingly, during 2001–2003 per capita income growth in the region was negative even as other regions in the world enjoyed positive growth.

As the region entered the new millennium not only did the Washington Consensus lose support but it also generated vibrant opposition in many quarters. With societies disappointed by the outcomes, policy makers found little or no ground to mobilize the political coalitions needed for additional doses of Consensus-style reforms.[26] Not surprisingly, the region entered into a period of structural reform fatigue, as economic reforms stalled in most Latin American countries around 1997 (Lora 2001 and Lora et al. 2004).

The puzzle then is what went wrong with the Washington Consensus? To this issue we turn next.

6. What Went Wrong?

Setting ideological differences aside, there is a wide range of economic views on what went wrong with the Consensus-style reform program. This variety of views should of course come as no surprise, for the same evidence examined from different perspectives can lead to different diagnoses. This section provides a flavor of the range of perspectives on the subject by classifying them into three typological views, each of which provides a distinct and nonreducible answer to the question of what went wrong, namely:

i. There was nothing wrong with the Consensus reform program itself. The problem was the faulty implementation of the reforms (including due to political economy constraints) combined with impatience regarding their effects.
ii. The Consensus reform program was fundamentally flawed. This view has two very different variants. Variant one: the Consensus failed to consider sequencing issues and threshold effects. Variant two: the Consensus was based on a simplistic and ultimately wrong understanding of the linkages between policy reform and economic outcomes.

392

iii. The Consensus reform program was not wrong in what it included but it did not include all that was needed. The Consensus was thus patently incomplete. It was based on too narrow a view of what matters for economic development and, as a result, left out essential areas for reform action.

Each of these contrasting views captures a relevant aspect of the debate, bringing out points that are mostly complementary but sometimes fundamentally at odds with each other. The reader should not make too much of this taxonomy of views, as there is no presumption that it represents a complete set nor that it is necessarily superior to potential alternative taxonomies. It should be seen essentially as a framework constructed from hindsight to help organize and discuss in an orderly fashion the salient aspects of, and discrepancies in, the assessment of the Washington Consensus.

6.1. Faulty Implementation and Impatience

According to this view, the Washington Consensus was fundamentally right in its principles, content and overall design. The set of Consensus-inspired reforms was fairly complete and reflects international "best practices" that are, by and large, of general applicability across developing countries and for a broad range of development stages. Moreover, in line with the econometric evidence presented, Consensus-style reforms were part of the solution and not the problem. Consistent with this view, Fernández-Arias and Montiel (1997) argue that "most of the enormous growth gap with East Asia (...) is explained by incomplete reform" and could be closed by "pushing further in the direction of the reforms that have already been implemented." A more recent study by the IMF (2005) blames the poor post-reform outcomes on uneven and incomplete reform implementation.[27]

Hence, supporters of this view argue that the shortfall in the outcomes relative to expectations was not due to flaws with the Consensus reform package itself but to the deficient manner in which it was executed. Reforms were unevenly implemented, hence the uneven outcomes. Where reforms were implemented more deeply and consistently (i.e., Chile) they were associated with impressive growth and poverty reduction outcomes. In the majority of countries, however, reforms, even when initiated, were insufficiently implemented or suffered reversals. In many cases, when laws were passed they were not adequately enforced or regulatory changes, institutional adaptations and capacity building did not follow. In other cases, key reforms were not even initiated (as in the labor field).

Moreover—this view contends—reformers were too impatient, unreasonably expecting results to materialize sooner than warranted. While the expectation of a rapid payoff was justified with respect to some types of first-generation reforms—especially in the macroeconomic stabilization arena—it was unrealistic for the more complex structural reforms that typically require long implementation and gestation periods. Looking back from 2010, a case can be made that the payoff of sustained reform did come for Latin America, when the global crisis of

2008–2009 hit. Countries such as Brazil, Chile, Colombia, Mexico, and Peru that persevered in implementing sound macroeconomic policies over the past fifteen years and that reacted with appropriate reforms to the crises of the late-1990s— by introducing greater exchange rate flexibility, developing local-currency debt markets, reducing currency mismatches and modernizing financial regulation and supervision—came out of the recent global crisis bruised to be sure, but without systemic damage. Those reforms helped reduce systemic vulnerability, prepared the countries to better face financial globalization, and enabled them to undertake countercyclical policies to cushion the effects of the external shock and avoid a systemic crises at home (Porzecanski, 2009; Rojas-Suarez, ed., 2009, and World Bank 2010a). This illustrates that patience and sustained implementation of Consensus-style reforms pays off in the long run.

This view does not ignore the costs of reforms, including those arising from transitory instability. But it notes that this is as it should be, since teething pains and even crises are part and parcel of the market-oriented development process.[28] The opening and competition that result from liberalization may increase instability in the short run but also help expose weaknesses and foster a cleansing process that ultimately strengthens defenses and stimulates further reform.[29] Over time, through pain and success, learning takes place and incentives are eventually set right, yielding durable results. Chile's strengths owe in no small part to a constructive reaction to the painful crises of the late 1970s and early 1980s. The message that naturally arises from this view is the need to persevere. Reforms must be sustained and consistent. And along the path to economic development a premium should be placed on letting market discipline work, recognizing that it sets in motion a process of "creative destruction" that involves short-term pain and long-term gain.

The emphasis going forward, this view would stress, should be on overcoming political resistance to reform implementation, as it is now well known that politics mattered much more than reformers anticipated. Much of the political economy constraints revolve around the collective action problem. That is, the difficulty of mobilizing broad support for reform given the *status quo* bias that emerges from self-reinforcing factors, including the fact that losses from reform have to be absorbed upfront while the (greater) gains accrue overtime, and the fact that losers are easy to identify and typically well-informed and well-organized (which boosts their capacity to lobby against reform) while winners (including future generations) are dispersed, unorganized and prefer to free ride.[30] Taking into account the political economy of reform implementation is essential to complement the technical soundness of reforms.

6.2. Fundamental Flaws

This view, in sharp contrast with the previous one, finds the Washington Consensus agenda to be seriously flawed in some fundamental sense. It involves two variants that are very different in nature.

The first variant is the sequencing critique. The original formulation of the Consensus was mostly silent on sequencing. It left open the question whether the outcomes would be similar, independently of whether reforms were implemented simultaneously or separately and, in the latter case, regardless of the order of implementation. A key focus of this critique, though by no means not the only one, is on premature financial market liberalization—the de-regulation of the domestic financial system and opening of the external capital account ahead of adequate regulatory strengthening. A wrong sequencing of reforms in this field can turn the normal pains of growing up into unnecessary suffering, as financial crises can rapidly wipe out gains achieved over several decades (Bhagwati, 1998 and Stiglitz, 2002).

Earlier versions of the sequencing critique to financial liberalization applied mainly to the domestic banking system. Weak banking systems are ill-prepared to operate prudently in freer financial markets and properly intermediate surges in capital inflows. As a result, they become prone to credit bubbles followed by credit busts (Gavin and Hausmann, 1996). Therefore, a minimum threshold of institutional strength—in terms of the legal framework, regulatory system, supervisory capacity, and accounting and disclosure standards—should be in place before liberalizing the financial system.[31]

In the second half of the 1990s, the critique was first applied to the domestic banking system.[32] Weak banking systems are ill-prepared to operate prudently in freer financial markets and properly intermediate surges in capital inflows, becoming prone to credit bubbles followed by credit busts (Gavin and Hausmann, 1996). A minimum threshold of institutional strength should be in place before liberalizing the financial system. This sort of sequence is of course easier to implement in countries where financial systems are repressed by administrative controls and the capital account is relatively closed. But what to do with respect to countries whose financial system is already liberalized? Some would counsel emerging economies to roll back capital market opening and "throw sand in the wheels," including through the use of Chilean-style disincentives on short-term "hot money" inflows. Some would even suggest that liberalization of capital flows should be managed on a permanent basis (Fukuyama and Birdsall (eds.), forthcoming 2010), as full financial integration might never be desirable (Ocampo, 2003; Stiglitz, 1999 and 2000; and Tobin, 2000). Others would advocate delaying further liberalization while attention is reoriented towards re-prioritizing reforms, in favor of strengthening in earnest the regulatory and institutional preconditions.

A later version of the financial sequencing critique—stemming from the so-called 'original sin' literature—focuses on currency and maturity mismatches in the balance sheets of borrowers. The "original sin" consists of the inability of emerging economy sovereigns and corporates to issue long-term domestic currency denominated debt, which begets the currency mismatches that, in turn, raise systemic vulnerability. In a first incarnation, this literature recommended the adoption of formal dollarization to bypass the "original sin" (Calvo and Reinhart,

2000; Hausmann et al., 1999). In light of the disastrous collapse of the Argentine currency board,[33] a second incarnation of this literature focused, instead, on sequencing—the need to develop the market for domestic currency denominated debt *before* completely opening the capital account (Eichengreen, Hausmann and Panizza, 2005). Proponents point to Australia as an example of a country that got this sequence right, one that is arguably also being adopted by the two largest emerging economies—India and China (Lane and Schmukler, 2006).

In general, sequencing arguments can also involve a reference to threshold effects—i.e., the notion that positive outcomes cannot be attained unless a minimum degree of implementation of an appropriate combination of complementary reforms is achieved. This perspective leads to the recommendation that reforms should be ordered so as to ensure that certain preconditions are put in place first to enhance the likelihood of success of subsequent reforms. Thus, the best designed fiscal rules would not work well in the absence of institutional preconditions that prevent, say, populist governments from arbitrarily breaking rules and contracts. This perspective also leads to the warning that there may be little or no gain (and maybe even significant losses) if a critical mass of complementary reforms is not implemented in a coordinated fashion (Rojas-Suarez, ed., 2009).

There are many more aspects to the debate on sequencing and threshold effects.[34] Trade liberalization in the absence of a safety net can undermine poverty reduction, and privatization short of an adequate regulatory framework may lead to monopoly pricing. In some cases, the resulting political backlash can also short-circuit the reform process itself. Initial uncorrected flaws may compromise implementation. In all, the "right" sequence is easier to define on paper than in the real world where reformers usually had to make do with second-best approaches in the face of political constraints. As such, sequencing remains largely an academic consideration.

Consider now the second variant of the view that the Washington Consensus incurred fundamental flaws. It contends that the main error was the Consensus' apparent assumption that a one-to-one mapping exists always and everywhere between reforms and economic outcomes. The reality is, however, much more complex and elusive. Even perfect sequencing could lead to faulty outcomes depending on their mapping to reforms. As noted by Hausmann, Rodrik and Velasco (2008), reforms that "work wonders in some places may have weak, unintended, or negative effects in others." The empirical evidence that specific reform packages have predictable, robust, and systematic effects on national growth rates is weak (Rodrik, 2005a).[35] Much of the variance that explains the difference in countries' growth rates is random, which implies that imitating successful reform experiences of other countries may not be wise (Easterly et al., 1993). In sum, contrary to the implicit understanding of the Washington Consensus as generally applicable, effective reform agendas have to be carefully tailored to individual country circumstances, both in their design and implementation sequence. The expectation that reforms would promise certain good outcomes almost automatically was simply wrong.

It does not necessarily follow from this variant that anything goes when it comes to growth determinants and the design of reform packages. A constructive and nuanced way forward is feasible under this view, as illustrated in Dani Rodrik's (2005b) "Growth Strategies" chapter in the *Handbook of Economic Growth*. While specific reform packages must be tailor-made, good economics highlights the crucial relevance of growth "foundations" or "first principles," notably the role of technological innovation and institutions such as property rights, sound money, fiscal viability and contestable markets (Growth Commission 2008 and Rojas-Suarez, ed., 2009). Although the mapping of first principles to specific reform packages is elusive and country-specific, it can be adequately served by diverse policy packages.

Moreover, growth strategies must be informed by the critical distinction between *igniting* and *sustaining* growth (Hausmann, Pritchett and Rodrik, 2005). Igniting growth in a particular country typically requires a few (often unconventional) reforms that need not unduly tax the country's limited institutional capacity. But the exact composition of these few reforms and how they can successfully be combined with "first principles" cannot be predicted easily—it varies from country to country. Sustaining growth is a different matter—it requires the cumulative building of functional institutions to maintain productive dynamism and endow the economy with resilience to shocks over the long term. A sensible growth strategy would search for the tailor-made agenda of few reforms that can ignite a growth process. Once ignited, growth itself can help align incentives in the political economy in favor of reforms that strengthen the growth foundations, thus setting in motion a virtuous circle that sustains growth over the long haul.

Putting together growth-oriented reform programs that are adequately adapted to a given country is then a much more difficult and complex task than the Washington Consensus led people to believe. But it is not an impossible task. To avoid getting things wrong, there is no substitute for deep country knowledge and experience. To use an analogy often mentioned by the late Rudy Dornbusch, good reformers are like good "country doctors" than can develop good diagnoses and suitable cures for individual patients whom they know well. Adequately designed and appropriately implemented reforms are more likely to be developed by well-trained, practically minded, and experienced economists that collectively have not only a good grasp of international reform practices but also experience in and strong knowledge of the circumstances of the country in question. These packages will, by definition, stay away from the mechanical application of 'best practices' and from un-prioritized laundry list-type reform agendas. They will also stay away from the pessimistic belief that nothing can be done where institutions are weak. Much help can be obtained in this process from a finer "growth diagnostics" method, one that focuses on the binding constraints to growth, rather than on the distance to "best practices," along the lines of the method proposed by Hausmann, Rodrik and Velasco (2008).[36] While not a silver bullet, this method can greatly complement the task of reform prioritization and design.

6.3 Incomplete Agenda

This third view agrees with the first one in stating that the Consensus reform program was not wrong in what it included. But it differs from it in claiming that the Consensus was patently incomplete, that it did not include all the relevant reforms needed to achieve sustainable and equitable growth. The Consensus simply had too narrow an understanding of what matters for economic growth and development.

Trying to assemble a comprehensive list of important reform areas left out by the Consensus is a rather futile exercise—for the components chosen for inclusion are not independent of the perspective adopted and the preferences of the researcher—and one that in any case lies beyond the scope of this chapter. In what follows, therefore, we illustrate this view using as guidance key flagship reports published by multilateral development agencies (World Bank, IDB, ECLAC and CAF) since the second half of the 1990s. Using headline publications from some of the institutions that supported (and at times actively championed) the Consensus during the 1990s helps to highlight the growing acceptance of this third view.

Among the many reform areas left out by the Washington Consensus are: (a) volatility; (b) institutions; (c) knowledge and technological innovation; and (d) equity.[37] What these areas have in common is the presence of significant market failures (due to externalities, coordination problems and imperfect information) which markets themselves cannot repair and that thus require active policy. They were not seen as part of Consensus-style reform agenda basically because the Consensus relied on well-functioning markets to solve the relevant development challenges and viewed any state interference in the economy with suspicion. Successful reformers, like Chile, also implemented important reforms in these other areas, thus supplementing the Washington Consensus.

Consider first *volatility*. By focusing on the first moment—the average or expected value of reform effects—Washington Consensus-style policies ignored the crucial relevance of the second moment—the variance of such effects. The fact is that volatility has an independent, first-order impact on economic development. This argument was forcibly put forward in the 1995 annual report of the IDB *Overcoming Volatility*. It discussed Latin America's proneness to volatility, driven by a high incidence of external shocks whose effects are magnified by shallow financial markets and inconsistent macro policies. Volatility is estimated to have reduced the region's historical growth rate by one percentage point, with particularly strong negative impacts on investment in infrastructure and human capital, and especially detrimental impacts on poverty and inequality. To overcome volatility, reforms need to put a premium on export diversification, financial market deepening and stable macroeconomic, particularly fiscal, policy.[38]

Subsequent reports of the World Bank and ECLAC drove home similar arguments and worries. The 2000 flagship publication of the Latin America region of the World Bank, *Securing our Future in the Global Economy,* raised policy issues from the macroeconomic, social, financial, labor and poverty dimensions. At ECLAC, Ffrench-Davis and Ocampo (2001) argued that financial liberalization brought with it the globalization of volatility and a new variety of crises linked to shocks to the newly deregulated emerging capital markets. Indiscriminate opening of the capital account led to macroeconomic and financial disequilibria, placing countries in a "frnancierist trap" of high vulnerability. To escape the trap, a relatively flexible exchange rate and comprehensive macroeconomic regulation is recommended.

Consider next *institutions*. The Consensus overlooked the institutional underpinnings of its proposed policies, with one key exception: establishing secure property rights which, in the spirit of De Soto (1989), should also be available to the informal sector. However, quoting Rodrik (2006), property rights "was the last item on the list and came almost as an afterthought." Williamson himself shared the view (see Birdsall and de la Torre, 2001) that property rights were added "mostly to get to a total of 10 items." In general, the Consensus was largely blind to institutions. It came at the end of the 1980s before what amounted to an institutional revolution in the development economics literature in the 1990s.

While institutions became firmly established among academic economists since the 1980s,[39] multilateral agencies jumped onto the institutional bandwagon starting in the late 1990s, as the realization grew stronger that the efficiency of markets and durability of reform effects needs appropriate institutional frameworks to avoid such problems as rent-seeking and policy reversals. In Latin America, this was illustrated in the IDB's 1997 report *Latin America after a Decade of Reforms* as well as the 1998 World Bank's regional flagship entitled *Beyond the Washington Consensus: Institutions Matter.* The former summarizes the evidence on the role of institutions in long run economic development, makes a case in favor of the feasibility of institutional reform, and offers a policy-oriented analysis of institutional reform issues in the financial sector, education, judicial systems and public administration. The latter develops an analytical framework and uses case studies to explain why policy reform processes that work in certain institutional environments may not work in others. The institutional literature also influenced the 2008 Growth Commission Report chaired by Michael Spence, which concludes that there can be no simple recipe for growth and sustainable development, implying that too much is country-specific to define any general policy consensus.

Consider now *knowledge and technological innovation.* If the Washington Consensus touched on this area, it did so indirectly—when it advocated the reorientation of public expenditure towards education and emphasized the need to remove barriers to FDI. The latter was intended not just to enhance competition but also to facilitate technological transfer. That the Consensus did not delve more deeply into policies related to technological innovation is somewhat surprising. After all, technological progress is at the heart of market-based growth and has been regarded as the main driver of productivity growth in economic theory since the times of Robert Solow's publications in the 1950s. The implicit assumption in Consensus-style reform agendas seems to have been that policies to promote export orientation and the opening to FDI would be sufficient to achieve the adoption and adaptation of new technologies as well as to eventually foster the capacity to innovate.

While the theme of knowledge and innovation was never absent from the academic literature, multilateral agencies sought to bring it squarely into Latin American development policy thinking during the early 2000s. An important precursor was ECLAC's 1990 report on *Productive Transformation with Equity*. Later on, the Latin American region of the World Bank devoted its 2002 flagship publication to the need to shift *From Natural Resources to the Knowledge Economy*. This publication was subsequently complemented by the 2003 regional flagship on *Closing the Gap in Education and Technology* and the work of Lederman and Maloney (2007). This body of research argues that the region's growth has not lagged behind due to a natural-resource curse but due to a major shortfall in technological adoption and innovation. The regional deficiency in "national learning capacity" is not independent of its gap in the quality of its education (Figure 13 shows LAC's backwardness in this regard), which along with entrepreneurship constitutes a key ingredient for innovation. A premium should then be placed on policies to diversify international trade and foreign direct investment flows, improve education (particularly secondary and tertiary), deepen the links between universities and the private sector, and foster the development of innovation networks.

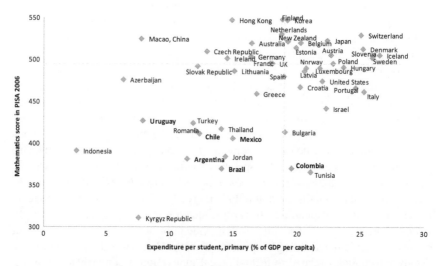

Figure 13 International Education Expenditure vs. PISA Scores (2006). Note: Public expenditure per student is the public current spending on education divided by the total number of students in the primary level. *Source: Program for International Student Assessment (2006) and World Development Indicators (2010).*

Around that time, the IDB and the Andean Development Corporation (CAF) focused on the role of knowledge and technology in growth from the perspective of competitiveness. They did so through their annual reports entitled, respectively, *Competitiveness: the Business of Growth* (IDB, 2001) and *Competiveness and Growth* (Sachs and Vial, 2002). ECLAC also launched a 2008 Report on *Structural Change and Productivity Growth.* To correct the low levels of factor accumulation and productivity in Latin America, policies should aim at alleviating credit constraints, modernizing labor markets, boosting human capital investment, easing infrastructure bottlenecks, and fostering the development of clusters and supply chains.

Consider finally *equity*. As noted, it was in the social arena where the disenchantment with the Washington Consensus was greatest. Williamson himself later declared (see Birdsall and De la Torre, 2001) that the Consensus policies he compiled were oriented towards achieving efficiency, not equity, and that he "deliberately excluded from the list anything which was primarily redistributive [because he] felt that the Washington of the 1980s (...) was essentially contemptuous of equity concerns."

When it comes to economic development, equity considerations are not simply a helpful corollary, but an essential ingredient, especially in unequal Latin America. For one thing, equity is in itself as important a developmental objective as growth—not least considering that excessive inequality of outcomes and high inequality of opportunity constitute an insult to our basic sense of justice. To the extent that reforms' uneven outcomes reflect unequal opportunities—across racial or ethnic groups and between those born poor as those born rich— their sense of unfairness also undermines the legitimacy of those reforms. Moreover, by failing to more explicitly deal with equity, the Washington Consensus neglected what is in effect a key impediment to growth. High income inequality not only hinders the impact of growth on poverty reduction but can itself contribute to low growth which, in turn, makes it difficult to reduce inequality. Institutions and policies in contexts with high poverty rates and heavy concentrations of income may themselves be a source of growth-impairing inefficiency (Aghion et al., 1999; World Bank, 2006; Levy and Walton, 2009; Demirguc-Kunt and Levine, 2009). Under those conditions, the interplay among political parties, business organizations and powerful large labor unions can result in rent-seeking and monopoly behavior that undermines the growth gains the reforms were meant to capture. Similarly, imperfect credit markets combined with unequal endowments of financial and human capital—typical of Latin America—are widely acknowledged as a constraint on growth, implying that inequality itself is worth addressing explicitly to minimize that perverse combination.

It was precisely in the failure to include an explicit concern with equity that Birdsall, De la Torre and Menezes (2008) find the most notable shortcoming of Washington Consensus-inspired reform packages. The omission undermined the benefits of and enthusiasm for market oriented reforms. In a booklet first published in 2001 under the title *Washington Contentious* and subsequently expanded into a 2008 book entitled *Fair Growth*, these authors discuss win-win policies that would serve the interests of greater equity while enhancing growth directly and indirectly. They reaffirm the relevance of fiscal discipline and counter-cyclical macroeconomic and financial policies. But they also emphasize new areas for policy action, including the establishment of automatic social safety nets; improving schooling for the poor; making income taxes progressive in practice; building a more supportive environment for small businesses; protecting worker rights and labor mobility; launching a head-on attack on corruption and discrimination; repairing land markets and establishing consumer-driven public services.

The equity theme was also bought to the center stage of the development policy debate through official publications by multilateral agencies. In its 1998 annual report *Facing Up to Inequality in Latin America* the IDB studied the resilience of the region's high inequality, attributing the gap mainly to wage differentials in a segmented labor market and underlying educational disparity. ECLAC focused on this issue in its 2001 *Equity, Development and Citizenship*, where redistributive fiscal policies were highlighted. Inequality was also tackled in the World Bank's 2004 regional flagship *Inequality in Latin America and the Caribbean: Breaking with History?* The report emphasizes the deep historical roots of inequality and its multidimensionality, affecting not just income but also the distribution of education, health, water, sanitation, electricity and telecommunication provision. It recommends using the redistributive power of the state through progressive taxation, basic service provision and transfers. It also advocates policies aimed at broadening asset ownership by democratizing education, improving land distribution, investing in public infrastructure and making labor markets truly inclusive.

7. Concluding Remarks

For all of its faults, the policies set out in Williamson's original Washington Consensus hold enduring messages. Countries that ignore them do so at their peril. If there is any consensus about the Consensus, it is especially with respect to sound macroeconomic policy, including not only fiscal discipline (still a challenge in most of the region) and transparent and steady monetary policy, but arguably also the logic of flexible exchange rates with a small dose of management. On these the Consensus aptly reflected the direction taken by most Latin policymakers since the late 1980s, by then already deeply allergic to the region's periodic and destructive bouts of inflation. This allergy was shared by citizens and voters virtually everywhere making it politically possible for small technically adept cadre to implement the appropriate stabilization policies in line with the Consensus (Naím, 2000). On these macroeconomic policies the controversy has focused not on the merits of the policies themselves, but on the role of the IMF and the World Bank in conditioning their lending not only on reasonable fixes to macro problems but also on privatization, trade and capital market liberalization and other structural policies, leaving aside the supportive institutional matrix to an extent that in many countries turned out to be politically toxic.

While the Consensus is typically criticized for its dogmatic adherence to market fundamentalism, the view that development must be market based has in fact endured—not only in Latin America, the original home of the Consensus, but throughout the developing world (Birdsall, forthcoming 2010). The reliance on markets to foster development is in effect a New Consensus among emerging markets and other developing countries, and it has survived well the crises of the second half of the 1990s and early-2000s as well as the global crisis of 2008–2009, including in Africa (Radelet, forthcoming 2010). To be sure, warring parties have engaged over the past quarter century in heated debates about the merits and shortcomings of the Consensus (defined variously as the original ten points, market fundamentalism, neo-liberalism or multiple variations of those). Yet beyond the differences, the great majority of developing countries— across the ideological spectrum from China to Chile—in fact adhere to a market orientation and indeed to a quest for safe integration into global markets.

So, on the one hand, the love-and-hate affair with the 1989 Washington Consensus might be over. On the other, for developing countries including across Latin America, the marriage of the state to markets is firmly in place. But a complex challenge that will test any new consensus going forward will be on how to manage and adapt that marriage in a shock-prone global economy. Global shocks widen the gap between private and social interests and increase the premium on global public goods and global collective action—as was brutally highlighted by the subprime crisis turned global. For Latin America, the limits and benefits of the role of the state in a global economy will once again be on the agenda, and arguably with a greater sense of urgency

We are grateful to the editors, Mauricio Cárdenas, Alan Gelb, Rudolf Hommes, Santiago Levy, Sergio Schmukler, and John Williamson for very helpful comments, and to Sandy Stonesifer for able research assistance. The views expressed here are those of the authors and do not necessarily represent the views of the Center for Global Development or the World Bank Group.

Notes

1 These classic arguments have been formalized theoretically in terms of principal-agent problems, scale effects, and externalities (Hoff and Stiglitz, 2001; and Murphy, Shleifer, and Vishny, 1989).

2 For Prebisch and Singer, the decline of the terms of trade for primary commodities was secular. It emanated from the combination of a low income and price of global demand for commodities, on the one hand, and the excessive dependence of the periphery on primary goods exports, on the other. It thus led to systematic resource transfers from the commodity-intensive periphery to the capital-intensive center.

3 ISI was politically attractive and ideologically appealing for key interest groups that were increasingly entrenched. Overvalued exchange rates ensured cheap imports of capital goods for the rising industrial class, along with protection of their consumer

products in the domestic market. Cheap borrowing on external markets and easy fiscal and monetary policies allowed for expanding job creation in urban areas, including in the public sector and state enterprises. By protecting activities oriented towards the domestic market and using an overvalued exchange rate to keep urban prices low, ISI policies acted as a tax on exporting agriculture. This dislodged the traditional power of large hacienda owners and contributed to increasing rural-urban migration, while creating a powerful new set of political constituencies in the rapidly growing urban areas (Lipton, 1977).

4 For example, Argentina and Brazil borrowed heavily to finance import-substitution while Mexico mainly to increase public spending. By contrast, public borrowing had little impact in Chile and Colombia.

5 The beginning of the Debt Crisis was marked by a fateful 1982 meeting in Washington D.C. when Mexican officials announced their payment difficulties to the US Secretary of Treasury. Mexican and Brazilian bond spreads skyrocketed 600 to 800 basis points. As the IMF offered Mexico U\$5 billion in emergency lending, Mexico nationalized the banks and announced that principal payments on the foreign debt would be suspended until 1984.

6 For analyses of ISI in Latin America see Hirschman (1968), Baer (1972), Balassa (1980) and Fishlow (1987). A more positive assessment is Thorp (1998) *History of Latin America in the 20ᵗʰ Century* and its companion volumes.

7 In terms of net external transfer of resources, Latin America and the Caribbean swung from inward net transfers of U\$11.3 billion in 1981 to net outward transfers U\$18.7 billion in 1982 and to an average outward transfer of US\$26.4 billion from 1982 to 1986.

8 The debt overhang is defined by debt levels that are high enough as to act as a 100 percent marginal tax on investment effort, thus undercutting growth. See Myers (1977), Krugman (1988) and Corden (1991).

9 The role of the international financial institutions, which pushed for the reforms, often conditioning their loans on reform progress, remains a matter of debate. Reforms would not have been implemented only in response to outside pressure—but the pressure was probably not irrelevant to their timing and depth, and in some cases to the backlash that they created.

10 See, for instance, the World Bank's World Development Reports *International Capital and Economic Development* (1985); *Trade and Pricing Policies in World Agriculture* (1986); and *Industrialization and Foreign Trade* (1987) as well as the Inter-American Development Bank's Economic and Social Progress Reports *Economic Integration* (1984); *External Debt: Crisis and Adjustment* (1985); and *Agricultural Development* (1986).

11 During the 1970s and 1980s, the East Asian Tigers took off while LAC stagnated and lost ground. The ratio of per capita income (nominal dollars) of the East Asian Tigers to that of the United States rose from less than 20 percent in the late 1960s to around 40 percent by the late 1980s. By contrast, the same ratio for LAC hovered around 30 percent during the 1970s and fell to less than 25 percent by the late 1980s (see again, Figure 1).

12 A fixed peg (or a predetermined path for the nominal exchange rate) was used in several LAC countries during the 1990s to rein on inflation in an *initially* less contractionary manner. On the theory of exchange rate-based inflation stabilization see Dornbusch (1976); Calvo (1986); Kiguel and Liviatan (1992); and Rebelo and Vegh (1995).

13 If pushed too far, a narrow and unduly technocratic view exposes the Decalogue to countless criticisms, starting with the obvious one that "consensus" is too strong a term, a point made by Richard Feinberg during the 1989 IIE Conference itself. Feinberg argued that, given the wide spectrum of views and personalities in Washington institu-

tions, a better term would have been "convergence." A similar criticism concerns the time horizon of the policies considered. Rodrigo Botero (Williamson, 1990) argued, that "there is a certain consensus on short-term policy issues, less on medium-term issues (...), and still less on the long-term issues." Moreover, one would be hard pressed to argue that some of the specific policies in Williamson's article—such as the recommendation to tax interest on assets held abroad—commanded strong consensus at that time. In a broader and deeper sense, this narrow, technocratic characterization falls short of the mark.

14 For example, on capital markets reform see de la Torre and Schmukler (2007), de la Torre, Gozzi and Schmukler (2006 and 2007). On pension reform see Mesa-lago (2002), Gill et al. (2004), Impavido, Lasagabaster and Garcia-Huitrón (2010, forthcoming). On labor and trade reform see Heckman and Pagés-Serra (2000) and Fajnzylber and Maloney (2005).

15 This heterogeneity is in part captured by Lora's (1997) classification of Latin American countries into four groups: early reformers (Argentina, Chile, and Jamaica); gradual reformers (Colombia and Uruguay); recent (or late) reformers (Bolivia, El Salvador, Nicaragua, Paraguay, Peru, and the Dominican Republic); and slow reformers (Brazil, Costa Rica, Ecuador, Honduras, Mexico and Venezuela). See also Morley et al. (1999).

16 The advance of the reforms is measured as the margin for reform existing in 1985 that was utilized in subsequent years—for trade, financial, tax and privatization policies (see Lora, 1997 and 2001).

17 The actual motives for privatization ranged from the search for efficiency gains to the need for fiscal revenues or pure rent-seeking.

18 Brazil did not carry out a Chilean-style pension reform but pension funds account for a significant portion of Brazil's institutional investor base. At the end of 2004, Brazilian pension funds assets represented about 19 percent of GDP.

19 There were also other important reforms implemented during the 1990s which lie outside the scope of the Consensus but are of importance in assessing subsequent economic performance in the region. Several countries, for instance, adopted new constitutions and moved decidedly towards fiscal decentralization.

20 The Dominican Republic was another notable exception during the 1990s, especially in terms of robust growth performance.

21 On the generally low total factor productivity growth in Latin America during the 1990s, see Loayza, Fajnzylber and Calderón (2005). While overall productivity in the region was relatively low, except in the case of Chile, major productivity gains were realized in many countries at the sector level, especially in agriculture.

22 In a well-known article, Dollar and Kraay (2001) find a robust empirical regularity that the per capita income of the poor increases proportionately to average per capita income.

23 To the extent that public goods provision is not incorporated into the income-based Gini measures, inequality may be overstated.

24 The situation in the unemployment front was varied but job creation was generally weak during the 1990s and informality tended to increase (Stallings and Peres, 2000; and World Bank, 2007).

25 This result was confirmed later on by Loayza, Fajnzylber and Calderón (2005) who, comparing 1986–1990 with 1996–1999, estimated that structural reforms and accompanying macro stabilization policies had a 1.9 percentage point average impact on growth for Latin America for the decade as a whole. Loayza, Fajnzylber and Calderón (2005) is, however, an exception among the studies that appeared after 1997.

26 Public opinion polls (Latinobarometro) of the early 2000 found Latin Americans resentful of market-oriented reforms, especially privatization and tired of high unemployment and stagnant wages.

27 Additional renditions of this sort of message can be found in Krueger (2004) and World Bank (1997).

28 Aghion, Bacchetta, and Banerjee (2004) show theoretically that countries undergoing intermediate stages of financial development are likely to experience greater instability that countries in either advanced or early stages of financial development.

29 Consistent with this hypothesis, Kaminsky and Schmukler (2003) find that financial liberalization is associated with more pronounced boom-bust cycles in the short run but leads to more stable financial markets in the long run.

30 Fernandez and Rodrik (1991) argue that there can also be a *status quo* bias in the presence of uncertainty with regards to the distribution of gains and losses. Alesina and Drazen (1991), focusing on fiscal adjustment, conclude that any efficient policy change with significant distributional consequences can be delayed by a "war of attrition." Lora (2000) finds that crises are significant predictors of reform while Lora and Olivera (2005) show that reformers can pay a significant price in the ballots.

31 A number of theoretical papers show that financial liberalization may be associated with crises (see, for example, Allen and Gale, 2000; Bachetta and van Wincoop, 2000; Calvo and Mendoza, 2000; and McKinnon and Pill, 1997). Empirically, several papers have found links between financial deregulation, boom-bust cycles, and banking and balance of payments crises (see, for example, Corsetti, Pesenti, and Roubini, 1999; Demirguc-Kunt and Detragiache, 1999; Kaminsky and Reinhart, 1999; and Tornell and Westermann, 2005).

32 A brilliant, pre-Consensus rendition of the sequencing critique can be found in Diaz-Alejandro (1984).

33 On the rise and fall of the Argentine convertibility system see Cavallo and Cottani (1997), De la Torre, Levy Yeyati and Schmukler (2003), Perry and Serven (2003), and Galiani, Heymann and Tommasi (2003). For assessments of the conceptual and empirical basis in support of exchange rate flexibility see, for instance, Goldstein (2002), Larraín and Velasco (2001), and Mishkin and Savastano (2002). Prior to the early 2000s, hard-pegs or dollarization, on the one hand, and exchange rate flexibility, on the other, were seen as competing, albeit equally respectable, alternatives for emerging economies seeking a safe integration into international capital markets (Calvo and Reinhart, 2002; Eichengreen and Hausmann, 1999; Fischer, 2001; and Frankel, 1999).

34 Graham and Naím (1998), for instance, see macroeconomic stability as a precondition for more extensive and gradual institutional reform. Rodrik (1990) argues for undertaking a few, deep reforms with narrow scope. Martinelli and Tommasi (1997), by contrast, note that radical or so-called bitter pill reform strategies can be optimal due to credibility problems and political sustainability considerations.

35 The lack of robustness is highlighted by, for example, Levine and Renelt (1992), Rodriguez and Rodrik (2000), and Ciccone and Jarocinski (2007), who show that the empirical results of regressions on growth determinants are sensitive to changes in country samples, control variables and econometric specifications.

36 The authors couch their argument in a second-best framework. They focus not only on the direct (negative) effect of the specific distortion, but on the additional interactions of this distortion with the other inefficiencies in the economy. Given the impossibility of reaching the first best, the authors suggest focusing on the country's most binding constraints, as this increases the chances that the benefits of relaxing a binging constraint will not offset by indirect adverse effects. For a discussion of the growth diagnostics method along with applications to a number of Latin American countries see IDB (2009). On the limitations of the method see De la Torre (2007).

37 A key area that was completely ignored by the Washington Consensus and yet is not in this list is environmental sustainability, particularly climate change. This topic is

not developed here because it is as much about global as well as domestic policy. The topic was until recently relegated to sector experts but Nicholas Stern (2008) decidedly brought climate change to the core of development policy thinking, arguing that greenhouse gas emissions represent the biggest market failure the world has seen. That climate change has been finally mainstreamed into Latin American development policy thinking is illustrated by the 2009 flagship report of the Latin American Region of the World Bank entitled *Low Carbon, High Growth: Latin American Reponses to Climate* Change. For a global perspective, see the 2010 World Development Report *Development and Climate Change.*

38 Follow-up articles to this report, which expand on the analysis and conclusions, include Gavin and Hausman (1996) and Gavin et al. (1996). They highlight the interplay of volatility with the region's precarious access to international financial markets and fiscal pro-cyclicality and propose as additional solutions regional integration and collective risk hedging. In a similar vein, Caballero (2001) proposes a simple organizing framework to study shocks, volatility, and crises in the context of weak international financial integration and underdeveloped domestic financial markets. He advocates longer-term solutions via financial market deepening and prudential regulation; for the short-run, however, he argues for the use of international insurance as well as contingent monetary, fiscal and labor market policies.

39 The seminal work was that of Nobel laureate Douglas North (1990), who defines institutions as a "set of rules, compliance procedures and moral and ethical behavioral norms designed to constrain the behavior of individuals." A pioneering application of the institutional approach to development was Engerman and Sokoloff (1997), who trace differences in economic development throughout the Americas to the nature of colonial institutions interacting with initial resource endowments. Hall and Jones (1999) present evidence to support the thesis that "the primary, fundamental determinant of a country's long-run economic performance is its social infrastructure." It was perhaps the contributions of Acemoglu, Johnson and Robinson (2001 and 2002) that gave institutions a definitive push in the development profession. To address the endogeneity of institutions and income, they used the now famous colonial settler mortality instrument and conclude not only that institutions are key drivers of growth, but also that they are responsible for the reversal of fortunes of once rich nations. In a similar vein, the empirical study by Rodrik et al. (2004) finds that institutional variables, rather than integration or geographical variables, matter the most for economic development.

References

Acemoglu, Daron, Simon Johnson and James A. Robinson. "Reversal of Fortune: Geography and Institutions in the Making of the Modern World Income Distribution." *The Quarterly Journal of Economics.* Vol. 117, No. 4. (Nov. 2002), pp. 1231–1294.

Acemoglu, Daron, Simon Johnson and James A. Robinson. "The Colonial Origins of Comparative Development: An Empirical Investigation." *The American Economic Review.* Vol. 91, No. 5. (Dec. 2001), pp. 1369–1401.

Aghion Philippe, Eve Caroli and Cecilia Garcia-Peñalosa. "Inequality and Economic Growth: The Perspective of the New Growth Theories." *Journal of Economic Literature.* Vol. 37, No. 4. (Dec. 1999), pp. 1615–1660.

Aghion, Philippe, Philippe Bacchetta and Abhijit Banerjee, Abhijit. "Financial Development and the Instability of Open Economies." *Journal of Monetary Economics.* Vol. 51, Issue 6. (Sept. 2004), pp. 1077–1106.

Alesina, Alberto and Allan Drazen. "Why are Stabilizations Delayed?" *The American Economic Review,* Vol. 81, Issue 5. (Dec. 1991), pp. 1170–1188.

Allen, Franklin and Douglas Gale. "Bubbles and Crises." *The Economic Journal.* 110. (Jan. 2000), pp. 236–255.

Bacchetta, Philippe and Eric van Wincoop. 2000. "Capital Flows to Emerging Markets: Liberalization, Overshooting and Volatility." In: Sebastian Edwards (ed.). *Capital Flows to Emerging Markets: Theory, Evidence and Controversies.* The University of Chicago Press. Chicago.

Baer, Werner. "Import Substitution and Industrialization in Latin America: Experiences and Interpretations." *Latin American Research Review.* Vol. 7, No. 1. (Spring, 1972), pp. 95–122.

Balassa, Bela, Gerardo M. Bueno, Pedro-Pablo Kuczynski and Mario Henrique Simonsen. 1986. *Toward Renewed Growth in Latin America.* Institute for International Economics. Washington, D.C.

Balassa, Bela. 1980. Process of Industrial Development and Alternative Development Strategies. The World Bank. Washington, D.C.

Behrman, Jere R., Nancy Birdsall and Miguel Székely. "Economic Policy Changes and Wage Differentials in Latin America." *Economic Development and Cultural Change.* Vol. 56, No. 1. (Oct. 2007), pp. 57–97.

Bhagwati, Jagdish N. "The Capital Myth." *Foreign Affairs.* Vol. 77, No. 3. (May/June 1998), pp. 7–12.

Bianchi, Andrés, Robert Devlin and Joseph Ramos. 1987. *The Adjustment Process in Latin America: 1981–1986.* International Monetary Fund and World Bank Symposium on Growth-Oriented Adjustment Programs. Washington, D.C.

Birdsall, Nancy, Augusto de la Torre and Felipe Valencia C. Forthcoming, 2010. "The Washington Consensus: Assessing a 'Damaged Brand'" In: *Oxford Handbook on Latin American Economics.* José Antonio Ocampo and Jaime Ros (eds.). Oxford University Press, New York.

Birdsall, Nancy, Augusto de la Torre, and Rachel Menezes. 2008. *Fair Growth.* Center for Global Development and Inter-American Dialogue. Washington, D.C.

Birdsall, Nancy, Augusto de la Torre, with Rachel Menezes. 2001. *Washington Contentious: Economic Policies for Social Equity?* Carnegie Endowment for International Peace and Inter-American Dialogue. Washington, D.C.

Birdsall, Nancy. Forthcoming, 2010. "The Global Financial Crisis: The Beginning of the End of the 'Development' Agenda?" In: Fukuyama, Francis and Nancy Birdsall (eds.). *New Ideas for Development after the Financial Crisis.* Johns Hopkins University Press. Baltimore, MD.

Caballero, Ricardo J. "Macroeconomic Volatility in Latin America: A View and Three Case Studies." *Estudios de Economía.* Vol. 28, No. 1. (Jun. 2001), pp. 5–52.

Calvo, Guillermo A. "Temporary Stabilization: Predetermined Exchange Rates." *The Journal of Political Economy.* Vol. 94, No. 6. (Dec. 1986), pp. 1319–1329.

Calvo, Guillermo A. and Carmen M. Reinhart. "Fear of Floating." *The Quarterly Journal of Economics.* Vol. 117, No. 2. (May 2002), pp. 379–408.

Calvo, Guillermo A. and Enrique G. Mendoza. "Rational Contagion and the Globalization of Securities Markets." *Journal of International Economics.* Vol. 51, Issue 1. (June 2000), pp. 79–113.

Calvo, Guillermo and Carmen Reinhart. 2000. "When Capital Flows Come to a Sudden Stop: consequences and Policy." In: Peter B. Kenen and Alexander K. Swoboda.

Reforming the International Monetary and Financial System. International Monetary Fund. Washington, D.C.

Cardoso, Fernando Henrique and Enzo Faletto. 1979. *Dependency and Development in Latin America.* University of California Press. Berkeley.

Cavallo, Domingo F. and Joaquin A. Cottani. "Argentina's Convertibility Plan and the IMF." *The American Economic Review.* Vol. 87, No. 2. Papers and Proceedings. (May 1997), pp. 17–22. Ciccone, Antonio and Marek Jarocinski. "Determinants of Economic Growth: Will Data Tell?" (June 2008). CEPR Discussion Paper No. DP6544.

Corden, W. Max. 1991. "The Theory of Debt Relief: Sorting out Some Issues." In: *Developing Countries and the International Economy: Issues in Trade, Adjustment and Debt.* H. David Evans and David Greenway (eds.). Routledge. London.

Corsetti, Giancarlo, Paolo A. Pesenti, and Nouriel Roubini. "What Caused the Asian Currency and Financial Crisis?" *Japan and the World Economy.* Vol. 11. (1999), pp. 305–373.

De la Torre, Augusto and Sergio L. Schmukler. 2007. *Emerging Capital Markets and Globalization.* Stanford University Press and World Bank. Washington, D.C.

De la Torre, Augusto, Eduardo Levy Yeyati and Sergio L. Schmukler. "Living and Dying with Hard Pegs: The Rise and Fall of Argentina's Currency Board." *Economía.* Vol. 3, No. 2. (Spring 2003), pp. 43–99.

De la Torre, Augusto, Juan Carlos Gozzi and Sergio L. Schmukler. "Financial Development in Latin America: Big Emerging Issues, Limited Policy Analysis." (2006). World Bank Policy Research Working Paper No. 3963. World Bank. Washington, D.C.

De la Torre, Augusto, Juan Carlos Gozzi and Sergio L. Schmukler. "Stock Market Development Under Globalization: Whither the Gains from Reforms?" *Journal of Banking & Finance.* Vol. 31, Issue 6. (June 2007), pp. 1731–1754.

De la Torre, Augusto. 2007. "Comments on Growth Diagnostics." LACEA. Bogotá, Colombia. http://siteresources.worldbank.org/EXTLACOFFICEOFCE/Resources/870 892-1197314973189/Growth_ Diagnostics.pdf

De Soto, Hernando. 1989. *The Other Path: The Invisible Revolution in the Third World.* Harper & Row. New York.

Demirguc-Kunt, Asli and Enrica Detragiache. 1999. "Financial Liberalization and Financial Fragility." In: *Annual World Bank Conference on Development Economics.* World Bank. Washington, D.C.

Demirguc-Kunt, Asli and Ross Levine. "Finance and Inequality: Theory and Evidence." (June 2009). World Bank Policy Research Working Paper Series No. 4967. World Bank. Washington, D.C.

Díaz-Alejandro, Carlos. "Good-bye Financial Repression, Hello Financial Crash." *Journal of Development Economics.* Vol. 19, Issue 1–2. (1985), pp 1–24.

Dollar, David and Aart Kraay. "Trade, Growth, and Poverty." (June 2001). World Bank Policy Research Working Paper No. 2615. World Bank. Washington, D.C.

Dornbusch, Rudiger. "Expectations and Exchange Rate Dynamics." *The Journal of Political Economy.* Vol. 84, No. 6. (Dec. 1976), pp. 1661–1176.

Easterly, William, Michael Kremer, Lant Pritchett and Lawrence H. Summers. "Good Policy or Good Luck? Country Growth Performance and Temporary Shocks. *Journal of Monetary Economics.* Vol. 32, Issue 3. (Dec. 1993), pp 459–483.

Easterly, William, Norman Loayza and Peter Montiel. 1997. "Has Latin America's Post-reform Growth Been Disappointing?" *Journal of International Economics.* Vol. 43, Issues 3–4. (Nov. 1997), pp. 287–311.

ECLAC. 1990. *Productive Transformation with Equity.* ECLAC, United Nations. Santiago de Chile.

ECLAC. 2001. *Equity, Development and Citizenship.* ECLAC, United Nations. Santiago de Chile.

ECLAC. 2008. *Structural Change and Productivity Growth: 20 Years Later, Old Problems, New Opportunities.* ECLAC, United Nations. Santiago de Chile.

ECLAC. 2010. CEPALSTAT: Latin America and the Caribbean Statistics. ECLAC. Santiago de Chile.

Economist Intelligence Unit. 2010. *The Economist.* London.

Edwards, Sebastian. 1995. *Crisis and Reform in Latin America: From Despair to Hope.* Oxford University Press and World Bank. Washington, D.C.

Eichengreen, Barry and Ricardo Hausmann. "Exchange Rates and Financial Fragility." (November 1999). NBER Working Papers No. 7418.

Eichengreen, Barry, Ricardo Hausmann, and Ugo Panizza. 2005. "The Mystery of Original Sin." In: Barry Eichengreen and Ricardo Hausmann (eds.). *Other's People Money: Debt Denomination and Financial Instability in Emerging Market Economies.* The University of Chicago Press. Chicago.

Engerman, Stanley L., and Kenneth L. Sokoloff. 1997. "Factor Endowments, Institutions, and Differential Paths of Growth Among New World Economies: A View from Economic Historians of the United States." In: *How Latin America Fell Behind.* Stephen Haber (ed.) Stanford University Press, California.

Escaith, Hubert and Samuel Morley. "The Effect of Structural Reforms on Growth in Latin America and the Caribbean: An Empirical Approach." *El Trimestre Económico.* Vol. 68, No. 4. (Oct. 2001), pp. 469–513.

Fajnzylber, Fernando. 1990. *Unavoidable Industrial Restructuring in Latin America.* Duke University Press. Durham.

Fajnzylber, Pablo and William F. Maloney. "Labor Demand and Trade Reform in Latin America." *Journal of International Economics.* Vol. 66, No. 2. (July 2002), pp. 423–446.

Fernándes-Arias, Eduardo and Peter Montiel. 1997. "Reform and Growth in Latin America: All Pain, No Gain?" Working Paper # 351. Inter-American Development Bank, Office of the Chief Economist. Washington, D.C.

Fernández, Raquel and Dani Rodrik. "Resistance to Reform: Status Quo Bias in the Presence of Individual-Specific Uncertainty." *The American Economic Review,* Vol. 81, Issue 5. (Dec. 1991), pp. 1146–1155.

Ffrench-Davis, Ricardo and José Antonio Ocampo. 2001. In: *Financial Crises in 'Successful' Emerging Economies.* ECLAC and Brookings Institution Press. Washington, D.C.

Ffrench-Davis, Ricardo and Helmut Reisen. 1998. *Capital Flows and Investment Performance: Lessons from Latin America.* ECLAC and OECD. Paris.

Ffrench-Davis, Ricardo. 2000. *Reforming the Reforms in Latin America.* ECLAC and St. Anthony's College. Oxford.

Fischer, Stanley. "Exchange Rate Regimes: Is the Bipolar View Correct?" *The Journal of Economic Perspectives.* Vol. 15, No. 2. (Spring, 2001), pp. 3–24.

Fishlow, Albert. "Some Reflections on Comparative Latin American Economic Performance and Policy." (1987). Economics Working Papers No. 8754. University of California. Berkeley.

Frankel, Jeffrey A. "No Single Currency Regime is Right for All Countries or At All Times." (September 1999). NBER Working Paper No. 7338.

Fukuyama, Francis and Nancy Birdsall. Forthcoming 2010. *New Ideas for Development after the Financial Crisis.* Johns Hopkins University Press. Baltimore, MD.

Furtado, Celso. 1963. Economic Growth of Brazil, a Survey from Colonial to Modern Times. University of California Press. Berkeley.

Galiani, Sebastián, Daniel Heymann and Mariano Tommasi. "Great Expectations and Hard Times: The Argentine Convertibility Plan." *Economía.* Vol. 3, No. 2. (Spring 2003), pp. 109–160.

Gavin, Michael and Ricardo Hausmann. 1996. "Securing Stability and Growth in a Shock Prone Region: The Policy Challenge for Latin America." Working Paper # 315. Inter-American Development Bank, Office of the Chief Economist. Washington, D.C.

Gavin, Michael, Ricardo Hausmann, Roberto Perotti and Ernesto Talvi. "Managing Fiscal Policy in Latin America and the Caribbean: Volatility, Procyclicality, and Limited Creditworthiness." (March 1996). Working Paper # 326. Inter-American Development Bank, Office of the Chief Economist. Washington, D.C.

Gerschenkron, Alexander. 1962. Economic backwardness in historical perspective: a book of essays. Harvard University Press. Cambridge.

Gill, Indermit S., Truman G. Packard, Juan Yermo and Todd Pugatch. 2004. *Keeping the Promise of Old Age Income Security in Latin America.* World Bank. Washington, D.C.

Graham, Carol and Moisés Naím. 1998. "The Political Economy of Institutional Reform in Latin America." In: *Beyond Tradeoffs.* Nancy Birdsall, Carol Graham and Richard H. Sabot (eds.). Inter-American Development Bank. Washington, D.C.

Growth Commission. 2008. *The Growth Report: Strategies for Sustained Growth and Inclusive Development.* World Bank. Washington, D.C.

Goldstein, Morris. "Lessons of Recent Currency Crises." Brookings Trade Forum. (2002), pp. 173–181.

Gunder Frank, André. 1967. *Capitalism and Underdevelopment in Latin America: Historical Studies of Chile and Brazil.* Monthly Review Press. New York.

Hall, Robert E. and Charles I. Jones. "Why Do Some Countries Produce So Much More Output Per Worker Than Others?" *The Quarterly Journal of Economics.* Vol. 114, No. 1 (Feb. 1999), pp. 83–116.

Hausmann, Ricardo, Dani Rodrik and Andrés Velasco. 2008. "Growth Diagnostics." In: *The Washington Consensus Reconsidered.* Narcis Serra and Joseph E. Stiglitz (eds.). Oxford University Press. New York.

Hausmann, Ricardo, Lant Pritchett and Dani Rodrik. "Growth Accelerations." *Journal of Economic Growth.* Vol. 10, Issue 4. (Dec. 2005), pp 303–329.

Hausmann, Ricardo, Michael Gavin, Carmen Pagés-Serra, and Ernesto Stein. "Financial Turmoil and the Choice of Exchange Rate Regime." Working Paper # 400. (1999). Inter-American Development Bank, Office of the Chief Economist. Washington, D.C.

Heckman, James J. and Carmen Pages. "The Cost of Job Security Regulation: Evidence from Latin American Labor Markets." (June 2000). NBER Working Papers No. 7773.

Hirschman, Albert O. "The Political Economy of Import-Substituting Industrialization in Latin America." *The Quarterly Journal of Economics.* Vol. 82, No. 1. (Feb. 1968), pp. 1–32.

Hirschman, Albert O. 1958. *The Strategy of Economic Development.* Yale University Press. New Haven.

Hoff, Karla and Joseph E. Stiglitz. 2001. "Modern Economic Theory and Development." In: *Frontiers in Development Economics: the Future in Perspective.* Oxford University Press. New York.

411

Inter-American Development Bank (IDB). 1984. *Economic Integration.* Inter-American Development Economic and Social Progress Annual Report. Washington, D.C.

IDB. 1985. *External Debt: Crisis and Adjustment.* Inter-American Development Economic and Social Progress Annual Report. Washington, D.C.

IDB. 1986. *Agricultural Development.* Inter-American Development Economic and Social Progress Annual Report. Washington, D.C.

IDB. 1995. *Overcoming Volatility.* Inter-American Development Economic and Social Progress Annual Report. Washington, D.C.

IDB. 1997. *Latin America After a Decade of Reforms.* Inter-American Development Economic and Social Progress Annual Report. Washington, D.C.

IDB. 1998. *Facing Up to Inequality in Latin America.* Inter-American Development Economic and Social Progress Annual Report. Washington, D.C.

IDB. 2001. *Competitiveness: The Business of Growth.* Inter-American Development Economic and Social Progress Annual Report. Washington, D.C.

IDB. 2009. *Growing Pains: Binding Constraints to Productive Investment in Latin America.* IDB, Research Department. Washington, D.C.

Impavido, Gregorio, Esperanza Lasagabaster and Manuel García-Huitrón. 2010, forthcoming. *New Policies for Mandatory Defined Contribution Pensions.* World Bank, Latin American Development Forum Series. Washington, D.C.

International Monetary Fund. 2005. Stabilization and Reform in Latin America: A Macroeconomic Perspective on the Experience Since the Early 1990s. Occasional Paper 238. International Monetary Fund. Washington, D.C.

International Monetary Fund. 2009. *World Economic Outlook: Crisis and Recovery.* International Monetary Fund. Washington, D.C.

International Monetary Fund. 2010. International Financial Statistics Online. Washington, D.C.

Kaminsky, Graciela and Sergio L. Schmukler. "Short-Rum Pain, Long-Run Gain: The Effects of Financial Liberalization." (June 2003). NBER Working Paper No. 9787.

Kaminsky, Graciela L. and Carmen M. Reinhart. "The Twin Crises: The Causes of Banking and Balance-of-Payments Problems." *The American Economic Review.* Vol. 89, No. 3. (June 1999), pp. 473–500.

Kiguel, Miguel A. and Nissan Liviatan. "The Business Cycle Associated with Exchange Rate-Based Stabilizations." *The World Bank Economic Review.* Vol. 6, No. 2. (1992). Washington, D.C.

Krueger, Anne O. "Meant Well, Tried Little, Failed Much: Policy Reforms in Emerging Market Economies." Remarks at the Roundtable Lecture at the Economic Honors Society. New York University. March 23, 2004. New York.

Krugman, Paul. "Financing vs. Forgiving a Debt Overhang." *Journal of Development Economics.* Vol. 29, Issue 3. (Nov. 1998), pp. 253–268.

Kuczynski, Pedro-Pablo and John Williamson. 2003. *After the Washington Consensus: Restarting Growth and Reform in Latin America.* Institute for International Economics. Washington, D.C.

Lane, Philip R. and Sergio L. Schmukler. "The International Financial Integration of China and India." (June 2006). Proceedings, Federal Bank. San Francisco.

Larraín B., Felipe and Andrés Velasco. "Exchange-rate Policy in Emerging-Market Economies: the Case for Floating." (2001) Essays in International Economics. No. 224.

Lederman, Daniel and William F. Maloney. 2007. *Natural Resources: Neither Curse nor Destiny.* Stanford University Press and World Bank. Washington, D.C.

Levine, Ross and David Renelt. "A Sensitivity Analysis of Cross-Country Growth Regressions." *The American Economic Review.* Vol. 82, No. 4. (Sep., 1992), pp. 942–963.

Levy, Santiago and Michael Walton. 2009. *No Growth Without Equity? Inequality, Interests and Competition in Mexico.* Palgrave Macmillan and The World Bank. Washington, D.C.

Lipton, Michael. 1977. *Why Poor People Stay Poor: Urban Bias in World Development.* Harvard University Press. Cambridge.

Loayza, Norman, Pablo Fajnzylber and César Calderón. 2005. *Economic Growth in Latin America and the Caribbean: Stylized Facts, Explanations, and Forecasts.* World Bank. Washington, D.C.

Lora, Eduardo A., Ugo G. Panizza and Myriam Quispe-Agnoli. "Reform Fatigue: Symptoms, Resons, Implications." (2004). IDB, Research Department. Washington, D.C.

Lora, Eduardo and Felipe Barrera. 1997. "Una Década de Reformas Estructurales en América Latina: El Crecimiento, la Productividad y la Inversión ya no son como Antes." IDB, Office of the Chief Economist. Washington, D.C.

Lora, Eduardo and Mauricio Olivera. "The Electoral Consequences of the Washington Consensus" (May 2005). Working Paper # 530. IDB, Office of the Chief Economist. Washington, D.C.

Lora, Eduardo and Ugo Panizza. "Structural Reforms in Latin America Under Scrutiny." (March 2002). Working Paper # 470. IDB, Research Department. Washington, D.C.

Lora, Eduardo. "What Makes Reforms Likely? Timing and Sequencing of Structural Reforms in Latin America" Working Paper # 424. (June 2000). IDB, Office of the Chief Economist. Washington, D.C.

Lora, Eduardo. 1997. "A Decade of Structural Reforms in Latin America: What Has Been Reformed and How to Measure It." Working Paper # 348. IDB, Office of the Chief Economist. Washington, D.C.

Lora, Eduardo. 2001. "Structural Reforms in Latin America: What Has Been Reformed and How to Measure It." Working Paper # 466. IDB, Office of the Chief Economist. Washington, D.C.

Maddison, Angus. 2006. *The World Economy: Historical Statistics of the World Economy.* Organization for Economic Cooperation and Development. Paris.

Martinelli, Cesar and Mariano Tommasi. "Sequencing of Economics Reforms in the Presence of Political Constraints." *Economics and Politics.* Vol. 9, Number 2 (July 1997), pp. 115–131.

McKinnnon, Ronlad I and Huw Pill. "Credible Economic Liberalizations and Overborrowing." *The American Economic Review.* Vol. 87, No. 2. (May 1997), pp. 189–193.

Mesa-lago, Carmelo. "Myth and Reality of Pension Reform: The Latin American Evidence." *World Development.* Vol. 30, Issue 8. (August 2002), pp. 1309–1321.

Mishkin, Frederic S. and Miguel A. Savastano. "Monetary Policy Strategies for Emerging Market Countries: Lessons from Latin America." *Comparative Economic Studies.* Vol. 44, Part 2/3. (2002), pp. 45–82.

Morley, Samuel A, Roberto Machado and Stefano Pettinato. "Indexes of Structural Reform in Latin America." (1999). Serie Reformas Económicas. ECLAC. Santiago de Chile.

Morley, Samuel A. 2000. *The Impact of Reforms on Equity in Latin America.* World Bank. Washington, D.C.

Murphy, Kevin M, Andrei Shleifer and Robert W. Vishny. "Industrialization and the Big Push." *The Journal of Political Economy.* Vol. 97, No. 5. (Oct. 1989), pp. 1003–1026.

Myers, Stewart C. "Determinants of corporate Borrowing." *Journal of Financial Economics.* Vol. 5, Issue 2. (Nov. 1977), pp. 147–175.

Naím, Moisés. "Fads and Fashion in Economic Reforms: Washington Consensus or Washington Confusion?" *Third World Quarterly.* Vol. 21, No. 3 (Jun. 2000), pp. 505–528.

Naím, Moisés. "Washington Consensus: A Damaged Brand." *Financial Times,* London. October 28, 2002.

Nellis, John and Nancy Birdsall. "Reality check: the distributional impact of privatization in developing countries." (Oct. 2005). Center for Global Development. Washington, D.C.

North, Douglass C. 1990. *Institutions, Institutional Change and Economic Performance.* Cambridge University Press. New York.

Ocampo, José Antonio and Jaime Ros. Forthcoming, 2010. "Shifting Paradigms in Latin America's Economic Development." In: *Oxford Handbook on Latin American Economics.* José Antonio Ocampo and Jaime Ros (eds.). Oxford University Press. New York.

Ocampo, José Antonio. "Latin America's Growth and Equity Frustrations During Structural Reforms." *Journal of Economic Perspectives.* Vol.18, No. 2. (Spring 2004), pp. 67–88.

Ocampo, José Antonio. 2003. "Capital-Account and Counter-Cyclical Prudential Regulations in Developing Countries." In: Ricardo Ffrench-Davis and Stephany Griffith-Jones (eds.). *From Capital Surges to Drought: Seeking Stability for Emerging Markets.* Palgrave MacMillan. London.

Perry, Guillermo and Luis Servén. "The Anatomy of a Multiple Crisis: Why Was Argentina Special and What Can We Learn From It." (June 2003). World Bank Policy Research Working Paper No. 3081, World Bank. Washington, DC.

Porzecanski, Arturo C. "Latin America: The Missing Financial Crisis." (October 2009). MPRA Paper No. 18974.

Prebisch, Raul. 1950. *The Economic Development of Latin America and its Principal Problems.* United Nations. New York.

Program for International Student Assessment (PISA). 2006. Organization for Economic Cooperation and Development. Paris.

Radelet, Steve. Forthcoming, 2010. *Emerging Africa: How 17 Countries Are Leading the Way.* Center for Global Development. Washington, D.C.

Rebelo, Sergio and Carlos A. Vegh. "Real Effects of Exchange-Rate-Based Stabilization: An Analysis or Competing Theories." *NBER Macroeconomics Annual.* Vol. 10. (1995), pp. 125–174.

Rodríguez, Francisco and Dani Rodrik. "Trade Policy and Economic Growth: A Skeptic's Guide to the Cross National Evidence." *NBER Macroeconomics Annual.* Vol. 15. (2000), pp, 261–325.

Rodrik, Dani, Arvind Subramanian and Francesco Trebbi. "Institutions Rule: The Primacy of Institutions Over Geography and Integration in Economic Development." *Journal of Economic Growth.* Vol. 9, No. 2. (June 2004), pp. 131–165.

Rodrik, Dani. "How should Structural Adjustment Programs be Designed?" *World Development.* Vol. 18 (July, 1990), pp. 933–947.

Rodrik, Dani. 2005a. "Why we Learn Nothing from Regressing Economic Growth on Policies." Harvard University Mimeograph. Cambridge.

Rodrik, Dani. 2005b. "Growth Strategies." In: *Handbook of Economic Growth.* Philippe Aghion and Steven N. Durlauf (eds.). Elsevier, Amsterdam.

Rodrik, Dani. 2006. "Goodbye Washington Consensus, Hello Washington Confusion?" *Journal of Economic Literature.* Vol. 44, No. 4 (Dec. 2006), pp. 973–987.

Rojas-Suarez, Liliana (ed.). 2009. *Growing Pains in Latin America: An Economic Growth Framework as Applied to Brazil, Colombia, Costa Rica, Mexico, and Peru.* Center for Global Development. Washington, D.C.

Rosestein-Rodan, P.N. "Problems of Industrialisation of Eastern and South-Eastern Europe." *The Economic Journal.* Vol. 53, No. 210/211. (Jun.-Sep. 1943), pp. 202–211.

Rostow, W.W. "The Stages of Economic Growth." *The Economic History Review.* New Series, Vol. 12, No. 1. (1959), pp. 1–16.

Sachs, Jeffrey D. and Joaquín Vial. "Competitividad y Crecimiento en los Países Andinos y en América Latina." (January 2002). Andean Development Corporation and Center for International Development, Harvard University. Cambridge.

Singer, H.W. "The Distribution of Gains between Investing and Borrowing Countries." *The American Economic Review.* Vol. 40, No. 2. Papers and Proceedings. (May 1950), pp. 473–485.

Stallings, Barbara and Wilson Peres. 2000. *Growth Employment and Equity: The Impact of the Economic Reforms in Latin America and the Caribbean.* ECLAC and Brookings Institution Press. Washington, D.C.

Stern, Nicholas. "The Economics of Climate Change." *American Economic Review: Papers and Proceedings.* Vol. 98, Issue 2. (May 2008), pp 1–37.

Stiglitz, Joseph E. "Bleak Growth for the Developing World." *International Herald Tribune.* Paris. April 10, 1999. P 6.

Stiglitz, Joseph E. "Capital Market Liberalization, Economic Growth, and Instability." *World Development.* Vol. 28, Issue 6. (June 2000), pp. 1075–1086.

Stiglitz, Joseph E. 2002. *Globalization and its Discontents.* W.W. Norton. New York.

Székely, Miguel and Juan Luis Londoño. "Sorpresas Distributivas después de una Década de Reformas: Latinoamérica en los Noventas." Working Paper # 352. Inter-American Development Bank, Office of the Chief Economist. Washington, D.C.

Thorp, Rosemary. 1998. *Progress, Poverty and Exclusion: An Economic History of Latin America in the 20th Century.* Inter-American Development Bank. Washington, D.C.

Tobin, James. "Financial Globalization." *World Development.* Vol. 28, Issue 6. (June 2000), pp. 1101–1104.

Tornell, Aaron and Frank Westermann. 2005. *Boom-Bust Cycles and Financial Liberalization.* The MIT Press. Cambridge.

UNICEF. 1987. *Adjustment with a Human Face.* Oxford University Press. New York.

Williamson, John (ed.). 1990. *Latin American Adjustment: How Much Has Happened?* Institute for International Economics, Conference Volume. Washington, D.C.

Williamson, John. "Democracy and the 'Washington Consensus.'" *World Development.* Vol. 21, No. 8. (Aug. 1993), pp 1329–1993.

Williamson, John. "Did the Washington Consensus Fail?" (2002). Peterson Institute for International Economics. Washington, D.C.

Williamson, John. "What Should the World Bank Think about the Washington Consensus?" *The World Bank Research Observer.* Vol. 15, No. 2. (August 2000), pp. 251–264.

World Bank. 1985. *International Capital and Economic Development.* World Development Report, World Bank. Washington, D.C.

World Bank. 1986. *Trade and Pricing Policies in World Agriculture.* World Development Report, World Bank. Washington, D.C.

World Bank. 1987. *Industrialization and Foreign Trade.* World Development Report, World Bank. Washington, D.C.

World Bank. 1997. *The Long March: A Reform Agenda for Latin America and the Caribbean in the Next Decade.* World Bank, Latin American and the Caribbean Region, Flagship Report. Washington, D.C.

World Bank. 1998. *Beyond the Washington Consensus: Institutions Matter.* World Bank, Latin American and the Caribbean Region, Flagship Report. Washington, D.C.

World Bank. 2000. *Securing our Future in the Global Economy.* World Bank, Latin American and the Caribbean Region, Flagship Report. Washington, D.C.

World Bank. 2002. *From Natural Resources to the Knowledge Economy.* World Bank, Latin American and the Caribbean Region, Flagship Report. Washington, D.C.

World Bank. 2003. *Closing the Gap in Education and Technology.* World Bank, Latin American and the Caribbean Region, Flagship Report. Washington, D.C.

World Bank. 2004. *Inequality in Latin America: Breaking with History?* World Bank, Latin American and the Caribbean Region, Flagship Report. Washington, D.C.

World Bank. 2006. *Poverty Reduction and Growth: Virtuous and Vicious Cycles.* World Bank, Latin American and the Caribbean Region, Flagship Report. Washington, D.C.

World Bank. 2007. *Informality: Exit and Exclusion.* World Bank, Latin American and the Caribbean Region, Flagship Report. Washington, D.C.

World Bank. 2009a. *Low Carbon, High Growth: Latin American Responses to Climate Change.* World Bank, Latin American and the Caribbean Region, Flagship Report. Washington, D.C.

World Bank. 2009b. "How Has Poverty Evolved in Latin America and How it Likely to be Affected by the Economic Crisis?" Mimeograph. World Bank, Latin American Poverty and Gender Group. Washington, D.C.

World Bank. 2010a. *From Global Collapse to Recovery.* World Bank, Latin American and the Caribbean Region, Spring Meetings Report. Washington, D.C.

World Bank. 2010b. *Development and Climate Change.* World Bank, World Development Report. Washington, D.C.

World Development Indicators. 2010. The World Bank. Washington, D.C.

31

WHAT SHOULD THE WORLD BANK THINK ABOUT THE WASHINGTON CONSENSUS?

John Williamson

Source: *World Bank Research Observer* 15, 2, 2000, 251–264.

The phrase "Washington Consensus" has become a familiar term in development policy circles in recent years, but it is now used in several different senses, causing a great deal of confusion. In this article the author distinguishes between his original meaning as a summary of the lowest common denominator of policy advice addressed by the Washington-based institutions (including the World Bank) and subsequent use of the term to signify neoliberal or market-fundamentalist policies. He argues that the latter policies could not be expected to provide an effective framework for combating poverty but that the original advice is still broadly valid The article discusses alternative ways of addressing the confusion. It argues that any policy manifesto designed to eliminate poverty needs to go beyond the original version but concludes by cautioning that no consensus on a wider agenda currently exists.

Ten years ago I invented the term "Washington Consensus" to refer to the lowest common denominator of policy advice being addressed by the Washington-based institutions to Latin American countries as of 1989 (Williamson 1990). While it is jolly to become famous for coining a term that reverberates around the world, I have long been doubtful about whether my phrase served to advance the cause of rational economic policymaking. My initial concern was that the phrase invited the interpretation that the liberalizing economic reforms of the past two decades were imposed by Washington-based institutions (for example, see Stewart 1997) rather than having resulted from the process of intellectual convergence that I believe underlies the reforms.[1] Richard Feinberg's "universal convergence" (in Williamson 1990) or Jean Waelbroeck's "one-world consensus" (Waelbroeck 1998) would have been a much better term for the intellectual convergence that I had in mind.

I have gradually developed a second and more significant concern, however. I find that the term has been invested with a meaning that is significantly different from that which I had intended and is now used as a synonym for what is often called "neoliberalism" in Latin America, or what George Soros (1998) has called "market fundamentalism." When I first came across this usage, I asserted that it was a misuse of my intended meaning. I had naïvely imagined that just because I had invented the expression, I had some sort of intellectual property rights that entitled me to dictate its meaning, but in fact the concept had become public property.

The battle of economic ideas, as McCloskey (1998) has argued, is fought to a significant extent with rhetoric. The use of a term with dual meanings and strong ideological overtones can therefore pose serious dangers not only of misunderstanding but also of inadvertently prejudicing policy objectives. Specifically, there is a real danger that many of the economic reforms favored by international development institutions—notably macroeconomic discipline, trade openness, and market-friendly microeconomic policies—will be discredited in the eyes of many observers, simply because these institutions are inevitably implicated in views that command a consensus in Washington and the term "Washington Consensus" has come to be used to describe an extreme and dogmatic commitment to the belief that markets can handle everything.

The objective of this article is to consider what should be done to minimize the damage to the cause of intellectual understanding, and therefore of rational economic reform, that is being wrought by the current widespread use of the term "Washington Consensus" in a sense different from that originally intended. Would it be productive, for example, to insist that the original usage is the correct one? Or should one simply refuse to debate in these terms? Is it possible to escape by declaring fidelity to some "post-Washington Consensus"? The first stage in answering these questions is a careful examination of the semantic issues involved.

The Original Version

My original paper (Williamson 1990) argued that the set of policy reforms that most of official Washington thought would be good for Latin American countries could be summarized in 10 propositions:

- Fiscal discipline
- A redirection of public expenditure priorities toward fields offering both high economic returns and the potential to improve income distribution, such as primary health care, primary education, and infrastructure
- Tax reform (to lower marginal rates and broaden the tax base)
- Interest rate liberalization
- A competitive exchange rate
- Trade liberalization

- Liberalization of inflows of foreign direct investment
- Privatization
- Deregulation (to abolish barriers to entry and exit)
- Secure property rights.

The need for the first three reforms is, so far as I am aware, widely accepted among economists. Nevertheless, when I reviewed the progress that Latin American countries had made in implementing the recommended set of policies several years later (Williamson 1996), it appeared that the least progress had come in redirecting public expenditure priorities. The other seven reforms have stimulated a measure of controversy and therefore merit comment.

In my original paper I specified interest rate liberalization as the fourth reform. I am now well aware that many economists have reservations about that formulation. As a matter of fact, I have such reservations myself: in Williamson and Mahar (1998) interest rate liberalization is identified as merely one of six dimensions of financial liberalization. Moreover, Stiglitz (1994) has argued that interest rate liberalization should come toward the end of the process of financial liberalization, inasmuch as a ceiling on the deposit interest rate (equal to the Treasury bill rate, he suggests) might provide a constraint on gambling for redemption. I find this argument persuasive and long ago changed my description of the fourth element of the Washington Consensus to financial liberalization. More recently Stiglitz (1998) has expressed a much more basic objection to financial liberalization, arguing that the success of some East Asian countries stemmed importantly from their policy of directing credit to particular industries rather than allowing the market to determine the allocation of credit. That argument is highly contentious, especially in the aftermath of the East Asian economic crisis of 1997–98.

My fifth choice—a competitive exchange rate—was not, I have concluded, an accurate report of Washington opinion. I suspect that by 1989 a majority of economists, in Washington as elsewhere, were already in favor of either firmly fixed or freely floating exchange rates and hostile to the sort of intermediate regime that in my judgment gives the best promise of maintaining a competitive exchange rate in the medium term. (My own preference remains an intermediate regime of limited flexibility, provided that excludes an old-fashioned adjustable peg, even if such a regime is more likely to spawn speculative pressures than a floating rate.) But note that the East Asian countries did by and large achieve and maintain competitive exchange rates, at least before about 1996 (and even after 1996 only Thailand failed to do so).[2]

My sixth reform was trade liberalization. Here I see little reason to doubt that I reported accurately on opinions in the international financial institutions and the central economic agencies of the U.S. government (although parts of Congress and the Department of Commerce are not noted for their dedication to liberal trade). But this is another area where critics can rightly claim that the policies that nurtured the East Asian miracle were, at least in some countries, at odds with the policies endorsed in the Washington Consensus. Much the same is true of foreign direct investment, except that the East Asian economies were less hostile to a policy of openness; only the Republic of Korea rejected most foreign direct investment during the years of the miracle.

Privatization commanded a lot of support in Washington, where it had been put on the international agenda by James Baker when he was secretary of the U.S. Treasury, in his speech to the World Bank-International Monetary Fund Annual Meetings in Seoul in 1985. Privatization was controversial in much of the rest of the world, where one's attitude to public versus private ownership had long been the litmus test for qualifying as left-wing or right-wing. Deregulation was rather less politically polarizing: it had been initiated by the centrist Carter administration in the United States, rather than by the right-wing Thatcher government that pioneered privatization in the United Kingdom. Deregulation, however, was not a policy that reverberated in East Asia, where the industrial policies pursued in some (though not all) countries ran very much in the opposite direction. The notion of the importance of secure property rights had come both from Chicago's law and economics school and from the work of Hernando de Soto in Peru. The concept was presumably offensive to those who resisted the advance of the market economy, but this breed was extinct in Washington by 1989 (if, indeed, it had ever existed there). My impression is that the institution of private property was somewhat more securely entrenched in East Asia than in most of the rest of the developing world.

So much for the content of my version of the Washington Consensus. What inspired it? In an immediate sense, it originated from an attempt to answer a question posed to me by Hans Singer during a seminar at the Institute for Development Studies: what were these "sensible" policies that were being pursued in Latin America (and that I was arguing justified approval of the Brady Plan to provide these countries with debt relief)? In a more profound sense, my effort was an attempt to distill which of the policy initiatives that had emanated from Washington during the years of conservative ideology had won inclusion in the intellectual mainstream rather than being cast aside once Ronald Reagan was no longer on the political scene.[3] Taking an even longer perspective, my version of the Washington Consensus can be seen as an attempt to summarize the policies that were widely viewed as supportive of development at the end of the two decades when economists had become convinced that the key to rapid economic development lay not in a country's natural resources or even in its physical or human capital but, rather, in the set of economic policies that it pursued.

Let me emphasize that the Washington Consensus as I conceived it was in principle geographically and historically specific, a lowest common denominator of the reforms that I judged "Washington" could agree were needed in Latin America as of 1989. But in practice there would probably not have been a lot of difference if I had undertaken a similar exercise for Africa or Asia, and that still seemed to be the case when I revisited the topic (with regard to Latin America) in 1996 (Williamson 1997). This doubtless made it easier for some to interpret the Washington Consensus as a policy manifesto that its adherents supposedly believed to be valid for all places and at all times.

Current Usage

The following is a selection of recent definitions of the Washington Consensus that I happened to stumble across. (I have undertaken no bibliographic research to compile this list.)

"A die-hard liberalization advocate (or a Washington-consensus believer). ..." (Ito 1999)

"... the self-confident advice of the 'Washington consensus'—free-up trade, practice sound money, and go home early. ..." (Vines 1999)

" . . . the Washington Consensus: policy prescriptions based on free market principles and monetary discipline." (Hamada 1998)

"The Washington Consensus had the following message: 'Liberalize as much as you can, privatize as fast as you can, and be tough in monetary and fiscal matters.'" (Kolodko 1998)

"The bashing of the state that characterized the policy thrust of the Washington Consensus. . . ." (United Nations 1998)

"This new imperialism, codified in the 'Washington Consensus'...." (Alam 1999)

"The Brazilian crisis has reignited the debate over the so-called Washington Consensus on the creation of a laissez-faire global economy." (Rajan 1999)

In none of these examples is my phrase used in the sense that I originally intended. On the contrary, when I coined the term in 1989, the market fundamentalism of Reagan's first term had already been superseded by the return of rational economic policymaking, and one could discern which ideas were going to survive and which were not (monetary discipline but not monetarism; tax reform but not tax-slashing; trade liberalization but maybe not complete freedom of capital movements; deregulation of entry and exit barriers but not the suppression of regulations designed to protect the environment).

How is it that a term intended to describe a technocratic policy agenda that survived the demise of Reaganomics came to be used to describe an ideology embracing the most extreme version of Reaganomics? The closest I can come to understanding this is to note that my version of the Washington Consensus did indeed focus principally on policy reforms that reduced the role of government, such as privatization and the liberalization of trade, finance, foreign direct investment, and entry and exit. It did this because the orthodoxy of the generation whose ideas were embodied in the practices being challenged in 1989 had been much more statist than was by then regarded as advisable, and hence the policy reforms that were needed at that time were all in the direction of liberalization. This need for liberalization did not necessarily imply a swing to the opposite extreme of market fundamentalism and a minimalist role for government, but such boring possibilities were repressed in the ideological debates of the 1990s. For it is certainly true that the Washington Consensus came to be used to describe an ideological position, a development that Naim (2000) argues resulted from the world's acute need for a new ideology to provide a focus for debate in place of the god that had failed. My qualifications about the Washington Consensus being an agenda for a specific part of the world at a particular moment of history were quickly forgotten, as the search for a new ideology, to endorse or to hate, was perceived to have succeeded. Ravi Kanbur argues that the staffs of the Bretton Woods institutions perceived themselves as storming the citadels of statism, which led them as a negotiating ploy to demand more in the way of liberalizing reforms than they really expected to achieve—a tactic that led citizens in the World Bank's client countries to identify these institutions with something closer to market fundamentalism than the institutions really believed in.

The term's use as a synonym for market fundamentalism appears to be the dominant, but not the only, current usage. Many Bank staff members, including those who wrote *Beyond the Washington Consensus: Institutions Matter* (Burki and Perry 1998), still use the term in the way that I intended, and I think most of them would endorse the reform agenda to which I had applied the term as a reasonably accurate and appropriate summary of what the Bank and other agencies concerned with the promotion of development were, and should have been, advising countries to do.

Joseph Stiglitz, formerly the World Bank's chief economist, recendy used the term in the alternative, neoliberal, sense (1999b). This at least makes it clear that he was not attacking his colleagues when he spoke of reviewing "the major ways in which . . . the 'Washington Consensus' doctrines of transition, failed. . ." (Stiglitz 1999a:4). He proceeded to question the priority given to rapid privatization and the lack of attention to establishing competition or building social and organizational capital, and later he spoke of "the standard form of voucher privatization promoted by the Washington Consensus. ..." I am not aware that Washington has ever displayed any particular preference for voucher privatization; certainly this was not a theme of the 1996 *World Development Report* (World Bank 1996), which dealt with the transition. I agree with Stiglitz on the substantive questions he raises: one can put too much emphasis on rapid privatization, and it is more important to do it right than to do it quickly; I agree that the great merit of privatization is that it can be used to further competition; I am skeptical about voucher privatization; and I think I agree about the importance of social and organizational capital, if I understand what the words mean. (I would describe them as social cohesion and good institutions, respectively.) What I do not understand is what is gained by describing these sensible ideas as refuting a doctrine described by a term that many people in the Bank regard as providing a useful summary of the advice the Bank dispenses.

Do Washington Consensus Policies Promote Poverty Reduction?

The answer, quite obviously, depends on which interpretation of the Washington Consensus one is referring to. The popular, or populist, interpretation of the Washington Consensus, meaning market fundamentalism or neoliberalism, refers to laissez-faire Reaganomics—let's bash the state, the markets will resolve everything. I would not subscribe to the view that such policies offer an effective agenda for reducing poverty. We know that poverty reduction demands efforts to build the human capital of the poor, but the populist interpretation fails to address that issue. We know that an active policy to supervise financial institutions is needed if financial liberalization is not to lead to financial collapse, which invariably ends up using tax revenues to write off bank loans that were made to the relatively rich. And some measure of income redistribution would be recommended by any policy that was primarily directed at reducing poverty rather than simply maximizing growth, but market fundamentalists rule out all income redistribution as plunder.

A plausible alternative concept would be that the Washington Consensus consists of the set of policies endorsed by the principal economic institutions located in Washington: the U.S. Treasury, the Federal Reserve Board, the International Monetary Fund, and the World Bank. I would argue that the policies these institutions advocated in the 1990s were inimical to the cause of poverty reduction in emerging markets in at least one respect: their advocacy of capital account liberalization. This was, in my view, the main cause of the contagion that caused the East Asian crisis to spread beyond Thailand and that resulted in a tragic interruption of the poverty reduction those countries had achieved (Williamson 1999). (I did not include full capital account liberalization in my version of the Washington Consensus because I did not believe it commanded a consensus, if only because I could not believe I was the only person in Washington who feared that capital account liberalization could precipitate a tragedy such as that which occurred in East Asia.)

My version of the Washington Consensus began with the proposition that the inflation caused by lack of fiscal discipline is bad for income distribution. The second reform specifically involved redirecting public expenditure toward primary health and education, that is, toward building the human capital of the poor. Tax reform can be distributionally neutral or even progressive. A competitive exchange rate is key to nurturing export-led and crisis-free growth and is hence in the general interest, including that of the poor. Trade liberalization, certainly in low-income, resource-poor countries, tends to be pro-poor because it increases the demand for unskilled labor and decreases the subsidies directed to import-competing industries that use large volumes of capital and employ small numbers of workers, many of them highly skilled. Foreign direct investment helps raise growth and spread technology, provided that import protection is not excessive, so that the case of immiserizing growth does not arise (Brecher and Diaz-Alejandro 1977).[4] The impact of privatization depends very much on how it is done: the sort of insider-voucher privatization that occurred in Russia allows the plunder of state assets for the benefit of an elite, but a well-conducted privatization with competitive bidding can raise efficiency and improve the public finances with benefits to all, including the poor. Deregulation in general involves the dismantling of barriers that protect privileged elites (even if some of them, like trade unionists, have difficulty thinking of themselves as an elite), and hence there is a strong presumption that it will be pro-poor. Private property rights are certainly a defense primarily for those who have private property, but the improvement of such rights is nonetheless very likely to be pro-poor because these are the people who find themselves unable to defend their property when property rights are ill-defined (for example, Hernando de Soto's squatters on the periphery of Lima).

I have omitted one of the ten reforms from the preceding list: financial and interest rate liberalization. This is the primary focus of Stiglitz's criticisms when he refers to something that I can recognize as akin to my version of the Washington Consensus. I have realized for some time (see Williamson 1996) that my first formulation was flawed in that it neglected financial supervision, without which financial liberalization seems all too likely to lead to improper lending and eventually to a crisis that requires the taxpayers to pick up the losses from making bad loans (Williamson and Mahar 1998). But should economists therefore endorse the view that directed lending as pursued in some—though not all—East Asian countries is pro-growth and thus ultimately pro-poor? On this issue, at least, I would have thought that the East Asian crisis, especially in Korea, should have tempered economists' enthusiasm for the practice. The high debt-equity ratios that resulted from directed lending were certainly among the causes of the financial fragility that deepened the impact of the crisis.

Thus most of the reforms embodied in my version of the Washington Consensus are at least potentially pro-poor. In some cases this conclusion is sensitive to the way in which reform is implemented: that is certainly true of tax reform, privatization, and, above all, financial liberalization. But I see no reason why the World Bank should back away from endorsing my version of the Washington Consensus in view of its reaffirmation of poverty reduction as its overarching mission. That is not to claim that the Washington Consensus, in any version, constituted a policy manifesto adequate for addressing poverty. My version quite consciously eschewed redistributive policies, taking the view that Washington had not reached a consensus on their desirability. But time has moved on, and we are now looking to *World Development Report 2000/01* for an outline of the policies needed to supplement my version of the Washington Consensus in a world that takes poverty reduction seriously.

The Semantic Dilemma

One can react to the semantic dilemma posed by the different definitions currendy in use in three possible ways. Consider these alternatives:

- *Insist on the original usage.* Insist that my version of the Washington Consensus is the only correct and legitimate interpretation, as a corollary of which the term will (with the qualifications noted above) be recognized as pro-poor. This alternative strikes me as both presumptuous and unrealistic: once a term has escaped into the public domain, one cannot dictate the reestablishment of a common usage. The likely result would be a perpetuation of the public confusion that I am attempting to address.

- *Abandon the term.* Refuse to debate in the terms that have been so compromised by the widespread adoption of the "populist" definition. I cannot imagine that this approach would end the populist use of the term; it would simply be a copout.
- *Endorse a post-Washington Consensus.* A more promising strategy has been adopted at least twice within the Bank. In 1998 the Latin America Regional Office of the World Bank issued a policy document that favored going beyond the Washington Consensus (Burki and Perry 1998). Stiglitz did almost the same, semantically at least, in urging a post-Washington Consensus in his lecture to the World Institute for Development Economics Research in January 1998.

When I first came across this approach, I thought it implied that the reforms included in the Washington Consensus were necessary but not sufficient for promoting development, an idea that seemed eminently reasonable. Clearly the Bank today would want to go further and endorse a wider array of antipoverty instruments than was able to command a consensus in 1989, when the most I thought I could legitimately include was the promotion of public expenditure on primary health and education.[5]

In their book, Burki and Perry (1998) explicitly refer to my version of the Washington Consensus and assert that the widespread implementation of the "first-generation" reforms it prescribed was paying off in Latin America in resumed growth and an end to high inflation. They noted that the reforms had not been equally effective in reducing poverty and inequality, which they argued demonstrated a "need to focus on improving the quality of investments in human development, promoting the development of sound and efficient financial markets, enhancing the legal and regulatory environments (in particular, deregulating labor markets and improving regulations for private investment in infrastructure and social services), [and] improving the quality of the public sector (including the judiciary) ..." (p. 4). This is an agenda dominated by institutional reform, which is indeed what has become known in Latin America as the second-generation reform agenda (Naim 1995).

It is not equally obvious why Stiglitz would want to propagate a post–Washington Consensus that implied endorsing and extending the original version, given his interpretation of what was included in it. In fact, the Stiglitz version of a post–Washington Consensus does not endorse any version of the original. He is advocating a policy package that is intended to supersede the Washington Consensus altogether. His new policy package is asserted to differ from the original in two dimensions.

First, he argues that the implicit policy objective underlying the Washington Consensus is inadequate. In addition to pursuing economic growth, the objectives should include "sustainable development, egalitarian development, and democratic development." In other words, he believes that policy objectives should include the state of the environment, income distribution, and democracy, as well as per capita gross national product. I find those objectives much more congenial than a single-minded preoccupation with economic growth, although I am not sure that the World Bank could formally endorse the pursuit of democracy (its Articles do, after all, forbid its involvement in politics).[6] Second, in addition to expanding the objectives, Stiglitz argues that it is necessary to pursue "sound financial regulation, competition policy, and policies to facilitate the transfer of technology and transparency" to make markets work in a way that will support development.

I have a somewhat different view of what should be added to the Washington Consensus to make it a policy manifesto supportive of egalitarian, environmentally sensitive development. I agree that financial regulation (prudential supervision) is crucial and that transparency is a useful complement to supervision in achieving appropriate conduct of financial institutions. Moreover, competition is a natural complement to deregulation in promoting a well-functioning market economy (although a liberal import regime is the most effective competition policy in tradables, as Srinivasan argues in his comment in this volume). I would not have included technology transfer in such a manifesto, although I would have no objection to including institutional changes that seemed likely to promote technology transfer if I were reasonably confident that I knew what these changes were (besides accepting foreign direct investment). Similarly, I would consider it desirable to include policies focused on improved environmental conditions, although I am not sure that I would know how to select policy measures at a comparable level of generality to my 10 original points. But my emphasis would have been different; I would have focused much more generally on institutions. To explain why, let me offer a brief history of postwar development thinking.

In the first wave of theorizing about economic development, from the 1940s to the early 1960s, economists saw the accumulation of physical capital as the key to development (as reflected in the Harrod-Domar model, the Lewis model, and the two-gap model). The second phase recognized that human capital provided another and more inelastic constraint on development, a constraint that explained why Europe and Japan had recovered from World War II so rapidly, when growth in developing countries had been lagging despite the adoption of development policies and the beginning of large-scale aid. The third phase, which started about 1970 with the work of Little, Scitovsky, and Scott (1970) and Balassa (1970), emphasized that the policy environment influenced the level and dominated the productivity of investment. The Washington Consensus attempted to summarize the outcome of this debate on the policies that were conducive to economic development. The major advance of the 1990s stemmed from recognition that the central task of the transition from communist to market-based economies involved building the institutional infrastructure of a market economy. This realization was complemented by a growing recognition that bad institutions can sabotage good policies. This viewpoint was reflected in Stiglitz's (1999a) remarks on the transition, in Naim's (1995) work on supplementing the Washington Consensus, in

Burki and Perry (1998), in the *World Development Reports* of 1997 and 1998, and in the World Bank's decision to launch a crusade against corruption.

What should one make of the idea of launching a post-Washington Consensus? I would not be happy at such a move if it were interpreted to imply a rejection of "the" Washington Consensus, although I would have no problem if it involved rejection of the populist, or market-fundamentalist, version. But it seems a somewhat odd crusade. The time of the original consensus, 1989, was an unusual period in that the ideological battles of the Reagan era, not to mention the cold war battle between capitalism and communism, were passing into history, leaving in their wake an unusually wide measure of agreement that several rather basic ideas of good economics were not only desirable but of key importance in the current policy agenda of at least one region—Latin America. Currendy, there is no similar coalescing of views, certainly not on the wider agenda that Stiglitz has laid out. (Consensus on egalitarianism? With aid fatigue threatening the future of the International Development Association? On environmental sustainability? In a world where the U.S. Senate refuses even to consider ratifying the Kyoto Protocol?) I agree, rather, with Tim Geithner (1999:8): "I don't think anyone believes there is some universal model that can or should be imposed on the world—Washington consensus, post Washington consensus, or not."

Resolving the Dilemma

Let me conclude by laying out my own ideas on how to resolve the dilemma.

- There is little merit in attacking abstract, undefined concepts that are interpreted to mean whatever the author momentarily decides they mean. It is better to spell out those concepts that are being criticized and debate policies on the basis of their merits.
- The World Bank should recognize that the term Washington Consensus has been used in very different ways. One summarizes policies that are pro-poor; another describes a policy stance that offers the poor very little and warrants no support.
- It is appropriate to go beyond the Washington Consensus by emphasizing the importance of the institutional dimension as well as of the sort of policies embodied in the original version of the Washington Consensus—policies that will promote an equitable distribution of income as well as a rapid growth of income.
- The hopeless quest to identify a consensus where there is none should be abandoned in favor of a debate on the policy changes needed to achieve a rounded set of objectives encompassing at least the level, growth, and distribution of income, as well as preservation of a decent environment.

The Bank will do the cause of economic development a great service if it can frame future debate in these terms. Admittedly my suggestions do not answer the pleas for a new ideology that would more adequately reflect the goals of the multilateral development banks and that might thus increase the chance of establishing local ownership of the sort of economic policy stance conducive to rapid and equitable growth. Let me plead in defense that I am not a suitable person to launch an ideology, inasmuch as Naim (2000) characterizes an ideology as a thought-economizing device and I actually believe that thinking is more desirable than economizing on thought.

Notes

This article was written as a background paper for *World Development Report 2000/01*. The author is indebted to the participants in a session at which an early version of the paper was discussed, notably Ravi Kanbur and Moisés Naím.

1 This intellectual convergence was the result of the collapse of communism, which resulted not from machinations of the Bretton Woods institutions, or even of the U.S. Central Intelligence Agency, but because socialism does not work except in a simple economy, and even then it seems to have worked reasonably well only when large numbers of people were inspired with revolutionary zeal.

2 Exchange rate policy is the one topic on which I have a serious difference of view with T. N. Srinivasan's comment that accompanies this paper. The term "competitive exchange rate" originated with Bela Balassa and signifies a rate that is either at, or undervalued relative to, its long-run equilibrium. I do not regard measuring the latter as an exercise in futility, see Hinkle and Montiel (1999) for evidence that other people in the Bank do not either. I dissent from the consensus Srinivasan proclaims that holds that only currency boards and freely floating rates offer viable regimes. For further details, see Williamson (forthcoming).

3 In trying to identify policies from the Reagan-Thatcher era that had not won consensus support, I wrote in 1996: "it [the Washington Consensus] did not declare that the only legitimate way to restore fiscal discipline was to slash government expenditure; it did not identify fiscal discipline with a balanced budget; it did not call for overall tax cuts; it did not treat as plunder the taxes raised to redistribute income; it did not say that exchange rates had to be either firmly fixed or freely floating; it did not call for the proscription of capital controls; it did not advocate competitive moneys or argue that the money supply should grow at a fixed rate" (Williamson 1997:50).

4 Growth of output of a heavily protected product can immiserize a country if the resources used in production exceed the social value of the output.

5 However, in commenting on my paper, Stanley Fischer (then the Bank's chief economist) argued that I could and should have gone further: "Emphasis on poverty reduction has increased in recent years and will continue to do so. [A good forecast.] The concern with poverty reduction goes beyond the belief that economic growth will reduce poverty, to the view that targeted food subsidies as well as the medical and educational programs to which Williamson refers, can reduce the number of poor people ... and should be used for that purpose" (Williamson 1990:27).

6 Some people might wish to add nation-building to the noneconomic objectives to be pursued by development policy (as was common in the 1960s).

References

The word "processed" refers to informally reproduced works that may not be commonly available through library systems.

Alam, M. Shahid. 1999. "Does Sovereignty Matter for Economic Growth?" In John Adams and Francesco Pigliaru, eds., *Economic Growth and Change.* Cheltenham, U.K.: Edward Elgar.

Balassa, Bela. 1970. "Growth Strategies in Semi-Industrial Countries." *Quarterly Journal of Economics* 84(1):24–47.

Brecher, Richard, and Carlos Diaz-Alejandro. 1977. "Tariffs, Foreign Capital, and Immiserizing Growth." *Journal of International Economics* 7(4):317–22.

Burki, Javed, and Guillermo E. Perry. 1998. *Beyond the Washington Consensus: Institutions Matter.* Washington, D.C.: World Bank.

Geithner, Timothy F. 1999. "The World Bank and the Frontier of Development Challenges." Remarks delivered to a conference on "Reinventing the World Bank: Challenges and Opportunities for the 21st Century," Northwestern University, May 14. Processed.

Hamada, Koichi. 1998. "IMF Special: Keeping Alive the Asian Monetary Fund." *Capital Trends* 3 (September).

Hinkle, Lawrence E., and Peter J. Montiel, eds. 1999. *Exchange Rate Misalignment: Concepts and Measurement for Developing Countries.* New York: Oxford University Press.

Ito, Takatoshi. 1999. "The Role of IMF Advice." Paper presented to International Monetary Fund conference on "Key Issues in Reform of the International Monetary and Financial System," Washington, D.C., May 29. Processed.

Kolodko, Gregorz. 1998. *Transition.* World Bank Development Economic Research Group newsletter, June.

Little, Ian, Tibor Scitovsky, and Maurice Scott. 1970. *The Structure of Protection in Developing Countries: A Comparative Study.* Baltimore, Md.: Johns Hopkins University Press.

McCloskey, Deirdre N. 1998. *The Rhetoric of Economics.* 2d ed. Madison, Wis.: University of Wisconsin Press.

Naím, Moisés. 1995. "Latin America: The Morning After." *Foreign Affairs* 74(July-August):45–61.

———. 2000. "Washington Consensus or Washington Confusion?" *Foreign Policy* (spring):86–103.

Rajan, Ramkishen S. 1999. "The Brazilian and Other Currency Crises of the 1990s." *Claremont Policy Brief.* Claremont College, Claremont, Calif. May.

Soros, George. 1998. *The Crisis of Global Capitalism.* New York: Public Affairs.

Stewart, Frances. 1997. "Williamson and the Washington Consensus Revisited." In Louis Emmerij, ed., *Economic and Social Development into the XXI Century.* Washington, D.C.: Inter-American Development Bank.

Stiglitz, Joseph E. 1994. "The Role of the State in Financial Markets." In Michael Bruno and Boris Pleskovic, eds., *Proceedings of the World Bank Conference on Development Economics 1993.* Washington, D.C.: World Bank.

———. 1998. "More Instruments and Broader Goals: Moving toward the Post-Washington Consensus." United Nations University/World Institute for Development Economics Research, Helsinki.

———. 1999a. "Whither Reform? Ten Years of the Transition." In Boris Plesovic and Joseph E. Stiglitz, eds., *World Bank Annual Conference on Development Economics.* Washington, D.C.: World Bank.

———. 1999b. "The World Bank at the Millennium." *Economic Journal* 109(459):F577–97.

United Nations. 1998. *Annual Report of the United Nations University*. Tokyo.

Vines, David. 1999. In an obituary for Susan Strange. Newsletter no 9. Economic and Social Research Council Programme on Global Economic Institutions, Swindon, U.K. Processed.

Waelbroeck, Jean. 1998. "Half a Century of Development Economics: A Review Based on the *Handbook of Development Economics.*" *The World Bank Economic Review* 12(May):323–52.

Williamson, John. 1990. "What Washington Means by Policy Reform." In John Williamson, ed., *Latin American Adjustment: How Much Has Happened?* Washington, D.C.: Institute for International Economics.

_____. 1996. "Are the Latin American Reforms Sustainable?" In Hermann Sautter and Rolf Schinke, eds., *Stabilization and Reforms in Latin America: Where Do We Stand?* Frankfurt: Vervuert Verlag.

_____. 1997. "The Washington Consensus Revisited." In Louis Emmerij, ed., *Economic and Social Development into the XXI Century.* Washington, D.C.: Inter-American Development Bank.

_____. 1999. "Implications of the East Asian Crisis for Debt Management." In A. Vasudevan, ed., *External Debt Management: Issues, Lessons, and Preventive Measures.* Mumbai: Reserve Bank of India.

_____. Forthcoming. *Exchange Rate Regimes for Emerging Economies: Reviving the Intermediate Option.* Washington, D.C.: Institute for International Economics.

Williamson, John, and Molly Mahar. 1998. "A Survey of Financial Liberalization." Princeton Essays in International Finance 211. Princeton University, Princeton, N.J.

World Bank. 1993. *The East Asian Miracle: Economic Growth and Public Policy*. New York. Oxford University Press.

_____. 1996. *World Development Report: From Plan to Market*. New York: Oxford University Press.